RUTH BENEDICT

STRANGER IN THIS LAND

AMERICAN STUDIES SERIES
William H. Goetzmann, Editor

RUTH BENEDICT

STRANGER IN THIS LAND

by Margaret M. Caffrey

UNIVERSITY OF TEXAS PRESS, AUSTIN

Requests for permission to reproduce material from this work
should be sent to Permissions, University of Texas Press,
Box 7819, Austin, Texas 78713-7819.

LIBRARY OF CONGRESS CATALOGING-IN-PUBLICATION DATA
Caffrey, Margaret M. (Margaret Mary), 1947–
    Ruth Benedict : stranger in this land.
    (American studies series)
    Bibliography: p.
    Includes index.
    1. Benedict, Ruth, 1887–1948.   2. Anthropologists—
United States—Biography.   3. Ethnology.   I. Title.
II. Series.
GN21.B45C34   1989   306'.092'4 [B]   88-20589
ISBN 0-292-74655-5

♾ The paper used in this publication meets the minimum requirements of American National
Standard for Information Sciences—Permanence of Paper for Printed Library Materials, ANSI
Z39.48-1984.

Permission to include the following materials is gratefully acknowledged:
    Excerpts from materials in the Ruth Fulton Benedict Papers. Courtesy, Vassar College Library,
Poughkeepsie, New York.
    Excerpts from *An Anthropologist at Work: Writings of Ruth Benedict,* edited by Margaret
Mead. Copyright © 1959 by Margaret Mead. Copyright © renewed 1987 by Mary Catherine
Bateson. Reprinted by permission of Houghton-Mifflin Company, Vassar College Library, and
the Institute for Intercultural Studies, Inc.
    Excerpts from materials in the Margaret Mead Papers (Mead Archive) at the Library of
Congress, Washington, D.C. Courtesy of the Institute for Intercultural Studies, Inc.
    Excerpts from materials in the Franz Boas Papers and in the Elsie Clews Parsons Papers.
Courtesy of the American Philosophical Society Library, Philadelphia.
    Excerpts from a letter in the Alfred Kroeber Papers. Courtesy of the Bancroft Library,
University of California, Berkeley.
    "In a Station of the Metro," by Ezra Pound. From Ezra Pound, *Personae.* Copyright 1926 by
Ezra Pound. Reprinted by permission of New Directions and Faber & Faber, Ltd.
    Excerpt from "Let No Charitable Hope," from *Collected Poems of Elinor Wylie,* copyright
1932 by Alfred A. Knopf, Inc.

Frontispiece photo of Ruth Benedict courtesy Vassar College Library.

Contents

To Ronda Sue Campbell

Preface and Acknowledgments

WHEN I STARTED THIS BOOK, only Margaret Mead's work on Benedict was available, and that not easy to find. Since then Judith Modell's fine work has appeared, and I have been a beneficiary of the opening of the Margaret Mead Papers and the revelations about Benedict's personal life in Jane Howard's *Margaret Mead: A Life* and those on the Mead-Benedict relationship by Margaret Mead's daughter, Mary Catherine Bateson, in *With a Daughter's Eye*. Thus this book is able to deal more frankly with Benedict's woman-identification and its impact on her ideas than any previously written works while integrating this material into the total framework of her cultural milieu.

Unlike Mead and Modell, who do not see Benedict as a feminist, I explore Benedict's life as a case history in cultural feminism, a feminism derived from other than political sources, focused on changing the values and beliefs that make up the framework of a culture rather than working for change through laws or the courts, with an emphasis on covert rather than overt change. This is a feminism that concentrates on internal questions such as definitions of masculinity and femininity, and questions of selfhood, of individuality, or of independence and stresses the necessity of changing inward attitudes of men and women and the "shoulds and oughts" of American society in order to cause radical social change.

Benedict was a poet as well as an anthropologist, and I reexamine the motivations of her poetry in a Modernist, feminist context in a way that previous biographers have not done.

Both Mead and Modell approached Benedict as anthropologists. They saw Benedict and her work from the perspective of one anthropologist looking at another. But Benedict's work went far beyond its origins in anthropology and deserves to be evaluated in terms of its place on the larger American screen. Benedict was one of the most successful intellectual women of the first half of the twentieth century in America. As an anthropologist she was a leader in her field. But she also lived at the center of the important intellectual currents of her lifetime. Her classic book, *Patterns of Culture* (1934), besides igniting the work of the Culture and Personality movement within anthropology, is one of the major works of twentieth-century American intellectual history. It marked a turning point in American culture between what we think of today as nineteenth- and twentieth-century ideas, and acted as a catalyst for the acceptance of the new ideas by articulating them in clear, compelling language as a coherent social philosophy, a new set of axioms by which people could orient their lives.

Her book on the Japanese, *The Chrysanthemum and the Sword* (1946), while of interest to anthropologists, was probably most important in terms of its effect on its American readership-at-large. The Japanese had seemed to most Americans the most alien society America had ever dealt with—seemingly inhuman and irrational in their actions. Benedict explained to Americans why the Japanese acted as they did, and besides having an acknowledged influence on American occupation policy-makers helped lay the basis for the return of Japanese society to the post-war community of nations. The book also showed Americans some of the basic traits of American culture in contrast and comparison with the Japanese, and pioneered an interdisciplinary methodology for culture-cracking that deserves to be further examined.

Benedict was also one of the best known writers on the race issue during the 1940's. She was not a scholar of race—i.e., she did not do original, creative work in the area of racial studies, as her mentor, Franz Boas, had, but she was an exceptional synthesizer and a clear, forceful writer who increasingly experimented with ways to popularize knowledge of race and racism. Besides numerous popular articles on race, she wrote a book for the general reader called *Race: Science and Politics* (1940). Benedict subsequently turned material from this book into a high school teaching unit on race and racism and a Public Affairs pamphlet, co-authored with anthropologist Gene Weltfish. The pamphlet later became a cartoon-movie, a comic book, and a children's book, this last again with Benedict and Weltfish listed as coauthors.

Because she was so intimately involved, Benedict's life becomes a vehicle for examining the intellectual and cultural history of the first half of the twentieth century as she moved through it. Ruth Benedict was born into the last years of the Victorian era, came of age during the Progressive years, and participated in inaugurating the Modern era of American life. Like many of the women of her generation she rejected the validity of Vic-

[viii]

torian claims upon her as a woman: the inflexible expectations, the narrowness of the allowed female roles, the parched sexuality. At the same time, like other intellectuals of her generation, she faced the necessity of wrestling with the implications of Darwinism and the challenge of creating a new intellectual synthesis from its contradictions. During the Progressive era thinkers both in Europe and in America laid the groundwork for a striking new view of society and the universe, a Modern view that would reach its apex in America in the 1930's and have reverberations into the present time, which some call the second stage of Modernism. Benedict did not participate in this work during the Progressive period because she was busy disentangling the contradictions between intellectuality and femininity that Progressive culture as well as her Victorian childhood had placed on her life. For many of her female contemporaries, the Progressive era offered a framework which resolved conflicts between women's role in the family and in society. "Municipal housekeeping" became a common catch-phrase of the time. Women who became social activists and reformers found a place in the mainstream of Progressive life. But Ruth Benedict, who was not a social activist, yet remained sensitive to the Progressive imperative of social reform, faced two conflicts. The first was a struggle to find a role for herself as both intellectual and woman in American society; the second was finding a place for herself as an intellectual activist in the struggle for social change. The Progressives had concentrated on changing the external elements of American life: politics, sanitary conditions in cities and factories, public health, social services. Benedict was predisposed from childhood to believe that the only lasting change was internal change occurring in the values and beliefs of people. This, in turn, would generate external social change. Before and during World War I she turned to feminism and then education as bases for social change. But her discovery of anthropology right after the war gave her both an outlet for the sheer intellectual play of ideas and a tool for intellectual social change. When she entered it, anthropology was at the point of replacing natural history as the source of scientific moral authority in America. It was also at the beginning of a period of expansion which eventually gave it a primary role among the social sciences. Benedict, using anthropology as a base, contributed through her writings toward creating a Modern framework of thought in pre–World War II America, one based on a relative intellectual system rather than an absolute one. Also, she, most successfully of the social scientists, resolved the contradictions of Darwinism, giving many of her colleagues and readers Archimedes' famous "place to stand" from which to move the universe.

Within anthropology her work was increasingly controversial because it raised questions about the identity of anthropology as a discipline and the direction in which it should go. Anthropology had identified itself as a science at a time when science meant total objectivity. Benedict's work reintroduced a subjectivity that threatened anthropology's identity as a science. Ultimately, the threat was too great, and although Benedict's work provided a set of orienting concepts for many within anthropology during her lifetime, this influence did not survive after her death, when the Culture and Personality movement faded out of the mainstream of anthropological research until revived as the subdiscipline of psychological anthropology in the 1960's. I examine the conflict and also trace in more depth than previous researchers the interdisciplinary interaction of anthropological and psychoanalytical ideas through the 1930's and 1940's, including Benedict's work with the Neo-Freudian Cultural School of Psychoanalysis.

Finally, from the perspective of one who helped shape it, this book explores the history of the concept of "culture," with all its connotations, which has become such an important one in twentieth-century America.

The subtitle *Stranger in This Land* derives loosely from a folk song about immigrants arriving as strangers to America. As I wrote, the idea of Benedict as such a stranger, a person not at ease with major elements in American society, seemed more and more appropriate, for she was not comfortable in mainstream America even though she was born into it. Moreover, Benedict chose roles as intellectual and poet that are traditionally outsiders' roles in American society, which places its intellectuals, artists, and poets on the margins of life. In her work she attempted to understand her alienation, and through her ideas she tried to create an America and later a world in which strangeness or difference would be accepted and where no person or country would be a stranger, but instead play an acknowledged, integral part.

I would like to acknowledge with gratitude the help of all those who contributed to the completion of this manuscript, beginning with Professor William Goetzmann, Dickson, Allen, and Anderson Centennial Professor in American Studies and History at the University of Texas at Austin and the editor of this series, who has been a constant source of encouragement and guidance on the road to publication. A special thank you goes to all those others who also read the manuscript and offered advice: Robert Crunden, American Studies Chair, UT Austin; William Stott, Jeff Meikle, Desley Deacon, and Emily Cutrer from American Studies; historian and biographer Robert Abzug; anthropologists Chad Oliver and Mary Jane Young. Anthropologist Judith Modell corresponded with me about Ruth Benedict and offered encouragement at a time when it was greatly appreciated, although our interpretations and ideas do not always agree.

A special acknowledgment is offered to those librarians who aided my search for information, particularly Lisa Browar, the former Curator of Rare Books and Manuscripts at Vassar College Library, Poughkeepsie, New York, and Nancy MacKechnie, the present Curator; Mary Wolfskill at the Library of Congress; Doris D. Finley, Reference Director, St. Joseph, Missouri, Public Library; Bruce M. Brown, University Archivist, Colgate University; Doris W. Waters, Genealogy/Local History at the Guernsey Memorial Library in Norwich, New York; Joel Brenckman of the Owatonna, Minnesota, Public Library; David Espenscheid, Library Director, Pillsbury College, Owatonna, Minnesota; Barbara M. Soper, Librarian at the Buffalo and Erie County Public Library; Claude Goodrich, Librarian, Los Angeles Public Library; Dorothy Potter, Librarian, Pasadena Public Library; and Sheila K. O'Neill, the Bancroft Library, University of California at Berkeley.

The staff at the University of Texas Press has been exceptionally helpful. I would also like to thank those anthropologists and others who corresponded with me or took time to talk to me out of their busy schedules. Finally, my deepest thanks to friends and family who put up with me from the start to the finish of this project.

Ruth at three and a half with her sister Margery, two years old. Photo by Wick of Norwich, N.Y. Courtesy, Vassar College Library.

Ruth's graduation picture from St. Margaret's School, Buffalo, 1905. Courtesy, Vassar College Library.

Ruth and Stanley with family members on their wedding day in 1914. Ruth's mother is standing next to her in the center of the photo. Courtesy, Vassar College Library.

Ruth and Stanley Benedict at Lake Winnipesaukee, N.H., in the early years of their marriage. Courtesy, Vassar College Library.

Ruth Benedict in her office at Columbia University. Courtesy, Vassar College Library.

Photographic portrait taken between 1930 and 1948. Courtesy, Vassar College Library.

The unique value of life histories lies in that fraction of the material which shows what repercussions the experiences of a man's life—either shared or idiosyncratic—have upon him as a human being moulded in that environment. Such information, as it were, tests out a culture by showing its workings in the life of a carrier of that culture; we can watch in an individual case, in Bradley's words, "what is, seeing that so it happened and must have happened."

RUTH BENEDICT
"Anthropology and the Humanities,"
1947 American Anthropological
Association Presidential Address

Prologue: The "Simple Theme"

WHEN SHE WAS FORTY-EIGHT, and newly famous as the author of *Patterns of Culture,* anthropologist Ruth Benedict looked back at her own childhood at the request of friend and fellow anthropologist Margaret Mead, who was then working on a study of life histories. In fragments not meant for publication Benedict wove the happenings of her childhood into a pattern which she felt defined "the simple theme"[1] of her own life: "from my earliest childhood I recognized two worlds . . . the world of my father, which was the world of death and which was beautiful, and the world [of my mother] of confusion and explosive weeping which I repudiated."[2] With these two worlds Benedict structured a life marked by the Apollonian-Dionysian duality she had used so effectively in her book to characterize the Pueblo and Plains Indian cultures. By doing so she compressed into this seeming simplicity a large unexamined bundle of causes and motivations intricate in their complexity. Before exploring Benedict's childhood in Chapter 1, it is important to understand Benedict's own extremely perceptive yet narrowly psychoanalytic interpretation of her childhood and the limitations of that interpretation. Because when examined, what she defined as a simple theme actually becomes a multiplicity of themes that kaleidoscopically illuminate her life and reflect the complexities of American society.

Her father, Frederick Samuel Fulton, had died when she was twenty-one months old. He was a young man of distinguished promise and just beginning to achieve success as a homeopathic physician and surgeon in New York City when he became ill in 1888. He had to give up his practice and return with his family to Norwich, New York, where his father was a prominent local homeopathic physician. There they lived with Ruth's maternal grandparents, the Shattucks, on their farm outside the town. Frederick's condition got no better and a year later he died there. The impact of her father's prolonged illness and death on Ruth Benedict was profound. "I have very little idea what he was really like," she wrote, "but the part he played in my childhood, and still plays, was none the less great for that" ("The Story of My Life," p. 97).

Ruth Benedict idealized her father. She thought of him as "a young surgeon with a passionate love of his work and of research" (p. 97). Her memories of him were of "a worn face illuminated with the translucence of illness and very beautiful. There is no dispute that my father was beautiful," she wrote, and by this she meant beautiful in a saintly way (pp. 97–98). In one of Ruth's earliest memories as a preschooler she had equated her father with Christ in a picture on the wall of her grandparents' farmhouse. As an adult she recalled, "I had thought the picture of Christ on the wall *was* my father, and I think I never stopped believing it as far as my emotions went" (p. 107). Besides identifying her father with Christ in the picture "Christ before Pilate," as a child, she also as a young adult identified him with El Greco's "Fray Felix Hortensio Paravicino" in the Boston Museum. The picture shows an emaciated, ethereal, saintly-looking man of God surrounded by radiance. Benedict called her visits to see the picture "acts of friendship and love for the man painted" (p. 98).

But if she idealized her father, she found her mother all too human. Her mother made "a cult of grief out of my father's death, and every March she wept in church and in bed at night" (p. 98). Benedict also remembered as a young child seeing her mother's face "set for the scene of grief any mention of my father always called up" (p. 99). Her mother's explosive weeping repelled her and had the same effect each time, "an excruciating misery" including involuntary physical trembling "which culminated periodically in rigidity like an orgasm. It was not an expression of love for my mother, though I often pitied her," she wrote (p. 98). "I did not love my mother," she added. "I resented her cult of grief, and her worry and concern about little things" (p. 99). Crying before anyone became one of the two important tabus of her childhood. The other one, also prompted by her mother's behavior, was against the expression of pain. Mrs. Fulton had a large amount of dentistry done before they left the farm when Ruth was six. "She had no tabu on expressing pain," wrote Ruth. "My feeling at these times was nearest to humiliation—and repudiation" (p. 106). In contrast, Ruth remembered when she was seven or eight "lying awake all night with a toothache and not calling anyone." She recalled also that when she was fourteen her mother burned herself with hot candy. Ruth vomited, but "it was her groans that upset me, not pity for her pain" (p. 106).

This contrast of her feelings toward her mother and her father reflected

Benedict's sense of her childhood as a struggle to come to terms with her father's death. "The story of my life," she wrote, "begins when I was twenty-one months old, at the time my father died" (p. 97). Ruth saw the death of her father and her mother's response to his death as catalysts leading to direct and indirect psychological conflicts which she spent her childhood and young adulthood resolving. When her husband died, Bertrice Shattuck Fulton wanted "desperately" for twenty-one-month-old Ruth to remember her father. According to what one of her aunts told Ruth, her mother "took me into the room where he lay in his coffin and in an hysteria of weeping implored me to remember." Ruth called this her "primal scene" (p. 98). The picture drawn is one of a confused and frightened small child not old enough to understand death or even most of what her mother was saying, overwhelmed by the weeping and raw emotion of the scene. It suggests that her fright and confusion created an enormous sense of vulnerability as in one stroke she experienced the loss of the two most nourishing and protective people around her—the loss of her father to death and her mother to grief. Such an experience also might have led Ruth to feel responsible in some "magical," non-rational way for her father's death. At any rate what Ruth described as occurring after this was on the one hand a massive withdrawal from life on many levels and on the other hand a striking out in anger at her powerlessness over a situation she could not change.[3]

Her simplest withdrawal was physical. "I was considered very 'touchy' about physical contacts," she wrote (pp. 108–109). Her Aunt Mamie Shattuck Ellis used to play a game with her when she was small in which Mamie threatened to hug Ruth while Ruth ran and hid behind chairs and sofas. The big scene of physical avoidance she remembered from her childhood occurred with Great-Uncle Justin Fulton, a fundamentalist Baptist minister and a man she disliked. He gave her sister Margery a fifty-cent piece one visit for kissing him, but Ruth "ran in terror from room to room and finally hid on the treadle under the sewing machine" (p. 109). Also she developed a history of leaving her mother's sanctioned bounds to explore the neighborhood on her own. "During my babyhood," she wrote, "running away figured as my family crime along with my tantrums" (pp. 100–101). Although this type of running away is considered within the range of normal behavior for preschool children, Ruth herself connected it with her father's death.[4]

She also withdrew from concern about her material environment. She called the small role material things played in her life "striking" and "particularly curious" when remembering her childhood because the family went from being comfortable to being "very poor" by the time she was eleven. There were strict economies in clothes and food. She recalled the "momentous occasion" of spending a dollar and fifty cents for a hat. "Each year in rotation," she wrote, "one of us could have a new coat" (p. 110). One of the family stories concerned her sister Margery describing the meat she had had for dinner at a friend's house. " 'It was brown on the outside and red in the middle. *It was good*' " (p. 110). Margery had never had roast beef before. "But," wrote Ruth, "I was never conscious of my clothes or of poverty." She could not remember "any rebellion against the skimpy wardrobe we could afford" (p. 110). She lived her "real" life on another plane.

On a deeper level, Ruth also withdrew from human relationships and emotional response. "Nothing seems to me more striking in my whole childhood than this small role that warm human relations played," she wrote (p. 109). Her withdrawal from human contact was noted by the family, who thought that she deliberately did not answer when called, which Ruth admitted was partly true. She wrote of herself, "No one in my childhood really got past my physical and emotional aloofness. They never got into 'my' world" (p. 109). She commented that it was curious "how small a part in my real life" her sister played; yet they were always together (p. 103). She maintained an emotional distance from her mother, writing that she did not love her. As far as friends went, she wrote that when she was nine or ten and became a leader of a group of schoolgirl friends, "For the first time people began to play some real part in my life—not very real, but at least occupying" (p. 107). Emotional withdrawal accompanied this withdrawal from human relationships. Although outwardly a "warm little girl," inwardly she felt numb (p. 108). She refused emotional response to what other people thought of her, whether she was ugly or beautiful, and found it "irrelevant" (p. 104).

She remained emotionally detached from her tantrums. She called them "outside invasions of my person," saying, "it seemed to me that devils swept down upon me," and refused to feel guilty for them (p. 108). The punishments the family would administer when she had tantrums "never registered in my consciousness" (p. 102). Not allowing herself to cry in public or to express pain were other ways of repressing emotions. Most tellingly, she wrote, "I can't remember any longing to have any person love me or frustration that I wasn't chosen," although her actions as a child belied her words (pp. 109–110).

But to Ruth the most all-pervasive withdrawal response was her flight from reality into an imaginative world. From her earliest childhood she had recognized two worlds. One was a mental world which she called "the world of my father" (p. 99), her calm, creative Apollonian retreat; the other was the everyday world which was the world of her mother, the Dionysian world of confusion, disorder, anger. These two worlds, she wrote, "stretched out in all directions" (pp. 99–100). When the everyday world became too much, she could always retreat to her "other world." "To this world my father belonged," she wrote. "I identified him with everything calm and beautiful that came my way" (p. 99). Among young children whose parents have died psychologists have noted a tendency to identify in some way with the dead parent, often by a kind of mental merging with him or her. This is sometimes helpful in the process of mourning and in personality development after such a loss, but can also lead to disruptive behavior and severe withdrawal and arrest at the developmental level the child had reached at the parent's death. In her imaginary world Ruth could avoid feelings of anxiety and loss and increase her feelings of self-worth by identification with her father. She created a world that was a place of beauty, happiness, rest, and peace, a world whose interior boundaries changed as she herself grew and developed. Its earliest manifestation was as a "beautiful country on the other side of the west hill where a family lived who had a little girl about my age" (p. 100), seemingly an alter ego of her own, living an ideally happy life. She and her imaginary playmate explored together the "unparalleled beauty" of the country over the hill. This imaginary world ended when Ruth was five and she climbed the west hill for the first time with her mother and aunts and found on the other side only Uncle George's farm, "familiar and anything-but-romantic territory" (p. 100). She never played with her imaginary playmate again after that. After this episode her imaginary world took shape mostly from Bible stories, and still later she began to fantasize "a world all inhabited by people of a strange dignity and grace" (p. 109) who did not walk as others did, but skimmed the ground in an unbroken line. They lived on a "lovely hill" (p. 109), and Ruth used to go and watch them. As she grew older she added to it out of William Blake's figures and Michelangelo's paintings from the Sistine Chapel. In this world "the deepest emotions of discovery, of recognition, of beauty" were "possibilities."[5]

This "happy world I lived in by myself" could be enjoyed only for "precious moments" before "the mundane world and all its confusions" shattered her contentment. She thought of these moments as her "pearls of great price," because the transition from her mental retreat back to reality was "likely to be stormy," inducing "ungovernable tantrums."

Ruth wrote, "I was violent either to myself or to anyone else within reach" (p. 100). In her tantrums she sometimes hit her sister, Margery, and her mother always worried that Ruth would hurt her. Her tantrums lasted on and off until she was eleven. Ruth wrote about them that by the time she was eight, "I knew what Dionysian experience was, I had had to take account of fury, an experience that swept over me from somewhere outside my control—as I figured—, lifted me like a tornado and dropped me limp at the end." Besides fury she experienced "muscular stiffness" and a "blind impulse of destruction" that swept over her. Her response to this violence was "disgust." She wrote, "After a periodic scene I was likely to vomit, originally probably a straight physiological reaction, but more and more even as a baby, an expression of loathing."[6] During adolescence the tantrums turned inward and became depressions. "All my ideology connects my tantrums and my depressions as two different manifestations of the same kink, one supplanting the other," she wrote (p. 108). Both she always called her "devils" and both were "protests against alienation from my Delectable Mountains," her "beautiful country," her mental world. Her fits of depression, which continued into her adult years, "were more acceptable than unwanted participation in the 'other' world that was not 'mine.'" That other world, the everyday world, "was all a very strange place inhabited exclusively by alien people" (p. 108).

Among young children death often causes anger, and a small child, unable to verbalize emotions, uses his or her whole body to express frustration, confusion, and anger. At twenty-one months, Ruth ordinarily would have been in a transitional period between the turbulent eighteen months, with its frequent tantrums, and the calmer two, when the child for a brief period gains self-control before becoming turbulent again at two-and-a-half. Since death of a parent contributes to arrest of development to the level reached at the time of death, it is possible that young Ruth was still experiencing tantrums as the "normal" response to the everyday world, which would have made it easier to fall back on tantrums as a way to express her anger and fear. There are certain developmental stages where tantrums naturally reoccur, for example, at two-and-a-half, three-and-a-half, four, four-and-a-half, and especially six. Ruth's need to express her anger could have led her to this familiar outlet, and even as an older child, in times of particular stress and tension she could regress to behavior patterns of an earlier time. Also, there has been some research that suggests that experiencing a parent's death while a child is "one of the most significant factors" in developing depression in later life. Anger becomes depression when the person turns from directing it outward on the world to inward upon the self.[7]

Ruth's death responses—withdrawal and anger—were exacerbated by a hearing problem, a result of infant measles that was not discovered until she was five years old. She wrote, "My hearing was pretty bad at this time, and doctors began taking out my tonsils and trying by various means to keep my eardrums intact" (p. 105). Her partial deafness contributed to her image as a rebellious child within her family because when she did not answer calls her relatives thought she did this on purpose. Sometimes she did, but sometimes she just could not hear them. Discipline and control become real problems with a child unable to hear well. Parents usually use language to keep children in check. This is less possible with a hearing-impaired child. Such children receive incomplete, often ambiguous speech messages, which can create, in Ruth's own words, a "world of confusion" (p. 99). Within a busy household, sound must often have come to Ruth in confused bursts. In a crowded room sound perhaps became a general murmur she strained to differentiate, often failing in frustration. Children also usually learn to turn their inarticulate rage into angry speech to release anger. But a child with a hearing problem may remain violent, uncontrolled, and respond physically, especially if the hearing impairment develops at a time when tantrums come normally in a child's development, as seems to have been the case with Ruth. An inability to understand or be understood could have led to her use of tantrums and striking out to express her rage and anger at the situation.[8]

But most important, a hearing loss can disconnect a child from life, detach him or her from the surrounding environment and especially from easy, normal contact with other people. It creates a sense of isolation, a sense that others live in a different world where the hard-of-hearing child is a spectator, not a participant. Sounds seem to come from a distance, mostly in a confused jangle if many people are around, and some sounds do not come at all. Her hearing loss probably contributed directly to Ruth's becoming a child who enjoyed being by herself, somewhat secretive, deliberately not answering calls or commands only imperfectly heard. Her hearing problem made it easier to ignore the world of everyday life around her—to live in the "world of her father" and deny the world of her mother and family, a world of chaos and confusion which her hearing problem helped create. Such a hearing loss, research suggests, also helped to detach her from the typical cultural and social roles expected of her as a female, because many role reinforcers are verbal. It made it easier for her to identify with her father rather than her mother.[9]

Along with her tantrums, Ruth suffered as a child from "bilious attacks," or psychophysical vomiting, which she said she did not have before her father died. These attacks occurred from the time she was two or three until she began to menstruate at age twelve, and became rhythmic by age seven or eight, returning about every six weeks, which was the same cycle her menstrual period kept for the first ten years. She wrote, "During these attacks, I lay in bed prostrated with vomiting for a couple of days." She remembered taking "these descents into complete misery" with "a very good grace." She wrote that "The third day, when I sat up in bed for my first poached egg, was always a high watermark of felicity, a day I think of with greater pleasure than any of the days when I was well" (p. 105). The link with the menstrual cycle and her own sense that these attacks had a different source than the tantrums with their vomiting suggest some physical, perhaps hormonal problem, especially since she later was not physically able to have children. But research on these phenomena also suggests that there was a psychological component to these attacks, especially a strong element of self-punishment. Such a purging of self would explain her obvious pleasure and sense of renewal, of purification, at the end of each attack. Perhaps also these attacks served as ways of getting attention from a busy mother, since Ruth remembered herself as a saintly patient, "excellent and uncomplaining" (p. 105).[10]

Besides withdrawal, anger, and illness, Ruth struggled in other ways as a child to come to terms with the fact of death. She searched for the positive aspects of death. She found great beauty in the faces of the dead she came in contact with. As well as the memory of her father's face, she recalled that when she was four her grandmother took her to view a dead baby in a tenant house. Ruth wrote, "I remember vividly her transparent beauty. She seemed to me the loveliest thing I had ever seen" (p. 99). The living suffered by comparison. The beauty of death seemed to her to be a reward for living decently, "for even death couldn't make that special transformation out of a face filled with loathing and pettiness" (p. 99). One could rejoice instead of grieve if a person had won a face filled with death's beauty.

When Ruth was nine, a servant girl who worked at a farm down the road, and who had been her friend, committed suicide. The adults of Ruth's family condemned the girl, and this troubled Ruth, who felt her friend was not wicked. Some weeks later her mother gave Ruth a book on the Romans and she read about the noble suicide of Cato for his country, which helped her feel that suicide was not necessarily wicked and, indeed, held overtones of honor. As a child Ruth thought often of lying dead herself, and when about six used to play "graves" in the barn. She made a cave in the hay completely hidden in the dark and used to go there by herself and "lie in the hot dark" (p. 101). Such play is considered normal among children, who use it to try to handle their feelings about death and come to an understanding of the meaning of death by playing out death and funeral scenes.[11]

Intriguingly, the two worlds of Ruth's childhood mirrored closely the dualities of nineteenth-century American Victorian culture, with its intellectual overlay of Apollonian rationality and order over social irrationality and chaos. In theory the rational objectivity of science quelled intellectual turbulence. Ordered standards of sexuality held in check the bestial nature of men and encouraged the calm passionlessness of women. It was an era that placed a premium on the ordered life, and if social reality did not reflect this necessity, social ideals did to a high degree. The immediate roots of this Victorian imperative for social control lay in the breakdown of social order as America entered the nineteenth century. In Colonial society social stability revolved around a securely hierarchical family pattern of mutual responsibilities and duties. With the new nineteenth-century emphasis on democracy and the impetus of the Industrial Revolution, this social order broke down. Hierarchy gave way to the uncertainties of equality; masters and the journeyman-apprentice group found themselves in confusing and disordered relations as they became owners and workers with opposing goals in the new factory economy.[12]

Moreover, the values of this new industrial era clashed with those of preindustrial society. They set the individual first rather than the family, and seemingly required selfishness, trickery, and sharp dealing to get ahead, thus challenging the primary importance of God and the Christian virtues in the successful life. There was a sense that order needed to be restored. Nineteenth-century America restored order by creating social ideals that compartmentalized life, separating home from workplace, church from daily life, and in the Doctrine of the Spheres compartmentalizing men from women. In the Doctrine of the Spheres Victorian society created as a social ideal a world separated into dual, complementary spheres for men and women: the "world of the father" distinct from the "world of the mother."

Colonial society also had divided life into men's and women's spheres, and, indeed, the practice extended back in time through the Judeo-Christian tradition, but much more informally and with significant areas of overlap. A Colonial woman could do any work, including traditionally masculine work, if it was for the good of the family or her husband agreed. Since home and workplace overlapped, with the shop often attached to the house, women more often participated in activities outside their sphere of home duties. Both men and women, being about the home, participated more evenly in child-rearing. Even religion recognized the overlapping of spheres. A woman might be a "deputy husband." The virtuous woman, on whom Colonial ministers were fond of sermonizing, was she who not only cared for the household, but

> considereth a field, and buyeth it: with the fruit of her hands she planteth a vineyard. . . . She maketh fine linen, and selleth it; and delivereth girdles unto the merchant. (Proverbs 31 : 16, 24)

But by the 1850's the social ideal of men's and women's spheres had rigidified so that the spheres were separated completely and any stepping over the boundaries caused internal and external social conflict. In the words of Catharine Beecher, "The Americans have applied to the sexes the great principle of political economy . . . by carefully dividing the duties of man from those of woman, in order that the great work of society may be the better carried on." Society, threatened by the new uncertainties and disruptive values, contained them by compartmentalizing them and balancing them with the old ideas and values of cooperation, religion, soothing passivity, and the solidity of the family in the woman's sphere. Women's sphere thus acted as a safety valve for the excesses of the men's sphere. In theory, as men moved between home and workplace, the stability of the family would serve to neutralize the potentially disruptive influence of individual choice.[13]

Women's world was the private sphere, the sphere of family and home. Men's world was the public sphere, the sphere of the individual and the workplace. Each had its own set of doctrines, expectations, and tabus. The mythology of domesticity made restriction to the home as woman's proper place a positive virtue, idealizing motherhood and lauding women's moral superiority over men because they were untainted by the competitiveness and amorality of the men's sphere. These ideas were bolstered by the Colonial tradition of women's secondary and subordinate role as helpmate in the natural order. By staying out of the men's sphere, by raising her children in the Christian environment she created, and by using her influence on her husband, the woman supposedly would be doing her part to make the total society a little better. These were the arguments of those who believed in woman's sphere. But those who examined the Doctrine of the Spheres more closely found restriction to the woman's sphere to be a potential prison that was intellectually and creatively deadening, that rewarded passivity and fostered illness, that ignored the chaos inherent in raising children, and that curtailed women's power and autonomy, relegating them to the position of children in relation to men. The ideology of domesticity called for the sacrifice of woman's individuality and creativity and promised her a nebulous authority in the home and moral influence in society through her husband and children in return for acceptance of compartmentalization within the private sphere.[14] By Benedict's standards, on the surface woman's sphere was Apollonian, but beneath the surface at its core it was Dionysian, non-creative, and destructive.

Total acceptance of the spheres represented a social ideal, not social reality, in which women, even the middle-class women to whom the social ideal applied most rigorously, worked outside the home, or kept their roles as deputy husbands, or entered the public sphere as members of church societies, moral reform societies, temperance and abolition societies. As a social ideal the Doctrine of the Spheres began to break up with the Civil War, for as men went off to war women entered the public sphere and found themselves competent to carry on. But the Victorian spheres remained a powerful social force into the Progressive era, an internalized set of standards each woman had to deal with and make decisions about in her own life. Ruth Benedict's use of this duality in her personal worlds suggests that she had to come to terms with these ideas as she was growing up. In her case she implied her rejection of the larger "world of the mother," by making a point of rejecting the Victorian ideal of femininity, the True Woman, in her autobiographical fragments.[15]

Historian Barbara Welter has analyzed the True Woman as portrayed in nineteenth-century women's magazines, gift books, and religious literature, and found that this paragon possessed four cardinal virtues desirable in women: purity, piety, submissiveness, and domesticity. In the last half of the nineteenth century each of these four virtues came to be identified with certain characteristics and exaggerated into a set of absolute behavioral "rules." *Purity* came to be associated with frigidity. The higher a woman rose in the moral sphere, the more the sensual was refined away from her nature. Lack of desire and lack of sexual response were touted as virtues that strengthened women's moral superiority over men. *Piety* meant self-sacrifice and scrupulous religiosity. Examples of this occurred throughout popular literature such as in the series of Elsie Dinsmore books published after the Civil War. In one episode Elsie, the young heroine, refused to violate the Sabbath by playing a non-religious tune on the piano. Her father made her sit at the piano without food until she obeyed him, but she triumphed by falling into a faint. In another episode she refused to read aloud to her father from a secular book on Sunday. *Submissiveness* meant acceptance of woman's inferiority before men and need to lean on them as the stronger sex. Women should be submissive, the nineteenth-century argument went, not because of their place on the hierarchy of the Great Chain of Being as Colonial society believed, but because they were inferior mentally, prone to nervous diseases and hysteria, and physically the frailer, weaker sex. Proofs of women's inferiority were popular topics in medical journals, books, and magazines throughout the last half of the nineteenth century. Finally, in the virtue of *domesticity* homekeeping and motherhood became over-idealized and sentimentalized, women becoming the sacred priestesses of the "haven in a heartless world." [16]

Ruth Benedict, reared in this culture, refused to follow these restrictive guidelines for womanhood. She rejected the Victorian ideal of frigid purity and of women's alienation from sex. As a farm girl she was in an environment where sex was taken for granted. Ironically, since religion was the bastion of purity, she credited the Bible with her knowledge of life. "I can't remember when I did not know about position in intercourse and about semen," she wrote. She knew of everything but menstruation, she continued, "for I learned it all in the Bible stories, and it was all part of a great and good reality that held, too, the best things I knew" (pp. 107–108). As for piety, Ruth grew up in a pious household, where the Sabbath was strictly observed, and where her grandfather led the family in prayer on their knees every morning around the breakfast table. She, however, did not emulate Elsie Dinsmore, at least once getting into trouble for profaning the Sabbath with secular work. She wrote, "I never identified my 'religion' with the authority of the family . . . so that I never had to throw off a yoke of religious submission" (p. 107). As for the ideal of womanly submissiveness, she disliked her Great-Uncle Justin because he was "a big, cocksure man" (p. 109) and she would not submit to being kissed by him even for a fifty-cent piece. Identifying with her father the way she did, Ruth saw herself as the potential equal of any man, not his inferior. Her refusal to cry in public or express pain underscored her rejection of feminine weakness both in ideal and actuality. Crying in any situation was considered normal, especially as women were considered the more emotional sex, and showing pain was not considered remarkable in a culture where women were the frailer sex. In fact, she accepted for herself at least part of the masculine ideal, which did not allow men to cry in public or to appear weak by crying out in pain. On domesticity Ruth wrote that learning how to sew and make clothes as a young girl was "terribly trying to me" (p. 110). It came very hard for her to sew her own underwear and shirtwaists as she was expected to. Her sister Margery learned to sew by making dolls' clothes but, Ruth wrote, "I'd never cared how my dolls were dressed" (p. 110), her indifference toward her dolls a commentary on her future potential for the sacred order of motherhood. Margery even made Ruth's doll a dress once because she was appalled at the state of the doll's clothing, "but it wasn't a distress I could appreciate," Ruth said (p. 111).

There were also cultural resonances in her preoccupation with death. Fascination with death permeated nineteenth-century America. Woman's Rights leader Harriot Stanton Blatch wrote of her childhood in the late 1860's and early 1870's that "The minds of the children of that time in America were much occupied with death, more than the elders realized." She recalled walking often to the cemetery and playing there, acting out stories about rifled graves or Lazarus in the Bible. More morbidly, Victorian Americans worried about premature burial, a subject that spawned a number of books, such as *One Thousand Buried Alive by Their Best Friends* (1890) by M. R. Fletcher, and the classic of the genre, *Buried Alive* (1895) by F. Hartmann. Late-nineteenth-century Americans surrounded death with prolonged, intense rituals. They memorialized their dead with elaborate monuments and minutely ritualized mourning periods. This was all part of a larger cultural phenomenon that made spiritualism or communication with the dead a lucrative profession, that fostered consolation literature as a means of bringing the dead closer to the living, and made cemeteries into rural parks for the living to play and picnic in. Benedict's fascination with death had a local base as well. Within Chenango County at the turn of the century as in other rural communities around America, there was a noted preoccupation with death and especially with suicide and the meaning of suicide reflected in the local newspaper, the *Norwich Sun*. Between 1900 and 1910 the rate of suicide in Chenango County was high, in 1908 the highest suicide rate of any rural county in the state. Author Helen Swick Perry in her 1982 biography of Harry Stack Sullivan noted the "peculiar fascination with suicide and homicide" in Norwich and Chenango County that "existed eighty years ago, and it exists today." [17]

So the "simple theme" which Ruth Benedict tried to set down grows more complex. In being as honest as she could when writing her autobiographical fragments, she saw a pattern dominated by one theme: the overwhelming extent to which psychological events determined her life.

[13]

This emphasis reflected her growing interest in and knowledge of psychology and psychoanalysis in the 1930's, and caused her to overlook other possibilities. She portrayed events growing out of ordinary child development as abnormal. She discounted the profoundly disturbing influence of her hearing impairment, a fact that by itself could possibly account for all the problems she indicated as psychological. She did not even consider a physical cause for her childhood vomiting, although there might well have been one. Nor did she recognize that cultural influences might be at work in her rejection of Victorian beliefs and values concerning women, or her fascination with death.

But in one sense the pattern Ruth Benedict wove when she was forty-eight did reveal, as she had striven to, the "simple theme" of her life to that point, a theme that lay at the heart of *Patterns of Culture:* the struggle between the individual and her culture, and the attempt to remain an individual when one is a misfit in a repressive culture with whose values one cannot agree.

1

Inner Circle, Outer Circle

ON ONE LEVEL, Ruth Fulton Benedict enjoyed a superior status in American society. Her background was securely Anglo-Saxon and evangelical Protestant, so she never had to contend with the marginality of being Jewish as many of her intellectual colleagues did, or face the discrimination accorded Southern and Eastern European immigrants as they flooded into America from the 1890's through the 1920's. Her family background put her among the upwardly mobile middle class. She never had to struggle for an education as many women did—it was given to her as a gift in recognition of outstanding intellectual abilities. She grew up surrounded by a family sure of its special place in society, a family in the tradition of the yeoman farmers from whom the American Republic had sprung, whose pioneer heritage stretched back to the *Mayflower,* and whose blood had flowed at Lexington and other Revolutionary battles. But paradoxically she saw herself as a marginal person in American society, an outsider and observer of American life rather than a participant. This among other things later led her into anthropology, which stressed the outside observation of cultures, and seemed to draw social mavericks and marginal people to itself. The roots of this paradox lie in her relation to her family, both in itself and as the surrogate of the larger culture surrounding her.[1]

On June 5, 1887, when Ruth was born in New York City, life held high promise for Bertrice and Frederick Fulton. New York society welcomed homeopathic physicians. The wealthy preferred the alternative theories and approach of homeopathic medicine which, while offering surgery and other specializations, emphasized fresh air, bed rest, proper diet, and low drug dosages, all much preferable to the bleeding, purging, arsenic tonics, skin blistering, and other heroic therapies prescribed by regular allopathic physicians. Homeopathy had become one of the three major medical sects in post–Civil War America, with an affluent set of patients.

Homeopaths were numerous and influential, especially in New England and in all large cities, where homeopathy appealed to urban middle- and upper-middle-class people seeking a respectable alternative to regular medicine. By the 1880's, New York City had become the major center of homeopathy in America.[2]

In homeopathic circles in New York, Frederick Fulton was known as an up-and-coming young man. After a distinguished undergraduate career and graduation with high honors from Madison College (later Colgate University) in 1882, he had attended the New York Homeopathic Medical College in New York City, one of the best homeopathic schools in America. He had graduated in 1885, winning the Faculty Prize for the highest standing in his class. In a competitive examination he then won the treasured appointment as resident physician at the Hahnemann Hospital, the teaching hospital attached to the medical school, which was well known for its surgical training. In 1886 he left the hospital expecting to develop his own prosperous private practice. That same year he gained appointment as visiting surgeon to the Laura Franklin Free Hospital for Children. The 1880's were a time of great excitement in surgery, the decade of its growth from a crude and dangerous practice with primitive antiseptic precautions into the most prestigious of all medical specialties. At the Laura Franklin Free Hospital, Fulton gained a reputation as a "judicious surgeon" of "distinguished ability."[3]

That same year Fulton became involved with several colleagues in establishing the *North American Journal of Homeopathy*. He served as editor of the Reports of Societies and Hospitals section and contributed editorial columns, original papers, and book reviews to the journal-at-large. Fulton's *Journal* colleagues knew him as a "fluent speaker" and a "forcible and ready writer," with a growing reputation for his strenuous devotion to work. His interest in scientific medicine had led him also to the study of tumors, and he had begun writing a book on the histology of tumors for which he himself was drawing the illustrations, an exacting and time-consuming process. Professionally Fulton could look forward to a position of growing prosperity, power, and leadership in the ranks of his colleagues, coupled with respect for his work as a medical researcher and scholar.[4]

Personally his life looked bright as well. With the establishment of his own private practice, he and Bertrice Shattuck were able finally to marry. They had been engaged for six years, but in the 1880's middle-class people did not marry until they could afford to set up a household, and they had accepted this as a given. On July 14, 1886, they were married on the

Shattuck farm by Frederick Fulton's uncle, the well-known Brooklyn Baptist minister, Justin D. Fulton, assisted by Fred's brother, Rev. Charles A. Fulton, himself a newly married man. A little over ten months later their daughter Ruth was born.[5]

Bertrice Shattuck Fulton had grown up on the Shattuck farm. The Fultons had moved to Norwich in 1876 when she was sixteen and Frederick Fulton was nineteen, and they had become engaged when she was about twenty and he twenty-three. As a young woman Bertrice attended Norwich Academy, and for most middle-class young women of her generation that would have been the outer limit of education. But, possibly influenced by the example of her older sister Hetty (or Hettie), who had attended Vassar for one year in 1871–1872, she enrolled at Vassar in 1881, graduating Phi Beta Kappa in 1885. The next year she taught at Miss Mittleberger's School in Cleveland, Ohio, marrying Frederick Fulton the summer after. Bertrice was the first member of her class to have a child, and Ruth became the Class Baby of Vassar '85.[6]

The future seemed full of possibility for the Fultons in 1887 when Ruth was born. But the next year something happened. Sometime around January 1888, Frederick Fulton became ill. According to Ruth Benedict he was infected during an operation. In the 1880's, a time when the germ theory was still being debated in medical journals, many surgeons still operated with ungloved hands. According to family history, Fulton was stuck with a dirty needle during an operation in which he was not wearing rubber gloves.[7] But his obituary by colleagues at the *North American Journal of Homeopathy* records a different version of Fulton's illness. It states that in the strain of his "untiring activity," and the stress of setting up and maintaining his own practice along with all the other work he was doing, "his nervous energy failed." This suggests that his colleagues considered him to be a victim of neurasthenia, which by the late nineteenth century had become the "predominant malady of modern culture," more prevalent in cities than in rural areas, more common among professionals and white-collar workers than among blue-collar or farm workers. The symptoms of neurasthenia were almost unlimited but the results were the same—the victim found himself or herself "without the reserve or imput [*sic*] of nervous energy necessary to keep a healthy balance." The primary prescription for neurasthenia was a rest cure which provided relaxation from the hectic and exhaustive pace of urban life, preferably through a return for a time to wholesome country living. Whatever the cause, Frederick Fulton could not shake off his illness. When Bertrice became pregnant again, they decided to return to Norwich. Their families, who lived in and around Norwich, offered economic and moral support, and it was these people of this farming community in upper New York state who surrounded Ruth in her formative years.[8]

Both sides of her family were prominent and respected in Norwich civic and religious life. Her paternal grandfather, Samuel J. Fulton, was a well-known physician in Norwich and the leading exponent of homeopathy in Chenango County. He had been born in Sherburne, New York, in July 1825, the son of one of the pioneer ministers in that area. He studied medicine with Dr. Amos Walker in Pontiac, Michigan, then graduated from a two-year course at the Western Homeopathic College at Cleveland, Ohio, in 1850. He practiced medicine in Michigan, and then Toledo, Ohio, where Fred Fulton was born. He thought for awhile of giving up medicine for business, then in August 1876 received a call to take up a practice in Norwich, where he spent the last twenty years of his life. He became a medical and community leader in the county. He had a reputation for a natural diagnostic ability, and other physicians, allopaths and eclectic doctors as well as homeopaths, frequently consulted him. For years he was the secretary, then president, of the county homeopathic association. He took "a lively interest in every public movement," and became "an earnest supporter" of anything that seemed to be for the betterment of Norwich. A devoted Baptist, he was known in his community for his extensive Bible study. He raised his children "in the religious atmosphere which marked his own early home life."[9]

His wife, Harriet Fisher Fulton, was born in England December 14, 1826, the third of eleven children, and came to America with her family in 1834 when she was seven years old. She attended a female seminary in Norwalk, Ohio, and afterward became a teacher at a preparatory school connected with the University of Michigan located in Tecumseh, Michigan. At Tecumseh she met and married Samuel Fulton, January 26, 1853. They had four children: a daughter, Ella, born November 29, 1853; Willie, who died in childhood and about whom no other information is available; Fred, born September 17, 1857; and Charles, born in December 1860. Like her husband, Harriet Fulton was "an earnest worker in all branches of the church," so long as her health permitted. But she apparently had severe health problems and was an invalid for years. During Ruth's childhood her Aunt Ella taught in the Norwich public schools. Later in her life, Ella became Dean of Women at the University of North Dakota. Ruth's Uncle Charles became a successful Baptist minister with churches in various cities during her childhood, ending his career with a church in Colorado Springs, Colorado.[10]

Bertrice's father, John Samuel Shattuck, was a prominent local farmer, respected by his neighbors and fellow farmers as both progressive and scientific. He had deep roots in the land. His family had farmed in Chenango County since the 1790's, moving into the area a few years after the founding of Norwich. He had been born there in 1827 and lived his life in the county. After his marriage on May 29, 1850, he and his wife lived in a house on his parents' farm, where their first child was born. Three years later they bought the Avery farm three miles south of Norwich on the Oxford-Norwich road, and from that time onward it was known to all the neighbors as the Shattuck farm. Shattuck was a respected deacon of the First Baptist Church and, according to his obituary, "a man of mark in his community." [11]

His wife, Joanna Terry Shattuck, born September 10, 1827, in New Berlin, New York, moved to the Norwich area with her parents at age eighteen. In 1850 she married John Samuel on her parents' farm. Four years later they were both baptized together into the fellowship of the First Baptist Church, and from that time their lives became "fully identified with their church in every department of its work." Joanna Terry Shattuck, as wife and mother, "won the crowning glory of true womanhood." A woman "amiable and lovable," she possessed a "strong character" in a time when character for a woman meant ability to endure, do one's duty, and adhere to the strictest of moral codes. She was a "sympathizing friend and neighbor and zealous church worker" but "her true kingdom was her home." [12]

Joanna and John Shattuck had four children, all daughters. Ruth's mother, Bertrice, was the second. Bertrice's parents and sisters were important figures in Ruth's life. In 1888, when Ruth's family moved back to the farm, all three sisters were unmarried and living at home. Hetty was thirty-seven while Mamie and Myra were twenty-one and twenty respectively. They had all attended Norwich Academy (Norwich High School) and all were active in the Baptist church. All three were interested in the family and family history. They were lively and assertive; always, though, within the limits allowed them by tradition and custom.

Hetty, after her brief sojourn at Vassar, had returned home to her father's farm, probably because of her health, and remained there. Her religious life was "deep and intense," marked by "conscientious zeal and undeviating devotion to every duty." She had a talent for teaching. For several years in Norwich she taught a Sunday school class for boys and young men noted for its size and high attendance rate. She had an "active and richly endowed mind" that she "cultivated by extensive and well-directed reading and study." She also had "an executive gift, that made her capable and reliable in every position which she was called upon to fill." Hetty, more than any of the others, became part of Ruth's immediate family in childhood, traveling with them to Missouri, Minnesota, and finally Buffalo, taking care of the house and family while Bertrice worked.[13]

After high school Mary, or Mamie, spent two years in study at the Boston School of Oratory, developing a talent for presenting and interpreting drama and literature. A woman of "keen intellect" and a "rare and vivid personality," full of extroverted enthusiasm and enjoyment of life, she was at a period of transition from school to the adult world. Before she married and moved to Buffalo in 1896, she left the farm and returned several times—for summer vacations and between teaching jobs in Columbus, Ohio, and the Mary Baldwin Seminary in Staunton, Virginia. When Ruth was eleven and Bertrice Shattuck Fulton moved her family to Buffalo, they lived in the top part of Mamie's house while her family lived below, a situation that continued until Ruth was grown.[14]

Myra, the youngest daughter, did not go on for any higher education, nor did she ever marry. She stayed home to care for her aging parents, and at their deaths she took over the farm and kept it going, becoming a farmer in her own right. She had a questioning and enquiring mind, whose "interests and ideas progressed through the years as the needs of the world changed." She became interested in genealogy and history, later in life becoming president of the Chenango County Historical Society. She had an "unassuming way" and an "ability to work quietly and humbly, without the slightest thought of self." Myra became Ruth's favorite aunt, and after she became an anthropologist, the farm became a refuge to return to every summer to work and visit with her aunt.[15]

This was the family circle Frederick and Bertrice Fulton returned to in 1888. They stayed with the Shattucks, probably because Bertrice was pregnant and to avoid the burden of an invalid mother-in-law. It is possible Fred practiced some medicine with his father in Norwich during these months, but overall it was a time of "disappointing retirement," lightened only by the birth of a second daughter, Margery, December 26, 1888. As a last measure Frederick Fulton took a voyage to the Caribbean which he hoped would restore his health, going to Trinidad as Ruth Benedict wrote, "in a vain attempt to throw off the fever that was killing him." But he developed Acute Bright's Disease (kidney failure) and died within two weeks after his return home, on March 26, 1889. He was thirty-one years old when he died. His wife, Bertrice, was twenty-eight, and left with Ruth, then twenty-one months old, and Margery, only three months old. Bertrice and the children stayed on the farm until the girls were old enough to start school, then returned each summer thereafter during the girls' childhoods. So the farm formed the early environment of Ruth Benedict's life—the farm, and the large farm family who gave her a sense of the acceptable values and limits of her world in the Victorian twilight of the nineteenth century.[16]

Late Victorian America was a country preoccupied with national identity and belief in the cultural superiority of the American-born, especially in the face of the flood of immigrants beginning to pour into the United States in the 1890's from Eastern and Southern Europe. Native-born Americans thought that Anglo-Saxons had a spirit of enterprise and resourcefulness, a special love of liberty, and a capacity for practical, reasonable behavior above that of other races. From native American stock came the yeoman-farmer, the citizen-soldier who had answered the call at Lexington and Concord, the philosopher-workman tilling the land and conversing knowledgeably on all issues. Both sides of Benedict's family took pride in a distinguished heritage. In an era when the yeoman-farmer remained the national ideal, the Shattucks had farmed land in Chenango County since 1799, when the first Shattucks had come west from New England to settle the wild new land. Family history said they had come in a bobsled with a cow tied behind to ensure milk for the babies en route. If Chenango County was now a settled agricultural district, still the pioneer tradition remained. The Shattuck family could congratulate itself on representing "a fair average specimen of the honest, independent yeomanry . . . the foundation strength and energy of the republic."[17]

In a country still conscious of its newness, the Shattucks took pride in the fact that they could trace their family line back to the Pilgrims on the *Mayflower* through Ruth's maternal grandmother, Joanna Terry Shattuck. In an era when social standing in America came either from wealth or membership in the Daughters of the American Revolution (DAR), the family could claim a lineage of distinction. Four of Ruth's forebears on the Shattuck-Terry side had fought in the Revolutionary War as privates and corporals. A fifth, Lt. John Shattuck, was one of the immortal few who had answered the summons to Lexington. On the Fulton side of the family her ancestry was equally distinguished. According to family history her great-great-grandfather, Samuel King Fulton, had had to flee from Canada after daring to drink a public toast to George Washington around the time of the War of 1812. Lord Cornwallis, then Governor of Nova Scotia and a distant relative, kept him from being sent as a prisoner to Bombay, India, for this. Her great-grandfather, John I. Fulton, fought in the War of 1812. In 1822 he was licensed to preach by a church founded by followers of Roger Williams, the great Colonial advocate of religious freedom, and became one of the pioneer ministers on the frontier of upper New York state.[18]

This family heritage remained a living one. Ruth once joked that she was allowed to be radical in Norwich because her grandfather had voted for Bryan in 1896. Democrat William Jennings Bryan campaigned for President as the defender of the yeoman-farmer, desiring a purge of alien corruption and a return to the simplicity and virtue of the old Republic. Bryan preached a politics of salvation an old-line Baptist could identify with, the forces of light facing the forces of darkness. In voting for Bryan Ruth's grandfather was voting for a return to the old virtues in which he believed. Among the women, Ruth's mother and her aunts Mamie and Myra became members of the DAR, and the two aunts remained active members until the ends of their lives. Both aunts became experts on Colonial furniture, glassware, and other antiques, which both collected and treasured in their homes, Myra especially "with the thought that they would give to other generations a knowledge of what had been used in the past." Benedict herself wrote as an adult, "My own grandparents were Puritans, and no better stock was ever reared in any country that I know of."[19]

Ruth Fulton Benedict's was a family conscious of its special place in the inner circle of American culture, secure in an identity and status as Americans that the millions of immigrants streaming in would struggle to acquire over painful years and sometimes through generations. In the receiving of this heritage Ruth participated in full measure. Many of the themes she wrote in high school showed that the Colonial and Revolutionary periods sparked her imagination. "Old Esther Dudley" tells the story within a story of a little baby given into a Colonial governor's wife's charge during a smallpox epidemic; in the end, the baby turns out to be the narrator, Esther Dudley. "The Perseverance of Sir William Phipps" is another story within a story, this one told about Colonial times during the American Revolution; the boy listening to the story is revealed at the end as John Quincy Adams, sixth president of the United States. In the story Phipps is a Tory, but admirable as a self-made man who starts as the son of a shepherd in England and becomes wealthy and a governor of Massachusetts because he perseveres. At the end John Quincy decides that when he grows up he wants to be brave like Washington and persevering like William Phipps, a sentiment uniting the best in the Tory past with the best in the Revolutionary past.[20] Benedict shared fully in the family heritage, although in the everyday world of the family, she learned early and on a basic personal level to regard herself as an outsider.

In the everyday farm world, life for women in the late nineteenth century went from dawn to dusk and beyond. Besides making most of the family clothing, farm women spent hours in their kitchens baking bread and cooking, peeling potatoes, snapping beans, shelling peas, canning and preserving fruits and vegetables, churning butter. In this life of constant and necessary household chores, children received their share to do as soon as possible. In such a bustle of work, it was hard for Ruth to find peace or privacy. One of her prized memories as a small child was of shelling peas for the family, which took a long time since there were so many to feed, "at peace on the front porch while everybody else was busy in the kitchen" ("The Story of My Life," p. 100). Another good memory was of sitting on the woodhouse steps, holding a sleeping kitten in her lap, looking out over the hills. She sought out refuges from the family— as an older child, the attic and an old elm tree out in a pasture. As a preschooler, the barn became her chief retreat—a place where she would go to be by herself and hide under a big beam where "one could make a cavern in the hay completely concealed in the dark," and lie there and think. The barn was also a familiar play area, a place for jumping in the hay and playing hide-and-go-seek. At age five she jumped off a beam in the barn and sprained her ankle. Ruth was encouraged to be an active child. As she later wrote, "The family could always understand jumping in the hay, but they could never have understood lying in the dark in the hay if there wasn't a hide-and-seek game going on" (p. 101). The former was understandable, normal, acceptable; the latter was strange, unreasonable, peculiar behavior, therefore condemned. The family, like the society it was an extension of, valued the sensible over the seemingly senseless. The young Ruth was a daydreamer with a series of vivid imaginary worlds as she grew up. This put her in conflict with the family emphasis on common sense.[21]

From Ruth's point of view, it was a family of people who clashed and jangled. As a preschooler she would go off in her mind with her imaginary playmate and sometimes they would visit this little girl's family, who lived "a warm, friendly life without recriminations and brawls," apparently unlike Ruth's own (p. 100). She mentions this one other time. She remembered days when she shelled peas on the front porch, "happy there in the sunshine . . . and I'd come into the kitchen where some fracas was going on among the aunts. Something in me was murdered—something that might have lived all that day."[22] The women were apparently a lively group, at times loud, each of whom did not hesitate to assert her rights, ideas, and opinions on the way things should be around the house, and probably in the world, and on the raising of children, especially Ruth. Ruth's response to this as a small child was either to assert her own will and anger in a tantrum or to slip away from the family to be alone. Running away and having tantrums were her "family crimes" as a small child. The family was incensed by them, not only because they occurred over and over, and caused inconvenience and disruption, but precisely because they did not fit the ways the family or Victorian society resolved conflict. They were outside the boundaries of the allowed and expected. In Victorian society, self-control was the goal—the development of an inner-directed character capable of meeting and defeating the threats to an orderly life. Family irritation at Ruth's tantrums multiplied precisely because they were "irrational" and showed her lack of self-control. "The family were constantly exercised about my ungovernable tantrums," she wrote, which "came on for no reason the family could fathom." After them she was "always punished and wept over" (p. 100). Her lack of inner-direction pushed her over the acceptable boundaries of action in the family and the standards set by Victorian society.

Her sister Margery's behavior, on the other hand, was reasonable and rational from an early age. The family showered its approval on her. Margery was "a cherubically beautiful child with no behavior problems" (p. 103) and the family "always talked of her beauty" (p. 104). The only time Ruth remembered hearing that she was beautiful came not from a family member, but from a visitor, when she was fourteen. "It is the single comment of the sort," she wrote, "I ever heard till I was thirty" (p. 104). Margery wrote "a neat round hand," but Ruth's was "hen tracks" (p. 111). Ruth was not considered "handy" around the house, not good at the practical details of sewing dresses and underclothes or the myriad household tasks that made up the world of the Victorian woman. One of the hardest jobs Ruth Benedict remembered as an adult was washing dishes at the farm, starting when she was about nine or ten. There were always thirteen or fourteen people at the table and it was Ruth's job to wash the breakfast and dinner dishes while her sister dried. This also meant carrying water to the house and heating it on the stove to wash the dishes, since interior plumbing did not become part of most farms until after World War I. "I think I have never since been so tired as I used to be when I finished," she wrote (p. 106). To keep from crying with weariness she kept a glass of water on a shelf and drank down the lump in her throat. If that didn't work, she went to the privy to cry in private. After doing the dishes she often hid in the attic to cry out the rest of her tears. "I would look at the aunts and think how terrible it was that everyone was as tired as I was" (p. 106). From an early age she knew that the lot of a woman was hard, wearying physical labor in the service of family over self, and she felt a misfit in it. When she was learning how to sew, "it came very hard. I don't doubt the family suffered" (p. 111).

Or if she did bring enthusiasm to sewing, it came at an "impractical" time. She remembered once when she was ten and "being put through my first hated paces in sewing," one Saturday afternoon she suddenly felt "that warm glow about making the pair of drawers I had to do next. All the week's work had been put away in the house" in preparation for Sunday, but she got out her bolt of cloth and began to cut. One of her aunts found her at work and indignantly made her put it all away. "She belabored me well and I was embroiled."[23] But, she wrote, "I fulfilled the family requirements after a fashion. They didn't expect me to be 'handy' anyway; Margery was the 'handy' one" (p. 111). The family, again like the society it was an extension of, valued the practical and the useful over the impractical, doing over dreaming, and the active over the mystical. The same was true in religion.

Religion was an important factor in Ruth's childhood. "I was brought up in the midst of the church," she wrote (p. 107), and also in the midst of a pious family. They kept the Sabbath strictly and prayed daily together. When Ruth called the picture of Christ on the wall her father, her grandparents were "shocked with the blasphemy," or at least the naïveté of her words (p. 99). The children went to church and Sunday school as a matter of course. From age eleven through adolescence Ruth and her sister earned five cents a week for church and a penny for Sunday school by learning three verses of the Bible a day and six on Sunday. They learned "dozens and dozens of chapters" (p. 111). Her fantasy world came from the Bible and she made an identification between Christ and her father: the one stood in some non-explicit way for the other. "The story of Jesus was 'my' world," she wrote, that is, the world of her father. "Christ was a real person to me," she added, "and my favorite company" (p. 107). She loved the story of Christ and felt she knew it better than the ministers before she was ten. Although she read extensively, no other books competed with the Bible. "The story of Ruth was better than *Ramona*," she wrote, "and the poetry of Job was better than Longfellow" (p. 111).

But it was not institutional Christianity that attracted her, or church creeds. Ruth's was not an intellectual religion, nor a practical one. "Theological doubts never raised their heads against me," she wrote. She never identified her religion with dogma or family authority, so she never had to work free from a "yoke of religious submission" (p. 107). Nor did she see charity or missionary work as the road to God. Hers was a mystical approach to religion. For her the gospels described a way of life and Christ took the place of the playmate over the hill she had given up when she was five. Prayer also became important. "Prayer was better than the playmate over the hill, but still it was much the same" (p. 107). Her grandfather used one phrase over and over again in every prayer that stuck in her consciousness: that the Lord should lead the family toward "the light that shineth more and more unto the perfect day" (p. 102). It was to this mystical aspect of religion that Ruth was irresistibly drawn. "My 'religious' life was from childhood a picture of retiring into a room where no one else came but myself," she wrote. "I never brought there anything from this world, not even God." This room merged in her mind with the hillside where the beautiful beings moved, "where all life could be full of recollection and of dignity," and where the deepest experiences of insight and beauty were possible.[24] Moreover, she had a childhood experience that tended to turn her from trust in ministers and institutional authority. Her Great-Uncle Justin Fulton, a respected minister and author, said that he had had a revelation from God that her father would not die, but of course he had died. The didactic, self-righteous style of fundamentalist Victorian Christianity epitomized by her Great-Uncle Justin revolted her. Besides, he always made her mother sad. "When he came to our house he always prayed on his knees with the whole family," she wrote, "and I was afraid my mother would weep" (p. 109).

Ruth lived on the edge of the appropriate and acceptable boundaries the family laid out as given and too often stepped outside them, to the active disapproval of family society. She failed, more often than not, to live up to family and Victorian standards of practical common sense, rational and orderly action, and competence. She learned early that approval would not come to her in great quantities from the family and by extension from the larger society it represented. The difference between her place in the family and her sister's epitomized the ways in which she always felt marginal. In the world of the family Ruth and her sister were compared with Martha and Mary in the Bible. Mary sat at the feet of Jesus and listened, while her practical sister Martha bustled about doing the necessary work of preparing dinner for Jesus and his disciples. Margery was the Martha, bustling around, a budding True Woman, while Ruth was Mary, the mystic, the non-domestic. But it was "handiness" and common sense the family valued, not mysticism. Margery became the "family favorite and pet" (p. 104), while Ruth felt the oppressive sense of losing out in the family's approval because she did not meet their standards. Margery, with her blond hair and sunny temperament, was the family child of light. Ruth, with her dark hair, secretiveness, and tantrums, was the child of darkness.

Ruth wanted family approval. She wanted her grandfather's approval enough to lie to him to retain it in one instance. In the hierarchy of Ruth's affections, her grandfather, John Samuel Shattuck, was "the one person who stood out for me above all others." He was a tall, spare man with a white beard, "a grand old man with strong, calm movements, a patriarch" (p. 102). Though after her tantrums Ruth brushed off the punishments administered by the rest of the family, "Grandfather's rising from his chair and going to the barn was a terrible memory. I did not have tantrums after that when he was in the house" (p. 102). This quiet rejection by the grandfather she loved was a more terrible punishment than the anger and physical punishments of other family members. On the other hand, to be singled out by Grandfather was an event to be cherished. One day as a small child she left the elder patch where her mother allowed her to play and took off for the flat, a long distance that meant crossing some railroad tracks, which was not allowed. When she got there she found her grandfather haying on the flat. He welcomed her "royally." He took her on the haywagon to load the hay and into the barn while he pitched in the hay. She rode up with the empty wagons when he came up for milking. At that point she had to tell him her mother didn't know she had gone down there. He smiled down at her and said, "Well, if she doesn't ask, we won't tell her." Ruth recalled this as "a high point in my life. I had a secret with Grandfather, and I could see that he liked it as well as I did." Her mother did ask, and Ruth said she had been playing in the elder patch the whole time. That evening after milking, when he came in to supper, her grandfather lifted her up and whispered, "Did Mother ask?" She wrote, "What could I do? I said no, and he smiled at me again" (pp. 102–103).

Ruth viewed her sister's place in the family's inner circle with an outsider's wistfulness which sometimes broke out into open rebellion as in tantrums she would strike at her sister. This happened often enough that their mother was "always worrying about my hurting her" (p. 103). One of her few remembrances of family approval occurred when she was around nine or ten years old. She had begun writing small pieces and "Uncle Will," William Ellis, a patent lawyer who married Aunt Mamie in 1896, offered her a dollar if she would copy ten of them into a notebook for him to keep. She felt "a great sense of pride and responsibility." The sense of approval even then was mixed. Uncle Will was a newcomer to the family, and her mother disapproved of his giving her so much money. She thought it wasn't a good idea to give Ruth "an inflated sense of what her scribblings were worth." But, Ruth wrote, "I think it was only fair to counterbalance for the moment my abiding sense of Margery's 'handiness'" (p. 111).

As a schoolgirl she wrote several short papers based on Henry Wadsworth Longfellow's narrative poem "Evangeline," the story of an outcast people, the Acadians, exiled from their homeland in Nova Scotia to Louisiana in a move which tore up families and caused unnecessary deaths and suffering among those who survived. She identified with the outcast Acadians, especially Evangeline, whose father died and who wandered continuously from place to place searching for Gabriel, her lost love. In what is apparently the earliest of the series, "The Passing of Gabriel," Evangeline has fallen asleep on an island after searching constantly for Gabriel, and he passes by on the water while she sleeps, in a "vain search for a land where he might forget his sorrow" at his alone and outcast state. Another, "The Home of Evangeline," describes the "home of peace, a harbour of love and helpfulness," from which Evangeline was exiled. A third of the series, "A Blessed Incident," tells the tale of a Shawnee woman outcast from her people for loving a white man who has been murdered by hostile Indians and her chance meeting with Evangeline one evening on her journey back to her people. The two outcasts share their stories and weep together, Evangeline comforting the Indian. "We seemed like beings apart," Ruth wrote, "watching from our small corner, the progress of the world." Into the Evangeline stories Ruth poured out her own feelings of exile from home, search for loving approval, and sense of solitariness through this heroine, sometimes girl, sometimes woman, "beautiful as the sun."[25] That this sense of being an outsider was conscious as well as unconscious is evident from her recognition of Mabel Dodge, the future Bohemian New York salon leader, as a fellow outsider. As Ruth wrote, Dodge was "The first person I ever saw who, I knew, belonged somewhere else than in the world I stood so aloof from. . . . I remember knowing that she lived for something I recognized, something different from those things for which most people around me lived" (p. 109).

Benedict's sense of singularity taught her to depend on her own ideas over those of others. Before she was six she decided to leave out the "Forgive us our sins" in the Lord's prayer in order to make herself responsible for her own actions. "I never discussed the matter with anyone . . . I hadn't discovered that there could be any authority over and above the fact that it didn't seem right to me," she wrote of the incident (p. 103). Margaret Mead suggested in *An Anthropologist at Work* (pp. 83–84) that Ruth Benedict as a child had a great many thoughts her family considered shocking or blasphemous and therefore she was thrown back into herself, because, as Benedict wrote, to tell people things that mattered to her might either hurt them or make them interfere, probably with the intent of changing her ideas to conform with theirs.

She did not accept as automatic sins those things that society or family said were wrong. She did not internalize the social guilt for her tantrums the family expected her to feel, the desire to get back into tune with social mores. She made up her own list of sins that involved a desire not to be right in the eyes of society, but to be right with herself. She felt guilt about her tantrums, "not because I was responsible for them and they were wicked," but because their violence spoiled her moments of internal happiness. This was a guilt toward herself, reflecting a desire to get back in harmony with the best in herself, not with society. She recalled going down to the old elm in the pasture with guilt on her soul. "There were the hills, and the grass, and the clouds, but I was guilty before them; I had lost the part of me that had communion with them." [26] She did not identify her own version of right and wrong with the authority of the family. Instead she saw right and wrong as fluid, and life as an "education in the complexities of ethics" (p. 103). She balanced her actions not on the Victorian absolute scale of right and wrong, but on the relative scale of what seemed right and wrong to her. When she was a preschooler it did not seem wrong to her to lie to her mother about where she had been playing, yet it mattered to her when she lied to her grandfather, because she had won approval under false pretenses. "He was one of my self-elected loyalties," she wrote, "and I'd been false to it." She punished herself by eating no supper. "Life was more complicated than I had supposed, and somehow, somehow after that, I must plan so that I wouldn't have to *lie to Grandfather*" (p. 103). When the girl down the road drowned herself, Ruth remembered that "everyone in my world had said this was a wicked act." Ruth could not agree with this. When she read of the suicide of Cato for the ancient Roman Republic she ran to her mother "with great excitement . . . Perhaps now I could convince my mother that the servant girl wasn't wicked either." She did not convince her mother, "But I gathered that different times and different countries didn't agree in the judgments they made."[27] The family's value judgments were absolute moral statements that Ruth could not believe in.

"I never entirely understood her—but I understood her so much better than did our Mother," wrote her sister Margery as an adult. To her mother Ruth must have seemed a puzzle, a frustrating child with a hearing handicap, odd ideas, and abrupt changes of temper and mood, who resisted her guidance and rules. But in some ways her mother was as much of a puzzle to Ruth, for as a role model Bertrice Shattuck Fulton's life gave ambiguous, conflicting messages to her daughter. Bertrice had attended Vassar at a time when this was a daring, pioneering act. There was doubt that women were equipped to handle the pressures of higher education. In 1882, while Bertrice attended Vassar, Henry N. Guernsey in *Plain Talks on Avoided Subjects* told Americans that too much mental activity by women could cause "ovarian neuralgia" resulting in the inability of the body to supply both brain and ovaries with blood and therefore threatening women's later ability to bear healthy children. Moreover women were considered susceptible to nervous exhaustion due to brainwork. Doctors saw educated women as potentially easy victims of nervous disease. Women who went to Vassar and the other rigorous schools for women frequently regarded themselves and were regarded by society as "strong-minded" women, claiming mental equality with men and vigorously pushing aside obstacles to the use of their mental powers; or as "dangerous" women, women out to upset the boundaries of ordinary society, to turn the world upside down. Vassar opened in 1865 with the purpose of giving women the advantage of rigorous higher education hitherto reserved chiefly for young men. Women in the 1880's still looked upon this as a challenge and many of the women graduates of these years did not marry but devoted their lives to careers in the public sphere. By going to Vassar, Bertrice Shattuck Fulton showed herself to be an uncommon woman of her generation, with courage, initiative, and intellectual drive.[28]

But Bertrice married quickly, one year out of college, and while she was married she followed the expected patterns of nineteenth-century wifehood and motherhood. While Frederick Fulton was alive she did not work outside the home, concentrating instead on her husband and children. At his death she grieved in the manner expected of her by her society. Nevertheless, she did not collapse into helplessness, as her vigorous later life shows. Although her mother's grieving seemed excessive to Ruth both in 1935 and as a child, it was not excessive by the standards of the time period in which it occurred. In an age of expected moderation and strict morality in life, of repressed sexuality and a passion for rational order, death practices became an accepted social safety valve—an area where excess emotion was allowed and expected, where sentimentality and evangelical fervor ruled. People were encouraged to grieve openly and loudly.

The late-nineteenth-century pattern of grief was public and social. People wore elaborate mourning clothes for long periods of time and decorated their homes with crepe and funeral wreaths. Funerals were public events at which anyone could stop and grieve with the family. Ruth Benedict went with her grandmother when she was four years old "in the casual neighborhood custom of that farming country," to a house where a baby had died, "and we saw the dead child as a matter of course" (p. 99). This was a widespread custom, and not only in the country. Harriot Stanton Blatch, a daughter of Elizabeth Cady Stanton and herself a feminist leader, recalled her own post–Civil War childhood: "My sister and her older group frequently attended funerals. They were merely passing, and seeing the signs of mourning, dropped into houses where the family was quite unknown to them. Sometimes they took me." The girls also wept with the grieving families, "honestly moved to tears." Sunday funerals became an established custom, in order to encourage larger numbers of people to attend. Some families even hired bands to attract crowds, and as a result strangers and sightseers often crowded cemeteries on Sundays in the 1880's and 1890's. As the century turned, this custom began to be debated critically in serious journals. By World War I many of these practices had faded, and after the war grief became a private and personal matter.[29] But when Frederick Fulton died, his contemporaries would have been extremely surprised if his young widow had not collapsed with grief. Nor would her annual grieving have been thought bizarre, but a sentimental and moving way of keeping her husband's memory alive. Her brief marriage and intense love remained the focal point of her life. Her remembrances kept their father alive for the girls, and it is likely that the pattern of her marriage became the model Ruth Benedict internalized as necessary for the fulfilled life: the expectation that marriage must be the product of a "great love," or it should not be entered into at all.

When Ruth and Margery were old enough to start school, Bertrice Fulton returned to work as a teacher, a job she had held in the year before her marriage. She held a series of teaching jobs, then became Superintendent of Circulation at a large public library. Yet when her children were grown she left this job to live with her daughter Margery's family, content to be a live-in grandmother and help take care of Margery's children. Thus Ruth got the idea that women should excel intellectually, attend college, work outside the home and be economically independent, but at the same time received the conflicting message that traditional wifehood and motherhood were the supreme goals and ultimate fulfillment of a woman's life, a message reinforced by society. It took Ruth several years as an adult to work out a solution to these conflicts in her own life.

As a child Ruth learned early that she would orbit in the outer circle of her mother's attention and approval, seldom gaining the inner circle for herself. When Frederick Fulton died, Bertrice Shattuck Fulton had a three-month-old baby to care for and was prostrate with grief. There was little room close to her mother for Ruth at such a time. During Ruth's childhood her mother was constantly busy, first at the farm and then with her teaching and library positions. Again, there was little time for closeness. As Ruth grew, genuine differences in temperament and interests tended to widen the gap between them as individuals. Ruth mentioned her mother had no appreciation of art, an area Ruth delighted in (p. 98). Her mother's sentimentality repelled Ruth, as did her worry over little things and her need for security. Ruth did not worry over small things or the material world, and did not internalize the romantic sentimentalism common among women of the late nineteenth century. Ruth found her mother's responses irritating, embarrassing, and exasperating, and it is quite likely Bertrice felt the same responses on her part toward Ruth. Bertrice Fulton's reasoning seems to have been more precise and practical than her daughter Ruth's. From the scant evidence available she seems to have been a woman who thought inductively, concerned with the orderly development of an idea and with the fine gradations of arguments, a woman who wanted all categories clear before joining battle. Her granddaughter wrote of her that she read copiously and loved discussing world problems, and the big dictionary came out almost every time their family sat down to dinner.[30] Ruth was the more intuitive thinker, not so concerned with details as with the creative inner leap to a whole concept. People with these two thinking styles tend to clash when they come into contact with each other. In spite of Ruth's image of her mother as an uncontrolled emotional hysteric, Bertrice Shattuck Fulton seems to have been temperamentally calm and rational. Her style of discipline supports this. Her method of handling Ruth's not answering her calls was not to scold or beat her, but to reward her with a penny for each day she managed to answer when called. Ruth's turbulence must have repelled Bertrice as much as her weeping repelled Ruth.

The pattern Ruth developed as a child toward her mother contained the conflicting desire to express anger and resistance, yet at the same time a need for her mother's approval, attention, and love.[31] Ruth remembered one time as a preschooler when she got in trouble with her mother for running away while her mother was away for a few days and refusing to tell her about it. Her mother determined that she would stay in the house as punishment until she talked. After several days of this, during which "the whole family were hard put to it," and after she had managed to leave the spigot open on the kerosene can in the woodhouse, her mother took her to the downstairs bedroom and told her she would have nothing to eat until she talked. Then her mother sat with Ruth the whole day, a caring, supportive act, until Ruth could tell her. All day Ruth struggled with herself. Finally, after dark, she got out the story, feeling relief "like physical drunkenness." Then, the reward: "Mother took me out to the dining room and we ate together alone by the lamplight" (p. 101). Ruth, angry that her mother had gone away in the first place, ran away though she had promised not to (resistance) and refused to tell her mother about it when she asked (further resistance). She kept up her resistance for several days. Then when her mother concentrated on her, sat with her, paid attention to her, she struggled past her anger and resistance to win her mother's approval and love.

Not answering when called was another form of resistance Ruth practiced. Lying is a common action for small children just learning their social boundaries, but can hold overtones of resistance. In the story about her grandfather Ruth's lying to her mother contained that kind of resistance to her authority to set bounds. In a small way, she had beaten her mother's rules.[32] The psychophysical vomiting suggests the same need to resist, yet gain nurturing attention. The tantrums constantly recurred, yet her mother's approval mattered to her. She tried most of the time to earn the penny a day for coming when called. When they moved to Buffalo, Margery took art lessons every Saturday and Ruth stayed home—time alone with her mother—and wrote "pieces" (p. 111). Writing became a way to gain her mother's approval and her mother became her first serious critic. But even this approval was qualified. As with the rest of the family, Ruth felt excluded from the inner circle of her mother's approval.

Bertrice Fulton stayed home on the farm, doing her share of the work necessary to keep the farm going and caring for her children, until Ruth was six and Margery almost five, when she got a job teaching science and Latin at Norwich High School in nearby Norwich.[33] Bertrice and the two girls lived in town during the week, with one or the other of the aunts as housekeeper, and returned to the farm on weekends. In Norwich Ruth first entered school and her hearing problem was discovered. This must have eased some family pressure, to find out that Ruth had an organic problem, not a moral one. But the discovery of the hearing loss again branded her as different, an outsider.

The next school year, 1894–1895, her mother took a job for more money teaching Latin, zoology, and physiology at St. Joseph High School, St. Joseph, Missouri. Taking Aunt Hetty as housekeeper, Bertrice and the two girls moved to St. Joseph, where they lived first at 1116 Edmond Street, then the next year at 1516 Charles Street, returning to the farm for the summers. The high school had an enrollment of 370 students and a faculty of twelve teachers including Bertrice Shattuck Fulton. She taught at the high school for two years, 1894–1895 and 1895–1896, when Ruth was seven and eight.[34]

St. Joseph was quite a change from Norwich. Norwich, founded in 1793, was the county seat of Chenango County. It lay on the Chenango River, about equidistant from Utica to the north and Birmingham to the south. The Chenango Canal ran through Norwich, connecting it with both cities, but in the 1890's Norwich was a town of only a few thousand people, the largest town in Chenango County, to be sure, but Chenango was primarily a farming county, a place with few towns at all of any size. St. Joseph was also a county seat, situated on a bend of the Missouri River in the northwest part of Missouri, 310 miles from St. Louis. But it was a bustling city, rapidly approaching 100,000 people, one of the largest cities in the state. By 1900 it would be touted as the "Electric City." St. Jo was Ruth's first taste of city life, her first exposure to immigrants who spoke other languages in stores and on the streets, who dressed differently and lived differently from her family. It was her first exposure to black people in any numbers. She might have seen them on the street but she did not go to school with them, since "colored" and white pupils attended separate schools. According to her comments in later life, she found elementary school "an arid, uncomprehended desert." The teaching was on "a dead-level of incurious indifference" that made schoolwork "a world apart from our eager, hurrying, investigating life outside. The hours of school were only marking time." Nevertheless, Ruth could read anything she could find by the age of seven and had begun to write verses and descriptions in words and drawings. One of her favorite authors was Jean Ingelow, a British poet and novelist popular in late Victorian America, whose writings she found in her grandfather's house. It was probably in Missouri that Margery began to attend school in the same class with Ruth, so that they went through school together. This must have served as a source of healthy competition, because here was an area in which Ruth could best Margery. Margery probably also helped make the classroom less of a desert by making the teachers' words in crowded classrooms comprehensible through her notes and comments.[35]

After two years at St. Jo, Bertrice Fulton received an offer of a higher paying job as teacher and Lady Principal at Pillsbury Academy in Owatonna, Minnesota. In 1887 Baptists had founded Pillsbury as a boys' school, but by the fall of 1896, when the Fultons arrived there, the school population had broadened until almost 50 percent of the students belonged to other denominations and Pillsbury had admitted girls. But the school's avowed purpose was still to prepare students for college and provide a firm base of religion and moral training. The 1896 Board of Visitors reported on the "quiet, deep devout spirit" of worship at the school and becoming a minister was still the greatest ambition of male graduates in the 1890's. Physically the school consisted of several buildings spread over a rural campus. A military program that had begun in 1890 usually attracted about half the boys, who drilled for two hours, two days a week. In 1896 the student body numbered 301, overseen by about a dozen faculty. The Lady Principal, second only to the Headmaster, oversaw the girls' program and acted as headmistress, disciplinarian, and moral confidante.[36]

In size Owatonna must have seemed far more like Norwich than St. Jo. In 1895 the population numbered 4,891, a figure that changed slowly. Owatonna was also a county seat, famous for its mineral spring rich in iron and sulphur, often compared with the Vichy springs in France. It lay in southern Minnesota on the Owatonna River. Supposedly Owatonna meant "straight" in some Indian language, a gentle joke because the river wound and twisted. Steele County surrounding the town was dairy and farm country much like Chenango County in New York. But, more like St. Jo than Norwich, a quarter of the population of Steele County was foreign-born, mostly German, Scandinavian, Czech, and Irish. In Owatonna itself, 1,152 out of 4,891 were immigrants in 1895, the largest group being the Germans with 608 and next the Danes, with 150.[37]

The academy was a cultural and educational force in the community, offering music recitals monthly for local citizens, as well as student debates, speakers, parades, and other public events. As Lady Principal,

Bertrice Fulton held a high social position in academy and town society. The academy yearbook, *The Sybil*, compared her to Aspasia, Pericles' hostess and mistress, renowned for her social skills, calling her house "the celebrated resort for the most eminent Pillsburians." The yearbook added that she was well liked and respected for her "high mental accomplishments." Bertrice, besides her job as Lady Principal, taught literature and English, helped girls compose orations, and judged public debates. She also presided over student social occasions. "By her instructions," *The Sybil* commented, she was making "first class women" of the students in her charge. "Let the name Bertrice S. Fulton be applied only to women with remarkable powers of mind and heart," the yearbook proclaimed.[38]

For one of the few times in her childhood Ruth Benedict found herself at the center of an inner circle. Through her mother's position she had status in the community. She also gained personal status. She wrote of her two years in Owatonna when she was nine and ten, "At school I was the leader of the little group of the élite" (p. 107) consisting of all the professors' children, who happened to be girls, plus other girls they decided to take in. At an age when girls bond to other girls to form cliques, she was the leader of the most prestigious clique in her school. She had the power to sway the group to admit new girls or cast one out. She had the authority to direct the group's activities. She blossomed in the attention and people in general began to play some real part in her life. She made friends among the other girls. Known as "touchy" and physically withdrawn in the family circle, she became friendly with the school janitor, a man of about forty who used to make purple illuminated title pages for the girls. Ruth thought he was very kind, "and the warmest person I knew. I liked to have him stroke back my hair and know how well he liked me" (p. 107).[39]

Pillsbury was in tune with the increasingly military tone of the nation as a whole. In April 1898, the cadets gave themselves wholeheartedly to enthusiasm for the newly declared Spanish-American War. Fifty-two volunteered as national reserves and on April 29 the two companies of cadets paraded through the streets of Owatonna in uniform with their band, carrying the American and Cuban flags, heartily cheered by a large crowd. At the town center they stopped and gave three cheers for the U.S. and Cuba, then did drills back to the campus. As the *People's Press* of Owatonna reported, "The air seemed pregnant with pent-up patriotism." The *Owatonna Journal* reported that same day, "Around the Academy halls there is but one topic of conversation and that is 'War.' Everything is war, war, war." Whether this played any role in deciding her future is hard to tell, but by the summer Bertrice Shattuck Fulton had decided to resign and accept a job as Superintendent of Circulation at the Buffalo Public Library. Several other reasons lay behind this decision. Pillsbury's enrollment had begun declining, and though the slippage was small in 1898, the future at Pillsbury looked uncertain and the Buffalo job offered greater security. The nationwide Depression of 1893–1897 had underscored the need for security. Moreover Bertrice's sister Mamie and her husband now lived in Buffalo and invited Bertrice's family to live in their house. The move provided a closer sense of family, both because of Mamie and because Norwich was only a few hours away instead of days. The library job promised Bertrice responsibility over a number of staff and the status of being a manager. The one disadvantage was the salary. She began at $60 a month, or $15 a week, which had to support their family of four, for by this time Aunt Hetty was a permanent member of the family. This was at least $10 a week less than she made as Lady Principal in Owatonna, and city living would be more expensive. In 1900, $18 a week was considered the minimum necessary to support the average family in the city. Bertrice Fulton's salary in itself was comparable to the average teacher's salary of $14 a week in 1900 and much higher than the average woman factory worker's salary of between $5 and $6 a week. In spite of this comparative disadvantage, after a summer on the farm the Fultons began their life in Buffalo in the fall of 1898, when Ruth was eleven years old.[40]

Buffalo seemed to offer wider opportunities than Owatonna. In 1905 it became second only to New York City in size in the state, with a population of 376,595. A rapidly growing city, with its share of civic pride and a large immigrant population, for middle-class Americans Buffalo offered modernity mixed with pastoral elements. Many streets were paved with the new asphalt, for example, yet they were shaded by trees that in many areas seemed to meet overhead from both sides of the street. Working-class and immigrant families lived on the East Side, while the middle and upper-middle class congregated around Delaware Avenue and the streets branching off from it. On one of these branches, at 48 Dorchester Road, lived the Fultons and the Ellises. The Public Library downtown, where Bertrice Fulton worked, was growing along with the city and boasted 320,000 volumes by 1909 and various collections including original material by Emerson, Whitman, and Lowell. To escape from urbanization, one could go down to Lake Erie on which Buffalo bordered, or go to the popular rural cemetery, Forest Lawn, or to one of the parks scattered around the city, or make the twenty-mile excursion to Niagara Falls on the U.S.-Canadian border. In itself Buffalo seemed a pleasant place to set up a home.[41]

But the move to Buffalo was a traumatic one for Ruth. Abruptly she found herself in the outer circle again. In Owatonna she had been a leader among the girls; in Buffalo she was not. She had to start over, try to make new friends in this new place. In Owatonna her mother had status and comparative wealth. In Buffalo, relative to the economic status of the people they knew and mingled with, they lived in straitened circumstances. From her point of view as a child, Ruth wrote, the family "had everything in Owatonna," and in Buffalo they were "very poor" (p. 110). Although she wrote that she didn't care about this, she cared more than she admitted. Aggravating her distress over the move was her sudden height. Ruth experienced a growth spurt and was about 5'8" by the age of eleven, freakishly taller than most of the girls and boys in her school class.

The year they moved to Buffalo, Ruth's tantrums became especially severe and recurrent. She called herself "unusually unaccountable," and at last there came a time when tantrums seized her every day or so. Her mother was "doubly worried" that she would hurt Margery. "After an especially bad week," she wrote, "Mother summoned all her forces." Ruth had had a tantrum on going to bed. She lay crying herself "to exhaustion" after it had passed, when "Mother talked to me solemnly and dictated a promise, which I repeated after her, never to have another tantrum." She went out of the room and came back with a Bible and a candle and selected a verse that "invoked the aid of Jehovah" for Ruth to read aloud (p. 108). Ruth later wrote, "God was very real to me in those days, and the whole scene went deep within me."[42] After this she never had another tantrum. Bouts of depression took their place. This story charts the apex of Ruth's resistance to, yet desire for, her mother's approval as a child: the end of a pattern characterized by tantrums and open rebellion and the beginning of the internalized pattern that replaced it in her adolescent and adult years.

As an adolescent, Ruth turned to writing as a solace and an outlet. She had begun writing early and remembered writing verses and descriptive sentences into a notebook on the train to and from St. Joseph. Her writing gained her attention from her mother and a measure of approval, perhaps tied in with the notion that in this she was like her father, who had been an editor of his college newspaper before directing his writing to medical topics.[43] Writing, in which she had to listen only to the words of her inner self, became an area in which she excelled at school, gaining approval and recognition outside the family as well as qualified approval within. Through her writing she released thoughts and feelings previously restricted to her inner world. Her sensuality came through in descriptions such as this: "Through numberless days of sunshine and spring the sun had made love to the earth, and lovely, lovely had been the days" (p. 111). Her feelings of aloneness and longing for love came out in the Evangeline stories. Her outsider's eye toward American society had full play in stories like "Lulu's Wedding" and "The Greatest of These," which she wrote her senior year in high school.

"Lulu's Wedding (A True Story)" tells the tale of Ruth and Margery's adventure into the working-class world to attend the wedding of the family servant girl, Lulu. Stereotypical stories of weddings portrayed brides as radiantly happy and their surroundings, even though poor, as transformed by love. Benedict rejected the sentimental stereotype for a bleaker view. This composition reveals an understanding of the underside of marriage and the non-romantic, realistic reasons women chose it—for security and status—and it debunks the culturally idealized mythology of romantic love. Lulu is marrying not out of love, but because she has found a man who is willing. She is sixteen, and even though he is twice her age, she consents because she doesn't want to "work out allez." The wedding environment, far from being transformed by love, reveals not only the scarcity of material things, but even more a deep poverty of the spirit, of imagination, of emotion. The girls enter "a stuffy little parlor of a rickety house" on a side street. The decorations are scant and hastily assembled. On a bureau stands a jelly glass filled with flowers and above the bureau is rigged a crude bridal arch of two planks studded with flowers and fern. The guests eat the bridal dinner in the kitchen in two shifts, quickly and with few words. Then they sit around in silence. The impromptu entertainment consists of a harmonica player and Margery speaking a piece. There is no lively conversation or joking, and little joy.[44]

"The Greatest of These" portrays a non-romantic mother-son relationship. The stereotypical mother-son story of this time sentimentalized the parent-child relationship—the dutiful, successful son returning to take the mother who sacrificed to give him opportunities in childhood from a life of poverty and drudgery to live her last years with him in ease and comfort. Benedict gave the stereotype a twist. The son returns successful, but has succeeded through graft and corruption in politics, for which he is admired by his fellow men, nevertheless. He wants his mother, portrayed as thin and rheumatic, but naïvely loving, to come and live with him and his new wife, but only because his wife wants her as a cheap, live-in housekeeper to do the household drudge work. Being on the margins of her family and social world gave Ruth insight into the underside of her culture beyond the idealized and sentimentalized view of the upper middle class to which she belonged, and especially prevalent among girls of her age group. These papers she wrote in high school show an uncanny ability to look upon her own society with a coldly objective eye. Whether because her hearing problem cut her off from cultural reinforcement or because of her mental hideaway, or because she felt repelled by her mother's sentimental ties to her father, she never became imbued with the sentimental romanticism common to girls of this time, and indeed, she had a healthy skepticism of sentimental motives. Some of her later journal fragments seem to suggest that Benedict was a romantic, sentimentally looking for an idealized great love. But these high school essays show she had a very practical appreciation of her culture and did not view life through sentimental clichés. Her position in the outer circle saved her from immersion in the genteel sentimentality common in her day.[45]

When Ruth was thirteen years old, Aunt Hetty died. Deaths had occurred before in the family. Dr. Sam Fulton, her grandfather, had died in December 1896, and her grandmother Harriet Fulton had died a year and a half later, in June 1897. But both these deaths had occurred while Ruth lived in Owatonna and were mitigated by actual and emotional distance. Aunt Hetty had lived with Ruth, Margery, and her mother for six years, since their move to St. Joseph, Missouri, when Ruth was seven. Hetty had been ill enough to go to the Lexington Heights Hospital in Buffalo for nine weeks in the spring of 1900. After she had recovered she had gone home to the Shattuck farm to recuperate. She stayed there through the summer, participating in the celebration of John Samuel and Joanna Terry Shattuck's golden wedding anniversary. A sudden relapse brought about her death on August 2, 1900.[46] Ruth left nothing written concerning this death, but it must have been an important event in her life—the first death of a person in her immediate family, whom she was around as she was dying, the first death she could participate in, coming at the beginning of adolescence.

In spite of their genteel poverty, ability and connections got Ruth and Margery into St. Margaret's School for Girls, a private Episcopalian college preparatory day school in Buffalo that catered to the upper crust of Buffalo society. Aunt Mamie, wife of successful patent lawyer William Ellis, active member of the Abigail Fillmore Chapter of the DAR and the Town Club, which promoted civic projects, renowned for her presentations of new books and plays to groups of women eager to keep up with the latest literature, knew the principal of the school, Miss Mary Robinson. Miss Robinson offered Ruth and Margery full tuition scholarships on condition that they win accreditation for the school to Vassar College by doing well on the College Entrance Board Examinations and later by making a good record at the college. In St. Margaret's, as in her family, Ruth found herself among both the inner circle and the outer circle. Accepted socially because of their family background, she and Margery made friends and participated in social activities. Yet Ruth and her sister were scholarship students, conscious of being poor in relation to most of the girls, and having to learn a new language of upper-middle-class adolescent etiquette and sometimes being caught out, as when Ruth felt humiliated at graduation time because she wore a white dress to an afternoon party and white wasn't a daytime color then (p. 110). Both girls did well at St. Margaret's, Ruth graduating with a 99 percent average for her years there and Margery with a 98.7 percent. In their senior year, the headmistress told Bertrice Shattuck Fulton that the school had a wealthy patroness who liked to send one girl a year to Vassar in memory of her husband, who had taken an interest in Vassar. Since the school could not choose between Ruth and Margery, both exceptional students, she had agreed to give them both four-year scholarships. The benefactor, who preferred to remain anonymous, was Mrs. F. F. Thompson, and for many years Ruth and Margery remained ignorant of their patroness' name. Bertrice Fulton received a letter from Mrs. Thompson's secretary saying, "Mrs. Thompson has been pleased to place your two daughters, Ruth and Margery Fulton, on her list of Vassar scholarships for September, 1905." With that assurance, Ruth and Margery made ready for Vassar, and Ruth took the first step away from her family and the inner and outer circles it had fostered.[47]

2

Vassar

AT VASSAR Ruth and Margery had four years of special freedom not allowed many young women of their time. They had tasted this freedom in Buffalo. Ruth and Margery had "steered their bicycles" toward St. Margaret's every day. The battle of the bicycle for women had been fought and won in the 1890's, and by the early 1900's, the bicycle for young women had created a new freedom. It meant freedom from constricting clothing and long skirts; freedom from restricted boundaries to explore the city and its bordering country roads; but, more important, it meant freedom from the old constraining ideas of femininity, freedom to be the new girl of the new century, epitomized by the athletic, independent Gibson Girl of magazine illustrations. Vassar offered Ruth this kind of freedom, as well as the freedom to develop an identity and an individual philosophy among exceptional role models. As a member of the class of 1908 put it, Vassar "kept me lit up mentally like a Christmas tree for four years." But inherent in the Vassar experience were conflicting ideas about the freedom of the intellect versus the social constraints of femininity with which each student had to wrestle and come to terms, a struggle that took many postgraduate years for Ruth Benedict to resolve. At Vassar, Ruth explored her options, enjoyed the social life and camaraderie of the school, found intellectual mentors, and formed important friendships.[1]

When Ruth and Margery Fulton entered Vassar the "college girl" was no longer the phenomenon she had been a generation earlier. In the twenty years between Bertrice Shattuck's graduation from Vassar and Ruth and Margery's entry, the number of young women attending colleges and universities had more than tripled. Social acceptance had risen proportionately. Where the college women of their mother's generation in many cases could expect puzzlement, ridicule, animosity, or the curiosity reserved for sideshow freaks, Ruth and Margery's generation no longer faced such sharp reactions to women's higher education from society at large. As Ruth and Margery entered college, the October 1905 edition of *Ladies Home Journal* detailed the "Madcap Frolics of College Girls," following this up in November with "What College Girls Eat." "When College Girls Make Merry" was an ongoing series in 1908–1909, the year Ruth and Margery graduated from Vassar, and that same year, in September 1909, *Good Housekeeping* regaled its readers with "College Girl Follies." Though college was not for every woman, or even most women, the "college girl" had become an accepted feature of American life. Ruth and Margery went to Vassar familiar with the popular images of college girl life and one of their first discoveries, wrote Margery, tongue-in-cheek, was that the "chief occupation of college girls was not to make fudge every night in their picturesque kimonas [*sic*] to the tinkling accompaniment of the mandolin. Upsetting, indeed!" she concluded.[2]

Under the surface, however, still lay doubts and fears about the higher education of women. The old arguments concerning possible illness and sterility still appeared among supposedly informed people. Only the year before Ruth and Margery entered Vassar, psychologist G. Stanley Hall told the members of the National Education Association that "Mental strain in early womanhood is the cause of imperfect mammary function, which is the first stage in the evolution of sterility." A. L. Smith wrote an article in the *Bulletin of the Academy of Medicine* in 1905 which claimed that during the menstrual period any excessive brain activity diverted blood and vital energy from the ovaries, causing extra menstrual pain and ultimately degeneration of the reproductive organs. But by 1905 the focus of debate had shifted from women's physical frailty to the still real fear that college-educated women could not be family women, that a college education, especially at one of the rigorous women's colleges such as Vassar, made women unfit for contentment in marriage and the raising of children. This fear gathered strength with statistics which showed a lower marriage rate among college women, especially graduates of women's colleges, than non-college women. At Vassar, for example, only 42 percent of all graduates of the classes from 1867 through 1896 had married by 1900. Among those college women who married, statistics revealed a tendency to postpone marriage after college for at least two years, and the tendency to have fewer children.[3] The argument ran that superior women such as these were neglecting their duty to the race to have superior children—the unspoken corollary being that poor and immigrant, presumably inferior, women were breeding prolifically and filling the nation with their inferior progeny. The argument reflected the cultural imperialism infecting America at the turn of the century. Although women's right to higher education had been established, critics deplored the educated woman's contribution to "race suicide."

In reply to this argument sociologist and later anthropologist Elsie Clews Parsons wrote an article in the *American Journal of Sociology* the year Ruth graduated from Vassar, using a famous study done in 1900 by Professor Mary Roberts Smith showing that in proportion to the number of years married, college women actually had more children than non-college women. But she acknowledged that the problems of college women versus the family were real, not because of higher education itself, but because of the prejudices of society toward college women. The first college women were outcasts, she wrote, stigmatized as inevitable spinsters. She speculated that even by 1905, nine out of ten women who took up a profession had to choose between marriage and career because of society's prejudices against married women.[4] If one wanted a career, the single life remained the primary choice. So society placed women in a double bind. On one level it told them higher education was acceptable as a way-station to home and family. On another level it said that women who went to college and seriously wanted to pursue their studies afterward had more chance of leading lonely, unfulfilled lives, since fulfillment came through home and family, and it was seldom possible for a woman to have both career and family life. Although they didn't realize it then, these were the choices facing Ruth and Margery as they entered Vassar in 1905.

The Vassar to which Ruth Fulton and her sister came had grown and changed from the time their mother was a student. Founder Matthew Vassar's original purpose, to educate women on an equal plane with men, remained the guiding force. To this end, the preparatory department, which in Bertrice's time had accounted for over half the student population, had closed in 1888, and special students had disappeared from the campus. Facilities had expanded. During Bertrice's student years most of college life centered on the Main Building, an imposing structure with transverse wings where students ate, slept, studied, and went to library, chapel, and most classes, all under one roof. By 1905 six other large buildings served as dormitories and only the senior class, by traditional privilege, lived in Main. An impressive Norman-style chapel had opened the year before Ruth and Margery's arrival, the stately new gothic library opened the year they entered, and various classroom buildings dotted the campus.[5]

Athletics, always considered a necessary balance to the nervous exhaustion inherent in the life of the mind, had changed and expanded. In Bertrice's day physical education consisted of the Dio Lewis system of calisthenics, riding school, croquet, and compulsory exercise, along with more informal activities such as walks around campus or in the countryside, sledding and ice skating in winter, and rowing on campus lakes. Reflecting less restricted ideas of femininity, by Ruth and Margery's day students played basketball, field hockey, and tennis, and took part in field and track events such as running and jumping. They could swim in the indoor pool, and when winter set in, indoor gym exercises became compulsory. The informal activities remained just as popular as they had in Bertrice's day. Special places to go included the walk to Cedar Bridge, the climb up Richmond Hill to the single pine tree at its top, and the hike to the top of Sunrise Hill, with its view of the Catskills to the north and highlands to the south. Ruth was sensitive to the Vassar landscape, "the green-black of the campus pines in the dusk, the Catskills, their horizon line diamond-cut against the sky," and enjoyed physical activities, especially walking and swimming workouts, but did not play on any teams.[6]

Course offerings had doubled between the 1880's and 1910, giving students a wider variety of subjects to study. In Bertrice's college days students' course schedules were fixed by college requirements, not individual desires. But, following the lead of Harvard, in 1903 Vassar instituted the revolutionary elective system that gave students an element of choice in their class schedules. Ruth took five courses her freshman year. Besides the required English and math, she chose Latin instead of Greek, physics over chemistry, and German rather than French as her modern language, a choice with reverberations into the future and her study of anthropology with German-born Franz Boas. She did well in German, probably because the teaching emphasis prior to 1910 was on reading literature in the original and not on conversational German, where her hearing problem would have put her at a disadvantage. In her sophomore year she took two English courses, history, Latin, one more semester of German, and, interestingly enough, a semester of music. She could hear music and stage productions if she sat at the front of a hall close to the stage and later in life enjoyed going to concerts and plays. It is also likely that the class studied the lives of famous composers, an area where she would excel easily. By her junior year she had decided to major in English literature, taking three courses in English, supplemented with philosophy and economics, a semester of history, and a semester of physiology. As a senior she took two more English courses, more economics, one semester of psychology, and the required semester of ethics.[7]

Since Bertrice's day, traditions had solidified. Vassar had its own rituals and ceremonies, its own pattern of events for each class, its own expectations for students. On its rural campus Vassar remained fairly isolated from Poughkeepsie, where it was nominally located. Campus life was much more important than the life of the town nearby. The original idea of the founders had been to promote a feeling of belonging to one large family, and that spirit remained an important force. The dorms had their own sense of family life, "their special gatherings in their own halls and parlors, their teas, their parties, . . . their impromptu performances, their services of song." But the greatest unifying force was the class. "We're the class of one nine naught nine," sang Ruth and Margery as freshmen, "We're the class that none can outshine." Alumnae called it "a sight to be remembered" as classes came "singing across the lawns" or walking down the broad paths in "impressive phalanx." Intramural games, contests, debates, receptions, special events, all rebounded to class honor and glory.[8]

Vassar offered students a life of structured freedom. A typical day began at 7:00 A.M. with the rising bell, breakfast at 7:30, and classes beginning at 8:30. From then until midafternoon, with a break for lunch, students alternated between the classroom, the library, and the study. From midafternoon until dinner at 6:00 P.M., they participated in sports or some form of required physical activity, and sometimes spent the time in "frivoling," walking, shopping, or visiting. Compulsory chapel services took place at 7:00 P.M. after dinner, and evenings were filled with studying, library work, club meetings, occasional lectures, and the impromptu and sometimes heated discussions in someone's room, the friendly joking and camaraderie, the "cozy spreads" of crackers, jelly, olives, and other snacks. These were "perhaps the best times of all," times when Ruth and her classmates looked forward with eagerness and high confidence to making a mark on the world. Saturdays were free days, so social events usually took place then or on Friday evenings. Sundays were "times of quiet and peacefulness," with morning services conducted by ministers of different denominations invited from around the country, with a voluntary evening service of Bible study and prayer. Vassar prided itself on meeting Matthew Vassar's own ideal of a college—religious, but nonsectarian.[9]

Beyond daily life, the school year had its own pattern. When they arrived Ruth and Margery received a copy of their "Freshman Bible." Vassar opened formally with a chapel service on a designated Friday evening. The weekend was used to settle in, and school began "briskly" on Monday. Various functions marked the school calendar: the annual outdoor reception for freshmen given by the Christian Association and the Students' Association; the anniversary of the Philalethean Society, the oldest of all societies on campus, the theater society that annually gave the four hall plays, great campus occasions in themselves; the great annual debate on a vital topic sponsored by T & M, the senior debating society; the Ice Carnival, a winter festival held at the lakes at night with bonfires and Chinese lanterns, costumes, music, and ice skating; Founder's Day in the spring with its songs, speeches, pageants, and plays; the great junior and senior dances; and, of course, Commencement season, with its crowds of visitors, Class Day, the Daisy Chain, reception, graduation exercises, and various dinners, ending with the Class Supper on Commencement evening, and afterward "the singing by the seniors at their tree and then the partings." [10]

Choosing a special class tree was an important sophomore prerogative. For their Tree Ceremony sophomores chose a night, dressed in costumes, met in secret, and moved stealthily with lanterns to the chosen place, either choosing a tree already planted or planting one. The freshmen traditionally tried to find out about the ceremony and disrupt it. Afterward, freshmen and sophomores partied together. The Class of 1909 dressed as fairies "in myriad colors," and chose a tree already in place. They wrote of it that it was tall, thin, didn't have many leaves, and in the winter looked sad. But the class was proud of its tree. It, like them, had survived to graduation. Class trees became class rallying points for meetings, singing, and rejoicing after athletic or academic victories.[11]

As important as the Tree Ceremony in the life of a sophomore was the Daisy Chain. For nearly a day during Commencement Week the entire sophomore class picked daisies, and for part of the next day they all worked at making a long, thick rope of them. A number of the "prettiest sophomores" were chosen to carry the Daisy Chain over their shoulders as the graduating class moved in procession from Main on Class Day. Standing two by two, they formed an aisle for the seniors, and after the seniors sat down, the sophomores wound the Daisy Chain around their chairs. Later it was placed around the class tree. As second-semester sophomore president Frances Tyer wrote for the class of 1909, tongue-in-cheek, "our beauty was beginning to be recognized." She continued, "What quite equals the choosing of the Daisy Chain!" She described how night after night following chapel the supposedly unconcerned sophomores, "exquisitely dressed" and acutely aware of being scrutinized, walked past the selection committee, "stumbling over the registers in our embarrassment." Thus one important sophomore event affirmed the social standard of femininity the rest of the curriculum sought to deny.[12]

The juniors had their own special events as well, but of all the classes, the seniors had the most privileges, the most rituals. The seniors alone lived in Main and had their own special Senior Parlor there to furnish and care for, the only class so honored. Senior Parlor dedication was another annual event in Vassar life. Seniors alone could use the parlor, and studying there was forbidden. The seniors sat together in the dining room, their tables stretching down the center the whole length in parallel lines. The seniors alone celebrated every class member's birthday during senior year, whether it occurred during the school year or not, giving each young woman her own cake and presents by her plate. Seniors went on an annual one-day trip to Mohonk, where they picnicked while other classes studied. And only the seniors took ethics, their one required course, from the president of the college, Rev. James M. Taylor.[13]

Taylor had become president in 1886, the year after Bertrice Shattuck graduated, and had stamped his mark on Vassar in the nineteen years since. During Ruth and Margery's years he became a controversial figure. His successor wrote of him after Taylor retired in 1914 that "he literally was the life of the campus." He had "exuberant vitality," and "his figure skating was admired. His gay laughter pervaded the whole college." As a person and as a personality he had the affection and respect of the students, who serenaded him on his porch and applauded his inspiring talks in response. He was fiercely proud of Vassar and its preeminent role in women's education and produced intensely loyal alumnae. But he was also somewhat of a dictator and a conservative. With the support of a conservative board of trustees, Taylor kept a tight rein on socially radical issues on campus. Against the wishes of some students and faculty he refused to allow women's rights speakers on campus and refused even to allow a suffrage club to form while Ruth and Margery attended Vassar. His well-publicized ideal for Vassar graduates was that they become "well-rounded" women. As his successor, Henry Noble MacCracken, described the ideal, Vassar women were to be "cultured but human, not leaders but good wives and mothers, truly liberal in things intellectual but conservative in matters social." He concluded, "And this most of them dutifully became." As a 1904 article in *Popular Science Monthly* reported, Vassar alumnae tended to favor low-profile club, philanthropic, and general educational work, much of it part-time and volunteer, that could be done while caring for husband and family. As MacCracken added, "They were to be 'leading' women, taking a part in all civic enterprise without ever losing their charm." Thus Taylor dealt with the social standard of femininity by encouraging women to use their intellectual powers and education in "feminine" ways, modestly and with a light touch, putting husband and family first.[14]

By the time Ruth and Margery entered, Vassar was beginning to chafe under Taylor's benevolently authoritarian rule. Students wanted to have a voice concerning college rules and often felt resentment at paternalistic policies. The Students' Association had been pushing steadily for more control over rules of life at the college, and this continued to be a source of friction. Taylor's clampdown on the suffrage issue caused open revolt, led by the Class of 1909. The leader of the revolt was Inez Milholland, whom MacCracken called "the statuesque Joan of the advancing young folks," and whom her own classmates characterized in the senior yearbook as "Fascinating,—but a trifle dangerous for household use." One of 1909's star actresses and athletes, she also did college settlement work and served as class president the second semester of junior year. Suffrage leader Harriot Stanton Blatch called her "beautiful, capable, eloquent," and legend had it that in her final ethics exam with Taylor she wrote two answers: "The World as Prexy Thinks It Is," and "The World as It Is." Reportedly he gave her an A. She had been influenced by militant suffragists in England, and when Taylor restricted the suffrage movement on campus, she organized suffrage meetings in a cemetery that bordered on the campus. As Margery Fulton Freeman later wrote, "We used to climb the fence, and meet in an old graveyard, just off the campus!" The largest meeting Milholland organized made the New York papers. Forty undergraduates, ten alumnae, and two male visitors sat on the grass and listened to Vassar graduate Harriot Stanton Blatch, Charlotte Perkins Gilman, author of *Women and Economics,* Helen Hoy, a Vassar graduate and corporation counsel for the Equality League of Self-Supporting Women, and Rose Schneiderman, a labor organizer for the Cap-Maker's Union and one of the great women of American labor history. Reportedly, Harriot Stanton Blatch, "in order to allay the fears of any member of the faculty who might chance that way, bore aloft a yellow banner on which was inscribed in large black letters, 'Come, let us reason together.'"[15]

Benedict indicated in later writings that she had attended suffrage meetings, although not when. She admired Inez Milholland, and Margery later wrote that in college they did the important things together, so it is likely she went with her sister. Ruth also had a reputation among her friends as an intellectual radical, and Margery Fulton wrote that suffrage was *the* burning issue of their years at Vassar. Milholland, definitely a presence in the class, gave Ruth one role model outside that of a "well-rounded" woman, that of an active feminist leader working for radical social change. This was a role that she must have studied carefully in the person of Inez before ultimately rejecting it for herself. She was not a speaker or debater by inclination, her hearing putting her at a disadvantage in a crowded auditorium. By temperament secretive, she believed in "sane, healthy half revelation, half concealment," as she wrote in a college paper. She was not attracted to the public display of self the role of a radical leader required, nor to the theater and spectacle of the role. Inez Milholland could handle a street meeting, give stirring speeches on platforms with suffrage leaders like Anna Howard Shaw and Harriot Stanton Blatch, march in parades, and cause a Republican parade to break ranks as she threw leaflets out a window at them. Ruth Benedict would look for other outlets to assert her need to act. As Nietzsche, who greatly influenced her, wrote, "it is the stillest words which bring the storm. Thoughts that come with dove's footsteps guide the world." She turned inward to the life of the mind and followed other role models.[16]

Her courses brought her into contact with a series of fine teachers, many of them women. As an English major she could not help but come under the influence of Professor Laura Johnson Wylie, head of the English Department, and to hundreds of Vassar students "the ideal of the inspiring and stimulating teacher." Henry Noble MacCracken called her one of the "really great teachers," her field being literary criticism. Wylie could be formidable, telling students to "speak up, yuh silly goop, yuh know the answer, yuh know yuh do," while, as MacCracken said, "her sharp but kind eyes flashed fire at the trembling freshman." She wanted her students to think. Another teacher in the English Department Ruth held in high esteem was associate professor and woman's suffrage advocate Florence V. Keys, a woman who had studied at several European universities in the spaces between college sessions and who encouraged her to apply "the social test of the value of all knowledge," an idea Ruth resisted while at Vassar. In her history courses she must have encountered Lucy Salmon, another of the "really great teachers," a dynamic woman who told her students, "You have a mind, use it." Margaret Washburn, who taught philosophy and psychology at Vassar, both of which Ruth took, urged her students to study original problems. MacCracken called her "unrivalled as a clear lecturer and inspiring guide in the seminar." She was also a feminist. The story was told of her that she had been "intrepid enough to

invade the sacred precinct of the men's smoker at psychological meetings." Uninvited, she sat and lit up a cigar. "None questioned her privilege to enjoy the smoker thereafter." For women of the early twentieth
century smoking became a prominent and pronounced symbol of women's
emancipation. The president of Bryn Mawr, M. Carey Thomas, when the
school could no longer be harmed by it, "determinedly smoked, and
urged other women to do so," making a great production out of it, "all in
order to prove women's emancipation." Margery Fulton Freeman identified smoking as one of the most-talked-of issues at Vassar when she and
Ruth were there. Smoking was not allowed anywhere on campus. Ruth
Benedict, while a college professor, smoked, a fact that journalists considered newsworthy about her. For whatever other reasons she smoked,
that symbolism must have remained present in the back of her mind.[17]

Ruth was exposed to many more women role models than her mother
had been. Ruth's teachers were women of the first and second generations
of female college graduates in America and among that small number of
the infinitesimally few who went on for higher degrees. They were "strong-
minded" women, "dangerous" women, conscious of themselves as pioneers and innovators. Their view of the role of academics was as activists
and reformers, producing social change first by their example and second
through their influence on students. They saw teaching women to think
as a truly radical activity. They were people vitally interested in ideas.
They encouraged intellectualism over a broad range, scorning the practical, applied, service-oriented new area of domestic education infiltrating
Vassar during Ruth and Margery's days there, although the domestic
wave did not crest until after their graduation. They presented Ruth with
an alternative to Inez Milholland in an arena of mental activism and intellectual innovation, with a set of guidelines for following through in the
examples of their own lives. These were women who as teachers created
in Vassar a place where sitting and thinking was respected, where ideas
were important in themselves, and where people were valued for having
ideas. But many of the women teachers had never married, had made the
choice between marriage and career and encouraged students to go on
and have distinguished careers, study for Ph.D.'s and not bury themselves
in marriage. There was a general sense among them that marriage was
the death of intellectual life.[18] Vassar created a paradox in which it
seemed that a choice had to be made between intellectuality and family,
and either way, something precious and fulfilling had to be given up. But
that was a paradox that did not confront Ruth until after she graduated
from college.

Meanwhile the Vassar experience proved to be a focal point in Ruth's life, a time in which she began to draw together the vocabulary of ideas which gave meaning and direction to her adult life. She read Walter Pater, Nietzsche, Charlotte Perkins Gilman, John Burroughs, Walt Whitman, George Santayana, and others current in the intellectual life of her day. In reading and studying the ideas of others, she recognized their thoughts as her own becoming conscious within her for the first time. Their words illuminated her own experience and environment. She sorted through the array of choices open to her in classes, discussions, and private reading, and began to see her own life in perspective, to perceive her own goals, to create her own philosophy. The foundation laid at Vassar remained a re-markably consistent base influencing the rest of her life.

In the writings of English literary critic Walter Pater (1839–1894) she discovered a kindred spirit who helped her overcome the "passionate blank despair" she felt at times at Vassar, while struggling to discover the meaning of life. The Conclusion to Pater's *Renaissance* she discovered as a freshman, late one afternoon when, as she said, she ended up creeping to the windowseat of her bare tower room to catch the last light to read by. "The book fell shut in my hands at the end," she wrote, "and it was as if my soul had been given back to me, its eyes wide and eager with new understanding." Pater wrote of life as "the concurrence, renewed from moment to moment, of forces parting sooner or later on their ways," of life as constant movement, "the passage and dissolution of impressions, images, sensations" leading to the "perpetual weaving and unweaving of ourselves." He wrote that the ultimate way to experience life deeply was to catch the present moment "at the focus where the greatest number of vital forces unite in their purest energy," and that "To burn always with this hard, gem-like flame, to maintain this ecstasy" of the present moment was "success in life." He told the story of Rousseau, who thought he had a mortal disease as a young man and asked himself how best to make use of the time remaining. He decided on "intellectual excitement." We are all under sentence of death, Pater wrote; we have an interval between and then no more. "Our one chance lies in expanding that interval, in getting as many pulsations as possible into the given time," to create a "quick-ened, multiplied consciousness." Thus Pater suggested to Ruth that life could be enhanced and made meaningful by what James Joyce later called "epiphanies," moments that should "rouse" and "startle" the human spirit "to a life of constant and eager observation." What one had to do, wrote Pater, was to be "forever curiously testing new opinions and court-ing new impressions, never acquiescing in a facile orthodoxy." Ruth wrote of Pater's Conclusion to the *Renaissance* that "It belongs to the very texture of my life." Pater's words echoed for her "the cry of my deepest necessity." She yearned to burn with "this hard gem-like flame"; to experience the "quickened, multiplied consciousness"; to use "the services of philosophy, of religion, of culture as well," to "startle" herself into "sharp and eager observation." [19]

Pater's words helped Ruth create a philosophy to deal with the issue of death in her own life. When she read Pater her mind was "in the clutch of its first perplexity at the aims of living." [20] Her mother had kept her father present in the lives of his daughters through vignettes, remembrances, and her grieving, especially the tragedy of his early death, a life of great promise unfulfilled. When Ruth began, as all adolescents do, to wonder about the meaning of life, she had to resolve the meaning of her father's life, because on it hinged the meaning of her own. It couldn't be a life lived for the future, one directed toward achieving in the world or striving after set goals, because one might not achieve them and die unfulfilled—her father's life bore witness to that. Yet a life lived in the present had intimations of *carpe diem*—giving oneself up to the ultimately hollow and unfulfilling dissolution of self in sensual gratification. Pater's words gave her an acceptable alternative way of living in the present. What was most important, and most fulfilling, was not to achieve goals but *to live well*. To live deeply in the present moment, to be intensely alive and aware from as many perspectives as possible, to experience acutely love, friendship, beauty, clear thinking, the best within herself and in the world without—these became her goals. The well-lived life contained many "pulsations," moments of special clarity, of ecstatic mystical experience, of deep insight—of Vision, in its ancient religious sense. Her purpose became to experience this Vision.

Pater also suggested that the uses of such personal vision led to the creation of a broad social vision of a new humanity and of new values for society, "the vision of perfect men and things." What was important was "Revelation, vision . . . the *seeing* of a perfect humanity . . . above the *having*, or even the *doing* of anything." What counted, wrote Pater in another essay, was "the power of conceiving humanity in a new and striking way . . . selecting, transforming, recombining the images it transmits." These were the ideas upon which Ruth began to sort out her past and select her future course. Pater also wrote an essay on the Greek god Dionysius which set up a duality between Dionysius, the god of chaos, and Apollo as the god of order and rationality. [21]

But Ruth Benedict later in *Patterns of Culture* credited Nietzsche as the source of her analogies of Dionysian versus Apollonian ways of life, and it was at Vassar that she discovered him, probably in her freshman or sophomore year. Friedrich Nietzsche, German lyric poet and philosopher, used the comparison in his book *The Birth of Tragedy*. He presented Apollo as the "'shining one,' the deity of light," a philosopher-god of "measured restraint" and "philosophical calm," free from wild emotions. Dionysius Nietzsche described as his counterpart, the god of ecstasy, of barriers broken down, with a "hidden substratum of suffering and knowledge." The ecstasy, with its "annihilation of the ordinary bounds and limits of existence," contained a forgetting of the past and the everyday world. When one became conscious of the everyday reality again it was "nauseating and repulsive." Apollo dispelled individual suffering and required of his followers self-knowledge and self-control. But it was the "mystical triumphant cry of Dionysius" that opened the way "to the innermost heart of things." Nietzsche linked Apollo and Dionysius to the duality of the sexes, while Pater suggested that the feminine had Dionysian qualities, the masculine Apollonian. As an anthropologist Benedict applied Nietzsche's comparisons to the Pueblo and the Plains Indians, characterizing the Pueblos as "Apollonian" and the Plains Indians as "Dionysian." As a young woman at Vassar she could only have applied Nietzsche's words to the experience of her own childhood, which began to make sense within this framework, although she rejected his concept of Dionysian ecstasy for herself in favor of the image of chaos.[22]

But it was Nietzsche's *Thus Spake Zarathustra* which she read again and again and marked with pencil. "There's a gaiety and intoxication about it that nothing else quite achieves," she wrote. Nietzsche advocated creative iconoclasm. The Self desires to create beyond itself, he wrote: "Creating—that is the great salvation from suffering, and life's alleviation." The creativity he advocated was the creation of new values. "Not around the inventors of new noise, but around the inventors of new values, doth the world revolve; *inaudibly* it revolveth," he wrote. But changing values involved the destroying of the old as well as replacement with the new. "False shores and false securities did the good teach you," he wrote, for the "good" could not create; instead they crucified the true creators. Those who "grave new values on new tables" were seen by the righteous as lawbreakers, who "[break] up their tables of values." He advocated the destruction of conventional morality and conformity because they suffocated creativity. He affirmed physical joy. He called for a renunciation of materialism and for his readers to develop God within themselves. All of these were qualities Ruth believed most important. *The*

Birth of Tragedy gave her a framework to understand her past; *Thus Spake Zarathustra* gave her a sense of freedom from that restrictive past and a purpose for living out her future. When the time came that she looked for such a purpose, she found it already there, in the words of Nietzsche. She would be one of those who created new values, who gave, as Nietzsche said, "a holy Yea unto life." [23]

Nietzsche said many other intoxicating things. He favored voluntary death, "which cometh unto me because *I* want it," making him "free for death and free in death," affirming her own feelings about death. He thought most actual marriages futile, but ideal marriage he called "the will of the twain to create the one that is more than those who created it—the reverence for one another," confirming her own skepticism about marriage but affirming the possibility that the ideal existed and could occur. Unfortunately, although iconoclastic about society, concerning women Nietzsche was a reactionary. He believed women's problems had one infallible solution—pregnancy; that women were made for the recreation of men and were man's "most dangerous plaything." He admonished women "always to love more than ye are loved," and when loving to make every sacrifice. "The happiness of man is 'I will'; the happiness of woman is 'He will,'" he wrote. Men had deep souls; women's souls were like "a mobile, stormy film on shallow water." [24] So Nietzsche reaffirmed the conflict between being a woman and being a creative intellectual in the crudest terms. Ruth could ignore these words in college and take what she wanted from him. As a college student she knew she was different from the mass of women and his words did not apply to her. Only after she left Vassar would she have to come to terms with being a woman just like any other.

Meanwhile, it was not Nietzsche's ideas about women but Charlotte Perkins Gilman's which had the most impact. Gilman's book *Women and Economics* was "the Bible of the student body" in Ruth Fulton's day. That Ruth was familiar with Gilman is obvious from later journal entries. Gilman rebelled against restrictions placed on women by society. She dwelt on ways women had been limited in the past, telling women that the only way to break away from these limits was economic independence from men. She peppered her book with analogies of male and female behavior of insects, fish, and other sea dwellers and animals in natural history, also using some examples from the "savage life"; hers was possibly one of the first such comparative books Ruth read. Gilman believed in social evolution as well as biological evolution. Because women were economically dependent on men, she wrote, men had become women's economic "environment." To survive, women had adapted to their "environment," becoming abnormally enfeebled in body, mind, and spirit, deprived of natural health, vitality, and intellect. Women had to become producers in society again before the abuses and abnormal, unnatural qualities attributed to women could be normalized to human standards. "Only as we live, think, feel, and work outside the home, do we become humanly developed, civilized, socialized," she wrote. "Woman should stand beside man as the comrade of his soul, not the servant of his body." Gilman reinforced the idea of the home as maimer of intellectual and spiritual growth. She attacked the sentimental idolatry of motherhood and the home, suggesting motherhood should become a "voluntary power," entered into by choice and with planning and training. She even suggested that babies might be better off part-time in another's care besides the mother's. Gilman believed in monogamous marriage, however, and saw it as the ideal toward which social evolution was striving.[25] Gilman's ideas helped Ruth to see herself in college as the shaper of her own life. She and many of her classmates planned to become career women after graduation. They considered marriage as a possibility, but saw themselves primarily doing creative, productive work which would gain them both self-fulfillment and economic independence from men. If the details of this plan remained hazy, still for these young women anything seemed possible.

Ruth nurtured a spirit of self-reliance not only through Gilman but also through nineteenth-century transcendental thought, which held self-reliance up as a fundamental American trait. By the turn of the century transcendental thought had diffused into many areas of American life. It promoted a reverence for nature manifested in the new environmental-preservation and outdoor-recreation movements; it influenced ideas on the immanence of God, the overarching theme of the new religious liberalism. Self-dependence for women, first iterated by transcendentalist Margaret Fuller in the 1840's and reiterated by an elderly Elizabeth Cady Stanton in her essay "The Solitude of Self" in the 1890's, seemed a natural part of this American development. By the early twentieth century a new sense of "feminine individualism" was recognized among women, "a woman's sense of her right to her own life," as a 1910 *Atlantic Monthly* article stated.[26]

Ruth read Emerson and Thoreau, but she came into direct contact with transcendental philosophy through a spiritual descendent of the original transcendentalists, nationally renowned naturalist John Burroughs. In her senior year Ruth joined the Wake Robin Club, the organization that one or two times a year went out to see Burroughs at Slabsides, his home in the woods, relatively close to Vassar. The name of the club honored Burroughs, for it was the name of his first volume of essays. It also described the purpose of the club, which began as bird-watching and broadened to an interest in all aspects of nature. By the time Ruth joined the club, Burroughs had been inviting Vassar women to Slabsides for ten years. He had them sign his guest book, tramped around the countryside with them, and as they left, would take "a curious-looking stick from his mantelpiece, playfully wave it over their heads, and cry after them, 'This is my magic wand. By its spell I make sure you will come again.'" As President MacCracken described one such visit in the 1910's, Burroughs "took us into the woods and gave us a lesson in how to see things; arbitus [*sic*] in bloom, birds and insects and the rest of his world," an activity that fit into Benedict's need to be roused and startled into perceptive observation in order to achieve a "quickened, multiplied consciousness." [27]

Burroughs kept up his connection with Vassar for the rest of his life. Besides inviting the students to Slabsides, he became a frequent visitor to the college during the winter months when he and Mrs. Burroughs boarded in the city of Poughkeepsie, coming out to visit faculty and hear speakers. As one student wrote, "He seemed almost a part of our College—an outlying part, to be sure, but still he belonged to us." MacCracken called him "a Vassar institution." He was an older man with a flowing white beard in 1905–1909, and in looks much resembled Ruth's grandfather whom she trusted and revered. He was an intellectual descendent of Emerson and Thoreau, and his transcendental approach to life and nature appealed to the mystic in Ruth Benedict, who wrote of "coming to recognize the intangible significance of the world about us that can be expressed only through the symbols of Nature." Burroughs' was a different, calmer, more Apollonian philosophy than Pater's and Nietzsche's. He wrote that "a certain balance and proportion" are necessary to life: "Excesses, irregularities, violences, kill." He advocated plain literature and simple living, "the taste for the genuine, the real." For a young woman prone to depressions, wondering at times what was the good of it all, Burroughs' words on happiness must have been consoling. He had his own periods of depression that he called his "blue devils," a phrase Ruth probably picked up from him and one that she used for her own depression for the rest of her life. He wrote that thinking of life as a whole, "the most one ought to expect is a kind of negative happiness, a neutral state, the absence of acute or positive unhappiness." He ended, "A kind of tranquil, wholesome indifference, with now and then a dash of positive joy, is the best of the common lot." Burroughs advocated "something to do; some congenial work," to keep busy and not let the blue devils feed upon themselves. Nietzsche also had said something similar: "Do I then strive after *happiness?* I strive after my *work!*" "Blessed is the man," wrote Burroughs, with some original work, into which he can "put his heart," which gives him "a complete outlet to all the forces that are in him." Or again, "Oh, the blessedness of work, of life-giving and life-sustaining work!" He told his readers, "When you feel blue and empty and disconsolate, and life seems hardly worth living, go to work . . . The blue devils can be hoed under in less than half an hour." Benedict used this advice, sometimes seeking catharsis in chopping logs for firewood. She also used intellectual work as a way out of depression.[28]

Burroughs also wore the aura of having been a close friend of Walt Whitman, about whom he enjoyed writing and telling stories. Burroughs called the countryside around Slabsides "Whitman land," because its qualities seemed typical of Whitman's: "Elemental ruggedness, savageness and grandeur, combined with wonderful tenderness, modernness, and geniality." To Burroughs Whitman exemplified, along with Tolstoy, the triumph of democracy in literature, one of the important issues among American literary critics at the turn of the century. Ruth shared Burroughs' interest in Whitman and wrote an essay about him published in the *Vassar Miscellany* her junior year. She saw him as democratic in making the ordinary world poetic and in celebrating himself as a democratic Everyman. His "most significant message" was "The broadly developed individual . . . the 'strong-possessed soul,'" which succinctly defined the kind of person Ruth wanted to be. She also praised his ability to find and interpret the "divinity of life," of God "unmasked in the husk of things." To Ruth, Whitman, like Nietzsche and Pater, symbolized release, spontaneous creative energy, and a sense of Vision.[29]

The whole question of the democracy of literature became of importance to Ruth, and she wrote two essays on the subject, as well as her Commencement Address, "The Appeal of the Dime Novel." Starting from Burroughs' idea that democratic literature raises the appreciation of the average reader rather than lowering the standard of writing, she wondered whether the clichéd, formulaic writing that appealed to the vast mass of reading Americans would ever become literature, or lead people to prefer literature instead of itself. One essay, "*Lena Rivers*, by Mary J. Holmes," explored the dime novel *Lena Rivers* as literature. She decided that for the uneducated for whom the conventional plots, one-sided characters, and clichéd emotional expression were new and not worn-out, trite, and tired, a dime novel could be a positive influence for good. After all, wrote Ruth, echoing Pater, "it is the quickened sense of life that is sought for, the multiplied consciousness" that is the goal of reading any book, whether classic or dime novel. Her second, prize-winning essay, "Literature and Democracy," whose title reversed that of a well-known Burroughs piece, "Democracy and Literature," investigated the effects of the "democratization of literature," characterized by the growth of the clichéd and formulaic best-seller. Again using Pater, she wrote that people bought such books because "they know they can find the intensity of life they most desire, dressed in the fashion they can most readily compre-hend." But she decided this time that reading best-sellers did not, in the end, attract people to better-written literature. Democracy joined with literature instead to produce literary insight into "the common lot, the common-place details," as Emerson had said it should. This new litera-ture, she suggested, led the upper classes to desire to know the lives of working people and the "disinherited," and desire "to better them so-cially and industrially." Perhaps, she went on, with physical and eco-nomic improvement they would desire better literature. She concluded that although literature had not invaded democracy, democracy had per-meated literature and made it a new thing.[30]

In writing about this issue, Ruth wrestled with her own developing ap-proach to the social responsibility her generation felt to improve society. The response of her sister and most of her classmates was to shoulder that responsibility directly following the ideas of the Social Gospel to render to the economic and physical needs of groups in society. An example of this approach occurred at Vassar during her years there, when the Students' Association built and furnished a small building as a "Club House" for the college maids, a place where they could cook for them-selves, rest, or have social activities.[31] Many Vassar students did college settlement work or mission work through the Christian Association. Benedict, as a member of this generation, also felt the pull of social re-sponsibility. But her response was indirect rather than direct, intellectual rather than social. Hers became the social responsibility of the writer to make affluent people aware of working and lower-class life in order to influence the upper classes to help the less fortunate. Her emphasis stressed the influence of the writer on the minds of people to change society. This remained the cornerstone of her philosophy throughout her life.

In college Ruth came into contact with one other writer who later in-fluenced her life—philosopher George Santayana. His five-volume set of books emphasizing reason in life had appeared in 1905, and Benedict later cited *Reason in Religion* as one she had read in college. She continued to read Santayana's books as they were published throughout her life. In contrast to Nietzsche, his was the voice of rationality, his cool Apollonian tone contrasting with Nietzsche's tendency to excess. Santayana introduced her to the two worlds of Platonic ideal and of reality, the dualism that she wove into her idea of herself and her life. Plato postulated a calm, ordered world of ideals, a world of the spirit above and beyond the actual world, where the potential inherent in actual life, things, and persons, often so poorly realized, was satisfyingly fulfilled. Ruth yearned for such a world and such fulfillment.

Besides developing a philosophy of life at Vassar, Ruth also made friends. A close friend was Marguerite Israel Arnold, whom the 1909 *Vassarion* characterized with the quote "Perplexed where he may likeliest find, True to his restless thoughts." Like Ruth, Marguerite seems to have been a freethinking spirit with a quick mind. She was from Ohio, a debater and member of T & M, on the *Miscellany* editorial board, and president of the Contemporary Club in her senior year. Professors Wylie and Keys were also honorary members. Ruth became a member of the Contemporary Club her senior year. Marguerite remained a close friend for years after their graduation from Vassar. Another friend was Agnes Naumberg, whom the *Vassarion* characterized as "Most forcible— feeble." She wrote satire and humor for the *Vassarion*, became a Commencement speaker, as did both Margery and Ruth, and was also a member of the Contemporary Club with Marguerite and Ruth. She called Ruth "a magnificent free thinker" during their college days in a letter to Margaret Mead after Benedict's death. Another friend was Polly Root from Chicago, where Ruth visited, meeting people from Hull House and acquiring a connection with Harriet Monroe, the editor of *Poetry* magazine, whom she sometimes jokingly referred to afterward as "Aunt Harriet." She also met and became friends with a woman of the Class of 1911, 1909's sister class, named Agnes Benedict. The 1911 *Vassarion* classified her with the words, "To bring in—God shield us! a lion among ladies is a most dreadful thing." Agnes went on after Vassar to become a social worker and author. Ruth probably had also been acquainted with her older sister, Florence Louise Benedict of the Class of 1907, characterized as "the gentle reader." The brother of these two Vassar alumnae was a young man named Stanley Benedict, whom Ruth would later marry, and whose last name would become her own.[32]

She remained close to Margery, as Margery later wrote, "going through all the experiences of life together, and discussing the significance of each, endlessly." Besides suffrage and smoking, these issues included marriage and whether to work and do something in the world or marry and raise children right away, and "relations with Negroes." Margery recalled that Booker T. Washington spoke at the college and "the Southern girls were *horrified* when some of the Northerners ate luncheon with him at the Inn!" Margery was very much a public leader, elected as class president the first semester of her freshman year, serving as the freshman representative on the Committee for Self-Government, an issue central to all the students, and playing the role of Maria in Sheridan's play *The School for Scandal.* In her sophomore year she was one of the select few chosen to carry the Daisy Chain, an affirmation of beauty and femininity as well as leadership. In her junior year she became Chair of the Christian Association's Japanese Mission Committee, a post she held through her senior year. This was good role training for her because sometime during her Vassar years she became engaged to Rev. Robert Freeman, the minister of their church in Buffalo until 1907.[33]

She chose in him a mature man, a man of perseverance and strong personality. He was nine years older than she and had come to America as a poor immigrant from Scotland at the age of eighteen. He preached in city missions and on street corners until, ordained as a Baptist minister, he received a call to become the pastor of a small church in Pennsylvania. He left church work to attend Princeton Theological Seminary and, while there, received a call to Ruth and Margery's church, the Delaware Avenue Baptist Church in Buffalo. He agreed to preach for the church part-time as long as he could go on with his studies and for two years commuted more than one thousand miles a week. In 1907, after his graduation from Princeton Theological, he became full-time pastor of the Lafayette Avenue Presbyterian Church in Buffalo, being reordained as a Presbyterian minister when he accepted the post. Margery and he intended to marry when she finished college, and chairing the Japanese Mission Committee was good training for a future minister's wife. The Japanese had been in the news with the Russo-Japanese War of 1904–1905 and President Theodore Roosevelt's peace-making efforts. "Japanese things are the fashion nowadays," wrote one magazine author in 1904.[34] Thus Ruth was exposed early to a culture which she later studied with great insight.

Margery's executive gift also manifested itself theatrically. She was on the committee to produce Shakespeare's *Much Ado about Nothing* her junior year and chaired the committee that produced *As You Like It* her senior year. That same year she also played Sister Clemency in the play

Sister Beatrice. She edged Ruth academically, becoming Second Commencement Speaker, while Ruth was Third, but Ruth won the Helen Furness Shakespeare Prize. Instead of participating in Shakespeare's plays, Ruth wrote about them, particularly *King Lear,* in a study of the fool as Lear's "sub-conscious self." Both sisters were elected to Phi Beta Kappa. The *Vassarion* characterized Margery as "Clearly a superior woman." Margery was a woman superbly in tune with her time and epitomized the ideal of the "well-rounded" woman President Taylor strove to produce. Ruth needed more time than Margery to discover her roles and niches in Vassar life. She tried public leadership, becoming the class second-semester freshman vice-president and in her sophomore year treasurer of the Christian Association, but these were secondary leadership roles. However, by her junior year she had found her place at Vassar as a writer rather than actress, athlete, debater, or class leader. She was not, like her sister and Inez Milholland, a leader by example and direct action. What all her experience at Vassar affirmed was indirect leadership through the influence of words and ideas on paper, her influence more subtle but just as effective.[35]

She did not write fiction, however, but analytical essays on intellectual topics, usually related to literature. Vassar taught her how to be a critic. In college she used this skill on literature. Later, she would use it on society. Her essays reveal that her interests were eclectic. She wrote about various literary figures such as Charles Lamb, Whitman, Chaucer, and about works such as Euripides' *Trojan Women* and Shakespeare's plays. At least two of these essays evidenced her early interest in differences manifested by peoples of the earth. In one, "The Racial Traits of Shakespeare's Heroes," she discusses differences between the English, French, and Italians as portrayed in Shakespeare's plays and in another, "The Sense of Symbolism," differences between the ancient Greeks and Hebrews. The *Miscellany* published several of these, and in her senior year Ruth became a member of the college yearbook editorial board.[36]

Ruth also in her junior year became chair and only member of the Christian Association's Devotional Meetings Committee, and in her senior year, chair of the Bible Study Committee, a large group of seventeen members. Rejecting again the Martha-role affirmed by Margery, she reaffirmed her own Mary-role, giving her leadership abilities to the mystical, intangible side of religion at Vassar. In a generation of students geared to social responsibility and in an organization devoted to philanthropic work, Ruth's main interest was in the spiritual and intellectual side of Christianity, not the succoring side. The *Vassarion* of 1909 characterized Ruth as:

A salad; for in him we see
Oil, vinegar, pepper and saltness agree.

Her classmates recognized her as a woman of many moods, a mercurial woman with smooth, tart, stinging, and salty qualities mixed together in one personality. Ruth was not a woman in harmony with time and self as Margery was, and this remained a basic source of tension between them. "My natural euphoria," Margery wrote, filled her with "such an instinctive love of life that I couldn't quite grasp the depths of her thinking, and my glib conventional answers were a constant source of irritation to her—." [37]

When Ruth and Margery graduated from Vassar in the spring of 1909, they left with the thought inculcated in them that "the graduate of this college dare not let her life be a failure; she is under bonds to do things in the world." They left buoyed up by the idea that all paths were open to them, that anything was possible. Ruth would learn in the years following graduation how little actually was possible. As one student wrote of the Vassar experience, "life would never be like that again," and once she left, it took her "some time to understand the limitations of the great mass of well-meaning, excellent people of whom the world is composed!" [38]

3

The Limits of the Possible

IN THE FALL OF 1910 one last year of college-like freedom opened up unexpectedly for Ruth. In September she was invited to join an already organized all-expenses-paid year abroad with two other young women, Katherine Norton and Elizabeth Atsatt, only ten days before their steamer was scheduled to sail. Both were from California, and as Ruth wrote, "I had never seen any of the people I was to travel with and hardly even knew the names of the two girls. But it has been splendidly worth the risk." The trip was paid for by Charles M. Pratt of Glen Cove, Long Island, a boyhood friend of Katherine Norton's father, and the patron and most powerful trustee of Vassar at that time. Ruth found Katherine "meditatively sober" and Betty a cheerful person with a contagious laugh. The three spent a month traveling in France, then three months living with a French-speaking family in Lausanne, Switzerland, followed by "two months of joy unspeakable" in Italy, three weeks of it in Rome, part of it living with an Italian family. After this they spent three months in Germany, one month traveling, and two months living with a German family in Dresden, giving Ruth a chance to practice her German and hear "a great deal of music." The tour continued with Paris and Oberammergau in June, Switzerland again in July, England in August, living with an English family, and from there, home.[1]

The trip went beyond Ruth's wildest expectations. She described Italy especially as "one glowing weeks-long realization of a dream I hoped to have that never disappointed, and never seemed empty," with its two months' "continuous succession of beautiful things." There was a sense of freedom to go anywhere, do anything. The three went on a two-day walking tour in Switzerland unchaperoned. It was "an exploration." They walked "for the joy of walking . . . we did not choose to know where we were going . . . We were free as the open road. We had only to look at the signpost and choose where we should go." This Whitman-like exuberance filled her days. Nor was she out of touch with old friends. She had the special pleasure of meeting Vassar friends Polly Root, whom she saw in Paris, and Marguerite Arnold, who was in Dresden at the same time Ruth's group was.[2]

The variety of countries exposed Ruth extensively for the first time to other cultures, other customs, and outside perspectives of America. She wrote of her Swiss family that "All their knowledge and their interests are of things Swiss—the canton, the army—above all else, the army," and that to them, even though they were middle class and presumably educated, America was "a great unknown." Their mental map of America consisted of New York, where everybody lived in forty-story apartment buildings, and California, which abounded with parrots and monkeys, and where people lived on rabbits and other small game which they shot in their front yards.[3] The year had a magical quality with its kaleidoscope of ever-new experiences, its freedom, its richly fulfilling beauty, its intensity.

The return to Buffalo was a let-down. Ruth's grandmother, Joanna Terry Shattuck, in ill health for several years, had died while she was in Europe. Ruth returned to life with her mother and to a society that placed restrictions on her mental and physical freedom. The world that had seemed so open in Europe began to shut down. Ruth began doing paid social work for the Charity Organization Society (C.O.S.) as a District Visitor and began to discover the limits of the possible. The C.O.S. had originated in Buffalo in 1877 and from there had spread to cities all over the United States. Unlike earlier social welfare organizations, the C.O.S. depended not on church sponsorship but on private philanthropy for its funding. It became the first large-scale secular movement for social aid, which it attempted to put on a scientific, efficient footing. The basis of the C.O.S. system was the division of a city into districts, the scientific investigation and compiling of files on everyone requesting aid, and the use of volunteer middle-class visitors, usually women, providing personal support on a family-by-family basis. By 1911 the paid caseworker, still usually female, was replacing the volunteer "friendly visitor." Each week the caseworkers visited a certain number of slum families assigned to them. They rendered what aid they could or facilitated the aid of other organizations or city departments.[4]

Their services ranged from providing glasses for a child with headaches, to placing children in foster homes, helping a man find a new job, arranging a summer trip to the country for poor city children, helping widows, arranging a stay in a tuberculosis sanatorium, providing emergency food, or helping a housewife manage money. Beyond this their purpose was to establish a human tie from the educated middle and upper-middle class to the poor and immigrant families they worked with and to provide them with a vivid example of what their lives or their children's lives could be. The underlying purpose of the visitor's job was "to bring the poor to share her own values and moral standards—to make them more like herself." Thus this woman to whom freedom was so important became the arbiter of others' lives; this woman suffocated by middle-class mores became the agent of constraining people's lives to middle-class values and morality; this woman to whom the world of ideas was crucial left that world for a job externally filled with detail, but internally empty.[5]

Influenced by Professor Florence V. Keys of Vassar, to whom she wrote, "your insistence on the social test of the value of all knowledge has changed ~~my outlook on~~ Even [sic] all my plans of life," she turned from Pater's message that to live meant intellectual excitement and the search for vision and gave herself instead to the obligations of social duty in the spirit of the social gospel. She wrote that after college she "disbelieved." She added, "I had much in me to contradict Pater; my early religion which tried so hard to make me a moral being, my pity for others that almost made me an efficient one. But I was not run into either mould."[6]

Ruth Benedict left two stories based on her experiences with the C.O.S. that give some idea of what the work was like. They concern a social worker named Emily and two cases she worked on. In one case Emily faces the frustration of the death of a little immigrant girl because there are no tuberculosis programs for children. She also faces the incomprehension of the child's mother and her desire to have her child at home in spite of the infectiousness of the disease and her lack of resources to care for her. In the other case, Emily helps coerce a man with tuberculosis back to the tuberculosis camp where he does not want to be; she fights the frustration of his lack of understanding of the seriousness of his disease and his shiftless disregard for his family. She also has to fight his wife's desire to have him home in spite of his drinking and the infectiousness of the tuberculosis. The stories reflect journalist Jacob Riis' words, "It is a dreary old truth that those who would fight for the poor must fight the poor to do it."[7]

Ruth did not want to coerce others to be good or to do the right thing. Moreover, the job brought constant pain for her as she empathized with the poor people she worked with, caught in webs of misunderstanding and ignorance, seeing their children die, losing their husbands to the tuberculosis camp for months on end, women starving themselves so their children could eat, whole families living on "water-bread" or potatoes, the weariness of the drudge work that never brought in enough money. She felt their humiliation at being poor—"the shame of a pauper burial," with "an insolent priest, a hurried mumble of prayer, and a rough lumber coffin." She knew the deep poverty of the spirit her people lived in and could not break out of. The job also brought the frustration of having only limited means of solving life-and-death problems, with help available often too little or too late. There was the helplessness of watching a child die of tuberculosis over several weeks because the hospital would keep her only two weeks when she needed care for six months; or of not being allowed to send groceries to a family in which the mother was living on cottonseed oil and mutton tallow because the husband had returned from the tuberculosis camp and was technically the provider, even though he wasn't working and was spending his days in saloons.[8] Beyond this, the job brought the frustration of being regarded as a meddler by the people she meant to help, who sometimes regarded her with open hostility and often passively resisted her aid. Underlying the difficulties of the job itself remained the fact that she had entered a field that was one of the few professional jobs open to women, and that it was a job that fit right into the traditional concept of women's sphere. Helping the poor was a logical extension of the traditional role which Ruth found stifling. The job required a Martha-like person, a role Ruth was unready to sustain.

After her year of happiness in Europe, "the pressing terror behind" returned. Margery wrote that "Ruth's 'blue devils' waged ever more powerful war upon her battling spirit." Ruth had entered, as she later wrote of Mary Wollstonecraft, "that desperate period of youth" in which she was unable to find "those inner cohesions, those dominating motives" her soul demanded, and felt herself "mocked by every hope of purposefulness" and every attempt to express herself. Margery, completely absorbed in her marriage, found that "At that point I seemed to fail her utterly, for she believed I had become but the witless reflection of my dominant husband." Outwardly Ruth showed none of this turmoil. But after a year with the C.O.S. she found a job in Los Angeles as a teacher at the Westlake School for Girls, run by Jessica S. Vance and Frederica H. de Laguna. In January 1911, Margery and Bob Freeman had accepted a call to the Pasadena Presbyterian Church in Pasadena, California. It is possible they were instrumental in helping Ruth find the job. Margery already had one child, a son, and was pregnant again, besides carrying on all her duties as a minister's wife, so Bertrice Shattuck Fulton decided to retire from her job at the Buffalo Public Library and move to Pasadena to live with the

Freemans and help Margery with the children and the household. Thus the family found itself transplanted to the West Coast, a far different climate and style of life than that of Buffalo. It was here, Ruth once wrote, that she became interested in the Japanese, Chinese, and Koreans for the first time.[9]

Ruth had a bad year at the Westlake School for Girls. In teaching she did not find the fulfillment in meaningful work that she sought. She was as much a chaperone for her adolescent students as a teacher. Her days, though full of activities, seemed "dreary and empty" ("Journal, 1912–1916," p. 132). She was outwardly fine, but wrote in her journal that "All my cheerfulness, my gaiety were part and parcel of the mask." She spent a year "terrorized by loneliness, frozen by a sense of futility, obsessed by a longing to *stop*." She wrote that "bitterness at having lived at all obsessed me; it seemed cruel that I had been born, cruel that, as my family taught me, I must go on living *forever*" (p. 119). She had a deep longing for understanding, but felt blind to others; she longed for the power of expression, yet had contempt for her own efforts. She longed to give service, but felt blocked by her knowledge of people's isolation from each other and "the futility of our helpfulness." She longed for friendship in her deep loneliness (p. 122). She seemed to keep her grip "only by setting my teeth and playing up to the mask I had chosen" (p. 119). Her life seemed without meaning or purpose. She struggled distraughtly to find some coherence in what seemed a vacuous life.

For Ruth life seemed "a labyrinth of petty turns" (p. 119) and teaching, like social work, "a make-shift time filler of a job" (p. 120) which she saw with a kind of dread might become her lifework by default. She considered it a second-rate job compared to those open to men. Even within teaching the average man made $36 a week in 1910 compared to $17 a week for the average female teacher.[10] "There are so few ways in which we can compete with men," she wrote, "surely not in teaching or in social work." If she and other women had to remain single and support themselves all their lives, "why were we not born men? At least we could have had an occupation then" (p. 120). She had discovered, within three years of leaving college, the limited possibilities open to women. The two most favored areas for women, teaching and social work, were female ghettos, limited in scope, salary, and status. She could not reconcile herself to a life in either area. In desperation she turned to the traditional dream of her generation: "a great love, a quiet home, and children" (p. 120). Perhaps, she began to feel, this was the purpose of her life after all, the true meaning of every woman's life, as her society had taught her. She had disagreed in college, but the promises of college for meaningful, independent work had not materialized. Her belief in the feminist principles of her college days, that women could be "the artificers of their own lives" was shaken (p. 131). But even if she accepted the traditional ideal, she wondered if the right man would ever come.

At Westlake three of the other teachers had been unmarried career teachers, no longer young, and she could see her future in their present lives. Her family laughed at home about her "course in old maids," but to Ruth it was "tragically serious." She saw them as barren, "tragically alone," crying in their hearts for husband and home. Yet they clung to the "ideal" they had learned in college, the ideal that said they must be independent, self-reliant women, and instead, to Ruth, they were only pitiful (pp. 120–121). In this she succumbed to the values of her day, in which women who did not marry were viewed most often as unfulfilled, pathetic creatures, stunted by the warping of their homemaking and maternal instincts. She feared she would be stunted too. She also compared her future to those of women she knew in Pasadena, ten years older than herself, no longer young, who would probably never marry. Of them she wrote, "They are fighting the ennui of a life without a purpose . . . doing their best—to trump up a reason for living." This is the constant plea of Ruth Benedict's journal entries—to find a meaning for living, a purpose for life, a pattern that made sense. "What is worth while?" she wrote. "What is the purpose? What do I *want*?" She had already found that there was "no virtue even in a pay envelope to make life seem worth living" (p. 121).

In the spring of 1911, while Ruth was teaching at Los Angeles, the largest suffrage campaign yet organized began in California, to gain the vote for women there on a state level, since the federal government could not yet be persuaded to act. For six months Californians were inundated with the issue: the newspapers highlighted it, there were speakers, billboard ads and electric signs, pageants, plays, parades, and high school essay contests all devoted to the pros and cons of women's suffrage. On Election Day the woman suffrage referendum carried by the small margin of 3,587 votes, making California the sixth Western state in which women could vote and giving the Woman's Rights Movement its largest victory to that time. Ruth wrote nothing of all this in her journal but around this time she read Olive Schreiner's *Woman and Labor*, the Bible of the international woman's movement, which had become an American best-seller by 1911, soon after it appeared in America. This work, more than Charlotte Perkins Gilman's *Women and Economics*, had a decided impact on her. Olive Schreiner, originally from South Africa and a British citizen, said the same things directly and in eminently readable prose that Gilman said in a form which her readers had to struggle to understand. Schreiner began as a novelist, and Ruth first learned of her through her most famous novel, *The Story of an African Farm* (1883), in which a woman overcomes the oppression of her life and rejects marriage when she becomes pregnant, defiantly stating that "a woman who has sold herself, even for a ring and a new name, need hold her skirt aside for no creature in the street. They both earn their bread in one way." Schreiner's depiction of a woman who preferred to have her child out of wedlock shocked British literary circles when the book came out.[11]

Schreiner called her central concept in *Woman and Labor* "sex-parasitism." Using analogies from natural history she showed that there were as many forms of relationships among male and female as there were species on earth, and in some of them the female dominated. But in the human relationship women had become parasites on men. Whereas in the past this parasitism had been confined to small aristocratic groups or classes, now it threatened to become a widespread social problem as more and more useful work was taken from the hands of family women in society. Even education of children had been taken away from the mother. Women, losing their share of the old occupations and not gaining their fair share of the new, sank to existing through "the passive performance of sexual functions alone." They became consumers rather than producers, and in their role as sex objects sought dissipating amusements, becoming "the most deadly microbe which can make its appearance on the surface of any social organism." Such widespread parasitism would result in the loss of vitality and intelligence in women and, as a result, the decay of the whole civilization. To reverse this trend toward parasitism, women needed to be allowed useful and productive roles in society again. No branch of labor or profession should be closed to women, she advocated. "We take all labor for our province!" she wrote, and demanded equal pay for equal work. Judge, legislator, statesman, merchant, scientist, there was "no post or form of toil for which it is not our intention to attempt to fit ourselves; and there is no closed door we do not intend to force open." When women were no longer dependent on men, then men and women could become equal partners, and changes beneficial to both men and women in all areas of life would occur.[12]

Schreiner spoke to women's issues broader than suffrage which Ruth was then working out for herself: love, divorce, motherhood, relationships between men and women. Schreiner affirmed the beauty and health of sexual love, in its esthetic, intellectual, and spiritual as well as physical qualities. Economic freedom and social independence for women would "for the first time fully enfranchise" sexual love between men and women, bringing about "a higher appreciation of the sacredness of all sex relations," not snuffing it out or leading to promiscuity as objectors to women's emancipation feared. Schreiner, like Gilman, believed in monogamy as the ideal for humanity, but she saw that readjustment to a higher ideal of partnership might make divorce necessary. Schreiner accepted the importance of motherhood for women, but not as their all-consuming life-work. "Deep and overmastering as lies the hunger for motherhood in every virile woman's heart," she wrote, not all women would or should be child-bearers. Even for those who had children, she wrote, child-rearing only took up part of a lifetime—"an episodal occupation." She demanded for women "an additional outlet . . . which shall fill up with dignity and value" the extra years. For those not child-bearers, she demanded "compensatory and equally honorable and important fields of social toil." Her underlying approach was not that women should become like men to be equal to men, but that women had their own contribution to offer as women, "a slightly different angle with regard to certain facts of human life," whose value would become apparent as men left them free to offer it. She expected the world to change as women's perspective on life based on their different experiences in living became as important as men's. Women's vision would lead society on new paths. She saw the ending of war as one of the first possibilities of the changed world-view.[13]

Schreiner gave Ruth a way to define feminism that peculiarly suited her past and philosophy. Schreiner defined the Woman's Movement in terms of a religious movement, one of "those vast religious developments" of the past that "changed and reorganized humanity." Like them the Woman's Movement stressed large goals to be attained, reaching beyond "personal life and individual interests," to bind women together into one body. Her overview of the Woman's Movement was complex and far-reaching. The Woman's Movement, she wrote, "breaks out, now here and now there, in forms divergent and at times superficially almost irreconcilable." One time, she continued, "it manifests itself in a passionate, and at times almost incoherent, cry" for a share in public and social responsibility, at another in a "determined endeavor" for self-development; in one country it focuses on "remunerative labor" for women, in another on "an effort to reco-ordinate [sic] the personal relations of the sexes"; in one individual it is "a passionate and sometimes noisy struggle for liberty of personal action," in another "fought out silently in the depths of the individual consciousness." While it seemed so diverse, the Woman's Movement did have a common goal—"the negation of all possibility of parasitism in the human female." The Woman's Movement, she said, was not a movement away from men but "*a movement of the woman toward the man, of the sexes toward closer union.*" The movement did not cause problems between the sexes, she stated, what did was the conflict between the old ideals and the new. "All before was fixed and determinate," she wrote, but now it became necessary to reorient the "ideals, manners, and institutions of the society to the new conditions." [14] Schreiner gave Ruth a way to define herself as a feminist outside the mainstream of political activism and a goal she would return to when her dark night of the soul eased.

After one year at the Westlake School she got a job in Pasadena teaching English at the well-respected Orton School for Girls, founded and directed by Anna B. Orton, a Vassar graduate from the 1880's whose father had been professor of natural history at Vassar for many years. Ruth found this school much more congenial, partly because in Miss Orton she found an unmarried older teacher and educator she could respect. "It really does count to be a Miss Orton rather than a Miss D——," she wrote in her journal (p. 124). With her as a model the future seemed less grim. "I am glad to put my effort into my English classes," she wrote, "glad to have the girls like their work and like me." She still wondered at the episodical character of life and especially happiness. She wrote, "A morning in the library, an afternoon with someone I really care about, a day in the mountains, a good-night-time with the babies [Margery's children] can almost frighten me with happiness. But then it is gone and I cannot see what holds it all together" (p. 121). But she found at least a partial answer to her need for a meaning to life in the idea of self-development: that the purpose of life was continually to enlarge the self, to keep learning and growing. Although the present seemed a series of disconnected episodes, they would all link together someday to produce a mature future self. Then her question became, what is the purpose of this future self? Falling back on traditional teaching, she wrote, "The great instinctive answer is for Motherhood." "Yes, I think I could accept that with heart and soul," she continued; then her natural skepticism reasserted itself: "but no girl dares count on Motherhood" (p. 122).

She still felt a lack of zest for life. She was unable to throw off her loneliness and believe in her work. She had a low sense of personal worth, yet wanted to believe herself valuable, "of untold worth and importance."

She saw this as "the one priceless gift of this life" and envied Walt Whitman his exuberant egoism. She wondered if "this sense of personal worth, of enthusiasm for one's own personality," belonged only to "great self-expressive souls" or to a mature time of life she had not yet reached. "Or may I perhaps be shut from it by eternal law because I am a woman and lonely?" (p. 123). For, she concluded, "The only thing you can give the world is what you *are*—yourself" (p. 124). So she got herself to the end of her first year at the Orton School, a year full of "tableaux, the innumerable themes," being faculty advisor to the school publication, the *Mustard Seed,* and final exams. But the thought of returning for another year left her unenthusiastic. "In a world that holds books and babies and canyon trails," she wrote, "why should one condemn oneself to live day-in, day-out with people one does not like, and sell one's life to chaperone and correct them?" (p. 126). She had come to an endpoint. If she was not going to teach, what then could she do?

The year ended in a crescendo of strain and pressure. Ruth was tied up at school from 6 A.M. to 11 P.M. with final exams and Commencement events when her niece Bertrice developed a life-threatening illness with which she and her mother had to cope, since Margery and Bob were away on a long trip. Finally everything was over. The baby recovered, the students left. Ruth talked with Miss Orton and told her how she hated the meals and chaperoning, and asked for a conditional engagement for the next year. Miss Orton listened and promised her better conditions for the next year. But more than that, she gave Ruth "a self-respect I had not had for months—years." Miss Orton showed her that she was valued; she respected Ruth's feelings and did not offer platitudes about building character by accepting life as it came as her mother and other members of her family would have done. Instead she told Ruth that if any part of life were so hard it threatened to neutralize the rest, it was "the most natural thing" to try to change it if possible (p. 127). Miss Orton sympathized with her as a young teacher and encouraged her to keep enlarging and broadening her life, soothing her fears that she would be limited to a gradually fossilizing life as a teacher. "I want you to have many interests," she told Ruth. "You have much to expect of life." Ruth wrote, "She talked with me as an equal who had a right to his own distastes, and tried to help me plan my year more pleasantly. God bless her!" (p. 128). Tentatively, Ruth made plans to return to the Orton School in the fall.

By July she was wavering. She and her mother had gone back to the Shattuck farm for the summer. Her grandfather and Aunt Myra were living there and would welcome her staying on. Her journal records fantasies of earning money off the garden and orchard, perhaps in time building a prosperous business. "I shall not need much money," she wrote. "I can't believe that joyless life is significant life. I want to plan and manage and learn and work among the out-door elemental things of life" (p. 128). In May she had written, "the farm is attractive but very pious" (p. 126). By July she felt, "This home is waiting for me with the out-door life I love, the leisure, the home-life. Why should I not accept it and thank God?" (p. 129). But she felt guilty turning away from her responsibility to society for her own "private enjoyment." As a result she planned "large work among the farmers and their children to salve my conscience. But I do not know—" (p. 129). Doors seemed to be shutting. "Social work, teaching, farming:—it's rather an undignified array for three years," she confided to her journal. "It bespeaks floundering and mismanagement." But, she reassured herself, her jobs had never been ends in themselves, only means to find a way of living according to "certain passionate ideals" (p. 128), to attain a zest for life such as Pater advocated and to find the way to understand the web of meaning behind the seemingly scattered events of her life. She couldn't do it teaching in boarding school "without endless waste and friction" (p. 129). Buffalo and the C.O.S. were "impossible." She couldn't go "vagabonding" because of the expense and finally, she wrote flatly, "Stanley's ruled out" (p. 126). She had reached an impasse in her life, with no satisfying way to turn.

Then in August, all the barriers broke with a vengeance. After three years of emotional turmoil, of internal struggles over conforming or not conforming to society's expectations of her as a woman, of hesitancy over what to do in the world, and the frustrations of what she was allowed to do, she surrendered. She fell head-over-heels in love and the whole world changed. "How shall I say it?" she wrote. "That I have attained to the zest for life? That I have looked in the face of God and had five days of magnificent comprehension?—It is more than these, and better." Stanley Benedict had come down to the farm for a week in July—"a glorious week of tramping and rowing and reading, of lying on the hilltops and dreaming over the valleys." When he came down again to spend two days before going to Europe, she discovered that she would rather be with Stanley "than anywhere else in God's universe." They rowed down to a place called Collins' Woods and she kept waiting for him to notice the transformation in her feelings, to see her gladness. "It was afternoon when I told him—I had hoped he would see for himself," she wrote. If his lack of insight disappointed her, his response to her words was entirely satisfactory. "He had been lying on the ground. He sat up and moved toward me, and said with a tenderness and awe I had never heard before, 'Oh, Ruth, is it true?' And then he put his arms around me and rested his head against me." They sat there and "in the same hushed voice," Stanley asked her to marry him and she said yes. "And so the whole world changed." She felt "wonderful beyond expression," and concluded, "Every day I have grown surer, happier" (pp. 129–130).

She had met Stanley in Buffalo around 1910—perhaps he was traveling there and paid a courtesy call to the family of his sister's friend. As he wrote to her, "our acquaintance has depended on such little things— there happened to be a moon the night I first saw you in Buffalo—so we could walk to the Museum—without it we'd not have met again—and so it's gone to the end." [15] Stanley Benedict was three years older than Ruth, born March 17, 1884. His father was a respected professor of philosophy and psychology at the University of Cincinnati, in Ohio, his mother a former teacher, writer, and daughter of a college professor. Stanley received his B.A. from the University of Cincinnati in 1906, while Ruth was a freshman at Vassar. He then attended Yale and received his Ph.D. in 1908 in physiological chemistry, later known as biochemistry. The next year he taught at Syracuse University, then spent a year as associate in biological chemistry at Columbia. In the fall of 1910 he received appointment as assistant professor of chemical pathology at Cornell Medical College in New York City, where he remained until the end of his life. In 1913 he was named a full professor and later became chair of the chemistry department. In 1912 he was one of the founders of a group which worked with the medical school hospital to apply biochemistry to cancer research. He was an early pioneer of chemotherapy for cancer, searching for chemicals that would inhibit cancer growth or kill cancer cells. He continued this research over several years. [16] This was one of the things that drew Stanley and Ruth together, for her father had also been working on the treatment of cancer before his death. She showed him her father's papers, and his response was caring and respectful. "I've been reading your father's papers,—and I do so wish he could have gone on," wrote Stanley. "He was willing to start at the beginning and build up a science. And he knew the difficulties and discouragements and wasn't afraid." [17]

In fact, there were many things about Stanley that probably reminded Ruth of her father. He was three years older than she, just as her father had been three years older than her mother. He had planned to be a physician, but had finally decided he wanted to research medical problems, not do general-practice work, and had turned to biochemistry. He was dedicated to his work as her father had been. But beyond that, he seemed to her to have qualities she painfully lacked. He was strong-willed, steady, and serious of purpose. He had found his meaning for living, the pattern and purpose of his life. In January 1913, he wrote her of having "the entire responsibility of several human lives on one's mind night and day," the "turmoil of excitement and endless worry over our cancer cases," and of struggling on, even though the research was "*mostly* made up of disappointments" and frustrations. His work had a heroic quality that hers lacked and that she desperately wanted, the potential to make a large and lasting change in the world. Stanley had his "zest for life." Ruth also found him compatible in important ways. Because of his background Stanley was at home in the world of literature and philosophy as well as the world of science. They both shared a love for the out-of-doors and a quick sense of humor. Moreover, Stanley was a determined young man in love and pursued Ruth with gratifying tempestuousness. He wrote warm, caring letters and at times was not above appealing to her fears and desires. He wrote, "And Ruth—your mask is getting thicker and thicker . . . You're so wonderful behind it—I believe . . . You shouldn't *have* to wear it at all, for it's certain to grow to be a part of you if you do—and then you'll be altogether alone, and it's so wrong for *you* Ruth." At New Years in 1913, he made the two-week journey from New York to California and back just to spend two days with her, one of which they spent canyon-hiking. When she wrote to him that their relationship seemed impossible and she wasn't sure she wanted to keep their promise to spend time in Norwich that summer, he replied that her letter, when he had time to think about it, "*may* make me mad." If that happened, then "wherever you go I'll be there, and get acquainted, one way or the other, whether you approve, disapprove, like it, or don't like it." Again, he wrote, "you've had the reins a long time, and you *have* bungled things, haven't you? So it's time I take them I think."[18] That summer, Ruth handed them to him.

Her surrender to Stanley was also a surrender of the Woman's Rights ideas that had activated her since her college days. In the same passage of her journal where she wrote about her love for Stanley, Ruth Benedict turned to the problem of being a woman, and surrendered, for the moment, Schreiner's and Gilman's words and ideas. "We turn in our sleep and groan because we are parasites—we women," she wrote, "because we produce nothing, say nothing, find our whole world in the love of a man.—For shame!" She concluded that the problem of woman's rights and the relations of men and women were too complex to be solved by "our little mathematical calculations of 'done' or 'not done.' . . . Do we care whether Beatrice formed clubs, or wrote a sonnet?" Was "individual self-expression" important to Mary Wordsworth as she created "the quiet self-fulfilling love of Wordsworth's home"? Women had "one supreme power—to love" (p. 130); by exercising this gift, she concluded, women justified their existence, gave meaning and purpose to their lives. Again in another passage she wrote, "Life lays a compelling hand upon us women. We thought once, in college perhaps, that we were the artificers of our own lives. We planned our usefulness in social work, in laboratories, in schools." Marriage was considered as a possibility, not a necessity. But "all the time we did not yet know we were women," with "a moral hindrance to our man-modelled careers as to a man-modelled costume of shingled hair and trousers.—We learn it at last—that the one gift in our treasure house is love—love—love." If women could not give their love, she went on, they might collect themselves and offer their "second-best" to the world, and might be honored and rewarded, but "the vital principle" would be gone from their lives (p. 131). Thus in the first flush of love Ruth surrendered to biological determinism concerning herself as a woman and to all the old ideas concerning women's submission to women's sphere which she had proudly scorned in her college years. This first flush faded fairly soon, and it is not unreasonable to conjecture that it was despair and loneliness that led her into this relationship.

After teaching one more year at Miss Orton's, a contented year in which she had "Stanley to write to, my work to do, my small busyness of preparation to fill my time" (p. 131), Ruth Fulton married Stanley Benedict in June 1914, on the Shattuck Farm. The wedding was marred only by the absence of her grandfather, John Samuel Shattuck, who had died October 12, 1913. Ruth and Stanley moved into Douglas Manor, a suburb of New York City, and Ruth settled down to the role of wife, with "all my duties of housekeeping and cooking and clothes providing and visiting" (p. 131). For that last year at Miss Orton's there had been no journal entries. But five months after her marriage she felt the need to talk to herself again, at first to express her overflowing happiness. "This year," she wrote, "I have Stanley to talk to, to play with, to passionately love, but no longer to write to" (p. 131). Her happiness spilled out. "I have so much, so much—life seems so incomparably rich these days. I have been happy, happy this summer as I did not think it was given to be unless one were very young or very blind." She marveled at her love, "its strength and depth and power of healing." She celebrated "this satisfying comradeship, this ardent delight, this transforming love—now that I have it," she wrote, "it is what gives meaning to all of life" (p. 132).

[77]

She looked forward to the winter before her "to accomplish anything I wish." With all her new responsibilities, she wrote, "I have such abundant leisure as I never dreamed of except in my year abroad" (p. 131). She planned writing projects. She wanted "for amusement and for Stanley" to write out "the chemical detective stories for which he supplies the plots" and she thought about trying to sell them to a magazine (p. 132). One of these exists in manuscript, "The Bo-Cu Plant," written in 1916, for which she used the pseudonym Edgar Stanhope, in which a plant causes hallucinations that lead to murder in a tropical country.[19] Besides the chemical detective stories Benedict wanted to revise and write other social work stories, but apparently did not write any more. She also wanted to study Shakespeare and keep a book of notes and read Goethe "intelligently" (p. 132). Instead of giving in to the idea of marriage as the death of intellectual life, she saw it as a springboard to creative work useful to self and society. But her "pet scheme" was to steep herself "in the lives of restless and highly enslaved women of past generations and write a series of biographical papers from the standpoint of the 'new woman.'" Originally, it was a book intended to justify her own reversal of ideas on women. She wanted to show that "nature lays a compelling and very distressing hand upon woman, and she struggles in vain who tries to deny it or escape it," as she herself had done. "*Life loves the little irony of proving it upon the very woman who has denied it,*" she added ruefully. Woman could only hope for success by working with "Nature's preconceptions of her make-up," rather than against them (pp. 132–133; italics added). By 1914 suffrage was becoming a major issue in American life, feminism a common topic of conversation. For the next four years, the heyday of suffrage fervor in America, culminating in the passage of the Nineteenth Amendment giving women the right to vote, Benedict worked on her manuscript. In writing it she struggled to work out her own ideas on the balance between feminism and biologically determined femininity and to synthesize a feminist philosophy that would include both.

Her journal began to reflect increasing restlessness as the intense love of the first year mellowed and she found life with Stanley was not the all-fulfilling purpose she had been seeking in her life. By November 1915, she was writing, "I am puzzled about my intellectual bearings. I have a sense of unswept mussiness in my incentives" (p. 133). In October 1916, she wrote, "Again another winter. It is hard for me to look with any satisfaction on the two winters that are passed—and now another" (p. 135). In an undated fragment from this time period she wrote, "Anything to live! To have done with this numbness that will not let me feel" ("Journal Fragments: 1915–1934," p. 136). In another she wrote, "How much hunger for a focussed. [*sic*] for effective action eats inward and leaves only a waste barrenness because no pivotal issues are articulated" (p. 140). Margery wrote that marriage only strengthened the power of Ruth's "blue devils," "and even I realized that she was almost beside herself." [20] She found suburban life suffocating. By 1916 she felt the "house and coal fires and course dinners," the "entanglements of our order of life," were swamping her talents "in mere amateurness," as they were a friend's, and longed to simplify their living style. "But that would trouble Stanley's work," she wrote, and for that reason "it isn't fair to begin with that" (p. 138).

She was having trouble writing, but by 1916 had refined her "series of biographies" to three: Mary Wollstonecraft (1759–1797), the English author of *A Vindication of the Rights of Woman,* the classic book that sparked the Woman's Rights Movement in England and America; Margaret Fuller (1810–1850), American Transcendentalist, author of *Woman in the Nineteenth Century,* the classic American argument for feminism; and Olive Schreiner, the contemporary author of *Woman and Labor.* Besides their intellectuality, all three women shared the mantle of freethinker and lived lives that reflected their radical beliefs concerning women's equality and sexual freedom. All three struggled in their lives with the traditional roles of women, with the demands of femininity versus those of feminism. They were, in the Nietzschean sense, "creators of new values." For them, as Ruth Benedict wrote of Mary Wollstonecraft, "life had no axioms." [21] They were all women identified as having done what she ultimately desired to do, women who had "justified" their lives, made an impact on their own time and on future generations through the power of their ideas. Her purpose for writing this book had changed also, from examining the supposedly biologically determined femininity they struggled against but could not escape, to the affirmation their lives gave other women. "I long to speak out the intense inspiration that comes to me from the lives of strong women," she wrote. "They have made of their lives a great adventure." They had proved "that out of much bewilderment of soul," steadfast aims could be accomplished (p. 140).

As early as 1915 she returned with great intensity to the philosophy of her college years. She recalled the impact Pater had had on her life, and his message came back to her as "the cry of my deepest necessity" (p. 135). Again in her journal writings she was troubled about the meaning of life, which she could not find in "the magic efficacy of service to mankind" as others could, nor in "God's infinity" (p. 134), nor, now, in the love of one man. She re-evaluated the idea of self-development as the purpose of life and decided that if it were not in isolation but part of some evolution of humanity toward a higher state, then it would be a cause to which she could give her loyalty. She felt trapped in a superficial existence. "And surely the world has need of my vision as well as of Charity Committees," she wrote in frenzied despair. "It is better to grow straight than to twist myself into a doubtfully useful footstool; it is better to make the most of the deepest cry of my heart: 'Oh God let me be awake—awake in my lifetime'" (p. 135).

Cracks had begun to appear in the marriage. Although both Benedicts loved the out-of-doors, Stanley was more in the Teddy Roosevelt master-of-the-wild tradition than the gentle approach of John Burroughs. One of his greatest pleasures was to run his motor boat on Lake Winnepesaukee in New Hampshire, where they spent all their vacations. Ruth hated the loud, noxious motor boat and loved canoeing, which bored Stanley.[22] Temperamentally, Ruth needed to talk out problems, analyze them, while Stanley preferred silence and the avoidance of potential arguments. But the area from which most problems sprang was their differing ideas about marriage. Ruth, following the ideas of Olive Schreiner and Swedish feminist Ellen Key, thought of true marriage as a comradely partnership in which intimacy and love deepened as each person asserted and fulfilled his or her own needs and desires. Ellen Key wrote of the need for "assertion of the personality in order to be able to give one's personality," and again, "Each of the twain shall be master of his own person and of his property; of his work and of his mode of life." Women's new freedom of choice, wrote Olive Schreiner, would lead to "a closer, more permanent, more emotionally and intellectually complete relation" between man and woman. This was Ruth Benedict's ideal for her marriage—not self-sacrifice, but a meeting on equal terms that would lead to an ever deeper and more profound union. There is a story that when she and Stanley started playing chess, she studied all the books she could find on the game and practiced until she was as strong a player as he. Even at a gameboard they must meet on equal terms.[23] So it was important to her that, just as he did, she must have her own "business in life" (p. 138), preferably writing. In an undated fragment probably from the fall of 1916 she wrote, "I must have my world, too, my outlet, my chance to put forth my effort . . . [to] realize my purposes seriously enough and work at writing with sufficient slavishness" (p. 136). She and Stanley argued that

Christmas. "I said that for the sake of our love—our friendship, rather—I must pay my way in a job of my own" (p. 138), she wrote. He shot back that this meant that she had discovered marriage in its turn did not hold her. She told him that she would prove to him "that whatever I could achieve in my own life was something added to our relationship with each other" (p. 139).

But Stanley had his own idea of the role his wife should play. He wanted a wife who would take care of his home and his social and emotional well-being, putting him and his concerns first. He opposed Ruth's working outside the home. He encouraged her to write at home, but expected her to make her writing secondary to his needs, and came to have less and less respect for her as her writing produced few results. He came to take her writing, which she called "the self I love," and of which she wrote, "The best seems to die in me when I give it up," less and less seriously (p. 142). He kept his work almost entirely separate from his home life—he did not like to talk about it, did not want Ruth to come to his lab, and brought few fellow workers home. She felt cut off from that part of his life which was most important to him. His two favorite hobbies—taking apart engines of all kinds, e.g., from pumps, boats, or automobiles, and playing with different chemical processes in a photographic darkroom—were not interests Ruth shared and led to more isolation. High blood pressure and a need for rest and quiet made him increasingly reclusive, and they moved farther out from New York to Bedford Hills. To Stanley, Ruth wrote, love was identity: "anything in me that was not in him was betrayal of love, and wounded him as desperately as malice could have."[24] In 1920 she wrote, "the more I control myself to his requirements, the greater violence I shall do my own—kill them in the end" (p. 143). But as time went on, she began to show him "less and less of myself." She felt herself to be playacting as the kind of woman he desired her to be, keeping her real desires and opinions to herself, repressing herself for the sake of their marriage and their love. She wrote, "He rejected *me*—all of myself I valued—and however calmly my outward self agreed and resigned itself to a course of action, it cut the roots of my life at their source." Her life became "a routine to keep suicide from becoming too strong for me in an unguarded moment."[25]

Just as she had struggled with the issue of marriage, so in marriage she struggled with the issue of children. Benedict grew up in a time when people idealized motherhood and believed in the existence of a maternal instinct in women. Even the most ardent feminists acknowledged the importance of motherhood to women while demythologizing the reality of it. Voices like Schreiner's and Gilman's said that not all women would or should be mothers and those who were not should not be regarded as second class for that reason. They stated that women should have work of their own, beyond child-raising. Ruth Benedict knew these theories and also traditional ideas on the sacredness of motherhood. One part of her longed to have children, believing with the rest of her generation in "the same underlying notion: the passionate belief in the superior worth-whileness of our children. It is stored up in us as a great battery charged by the accumulated instincts of uncounted generations" (p. 141). She and Stanley argued over having children. In one argument, he said nothing would ever hold her interest. Children might for a year or two, but no more (p. 138). Later they discovered that she probably could not have children. There was a chance, if she had an operation, but Stanley considered the risk factor too great for Ruth and refused to give his consent. One of the underlying assumptions of major writers about Ruth Benedict has been that having children was so important to her that when she found she could not have them she never felt fulfilled, there was always something lacking, and out of this lack she turned to anthropology, which could only be an inferior substitute for motherhood in her mind.[26] As Benedict herself, very much a person of her time, wrote, "When there are no children, unless the instinct is somehow employed, the battery either becomes an explosive danger" or loses power (p. 141). But the evidence shows that she had begun to study anthropology before she learned of her potential childlessness, and her journal entries clearly indicate her ambivalence about having children before she discovered she could not. They show that even if she had had children, she would have turned to something else later in life. She realized child-rearing would not fill her life, would be intense only for a few years and part-time thereafter, and that a mother could not live vicariously through her children, but had to follow her own visions.

A journal entry in November 1915 records her doubts about having children. The "radiant faith" people had in their children, she wrote, seemed to have come from "a mocking Master of the Revels." One gave up too much to have children, she went on, "the dreams that slipped from us like sand in the hour glass," the work laid aside during their birth and rearing, giving up one's own success for the hopes of one's children's future achievements. The "master stroke of the irony, the stabbing hurt of it" was that society saw this as "noble and self-less" when truly it was madness, "that last infirmity of noble minds" (p. 133). Again, she wrote that Pater's "high level of life" was one to covet for future children, yet that level of life was also "our consummate duty to attain—and not in these friends, these children of ours; in ourselves" (p. 134). She wrote that she had to have her world too; yet, "If I had children or were expecting one, it would call a truce to these promptings, I suppose. But surely it would be only a truce—it would sign no permanent terms of peace with them." She had obviously been thinking about this issue, for in the next paragraph she wrote that there was no "misreading of life" that hurt people so much as the idea that in their children they could carry out their dreams. She added that it was unjust for the child to be born and reared to be the "creation" of its parents. The child "is *himself*" and may be the very opposite of them both. "No," she concluded, "it is wisdom in motherhood as in wifehood to have one's own individual world of effort and creation" (p. 136). In 1923, she re-expressed her ambivalence about having children when she wrote of her "wish for children—and dread they may not want the gift." She was not sentimental about children. When Esther Goldfrank at the Anthropology Department at Columbia married a widower with five children, she wrote in her diary, "I don't envy her." [27]

In an undated poem/prose fragment in the style of Nietzsche, Ruth Benedict expressed her ideas on motherhood and the role it should play in a woman's life. In the piece she created a "Woman-Christ," whose life, unlike the original Christ's, knew sexual passion and motherhood. A woman pressed forward in the crowd as the Woman-Christ talked and showed her her son, saying, "He is my work, my creation, my immortality. Show me now how I shall fashion him that he may bring to pass the dreams I dreamed and could not realize for the strength I lavished upon his rearing." Benedict wrote that the Woman-Christ looked on her and loved her. But then she said to the woman, "You cannot fashion him to bring to pass those dreams you dreamed . . . The boy, your son, he is *himself*." Those dreams dreamed by his mother, the Woman-Christ went on, "he may denounce as hollow and as false." You gave him life so he could achieve *his* dream, said the Woman-Christ. "Those visions which you saw, they were given for the guidance of *your own* life, you had no other, nor can attain one. Go! Live the life you covet for your child:—not vicariously; in your own person shall you attain unto it." She affirmed here that the work of a woman's life was as important as bringing children into the world, not inferior to it. In a poem written circa 1926 and published in 1928, Benedict wrote of a woman seduced by passion into a marriage which resulted in six children, but also the death of her own hopes and dreams. The poem ends,

> She bowed her to the treason of the blood
> That had despoiled her heaven, and she bore
> Six sons and daughters to a doughty spouse.
> What madness worked within her that the bud
> Of any April apple-tree was more
> Than all her children in that comely house?

The memories of her own dead dreams, revived each year for a time, are more important to her than having six children. Written after Benedict found she could not have children, this certainly does not express "pathetic resignation" to this fact nor does it give one the impression that she felt there was "no possible compensation for not having a child."[28]

In fact, Benedict used her inability to have children, which initially must have been a mixed source of great pain and of relief for her, to ease her entry into the academic world, not one to encourage the entry of married women into its ranks, just as she later used her status as a married woman to give her words more weight than an unmarried woman might command. Dropping her high personal privacy barriers, she let her colleagues know that her attention would not be divided from anthropology by child-raising. "I don't have children, so I might as well have Hottentots," she told Esther Schiff Goldfrank when she first met her at Columbia.[29] But a deeper motivation also seems to underlie this remark. In putting anthropological research and writing on the same plane as having children, Benedict indicated not the need to fill some deep maternal void, but her actual deep need for immortality in some form. She had equated children with immortality in the "Woman-Christ." Her journal entries suggest that she wanted to have children in the same way that she wanted publication of her book on the three women. With her subconscious identification with her father, she seems to have expected to die young. Because of this orientation toward early death she saw children and her writing as forms of immortality, as ways to go on, to make a difference on earth after death. Yet rationally she knew, and kept repeating over and over in her journal, that one cannot live through one's children, one has to live one's own life, fulfill one's own dreams. She also used the cultural expectation that women live through their children as a coping mechanism to help her live her own life. She had been using fantasies about the nearness of death to help her get through the days. But as she grew older she gave up her death fantasies and told herself "this is my daughter's life posing as mine," her life that would be perfect, her abilities that would find scope, her insight that would be true and valid, she who had to speak out her beliefs, "who shall not miss the big things of life" (pp. 140–141). So Ruth Benedict helped herself to carry out her own purposes and ideals.

Meanwhile during the nineteen-teens she continued writing her biographies. With this work she struggled to understand herself and to synthesize her own philosophy of feminism. Besides Gilman and Schreiner, her ideas were influenced most by Swedish university professor and author Ellen Key. She had discovered Key's work sometime after it had become available in America in 1911 and 1912. Key managed to translate the ideas of Nietzsche into feminist terms. Agreeing with Nietzsche, she attacked conventional morality, saying that a great part of the work of each generation was the clearing away of the dead rubbish of conventionalism, the dead conceptions of right and wrong. She lauded Nietzsche for his "most profound conception of parenthood and education as the means whereby humanity will cross over the bridge of the men of today to the superman," then expressed her own ideas on the parenthood and education that would lead to this result. Key also managed to combine freethinking with conservative ideals. She affirmed the necessity of free choice for women in all areas of work, but added that nature would limit this choice herself and most women would choose to be mothers. She affirmed motherhood as the sacred calling of women but believed all mothers should be honored, even those pregnant out of wedlock and socially shunned, since she believed children should be conceived in love. She advocated that mothers be paid a salary by the state, thus having their work recognized like any other profession. She suggested the idea of psychic motherhood in which she saw the maternal instinct as giving women power to become spiritual mothers consciously dedicated to improving the race. This may have later opened for Benedict a type of motherhood in which she could participate and which reinforced already important goals in her life. Key upheld monogamy as the highest ideal relationship and the tendency of the evolving human race, but advocated "free love" unions of couples without marriage, believing the relationship bond should be internal, not external. As she wrote in *The Morality of Woman and Other Essays* (1911), "Love is moral even without legal marriage, but marriage is immoral without love." Key combined the Romantic ideal of "a great love" on an intellectual and moral plane with a corresponding erotic love to create a new ideal in which spiritual and erotic love blended, "to free each other and to develop each other to the greatest perfection."[30]

In *The Woman Movement* (1912), her *magnum opus* on feminism, Key concentrated on what she called the "psychological sphere" of feminism. She noted the importance of opening jobs to women and of the suffrage, but stressed the need for women to have jobs they liked and did well—meaningful work rather than drudgery. Key saw the Woman's Movement as a series of stages. The first concentrated on education for women, the next on getting women into professions and changing laws, then women's suffrage. But suffrage was not the Alpha and the Omega. It was the jumping-off point to attain wider and more fundamental goals for women. The next stage, beyond suffrage, was that of "self-development." The first stage of emancipation was of *"women in the mass"* working for joint, common ends. Then came "the task of the present 'radical' feminism," which would lead "each individual woman" to the "free heights" where "feminine individuality can choose her own path of life, perhaps at variance with all others; can choose it in freedom, answerable only to her own conscience." The first movement was "collective work," the second must be "the personal concern of each single individual." From political feminism, women were called to the next stage, cultural feminism; from external reform of society to internal reform of self, and through self, of culture. Only in this way, by clearing out the dead rubbish of conventionalism from people's minds, could society be radically changed. Key saw education as the way to accomplish this, starting with small children to achieve "a liberating of the personality." "To develop woman's personality from within—that is the great woman question," wrote Key. "To free women from conventionality—that is the great aim of the emancipation of woman."[31] Key developed her ideas about femininity and feminism in many American magazine articles and was a well-known feminist theorist in the United States during these years.

Grappling with Gilman's, Schreiner's, and Key's ideas, Benedict in her journal entries tried to clarify her own position on feminism. Like Key she felt work issues and suffrage were only "initial." She wrote, "The deeply-sundering issue in feminism doesn't lie any longer in paid labor vs. parasitism." The new issue was freedom of choice, "Initiative to go after the big things of life" (p. 145), as each woman perceived them; for some, political activity, for most, motherhood, love, social activity. Benedict believed in suffrage and economic independence for women, through her own experience preferring that women should have the opportunity for quality work rather than quantity work. "Our factories are filled with women and girls," she wrote, "and their experience is as nothing—nothing—in their development" (p. 145). Women must have work with value beyond that of a paycheck. She believed in dress reform, that women should be allowed by society to dress neutrally and not in clothes that emphasized them as sex objects or femininely helpless or delicate. She believed that conventional marriage needed to be readjusted away from women's dependency toward equality among partners and the stigma on divorce abolished. She thought prostitution and illegitimacy needed to be honestly faced and hypocrisy about them done away with, and following Ellen Key, that women should be economically compensated as child-bearers. All of these, she thought, were "part of the great objective." But the ultimate goal, she wrote, "remains an inward affair, a matter of attitude." Radical feminists had the duty to attack the "sanctities." This was the area "where women have the great stakes." The goal was "fine, free living in the spirit world of socialized spiritual values" (p. 146) for both men and women—that meant freedom from stereotypes and damaging cultural values, freedom from the conventional ideas of femininity. Like Key and Schreiner, Benedict saw men and women as very different, and these differences needed to be explored in cooperation on an equal plane. She saw herself as a fighter in "the depths of the individual consciousness, that primal battleground, in which all questions of reform and human advance must ultimately be fought and decided," as Olive Schreiner had written.[32] She recognized as central to her own approach to feminism the emphasis on covert as opposed to overt change, the necessity of changing inward attitudes to cause radical social change, and individual action over group activism. She saw herself working within the next stage of feminism, the "psychological" stage, even before suffrage was fully accomplished. In her capacity as a writer she defined herself as of the Woman's Movement but outside the political wing.

Her own definition of feminism did not depend on politics. She wrote of it that "no one who has subjected himself to a half dozen of its meetings could have an iota of hope for it left." Feminism in spite of all the analysis of it could not be reduced to a system. She wrote that feminism was "a passionate cry to be awake, awake in our lifetime," that found expression in one blind alley after another, a "passionate determination" to live life at its full value. She intended her book to bring feminism home to the masses, to be a popular rather than a scholarly book. She saw her book contributing to the internal development of feminism in her readers, the development necessary to change society to a more feminist perception. Feminism had no heroes to rally round, she wrote, and to "the uninitiated," this "lack of a flesh and blood incarnation" was a "perplexing obstacle." Feminism's well-springs were not dry or complex arguments on economics and theories of biology, she continued, because feminism did not live by its logic. "Once adventure thro' the life of one woman who has been profoundly stirred by a great restlessness and you will comprehend more than from a library of theorizings," she wrote. "The urge, the power of this woman's movement" came from women's "bright stinging realm of their dearest desires, their deepest loyalties, it is a passionate attitude toward their own lives . . . to hazard themselves and to risk the maiming, but somehow to attain to something that may conceivably be called living." In her draft notes for an introduction she called being a woman the great adventure of her time—so undiscovered, facing such wholesale reversal of conditions, with confusion to the soul. Exploring and discovering new meanings of what it meant to be a woman would be difficult: "Nowhere else have those upon the quest so much in themselves to contend with." Women had "notoriously seen their life's navigation marked out for them in one or another of two broad, black lines traced across an inherited chart." They had to learn to re-see life as a chance for "vigorous living, much lavish expense of spirit, much 'extraordinary generous seeking'—that vision has become the crying necessity among women." That vision is what the three women in her biography had in common, and they were its standard bearers. Ultimately hers was a mystic's approach to feminism, seeing the wellsprings of the movement as a passionate vision made flesh in the lives of Mary Wollstonecraft, Margaret Fuller, and Olive Schreiner, a vision which she hoped to implant in the souls of her readers. "Unless we, as women, take part on the lists of spiritual adventures . . . unless we are willing to create new goals," she wrote, "our lives today have only a worn-out significance." [33]

She wanted her book to have an impact on society, but its impact on herself was already profound. In her notes for an introduction to *Adventures in Womanhood* she highlighted a quote from William James: "and in picking out from history our heroes, and communing with their kindred spirits . . . Each of us may best fortify and inspire which creative energy may lie in his own soul." By writing about them and researching their lives she communed with them and with herself, keeping her creative energy alive in what became more and more a restrictive, isolated marital relationship. She got from her biographies "in the heat and depression" of her own struggle, the belief again "in the existence of great ends which their lives have already served,—which, if we are worthy of their comradeship, our lives may also serve." [34]

Benedict never wrote anything on Olive Schreiner. She researched Margaret Fuller's life and finished a manuscript on Mary Wollstonecraft's life. Both Fuller and Wollstonecraft dealt with the issues of marriage and children in their own lives as well as career and public usefulness, the same problem Ruth was struggling with. Both suffered early, untimely deaths as her father had, yet both accomplished significant work through their writing and their ideas. Unlike the unfulfilled promise that had haunted her father's short life and unexpected death, their lives had been fulfilled, had achieved meaning. In the lives of Fuller and Wollstonecraft Benedict found many parallels to her own. She wrote of Fuller's childhood, "A child living absolutely to herself . . . and filled with the heroic lives of the Romans, finding relaxation in watching the [NE] sunsets through the dark frame of garden gate," a passage that could have described her own childhood as well. Or again, her draft description of Fuller as an "awkward, overstimulated girl, cruelly [stultifyingly] [sic] repressed in N.E. household, suddenly erupting into a world of girls. where [sic] She felt herself master," suggests the farm and Owatonna. In her notes she copied Fuller's cry that her mind was being used up by ounces: "I wish pailfuls might be poured into it." [35]

For Ruth Benedict, Mary Wollstonecraft was a woman who "made no apologies for her brain," who risked supporting herself by writing, who dared discuss in print the entrapment of women's lives by society, who first expressed an idea that was a passionate belief for Benedict: "that women are more than men's playthings, that they have lives and understandings of their own, and that anything short of a full development of their powers is a duty left undone." As with herself, Benedict saw that in Mary Wollstonecraft intellectual pursuit, even when successful, was not enough. Like Benedict herself Mary Wollstonecraft came crashing against the barrier of her supposed biological needs for fulfilling love. She had loved beyond prudence, through emotional chaos, and finally attained peace with her womanly nature. She wrote that woman's first duty was to herself as a rational creature, but did not disparage marriage or motherhood. She held woman's next duty after care for self to be motherhood, and she held to the ideal of marriage while castigating the reality. Mary Wollstonecraft was a woman whose emotional needs were Dionysian, leading her to place her friend Fanny above all else in her life, leaving everything to go to her when she needed her, and later plunging herself headlong into the chaos of her abortive affair and illegitimate child with Gilbert Imlay which almost led to her suicide. But Wollstonecraft finally at the end of her life achieved an Apollonian peace in herself and within her relationship to William Godwin. She gradually won "a quiet, pervading happiness" toward the end of her brief life, as she came "at last into the powers of her tranquil maturity." To Benedict, whose own emotional life was often chaotic and full of turmoil and who strove to attain Apollonian peace in her own character, Mary Wollstonecraft's life was "a guarantee, a promise" that, though the price would be high, the goal of Apollonian balance could be attained.[36]

The same is true for Margaret Fuller's life. She led a Dionysian emotional life until her last years, when she found Apollonian content and entered a peaceful rather than a passionate relationship with Ossoli. "I feel so refreshed," Fuller wrote in her last year of life, her child and Ossoli diffused "such a power and sweetness over every day"—this Ruth copied into her notebook. In the lives of these women Ruth found the promise that someday she would achieve her own "tranquil maturity," her own Apollonian balance. She found the promise that an early death did not have to mean a meaningless life. For these were women who, as she wrote of Mary Wollstonecraft, did not "catch a character" from the society they lived in, but "spread one about" them. Ruth Benedict found the fact that they could do this in their lives a promise that she could do it in hers. On the cover page of the "Mary Wollstonecraft" manuscript Benedict sent to Houghton Mifflin she used this quote from Nietzsche: "What wonder that even ye have failed and only half-succeeded, ye half-shattered ones! Doth not man's *future* strive and struggle in you?—man's . . . profoundest . . . prodigious hopes." Thus she also hoped to influence her generation.[37]

After she finished the Mary Wollstonecraft manuscript, the coming World War drew her back into social work. She thought she had finished with "the meddling of social work," but spent the whole year of 1917 at it, organizing day nurseries, probably for working mothers. She felt good about it. "I've called an organization into being that's doing good work, and needed work," she wrote. "A dozen other women are working well who otherwise wouldn't have had a niche to work in." But it wasn't this "efficient, philanthropic self" she loved. "The other day when I was getting up an open meeting and spending the day at the telephone, I wept because I came across a jumbled untouched verse manuscript . . . oh, I long to prove myself by writing!" (p. 142). Nevertheless she did Home Service work for the Red Cross in 1917–1918, then in the fall of 1918, influenza nursing and office work with the Henry Street nurses in New York City. Stanley, at the same time, was researching the biochemistry of poison gas and was himself badly gassed, increasing his need for isolation.[38] Her manuscript ultimately was rejected by Houghton Mifflin, but by then her motivation for writing the biographies was expended. As World War I came to an end and women received the right to vote, she felt that the feminist movement, as a collective public political movement, was over. "In a world at war for three years," she wrote, "we can hardly drag back from oblivion the vital questions that were life and death to us that early summer of 1914." Feminism had "its battle-cry then, its militants, its warring camps." Now, as a world-wide movement, feminism was "nonexistent." But war had called woman "out of her ease and indifference and given her work and responsibility." It was time for a reevaluation of life and its values, and women must be ready. In the postwar period, women would play "an unprecedented part." The old goals of the Woman's Movement were satisfied at a basic level. "The vote, labor and the training for labor, love and the right to well-born children" were no longer "grudgingly doled out" to women after "bitter campaigns, but are commanded as her duty." The old goals were gone. Post-war, women must be "brave to create new goals," and the new feminist goals would be internal ones, "a challenge to play a full human being's part in the new democracy of peace that is to come."[39]

4

The Search for Place

THE 1920'S BECAME a period of intense seeking for Ruth Benedict. On one level she continued a personal spiritual quest for vision begun in young adulthood as she retreated farther and farther from institutionalized religion. On another level she continued her quest to transform the spirit of society, begun in her feminist biographies, by seeking new goals and new values to undergird society. On a third level she started a public quest for an intellectual community in which she would have a place and which would serve as the medium through which to influence social change. On the fourth and deepest level, as her marriage to Stanley Benedict slowly died, she continued an ongoing private quest for fulfillment, particularly through a growing intimacy with Margaret Mead which brought her to serious choices concerning her own life. All of these themes wove in and out of her life in the 1920's, culminating at last in her enduring classic, *Patterns of Culture*. The simplest and most basic of the four themes was her search, in the words of Archimedes, for a place to stand from which to move the world.

With the end of World War I and before later disillusionment, a millennial sense pervaded America. The war had been, as Benedict wrote, a "tornado of world-horror." Not only to her, but to all American intellectuals, the end of the war meant a chance for a new heaven and a new earth. "Our vision flashed like strong birds flying," she wrote. Then in 1920 women won the vote, and Benedict perceived the Woman's Movement as stepping forward into the next stage, the psychological stage, the battle for women's and men's minds and beliefs. A new America waited to be forged, a more liberated, feminist America, and Ruth Benedict wanted to have a hand in its shaping. She turned from feminism to a broader realm of influence, the realm of progressive education, as the new arena in which to battle for feminist values in society. Ellen Key had written that education fostered conventional womanhood and gradually erased the individuality of all children. A new system of education was necessary, Key wrote, that should work against the shaping of children's minds into rigid forms and assure the free development of the personality; education that encouraged discovery, beauty, and self-initiative, and fostered instead of extinguishing children's enthusiasms; a system that created an "intense feeling of life," a wholeness, a sense of complete development of a child's potentials—these were the ideals Key set forth to be worked out in more useful forms by others.[1]

Benedict believed education had the potential to change underlying attitudes and beliefs about men and women. In the broader arena she thought education might have the power to abolish conventional ideas in all areas. She decided, in essence, to become an educational philosopher. To this end she first went back to school. She had discovered educational philosopher John Dewey. An article she wrote for the *Vassar Quarterly* in July 1918 expressed her enthusiasm for Dewey's ideas and her own desire to use education for social change. She wrote that it was time to "recast in accord with the new demands the conventional material of school instruction." She emphasized as Dewey had that education consisted of all the experiences and judgments made while taking part in purposeful activity, and that teachers should make use of children's curiosity and delight in doing things. The traditional 3 R's could be integrated into the day's activities, especially those that encouraged cooperation: measuring and math for building play houses; physics in pushing and pulling; writing for recording activities; speaking and reading in performing plays; more reading to find out how others had done the same activity. She told her Vassar readers that never was there "such a chance for the lay-sister to further a program that has as its stakes the future of the race," and as its material, "the youngest plastic child." The war had created a time when people found it easy to spend themselves for others. "To keep our sanity," she wrote, "we must feel that we are somehow doing something for the cause of democracy—[even] if it is only turning off sweaters." But democracy, as readers could see from the tragedy in Russia and city politics at home, was still only in "a long humble process of evolution. The only way we shall achieve it is through education," she wrote. "The cause of democracy is bound up with the cause of the little child." The school, especially the early grades, was the "strategic point in this crisis of unprecedented hopes and ideals." She urged her readers to read Montaigne and John Dewey and visit "schools of tomorrow" themselves; to work on school boards and sponsor private "new hope" schools, and especially to consider the new education as a vocation. "It is the strategic moment,"

[93]

she wrote. The work of "winning democracy" needed the school as its backbone. That fall, 1918, and spring, 1919, she studied with John Dewey at Columbia University.[2]

She was thirty-one when she decided to go back to school. Her age is significant, because it was the age at which her father had died. Psychologists have studied two modes of response to death: participating in death, or overcoming it. Those who participate become partners in the death process. They may wish for death, find daily life colorless and full of drudgery, and the future bleak, as Ruth Benedict did. They see death as a relief. Those who work to overcome death strive for immortality or a satisfactory life on earth.[3] Through her childhood and young adulthood, Ruth Benedict's primary response to death was participatory. She identified with her father and tried to live as much as possible in the "world of her father." She looked for the positive side of death which made it a friend, not an enemy. In her fantasy life while growing up she pretended each day that she was doing activities for the last time, because the next day she would be dead. Holding death as near and expected enabled her to create a façade of liveliness and enthusiasm. In college she developed a philosophy that enabled her to accept the possibility of an early death, that stressed living intensely in the present moment, not planning for the future, and living well rather than accomplishing something in life as the greatest success. Her journals record her recurring sense of the blankness of life and longing for death's relief. But as she approached the age at which her father had died, she grabbed at some way of overcoming death, of reaching for immortality: first through her writing, and when that was not succeeding, through the thought of having a child. When she passed her thirty-first birthday and did not die, as possibly subconsciously she expected to,[4] she took a significant step away from her extreme participation in death. She began to plan for the future; she began to plan for a career. She returned to school.

For many years her depressions recurred, and then life seemed flat and stale, death an inviting release. Death remained in her future as a welcome friend. But the balance had shifted significantly, and the importance of a satisfying life on earth gradually increased in value. "If I can just live till I'm fifty, I'll be peaceful," she once said. A career became a means to distance herself from thoughts of death and lift herself out of suicidal depression by throwing herself into work. She used to say wryly in her early years in anthropology, "I haven't strength of mind not to need a career," a disparaging way of explaining her late return to school, and an ironic truth. But the shape of her later career also suggests she felt a need to give

meaning to her "extra" years of life—to overcome death by leaving
something of herself behind. The massive slaughter of young men during
World War I had an effect as well. This large number of lost youth seemed
to demand "some new lovelier life fashioned from that death." For Benedict this meant planning for a future that abolished war and encouraged
democratic tolerance and freedom of choice. But this future had to be
shaped by present thinkers.[5]

Progressive education remained a life-long interest of Benedict's, but in
the fall of 1919 John Dewey went on sabbatical to California, Japan, and
then China, and her life took a new turn. She decided to take a course
called "Sex in Ethnology" taught by Elsie Clews Parsons at the New
School for Social Research. The New School had opened in New York in
the spring of 1919 as an experiment in unconventional higher education.
Discarding the academic emphasis on course programs, grades, and degrees, its founders emphasized the liberalizing importance of learning itself, offering courses by some of the most brilliant minds in the United
States, including economist Thorsten Veblen and historians Charles Beard
and James Harvey Robinson. The "novel venture" of the New School excited "every liberal in the city," wrote Alvin Johnson, who became New
School director in 1923. Margaret Mead aptly described the New School
as a place then "in a ferment of ideas taught by brilliant people," many of
them social or political mavericks. The New School aimed its program at
older students "delayed or sidetracked in choosing a career," who went
there to explore new fields.[6]

Parsons was a well-known and highly respected sociologist who around
1915 had discovered anthropology and switched her interests to that
field. She was also well known for her shockingly unconventional ideas
on women, the family, and society. Born Elsie Clews into New York's elite
social circles, as a young woman she rebelled against the narrowness
of society's and her family's expectations for her. She fought her way
through her parents' objections into Barnard College, through graduate
work, and to a Ph.D. in sociology at Columbia in 1899. She became a
teaching assistant and then a lecturer at Barnard with the help of her
mentor, Franklin Giddings, one of the top names in sociology of his generation in America. She continued to teach after her marriage to lawyer
Herbert Parsons and through the birth of two children. They had six children in all, four of whom lived to adulthood. After her husband's election
to Congress she quit teaching and channeled her energies into writing articles and popular sociology books on social issues, with particular focus
on women. She wrote her most notorious book, *The Family*, in 1906,

while Ruth was at Vassar. Later popular works included a widely read book called *The Old-Fashioned Woman* (1913), which used examples from primitive societies to awaken her readers to the lack of respect for women in modern society, and *Fear and Conventionality* (1914), which examined the influence unconscious internalized systems of conduct had on the individual, demonstrated how people were lock-stepped within these systems, and showed society's intolerance of those who are different. These and other books she wrote prior to 1919 were considered shocking in their frank discussion of tabooed subjects and their open advocacy of unconventional solutions to social problems. In *The Family,* for instance, far ahead of most people in 1906, Parsons advocated birth control, trial marriage, and sex education for girls. In the same book she wrote openly about venereal disease and advocated making its transmission in marriage a penal offense. She also argued that women should take their place in all areas of society hitherto reserved to men, including the suffrage. As a result of the shocking aspects of *The Family* and *The Old-Fashioned Woman,* Parsons was stricken from the Social Register, "a decision that certainly did not disturb her," remarked anthropologist Esther Schiff Goldfrank.[7]

Even if Benedict was not familiar with her books, the reputation of Elsie Clews Parsons as freethinker, feminist, and pacifist during World War I would have attracted her. The title of the course probably invited her too, as it implied the study of sex differences between men and women and among different societies. Once in the class she found Parsons' approach different from her own. Parsons' sociological books had been broad-ranging, suggestive studies. But even these books showed her to be an inductive thinker, one who concentrated on presenting a mass of details and built general ideas from them only at the end. When she began again in anthropology under the tutelage of Franz Boas, the preeminent anthropologist in America, her approach became even more cautious. She tried to be as neutral and painstaking as possible, drawing no conclusions until the data provided them, which often never happened. Ruth Benedict was a "top-down" thinker with a deductive approach. She saw data as pieces of a puzzle that one filled with insight. The whole purpose of collecting data, the creativity of it, came from drawing general conclusions. Though Benedict did not like Parsons' approach, she did like anthropology and took another course the next semester with Alexander Goldenweiser. With him, the possibilities of anthropology opened up to her.

Goldenweiser was a protégé of Professor Franz Boas, head of the Department of Anthropology at Columbia University. Goldenweiser came from an upper-middle-class Russian Jewish immigrant family. He was a colorful personality and a charismatic speaker, cosmopolitan and gifted. A humanist with a broad range of interests, he was described as "the most philosophical" of American anthropologists. As a scholar he was more interested in theory than fact, in making wholes out of fragments, in tracing patterns. He was teaching at the New School because he had been dismissed at Columbia, against the will of his mentor Boas, who, although he could not prevent the dismissal, had found Goldenweiser this job. Goldenweiser, as Margaret Mead wrote of him, was "always involved in complications," either with women or over money, and one of these contretemps finally brought about his dismissal from Columbia in 1919. In these years he was a creative, productive scholar. He was also, as Benedict described him, "a rare teacher." His lectures were only a small part of his teaching, she wrote. He suggested books and articles and talked them over with her after she had read them. He suggested topics to investigate and gave her criticism. "He did not stint time nor patience," or try to restrain a student's interests, she wrote; "he liked neophytes." He also held extracurricular discussion groups and informal seminars on current literature in the social sciences and "talked constantly of closer raprochement [sic] among the different disciplines." Although she did not mention this, he was interested also in psychology and the psycho-analysts and brought their ideas into his classes.[8]

After working with Benedict for a year, Goldenweiser suggested she become a graduate student at Columbia and sent her to Boas. Elsie Clews Parsons added her recommendation and support as well. So in the spring of 1921 Ruth entered the Ph.D. program in anthropology at Columbia University and took classes with Boas, Goldenweiser, and Robert Lowie, one of the best of Boas' former students and a contemporary of Golden-weiser's. Lowie's upper-middle-class family had emigrated from Austria to New York when he was ten years old. As an anthropologist he had had extensive experience working with various American Indian tribes, espe-cially the Crow. Lowie was urbane and well versed in literature and phi-losophy, liberal-minded and a believer in Women's Rights. As a teacher he favored a careful, disciplined review and consolidation of available facts.[9]

In anthropology Benedict found a community of minds she respected. She found people who shared her values—the belief in freedom of choice, an almost fanatical tolerance of differences, and a dislike of the tyranny of convention combined with an attempt to understand and overcome it. In anthropology she also found a community that shared her sense of difference, of looking on America with an outsider's eye: Boas, Goldenweiser, and Lowie because as immigrants they were "marginal men," living between two cultures; Parsons because as a feminist she was conscious of women's marginal status in American affairs and as a person had different values from those of people in her upper-class milieu. Benedict also discovered "*just* the kind of material I felt it was most important to study: the ways of life that different societies had built up for themselves," ways she increasingly realized were not haphazard bits and pieces but "interrelated and coherent." [10]

In anthropology she also discovered a discipline in which women had created a place for themselves. This included women like Matilda Coxe Stevenson who began as part of a husband-wife team in the late 1800's and after her husband's death continued her own study of Zuni culture. After visiting the American West and meeting James and Matilda Coxe Stevenson, Edward B. Tylor, English author of *Primitive Culture,* had suggested in an article in *Science* in 1884 that women made excellent investigators. On a husband-wife team "really half the work of investigation seems to fall to her," he wrote, because women could get close to and study women and children, where men could not. He called this a lesson to anthropologists "not to sound the 'bull-roarer' and warn the ladies off," but to "avail themselves thankfully of their help." There were also women who had gone by themselves to study Indian tribes, such as Alice Cunningham Fletcher, who, when she first discovered Indian music, went alone among the Omaha and other tribes for several years recording songs and later became well known in anthropology for her comprehensive work *The Omaha Tribe,* written in collaboration with colleague Francis LaFlesche. Fletcher became president of the Anthropological Society of Washington, D.C., in 1903. The society had begun admitting women in 1899 when forty-nine women became members. Women also became charter members of the American Anthropological Association when it organized. Benedict learned of these women and later used the work of Stevenson, Fletcher, and other women in her dissertation on the Guardian Spirit in North American Indian culture. [11]

In Franz Boas she found a person she could admire, and a professor who accepted women as students and potential colleagues on a par with men. When they first met she was thirty-three, and he was sixty-three and had been a central force in American anthropology for over twenty years. During those years he had trained most of the young anthropologists working in linguistics, ethnology, and physical anthropology. From his own training as a physics Ph.D. with a minor in geography and a lifelong interest in natural history he brought to anthropology rigorous expectations of proof, a serious skepticism toward generalization, and a scientist's neutrality toward explanations as only useful hypotheses until research showed no other answer possible. "You don't just *have* theories," he told students; "your materials furnish your theories." His motto was "icy enthusiasm," described as an "ardent, unsparing drive for understanding, completely controlled by every critical check." Scars on his face, reportedly from dueling as a student over anti-Semitic remarks, testified to his uncompromising stance toward what he believed was right. All his life he was a "fighter-for-truth." As Robert Lowie wrote, "In science he was not daunted by 'authorities' nor in life by public opinion. He stood by what he saw as right, and let consequences go hang." The liberal ideals of tolerance, freedom of thought, equal rights for all, and individual liberty that had permeated the German Revolution of 1848 were "a living force" in his home as he grew up and remained the ideals of his mature life.[12]

The war years had been troubled years for him. Born and raised in Germany, proud of his heritage and with family still there, Boas was upset by the xenophobic hatred for anyone or anything German and outspokenly opposed America's intervention in World War I. Moreover, Boas described himself as a pacifist with one exception. He recognized the right of revolution, that is, the use of force when freedom of discussion and free choice were denied. He thought the war a horrible, senseless mistake that would not solve international problems but instead caused problems as authorities in America used the war as an excuse for the restriction of individual liberties and academic freedom. The Columbia Board of Trustees, with the whole-hearted support of Columbia President Nicholas Murray Butler, ordered an investigation into faculty political opinions during the war, to which Boas responded by reading a statement of principles in his classes and trying to get it printed in the *New York Evening Post*. In his statement to his Barnard class he spoke forcefully against the movement to restrict freedom of thought, and especially for the need to protect "non-conformist thought." He advised his students to examine critically the underlying motives of such repression. In this statement he also articulated a philosophy which governed his whole career and which later proved especially attractive to Ruth Benedict. To achieve true freedom, he stated, meant rising above "the fetters that the past imposes upon us" and learning to understand "the obscure emotional motives that determine our conduct and our way of thinking." This required

"hard mental work and the willingness to overcome emotional resis-
tances," to accept the discovery that some "cherished ideas" were only
"traditional phrases without any kind of rational significance." It was the
job of the anthropologist to bring these unthinking habits and unexamined emotions to consciousness and examine them. The basis of the
anthropological approach was "the willingness to take the position of the
non-conformist, not to take anything in our social structure for granted."
This philosophy meshed with Ruth Benedict's desire to throw off the fetters of her fundamentalist, Victorian past and understand social conventionalism in order to undermine it. But Boas' liberal stance led to tension
between him and the Columbia administration which created funding
difficulties for the Anthropology Department. Undergraduate courses in
anthropology were phased out due to a dispute with the administration
over assistants. Only the undergraduate course at Barnard and graduate
courses at Columbia remained, with very few anthropology graduate students. By the end of the war Boas was in a position where he had to re-
build anthropology at Columbia almost from scratch. He himself was the
only faculty member left in the Department.[13]

Boas had not only alienated the Columbia administration during the
war, he had also alienated parts of his own profession, a situation that
came to a head at the annual American Anthropological Association
(AAA) meeting in December 1919. Boas had deeply regretted the loss to
science during the war years, both in the disintegration of international
scientific cooperation and in the loss of good young men as students. But
he became especially inflamed when he found out that some American
anthropologists had undertaken a secret mission to Mexico and Central
America for the American government. He saw this as a prostitution of
the basic principle of the neutrality of science. After the war ended he
wrote a letter to *The Nation* condemning this activity and chastising the
four men involved. The letter, headlined "Scientists as Spies," acted as a
spark to set off long-smoldering anger against him within anthropology.
The Association censured Boas at the annual meeting in 1919, expelled
him from the executive council, and pressured him into resigning from
his position as one of the liaisons between anthropology and the National
Research Council, a potentially large source of funds for anthropological
research. As a result Boas faced the necessity of rebuilding his position of
power within the anthropological community as well as in the university
community, although his senior status and professional reputation remained intact.[14]

By the time Ruth Benedict entered Columbia in 1921, Boas had come some distance in rebuilding the Department. Physically it remained small, occupying three rooms (703–705) on the seventh floor of the Journalism Building. But it had begun growing again. Although he had not persuaded the administration to add another regular faculty position, Boas added classes through the extension program, to be taught by three other anthropologists: Bruno Oetteking, Pliny Earle Goddard, and Robert Lowie. Oetteking was a rather formal, German-born physical anthropologist who in 1921 had just become Curator of Physical Anthropology at the Heye Foundation Museum of the American Indian in New York. Pliny Earle Goddard was Curator of Ethnology at the American Museum of Natural History in New York. He taught a course in technology at the Museum for the Department and worked to keep communication open between the two institutions. He smoothed the way, making the Museum available for class lab trips and giving students temporary research funding and working space. Robert Lowie was teaching in Extension as a stopgap between jobs. He had lost his job at the American Museum of Natural History due to personnel cutbacks there in 1920. In the fall of 1921 he left Columbia with Boas' blessing to become an associate professor of anthropology at Berkeley, under Alfred Kroeber, Boas' first and most successful Columbia student. Goldenweiser served as an outpost of the Department in the New School, recruiting students like Melville Herskovits and Ruth Benedict and teaching courses Boas accepted for graduate credit.[15]

Goddard, an enthusiastic admirer of Boas, had introduced Elsie Clews Parsons to him around 1915. After the war Boas found in Parsons not only a colleague but an alternate source of funds for Department work. Until her death, Parsons paid for his secretary out of her own family wealth. She paid expenses for many student field trips, especially to the Southwest, made good funding deficits in the publication of the *Journal of American Folklore*, funded the publication of articles, and contributed to publication of collections of folklore through the American Folklore Society's Memoir series. In the early 1920's she concealed her philanthropic activity behind the name of the Southwest Society.[16] Without her generous allocation of her personal fortune to anthropology, especially in the early 1920's, the Department at Columbia would have been strangled in its post-war rebuilding.

Among his graduate students Boas had begun to collect the nucleus for a new generation of anthropologists. Students already at Columbia when

Benedict entered in 1921 included Gladys Reichard, who had taught several years, then returned to college to get her B.A. She entered the Department immediately after receiving her undergraduate degree in Latin at Swarthmore in 1919, at the age of twenty-six. Reichard later became known for her field work among the Navaho. Another student was Melville Herskovits, who entered the Department a year before Benedict in the spring of 1920 at age twenty-five, coming from the New School as Benedict had done. Herskovits later became famous for his study of black culture in America and around the world. A third student was Esther Schiff, a 1919 Barnard graduate in economics, slowly shifting from Department secretary to full-time graduate student. As Esther Schiff Goldfrank she became known for her work on the Southwest which challenged Benedict's theories on Pueblo culture. With these students Boas rebuilt the Department psychically as well. Students, even graduate students, had a tendency to be awed by Boas' acute critical judgment and overwhelming knowledge. He had a reputation for being a demanding teacher, expecting students to take responsibility for learning, to be productive rather than receptive, to reach beyond themselves. He expected his students to become familiar with international scholarship as well as American. For those who met his demands his greatest strength as a teacher was that he continually generated new ideas and opened paths to new problems. As Lowie wrote, he did not "merely refute a given view and drop the matter." Instead he gave the problem "a distinctive twist that led to novel insights and stimulated research along untrodden paths." He gave his students a sense that there was "a vast possible panorama, a landscape with only tiny points of illumination *yet*," in which each study and problem added to the light. The goal, which stretched beyond their lifetimes, was to light "all that vast landscape." He excited students' minds—but they also found him difficult to approach. He seemed stern, impersonal, at times forbidding, a man of austere presence. By means of intense discussions in the seminar, which everyone had to take and which Boas taught; by means of anthropological lunches every week; and by accepting the title "Papa Franz," he gradually re-created a sense of the Department as an anthropological community, almost a family, a tightly knit group with a sense of fellowship, a sense of responsibility to each other, a group with high standards, bound by a sense of purpose.[17]

Into this community, in the spring of 1921, Ruth Benedict entered as an outsider. She had not found an intellectual community at the New School in spite of attending for a year and a half. At this time she was deeply shy, somewhat uncertain and awkward with people, and with a

tendency to stutter. She was a gentle, tentative person, "just deaf enough
to miss a great deal of what was being said before others recognized it,"
which made conversation in groups difficult and fatiguing. She was also a
very private person who did not advertise her life or her difficulties to the
world. Esther Schiff Goldfrank, then Boas' secretary, recalled Benedict in
her early student days as "aloof, nodding assent or smiling quizzically at
some passing remark, unaggressive in manner, a person of few words."
Before she found herself at home in the Department she underwent three
experiences that served as rites of passage for her to insider's status within
the anthropological community.[18]

The first took place with the publication of her first paper. Benedict
read "The Vision in Plains Culture" at the annual meeting of the AAA in
December 1921, and although it was her first professional paper, it was
chosen to lead off the January–March issue of *American Anthropologist,*
the major magazine of anthropology in America, a mark of distinction
and a debut that foretold a promising career ahead. The paper dealt with
the multiplicity of ways the phenomenon of the vision had manifested itself in various Indian cultures. Benedict had taken a more difficult subject
than the usual ones—not a concrete item such as a canoe, which could be
followed from culture to culture easily, but rather a state of mind. She had
handled it well. Her article presented a thorough, objective, scholarly
analysis of the various vision elements that met the standard of scientific
neutrality held by Boas and the meticulousness of Robert Lowie, who
emphasized thoroughness of data collecting and caution toward general
theorizing, and for whom she had written the paper originally. The publication of "The Vision," and its approval and acceptance, marked Benedict's first step from amateur to professional and gained her respect as a
serious scholar.

Her dissertation, "The Concept of the Guardian Spirit in North America," was a second, more important rite of passage, from student to colleague, even if a most junior one. It took Ruth Benedict only three se-
mesters to finish her Ph.D., which was formally conferred on her a year
after that when her dissertation was published. Boas, "with his customary disregard for administrative rules," got her credit for her New School
classes, which helped to speed up the process. With the publication of her
dissertation in 1923 she officially became Dr. Ruth Fulton Benedict, for
in both papers she used this feminist form of her name. She was one of
forty women in the social sciences in the United States to receive a Ph.D.
that year. Lowie wrote to Franz Boas that her dissertation struck him as
"an excellent piece of work" when he read it in manuscript and he hoped

it would be published soon so he could refer to it. He added that she seemed to have gone much deeper into the subject than Paul Radin, a contemporary of Lowie's who had written on American Indian religion. Goldenweiser used her material and credited her for her scholarship in *Early Civilization* (1922). In June 1922, linguist Edward Sapir, a contemporary of Lowie's, wrote to congratulate her. "Dear Mrs. Benedict," he wrote, "I read your paper yesterday in one breath," stopping only for supper, "most necessary of distractions." He called the dissertation "a very fine piece of research," and a "notable addition" to the body of work anthropology owed to Boas. He ranked it with Goldenweiser's totemism paper and T. T. Waterman's "Exploratory Element in American Mythology," both considered ground-breaking pieces, but called her work "decidedly more inspiring." In 1922, when Benedict and Sapir apparently began corresponding, Sapir was head of the Division of Anthropology with the Geological Survey of Canada and had a reputation as an outstanding linguist. Boas himself considered him the most brilliant of all his students, so praise from him was praise indeed.[19]

Benedict's article and her dissertation had both been based on library research. That summer of 1922 ushered in her third and most important rite of passage into anthropology: her first field trip. She went to the Morongo Indian Reservation in the San Gorgonio Pass near Banning, California, to study the culture of the Serrano Indians, one of the several groups of the Southern Californian Shoshoneans. She worked under the "introductory tutelage" of Alfred Kroeber, head of the Anthropology Department at Berkeley, and the man Boas considered his best overall student and heir-apparent in anthropology. Kroeber, like Benedict, had come into anthropology from the study of English literature. He was cultured and humanistic, with a breadth of mind that matched her own, and they shared similar anthropological interests. Moreover, they shared something else—Kroeber had contracted Ménière's syndrome whose symptoms over a period of years from 1915 to 1922 or 1923 included vertigo and hearing problems, finally resulting in total deafness in his left ear. Who better could have directed Ruth Benedict in the field than a man who understood her problems with an insider's view and could therefore suggest effective ways to overcome her hearing problem and be productive? In return she may have helped him understand life with a hearing handicap and how to make the best of it. At any rate she always referred to Kroeber's help "with gratitude for the sensitivity of her initiation." Her summer in California inaugurated three decades of continuing intellectual exchange with Kroeber and gave her an opportunity to meet and make connections with other members of the Anthropology Department at Berkeley. Boas was also in California for part of that summer teaching summer school at Berkeley and thus available for consultation as well.[20]

Her first field trip was a salvage operation among a people whose distinctive ways of life were slowly being lost as they adapted to white civilization. She worked with informants, old men and women, who remembered something of the past. These were people who spoke English and whom she could work with individually, preferably in some quiet place where her hearing difficulties would be minimized. The style of field work at this time, which emphasized gathering information about life in the past from native Indian informants, worked to her advantage in this situation. She studied the way the Serrano used to live, the foods they had eaten and how they prepared them, the ceremonies they had observed, their kinship organization, how the tribe dealt with puberty and marriage, and their economic system. She learned the procedures for obtaining information and how to interpret information so obtained. She experienced first-hand the work that made anthropology the special study that it was and had her baptism within the profession.

In the fall she came back to a department and a discipline in which she was no longer an outsider. She had become part of the small, tightly knit community that was anthropology, securely anchored in the Columbia Department and linked to the outposts in California and Canada by ties of new friendship. Information about her was included in the news network that circulated by mail. Boas wrote her in September, before the semester began, "My dear Ruth," and went on, "Gladys writes that you got interesting results [on the field trip]. I am glad to hear it." She became a link in the news network herself, writing the latest from the Department to Gladys Reichard, who was working in California for the winter, and to Edward Sapir in Canada. Esther Schiff sought her advice that fall about the wisdom of marrying a man with three sons. Benedict returned in that fall of 1922 to a job as Boas' teaching assistant in his Barnard class, a class he usually found exciting due to the high caliber of student it attracted. She continued to attend classes, especially the seminar, which drew all the students together with Boas, although her hearing problem probably made it more difficult, fatiguing her and increasing the stress of class situations.[21]

On the other hand it may have worked for her from the beginning. If Boas knew she was hard-of-hearing, as is quite possible since Parsons, Goldenweiser, or Benedict herself might have told him, he would have gone out of his way to speak to her and make sure she understood the material, since he was always ready to help people when shown that they needed help. Or if, because of his strong German accent and partial facial paralysis from a cancer operation in 1915, she could not understand him well in lecture, she may have developed a pattern of going to him and talking over class material. This last seems most probable. This was the pattern she had used with Goldenweiser and apparently with Elsie Clews Parsons. A letter Benedict wrote to Boas in September 1923 suggests this. All that summer she had worked on mythology, she wrote, "and I don't suppose a day has ever passed that I haven't wished fervently I could ask you some question, or wondered what you thought of some difficult coincidence in the stories." But she did not accept his ideas verbatim. A diary entry for January 1923 recorded: "Seminar—*Contra* Dr. Boas on culture areas. He's such a godsend. Argued with him again about the Races book." Whether her hearing was the cause or not, Benedict successfully broke down Boas' formal reserve and established a communicating relationship. That she was in her thirties and a married woman probably also helped overcome his reserves. In the fall of 1922, working closely with Boas and talking with him, Benedict had drawn close to the center of the Departmental community.[22]

But in spite of her acceptance in the Department, she remained marginal in the academic community. Her teaching assistantship was only for one year. The question remained, what would happen then? Boas was giving up his Barnard class the next year and had persuaded the Barnard administration to appoint a full-time instructor to replace him. Benedict had hoped to be that person, but Boas chose Gladys Reichard to succeed him at Barnard. Reichard was thirty years old and single, and Boas saw her as needing the full-time job more than Benedict. In her diary for February 13, 1923, Benedict wrote, "Worst sick headache I've had in years." She knew her subconscious had staged it, she went on. "I suppose it's hanging on to the idea that I can teach at Barnard—which my conscious self has known I couldn't do, always."[23]

But Boas was not unmindful of Benedict's future. On that same day he wrote to Lowie, "I am not sure what Mrs. Benedict will do next winter, but I am hoping for arrangements which will enable her to carry on research work in the field in which she is interested." Earlier, on February 9, he had written to Elsie Clews Parsons, suggesting that Ruth Benedict become her research assistant, since she had been looking for someone to help her. He suggested that Benedict could do research Parsons needed done, and at the same time work on her own independent project, "one of the big problems of the Southwest," the question of comparative mythology. This would give a "young" anthropologist the opportunity for research work and be a contribution to the work of anthropology as well. Parsons replied that she liked his suggestion. The idea didn't quite fit her personal need, "for there is work merely for a copyist which I would not give her," but there was the mythology plus work on kinship terms for a paper she was doing, and other subjects would develop. "I wish you would talk over the matter with her—amount of time, pecuniary arrangement, etc.," she concluded.[24]

Ruth Benedict's diary for February 12 records, "Dr. Boas talked to me about a fellowship in SW folklore. He'd had a letter from Mrs. Parsons falling in with his suggestion." The day after this she had her worst sick headache. She resisted the job in her disappointment over not gaining the Barnard position and because it was a stopgap position. It led nowhere and did not give her the professional recognition and security she desired. Possibly also she did not look forward to working with Parsons because of the large differences in their approach to anthropology. Boas had told Benedict to talk to Parsons, but she couldn't. She discussed the offer with a close friend and "it seemed more possible." Finally her diary records:

~~Couldn't~~
/~~Wrote Mrs. Parsons I'd take the job~~. Wrote Mrs. Parsons I was interested.

After lunch the next day with Pliny Earle Goddard she recorded that he had talked of Boas' worry about her. Goddard said that Boas "supposed there'd always be these driblets of research but that was all he could see ahead for me." She got angry: "I feel some capacity for making a place for myself, thank you!" But on the elevated railway afterward she felt "weary, and plain wept with vexation." She looked ahead and saw this as the pattern of her future and it depressed her. But Mrs. Parsons offered a thousand dollars for the study of Southwest mythology and Ruth Benedict took the job.[25]

She kept the fellowship for the next two years. But she remained on the fringes of academia, as she had feared, for the next several years. Her work for Parsons developed into the creation of a concordance of Southwest mythology and folklore, i.e., gathering tales, abstracting them, and listing incidents. The concordance, as originally planned, would be a reference tool for all workers in the Southwest, consisting of abstracts of the collected folklore of the Southwest, including pueblos, nomads, and village peoples, all arranged for comparative purposes, with some references to outside areas. Boas envisioned it for Benedict as leading to a study of Zuñi mythology similar to his own work with Tsimshian mythology in which he had shown how Tsimshian folklore reflected Tsimshian culture. Benedict worked hard at it through 1923–1925. She spent the summer of 1923 in New Hampshire studying mythology five days a week, gathering background from all over the world, writing Boas that it was "much more enjoyable to work out in a canoe than in the Columbia Library." She got Mel Herskovits in New York to buy her a Spanish dictionary and grammar so she could learn enough Spanish to read untranslated Southwestern tales. In the fall she wrote to Sapir of her planned work in mythology and he congratulated her that "we are going to get a really fruitful treatment of American mythology from you." During 1923–1924 she worked hard on the concordance in the Columbia library, carefully collecting mythological incidents and themes from different tribes, collating them together, and noting the distribution from tribe to tribe on thousands of little slips of paper. The concordance work and her own studies led to her next field trips: to Zuñi and then to Zuñi and Cochiti pueblos in the summers of 1924 and 1925. In Zuñi she found several things to attract her: it was a matrilineal culture—lands and homes passed from mothers to daughters, and husbands and sons worked for them. It was a culture which expected even more conformity from its members than that of her childhood. Where better to observe the role of convention within a culture than in the most convention-bound culture known among American Indian peoples. Many anthropologists had spent time in Zuñi, from Matilda Coxe Stevenson in the nineteenth century to people Benedict knew, such as Parsons, Kroeber, and Leslie and Erna Gunther Spier. Boas had spent a few weeks in Zuñi in the summer of 1920. Most important, the pueblos of the Southwest constituted some of the few still primarily intact American Indian cultures. Ruth could see for herself how the folklore and mythology expressed or did not express facets of Zuñi life and thought.[26]

The trip to Zuñi in 1924 was Benedict's first immersion into a living, native culture, unlike the Serrano one still intact and largely unassimilated into white society. She planned to eat what food supplies were available and stay in lodgings provided by a native family. That same summer, Ruth Bunzel, Boas' second secretary-turned-graduate-student, also decided to go to Zuñi to study pueblo pottery at Boas' suggestion. Bunzel, nicknamed "Bunny," had graduated from Barnard in history in 1918 and had replaced Esther Schiff as department secretary in the fall of 1922. In 1924 she was twenty-six and Benedict thirty-seven. Bunzel and Benedict went to Zuñi together, thus providing each other with companionship and moral support, and mitigating the effects of culture shock. Benedict brought to the trip her experience in anthropology and with the Serrano; Bunzel brought support by her presence to a woman who knew the problems inherent in her hearing handicap. Bunzel wrote to Boas two days after their arrival that their contact there had left Zuñi before they had arrived: "Our hearts went down into our toes when we got here and actually found her gone, and our letters lying undelivered in the post office." They arrived at a time when anthropologists were in disfavor at Zuñi because some had attempted to photograph the mid-winter ceremonies. Their cameras had been broken and they had been expelled from Zuñi. Benedict and Bunzel contacted Flora, a suggested Indian informant who spoke English and worked for the government school, and who belonged to an important family in the pueblo. Bunzel wrote to Boas that Flora received them "like princes," and they rented a house from her on the edge of the village. "We have the unexpected luxury of a bed (not wholly unpopulated, of course) and a table; and we manage beautifully," Bunzel continued. Flora's mother was a potter, so Bunzel was working with her. Flora herself was "a good story teller and a good interpreter," and Ruth Benedict seemed to be "getting along very well with her tales." Flora was talking and Ruth transcribing as Bunzel finished her letter. Nevertheless, Bunzel later recalled, "For the first week it seemed doubtful that we would be able to remain, but through a mixture of caution and luck we survived." [27]

Benedict would bring people back to the house and interview them, paying them money for their time as was the anthropological custom. Flora remembered her as especially generous in that way. She also called her "a deaf," adding, "She always put her right hand on her ear while she talked with somebody and often asked them to speak louder." Benedict took her collecting very seriously, on one day spending eleven hours taking dictation on Zuñi folktales and myths. But she also observed the life around her, needing to know how to relate this still living and growing mythology and folklore to the lives of its creators. Since Bunzel was also there, the two of them could pool their experiences and observations and doubly gain. Benedict's awareness of Zuñi life comes through in such remarks as this in a later letter: "In Zuñi you would never sit out unless it was about to rain because no shade is thought proper in Zuñi." If Benedict had any reservations about herself as a full-fledged anthropologist because of the ease of conditions on her first field trip, they were dispelled after that first summer of roughing it in Zuñi. The trip had another result as well. Benedict and Ruth Bunzel became fast friends, a friendship that would span their lifetimes and professional careers. When her book, *Pueblo Potter,* appeared in 1929, Bunzel, on the Acknowledgments page, warmly expressed her indebtedness to Franz Boas and added, "only less is her debt to her teacher and co-worker, Ruth Fulton Benedict."[28]

On her second field trip to Zuñi the next summer Benedict wrote, "I've discovered in myself a great fondness for this place." She loved the landscape and felt comfortable there. "Nick [Flora's husband] and Flora both eat out of my hand this summer," she wrote. Katherine Norton Brenner, who had gone to Europe with her so long ago, now recuperating from an illness in Santa Fe, visited her there. Ruth Bunzel came a few days before she left Zuñi for Peña Blanca. They went hiking under the sacred mesa, "along stunning trails where the great wall towers above you always in new magnificence. . . . When I'm God I'm going to build my city there," she joked. At Peña Blanca she stayed with a Mexican family, in "a clean room under a tin roof" and her diet consisted of milk and tomatoes, bread and butter. She planned to spend six hours a day there with an informant coming from Cochiti but that did not work out because he did not know enough. She decided to go to Cochiti and use him as interpreter. This was a time when Cochiti was supposed to be a hostile place for anthropologists, so she felt some worry but wrote, "I never do seem to find the spiked fence Elsie talks about [for Zuñi]—and Papa Franz for Cochiti too." So she forded the Rio Grande in a cart and went to Cochiti, where rice and raisins became her staple foods, supplemented by canned soups from "one of these little rows of shelves they call 'stores.'" From experience she knew that "Presently the Indians will begin to provide, and I'll be eating field corn with the rest of them." She rented a house from an old Indian graduate of Carlisle Indian School who spoke precise English, and she suffered the usual run of bugs, sleeping on the roof to avoid the worst of them. Callers deluged her, mothers and "innumerable children who've heard I have candy," and men, including one who kissed her hands "six times with much heat" and whom she discouraged by bribing a little girl to come over and stay with her for a night. Her diet improved with the discovery of three small boxes of Aunt Jemima pancake flour at one of the stores. "The whole village vies to sit with me for a seance," she wrote, since she paid them, and her interpreter dispensed appointments like "a poor fund." She averaged eight hours of dictation a day, then nine toward the end.[29]

She made one more field trip in the 1920's—in 1927 to the Pima, a tribe which neighbored the Pueblos and which lived under the same geographic conditions. She apparently chose them because they presented a contrast to their neighbors in Zuñi, but the amount of contrast between the two groups she found totally unexpected. Here she obtained songs, orations, and long ritualistic myths that were known only to a handful of old men and would have been lost at their deaths. This same summer she returned to Cochiti on the Rio Grande and obtained accounts of more esoteric tales withheld on her first visit. She also included a trip to the Mojave to investigate some special problems of their relationship system. The field trips gave her a great deal of folklore and mythology. For Zuñi alone she had collected a thousand pages. But by 1926 Benedict was seeking to get rid of the concordance work. She apparently had done a great deal of it. She had created extensive card indexes on the distribution of incidents, had abstracted culture from the tales, especially for the Hopi, and had completed a typed outline of story plots for the Pueblos. But by 1926 she was so busy with other projects that she no longer wanted to give time to this one, which was tedious and mechanical in many ways.[30]

By 1924 she was trying for professional legitimization through national fellowship recognition. The 1920's saw the development of nationally coordinated science and social science programs that led to planned projects and dispersal of funds on a scale never before known in scientific circles. One of the first and largest programs was that of the National Research Council Fellowships. The National Research Council (NRC) had begun in 1916 with the purpose of coordinating cooperation between the government and educational and professional organizations to encourage scientific research and the use of research in industry and national defense. Representatives from major scientific organizations like the American Anthropological Association composed the membership, and anthropology was one of the seventeen original committees. The NRC in wartime became the coordinator of the nascent "government-educational-industrial research complex" and with some reorganization continued that role after the war. In 1923, funded by the Rockefeller Foundation, the NRC established its NRC Fellowship program. A fund of $325,000, a huge sum then, was set aside for fellowships in the biological sciences, including anthropology and psychology. NRC Fellowships supported Melville Herskovits from 1923 to 1927 before he received a tenure-track job as assistant professor at Northwestern University in Illinois. Margaret Mead received an NRC Fellowship to work in Samoa. But Ruth Benedict, although she applied in 1924, received nothing on the grounds that she was over the age limit. Elsie Clews Parsons interceded and wrote to the selections committee concerning this action and received the discouraging reply, which she passed on to Benedict, that the board did not consider candidates over thirty-five (Benedict was then thirty-six, and would be thirty-seven that June). The purpose of the fellowships, the letter continued, was to develop researchers "with the idea of assuring the succession to university appointments." The NRC representative went on, "It has been our experience" that someone not established in university work by age thirty-five "is not very promising material for development."[31]

Another source of funds after the war was the American Council of Learned Societies (ACLS), which began in 1919 as a U.S. branch of the International Academic Union. It was a federation of major societies, including the American Anthropological Association, formed to represent scholars in the humanities and social sciences. The ACLS later gave Boas large grants for linguistic studies, but when Ruth Benedict tried for $500 for her work on Zuñi mythology in the spring of 1926, her proposal was turned down as too narrow. Another major funding source remained. The Social Science Research Council (SSRC), incorporated in December 1924, represented a coming together of the major organizations of the leading social sciences. Anthropology became associated with it in 1925, and by the next year anthropologists were applying for SSRC Fellowships. Ruth Benedict applied in the spring of 1926, but again was refused. Edward Sapir urged her to reapply the next year, "Only, *for God's sake*," he wrote, "don't make it so remote and technical as last year." Both she and Ruth Bunzel should get fellowships if they applied. "Hurry," he concluded. Bunzel did get an SSRC Fellowship, which was thereafter renewed, but there is no evidence that Ruth Benedict even bothered to reapply. After 1926, she turned away from fellowships as a possible path to professional recognition. Ironically, her best temporary job of the 1920's occurred as the result of a fellowship. Gladys Reichard received a Guggenheim Fellowship to study anthropological material in Europe for 1926–1927 and Ruth Benedict received her teaching position as instructor at Barnard and a $2,000 salary while Reichard was away.[32]

By 1925 she had begun to receive some status at Columbia. She had taught a course in fine arts for the graduate school in 1923–1924. Apparently beginning in the spring of 1925 Boas got her appointed as a lecturer without pay, which meant teaching status but no steady economic support. This was not unusual. Both Melville Herskovits and Pliny Earle Goddard from the American Museum of Natural History were appointed in this fashion as well. It meant that they could teach through the extension program. More important, she had begun to receive some status within anthropology. In the spring of 1925, Boas relinquished editorship of the *Journal of American Folk-Lore* (*JAFL*) and the American Folklore Society's Memoir series to Benedict. Boas had wanted to get out of the job for several years, feeling overextended. Then his assistant, who did all the technical work, died in October 1923. Ruth Benedict took over her job with the title of assistant editor in 1924, which gave her the experience to become editor in 1925, while Boas remained as an associate editor. This move gave Benedict her first solid professional status in the academic community. She needed it to reinforce her own self-esteem and as public recognition that she was more than just a "hanger-on" in the Department and in the university. The role of journal editor guaranteed her automatic respect from other academics. Other marks of recognition occurred. In 1925 she was elected to the Council of the AAA. By 1929 her AAA colleagues had chosen her to serve on the three-person Executive Committee of the Council, which actually ran the organization, along with S. K. Lothrop and J. R. Swanton, and she served again in 1930.[33]

By 1927 Boas began trying to get her some kind of permanent appointment in the Department as well. In March 1927, he wrote to the Rockefeller Foundation to sound them out on funding both to establish positions for women academics at women's colleges and to establish a new position, that of "associate," in coeducational universities, "primarily for research but also for teaching of advanced students," as women were doing already at Columbia, specifically, of course, Ruth Benedict. Nothing ever came of this, and by fall Boas became much more explicit. In a letter to Dean Frederick J. E. Woodbridge of the Graduate Faculties, November 30, 1927, Boas wrote that he wanted to develop religion as an area study in anthropology with three courses at Columbia and one at Barnard. To do this, he continued, it became necessary to appoint Dr. Ruth Fulton Benedict, who would teach these courses, to an "adequate position." Negotiations over this went on into the spring of 1928, but the dean ultimately refused the request. As Margaret Mead later wrote, "the idea that a woman might become a member of the faculty did not then occur to the administration." Dean Woodbridge wrote Boas that at that time it was impossible to provide "a regular position" for Dr. Benedict in the Department, and suggested Extension courses as the most workable solution.[34]

Benedict by then already received money for co-teaching with Boas and also for her own classes in Extension. She had taught through the Extension program for several years. Extension was Boas' answer to the lack of faculty positions in the Department and also to the problem of what to do with former students who needed a base while searching for a full-time job. Extension courses kept a person alive in academia, but just barely, as Benedict was well aware. She wrote to a colleague in 1928 that her policy was to teach no more than one course a year in Extension for three reasons: first, because "it gives me no position except Lecturer"; second, the fees were not a living wage, just intended to supplement a regular salary; and last, teaching the same course in the Department meant "a more homogeneous group of students" and permitted higher-quality work. Through these years of temporary work she was sensitive to her vulnerable position in academia and to the marginality of her status. She held standards for herself as a professional that included the necessity of a regular academic position with a steady salary.[35]

Although Boas did not succeed in 1927–1928 in establishing Benedict in the Department, he arranged for her to be in charge of and teach the anthropology summer school courses beginning in 1928 and continuing through 1930, at a salary of $700 per summer. "Professor Boas says you are the dictator," one of her colleagues wrote her in 1930 about the summer session. In 1929 Franz Boas tried again to have Benedict appointed to the Department. Writing to President Butler about the future of the Department, he recommended Alfred Kroeber or Robert Lowie as his successor, Sapir for linguistics, and "for the junior position" in ethnology, "I should like to see Dr. Ruth F. Benedict appointed who, for a number of years has proved a most valuable help in the work of the department." This request simmered on the back burner into 1931.[36]

Then things changed. By 1931 Howard Lee McBain had replaced Woodbridge as Dean of the Graduate Faculties at Columbia. He proved much more sympathetic to the Department's needs and to the presence of women on university faculties. The wheels of academia, which had ground to a halt in 1929 on both the Department's and Ruth Benedict's future, started turning again. McBain authorized Boas to recruit Kroeber and Sapir for the Department. In writing to Kroeber Boas told him Ruth Benedict had an appointment as lecturer, but "I am hoping to get for her the position of Assistant Professor." He went on, "Most of her work is being done nominally in Extension, but is actually departmental work." At first Columbia decided to appoint Benedict as a paid lecturer at $3,000 a year for 1931–1932. But Boas interceded and gave up an unfilled position for an associate professor, which would have cost Columbia more money, in exchange for Benedict's appointment as assistant professor. In June 1931, two days before her forty-fourth birthday, Ruth Benedict accepted her appointment as assistant professor at Columbia at an annual salary of $3,600 a year, supplemented by Extension courses worth $1,000 more.[37] This was important, since she and Stanley had separated by then. Now her financial position would be steady; it would be no struggle to earn enough to be independent. But, more important, the salary symbolized her worth as a person. Through the 1920's Benedict had remained caught within a cycle of irregular academic positions: teaching in Extension, co-teaching the seminar with Boas, handling summer school, and receiving a small salary from *JAFL*. At last she had attained a position which gave her academic security and professional credibility. She had found a fulcrum and a place to stand. Now she could begin to move the world.

5

The Social Quest

RUTH BENEDICT SPENT the 1920's in a spiritual quest to transform society through a search for new goals and new values with which to underpin it. In anthropology she found the medium and the focus for her quest for social change—the idea of culture and the importance of culture as a determiner of human life. Through her work during the 1920's she significantly influenced the definition and shape of the concept of culture. Her studies in mythology and religion were significant scholarly contributions in themselves, but all her work in these areas led back to one focus—the role of culture in human life and the dynamics of cultural change. Her studies in mythology, her thinking about religion, her participation in the 1920's social science debate on culture, all culminated in the multifaceted social vision of *Patterns of Culture.*

While groping for an outlet for her energies prior to her immersion in anthropology, Ruth Benedict spent at least one winter working hard at rhythmic dancing, possibly inspired by the work of Isadora Duncan, to whom dance was an outlet for women's spirituality, a return through movement to the spiritual wellsprings of being. But dance turned out to be a spiritual dead end for her. In the summer of 1919 she went to a rhythmic dance camp, but she didn't find answers to the questions she was asking. She found the work of the dancers exciting and worth learning from but was irritated by their "false exclusions," "muddleheadedness," and "holier-than-thou-ness." Among the "riches they cast overboard," supremely important to Benedict, were "hard thinking" and "concern with the life and organization of this world." [1]

This last was so ingrained into the Progressive ethos that no one who came of age in that era could ignore it. Most of Benedict's generation perceived their task as somehow working to create a better society by means of external change: replace crooks in government with reformers; pass laws regulating and cleaning up the food and drug industries as well as other problem areas; clean up the urban environment to create a clean moral atmosphere. But Benedict's perception was different. Her childhood had predisposed her to the belief that the world of the mind was the most important world. This had been reinforced at Vassar, where she had learned that intellectual pursuits *were* activist from the women who taught and thought there. Her foray into "municipal housekeeping" as a social worker in Buffalo had taught her the limitations of do-gooding and of changing people through external means. Her experience reinforced her already instilled belief that real social change had to come through internal change, a change of heart, mind, inner attitudes and beliefs, or the intangible mores of society. She saw external change for the most part as useless or impossible until this internal change came. The Progressive prod to activism came out in her as intellectual activism—change through the power of the written word to alter people's ideas and perceptions of themselves and society. Thus she took up the Progressive imperative to "make society better," not through social activism, but by changing the ideas upon which society's actions were based.

As did others of her generation, Benedict first reacted against the Victorian society of her childhood. Following the ideas of Nietzsche and other radical thinkers, she began with a desire to free society from "conventionality," what she perceived as the suffocating dead weight of custom and tradition from the parochial and rigid Victorian past still influencing the present. Feminism attracted her because it was a bold struggle against conventionality and promised the creation of new values that would revolutionize society as its goal. Margaret Mead wrote that "Woman's suffrage, as a great issue, had bored her." Of course political feminism did not appeal to Benedict. She didn't see the vote, an imposed, external social measure, as important or lasting change. The failure of the vote to change society in the 1920's only confirmed for her the necessity to change internals, not externals. Moreover, such change seemed possible. She wrote in her journal after 1915 that in the world of ideas "the majority are lost and astray unless the tune has been set for them, the key given them . . . the spring of their own personalities touched from the outside." There was no use talking about "Reform," she continued. Society would be "very obedient when the myriad personalities that compose it have, and are aware that they have, an object in living."[2]

After the war, when political feminism phased out, Benedict looked for a movement or a discipline through which to carry feminism internally into society and which also worked to free society from conventionality and conformity, which Edward Sapir once called "a shop-word from your inventory of protest." Progressive education and educational philosophy first attracted her, but she ultimately discovered anthropology as more intellectually stimulating and suited to her needs. For anthropology showed the relativity, the changeability of convention from society to society and the variety of roles men and women could assume in relation to each other. Anthropology struck at the heart of the old social system, at its assumption of the absolute righteousness of its ways and the superiority of its white, Anglo-Saxon base. Boas and his students made no moral judgments about differences in custom from culture to culture. Instead they accepted them as alternate possibilities of human life formed from the particular circumstances unique to each culture's history. Nor were some cultures regarded as better than others. Boas taught that each culture deserved equal respect with every other culture. On one level anthropology promised Benedict the tools to understand the spiritual experience of a society, to explore the social manifestations of spirituality at the same time she was exploring spirituality privately in her own life. On another level anthropology, while a conceptual study, offered future practical applications. Based on the authority of science, it had the potential to lead to internal social change in American society. Critical analysis of the traits of other peoples, Boas had written as early as 1888, would in the end allow for the viewing of "our own civilization objectively." This would enable people to discover both the strengths and the restrictions and limits of American culture, which they did not feel because they were immersed in it. As Benedict wrote of Boas, "The study of the mental life of man in other cultures was to his mind one of the best pedagogical means of making men 'free.'" Once people were conscious of culture, i.e., the unconscious baggage of learned behaviors they carried around with them, they could work to change life and make it better, because what one has learned can be unlearned or readjusted for new purposes.[3]

Anthropologists also studied other cultures hoping to establish the regularities of social dynamics, for if such existed they could be manipulated to produce desired social change. Clark Wissler, Curator of Ethnology at the American Museum of Natural History in New York, as early as 1920 in his outgoing speech as President of the American Anthropological Association stated that when people in Western civilization became culture-conscious, this would be followed by "the realization that problems in culture can be met by the application of the appropriate scientific technique." In *Man and Culture* (1923) he wrote that when humans came into "even a partial understanding of what culture is," with this advance they could "begin to manipulate not merely isolated individual behavior, but group behavior." What was needed, he wrote, was a systemization of all present knowledge of culture in order to "apply to current problems the principles so formulated." Wissler voiced what many anthropologists hoped. Boas, in his suggestively titled book, *Anthropology and Modern Life* (1928), wrote that consciousness of anthropological principles "illuminates the social processes of our own times and may show us, if we are ready to listen to its teachings, what to do and what to avoid." Although he did not believe in overall cultural laws and wrote critically of the "attempts to reduce all social phenomena to a closed system of laws applicable to every society," Franz Boas did believe limited laws of social conditioning could be found. By 1930 he was writing, "It seems possible that laws exist that determine the development of a given culture in a definite direction."[4]

The search for cultural laws was not limited to anthropology in the 1920's. All the social sciences were affected by its lure. Many social scientists thought workable means for controlling society would become possible in the near future. In 1922 Barnard sociologist William Fielding Ogburn, a familiar associate of the Columbia Anthropology Department, published his famous work *Social Change,* in which he surveyed ideas about why changes occur or do not occur within societies. In his closing remarks he noted that changing the course of a culture was more difficult than expected, but that relatively minor changes judiciously applied could have major effects. "These changes," he wrote, "though difficult, may be looked forward to as feasible, if not now, certainly in time."[5] In economics, researchers looked for economic regularities. Psychologists had begun to discover ways to manipulate individuals through behaviorism. In psychology a new area of study developed to look for group laws of human psychology, called social psychology. In American society itself there was a renewed interest in social control. Books with titles such as *Influencing Human Behavior* (1925) by H. A. Overstreet or *Man the Puppet: The Art of Controlling Minds* (1925) by Abram Lipsky reflected this popular curiosity over social control through psychology. People became sophisticated about the idea of propaganda, and the 1920's saw the development of high-pressure advertising, associating products with emotion-filled symbols to provoke an automatic response or appealing to deeply rooted human urges such as sexuality to sell products.

All of this reflected the internalization of Progressivism that occurred in America after World War I. By 1922 America was in reaction against the naïveté and optimism of pre-war reform, which had raised high hopes but had produced hit-and-miss results on a relatively small scale. Crusading was out, do-gooding scorned. Progressivism, as a political movement, seemed dead. The impetus to change external forms and structures of society through law, clean-up, and direct-impact aid had dissipated in the aftermath of war. But underneath this overt rejection of Progressivism, Progressive motivations and goals remained important driving factors. Pragmatism, for instance, the most important philosophy of the Progressive era, had gone from being an overt philosophical system to an internalized set of unconscious assumptions about life and society. These assumptions included acceptance of the changeability of values, the importance of a scientific approach, and the affirmation of human ability to change society. Pragmatists believed that values came from within the context of action instead of being imposed from an external set of absolute givens. Therefore it was possible for values to change. Pragmatic philosophers had also emphasized that science was the key. When science and values combined, it would be possible to pick out and discard obsolete or unreal values which developed outside the context of action. In a world constantly changing to the point of chaos, Pragmatists also contended that human beings were not helpless but instead were responsible actors. In a world so unfinished there was room both for the unpredictable and for additions and improvements by humans. Although people did not have complete freedom of choice, they could engage in experimental activity, and they could change the direction in which events flowed at crucial points. The redirecting might be helpful or detrimental, the Pragmatists concluded, but it was human responsibility to act.[6] This philosophy had done its share to motivate Progressive reform. It now went underground, and Progressivism itself became covert, a cultural force rather than a political one.

In the social sciences this meant that social reform went from explicit to implicit expression, from being a direct result of social science research to an indirect one. It was believed that reform had failed because of the excessive optimism and idealism of people operating without understanding what they were trying to change. Expertise was required. Once "the facts" became available and the regularities were established, intelligent choices could be made, and effective reform ordered toward creating a better society could begin, with the possibility of producing lasting results. For this to occur, the methods of science, pursued with the utmost objectivity, were necessary. Ironically, this meant that, while the social sciences rejected Progressivism, they continued to use the methodology developed during the Progressive era. In reaction to nineteenth-century value judgments and moral assumptions, social scientists had vowed by the nineteen-teens to give up armchair theorizing, introspection, and impressionism, that is, the making of generalized judgments from an extremely small number of scattered cases, or even one case, since these were the methods by which nineteenth-century thinkers had arrived at their ideas. They opted instead to study humanity objectively, i.e., by using concrete, verifiable data and by emphasizing the study of overt, external behavior which others could reobserve in order to check research results. They stressed particularity, i.e., dealing with specific facts, rather than concepts; the particular case, not the general. They emphasized an operational approach, the study of how something actually operated in practice rather than in theory, which involved the use of rigorous, verifiable observational methods.

In economics and political science this meant studying the actual operations of organized economic groups and forms of government. In sociology it led to direct observation of social groups and the development of participant observation—for example, one sociologist lived as a hobo and wrote a descriptive account of that life without passing judgment on it. Psychologists began studying overt behavior and developing psychological testing and experimental psychology, which studied the behavior of rats in mazes. For anthropologists the new approach meant the development of field work, actual living in and observing the daily workings of primitive cultures, interviewing members of these cultures to understand their point of view. It also included writing descriptive accounts of primitive cultures without making moral judgments. It meant collecting vast amounts of raw data, ranging from the collection in physical anthropology of thousands of strands of hair to the need in cultural anthropology for all possible existing variants of myths and folktales, or in linguistics of all possible vocabulary words, grammars, and ways of pronunciation. With objectivity, particularity, and an operational approach, social scientists in the 1920's felt confident they would succeed where political Progressives had failed. Through knowledge they would find a way to manipulate and regulate change in human societies. For many the purpose specifically was to promote change in American society.[7]

In the last sentence of her dissertation Ruth Benedict showed herself conscious of these goals. She spoke of the need to abandon the "superstition" that culture for all humankind was "an organism functionally interrelated," i.e., a *closed system* as the nineteenth-century evolutionary anthropologists had proposed. Without this change, she concluded, "we shall be unable to see our cultural life objectively, or to *control its mani-*

festations." In a 1922 letter Sapir spoke of Benedict's desire to "evangelize" for the idea of culture. Benedict and Sapir discussed Ogburn's *Social Change* when Sapir visited New York in the spring of 1923. Ogburn had introduced the idea of "cultural lag." He showed change in culture as uneven. Part of a culture changed, but another part needed to catch up with this change. Mores, he wrote, lagged behind actual conditions. That same year Benedict read John Dewey's *Human Nature and Conduct* (1922), which emphasized the inertia of custom. "Habits of thought outlive modifications in habits of overt action," he wrote. The key to lasting social change then seemed to lie in showing people that their actions were often directed by culture and making them aware of the arbitrariness, the illogical absurdity of some features of their own culture.[8]

By that spring Benedict had already become engaged in the project of making America culture-conscious by writing popular articles for placement in various magazines like the *Nation,* the *New Republic, American Mercury, Scribner's, Harper's,* and *Century* in order to make anthropological ideas an important factor in American life. Barnard senior anthropology student Margaret Mead wrote her grandmother that Mrs. Benedict belonged to a "press committee which tries to popularize Anthropology and make at least a few of its ideas common coin."[9] In this she followed the lead of Boas, who wrote hundreds of letters and articles to widely read magazines and papers throughout his career. He wrote his early classic, *The Mind of Primitive Man* (1911), for a popular, educated audience and later wrote *Anthropology and Modern Life* (1928) for the same audience. Robert Lowie's pen was familiar to the readers of H. L. Mencken's *American Mercury* throughout the 1920's, and Edward Sapir, Alfred Kroeber, and other students of Boas each published several popular articles during this decade on anthropology and related topics. Benedict left several manuscripts unpublished during her lifetime that show her own efforts at popularization. The earliest, "Cups of Clay," no longer exists, but the material was later incorporated into *Patterns of Culture.* Apparently it dealt with becoming culture-conscious, trying to show its readers that there is a fabric of standards, beliefs, rituals, and institutions that shape and give meaning to life. She elaborated on the words of one of her informants, a Serrano Indian chief, "God gave to every people a cup, a cup of clay, and from this cup they drank their life." He continued, "They all dipped in the water, but their cups were different. Our cup is broken now. It has passed away."[10]

At the time Ruth Benedict entered anthropology, the concept of culture was acquiring new importance. The "nature-nurture" debate had been going on since before Englishman Francis Galton coined the term in 1874, but nature had always held the dominant place. Into the twentieth century the majority of scientists assumed that inherited traits or characteristics were more important than influences from without that affected people after birth. In the nineteenth century this had locked thinkers into a type of biological determinism which came to seem more and more of a trap as the Progressive era advanced. For example, they and society in general assumed that masculinity and femininity were biologically determined, just as gender was. Just as biological secondary sex characteristics such as facial hair in men or breasts in women appeared at puberty, so did the character traits of men and women. Society assumed that masculine and feminine qualities like dominance in men and the instinct for nurturing in women came into their own at puberty. There was nothing anyone could do to control or reject these changes because of their inherent, biological nature. In the same way society considered criminal tendencies to be innate and subject to heredity, as were insanity and racial inferiority. But during the Progressive era environment came to be viewed as a shaper of character at least as important as biology and in some cases even more so. A substantial number of thinkers and educated people came to see criminality, poverty, and racial inferiority as the results of environmental pressures on individuals: growing up in a bad neighborhood, living in slum conditions beyond the individual's control, losing a job and being unable to find one due to widespread economic problems, having a poor education. The first thirty years of the twentieth century saw the playing out of a great debate to see which would triumph in the American thought system: nature or nurture, biology or environment. In anthropology the debate took the form of deciding which was a more important influence on human development, "race" or "culture," inherent characteristics or learned behavior. In the process new ideas of culture and new questions about it appeared.

Culture in general in the nineteenth century had meant the fine arts of civilized nations. Then Englishman Edward Tylor, in *Primitive Culture* (1871), created a broader concept of culture as all the learned behavior "acquired by man as a member of society," including "knowledge, belief, art, morals, law, custom, and any other capabilities and habits." [11] This definition of culture became the basis of anthropological study. But beyond the above straightforward definition of culture, Tylor's concept carried a load of intellectual baggage that Franz Boas and other American anthropologists could not accept by the turn of the century. Tylor's idea included the element that human culture was somehow an organic whole, a vast, absolute, closed system, all humankind progressing together at various stages of development. He believed cultures evolved linearly from lower to higher states, from savagery through barbarism to civilization, with Europe and America the highest forms of culture so far evolved. He equated primitives with children in their moral and intellectual condition and assumed that evolution ran from simple cultures toward complex. He saw culture as the result of immutable laws beyond human ability to change.

Boas and his students spent the first twenty years of the twentieth century disproving these theories through studies of the diffusion of cultural artifacts such as canoe design or tattooing and of cultural traits such as language or the use of the vision or guardian-spirit idea in religion. The diffusion studies disproved the idea of culture as a purposeful universal organic evolution of humankind by showing the chance processes historically involved in a trait's movement from culture to culture. Actual studies of tribes revealed that some "primitive" cultures were more complex than so-called more advanced cultures in areas like language or social organization.

During the early years of the twentieth century anthropology was classed as a biological science, as was psychology. But at that time a movement began within biology that went against the idea of culture as learned behavior and linked cultural achievement to race. Following the Lamarckian idea of the inheritance of acquired characteristics, a broadly popular scientific concept in the late 1800's and later, and embracing Social Darwinism with its imperative of survival of the fittest and its idea that hereditary forces determined human development uninfluenced by cultural environment, the proponents of the eugenics movement believed that biological heredity determined whether or not a race continued to develop and evolve to higher levels. They believed that the degree of culture depended on original mental and physical endowment rather than the ways a people lived. They therefore founded eugenics as the science of "race improvement," planning to better the race culturally and physically through controlled breeding programs, including sterilization of the "unfit." By 1910 eugenics had become a major social influence in the United States.

In a direct attack on the eugenics idea, Boas in his book *The Mind of Primitive Man* (1911) had affirmed that culture was a result of a variety of external conditions acting upon general human qualities, and not an expression of innate or hereditary mental qualities. According to historical anthropologist George Stocking the "whole thrust" of Boas' thought was to differentiate the ideas of race and culture, to "separate biological and cultural heredity," and beyond that to emphasize the importance of cultural processes, an area neglected in the past, and to free the idea of culture from its racist and evolutionist anchors/survivals, so that as Stocking concluded, culture could become "completely independent of biological determinism." In a 1916 article in *Scientific Monthly* Boas attacked eugenics as an extreme pseudo-science in which "nature not nurture" had become a dogma. As a result of eugenics' extreme doctrines, Boas said, anthropologists and biologists had come to a "parting of the ways." [12]

The major coups de grace were given to the idea of culture as innate and hereditary the next year in Alfred Kroeber's article "The Superorganic" and Robert Lowie's book *Culture and Ethnology.* Kroeber described culture as wholly non-biological, free from the constraints of physical evolution and biological determinism, and affirmed that culture, not heredity, was the primary influence on human beings. He called this recognition of the overwhelming importance of culture in human life "as fundamental a shifting of mental and emotional point of view . . . as when the Copernican doctrine challenged the prior conviction of the world." Culture, he contended, was a product of social evolution which was of a different order than physical evolution, and the two had often been confused. He used the example of bird flight versus human flight to highlight a basic difference between the two. In organic evolution birds became able to fly through loss or modification of existing organs and faculties. In social evolution humans learned to fly by accumulation; i.e., all the original human qualities remained but something was added to them, the invention of the airplane. Another example arose from the differences between human and animal responses. Instinctively an animal knows its own language, how to hunt, its sex patterns. Even if a dog were raised with cats, he stated, it would bark, not hiss, and would respond to a bark even if it had never heard one before. But the contents of human minds come through tradition, what is handed down, from one generation to another, and tradition is not instinctive, it is external to the organism, learned from without. A Frenchman raised in China would not instinctively speak or understand French. Kroeber said that the human organism, unlike animals who were locked into instinct by heredity, was like a piece of paper that can carry thousands of marks of different force and value and can be erased and reinscribed. He agreed that humanity was both organic and social but called it a "cardinal mistake" to confuse the two. He called the attempt to treat the social as biological or culture as hereditary "essentially narrow minded" and absurd. He attacked the eugenics movement as "a confusion of the purposes to breed better men and to give men better ideals . . . a biological short cut to a moral end" that was inherently impossible. Edward Sapir, in an article following Kroeber's later in the year, disagreed with his view of culture but applauded and affirmed the rightness of his stand on the importance of culture as opposed to biology. Goldenweiser did the same.[13]

Kroeber's article was published in *American Anthropologist* and aimed at his colleagues in anthropology and related areas of study such as sociology and psychology. Lowie's book *Culture and Ethnology* (1917) he called "an attempt at popularization," to acquaint educated lay people with some of the principles and problems of modern ethnology. On the first page of the first chapter Lowie identified culture as a "fundamental" concept as important as the study of life in biology and electricity in physics. He emphasized in Chapter 2, "Culture and Race," that while race remained a relatively stable factor, culture changed significantly through time in the same race, producing within a few hundred years a change from barbarian to civilized status in Western European culture alone. Lowie also argued that cultures were not linked to specific races, citing the takeover by the Japanese of Western European culture. "Culture cannot be adequately explained by race," he wrote, adding that "the same race varies extraordinarily in culture even within a very narrow space of time." In Chapter 1, "Culture and Psychology," Lowie reaffirmed culture as *learned* behavior and therefore separate from psychology, which dealt with *innate* traits. Culture dealt with the influence of *society*, while psychology dealt with the *individual*. Thus Lowie affirmed fundamental distinctions between anthropology and psychology which helped firm up the boundaries of anthropology as a distinct discipline in its own right.[14]

By 1917 anthropology was in the process of becoming a profession, establishing its own standards, its own methodology, its own distinct identity. Part of this meant rejecting dependence on the parent field of biology and striking out on its own as a discipline. As the study of culture increasingly became the key to anthropology's identity as a discipline, Boas and his students proclaimed their intellectual independence by veering away from biology and developing several variations on the idea of culture which proposed the dominance of cultural determinism over biological, of nurture over nature.[15] If culture was to be the anthropologist's focus of study, then the concept needed to be clarified, revised, and extended to fill the role. Boas and his students began to debate among themselves the various facets of culture, its nature and its properties. The farthest-reaching ideas came from Kroeber, Sapir, Lowie, and Boas himself. Theirs were the ideas circulating about the concept of culture in the Columbia Department of Anthropology as Ruth Benedict began her life there.

Kroeber became the first to strike out boldly in new directions. In "The Superorganic," besides placing culture firmly outside biology, Kroeber attempted a new definition of culture. Culture, the vast body of learning passed down to humankind from generation to generation, had acquired a life of its own in the process, he wrote; it had become the "superorganic." Society was not "merely a collection of individuals," but "an entity beyond them." He remained fairly vague about the nature of this entity, except to see it as having "majestic order" and purpose, permeating the lives of individuals but "in its very essence non-individual," uncontrolled and uncaused by individual effort. He referred to it as a "progress of civilization," or "march of history," which was "independent of the birth of particular personalities." He stated that forces in culture demanded certain ideas and inventions at certain times, citing the commonness of parallel discovery to show that it didn't matter who the discoverer was. Although the article stopped short of saying so, Kroeber implied an absolute cultural determinism at work upon humanity which individuals could not affect, as much a trap in its own way as the theories of the biological determinists. By 1920 Kroeber was writing of culture as a kind of group-mind, a "super-psychic" or "super-individual" with "an existence, an order, and a causality as objective" as that of the physical world.[16]

Edward Sapir took the opposite approach and focused on the importance of individuals as determiners of culture. He rejected Kroeber's superorganic because it left no scope for the individual. As he said, Aristotle, Jesus, Shakespeare, and others were not merely "the cat's paws of general cultural drifts." He agreed that social traditions molded the contents of people's minds, but social traditions were not the same everywhere. They underwent selection, and it was in this area that the individual played a role, for "it is always the individual that really thinks and acts and dreams and revolts." In his first published letter to Ruth Benedict, Sapir wrote of the necessity to discuss the relationship between psychology and culture. "I should like to see the problem of individual and group psychology boldly handled, not ignored, by some one who fully understands culture as a historical entity," he stated, adding, "I hope you will do just this one of these days . . ." Goldenweiser agreed with him that Kroeber had gone too far and that there must be some place for the individual in culture.[17]

Taking another tack, Robert Lowie concentrated on the particularist nature of culture, viewing cultures as products of their particular histories rather than more general causes. He wrote that "Cultures develop mainly through the borrowings due to chance contact," and in the last lines of his book *Primitive Society* (1920) called civilization "that planless hodge-podge, that thing of shreds and patches," and added that students of it dreamt of a "rational scheme to supplant the chaotic jumble," but none was yet known. Boas, not one to theorize openly, by 1919 had decided that the summation of diffused elements did not comprehensively describe culture, and that he was against "the mechanistic theory of cultural diffusion." He quietly began to search for ways to study the "inner development" of cultures, to understand the nature and role of "inner forces."[18] As she came to know the various approaches, Benedict began to develop her own ideas about culture and its role, especially after her return from her Serrano field trip.

For Ruth Benedict herself the words of her Serrano informant on the "cups of clay" had acted as a powerful statement about the concept of culture. On her field trip to the Serrano she had observed the erosion of what had once been a cohesive way of life. "A great deal of the old meaning, both in social organization and religious practices, is undoubtedly lost," she wrote. She found that no shaman or priest survived. The tribe depended on a shaman of the desert Cahuilla tribe for some of the old dances and rituals. The great magic by which a shaman could summon power and transform himself into a bear in the bear dance was lost. Her Serrano informants had to use guesswork to give the meanings of some ceremonial songs. Of the nine bands of Indians who had cooperated in the annual Serrano ceremonial observances fifty years earlier, two bands of Serrano had become extinct several years before Benedict's field trip and the last person of a third group, the Mamaintum, had died recently. The most sacred possessions of the Serrano were feathers kept in a sacred place during the year and brought out for the week-long ceremonies. But, Benedict wrote, "the feathers are falling to pieces now," and the last man who could do the feather dance had died twenty-five years earlier. Benedict, ever a realist, saw that the Indians had adapted, had become Christians and orchard farmers of peach and apricot trees on irrigated land. But for the first time she experienced a culture overwhelmed by another and felt deeply the fragmenting of a culture that had lost its internal cohesion. With the Serrano chief's words she gained a new consciousness of the concept of culture. Underlying her dissertation had been the idea of culture as a summation of diffused elements organized into a social pattern made up of those elements a specific culture had singled out, recognized, standardized; a pattern that then influenced how an individual in the culture perceived or used a particular trait. This had the virtue of being open-ended, but at best remained a partial and incomplete concept. With the statement on "cups of clay" for the first time she understood culture as the internal life of a people, what she at that time might have called the soul, or later, the psyche, of a society. With the loss of rituals, obligations, the succession of ceremonials, and standards of right and wrong, she wrote, the Serrano had lost something as important as life itself, "the shape and meaning of their life." Nietzsche had used the cup as a metaphor for individual personality. Here, for the first time, she heard it used as a metaphor for group personality. The statement provided her first glimpse of a holistic view of culture free of the absolute determinism inherent in Kroeber's. She glimpsed how the diversity of cultures could be reconciled with an integrated wholeness, not in the nineteenth-century evolutionary sense with its closed systems, but in a totally new way.[19]

Upon her return to Columbia in the fall of 1922, Ruth Benedict searched for an area within all the various branches of anthropology in which to begin serious study. She was not drawn to archaeology, physical anthropology, or material culture. The study of language might have interested her, but her partial deafness made it hard for her to catch pronunciations or sound variations. Instead, by temperament and by life experience she was attracted primarily to the study of the subjective side of humankind manifested in art, religion, and ethics. She was drawn secondarily to the anthropological area of social organization, which included the study of family forms, marriage, and sexual relations. For her first serious study as a full-fledged anthropologist she turned to mythology, for several reasons. Myths, as tales of the supernatural world, offered access to the supernatural experience of a society, an area she felt a need to understand both as a person and as a social scientist, for she saw social spirituality as a key element in producing new ideals and values for a society. Boas had called mythology, theology, and philosophy "different terms for the same influences which shape the current of human thought." Myth and religion had "constantly cross-fertilized each other," she later wrote, and in fact among some peoples myth was "the keystone of the religious complex." If she were to understand the religion of her upbringing and its hold on society, she needed to understand its roots in myth. Mythology also had connections with literature, the focus of her undergraduate study. Again mythology offered access to a fuller understanding of culture. Indeed, within mythology Benedict began exploring the covert underpinnings of culture and the ways these manifested themselves directly and indirectly. Besides, as she later wrote, folklore was the field that had been used since the time of Tylor "to document the parallelisms of primitive and modern culture."[20] Finally, the study of mythology offered a Modernistic approach to culture, for to understand mythology one must step outside one's own cultural expectations and put oneself in a strange and foreign world-view, see things in a totally new way. One must grasp the complete relativity of cultural perspective.

Benedict came of age in America during the period when Modernism swept intellectual circles with new excitement. Modernism began as a rejection of old ideas and values as exhausted, leading to experimentation and a search for new ideas and values to give meaning to life and art. Moderns rejected the nineteenth-century cultural web of Romanticism and Victorianism, with its emphasis on absolute values in areas ranging from science to morality, for a more relative world view, a view that received scientific authenticity in 1905 with the publication of Albert Einstein's Special Theory of Relativity in physics, and later, his General Theory of Relativity. For centuries scientists had believed that space and time were absolute concepts, immutable and unchangeable. Einstein found that time and, by inference, space were relative, depending on an observer's point of view. In 1908, mathematician Hermann Minkowski announced a new principle, based on Einstein's theory, called "space-time." His colleague and fellow mathematician Hermann Weyl explained Minkowski's idea of space-time by saying that "the scene of reality" was no longer a three-dimensional space, "but rather *a four dimensional world,*" and scientists and artists began to try to explain "the fourth dimension."[21]

Close to the same time in America, Franz Boas was shaking the absolute foundations of biological science. Physical anthropologists and biologists had always believed the size of the head unchangeable, an absolute given, which had been used to support theories of white racial superiority and the superiority of men over women. Boas found, in a study of immigrants and their children, that head size actually changed among the children, presumably because of the change in environment from Europe to the United States. What had been seen as absolute was shown to be relative. The publication of Boas' results in "Changes in

Bodily Form of Descendants of Immigrants" (1910–1913), a report for the Dillingham Commission of the 61st U.S. Congress, dealt a severe blow to the idea of unchanging racial features and sent shock waves through biology and related areas.[22]

The findings of science fit the ideas of various philosophers and writers, some of which Ruth Benedict had read in her college days, who had espoused a relative point of view in society and morality. Pater had written in the 1890's that "modern thought" differed from ancient in its "cultivation of the 'relative' spirit in place of the 'absolute.'" To the modern spirit, he wrote, nothing could be known "except relatively and under conditions." Or again, "Hard and abstract moralities" were not "eternal outlines," he wrote, but "a world of fine gradations and subtly linked conditions, shifting intricately as we ourselves change." Nietzsche had written, "Much that passed for good with one people was regarded with scorn and contempt by another." He then gave some examples of this and concluded, "Verily, men have given unto themselves all their good and evil . . . it came not unto them as a voice from heaven." Like Pater and Nietzsche, Charlotte Perkins Gilman had reaffirmed the relativity of values. "Virtue is a relative term," she wrote. "Human virtues change from age to age with the change in conditions."[23]

During the time Einstein was developing relativity in physics and Boas was encouraging it in biology, William James and John Dewey were developing it in philosophy in Pragmatism, a favorite topic of Goldenweiser's along with current art movements and psychoanalysis. The Pragmatists accepted no absolute values. There could be no set of fixed values because conduct determined values and conduct altered constantly. Resolving problems depended on taking into account all the circumstances of a particular situation at a given time as far as possible. Thus values depended not on an absolute standard, but on the point of view or position of the observer. The Pragmatists determined that there was no all-embracing, absolute reality as the framework of life. Instead all experience was an ever-flowing stream of change and movement. Reality was not fixed; it shifted with shifting contexts. Nothing was static or permanent. What seemed to be was just changing very, very slowly. Thus change replaced the old static frame of absolutes as the new reality. Change became the constant element of life—it became part of the life process itself.[24]

What occurred, for those like Ruth Benedict who felt the force of the relative arguments, was a changed world-view. This new world-view did not strike everyone at once but permeated gradually and is still permeating through society, working its effects first on one, then another. But among those who felt the change a sense of historical discontinuity occurred. The old formulas would not work in a world where the uncertainty of relativity replaced the static, global framework of absoluteness, no longer allowing fixed reference points from which to determine reality. In this world the development of the new concept of space-time signified that an idea, person, or event could have meaning only in context, in relation to other ideas, persons, and events. Reality awaited re-creation. The world waited to be reinterpreted and re-understood within the new perspective of shifting images. Creative people in all the arts—literature, music, painting, dance, and the even newer film—began to take up the challenge of the new relativism and create a new art for a new age. Cubist and Futurist painters in France and Italy developed "the artistic equivalent of space-time."[25] The Cubists tried to see and portray objects simultaneously from all sides, above and below, inside and out, around and through. In their first phase shortly before 1910 they achieved this effect by breaking up the surfaces of the natural form into angular facets. Each object in a painting was divided into many angles, and each angle created for the observer a new frame of reference from which to view the picture. Around 1912 they developed the collage. Artists used paper, sawdust, glass, sand, newspaper, cloth scraps, handwriting, and single written words together in one picture to express the different perceptual references which constituted the whole. As the Cubists explored what they called "the fourth dimension"[26] through spatial representation, the Futurists developed an approach based on movement research. They distorted and multiplied objects to create a multiplicity of perspective based on speed and vibration. Benedict was in Europe in 1910 when the new art was scandalizing European audiences. She was living in a suburb of New York when the Armory Show of 1913 created its shocking impact on the American art world, especially Marcel Duchamps' Futurist portrait, *Nude Descending a Staircase*.

Space-time in physics meant that space and time no longer existed independently but were interconnected, each depending on the other for existence. Transferred from science into Western culture, the new space-time concept challenged artists to represent all time in a single piece of space or, conversely, all space in a single moment of time. For some the idea of simultaneity offered a way to present space-time artistically. The Imagists in poetry achieved this by superimposition of image on image, the simultaneity of one idea set on top of another in words, as in Ezra Pound's famous piece, developed from the example of Japanese haiku:

The apparition of these faces in the crowd;
Petals on a wet, black bough.

Pound expounded the Imagist doctrine that an image "presents an intellectual and emotional complex in an instant of time" and that this gives a sense of "sudden liberation . . . from time limits and space limits." The Imagists achieved a sense of instantaneousness by discarding transitional and developmental passages. In using simultaneity, in trying to express as one totality two disparate elements, just as space-time made one unity of space and time, creative people tried to relate formerly unrelatable images and ideas. Their object was to create a new perception of wholeness out of dissonance. For the challenge of the new relativity was how to deal with the chaos this new way of thinking made of the universe, a universe where disorder and dissonance ruled.[27]

Darwinism, which had swept through intellectual circles by the late nineteenth century, had introduced chance as an important element in the equation of life. On the surface the world seemed an ordered place through time; or at least, if not ordered, in the process of becoming so through progress and evolution. But implicit in the idea of evolution was the necessity of dealing with chance as a major force in life, and by the turn of the century this had become a crucial issue. If chance or accident made one species human and another into apes, then one had to accept that order and rational development were not the guiding principles of the universe, that irrationality might be, and that at the very least a place must be made to include chaos and chance in the philosophy of life. Relativity meant chaos—it introduced disorder into the previously well-ordered areas of science, philosophy, and art.

But relativity also provided thinkers, scientists, and creative people with a lever with which to deal with the immanence of chaos, for Moderns, unlike their predecessors, accepted chaos as a major element to be explained and dealt with in itself. The message of relativity was that there was order in disorder and plan in seeming chaotic chance, but that one required a new vision to perceive it, and this was embodied in the relativistic point of view. The Moderns accepted dissonance, paradox, and the juxtaposition and superimposition of seemingly polar opposites with the expectation that by including all the possible points of view they would discover a new form of order, one which revealed more of the universe and the meaning of life than had ever been clear before. The Moderns were essentially integrationists, striving to create a synthesis out of the seemingly disparate elements of life, having faith that in spite of appearances, a complex yet ordered pattern underlay the seeming chaos. The new arts, while shocking people's sensibilities, displayed how order could be re-established within a relative framework. Thus Cubist paintings displayed visual dissonance. But if an observer had the key to viewing them, order reappeared. Much of the new poetry seemed like unintelligible gibberish. But if one understood what the poets were trying to accomplish, that gibberish suddenly made a new kind of sense. The same thing was happening in all the arts.

That Benedict knew and thought about these ideas is certain. In the period between 1914 and 1917 she wrote that Mary Wollstonecraft was as incomprehensible to the eighteenth century as "the fourth dimension to a class in fractions." In a 1930 letter she wrote that studying a living culture "one could give a [s][sic] nearly a Proustian picture as one can achieve." By 1920 these ideas were common coin in the American intellectual community. The years 1919–1921 saw the popularization of Einstein's General Theory of Relativity in America. This theory, created in 1915, contained the prediction that if general relativity were true, the rays of light from a star would bend when passing the sun by an amount twice the size of that indicated by Sir Isaac Newton's principles. This prediction could be tested under eclipse conditions, and a major solar eclipse was expected in 1919. A British expedition photographed the eclipse and confirmed Einstein's prediction. The drama of the eclipse and of international cooperation between scientists of Britain and Germany in the project so soon after World War I caught the imagination of the public, especially in America, and made relativity a topic of popular discussion and media coverage. Einstein's ideas suddenly stood out in relief due to the world-wide barrage of publicity beginning in 1919.[28]

As historian Edward Purcell has chronicled, another result of the drama of the eclipse was that the idea of "non-Euclideanism" became popular in America. For 2,100 years the geometry of Euclid had seemed the ultimate mathematical and logical system, the ultimate fixed frame of reference, accurately describing the physical world. In the nineteenth century, however, three "non-Euclidean" geometries were invented by three different mathematicians. Einstein used one of these, Riemann's geometry, to deal with gravitation and the deflection of light rays in his theory of general relativity. After the eclipse, scientists and nonscientists alike saw that at least one non-Euclidean geometry worked, thus showing that Euclidean geometry did not completely describe the physical universe, and that geometry, the symbol of unshakeable logic and absolute rationality, had become as relative as everything else. Even before the eclipse Benedict had written in "Mary Wollstonecraft," "For her, life had no axioms; its geometry was all experimental." Non-Euclideanism came to stand for unconventional ways of doing things, for provocative ideas, for the juxtaposition of two or more highly unrelated concepts. Non-Euclideanism became the social science equivalent of the concept of space-time.[29]

Non-Euclideanism significantly affected ideas in many fields. Lawyers and social scientists tried to become aware of non-Euclidean possibilities leading to better laws or understanding of society. For example, John M. Clark in 1924 tried to work out what he called a "non-Euclidean economics." Robert Lowie wrote that knowing the differences between societies, based on different world-views, beliefs, and value systems, "enlarges our notion of social potentialities as the conception of n-dimensional space enlarges the vision of the non-Euclidean geometrician." Edward Sapir wrote in 1924 about the "relativity of concepts" which were "not so difficult to grasp as the physical relativity of Einstein . . . [or] psychological relativity of Jung." He continued, "What fetters the mind and benumbs the spirit is ever the dogged acceptance of absolutes." Anthropology, by its very essence, was the preeminent non-Euclidean science, the field where Modernism could have its widest scope. Its emphasis on the relativity of cultures dealt a sharp blow to belief in absolute systems. In revealing the various possibilities of cultural choice made throughout the world, anthropology graphically affirmed the plasticity of human nature. The study of other cultures demanded acceptance of different perspectives of the world, as Cubist paintings did of objects. It accepted a reality based on the subjective viewpoint of the individual in his or her culture. Moreover, the study of other cultures placed new, non-Euclidean alternatives for living and for solving problems before American society.[30]

Boas and his students spent the first twenty years of the twentieth century in the tasks of the first stage of Modernism: the abandonment of absolutes and the acceptance of infinite multiplicity. They tore down the ideas of universal evolution, universal cultural stages, unilinear progress, and showed the seeming disorder of human development, in which less technologically developed peoples could be more complex socially or in language sophistication than Western societies. They showed that societies did not move from simple to complex as evolutionists like Bureau of American Ethnology chief John Wesley Powell had formerly thought, but contained both simple and complex elements in greater or lesser degree. In the movement of traits, tools, and designs from culture to culture they charted the influence of chance. These studies showed that primitive societies did not have the absolute stability necessary to the evolutionists' and universalists' theories, but that within cultures, culture traits were in a constant state of flux. They emphasized the diversity, the variety of possibilities that occurred from culture to culture, shattering the simple, absolute ideas of their nineteenth-century predecessors and contemporary colleagues in Europe who argued for another absolute system, a horizontal evolution with culture disseminating over time from one central spot on earth, or perhaps two or three—a system which necessitated the absolute stability of culture traits over long periods of time to be plausible. In place of a closed, fixed system of human development, they created an open-ended system that accepted relativity and, for the moment, disorder, dissonance, and chaos.

During the nineteen-teens Boas and his students moved into the second stage of Modernism and began looking for new ways to reintegrate what they had broken down. They began to look for patterns among the chaos—limited patterns, not general ones—patterns that fit an open system, not a closed one. They struggled over the idea of "convergence," or the production of similar traits in highly unconnected cultures where diffusion could not be a factor, as suggestive of a possible underlying integrative force. Trying to strengthen the concept of convergence in 1913, Goldenweiser suggested in what he called his "principle of limited possibilities" of culture development, that out of the unlimited possibilities for cultural variation "a culture would always embrace a limited set," just as each culture did in language, and thus the "chaos of cultural traits" easily yielded to order. But his was not an open system, since he used the principle to emphasize that the same culture patterns repeated again and again and that cultures made the same choices from all the open possibilities, thus being locked into a restrictive framework. His concept was also considered highly theoretical and was not backed by concrete cultural examples. Nevertheless it presented intriguing ideas. In *Patterns of Culture* Benedict later stood this concept on its head and created from it "a principle of unlimited possibilities." In a more successful attempt at limited integration, in 1917 Clark Wissler in his book *The American Indian* firmed up and systematized the idea of "culture areas" by defining and mapping ten North American and five South American culture areas in which cultures shared common factors.[31] That same year Alfred Kroeber wrote his article "The Superorganic," which attempted to provide an integrative view of culture and which sparked other integrative culture concepts.

Thus, Ruth Benedict entered anthropology at a time of transition from an emphasis on analysis, or the breaking down of general ideas, to a period in which reintegration became the primary aim. Her early work reflected this. The theme of her 1922 article "The Vision in Plains Culture" was that, although an overall common vision pattern had been assumed by armchair anthropologists in the past, in fact no such overall, fixed pattern existed. She emphasized the extraordinary diversity of elements in the vision complex from tribe to tribe, each with its separate distribution and importance, each accepted by one culture in one way, or almost entirely modified in another culture. She showed the dissonance underlying the assumed simple order: that where patterns had been assumed, there were none; where elements were thought to be connected, they were in fact disparate. In ending her paper she warned against the "false simplicity" of general studies of religion and affirmed the "heterogeneity" and "indefinite multiplicity" of ways the religious experience appeared in cultures, implying in conclusion that there were no absolutes for religious experience.[32] In all of this she contributed to the tearing down of the old absolute ideas and affirmed an element of chance in the development of religious outlets. At the same time, while she was doing this, she accepted limited patterning within an open-ended system by speaking of the distinct patterns of religious experience found within tribes, and affirming that each individual searched for a vision within his or her own cultural expectations of how that search should go and what the result should be.

In the same way in her dissertation on the Guardian Spirit she emphasized that humans built up culture out of "disparate elements, combining and recombining them"; that traits correlated with the vision–guardian-spirit complex were not organically associated with them but entirely "fortuitous"; and that until humans gave up the idea that culture was a universal organism and that there was an overall, absolute pattern, they would never see clearly how culture actually worked, being blinded by theories laid upon it. But underlying this emphasis on disintegration lay an acceptance of the limited idea of "social patterning—of that which cultural recognition has singled out and standardized," not a closed system, not fixed or absolute in itself, but rather material handed down through generations and subject to diffusion. All of this reflected a Modern view of the world. But beyond this, Benedict perceived the abandonment of absolutes and the acceptance of the relativity of reality as the first step toward realistic social control. For until then, she wrote, "we shall be unable to see our cultural life objectively, or to control its manifestations."[33]

Progressive and Modern motivations mixed also on her return from the Serrano field trip. She felt the urgency of the anthropologist's task to preserve the record of disappearing cultures in a do-gooding sense, because the Progressive ethos demanded action in the face of loss, but also because part of the human heritage of alternate possibilities was about to be lost forever, the vast pool of relative social alternatives narrowed and limited by the loss.[34] All of this background colored Ruth Benedict's plunge into the serious study of mythology.

6

Mythology, Religion, and Culture

THE QUESTION Benedict chose to pursue might be phrased as "Where is the purpose in mythological chaos?" Myths were noncohesive, disordered, dissonant, and illogical, just like Cubist painting. The internal lack of order in mythology intrigued her. By the spring of 1923 she found herself committed to an external ordering of mythology in the Southwest Concordance project. She also committed herself to the much more congenial task of coaxing purpose from chaos. Various theories had been proposed to explain mythological plots, motivated, as Benedict later wrote, "by a desire to find a rational explanation for their abhorrent and fantastic content." These included the ideas of myths as allegories based on puns in Aryan languages on the names of gods and heroes; myth as fantasy concealing historical fact; myths as nature symbolism, reproducing natural phenomena in metaphor, e.g., the death and rebirth of the hero actually signifying the passing of winter and coming of spring; myths as explanations of why things happen in nature and culture; and the most recent, myth interpreted by psychoanalytic ideas to reflect fixed sexual symbolism taken from analysis of individual dreams, e.g., fire as the sex act, water as birth, whetstones, knives, and snakes as male genitalia. All of these failed to explain mythology adequately.[1]

The first explanation did not hold for myths outside the Aryan language group, nor did it explain many within that group. The second was too speculative, as fantasy could be linked to many historical facts with little justification. As for the third, explanations from cultural events such as marriage or war could be just as explanatory as nature. Anthropologist T. T. Waterman had shown in examining Indian tales that explanations of why things happened were often tacked onto stories as afterthoughts and did not form the reason for the development of the stories themselves. Myth as psychoanalytic symbolism often clashed with the actual symbolism of a region, e.g., where the snake was a symbol of immortality rather than a sexual organ; and psychoanalytic theories suffered from being culture-bound, projecting urban twentieth-century Western standards onto primitive peoples.[2]

Benedict rejected this search for fixed laws concerning mythology. For her the most important reason to study myth was as an entry point into culture, to help understand individual culture patterns and how culture worked, with myth in constant and intimate interaction between new elements from other cultures and the local culture which determined how the new would be perceived and used. Boas, in his study of Tsimshian mythology, had shown it to reflect Tsimshian culture and had used mythology to produce the "autobiography" of a people. Ruth Benedict intended a similar study for another specific case, Southwest mythology, following Franz Boas' idea, as Benedict later wrote of him, that "you might find the universal in an adequate study of one particular subject if you devoted yourself to unraveling processes." She intended to study how traditional material in tales reflected and perpetuated the ethics or morality of a tribe. As she wrote later, tales crystallized "forms that are locally favored or insisted upon" and acted as one of the "important available sanctions to the mores of the group."[3]

So her first idea was to reject the necessity for a rational explanation of myth plots. The plot itself was not important; the sanctions within the plot were. But here she ran into a snag. Mythologies often contained dissonant, seemingly nonfunctional, even irrational material, including not only material objects a culture had never used but also ideas that clashed with values present in the culture. She realized mythology was not the clear window on culture it had appeared on the surface—something else was going on. Edward Tylor had explained this variant material as survivals or partial survivals from a past time that were no longer functional or no longer of major importance in the culture, carried into the present by sheer inertia.[4] Some anthropologists, such as Paul Radin, a student of Boas' first generation and a colleague of Benedict's, continued to believe this theory. Benedict began by accepting this idea as a starting point, that the "something else" in the myths was historical or traditional material, either residues of an earlier period of integration, or material accepted into the mythological structure through diffusion. Her first idea was that historical or traditional material was the source of conventionality in cultures, and she planned to study the inertial effect or cultural lag this material exerted on the cultures which accepted it.

In the spring of 1923, in a short article in the *Journal of American Folk-Lore* she asked field workers to annotate folk material they gathered as to the differences between what the folklore said and what the people actually believed and practiced. She cited for example a Paiute story which talked of cremating a dead companion at sunset, adding that the Paiute never burned their dead—the cremation was "traditional" material. Similarly, she had been told by the Serrano many times that they had no concept of an afterlife; yet their mythology contained an Orpheus tale with considerable detail on the way of life of the dead. Benedict was convinced that "there was no contradiction in their minds." Knowledge of what was true for a culture in folklore and what was not was necessary in order to understand the material correctly, she said. She stressed that this was not an intrusion of outside point of view but a necessary other dimension in understanding the story's meaning to the people who told it. Otherwise, she concluded, it would be impossible to study "the hold which traditional material has upon mankind." Implied here was the idea that traditional material reinforced and perpetuated out-of-date ethics and morality. Once one understood the hold of this conventional material acting like a dead weight on a culture, one could act to release the hold. That fall she wrote to Sapir about her ideas and he replied, "I am sure you are right about the overwhelmingly historical or traditionally moulded character of mythology in all cases," but went on to ask her what she thought of applying psychoanalyst Carl Jung's idea of "primordial images" to mythology, saying, "Jung would get small comfort from you, I'm afraid." Benedict rejected the archetypal approach to mythology largely because the idea of the archetype harked back to a closed system with fixed laws. This was her criticism of those trying to find an archetypal tale.[5]

She went to Zuñi to build a body of raw data in folklore and mythology on which to base her study, to understand the culture behind the myths on an intimate level, and to begin to study one mythological system in depth, following Boas' theory that case study led to general principles. Reporting to the Columbia administration on her first field trip to Zuñi, Boas wrote that Benedict had investigated Zuñi folklore to determine how much folktales were "a reflex of the social conditions of the tribe," an investigation directed primarily against recent psychoanalytic theories about folklore based on the ideas of Freud and Jung. She expanded her ideas on mythology and folklore by giving reports in the seminar during the fall and spring of 1924, in which she emphasized the ethical character of mythology and the unimportance of plot.[6]

But by 1925 Benedict's ideas had begun to change. Through her work on Hopi mythology, abstracting culture from the tales, she had discovered that the myths' diversity of incident was a "self-sufficient rebuttal of their historicity." Meanwhile her work in Zuñi had shown her that Tylor's idea of survivals did not fit within a culture where mythology was still alive and functioning. This threw in doubt the whole question of whether one could study culture through mythology in any meaningful, not severely limited, way. But she believed that culture was "the fundamental factor" to deal with in mythology. Her problem became to explain, as she later wrote, the impression that folklore "tallied with culture and yet did not tally with it." So she made a shift of viewpoint. She had read *How Natives Think* and *The 'Soul' of the Primitive* by French psychologist-anthropologist Lucien Lévy-Bruhl. She rejected his main thesis that primitive peoples think nonrationally as opposed to civilized peoples, who think logically. But reviewing his books fed her own interest in human irrationality as a part of life. Instead of trying to explain out-of-phase material as no-longer-functioning survivals from the past, she accepted the presence of the irrational in mythology as belonging there. She decided that in spite of their seeming chaotic nature, non-fitting elements had a function within myths. The problem became then to find what that function was. As she wrote in the *New Republic* in 1929, "Man's irrationalities must be studied scientifically," by asking questions like "Do the various forms they assume help us toward an understanding of the person or people of whom they are characteristic?"[7]

At first, drawing on her background in literature, she saw myths as primitive analogs of modern novelistic fiction and their plots as the play of imagination from a non-Western perspective which would make sense if one understood the culture from which they arose. By that time she had read and been deeply impressed by English anthropologist W. H. R. Rivers' book *Instinct and the Unconscious* (1920; 2d ed. 1922), in which he critiqued Freud, rejecting many of his conclusions but accepting much of the structure Freud set up to explain the workings of the mind. Rivers gave a clear exposition of the concept of the unconscious, repression, sublimation, rationalization, and other Freudian mechanisms for understanding the mind. Benedict had read British anthropologist A. R. Radcliffe-Brown's *The Andaman Islanders* and Bronislaw Malinowski's *Argonauts of the Western Pacific* in seminar. Radcliffe-Brown had spoken of the need to understand the role myths play "at the present time in the mental life" of a people. She was familiar with the use British-based anthropologist Malinowski had made of function. By 1926 she was exploring these ideas in relation to myth. She helped Otto Klineberg, then a student, put together a positive rather than a negative report on psychoanalytic treatment of myth. He thought it was impossible at first, but, Benedict wrote, "with the help of Malinowski's work and of suggestions we cooked up" Klineberg gave "an exceedingly interesting report." Among the suggestions was the use of the idea of repression, i.e., mythological material reflecting ideas or actions repressed in the actual culture, and myth as compensation for an inhibition—people making fun of their taboos. She wrote that Boas objected and got very excited and the seminar class had a good discussion.[8]

In spite of Boas' reservations she continued to develop her ideas about myth along these lines, with the result that she came to see important elements in myths that were seemingly unconnected to the culture acting as a form of "wish fulfillment," enhanced by the play of imagination allowed by story creation, that allowed exaggeration, abolished space and time, and personified animals and things. At first, in *Tales of the Cochiti Indians* (1931), she saw these wish fulfillments as added to the tales by individual storytellers. But then she made a quantum leap to see myths themselves as containing the collective wish fulfillments of a culture. Since the wish fulfillments of various cultures differed, she wrote, strongly varying myth cycles developed. Mythological themes incorporated the "dominant daydreams" of their tribe, or culture area, or group. Thus she came to see mythology as "a means of expression by a social group of its own attitudes and cultural life," not primarily straightforwardly, but internally. By 1935 in *Zuñi Mythology* she was calling "wish fulfillment" a "compensatory daydream" and writing, "Other contrasts between custom and folkloric conventions must be explained as fundamentally compensatory." This idea—a non-Euclidean response to the irrationality inherent in mythology—included the fulfillment of wishes but went beyond it to see in myths themes or elements acting as "compensatory mechanisms," providing an outlet for those things a culture represses and does not allow to be acted out.[9]

Another question important to her was the role of the myth-teller. By understanding the role of the myth-teller she could begin to understand the interrelationship between an individual and his or her culture, including how much influence each exerted upon the other. Partly her interest in this issue came from the temper of the 1920's, during which the individual, or the self apart from society, became a focus of speculation and thought; partly it occurred in reaction to her own experience growing up as an individual in a restrictive society. Two questions concerning the individual seemed important to her in the 1920's: First, does culture determine an individual's actions or can one free oneself from a restrictive society and create in one's own way? Next, if individuals affect society, how do they act to create change in a positive way and how do they cause change in negative ways? Underlying these general social questions for Benedict lay her own concerns: how she as an individual could deal with a culture in which she felt a misfit due to its restrictiveness and how she, one individual, could influence society to develop new values and new ideals. But questions about the individual had also become important problems in literature and in all the social sciences. In anthropology specifically, in order to understand the role culture played in human life, it was necessary to know how the individual was acted upon or in turn acted on culture. Franz Boas had sent Ruth Bunzel to Zuñi together with Ruth Benedict in 1924 to study that very problem through an examination of pueblo potters and their influence or lack of influence on pottery styles. Ruth Benedict took up the same study in the area of mythology.

She decided that "in the last analysis" all folktales were individual creations, not communal, and "determined by cultural conditioning," that is, that the myth-teller acted within the boundaries of what was considered creative or noncreative for the group, and this varied from culture to culture. She found that the path of the individual was not totally determined by the culture. The myth-teller, as a creative individual, also acted as an element upon the culture. But this individual creativity then had to be accepted or rejected by the culture as a whole, based on its "cumulative social traits and preoccupations." The culture accepted from individual effort what it perceived as worthwhile from its own point of view, things that fit in some way with everything else, a process "with which the individual has comparatively little to do." The myth-teller in turn reshaped tales to fit within the expectations and boundaries of her or his own culture and generation, and in a sense acted as a kind of social psychiatrist, bringing forbidden ideas hidden in the unconscious of the people into the light of day and dissipating their impact. In this role of social psychiatrist the myth-teller also mediated the intermingling of the traditional and the new in ways by which they then could be accepted or rejected by the culture. When individual creativity was accepted as a standard, Benedict wrote, the individual could have much more impact on his or her world.[10]

This also had implications for modern society. From the beginning of her study of folklore and mythology Benedict had been interested in the hold traditional elements had on humanity. As she wrote, "Individual expression is still largely curtailed in . . . marriage and education, by an emphasis on the value of conformity to traditional standards." In folklore that emphasis also held. But although literature in earlier centuries had also been "traditionally determined," in modern society "individual creativeness is now indispensable for popular approval." In this area the individual writer could have an impact on society, changing its standards and values. The study of its now-dead folklore, she wrote, helped contemporary society understand "the changes that occur" when a culture trait, not necessarily literature, but even "marriage or education," ceased to be bound by traditional standards and became an area of "individual responsibility," a trend that to many educated people seemed to have the potential of occurring within the decade. The study of folklore made "more vivid than any other discipline" the contrast between behavior as a manifestation of traditional cultural standards and behavior sparked by individual creativity. This process of contrast could also be applied to other culture traits in modern society as a device to make people culture-conscious, while individuals might act as myth-tellers to suggest alternatives to the bonds of tradition.[11]

Mythology proved only one avenue through which Ruth Benedict continued her social spiritual quest. Religion itself, which she called the "slow and halting exploration of the spiritual life," remained, as it had from the beginning, a major focus of her inquiry. But religion, like mythology, proved to be more important to her for its potential to make people culture-conscious and as a pathway for exploring the impact of culture itself than as an abstract study of the social side of spirituality. As Boas wrote, "Religious beliefs pervade the whole domain of cultural life, for technical, economic, legal, social, and artistic manifestations are filled with beliefs and actions that have a religious background." The important point for Benedict, as she wrote in an unfinished book manuscript in the 1920's, "The Religion of the North American Indians," was that "the chief values of the peoples will be also the chief concerns of their religion." Religion then, like mythology, was a way to explore existing values, often unconscious, bring them to the surface, and examine them in contrast with the values of others in order to create new values and ideals. Studying the religion of the North American Indians, as did all cultural studies, made clear "the make up and behavior of our own ideas. It gives them to us in perspective."[12]

For Benedict a primary purpose for studying the religion of the North American Indians was the sharp contrast it provided with Judeo-Christianity. The emphasis on the ecstatic vision and the search for the guardian spirit on the Plains contrasted sharply with the rational approach of middle-class American Protestantism. The idea of a boasting, fault-filled animal trickster bringing customs to a tribe or shaping the world clashed jarringly with the idea of an omnipotent, good God and an evil Satan, and opened to question the necessity of the fundamental opposition of good and evil so central to Christianity and Western culture. Among the Indians, religion was identified with power. A religious person was one who acquired power through religious rituals and ceremonies. But in Christianity, wrote Benedict, religion was identified with myths. "The Christian cosmology has been selected as the substance of religion," she wrote. People who "found" religion "embraced a certain mythology." Those who "lost" religion stopped believing in the mythology. The contrasts between Judeo-Christianity and North American Indian religion, besides advancing her own knowledge of spiritual experience, revealed clearly the relativity of religious perspective and the religious provincialism of Christianity.[13]

Moreover, in Western culture, religion remained the repository of morality, an area of definite cultural lag in 1920's America. By the middle of the decade there had been a resurgence of fundamentalism in American religion, culminating in the highly publicized Scopes "monkey" trial over the teaching of evolution in public schools. Religious censorship fell not only on science but over society, and an authoritarian spirit replaced the liberal theology of the Progressive era. "Prohibition" became the order of the day. The Ku Klux Klan revived and promulgated racism and terrorism in the name of morality. To liberal-minded people like John Dewey, religion in the 1920's seemed "petrified into a slavery of thought and sentiment" and "perverted into something uniform and immutable." Against this authoritarianism an "anti-Puritan" revolt broke out among American intellectuals, who identified as Puritan any fixed, arbitrary standards of taste and morality and rejected them. George Santayana wrote in 1927, "I ask myself sometimes, is not morality a worse enemy of spirit than immorality?" Because of the uses to which it was being put in 1920's America, Benedict wanted to "secularize" morality, to remove it from the religious frame so that the "moral" could be judged on its own merits and not from an arbitrary absolute background. Most religions, she discovered, did not have the thorough identification with morality that Christianity had. Religion historically was more often used to gain success in this world than to pursue ideal ends. In many religions leading a better life was not the "reason for seeking relationship with the supernatural." Among differing peoples it was "far commoner," she wrote, for "any local form of morality to be upheld without recourse to religion." There was no innate reason to keep the two entwined.[14]

Benedict began her book on religion about the same time that she began studying mythology. Sapir wrote to her in 1924, "I have been disappointed not to get your Religion by now." During the years she was writing it she was also teaching classes on religion for the Department and saturating herself in research on the nature of religion and its various manifestations. She apparently submitted the manuscript to Knopf and was turned down. By 1930 the topic had broadened from the North American Indians to "The Religion of Primitive Peoples." But even though she had been working on the subject for at least six years, Benedict did not feel that she had a manuscript in shape to publish when a publisher expressed interest in that year. Looking at the chapters of the earlier book left in manuscript it seems clear that the book never came together for her because her own perspective about what she wanted to write was unclear. When Sapir did finally read the manuscript he wrote on it a short comment on its incompleteness, saying it left out things such as dance and ritual drama which were as important in North American Indian religion as the vision. As an approach to religion as a topic it was incomplete, which is probably why the manuscript remained unfinished.[15]

What she discovered as she wrote was that she wanted to do a book that secularized morality, that focused not on religion, but on ethics. The history of religious development, she wrote in the manuscript, was "a progress in secularization," helped along by increasing scientific knowledge. John Dewey articulated her goal well in an article on "Anthropology and Ethics" (1927). He wrote that the link between morality and religion had been "broken into more than once by the rise of philosophical and scientific criticism," and as a result moral ideas were "enlarged and altered" and stated "independently of particular religious beliefs." In a seminar report in 1924 she had stated that the "observance of patterns of behavior is morality and philosophizing about it is ethics." She wanted to write a book on religious "standards and attitudes" rather than religious practices. Religion "inevitably" regarded as immoral anything that did not fit "its own customary arrangements and institutions," she wrote. "The approved and ethical action will be that which is customary." Specific acts had no "special moral quality" inherent in them. They became virtuous by "blanket approbation" given to traditional patterns of behavior. She wanted to make people aware of this, to foster a relative ethical system, to help free morality of its reactionary restrictions and revise it to harmonize with the world as it should be, a place of individual freedom and tolerance for the outsider, trusting that once the internal changes in belief and mores had occurred, they would be reflected in external social changes. She agreed with John Dewey that the essence of social action was "To foster conditions that widen the horizon of others and give them command of their own powers, so that they can find their own happiness in their own fashion." But most religious standards and attitudes, she wrote, "are those of the society in which we are born and bred . . . We analyze our attitude toward women, our competitive economic system, our organized religion" as though they were individual phenomena and rose from "man's essential nature," when actually they are the result of "our social heritage of custom." Thus in the last analysis, as she finally discovered, she wanted to write a book on *culture*.[16]

The debate over culture had continued through the 1920's within anthropology and the other social sciences. The biology versus culture argument continued to find space in books and journals, though increasingly, as in William Fielding Ogburn's *Social Change* (1922), emphasizing the role of culture over biology. But the questions that occupied most time and space concerned the nature of culture: what it was, how it operated, how it changed or resisted change, what was the role of the individual in culture. The concept of culture became the key to ordering the chaos of human development. But what this concept included remained unclear. Alexander Goldenweiser wrote of *Early Civilization* (1922), meaning culture. Clark Wissler organized culture in *Man and Culture* (1923) as a collection of traits and complexes organized within culture areas with a center and margins. Edward Sapir in 1924 wrote of "genuine" and "spurious" cultures, envisioning genuine cultures as harmonized wholes, spurious cultures as "spiritual hybrid[s] of contradictory patches."[17]

All anthropologists and social scientists used as their basis Tylor's definition of culture as learned behavior. This meant culture was plastic as no genetically controlled behavior could be, thus opening far-ranging possibilities for the betterment of society through cultural change. But how to reconcile accident with purpose remained the underlying problem. Anyone who worked with field data realized the role accident or chance played in bringing traits together. Yet there was a sense of possible integration in the data too. The problem was to find a solution that accommodated both purpose and chaos. Wissler tried by creating a theory in which the culture pattern was innate, i.e., linked to human hereditary nature biologically, while the cultural content was accidental. The Boasians rejected Wissler's theory because of its link with the innate. In *Man and Culture* Wissler also upheld Nordic supremacy, so anything he said was highly suspect. Sapir tried for a solution in "Culture, Genuine and Spurious," with the idea that "genuine" cultures had purpose, while "spurious" cultures were the result of chance and therefore chaotic. But the argument was vague, incomplete, and easy to poke holes in. Boas later, in *Anthropology and Modern Life* (1928), discussed the problem of purpose and chance, coming down on the side of accident. But he did see a hope for progress in ethical conduct, as larger groups were included in the rights of society, and for "an increasing social control" as a result. Some anthropologists went to one extreme and saw culture only as a collection of traits brought together by historical chance, while others held it to be a superorganic entity (as proposed by Kroeber), or a collective mentality (as described by Lévy-Bruhl), or even a collective unconscious (borrowing Freud's and Jung's terminology) and thus subject to some form of "social" psychology, analogous to, but on a different plane from, individual psychology. The nature of social psychology, like the nature of culture, remained open to the broadest speculation.[18]

By 1926 the effect of outside influences had significantly sharpened the debate on culture and refined its nature. The first such influence was the introduction of English functional anthropology into American thought in the work of Bronislaw Malinowski and A. R. Radcliffe-Brown. Both were leaders in the English revolt against nineteenth-century evolutionary anthropology, a revolt which did not occur in England until after World War I, much later than in America. The English movement took a different twist. Where the Americans emphasized the influence of history and diffusion, both Malinowski and Radcliffe-Brown advocated a functional approach to the study of culture. Both rejected Tylor's idea of survivals continuing to exist in society, instead taking the position that everything functioned in a society, every element had a purpose even if it seemed not to, and one just had to figure out how that seemingly unrelated part fit in. Malinowski and Radcliffe-Brown approached the idea of function from different perspectives. Malinowski's system emphasized the reciprocal relation between elements in a culture, how each part of the culture fit together with every other part. Radcliffe-Brown, following the ideas of French sociologist Emile Durkheim, advocated the idea of social structure as the central focus. He considered the idea of culture to be a vague, amorphous concept and preferred to limit his definition of social study to the narrower base of social organization, a system of subgroups, clans, moieties, and other groupings for which he used the analogy of an "organism." Each part of the social organization functioned in relation to the whole. Though the individuals involved changed, as did cells in an organism, the internal relations between social structures continued, as did those of organs within an organism. Radcliffe-Brown's system, like

Kroeber's superorganic, allowed little leeway for the individual, whose actions in his system were determined by the social structure of the society. Benedict met Radcliffe-Brown when he visited New York in the late 1920's, and she and the other anthropologists at Columbia all knew his work. What was important to him was not the origin of a custom but its meaning in the lives of a people. "We have to explain why it is that the Andamanese think and act in certain ways," he wrote. The meaning of each custom was related to other customs and "their general system of ideas and sentiments." [19]

Benedict also knew Malinowski's work and liked him when she met him in 1926. She wrote of him, "He has the quick imagination and the by-play of mind that makes him a seven-days' joy." Like her, in lectures and in conversation he often used examples from modern societies, and he talked amusingly of British social customs. Like her he was interested in a broad range of topics and saw no conflict between science and the humanities. Like her, he enjoyed shocking people, particularly those he thought over-conventional, but unlike her, he had the expansive personality to do so often and publicly. With women colleagues he was "a continental gentleman . . . gallant and flirtatious," but, unlike many of his contemporaries, "completely serious" when discussing their work. In 1926, while in the United States, he had visited the Hopi and done some field work there, so he and Benedict had a common ground for discussion. [20]

Benedict found his exploration of psychoanalytic ideas in culture interesting, though not the use to which he actually put them. Like most American anthropologists, Benedict appreciated the integrative element of functionalism—the interrelation of cultural elements. From her approach to mythology in the late 1920's it seems clear that Benedict had decided that functional ideas had a place in anthropology, though not the central place Malinowski and Radcliffe-Brown wanted to give them. But again like most American anthropologists in the late 1920's, Benedict had major problems with the British functional approach. Because the revolt had occurred so much later in England, the British anthropologists seemed to many American anthropologists to be working through ideas and approaches already worked over in America and either accepted or discarded. During his visit Malinowski stimulated American anthropologists, but along with this went a sense that he was "capitalizing on the obvious," that he was promoting "as new and startling" ideas that Boas and his students either had long quietly accepted and practiced or had rejected as impractical. [21]

Next, functionalism ignored or discarded as irrelevant the influence on culture of history and diffusion, both of which American anthropologists had shown to be significant influences in cultural development and change. But, most important to many American anthropologists and especially to Benedict, functionalism represented a closed system in dealing with culture. It rejected acceptance of irrational or disorderly elements in society and tried to stuff all elements of culture into a tight little box labeled "organism" by Radcliffe-Brown and later explained by Malinowski as integrated institutions always serving human needs. Radcliffe-Brown and Malinowski's approach essentially was not Modern. In itself the idea of functional integration, especially as propounded by Malinowski, was exciting. As a system British functionalism hearkened back to the absolute, closed systems of the nineteenth-century anthropologists, brought up to date and articulated in contemporary form. It was an approach to life and thought familiar to Americans from the Progressive era, when Americans explained anything from business to government to architecture and cities as "organisms," a style of thinking that had gone into disrepute in America after World War I. Ironically Benedict and other American anthropologists saw British functionalism, which was itself a reaction against overarching theory and ideal systems, as being too idealized and theoretical, and not dealing with how society actually operated in practice, which was often illogical, disordered, and irrational.

In reaction to British functionalism and in search of a more Modern solution, American anthropologists in the late 1920's looked around for an alternative approach to culture. They were intrigued by the potential of another European influence, Gestalt psychology, to create a workable social psychology and an integrated concept of culture. German psychologist Kurt Koffka in *The Growth of the Mind,* translated into English in 1924, introduced the Gestalt idea of configuration to American social scientists on a broad scale for the first time. Like the idea of function, that of configuration emphasized the potential interconnectedness of traits or activities. Koffka spoke of a configuration as a "coexistence" of traits in which each "carries every other." He explained the classic chicken experiment conducted by Wolfgang Köhler, the founder of Gestalt psychology. Chicken food was placed on dark grey and light grey sheets and the chickens were allowed to eat from the light but not the dark sheets. When this behavior was established, another piece of paper was introduced, brighter than the light grey. If the stimulus-response theory held, the chickens should have eaten the food on the light grey sheet and ignored the new paper. But the chickens ate from the new paper fifty-nine times out of eighty-five, a much greater proportion than chance. Köhler concluded that the choice was determined by learning the light-dark pattern rather than the specific color of the paper. The behavior thus depended on the response to the "characteristics of a configuration" rather than just an actual event. Köhler did a similar test with children and candy using a light-covered and a dark-covered box and the result was similar to the response of the chickens. He concluded that people learn and act in response to the configuration, i.e., in response to an underlying pattern called forth by the specific event.[22]

The Gestalt idea of configuration fit neatly into the idea of "pattern" used since the nineteen-teens by Boas and his students, and also with other ideas circulating among the Americans. "Pattern" was earliest used simply and descriptively by the Americans as shorthand for "behavior pattern," i.e., a sequence of expected events in behavior. From there it was just a step, but an important step, to enlarge the definition into "social pattern," a step taken by Robert Lowie in his article "Plains Indian Age Societies" (1916) and elaborated by Leslie Spier in "The Sun Dance of the Plains Indians" (1921) and by Ruth Benedict in *The Concept of the Guardian Spirit in North America* (1923). The idea of social pattern meant a pattern formed by the inertia of tradition; customs and beliefs passed down through generations forming a distinct pattern able to mold culture traits to itself through its inertial force. By 1923 Wissler in *Man and Culture* was calling this channeling of the new by a culture "pattern phenomena." But there was no sense of the pattern as a superorganic entity. Wissler broadened the scope of pattern by introducing the idea of a cultural pattern which he called a "universal pattern" underlying all specific cultures. Here he meant a pattern as an organizing principle like the plan of a house or a "skeleton of culture," an outline in which each culture contained the same categories of elements to deal with—"speech, art, religion, etc." Kroeber later called Wissler's idea "like a table of contents in a book. It guides us around within the volume rather than giving us the essence or quality of it." Wissler also conceived of this pattern as innate and genetic, a concept generally rejected by American anthropologists absorbed in releasing culture from biology. In an article about Wissler's universal pattern, Melville Herskovits and Malcolm Willey stressed the necessity of understanding that cultural patterns were "capricious in the extreme," which was essential knowledge to anyone undertaking problems of "social control or amelioration." Social scientists speculated on the future use of culture patterns for social betterment but did not actually know how they worked yet. Patterns were not necessarily linked by function or logic. Many seemed to be the random result of particular historic events, or to contain within themselves elements that in no way seemed to fit together purposefully. But with the new psychology and emphasis on the group as entity in sociology there began a slow groping toward the definition of a "mental pattern."[23]

The basis for such an idea already existed in American anthropology. Boas often emphasized "the psychological setting of a custom" to his students and wrote approvingly in the obituary of his student Herman Haeberlin in 1919 that he had "grasped the psychological basis of culture as a unit." Haeberlin had been influenced by the work of German psychologist Wilhelm Wundt, whose ideas on folk psychology were well known to Boas and his students. Wundt postulated that the group always actively cooperated in producing attitudes and ideas. Before that Goldenweiser had proposed that the outer activities and psychic states of people coordinated in some way. Wissler in 1923 introduced the idea of the "culture-complex," a collection of culture traits integrated together. The backbone of the culture-complex was "a core of ideas and beliefs, actuating a people and in a large measure controlling their career." Material culture differences reflected differences in beliefs and ideals. Thus a horse culture-complex might include not only the horse but habits of use, equipment, social distinctions, literary ideals, or religious customs, and these would vary from culture to culture to reflect the beliefs and ideas of differing peoples. Almost anything could form a culture-complex. Wissler mentioned wild rice, tobacco, and maize among material objects, and exogamy and sun worship as non-material focuses for various traits. Anthropologists used the culture-complex idea extensively, and Ruth Benedict talked about the vision–guardian-spirit religious complex. Borrowing from sociology the idea of group norms and individual variation from the norm, Wissler wrote that these trait complexes formed distinct "patterns," i.e., trait norms or standard group norms, with individual variation within tribes. Wissler suggested that integration within culture-complexes might ultimately be explained by some underlying ideal that linked all the traits. He used an example from American culture of machines being surrounded by beliefs and attitudes concerning economics, social organization, religion, and other cultural traits, all linked through an "inventive ideal." But this was highly speculative, the culture-complex idea itself was limited, and Wissler was unsure how or even whether various culture-complexes came together to form a culture.[24] In 1924 anthropologist Wilson D. Wallis wrote an article called "Mental Patterns in Relation to Culture," in which he suggested, in line with the various theories of group mind going around, that groups such as nations had distinctive mental patterns in which parts were linked. That same year Sapir called genuine culture "the expression of a richly varied and yet somehow unified and consistent attitude toward life, an attitude which sees the significance of any one element of civilization in its relation to all others." The Gestalt idea of configuration fell on open minds in America. A configuration was a form of pattern that linked facts and events with the attitudes and beliefs underlying them.[25]

Benedict knew of Koffka's book from discussion with Edward Sapir and Margaret Mead. Mead had discovered it in 1924 and loaned it to Sapir. Sapir wrote Benedict in April 1925 that he had been reading Koffka and "It's the real book for background for a philosophy of culture, at least your/my philosophy." He called it an "echo telling me what my intuition never quite had the courage to say out loud," and fantasized about its "fascinating and alarming possibilities" in the areas of "behavior, art, music, culture, personality, and everything else." Moreover, Koffka's book was widely read in the social science community at large. Benedict had also read Köhler. In 1926, in her SSRC grant application, Benedict proposed to study the "culture-configuration" and "the emotional bases" of primitive folklore, including "a consideration of the particular psychological set of the group." She proposed a comparative study to estimate "the role which the cultural patterns of the group play" in the development of myth. By 1927 Wallis was writing that Gestalt psychology made possible the conception of "a mental pattern applicable to a given group . . . in which the parts are interwoven and interdependent." Around the same time Sapir was calling social pattern "a psychological attitude or mode of procedure," and writing optimistically about the future use of configurations. Goldenweiser was talking of culture pattern as "a preexisting scheme or configuration of traits," and was also optimistic about the use of Gestalt psychology.[26]

That same year, on her summer field trip to the Pima tribe in Arizona, Ruth Benedict made the mental breakthrough that set the new definition of pattern being developed into its final form, and that brought the beginnings of a solution to the problem of how to integrate purpose and chance in culture. The Pima, Zuñi's nearest neighboring tribe to the southwest and with easy contact available between the tribes, had a culture so far apart from the Zuñi that Benedict was shocked. She wrote to Boas that the contrast between the Pima and the Pueblos was "*unbelievable*." The central ceremony of Pima life was the brewing of a cactus beer which first the priests, then all the people drank in order to achieve religious exaltation. "Intoxication," she later wrote, "in their practice and in their poetry, is the synonym of religion." The Nietzschean contrast between Apollonian and Dionysian came to mind to describe them—the Apollonian Pueblo, the Dionysian Pima, and by extension the Dionysian Plains tribes she had spent so much time studying. She worked out her ideas the next winter and put them into a seminal paper, "Psychological Types in the Cultures of the Southwest," which she read at the Twenty-third International Congress of Americanists in New York in September 1928. Her paper became the first concrete display of the new meaning of "Pattern." The title itself, like Kroeber's "Superorganic," was a play on meanings. Psychoanalyst Carl Jung had written a book, *Psychological Types,* that had become one of the best-sellers of the early 1920's among the educated American public. People turned his idea of introverts and extraverts into a parlor game and tried to catalog each other at parties and in casual conversation. But Jung's system was essentially a closed one, based on temperament, not learned behavior. Benedict turned his title around and used it to describe her cultural, open system.[27]

She wrote of the Pueblos as Apollonian, distrustful of excess or ecstasy, highly ordered, highly controlled through ritual and formal detail, and full of sobriety; and of the Pima and related Plains and Southern California neighbors as Dionysian, seeking to break out of ordinary existence through excess and ecstasy, to break through to a new plane of existence using alcohol, drugs, torture, orgies, the vision. The use of literary comparisons to express psychological differences was creatively non-Euclidean. She used Apollonian and Dionysian to mean "fundamental psychological set[s]," or "two diametrically different ways of arriving at the values of existence." What she was saying was that cultural activities, even cultural beliefs, were a response to an underlying mental pattern discernible in the activities and beliefs of a culture. This mental pattern was not a set of specific traits, but instead a perspective of vision, which provided for choosing among cultural traits amenable to it, modifying clashing traits to conform with it, and creating new traits from within according to its parameters. This psychological mind-set served as the ideal for the culture, providing the standard or norm for the group around which individual variations inevitably occurred. Moreover the pattern allowed to individuals differed from culture to culture as the underlying viewpoint of the cultural ideal changed. With this concept, Ruth Benedict had found a way to integrate purpose and accident in culture. The underlying psychological mind-set provided direction to the culture, for everything in it was worked out in relation to its terms. But the specific content of the culture was due to accidents of time and place. Though many parts of culture did not seem functional in relation to other parts, they actually did function together in the culture as different expressions of the way the underlying psychological mind-set manifested itself in actual social behavior. The "fundamental psychological set," she wrote in ending the paper, created "an intricate cultural pattern to express its own preferences." [28]

Her paper caused a stir at the Congress. After she read it, Kroeber asked her, "How does the old man take a paper like that?" Sapir told her it was "a good lecture and a good point." Archaeologist Alfred Kidder came up to tell her that Pueblo art and material culture supported her thesis. Wissler "scowled through a great deal of it and I haven't seen him since," she wrote. Anthropologist Hortense Powdermaker and a German professor from Hamburg told her it was the most important paper of the Congress. Elsie Clews Parsons was "speechless and rose to make all sorts of pointless addenda when she recovered her breath." By December however, Parsons was willing to admit it was "a very good paper." Benedict had asked her to read the paper prior to publication. Parsons went over it carefully and made some suggestions which she thought were further arguments along the same lines strengthening the paper. "Pretty good to fetch conviction to Elsie on so alien a point," Benedict wrote. But it wasn't really that alien a point. In a review in 1925, Parsons had characterized the Hopi as "objective-minded" and their neighbors the Plains Indians as "subjective-minded," creating a duality very similar to Benedict's. [29]

Benedict's characterization succeeded because she voiced a condition that investigators of Zuñi had intuited at a gut level but had not reasoned into words. "Pattern" had reached its final metamorphosis. In 1930 Boas wrote in his article on "Anthropology" in the *Encyclopaedia of the Social Sciences* that more essential than the interrelations between aspects of culture was "the unification of culture according to definite patterns," which he explained as "fundamental attitudes that dominate the thoughts and behavior of the society." He gave Benedict's idea his stamp of approval, writing in pedantic professor-ese that she had described "in a most instructive manner" the "'Dionysian' orgiastic pattern" of most Indians and the "'Apollonian' formal pattern" of the Pueblos. He qualified, "In many cases the general cultural pattern is weak and the culture seems to us thin." But even then the strong influence of pattern could still be felt in aspects of a culture such as art styles or local versions of myths and folktales, in social organization, or in religion. By 1930 "pattern" in the new meaning had become for American anthropologists what "function" had become for British anthropologists—a guiding principle around which anthropological study could organize.[30]

In 1930 or 1931 Benedict wrote another paper carrying forward her ideas on "pattern," which she called "Configurations of Culture in North America." She began with a critique of the British functionalists, who had the right goal, to explain human culture as "organic and functioning wholes," but the wrong approach, because although they showed traits as functioning, they did not deal with the nature of the whole in which they functioned or with how the traits interrelated with the total culture. The functionalists, she wrote, did not ask some very necessary questions. She described the paradox that primitive cultures are "so overwhelmingly made up of disparate elements fortuitously assembled from all directions by diffusion," yet again and again are "integrated according to very different and individual patterns." The functionalists did not deal with the element of accident in culture, while Benedict's work did. Order appears, she wrote, because "the assembled cultural material is made over into consistent patterns in accordance with certain inner necessities that have developed within the group." The "configuration of culture itself" expresses "these varied readings of life." These "fundamental and distinctive" configurations "pattern existence and condition the emotional and cognitive reactions" of people in a culture. Each configuration specializes "in certain selected types of behavior" and rules out opposing types. The configuration is a psychological set that has become institutionalized over generations, with power to shape the culture itself. In becoming institutionalized it becomes the "*ethos*," or guiding principles of a culture, the ideal toward which the people of the culture strive.[31]

In the "Configurations" paper Benedict made a further distinction between cultures, identifying dual configurations of realists and non-realists or, using William James' terminology, "tough-minded" and "tender-minded" cultures. Most cultures, she concluded, had been non-realist, based on non-realistic notions. The tough and tender-minded categories cross-sectioned the Apollonian and Dionysian. The Plains culture she classed as realist although Dionysian and the non-Pueblo Southwestern tribes, the Shoshoneans, and the Northwest Coast tribes as non-realists with "tender-minded" awe and horror before dark and mysterious forces like death, childbirth, menstruation, sorcery, even the mystic power of names. Realist cultures institutionalized "death as loss, adolescence as an individual's growing up, mating as sex choice, killing as success in a fight," and so forth, while non-realist cultures surrounded these and other activities with dark and contaminating forces, made them crisis situations fraught with danger. In this paper she also described another configuration in depth, adding to the Apollonian Pueblos and the Dionysian Plains tribes the pattern of "the pursuit of personal aggrandizement" in the North Pacific Coast culture, which approached "an institutionalization of the megalomaniac personality type." These tribes played the game of prestige with the result that the inferiority complex became institutionalized, she wrote, and a great range of insults in words and actions threatened the "ego security of the members of this paranoid-like civilization."[32]

Her summation revealed the main points of the configuration/pattern concept of culture. By 1931 she was ready to be more open than in "Psychological Types." She wrote that cultural configurations were to group behavior as personality types were to individual behavior. Cultures became "individual psychology thrown large upon the screen, given gigantic proportions and a long time span." The crux of the process was "the selective choice of the society." As for the question of the individual in society, "the group has already made its cultural choice of those human endowments and peculiarities it will put to use." Most persons, she wrote, were in accord with their culture. The misfit was "the person whose disposition is not capitalized by his culture." Gifted individuals could bend their culture in the direction of their own capacities, but the configuration transcended its individual elements. As for configurations themselves, they were not necessarily noble. Stability and harmony, she argued, could belong to cultures built on "fantasies, fear-constructs, or inferiority complexes and indulge to the limit in hypocrisy and pretensions." Nor did she say that every culture had a configuration, or a "dominant drive," only that enough evidence suggested that it was an area of study that needed to be further investigated.[33]

To call the Kwakiutl megalomaniac and paranoid was again creatively non-Euclidean, borrowing terminology that psychoanalysis used about individuals and applying it on another level to a culture. It took great scholarly courage. Her two articles were academic risk-taking of the highest order, first because they theorized as well as described, and second because they theorized in the direction of the new psychology which Franz Boas frowned upon, which could have risked her personal as well as her professional relationship with him. But her articles pointed anthropology in a new, Modern direction, which in the 1930's came to be known as the study of Culture and Personality. But that was for the most part still in the future.

Her studies of mythology, religion, and culture in the 1920's, while overtly scholarly, remained covertly social. They dealt with the important contemporary problems of American society, questions both Progressive—how to create a better society—and Modern—how to deal with the problem of chance in the universe. In mythology she investigated purpose in chaos, the role of the individual in changing or reinforcing social attitudes, and how to promote social change. Religion she studied conscious of its role as a force of convention and reaction in American society, ultimately desirous of changing the role of religion in America by divorcing morality from religion and giving it the rational basis of science. Culture became the vehicle for directed social change. In finding scholarly answers to scholarly questions, she actually sought answers applicable to society at large and to questions that had become the burning issues of the decade.

She continued one overtly social activity: the popularizing efforts that had begun with "Cups of Clay." In this Benedict may have drawn on the example of Elsie Clews Parsons' earlier books like *The Old-Fashioned Woman*. By comparing primitive with civilized customs, Parsons attacked conventionality and exposed the absurdities of American traditions and customs, showing them to be no more logical or "right" than those of other peoples, whether savage or civilized. "The debutante's skin is generally 'improved,'" she wrote. "Sometimes it is tatooed or cicatrised. Sometimes it is painted, sometimes merely powdered." Benedict throughout her life used this type of satirical, consciousness-raising style in her own popular writings, not only about women, but also on economics, social relations, and other aspects of culture. In 1925 she wrote a popular article, unpublished during her lifetime, called "Counters in the Game." She looked at American materialism from an Indian standpoint. The Indians found it ludicrous that whites spent so much time and energy buying land when they could be purchasing much more valuable songs or visions or, as on the Northwest Coast, could engage in cutthroat competitions to give all their goods away. All of these activities, Indian and white, had the same underlying base, she wrote, the desire to accumulate prestige. The white way of buying land and accumulating wealth was only one of many possible methods to achieve this. She wanted Americans in general to become more conscious of the actual motivations of their culture that lay below the rationalized, commonly accepted ones. Her purpose, as with "Cups of Clay" earlier, was to startle people into becoming culture-conscious and to make them examine the "givens" of their own culture. She made 1920's materialism look absurd, and made Americans view their life from an outside perspective. She stressed the relative point of view by giving equal value to the methods and opinions of whites and Indians and found order in seeming irrationality, showing that people could act from motives another group considered absurd, but which were from their own perspective quite normal.[34]

Another article she wrote around the same time continued this consciousness-raising purpose. She wanted to show Americans the absurdity of the ultimate savagery, war. In "The Uses of Cannibalism," modelled on satirist Jonathan Swift's "A Modest Proposal," she suggested that cannibalism be substituted for war in Western society. She used anthropological examples to show how cannibalism could be rationalized into a positive good, just as war had been. Like war, it would encourage group solidarity, validate and encourage heroism, endurance, and self-control, lead to positive ethical values such as the supreme cherishing of the dead, help channel aggression in society, and be a source of patriotism. She also wrote another popular article in the 1920's called "They Dance for Rain in Zuñi," to show that for the Zuñi dancing was a form of praying, a spiritual experience far from the secular activity of the Charleston or the "Black Bottom." Each of these articles was an attempt to make anthropological ideas "common coin" among the educated public and to alter people's perception of their culture. Each remained unpublished. Finally, in 1929, *Century Magazine* ran a series on what the different sciences had to offer modern thought and, as Ruth Benedict wrote, instead of her soliciting them, "they sent a woman up to ask me to do anthropology." The result was her article "The Science of Custom," her credo on anthropology and on life as the 1920's closed, which, somewhat modified, later became the first chapter of *Patterns of Culture*.[35]

Primitive peoples formed great, almost inexhaustible, natural laboratories for the study of culture, she wrote. By studying culture in miniature one might learn how the complex whole of learned behavior passed down from generation to generation influenced everyone born on the earth. She affirmed the importance of nurture over nature, by 1929 a generally accepted idea in the social sciences, talking of the "small scope of biologically transmitted behavior and the enormous role of the cultural process." She startled her readers out of their culture-bound ideas about the effect of biology by showing how adolescence and the maternal instinct, both accepted as biological givens with certain consequences, differed from culture to culture. She even showed that emotional responses were culture-bound, using jealousy as an example. She treated the universal evolution of culture and the supremacy of Western society as discredited, closed issues. She emphasized the effect of culture on the individual rather than its opposite, as Sapir would have done. "No man ever looks at the world with pristine eyes," she wrote. "He sees it edited by a definite set of customs and institutions and ways of thinking." Individuals affect culture in the same amount as a baby influences his family's language, she said, using an example from John Dewey. The baby instead is coopted into the family's language. She agreed that the individual does influence culture, but insisted that influence is small compared to the influence culture exerts on the individual. "The traditional patterns of behavior set the mold and human nature flows into it," she wrote. She got in a dig at the British functionalists, calling it "beside the point to argue from its important place in behavior, the social usefulness of a custom." There seemed to be little logic in what cultures emphasized and what they didn't. What had been created were "great superstructures of the most varying design, and without very striking correlations with the underpinnings on which they must each and all eventually rest." Cultures had grown up with "the useful and cumbersome together," and were not perfect systems. "Not one of them is so good that it needs no revision," nor so bad that it could not meet the needs of itself and its members in some imperfect way, she wrote.[36]

What did all this have to do with contemporary society? First, she stated, "What we give up, in accepting this view, is a dogged attachment to absolutes." Passionately she asked, "For what is the meaning of life except that . . . we shall make of it always a more flexible instrument, accepting new relativities, divesting ourselves of traditional absolutes?" Next she discussed how necessary it was for the general population to become culture-conscious. Because culture was "automatic . . . outside the field of conscious attention," changes taking place had so far been blind. "Gradually," she wrote, "in so far as we become genuinely culture-conscious," change "shall be guided by intelligence." She affirmed that what was needed in the future was "a reinstating and reshaping of the spiritual values of existence" to balance the present stress on material values. Based on the relativity of culture and an acceptance of relative standards of right and wrong, a more "tolerant and objective" view of human life could grow. These were the social goals Ruth Benedict held for America in the 1920's. These were the goals she knew she wanted to communicate to the American people. By 1931 she was ready to promote these goals on a larger scale.[37]

7

The Personal Vision

IN THE EARLY YEARS of her marriage Ruth Benedict had an epiphany which marked the distance she had come from formal religion. She went one Sunday while in New Hampshire to a Second Advent camp meeting. It seemed to her "the *reductio ad absurdum* of the religion even of those I respected." She found the camp ground filled with "close-lipped people to whom the universe was about as rich and various as it is to a cat after mice." She felt their minds and souls were "knotted and tied against the very notion of infinity." By no stretch of the imagination could she conceive that "finite man was here rising toward the infinite." It seemed to her now that she understood that "such in its essence was even the religion I respected—it was always fundamentally a paralyzing, a limiting, a mocking finite, of the Infinite." She tried involving herself in religion by teaching Sunday school in Douglas Manor, but lost her place when she assigned her class to look up Jesus in the *Encyclopaedia Britannica*.[1]

As formal religion ceased to have meaning for her, she searched in many diverse directions for spiritual guidance. "The trouble with life," she wrote, "isn't that there is no answer, it's that there are so many answers." The words of Christ, Buddha, Thomas à Kempis, Browning, Keats, Spinoza, Thoreau, Walt Whitman, Elbert Hubbard, and even Teddy Roosevelt, by turns fit her needs, but never completely. She had come to see that "for ourselves we must build up our own answer, that not even a Kant or a Christ can answer it for us." She tried writing out her own ideas of the spiritual life. In one such effort she divided the mind into two kingdoms: that of knowledge, where reason gave understanding, and that of wisdom, where detachment gave understanding. "This detachment," she wrote, "is the life of the spirit." She called it the "life of the artist and the life of the mystic," a spiritual life with no dogmas, no duties, its essence its immediacy "without the distractions of belief or anxiety." She called it a "final synthesis of knowledge" and "a laying aside of knowledge." Religion, grief, artistic creativeness all had helped keep the spiritual life alive, often accidentally, she wrote, by providing arenas for detachment from the world. As institutionalized religion fell apart in her life, part of her spiritual energy turned to feminism, which Olive Schreiner had characterized as analogous to a wide-sweeping religious movement, and led her into writing her biographies, her spiritual feminist testaments. Part of it went into dance and also poetry, which she began writing in these years under the pseudonym "Ruth Stanhope." "The poems were just saying 'ouch' because someone had stepped on one's foot," she said of her early verse.[2]

Then she discovered anthropology. As other women of her generation turned to oriental mysticism or ancient Greece for spiritual roots, she turned for awhile to the religion of American Indian cultures, hoping to find a personal spiritual focus for herself as well as an understanding by contrast of the spiritual base of society. So she studied the vision quest and the guardian spirit complex in which the vision was fundamental. For she had written once that "contiguous to our lives" existed a life of the spirit, "something so strenuous" that next to it the Arthurian quest for the Grail was only a shadow of reality, and "something so costly" that few dared pay the price. Yet that was what she wanted. "That is the only thing in life that interests me," she wrote, and only the world's growth toward the life of the spirit could "excuse its existence." She added, "And that can only come about by individual quest." In the vision quest she found a way that fit the pattern she described: a glimpse into the spiritual world necessarily strenuous, gained at great physical and psychic cost. At the heart of the Indian vision lay the vision of Pater, for the distinguishing characteristic of the vision was "a feeling of significance, a 'thrill' of greater or less intensity," Pater's "hard gem-like flame." In a religious complex that recognized the vision as its "fundamental and typical religious fact," Ruth Benedict privately sought the mystic heart of religion.[3]

She did not find it. She was attracted to the vision as the basis of religious experience because it was so diametrically opposed to the rigid structure of beliefs and dogmas that had filled her own religious experience growing up and which for her was the basis of Judeo-Christianity. But by the early 1930's she was thinking of visions and ecstasy as "borderline psychological states," and she had discovered in the writing of her dissertation that people see in visions what their culture teaches them to expect. As she studied the concrete facts of primitive religions she drew further and further away from a mystical approach to religion. By the late 1920's she no longer saw it as something "sacred" or mysterious, but instead as something with very matter-of-fact roots in daily human experience. From her original view of the supernatural as "the existence of wonderful power," which charged the universe like electric voltage, she moved to the more prosaic concept of the supernatural as a product of human imagination built on two foundations: human experience with things and human experience with people. The former was usually known as animatism or belief in *mana,* the magic impersonal power of objects or acts; the latter was animism, the belief in spirits or in a personalized universe.[4]

She saw animatism or the use of magic power as impersonal acts or rites of wish fulfillment and emotional release projected onto objects such as amulets or magic formulas. She saw animism as a projection of human relationships onto the natural world. If the universe were personalized, then one had to use behavior toward it that one would use toward another person—love, punishment, reverence, bribery, flattery, hospitality, command, sex. Various religions then were on a continuum between these two poles of behavior toward things and behavior toward people. In the same way, power ascribed to gods took shape from people's experience in the human world, not from some supernatural fiat. Primitive peoples saw their gods as having the powers they themselves had—larger than life, but sometimes limited, and with the faults of humanity larger than life as well.

She found some aspects of religion considered vitally important in Western culture not necessarily religious at all in other cultures and often found in "secular connections." Pageantry was the secular side of ceremonialism. The "non-religious aspects of border-line psychological states are obvious to anyone in our civilization," she wrote. Dogma and belief, taken as the fundamental basis of modern Christianity, were not actually basic to religion but "superstructure" grown over the behavior of a culture. In primitive cultures cosmology, the delineator of dogma and belief, acted as a commentary on the life of the people, set out the virtues and vices of a culture, and gave free play to the wishes important in that culture. Cosmology then was important "for its help in understanding an individual culture," not the supernatural. Nor was the basis of Christian cosmology, the conflict between good and evil, a usual theme of cosmologies, which showed gods as good or bad according to circumstances. Most moral systems were secular and not involved with religious sanctions. "Ethical religions," those that used religion as a sanction for ethical conduct, were rare and tended to a "puritanical code of morals." For most primitive societies the goal of religion was not to live virtuously or look to the eternal, as in Christianity, but to attain success in this world, a secular rather than a sacred goal, and among the Plains Indians, the goal more often than not was success in battle.[5]

Benedict's ideas reflected her own increasing disillusion with the "sacred," with the provincialism of Judeo-Christianity which had taken itself as the measure of all other religions, the center of the religious universe, the sun around which all other religions revolved and against which they must be judged. She believed increasingly in the necessity of secularizing morality and removing it from the dead weight of religious authority in order to further human progress. Her disillusion with religion was profound. "Isn't it unbearable that that is all about nothing?" she said upon viewing the great cathedral of Notre Dame across the Seine in Paris in the summer of 1926. In a poem written in the 1920's and published in 1930 she likened contemporary Christianity to the "Dead Star" of Bethlehem, whose light shone on through the power of inertia even though the star itself, that is, the original energy of early Christianity, was long dead. She likened modern Christianity to a

... gleam ... fathered of the dead,
A goblin birth, having no source in heaven
Nor in men's eyes, a disinherited
And phantom thing, that soon shall scatter even
Its slight and tapered essence, and the dark
Close down at length over its gutted spark.[6]

Through the 1920's, as Ruth Benedict explored religion and confronted the question of life after death, part of her personal spiritual energy went into an exploration of death itself. She continued the interest in death she had had since childhood, but with a difference. Through the study of death practices and ideas about death in many cultures she created an intellectual distance between herself and death. As if death were a dangerous electric current, she surrounded it with insulation so that it could be handled with safety. She grounded death in reality, through the matter-of-fact anthropological approach removing herself from the immediacy of her concern. Her study of death was a way of putting it aside, out of the central focus of her life, so she could get on with the business of living. As early as 1923 she had written a paper, since lost, on "The Origin of Death in Mythology," which later became a topic in her mythology class. In "Psychological Types" she spoke briefly of the Pima and Plains Indians' ideas of suicide and of the Pueblos' lack of comprehension of suicide, apparently struck by this. "Again and again I have tried to convey the general idea of suicide to different Pueblo Indians," she wrote, adding, "They always miss the point." This passage reflects her own interest and concern over the subject of suicide since childhood.[7]

But it was into her "Configurations" paper that she poured all her gathered knowledge of death, for this is a paper largely concerned with death practices, grief, and cultural sanctions on the killing of others. She stressed the relativity of death practices. There was no one "right" way to approach death. Reaction to death came out of the cultural configuration of the people involved and death was re-interpreted with each culture according to its "psychological set." She identified two basic responses to death: death as a loss situation, i.e., a direct approach to loss, and death as a danger situation, i.e., one of fear of contamination or return of the dead. The former she called "realist," the latter non-realist or "romantic." By reducing death to the impersonal study of its material and social processes she took it out of her own emotional realm and translated her emotional involvement into intellectual understanding, robbing death of much of its power in her life. She identified herself as a "realist" on death, not one focused on the irrational power in death but able to deal with it rationally as a part of life, not as a danger but as a loss. Through the study of grief processes she also had an opportunity to gain insight into her mother's early grief. She could deal with it not as hypocrisy but as a legitimate approach to grief which she found institutionalized among Plains Indian cultures. She realized that the free excessive expression of emotion in grief could reflect a realistic direct approach to loss and not a romantic one, and indeed did so among the Plains Indians. This probably helped her to understand her mother better, because essentially Bertrice Fulton seems to have been a realist in her approach to life, and her Dionysian grief must have seemed somehow out of phase with her personality and so doubly disturbing to a child. Benedict discovered that one could be realistic, yet Dionysian in grief, as her mother apparently was.[8]

Another thing she discovered in her study of death was that there was no ethical reasoning involved in cultural sanctions on killing people. The only rhyme or reason seemed to be to deal with murder or other forms of violent death by justifying, rationalizing, or condemning them in terms of the cultural pattern. Among the Northwest Coast Indians, she wrote, using the most outrageous and absurd example for her readers that she could find, killing another became part of the dominant pattern of raising one's personal prestige and humiliating one's fellows in the process. The death of a relative became an insult to be wiped out by the death of someone of another tribe, even if the relative had died of natural means. One also gained prerogatives through the death of a person one had killed.

Thus head hunting had become an established institution. In studying the justifications for murder among various peoples, she saw clearly that the justifications for social killing in war had no real base, that war did not rise out of some real need in a culture but had become a social habit wreathed around with essentially spurious arguments for its validity as a social process.[9]

With the writing of the "Configurations" paper and her book, *Patterns of Culture,* by the early 1930's Benedict had apparently worked through her own preoccupation with the personal aspects of death in anthropological study and in her own life. During the 1920's her major concern was with personal aspects of death in culture—grief, fear of ghosts, pollution, funeral practices, the place of the dead in the life of the living. But she was also concerned with social aspects of death, both in the personal forms of murder and suicide and in the mass form of war, as seen in "The Uses of Cannibalism" (1925). This social aspect became dominant in the 1930's and 1940's, with the expectation and then the occurrence of World War II. Her interest in death turned from personal exploration to a study of what she saw as the institutionalization of murder called war.

In the 1920's Benedict's confrontation with death and life beyond death also emerged in her poetry. For during this period poetry had developed from a minor interest to vie with anthropology as the major interest in her life. Poetry became an outlet for personal spirituality as formal religion gradually lost this function for her. As she wrote in 1929, the "spiritual rewards of life" came not necessarily or primarily from religion, but from "all enthusiastic dedications of the self," which especially meant poetry. There was also a sense that society needed the new vision of poetry. As Louis Untermeyer wrote in *American Poetry since 1900* (1923), "We are in the midst of one of those tremendous spiritual upheavals when, as in every crisis, the mind of man . . . flashes into poetry." For Benedict poetry became an arena of personal vision for the world. She wrote poetry both for herself and for those who would read it. Publication was vitally important to her as a poet because her poetry was a way of giving something to society, a vivid perspective on life, a vision which would provoke her readers to new insights about themselves and help them to know themselves a little better, a little more clearly. Within poetry she sought for herself an integration of the pull between self and society which was one of the underlying tensions in early twentieth-century American society.[10]

Individualism had been a prized quality in nineteenth-century America while it remained an essentially agrarian society. The idea prevailed that as each man pursued his own particular good, the general community would prosper. As Adam Smith had stressed in 1796 in *An Inquiry into the Nature and Causes of the Wealth of Nations,* individuals were led by an "invisible hand," i.e., the force of natural laws, to promote the public interest while trying to promote their own. This idea permeated nineteenth-century American public life. But with the passing of America from a rural society to an urban one by the twentieth century, this concept of individuality and the individual's relationship with society no longer held. As President Charles Eliot of Harvard wrote in a widely read essay, *The Conflict between Individualism and Collectivism in a Democracy* (1910), "An agricultural population . . . may continue to exist without much attention to the interest of the group." But when thousands of men, women, and children lived crowded into small areas, "close attention to the collective welfare is the only way to make the individual reasonably safe." During the Progressive era the necessity of coming to terms with the new urban collectivism meant modifying the meaning of individualism to fit the new situation. The compromise that emerged portrayed the individual as part of society, unsubmerged by society, yet working for the good of the whole; while society, by protecting public rights, actually worked for the best interests of the individual as well. Agrarian individualism became recognized as selfish individualism, the new concept as unselfish individualism. Sometimes an individual had to give up something for the good of the whole.[11]

At the same time the resurgence of feminism during the Progressive era led women, who during the nineteenth century in general had been excluded from the public idea of individualism and urged to sacrifice their personal interests for the good of their families, to desire self-satisfaction and individual personal fulfillment in nineteenth-century terms. Paraphrasing Adam Smith's argument, feminists wrote that women's fulfillment of their personal goals and needs worked ultimately for the betterment of their homes and families and that self-sacrifice destroyed not only women, but their families as well. Elizabeth Cady Stanton's essay "Solitude of Self" (1892) was the classic statement of turn-of-the-century feminism, buttressed in 1898 by Charlotte Perkins Gilman's argument for women's economic individuality and self-fulfillment in *Women and Economics.* This philosophy became part of a larger affirmation of the individual with roots in psychology, particularly psychoanalysis, which emphasized the necessity of satisfying individual needs and expressing individual gifts whose repression might otherwise lead to mental illness. By 1920 these ideas had upset the Progressive compromise on the harmonious relation of the individual and society, between individual and social rights. There was also a reaction against "unselfish" individualism and a desire to return to the clear-cut individuality of nineteenth-century America. American culture in the 1920's reflected the stresses between the individual and society: alienation of individuals from the values of their society, belief in the necessity for individual fulfillment, the search for individual pleasure over the good of the whole exemplified in the flagrant disregard of Prohibition.

Ruth Benedict was caught up in this rapidly moving turmoil of ideas. As a person who came of age during the Progressive era, she internalized its public ideal of unselfish individualism, the necessity for the individual to have and display social responsibility. As a woman influenced by feminism she accepted the idea that women had a right to personal fulfillment, a fulfillment that would enhance, not harm, family relationships. She harmonized these potentially conflicting ideas by melding them into a new guiding principle: personal fulfillment must also lead to the betterment of society in some way. She justified her writing because of its potential impact on others. When she saw no hope for publication of her feminist biographies she abandoned them. She justified going back to school first in terms of bettering her relationship with her husband, and then, in spite of the disapproval of her husband and continuously worsening relations with him over her professional life, in terms of the social good that could be done, first, if people were reeducated; then, when she discovered anthropology, when they were made culture-conscious. Sapir wrote to her in 1925, "Must everybody contribute his share toward the saving of humanity? That is your faith and an inhuman absorption in a purely intellectual pursuit will never satisfy you." [12] She approached poetry with the same rationale. By fulfilling her personal gift for poetry, by fulfilling herself, she would also have a worthwhile public impact through the ideas and visions expressed therein, for good poetry, like good literature, although it directly touched relatively few, added to the store of the race's spiritual resources. For a time in the 1920's, publication of a book of poetry seemed to her to be the way to have the most impact on society, to integrate the conflicting demands of responsibility for self and for society. She shared a poetic vision with colleagues with whom she gradually formed part of a poetic network. They strove to create a special form of communication in poetry consistent with the new ideas of a new century, a Modern poetry with its own rationales, its own goals.

Several people contributed to Benedict's growth in poetry. In the early 1920's Benedict began to know Edward Sapir not only as an anthropologist but also as a poet. He had had a book of poetry, *Dreams and Gibes,* published in 1917, although it was reviewed unfavorably in *Poetry* magazine. He had also succeeded in having some poems published in various American magazines. The fact of publication may have marked him as a serious poet for Ruth Benedict and one with whom poetry became a natural topic of conversation. When he wrote to congratulate her on her dissertation in June 1922, they were already discussing poetry—his poetry, that is. Apparently she had asked him in her letter whether he was writing poetry, for he replied, "No, I have not written any poems lately," and went on to talk about a poetry book manuscript rejected by a publisher and expressed his wish to build up a body of work over a period of years worthy of being published. "One *really good* book of verse would be an achievement," he said, articulating a goal he and Ruth Benedict shared together over the next several years. He also sent her a copy of a poem to appear soon in the *Nation.*[13]

By 1924 they had progressed from "Dear Mrs. Benedict," to "Dear Ruth," and she had relaxed the deep privacy of her nature enough to show him her poetry too. This common bond in poetry became one of the main themes of their correspondence and one of the important links of their friendship. He encouraged her to take her poetry seriously. "You have the stuff and the go," he wrote, "a unique feeling for majesty and austere irony, great boldness of conception, and the beginnings, at least, of a very original diction. . . . You must take this business of writing verse far more seriously than you do or pretend to do, Ruth." In 1925 he wrote, "Zuñi myths are important toys, of course, but your verse, even when you're not pleased with it, is a holier toy." In March 1926, he told her it was no secret that he saw her poems as "infinitely more important than anything, no matter how brilliant, you are fated to contribute to anthropology." He had written the same message in a poem called "Signal (To A.S.)" in 1924:

> Throw fagots on the fire!
>   Give the mad tonguing play
> Path for the flame's desire,
>   Shoulder the smoke away.

Here he used image and symbol to tell her to let loose her creativity, to clear away the smoke of hesitancy. "Don't affect an apologetic Muse, dear," he wrote. "Stand up and sing." He helped her resist discouragement over magazine rejections. "There are hundreds of reasons for rejecting first-rate poems and dozens for accepting rotten ones," he wrote. She had the necessary quality, he told her. She needed to keep sending out poems because success was only a matter of persistence.[14]

Besides encouragement, he gave her serious and honest criticism of each poem she sent him. Donning his "professorial robes," he gave her a detailed technical critique of her use of words, rhyme, meter, and occasionally, though not often, content. He began as her mentor, but they quickly became poetic equals. They shared judgments of what to include in possible poetry book manuscripts and planned an anthology of contemporary poems they liked best. As a scholar of language Sapir had a deep interest in the form, movement, and precision of words in poetry which he communicated to Benedict. "Look to your form and rhythm," he wrote. He encouraged her to pare down her words, her images, to get rid of filler and loose verbiage: "Let every asperity *which is not the embodiment of the essential feeling* be shunned like the plague."[15]

This was the same message she was getting from another source. Through Margaret Mead sometime in 1923 she met Mead's former college roommate, poet Léonie Adams, whose poems "gave her pure delight" with their unexpected use of word-play and turns of phrase. But what most excited and moved her were the underlying emotional messages the poems conveyed. Sapir called this "the subtler feeling value of words and phrases," deficient in him but similar to what he felt from "haunting passages of music that you evidently get from Miss Adams' verse." Benedict and Adams became friends, and through Adams both Benedict and Mead met Louise Bogan. Adams had been working as a waitress when Mead, working as Professor William Fielding Ogburn's graduate assistant in 1923–1924, got her a job cataloguing for a research project in Ogburn's office at fifty cents an hour. Adams had met Bogan in the fall of 1923 and the two had immediately liked each other. Bogan told Adams that her poem "Death and the Lady" in the *New Republic* had "struck her between the eyes." At Mead's urging both Bogan and Louise Townsend Nicholl, poets associated with the little magazine *The Measure,* came to work on the project.[16]

Bogan had had her first book of poetry, *Body of This Death,* published in 1923 to critical acclaim. She and Nicholl were insiders on *The Measure,* one of the important little magazines of the 1920's. Little magazines, in defiance of the mainstream world of business and convention, stressed poetic quality over mass taste and ran on shoestrings, providing a forum for most of the young poets and poetic movements after 1912. Most of them had a brief life-span and *The Measure* was no exception, appearing monthly from 1921 to 1926. But it has been called "one of a few important American poetry magazines," and according to Louis Untermeyer, it was "to New York what Miss Monroe's monthly [*Poetry*] is to Chicago." Through Mead or through the Anthropology Seminar which all three attended in the fall of 1924, Benedict met Eda Lou Walton, who had been affiliated with a California group of poets led by Witter Bynner, two of whom, Genevieve Taggard and Rolfe Humphries, were on *The Measure*'s executive board. Walton was also a friend of Idella Purnell, the founder and editor of a little magazine called *Palms* published quarterly in Guadalajara, Mexico, in English and distributed in the United States. Originally from New Mexico, Walton became interested in studying Navaho chants while in California and ended up retranslating them into English in a book called *Dawn Boy* (1926), which received critical approval.[17]

Benedict identified herself especially with Bogan and Adams as a poet. Sapir wrote her, joking, that he had thought himself one of the "Simple Simon school" of poetry, "and here are you severe and lofty-dictioned Parnassians—you and Léonie and Louise Bogan . . . —and where do I come in?" Louis Untermeyer, who published Benedict's poetry in his prestigious yearly anthology *Modern American Poetry,* in the 1920's, identified her with the Lyricists, particularly Adams and Bogan, who had the most impact on her growth as a poet. They, in turn, were linked in the minds of their contemporaries with Elinor Wylie and Edna St. Vincent Millay, and indeed all knew each other's poetry and were friends and acquaintances of varying degree. Though they were quite diverse they were all tagged together by the term "Lyricists" or "Lyrists" through the 1920's, Benedict along with them. Although the Lyricists have become a footnote in American literary history, in 1923 Amy Lowell saw them as harbingers of the next generation of poetry in America. Her own generation had been that of the Imagists, who concentrated on producing precise images of people, events, and things as an artist produced a picture in paint on canvas. They experimented with free verse, hoping to free a new poetic creativity in the process. In 1923 Lowell saw two distinct movements among the younger generation of poets: those she called the Secessionists, whom we today know as Dadaists, and the Lyricists.[18]

Both were movements in reaction to Imagism, at opposite points from each other. Dadaism rejected the precision of the image for extreme, often absurd, obscurity, rejecting the surface facility of Imagism for deeper meanings to be found by contacting the unconscious or subconscious. Dadaists also took free verse to its absurd extreme, freeing themselves from all formal limits. Lyricists rejected the free verse of the Imagists out of a sense that free verse was exhausted. They returned to an emphasis on the importance of form in poetry, turning to Elizabethan and seventeenth-century metaphysical poetry for models. As Louise Bogan wrote in *The Measure* in 1925, at a time "when everyone is writing free verse," young poets need "the courage to learn the heft and swing of English poetry in the tradition," not to become facile imitators, but as a springboard into a new, original poetic expressiveness. She described the exhaustion of the state of contemporary poetry, with poets "posturing in a stale gallery of mirrors [Imagism] or with one ear to the ground, alert for rumors." Like the Dadaists, the Lyricists attempted to break away from the limitations of form. They did so by deliberately disciplining themselves within certain poetic forms in order to break through and beyond them. Theirs was a Modernism of subtle experimentation within disciplined forms, a breaking out through using unexpected old meanings for words, or creating new meanings by putting words in new contexts, creating new metaphors, playing with adjectives as nouns, making new connections between words, subtly altering rhyme and meter to create a new form within the illusion of the old. Benedict began to use these principles in her own poetry. Like Bogan and the other Lyricists Benedict returned to traditional verse forms to try to use them to go beyond the limits of form. Although critics today have had trouble perceiving the Lyricists as Modern, they were seen by their contemporaries as a Modern movement growing out of the post-war feeling that life and poetry had become exhausted and needed revitalization through new forms.[19]

Modernism in the arts both fed from and reacted against the arts and aesthetic of the late nineteenth century. Modern arts, influenced by the new relativity, were characterized by subjectivity, by reality as perceived rather than as independently existing outside the mind. As Moderns, Benedict and her friends were concerned with exploring "the invisible deep structure beneath the visible surface of things." Their approach was a subtle one. Where the Dadaists dealt in broad strokes, the Lyricists narrowed and sharpened their vision. They chose a form, the lyric, which had flexibility and a traditional link to subjective states, as a vehicle for the expression of emotion for both poet and reader. They combined the Imagists' insistence on the precise use of words with the transferences and correspondences of the French symbolists to capture both sensations and associations in their use of objects and nature within poems. As one critic wrote of Elinor Wylie, by "saying one thing with exactitude" Benedict and her friends tried to convey "the echoes of oblique meanings." They tried to make "the emotions carry the weight of an overburdened mind," wrote critic Morton Dauwen Zabel. Their images suggested not only sensory experience "but also the subtle associations of intellectual experience." The result, he wrote, was "a merging of mind with sense, of abstract thought with physical reality, which leads to a strange exotic flowering of language." He concluded that poetry again became "(in Mr. Eliot's phrase) an elaborate 'mechanism of sensibility,'" of acute consciousness, intense awareness. As the Expressionist painters did with paint, Benedict and her colleagues tried to create "the texture of feeling and not the naked fact." They tried to tap their own subconscious minds and use words to communicate non-verbally and directly with the unconscious of the reader. Edward Sapir later used the term "condensation symbolism," which seems to describe what Benedict and her friends were trying to do. He defined such symbolism as striking "deeper and deeper roots in the unconscious" and diffusing "its emotional quality to types of behavior or situations far removed from the original meaning of the symbol." Through the power and the pattern of emotional response they explored the subjective side of human life and examined the inner dynamics of self. Through the personal voice they tried to express universal insight, to create an epiphany for the reader, an "instant of recognition" as Louise Bogan wrote.[20]

As poetry of the unconscious, Lyricist writing was necessarily obscure and ambiguous in its meaning, a quality which suited Ruth Benedict well. She had written in college of the "sane, healthy half revelation, half concealment" that she hoped would develop in modern poetic symbolism. Her own deep need for privacy responded to the idea of a poetry both personal and detached. Bogan expressed Benedict's philosophy well when she wrote, "At its best a poem cannot come straight out of the heart," but must break away "in some oblique fashion" from the direct experience of sorrow or joy—"be the mask, not the incredible face." In the early 1920's this obscurity was appreciated. A. Donald Douglas in the *New Republic*, December 5, 1923, called it obscurity "in all its dignity," and praised Bogan's poems for not presenting words "like glass beads traded to worshipful savages." The understood intention was for the meaning of a difficult poem to tantalize the reader, then finally "explode" on the reader's consciousness after several readings. Critic Llewellyn Jones in 1925 called Bogan's writing of inner experience in natural symbolism instead of directly "a sort of dream imagery," in which the poems had to be read for "the emotional drama which the imagery symbolizes [rather] than for any explicit story with a physical locale." This became true of Benedict's poetry as well.[21]

In exploring the deep structure below the surface of life, Mead, Benedict, Bogan, and Adams took many paths. All of them were aware of psychoanalytic concepts. Margaret Mead wrote that Léonie Adams told her friends her dreams "that later were transformed into poems." The Dadaists and later the Surrealists used automatic writing to tap the unconscious. But Bogan had contempt for "surrealist rubbish," saying "anyone of us could write that kind of thing in the middle of the night with our hands tied behind our backs." Bogan's approach was more disciplined, her poetry the product of an interweaving between consciousness and the unconscious, her poetic philosophy and intensity reinforcing Benedict's own. Bogan wrote, "Poetry is an activity of the spirit; its roots lie deep in the subconscious nature, and it withers if that nature is denied, neglected, or negated." She described her poems as the "free setting down of memory and desire." She talked in later life of repressing the actual facts of an event or happening, absorbing the event and forcing the mind to recreate the event in symbols which then became the poem. Poet Theodore Roethke called Bogan's poem "Medusa" in *Body of This Death* "a breakthrough to great poetry, the whole piece welling up from the unconscious, dictated as it were." Mead recalled that Bogan often talked about "perception itself—the way impressions of the external world and insights into people sink into the mind and become part of its texture." It was this texture that she was intent on reproducing in her poems. This was also what Benedict was trying to do. Bogan's intensity also attracted Benedict, evoking Pater's dictum to burn with a hard, gem-like flame. Yet poetry as expounded by Bogan was also a way to wrestle with the Dionysian in oneself and to achieve Apollonian calm. The poet, she wrote, "sets out to resolve, as rationally as he may, the tight irrational knot of his emotion." In a poem, "the poet makes a world in little, and finds peace." [22]

Bogan and Adams had another aspect that attracted Benedict: they wrote about women's issues, about being women, about life from a woman's perspective. This was characteristic of all those tagged with the Lyricist label. Amy Lowell had written in 1923 that while the older movement was "innately masculine, the new one is all feminine." She did not mean feminist, and not all the Lyricists were avowed feminists. Edna St. Vincent Millay certainly was and with the publication of *A Few Figs from Thistles* (1922) and *The Harp-Weaver* (1923) became the symbol and spokesperson for the "new" woman in the public mind, writing on self-reliant women often turning the tables on men in love. Bogan and Adams were feminists as well, although they expressed it more subtly in their poetry than Millay. Literary analyst Deborah Pope has shown how Bogan's first book, *Body of This Death* (1923), can be read as a woman's inner journey or spiritual quest toward selfhood. The journey starts by revealing in several poems the boundaries and limits put on a woman's life and felt by women: the sense of paralysis induced through outside causes or internal socialization through which they lose the ability to act, the frustrated anger and rage which result. Various forms of escape are tried, through travel, or through another person, but they fail. The last of these poems in sequence is the famous "Women," detailing women's internal barriers to self-achievement and self-worth. At this point, the quest for outside deliverance is given up—escape from the "body of this death," the compression and containment of women's spirits, must come from within. The following poems to the book's end detail women's ability to change, to choose, to throw off their restraints and become new women with a new self-reliant vision.[23]

Although she differed from Bogan in many ways, chiefly in her use of the gentler emotions in her poetry, Léonie Adams, like Bogan, exhibited a single character in her poetry, a woman speaking from her perspective as a woman, with a woman's perceptions. Of Elinor Wylie one critic wrote that she felt that stirring within her "that would sever its bonds and be off," and she wrote of herself,

> I was, being human, born alone,
> I am, being woman, hard beset;
> I live by squeezing from a stone
> The little nourishment I get.[24]

Wylie's work was not overtly feminist, but like the others she wrote poetry based on women's perceptions of life and the world. Like Bogan, Wylie wrote poetry of revolt against constraints, and with searching perception of the upper-middle-class world that bounded and limited women. Benedict seemingly concentrated her own perception as a woman in the struggle between matter and spirit, and conformity versus individuality.

Millay, Bogan, Adams, Wylie, and Benedict had one thing in common that tied them together in spite of manifest differences. They chose to write in a traditionally "feminine" verse form and one identified with women, the lyric. They chose to deal with emotion, the traditional province of women, trying to create a workable synthesis of emotion and intellectuality, the subjective and the objective. As Georgia O'Keeffe was doing in painting in the 1920's, turning the traditional "minor" art of flower painting by women into "major" art, these women took the "minor" poetry of the lyric and determined to create "major" art.

[176]

Elinor Wylie spoke for the Lyricists in an essay in the *New Republic* in 1923 in response to criticism that the lyric poets expended great effort to create very small art. Adopting a tone of mock humility, she played the genteel upper-middle-class woman agreeing with male pronouncements. In her mind's eye she saw the Lyricists "hunched over our filing and fitting," "dwindled" to the size of a picture in a camera obscura, "excellent workmen for the most part, but a thought too intent upon the binding." The title of the piece, "Jewelled Bindings" punned on binding as form, like the binding of a book that surrounds its contents, and bindings as chains, what she called the "spiritual bonds" that "constrict the essence of contemporary lyric verse," and by implication the lives of women as well, bindings the women dealt with in their poetry. She compared the Lyricists to "the bright and singing" birds of eighteenth-century snuff-boxes, confined, gilded toys that popped out and sang when the box was opened, thus parodying ideas of women as decorative ornaments rather than serious artists. But instead of "powdery dryness," the modern boxes had birds who repeated "a fine variety of tunes, melodious, bitter, passionate, or intellectual." For this type of singing, she continued, "a small, jeweled receptacle of two or three well-polished stanzas is no bad thing." She agreed, with mock humility, that it seemed "comfortable and fitting." What this meant in the materialistic terms of the 1920's was that the "small, jeweled receptacle" had more value than many a larger "box" in which poetry was contained. The Lyricists' "little" verses, "brilliant and compact," like small poetic diamonds or pure gold and silver were of infinitely more worth than the dross being produced in large, sloppy forms. "I think rather that we have found a manner which very justly encloses our matter," she wrote, "a letter which very nicely defines our spirit." The "bindings" of the lyric echoed the bindings of women's spirits. The Lyricists used them to call attention to these bonds and to transcend them. The description of the lyric had traditionally defined women's spirits— emotional rather than intellectual, shallow and facile rather than deep, delicate and refined rather than strong. It seemed only fitting to use the lyric, as O'Keeffe was using the flower, to redefine women's nature and women's spirit, still feminine, but a term defined anew by women rather than imposed by men. The women did not think of their art as minor. "Why were women born with ambition!" Louise Bogan wrote in 1924. "I wish I could sit and tat," she continued, "instead of wanting to go and write THE poem . . ." They had no smaller intent in mind than the realignment of poetic categories themselves, the recreation of the lyric form as "big" art.[25]

Benedict's poetry changed significantly between 1923 and 1924. Poetry written in 1923 was still just saying "ouch." In poems like "Of Graves," "Release," "New Year," she used a simple, extremely personal poetic voice, speaking of "My grandmother," writing "I shall lie once with Beauty," using "my," "mine," "we." Her predominant forms were simple rhymes seemingly influenced by Emily Dickinson, whom she admired, and occasional free verse, but form was important only to convey the message of the poem. Her concern was to unfold the meaning of the poem gradually through two or three stanzas. She made a narrative of a whole poem, describing a situation rather than letting images reveal it, as in this second verse of "New Year":

I'll walk your desert quite
Self-possessed
Never Nor once cry pity
At your worst any jest;

By 1924 her poetry had become more intellectual, symbolic, obscure yet precise. Her poetic voice was less overtly personal, more universal—no longer just saying "ouch" on paper, but a disciplined distillation of personal experience and emotion expressed in universal terms. She had become conscious of form and of the necessity for precise images symbolic of emotional states. "Toy Balloons," written in 1924, displays the change in her poetry. She detaches from the personal "I," using "He" instead. She turns to the precise image of toy balloons to talk symbolically of human visions, human dreams. Again, in "Withdrawal," written in 1925, the change has become even clearer. She uses the personal "I" but detaches by focusing emotional attention on nature images:

All day the rain caressed my straining trees
With slim white hands upon their naked flesh;

provoking in the reader's mind the sensuous image of tempestuous passion—distanced from the poetic voice, yet alive and vivid.[26]

Using her perspective as a woman, she explored the duality of spirit versus the material, a problem given new meaning in the context of the 1920's. An underlying theme in many poems is the necessity of giving up the easy life and conformity and choosing pain, discomfort, and intensity in order to struggle for something great, for a creativity and spiritual richness of life beyond the ability of material goods to supply. In veiled terms she wrote of the impact of the war, explored passion and the life of the spirit, and tried to convey a vision distilled from the experiences of her own life and the conclusions of her own thought. Religious imagery in her poems acted as a counterpoint to her impersonal and dry anthropological study of religion, and in poetry she created an emotionally based counterpart of her analytical study of death, releasing pent-up fears, anger, and longing for death in disciplined emotional bursts. In the early poem "Of Graves," for example, she wrote of her grandmother's acceptance of her own someday death, which helped her calm her own fears of death:

> And days I shiver swift and strange,
>   This still is what I see:
> Sunlight and rabbit in the grass.
>   And peace possesses me.

She wrote of death as the citadel, the refuge to be gained from the morass and confusion of the actual world. She used death as a metaphor for her desire for permanence in life, for a settledness that seemed elusive, writing of its "unwavering landscape, not the sport/of seasons." She longed for death as for a lover, with "embrace/Ultimate, irretrievable, complete." But the last poem in her collected poems in *An Anthropologist at Work*, published originally in 1934, suggests that she had worked her way through to a new calm acceptance of, and detachment from, her intense connection to death. It concerns one who has died and not found in death the expected refuge. The Lazarus-figure had found the secret of the world in the clarity of seeing that

> . . . Death unfolds
> Nothing but this, no angel's song,
> No beauty at the bone.

Understanding this, the figure chooses to accept life over death:

> Clear-eyed the tenemented ghost stands up
> And rolls away the stone.

In the same way Benedict by the 1930's had turned away from her personal preoccupation with death to a "clear-eyed" acceptance of life, with all its impermanence, chaos, and confusion.[27]

By 1925 Bogan, Adams, and Mead formed an important part of Benedict's poetic support group along with Sapir. All of them shared poems for comment and appreciation. Hints of this sharing appear in Bogan's letters to Benedict. She wrote of sending Benedict two poems she had just done and one other she was too unsettled to show her when they visited, and asked her to share them with Margaret Mead. She told Benedict that she was exasperated with Léonie for not sending her new work. She commented on Edna St. Vincent Millay dropping by a copy of her new book and asked Benedict if she had seen Elinor Wylie's new sonnets, which Bogan thought were the best works she had done yet. She sent Benedict a sonnet she thought good when she wrote it, telling her, "Please be *perfectly* critical about it." She ended a letter, "Do write, and send poems if there are some." Of Benedict's own poetry shared with her, she gave high praise to "But the Son of Man," asking her if she'd tried to get it published yet. During 1926 Adams, Bogan, and Benedict belonged to a larger poetry group. Benedict noted in her diary meeting Eda Lou Walton, Louise Bogan and her husband, Léonie Adams, and another poet, Berenice van Slyke, and her husband for dinner, then going to what she called "Poetry group" to hear Louise read. Apparently Benedict herself read her poetry to the group later that spring.[28]

In 1925 her first poems were published in *The Measure*. Her poetry was published subsequently through the next few years in *Poetry, The Nation,* and *Palms*. Eda Lou Walton included her work in a poetry anthology she edited called *The City Day,* and Louis Untermeyer included her work in his *Modern American Poetry* anthology, writing of her as "interesting but influenced; her cadences do not conceal the accents of Léonie Adams and Louise Bogan. Her metaphysics are her own." She published under a pseudonym, Anne Singleton, largely out of her deep need for privacy, but also perhaps partly because using a pseudonym helped free her from the constraints of her conscious personality as Ruth Benedict to reach the subconscious buried deep in her mind and allow it free play. This is suggested by Benedict's use of an earlier name, "Sally," as Margaret Mead wrote, "for the self who came and went and who would 'dictate' lines only when it suited her." As others turned to automatic writing or hypnosis to tap the subconscious, as Louise Bogan experimented with repressing facts to cause symbols to well up from the unconscious, perhaps Benedict used a persona to achieve the same end. W. H. R. Rivers, in *Instinct and the Unconscious,* had talked of double personality as a reflection of the unconscious. Perhaps Benedict used a persona or alternate consciousness to bypass the gatekeeper of the unconscious and cause buried material to surface for use in poetry.[29]

But basically the use of the pseudonym created a public yet private face for her. Anne Singleton was not just a mask to hide behind. By using this persona Benedict could reveal her deepest emotions, her most private values, her truest personal vision. She could explore publicly her own free-thinking ideas about philosophical questions on the meaning of life, love, and death while protecting herself from total vulnerability to possible adverse reaction to her feelings and ideas. Ruth Benedict was the public Ruth who outwardly conformed to the expectations of society. Anne Singleton was the public Ruth who could express the long hidden thoughts of the private Ruth safely. Benedict wrote that in her childhood the development of her two worlds led in turn to the development of two selves: a hidden inner self and a public outer self. As a child she became reluctant to talk about her "other" world or the things that concerned her most closely to anyone. She believed the things that mattered "must always hurt other people to know or make them interfere, and the point was to avoid this." She decided one day while lying in the haymow in the barn "that if I didn't talk to anybody about the things that mattered to me no one could ever take them away." Throughout her childhood and young adulthood she found it important to present an outer face to the world, while keeping her "real" self hidden. When Benedict first saw the Grand Canyon as an adult, her first impression was of "the effort of the river to hide, a torturing need for secrecy which had made it dig its way, century by century, deeper into the face of the earth." The Anne Singleton persona was an intermediate step toward reconciling the public and private parts of her personality. As she grew toward her forties her concern for such deep secrecy lessened. She decided that "being oneself was too big a job to keep the seal of secrecy on always, and other people could take it or leave it." As her compulsion for privacy lessened, her need for the Anne Singleton pseudonym lessened as well. By the 1930's she was publishing poetry under the name Ruth Benedict, taking the final step toward creating an honest public persona, one which became with time her greatest persona of all.[30]

In 1928 Louis Untermeyer accepted a manuscript of her poems for serious consideration by the publishing house of Harcourt, Brace and Company. He sponsored her book, but it was turned down on the basis that it would appeal primarily to too small and limited an audience. The obscurity that had seemed a breakthrough at the beginning of the decade now seemed too handicapping. The materialism of the late 1920's had turned people from an appreciation of the obscure to a need for realism and clarity, a trend the Depression of the 1930's later intensified. The Depression also turned poets to writing epics and narratives, and the lyric returned to a minor place in the literary canon. Léonie Adams wrote Benedict from

Paris, "I am sorry Harcourt didn't take the poems but I feel more and more that such things are accidents and of no mortal consequence." Benedict's response was, "They aren't good enough to give one's life to." [31]

In her mind she had justified her poetry as she had justified her feminist biographies, through their potential impact on others. In poetry she tried to project a spiritual statement meant to influence others. Poetry may also have seemed to her a way to live on after death. As Santayana wrote in *Reason in Religion* (1905) which she had read in college, "he who lives in the ideal and leaves it expressed in society or in art enjoys a double immortality . . . he can say, without any subterfuge or desire to delude himself, that he shall not wholly die." [32] Rejection of her book manuscript robbed her of hope of achieving either of these results. She continued to write poetry for herself and to publish in magazines in the early 1930's, but turned to other outlets. Her spiritual impulse became subsumed into the study of the psyche in the 1930's. But, most important, her personal spiritual quest merged with her social spiritual quest in the writing of *Patterns of Culture*. Like American society in the 1920's Benedict's exploration of poetry reflected the struggle of personal vision with social vision for the important place in her life. She resolved this conflict in terms of social vision, but found that within social vision her personal vision, as in an Imagist poem, could be integrated. She wrote poetry as an outlet of personal vision for the world. This vision highly colored the writing of *Patterns of Culture*.

8

The Personal Search

PROBLEMS IN HER MARRIAGE to Stanley intensified as Ruth Benedict found a place for herself in the Anthropology Department at Columbia. He continued to be unhappy about and unsympathetic toward her desire to have a career. Although he occasionally made a gesture in the early 1920's, such as the time he went to hear Edward Sapir speak at Cooper Union, for the most part he refused to meet her colleagues. Sapir called him "the shadowy Stanley." Esther Schiff Goldfrank recalled that at an all-day picnic at the Benedicts', attended by Franz Boas and other department members, Stanley Benedict spent the day in his darkroom, using the developing of pictures as an excuse not to participate. Ruth's schedule contributed to the lessening of intimacy. She took a room near Columbia University and only went home to Bedford Hills on weekends. Stanley occasionally spent the night with her in the city, but by 1923 they were talking of divorce. She wrote, "It's as if we inhabited the opposing poles." They played a lot of go-bang together that year, as if reduced to the easy pseudo-intimacy of games. "My program is to fill the twenty-four hours each day with obliviousness, with work," she wrote, "—And oh, I am lonely—." [1]

Into her 1923 diary she wrote a poem which seemed to express her sense of their relationship and their future:

We'll have no crumb in common
In all our days
We shall not make
A dream come true by naming it together;
Nor go full-fortified
From touch of lips.

These are sweet things.
To us they are as words

Rhymed in proud cadence
By a jesting fool.

We have but this: an hour
When the life-long aimless stepping of our feet
Fell into time and measure
Each to the other's tune.

Her marriage seemed to be becoming, in Nietzsche's words, "one long stupidity . . . the poverty of the soul in the twain . . . a small, decked-up lie." There were still good times. She and Stanley enjoyed the out-of-doors together. They had times of closeness, such as the one inaugurated in 1925 when Stanley made her cover with postage stamps the names of all the authors in a magazine carrying her poetry, and was able to pick out her poetry from the rest. But her poetry did not ultimately become a springboard to intimacy because he didn't particularly like what she wrote. Their lack of mental and emotional intimacy led to sexual estrangement as well. Stanley apparently fell in love with another woman, and Ruth wrote that it wasn't this that bothered her but that they "couldn't get within a thousand miles of each other." In 1930 she wrote that Stanley found her "especially undesirable, and I've lived with him now for four years on that basis." In a 1925 poem she wrote, "The worst is not our anger," but rather "Hearts / Grown icy with the bitterness / Of calculated hurt." Thus, she wrote,

. . . . Love departs . . . nor leaves behind
One red-lipped fagot of the fire
Of her incredible and dear desire.

"No longer any grief," she wrote, "to see love crucified"

Down the vain ways where love has died.

Perhaps it finally came down to the difference in temperament expressed in "Sight":

He said, "Reality will be at last
A heaven-scaling mountain on your path,
And you'll ignore it in your puny wrath
And brain yourself still trying to get past.
Is it not anything to you this roof
Will last our life-time, and will keep us warm
On every winter night, that you must form
These dreams of bliss that bide no mortal proof?"

But she could only wonder at his sight
That made of these four walls reality
The equal of her dreaming. Stare as she might
She could not see them for the urgency
Of tortured promises that starred her night
With their implacable transplendency.

Inexorably, through the 1920's, they drifted apart. They finally separated in 1930.[2]

Benedict had already begun facing other choices in her growing intimacy with Margaret Mead. They met in the fall of 1922 when Mead was a senior at Barnard taking Franz Boas' anthropology class and Benedict was the teaching assistant for the course. Mead was a well-known student, editor of the Barnard newspaper and member of a group of students who called themselves the Ash Can Cats, who considered themselves daring, high-spirited, sophisticated, and liberated. They "made forays," as Mead later wrote, into radical activities. That November of 1922 Mead and her friends caused a stir at Barnard when they dressed in red, decorated their table with red flags, flowers, and candles, and sang the "Internationale" in the dining hall for the fifth anniversary of the Russian Revolution. They followed Edna St. Vincent Millay's dictum, "My candle burns at both ends," and ardently embraced and examined every freethinking concept that came along, from political radicalism to Freudian ideas on sexuality.[3]

Benedict was quiet, shy, and, according to Mead, "always wore the same dress." Although she did this in response to the double standard which allowed male professors to wear the same suit over and over to every class without comment, it was a point against her with Boas' class of young, appearance-conscious women from Barnard. Many students were also put off by Benedict's hesitant speaking style and stumbling presentation, but Mead became one of the first to discover, as a later student put it, that "between the uh and the ah" often came "a bombshell of light which changed everything." Mead found Benedict's explanation of the Sun Dance model in the Plains Indian Hall of the American Museum of Natural History particularly halting—but also "particularly exciting." She listened avidly in other classes as Ruth Benedict compared the Inca Empire to a communist state or explained that the Crow Indians invested in visions as Americans invested in stocks. Mead and another student, Marie Bloomfield, set out to get to know Mrs. Benedict.[4]

Instead of meeting at the museum, as the other students did, Mead and

Bloomfield during that first semester began meeting Benedict at Columbia and riding down and back on the Broadway streetcar with her as a chance for conversation. Benedict invited both to the seminar where she reported on John Dewey's *Human Nature and Conduct,* and they found her "combination of shyness and inarticulateness devastating." Mead wrote that it took years before Benedict mastered her shyness and spoke fluently and with authority. But to Margaret and Marie she communicated her "vivid delight" in topics like Northwest Coast art and the Toda kinship system and gave life to Boas' course. Benedict must have been amused and flattered by the interest of these two women fifteen years younger than she. Mead wrote that she was slowly getting to know Ruth Benedict when something happened that caused Benedict to lower her extremely high personal privacy barriers and set aside the formal student-teacher relationship adopted from Franz Boas. Benedict wrote in her diary for February 8, 1923, "Marie Bloomfield's suicide in papers. . . . It bowls me over completely. Wrote M. Mead—She came to my room before bed time." She concluded, "Someday I hope I'll be able to go through with things just in the way Dr. Boas does." [5]

Mead felt a responsibility in Marie Bloomfield's death. She had helped Bloomfield return to the dormitory after six weeks in the hospital with the measles, apparently in a depressed condition, then had left to have lunch with a friend who came out of a physics exam hysterically blind. Mead, caught between two people who needed her, made the choice to stay with the friend who had lost her sight, which she did regain. But this meant that Mead left Marie by herself in a deserted dormitory over the weekend. On Monday, when she did not show up for dinner, it was discovered that she had killed herself by taking cyanide. Mead felt that if she could have stayed, Marie "might not have been driven by such desperation." To compound the weight of her guilt, the college administration pressured her to believe and tell others that Marie had been insane, which Mead resisted as a callous and libelous slander of Marie's memory. Only Ruth Benedict seemed to understand. When Mead went to see her they talked out Mead's feelings and fears. Mead wrote, "She was the one person who understood that suicide might be a noble and conscious choice." Benedict lightened her sense of guilt. She opened up and talked to Mead of her own friend who had committed suicide when she was a child and her wonder at why Cato's suicide was considered noble while her friend's was not. From that point on, Mead wrote, "I began to know her not only as a teacher but also as a friend." Even though the privacy barriers had been breached and they now began talking on a deeper level about anthropology and their own lives, the relationship retained a formal aspect. Mead wrote, "I continued to call her 'Mrs. Benedict' until I got my degree and then, almost imperceptibly, our relationship became one of colleagues and close friends."[6]

Ruth was everything Margaret was not. She was tall; Margaret was small. Ruth was athletic. She enjoyed swimming and walking and had seriously studied dance for a year. Anthropologist Raymond Firth described her as "willowy." Margaret hated exercise but admired the grace and discipline of dance.[7] Margaret was attracted to Ruth's quick wit, which she felt she somewhat lacked. Ruth was quiet, Margaret exuberant; Ruth contemplative, with a mystic strain in her personality, while Margaret was practical, rational, earthy. Margaret was upbeat, optimistic; Ruth downbeat, with a tendency to prepare for and expect the worst from situations or people. Ruth had her Ph.D. and was forging her own career as Margaret aspired to do. Ruth, on her side, was warmed by Margaret's admiration and saw her, fifteen years younger, at least at first, as somewhat of a daughter to be helped with problems and career choices. Often deeply depressed, she appreciated Margaret's outgoingness, her sunny personality, her energy, her intensity toward living. Though they were attracted to each other by differences, both were fanatically tolerant freethinkers with a radical bent of thought and both were of superior intelligence and attracted to intelligence in others. Both thought ideas important and valued creative, original thinking. Both felt a need to be useful, to make a difference in the world.

Through the spring of 1923 they met and talked of anthropology, of Dr. Boas, of Benedict's own field work with the Serrano. Benedict conveyed to Mead a sense of urgency in anthropological work because cultures were being irrevocably lost, as Benedict had seen at first hand among the Serrano. This sense of urgency, of doing work that mattered, coupled with her admiration for Benedict, tipped the scales for Mead and made her decide on a career in anthropology. They speculated together on what in societies derived from biology and what from culture. The evidence from older field work showed that many "conflicts," as Benedict wrote, "which we in our culture in 1923 regarded as the inevitable lot of human nature were by no means universal." They mapped out plans to investigate them in the field "so that someday we might really *know.*" Benedict talked to her of "Cups of Clay" and about the need to popularize anthropology. In March 1923, Mead wrote her grandmother that anthropology was her "chief enthusiasm." That same March, Benedict wrote of Mead in her diary after a talk with her about her future, "She rests me like a padded chair and a fire place. I say it's the zest of youth I believe in when I see it in her. Or is it that I respond understandably to admiration?" On Mead's entering anthropology, Benedict wrote, "I hope she does it. I need a companion in harness!" That spring when Mead's father refused to support her in graduate school the next year and she did not receive the fellowship she had applied for, Benedict surprised her with a $300 check and accompanying note, "First Award No Red Tape Fellowship," the first of many times Benedict helped her students out financially.[8]

During the next two years Benedict attended classes even though she had finished her Ph.D. in her desire to learn all that Boas could teach. Mead usually sat beside her in seminars, and her notes made it easier for Benedict to follow the parts of the discussion she could not hear. Out of class, Mead wrote, "we spent hours telling each other stories about people whom the other had never met, wondering and speculating why they had done or felt or thought what they seemed to have." They spent hours talking about ideas. Mead showed Benedict her poetry, Benedict revealed herself as a poet, and they began sharing poems and ideas about poetry. In these years Benedict and Mead made the final transition from teacher and student to colleagues and friends. Sometime during this time they also made the transition from friends to lovers, a decision they confirmed while visiting the Grand Canyon together in the summer of 1925, a short visit, for Mead was on her way west to catch the boat for Samoa and Benedict was at the beginning of a summer's field trip among the Zuñi and Cochiti.[9]

Such a choice was not unknown to either, nor did it seem to be a relationship in competition with their marriages. Into the early twentieth century, American society encouraged women's passionate romantic friendships. During the nineteenth century, relationships between women that included kisses, embraces, passionate protestations of love, and sleeping together were considered innocent by society and by the women themselves, who, vowing passionate love in one sentence, would voice their fervent faith in Christianity in the next and news of their husbands in the third. Emotional involvements between women, which often led to some degree of physical affection, were accepted by society. They did not challenge the natural order of things. Most women married and carried on romantic friendships within the framework of caring for household and children. Society itself encouraged the formation of same-sex friendships with its focus on the Doctrine of the Spheres as its social ideal. Since men and women had less and less in common, they were encouraged to look for intimacy among those who shared their spheres and who understood their lives and problems. Moreover, it is only since World War I that love has been linked with sex as a romantic ideal in American society. During the nineteenth century the most important component of love was its spiritual element. Sex was considered an animal instinct belonging to the lower nature of humans, and the goal was to strive for a love beyond sordid physical attraction, one that raised humans above the beasts and set them on a plane with the angels. Such a love ennobled both the lover and the loved. Such a love made each a better person and stimulated both to grow finer, less selfish, more generous, stronger, more honest, and closer to God. This deep spiritual love enabled both to tap the best in themselves. As late as 1912, feminist Ellen Key could write that true love "liberates, conserves and deepens the personality," inspiring great works and high aspirations, while mere sensual love "enslaves, dissipates and lessens the personality." By the 1890's, love among women had been accepted not only spiritually but socially through the institution of the "Boston marriage." This was a phrase used in New England to describe the common phenomenon of a long monogamous relationship between two unmarried women, usually women with careers or personal wealth, who shared their lives.[10]

Throughout the nineteenth century and up until World War I, romantic friendship among women was celebrated in popular literature. Literary historian Lillian Faderman provides many examples of this in her book on women's friendship, *Surpassing the Love of Men*. Well-known short-story writer O. Henry wrote "The Last Leaf," in 1906, while Ruth was in college. It is the story of two women who meet in New York as struggling young artists and live together. They are deeply attached to each other. When one falls seriously ill she loses her will to live and resolves to die when the last leaf falls off the tree outside her window. Her friend tells her, "'Dear, dear! . . . Think of me if you won't think of yourself. What would I do?'" The enduring nature of the women's relationship is implicit and accepted throughout the story. "The Lass of the Silver Sword" ran serially in the children's magazine *St. Nicholas* in 1908–1909. It concerns two girls in a boarding school. The younger, Jean, had "fallen in love with [Carol] at first sight." Jean left anonymous gifts of candy and flowers for Carol, and wrote "poems, stories, and *odes*" to Carol in her notebook which two other girls discovered and showed to Carol as a prank. Carol, instead of exhibiting anger or rejection, was openly delighted, and the two became good friends. They exchanged physical affection openly in a way women after World War I would hesitate to do. "Carol came in, caught Jean, whirled her around, pulled her down on a cot, and gave her a warm kiss." Later she pulled Jean "into her lap and hugged her tight." All the other students knew they were devoted to each other and no one thought them odd. They both became recognized school leaders. A woman writer looking back at her own schooldays from the vantage point of 1930 recalled, "there still remained a genuine and important outlet for eroticism, without any guilt attachment."[11]

In women's colleges romantic friendship had become a tradition. College women wrote poetry to and about each other. They exchanged tokens of affection such as flowers and notes, and gestures of affection, walking with arms around each other or holding hands, kissing, hugging, and openly enjoying their attachments to each other. They wrote matter-of-factly to parents and friends of these relationships. It was generally assumed that these friendships would later be superseded by marriage. But while at college the young women turned to one another. Faculty women turned to each other as well. Twosomes had become established institutions on women's college faculties by the late nineteenth and early twentieth centuries.[12]

Ruth Benedict had grown up in a late Victorian society that still affirmed women's romantic friendships. The atmosphere at St. Margaret's, where she attended high school, was permeated by schoolgirl crushes on female faculty members and students' attachments to each other. She wrote in her autobiographical fragments of "the youngest Becker daughter," who was "one of the first of those people who have been romantically devoted to me," when she was fourteen years old. She attended a woman's college, where, even if she herself formed no romantic friendships, she must have been aware of others who did. A few years after Benedict's graduation from Vassar, Edna St. Vincent Millay entered and formed her own romantic friendship there. In 1921 Millay wrote a play, *The Lamp and the Bell*, commenting on and celebrating college women's love for each other. The play, written to be produced at Vassar, thinly disguised the academic setting as a medieval one. Benedict herself apparently had a quiet crush on at least one woman faculty member while at Vassar which influenced her post-college career. In her feminist biography she wrote sympathetically of Mary Wollstonecraft's relationship to Fanny Blood, recognizing hers as a romantic friendship which, as her husband William Godwin wrote, remained the "ruling passion of her mind" while Fanny lived and in ways after her death. What is striking is the lack of sentimentality in Benedict's portrait of their friendship. She wrote that a love that began as "adoration before an idol" became over the years protectiveness as Wollstonecraft learned the weaknesses of her friend. But her love and her loyalty never wavered. "She had never demanded perfection," wrote Benedict, and Fanny Blood remained Wollstonecraft's "precious adventure in romance." Always a component of realism surfaces in Benedict's writing—love exists in the acceptance of human weakness and limitations, not on some ethereal sentimental plane. Margaret Fuller also wrote about a woman whom she loved "passionately," a love that was for her "a key which unlocked many a treasure which I still possess." [13]

Margaret Mead had grown up at the end of this same tradition of romantic friendship. But by the time she attended college a significant change had occurred, a change expressed well in a 1928 novel, *We Sing Diana*, by Wanda Fraiken Neff. Her leading character, a student at a woman's college in 1913, found all around her participating in romantic friendships, which were thought of as "the great human experience." Extreme crushes on a certain female teacher existed to such an extent that she was nicknamed "The Freshman Disease." When the heroine came back to the college in 1920 as a member of the faculty, she found the students full of Freudian vocabulary and everything explained by sex or lack thereof. "Intimacies between two girls were watched with keen, distrustful eyes." Students marked out "the bisexual type, the masculine girl searching for a feminine counterpart, and . . . ridiculed their devotions." Mead wrote of her own college days as full of Freudian discussion, adding that she and her friends also learned of homosexuality from upperclasswomen and alumnae friends. "We worried and thought over affectionate episodes in our past relationships with girls," she added, wondering if they were "incipient examples." [14]

By 1920 in America the ideal of romantic love was being replaced by that of romantic *sexual* love. This included not only the "joy of sex" but the idea that sex expressed the deepest intimacy, and that the deepest love automatically required some kind of sexual component. But if love now included sex, then love between women, formerly accepted as innocent, became tainted with the possible presence of Lesbianism. In 1912 Ellen Key could still praise women's friendship with other women as "a valve for unused feelings," saying that women found in these friendships "the qualities which set their spiritual life in the finest vibration of admiration, inspiration, sympathy and adoration." But she felt constrained to add that she was talking of "entirely *natural spiritual conditions*," because there was too much discussion of "'Sapphic' women." It was possible they existed, Key said, but she herself had never met one. [15]

The image of the "Sapphic" woman was a low one. The early German "sex expert" Richard von Krafft-Ebing and later the Englishman Havelock Ellis portrayed Lesbians as sick, tortured women, prone to murder or suicide. French and German writers portrayed them in fiction as morally corrupt, prone to jealousy, violence, and vice of all sorts. Freud viewed homosexuality and Lesbianism as neurotic, a sickness from which the victim needed to be cured. To be a Lesbian was definitely to join the ranks of the abnormal. Women loving other women by the 1920's faced a society which made them question that love. But the widespread existence of women's intimate friendships in the first twenty-five years of the twentieth century was revealed in a 1929 study by Katharine Bement Davis, *Factors in the Sex Life of Twenty-Two Hundred Women*. Her study, conducted nationwide on women from the supposedly "normal" population, found that 41.4 percent had had "intense emotional relations with other women . . . accompanied by hugging and kissing" and that over half of this group had had experiences that were overtly sexual or that they thought of as sexual. The custom continued, but how women perceived their friendships and how they were perceived by society had changed, and each woman now had to chart her own course within the new social dictates.[16]

Ruth Benedict was knowledgeable about sex, sensual, and delighted in physical sexuality. "When touch seems such a sweet and natural human delight," she wrote in her journal, "I resent sorting it out even in favor of my dearest dream of achieving some sort of dignity in living." Another passage, dated March 22, 1930, revealed a period of sexual frustration. She saw herself as "a lonely woman whose sex demands could get out of hand at a moment's provocation—*are* out of hand on a day like this." Her poetry reflects her openness, as she wrote fantasies likening beauty to a woman:

> I shall lie once with beauty,
> Breast to breast;
> Take toll of you, year;
> Once be blessed—[17]

Mead was no stranger to intense relationships with women. Letters in the Mead collection at the Library of Congress indicate that she was carrying on a passionate romantic friendship with a contemporary from Barnard during her senior year, the same time period in which she was getting to know Ruth Benedict, the same period in which she was planning her wedding to Luther Cressman, which took place the summer after graduating in 1923. Mead, by her college years, had apparently internalized the new ideal of romantic sexual love to a high degree and expected passionate love to include sexual passion. Mead's daughter wrote of her that she was "inclined to see sex as a natural expression of intensity of relationship." [18]

After the Grand Canyon trip, Mead and Benedict planned to meet again if possible in Europe for the Congress of Americanists to be held in Rome the next summer, 1926. Ruth traveled to Europe with Stanley, who attended a professional meeting of his own in Norway, where they traveled the fjords and saw spectacular scenery. She also visited England and through contacts there visited slum areas which greatly depressed her. When the time finally came to meet Margaret in Paris she received what must have been shattering news: on the boat from Samoa to Europe Margaret had met and fallen in love with Reo Fortune from New Zealand. A journal entry from those days reflects her mood. She returned to her old companion, death, for comfort in her disillusion and despair. "Passion is a turn-coat," she wrote, "but death will endure always." However, when they met again in Rome, Margaret, who had by then chosen to stay with Luther rather than Reo, must have convinced her that nothing had changed for them. "We had a week together in Rome," wrote Margaret, an intimate week in which they argued energetically over the Sistine Chapel, "whose outsized demigods repelled me and delighted her," and, sitting by Keats' grave lost to time, got locked into the cemetery and had to ring the special bell to be released. Ruth had cut her hair, an act which signified the New Woman in the popular mind and probably had connotations of freedom for Benedict herself. Her hair had turned prematurely white, "a silver helmet of white hair," and Margaret found her strikingly beautiful. They returned together on the steamer from Europe and plunged into a year of close collaboration teaching the Barnard course in which Margaret assisted Ruth. [19]

It is difficult to say what pertains to the Mead-Benedict relationship in Benedict's poems because of their inherent concealment and mixture of actual experience with the play of imagination. But Mead wrote that "Many of our poems grew out of our relationships to one another," and in examining Benedict's poetry from the mid and late 1920's we gain glimpses of feeling and issues important to them. "Reprieve" deals with the age gap between two lovers, "The untoward circumstance of age or birth." It goes on to counsel not worrying over things that cannot be changed, to enjoy the time given. Several of Benedict's poems deal with the problem of permanence. Benedict valued permanence. She wrote that casual shiftings were repulsive to her—"it seems to me that every chance love's got for dignity and distinction depends on a *belief* in its permanency." But with Mead she found herself in a relationship with no indication of permanency, and her poems reflect her ambivalence: at times the outright rejection of permanence ("Preference"), the acceptance of the fact that one can expect no permanence in life ("This Breath"), or the positive side of impermanence. She wrote of "Love That Is Water," and like water

> . . . slips lightly, flawless, from our confines,
> Shaped to no permanent feature, fluid as air . . .

If love has no permanence, it also has no bonds of convention to shape it into rigid forms. It occurs in its purest form outside of binding structures. Permanence then for Benedict had to do with the realm of the spirit, and several poems deal with the clash of spirit and flesh or spirit and material world. In "Earthborn" she wrote:

> I have put spirit from me as a cheat
> No longer to be borne. Shall flesh be less
> Than this impalpable wherefrom I eat
> No food of comforting, or ever bless
> As once your wandering hands? . . .
> . . . .
> . . . . Nay! Rather know
> I have such need of you as petals shed
> Before the wind one burning hour ago.

In other poems she stresses the element of spirit. In a poem written for Mead she brought the two themes together. She likened Mead (or perhaps herself) in the poetic device of gender reversal, to Gabriel, the soulmate of Evangeline with whom she had identified as a child. In Longfellow's poem Evangeline and Gabriel were star-crossed lovers, searching always for each other, never finding peace or a home together. The beginning lines of Benedict's poem reflect this lack of permanence:

> He wrought a pitiful permanence
> From jagged moments, and dismay,
> And tears more purposeless than pain.

But out of this lack of permanence Gabriel walks with the stars in their "crystal citadel." [20]

Some poems deal with freedom. "Unicorns at Sunrise" tells someone to "Be free/As unicorns." In another poem Benedict writes more dolefully

> We shall go straitened upon sundered ways;
> Be lonelier than ghosts who may not lay
> Cheek upon rose-flushed cheek, nor ever say
> The word the living weep for all their days.

But she ends the poem saying, "Go. I shall not call."[21]

Some poems express delight in love. "For the Hour after Love" whimsically muses metaphysically that passion ends in sleep, in a let-down after ecstasy—but it is so delightful that duty can't compete with it, for what can "compete / With sleep begotten of a woman's kiss?" Another poem seems to express this delight:

> Had I the green and silver laughter of the birch tree,
> The thousand dancing laughters of her lips,
> Had I the milk-white fairness of her body,
> The quiet of her brooding fingertips,
>
> I should be glad I'd lifted dark sod into the light,
> And that the dust of women was sweet again
> In me. I pray you then for my burial
> Find out a birch. You shall have answer then.[22]

Two poems can be taken as responses to a world grown unsympathetic to women loving women. "In Parables" runs:

> Once having sight, seek not
> Dear blindness any more.
> Our eyes are open; here
> Is the estranging door.
>
> Men have told long since
> This parable;
> Of the great darkness then,
> The merciful,
>
> When lay as lovers lie
> In passionate reach
> The sweet-fleshed earth and sky
> Close-bosomed each to each.
>
> Light flowered that day
> The violent sea

Drove salt between their lips
Idolatry.

Cursed with unblinking light
We too endure
They drink, men dreamed, this gall
Of forfeiture.

This can be interpreted to mean that women's realization of their love for each other leads to estrangement from society. Using the imagery of the Maori creation myth in the next two stanzas, Benedict writes of how the earth and sky lay as lovers innocently in the dark, a love that became "idolatry" in the light. In society's light women lovers too are cursed, but endure, although men "dream" they forfeit their rights in society. Another poem that can be interpreted as a realization of the world's probable response to her relationship with Margaret is "Our Task Is Laughter":

Being then branded, do not weep for this
What have they cherished behind fast-turned key
One-half so precious as this injury
That leaves us still together? Here only bliss
Is for our taking, stripped of the artifice
She wears to guard her dear absurdity—
For those whose wisdom is an old decree;
Who cannot know the folly of a kiss.

The answer to this disapproval, she goes on, is laughter, and "We must learn to wear / Its farthest implications in our souls." [23]

By the mid-1920's, study of the misfit had become an important issue generally within the social sciences. Sociologists studied the "marginal man." Psychologists and psychoanalysts studied the "abnormal," looking at the ways humans fell mentally out of step with their society. All of this grew out of the general effort to understand the interrelationship between the individual and his or her culture, how much influence each exerted on the other. But more than that, for those struggling with the Modern viewpoint, individuals, especially misfits, constituted the random element within societies, whether they were geniuses, criminals, immigrants, or minorities not tied into the majority value system. All had the capability of producing unpredictable positive or negative effects on society and the capability of creating chaos. Benedict found the study of misfits congenial to her personally, having felt herself a misfit in American society since early childhood. Now she and Mead were faced with the questions the new psychology raised about their love—were they sick, were they neurotic, were they abnormal, did they deserve to be social outcasts? Within this general context and within the specific context of their feelings toward each other, during 1926, when Mead and Benedict worked together at Barnard and Mead wrote *Coming of Age in Samoa,* they began to explore the idea of deviance and ultimately subtly attempted to change the idea of the deviant from a totally negative one to one possessing positive value.

Chapter 11, "The Girl in Conflict," in *Coming of Age,* written in the autumn of 1926, dealt with misfits in Samoan society, who they were and how they clashed with or deviated from the "normal" in their culture, "a question which Ruth Benedict had taught me to ask," as Mead later described it. While dealing with misfits, Mead also raised the question of the deviant. The word "deviant" had ugly connotations in American life. She attempted to expand the meaning of the word in a positive direction. She placed deviants into two groups: those deviating upward (positive deviancy) and those deviating downward (negative deviancy). The former consisted of those who "demanded a different or improved environment, who rejected the traditional choices." In exercising more choice than usual they came to "unconventional and bizarre solutions," but freely, adhering to a "different standard" from that accepted by society. The downward deviant Mead called the delinquent, because this person, unlike the other who rejects the group norms as her norms, internalizes them and "violates the group standards which are also her own." They were people who could not develop new standards but could not live by the old. In a footnote she clarified that delinquency cannot be defined by a culture in terms of acts alone; attitude has to be taken into account as well. A girl who steals and believes stealing wrong is delinquent, she wrote. Another, giving away her own clothes and her family's too, "may be a menace to her family and to a society based upon private property," but is not delinquent as the first girl is. "She has simply chosen *an alternative standard.*" [24]

In an even more telling comparison Mead spoke of the girl who commits "sex offenses" as being delinquent when she does so with shame, guilt, and a sense of wrongness even as she continues her course of action until she becomes a social problem. But the "young advocate of free love who possesses a full quiver of ideals and sanctions for her conduct, may be undesirable" but is not delinquent. This indicates that Benedict and Mead had decided that women who loved women, dubbed Lesbians by society, were healthy when they accepted their love as an alternative standard to that of the mainstream. Women-loving women became unhealthy when they internalized society's condemnation of them and the sinfulness of their love. Then they began to have social problems, such as drinking, or themselves became social problems through their self-hating behavior. It seems clear that Benedict and Mead saw their love as healthy, saw loving women as an alternative standard with an ethics of its own not to be condemned by society as wrong, but accepted as different yet worthwhile. The deviant, Benedict wrote in her "Configurations" article, was "not some one type to be specified and described on the basis of a universally valid abnormal psychology," but instead represented "the type not capitalized in the society to which he was born." This was a brave stance in a society so hostile to Lesbianism and homosexuality. Even the anthropologists they knew, a group by profession open to different standards and mores, had little good to say about the topic. Lowie called berdache, the practice among the Plains Indians of men assuming women's clothes and roles, a "pathological variation." Professor Boas wrote of homosexuality as one of the "abnormal sexual habits." Edward Sapir, who had become a close friend of both Mead and Benedict, wrote in a 1929 article of homosexuality as "unnatural," adding "the cult of the 'naturalness' of homosexuality fools no one but those who need a rationalization of their personal sex problems." [25]

Through their poetry and mutual sympathy Sapir and Benedict had become close in the early 1920's. Facing his wife's illness and eventual death, as well as other family problems, feeling out of touch with his profession in Canada, Sapir needed a friend. Benedict, struggling to find a place in anthropology, facing slow estrangement from her husband, also needed a friend. Benedict was attracted to Sapir. He was in deep trouble which called out her sympathy; he was brilliant and articulate. Her 1923 diary gives glimpses of her feelings. Sapir was in New York to lecture and get medical treatment for his wife that winter. After a casual talk with him she wrote, "I must remember afterwards how simple happiness is—." But they apparently never became involved. As far as men were concerned, Benedict was fixated on her husband and wrote of her dislike of the thought of having an affair. Also, the variety of the published Sapir-Benedict correspondence reveals a friendship based on a passion for poetry, with whatever sexual tension existed between them kept at bay by an impassioned yet impersonalized discussion of poetic form. [26]

Mead, however, did become involved with Sapir after his wife's death, to the extent that he asked her to divorce Luther and marry him. He also tried to persuade her not to go to Samoa and, when that did not work, wrote to Boas recommending he not allow her to go. Margaret decided to end the affair by getting Sapir to reject her as unworthy of his love. She persuaded him that she could never be faithful to him alone after marriage, and that kind of faithfulness was important to him. He finally ended the relationship by letter toward the end of Mead's stay in Samoa. It was in discussing this relationship at the Grand Canyon that Mead and Benedict decided they preferred each other to him. When Sapir's 1929 article was published, Benedict wrote him an angry letter ostensibly over a supposed quotation but more hurt probably by his negative statements on homosexuality. She must have been saddened by his reply, which read in part, "What values I possess I hope to keep as clear as I can . . . I am too old to learn to be different, too young to be indulgently or wisely indifferent . . ." By 1929 Sapir too was beginning to turn from poetry as an important factor in his life. He had become a professor at the University of Chicago and had remarried. He seemed to be getting caught up in the round of academic politics and enjoying it. For all these reasons their friendship cooled in the 1930's, though it never died.[27]

Both Sapir and Mead must have appeared to Benedict as like the romantics or non-realists she describes in her "Configurations" article, "elaborating danger situations" and displaying "awe before dark and uncanny forces" surrounding life, particularly the forces of the psychic unconscious, while she categorized herself as a realist, a person with an "ineradicable drive to face the facts and avoid hypocrisy." Concerning names she wrote that Plains Indian names were not "a mystic part and parcel of one's personality; they are realistic appellations much in our own sense." In the same way for her, using the pseudonym Anne Singleton was matter-of-fact, but to Sapir it was fraught with danger. "Pen names are an abomination," he wrote. "You know how I feel about even toying with the idea of dissociation of personality. I hate it." She apparently wrote him a letter in praise of individuality and he saw danger in this. In his reply he wrote that there was "something cruel" in her "mad love of psychic irregularities." He continued, "Do you not feel that you extract your loveliness from a mutely resisting Nature who will have her terrible revenge?" The danger Sapir saw for Mead in Samoa was not so much physical as a mental breakdown. Mead had the same sense about Benedict's pen name as that expressed by Sapir, an uneasiness before a potential double personality. She also tended to surround the problems of her friends with a psychoanalytic atmosphere. Her first husband, Luther Cressman, said of her that she tended to "dramatize situations and give a symbolic importance to them." When she had trouble with her eyesight, he said, she attributed it to the stress of the troubles in their marriage, but it turned out to be caused by her glasses.[28]

For Mead and Benedict, in any case, more important than their physical relationship was their deep intellectual collaboration during the late 1920's. For both Mead and Benedict the relationship retained the flavor of a nineteenth-century romantic friendship, with an important measure of physical affection in which both took delight, but with an emphasis on intellectual, emotional, and spiritual intimacy as the lasting qualities. After all, they made the decision for the relationship at a point in time when Margaret would be in Samoa for at least one year, possibly longer. When they met again in Europe and returned together on the boat home they began a period of intellectual collaboration that was creative for both. They worked on the question of the person who did not fit into the cultural pattern that developed into the discussion in *Coming of Age*. In the summer of 1927 Benedict had her insight into the Pima that led to the development of her Apollonian/Dionysian model. That same summer, with her marriage rapidly disintegrating, Mead went to Germany, overtly to study in museums and also covertly to see Reo Fortune again. That next winter, 1927–1928, Mead wrote *Social Organization of Manu'a*, a more technical monograph of her Samoan experience. She and Benedict "spent hours discussing how a given temperamental approach to living could come so to dominate a culture that all who were born in it would become the willing or unwilling heirs to that view of the world." Benedict wanted an open-ended solution; Margaret looked for one that would tie up all loose ends neatly. In their talks "echoes" entered from Koffka and Mead's conversations with Sapir and Goldenweiser in 1924 at the Toronto meeting where Sapir was enthusiastic about Jung and about an article by C. G. Seligman concerning certain pathologies having more scope in some cultures than in others. Mead wrote that she "supplied the psychological materials" and experience with a living culture in Samoa to challenge or confirm a point while Benedict "tested and retested her emerging theory" against her own experience of the Southwest Indians and her reading on American Indian religion. Mead's chapter on "Dominant Cultural Attitudes" in *Social Organization of Manu'a* written that winter was the first paper to use Benedict's ideas. "None of her theoretical phrasings were included in my chapter," Mead wrote, "but every detail of the phrasing was thrashed out between us." In that chapter Mead wrote of Samoan culture developing like that of a human personality making choices between many interests to form a coherent whole. "Human societies," she wrote, "left to themselves, will select parts of their heritage for elaboration . . . until a coherent individual culture has been developed." So the Samoans had developed a "formal social personality," with careful observance of all the prescribed courtesies.[29]

By the winter of 1927–1928, when Margaret wrote *Social Organization,* she and Luther Cressman had separated and Mead was living with three college friends. She had decided on her next field project to Manus and had also decided to marry Reo Fortune. That summer of 1928 Benedict taught summer school at Columbia and came to live with Mead. All of her roommates had left and they had the place alone. Mead wrote to her mother that she was going to Mexico rather than Nevada for her divorce "and spending the extra money to be here with Ruth this summer." In a sense this summer must have been a climax of their relationship and a farewell. Through 1927–1928 Benedict may have had hopes that their relationship could be more. After all, Mead was in New York, Fortune in Europe, and a lot could happen as time passed. Whatever hopes she might have had of their living together were fulfilled briefly and bittersweetly in the summer of 1928, then dashed totally as Mead went off to Manus, marrying Reo Fortune in New Zealand on the way there. They then spent the next two years in the field together. Fortune, of possessive and jealous temperament, would not have looked lightly on Margaret's relationship with anyone else during their marriage, and to please him it seems likely that Mead stayed within bounds until the break-up of their marriage in 1934. Thus the physical element of Mead and Benedict's relationship went into eclipse through distance and choice. But the romantic friendship remained steady through all the years of their lives. What Mead mourned at Benedict's death was the loss of the only person who had read everything she had ever written, and all of whose work she in turn had read, an intellectual intimacy that had withstood the break-up of many other relationships in each of their lives.[30]

For Margaret Mead theirs was a spiritually permanent relationship but not a socially permanent one. Mead had a pattern of falling in love with more than one person at a time, a pattern of double relationships throughout her life. She said once, "I've never known the kind of union that made me want to exclude other people." Only if the other person cared did she honor the desire for exclusiveness. "But I've never wanted to belong to another person, nor would I ever want anyone to belong to me." In the 1920's there were other reasons for their not living together. The age gap bothered Margaret. She felt Ruth saw her as the child she had never had. "I worried that she'd lose interest in me because of the age discrepancy," she later said. Mead also cared too much about her position in society to become an open Lesbian. There was no social sanction for Lesbianism. One became a pariah, an outcast if it ever became known. Mead, more than anything else, wanted to make a contribution to society. She wanted to bring about "change in the world." Sensitive as to how she would be received, she once wrote that she stayed out of active politics because divorce made her "too vulnerable since I might damage any cause I would be expected to promote or defend." How much more damaging a charge of Lesbianism would have been. Her words and ideas would not have been listened to, she would have carried no authority to create change. Her daughter relates a story that highlights Mead's sensitivity and protectiveness toward her professional life. Mary Catherine Bateson had a "partially conscious romance" with a woman during her adolescence. When she revealed it to her mother, Mead's first reaction was concern that Mary Catherine had not thought about possible damage to her mother's career if the relationship had become public. She valued her role in American public life too much ever to threaten it by taking the step into Lesbianism. Not placing herself in a position to become a social or professional outcast was one of the few imperatives of her life. Moreover, Mead seems to have been a true bisexual, attracted both to men and women, unwilling to sustain a social relationship exclusively with any one person over long stretches of time. In addition, the relationship with Benedict was not Mead's first involvement with a woman although it became a most significant one over time. Finally, marriage was expected to parallel romantic friendship in the American tradition. Both of them were married. Even the famous novel *The Well of Loneliness* (1928), the most sympathetic portrait of Lesbians during that time period, ended with the woman heroine sending her lover into the arms of a man, for all three recognized heterosexual marriage as the path to a happy, untormented life.[31]

But for Ruth Benedict her relationship to Margaret Mead acted as a revelation. It apparently affected her so deeply that from that time forward she became a woman-loving woman, willing to try a relation socially as well as spiritually with another woman. Benedict desired permanence, "human intercourse that can only come out of much more complicated arrangements than spending a night together." She separated from Stanley as the decade of the 1930's began. By the summer of 1931, when she had achieved financial independence and professional security with her job as assistant professor at Columbia, she met a woman with whom she was willing to take a chance on sharing her life. Her name was Natalie Raymond and she came from California. Apparently Benedict met her there while visiting her sister's family. The first mention of her in the Benedict correspondence was from a member of her student field trip in the summer of 1931 sending regards to Natalie, who had visited the group that summer. When another of the group asked about her, Benedict replied that Natalie had decided to come to New York and study at Cornell Medical School. Nat made quite an impression on the Mescalero group, one writing Ruth Benedict to joke, "is that very vigorous young lady, Natalie, still storming about New York, menacing the lives of all gentle and well-behaved young men, dogs, and cats?" Natalie moved in with her and shared her apartment. Benedict wrote of her in 1934, "loving Nat and taking such delight in her I have the happiest conditions for living that I've ever known." Understanding the outcast position this put her in with society, especially if it became widely known, made one of the goals of Benedict's work a change of social attitude concerning homosexuals. She wanted nothing less than a redefinition of the categories of "normal" and "abnormal" themselves.[32]

Her first target was psychologists and psychiatrists who as a profession defined homosexuality as an illness and a pathological state. She later wrote that in 1930–1931 she saw writers in abnormal psychology constantly confusing "adequate personality adjustment and certain fixed symptoms." She wanted, she wrote, to "break down the confusion" by showing that in other cultures "adequate functioning and fixed types of behavior" were not related. She wrote that she wanted to "drive" psychologists toward changing the definition of abnormality. For them in 1932 she wrote "Anthropology and the Abnormal," published in the *Journal of General Psychology* in 1934, before *Patterns of Culture* appeared. She began by getting her readers to question normal and abnormal as absolute categories, stating that people labeled abnormal in Western culture would function "at ease and with honor" in other well-studied cultures. She used trance or cataleptic states as her first major example. People who went into trance or catalepsy were considered abnormal in Western culture, she wrote, but in certain American Indian societies the trance experience was the door to prestige as a shaman or tribal leader. So, she went on, with homosexuality. In modern Western culture those with a tendency to same-sex love were exposed "to all the conflicts to which all aberrants are always exposed," and the instability resulting from this stress and conflict tended to be equated with homosexuality. But if the conflict with society did not exist, as it did not in ancient Greece, then homosexuals would not be regarded as abnormal. "Wherever homosexuality has been given an honorable place in any society," she wrote, "those to whom it is congenial have filled adequately the honorable roles society assigns to them." In ancient Greece, homosexuality was seen as a "major means to the good life." She then explained the American Indian institution of berdache, men who took the dress and the occupations of women at puberty, and who sometimes married and lived with other men. They were regarded as good healers of certain diseases in some tribes, social organizers in others, leaders in some women's occupations in others. They had a recognized place in society and were not viewed as outcasts. She continued her article with a brief description of Dobu and the person considered abnormal there, "of sunny, kindly disposition who liked work and liked to be helpful." This was considered "silly and simple and definitely crazy." Next she described the Kwakiutl Indians of the Northwest Coast, a society that encouraged "delusions of grandeur" and a "paranoid view of life," where to be a megalomaniac paranoid, an illness in Western society, was "an essential attribute of ideal man." All of these examples, she wrote, "force upon us the fact that normality is culturally defined."[33]

Normality means that part of human nature fostered by a culture; abnormality means that part of potential behavior a culture does not use. The normal is "that which society has approved," that falls within the range of expected behavior for a society. Most individuals shape their behavior to the expected range. In a society institutionalizing homosexuality, she wrote, most people would be homosexual. Those individuals who do not fit their cultures, either temperamentally or as a result of childhood experience, are deviants, "no matter how valued their personality traits may be in a contrasted civilization." Such an individual can successfully participate in the culture "only by doing violence to his whole personality"; the alternative is to be branded abnormal because "he has betrayed his culture." Such an individual is one on whom the culture "has put more than the usual strain." Adaptation includes "a conflict in him that it does not in the so-called normal."[34]

She suggested that professionally it was "fundamentally important in successful mental hygiene" for psychologists and psychiatrists to encourage "tolerance and appreciation in any society toward its less usual types." Patients also needed "education in self-reliance and honesty." When the patients realized that their problems were not internal but due to "lack of social backing," they could learn to "achieve a more independent and less tortured attitude" and to function adequately. She made the point that acceptance of the relativity of normality could lead to the conscious changing of normality within a society. As in ethics, so too with abnormality, "all our local conventions of moral behavior and of immoral are without absolute validity." Psychoses and neuroses were not absolute but derived from cultural conditions—and cultural conditions could be changed. Benedict wrote "Anthropology and the Abnormal" for a special population, but she also felt the need to get the general educated public to question the definitions of normal and abnormal, to strike a general blow against homophobia. This became the final impetus to the writing of her masterwork, *Patterns of Culture,* the final thread weaving together the themes of her work and her life.[35]

9

Patterns of Culture: Between America and Anthropology

PATTERNS OF CULTURE, Benedict's classic work, was a culmination of all the searching and questioning she had done in the 1920's. It was written out of a secure feeling of belonging to an intellectual community which would take her words seriously. It was written out of a sense of social responsibility, a desire to lead society toward new values and new goals. It was written in response to questions asked in anthropology, the other social sciences, and society in general concerning the importance of biology versus culture, chaos versus order, the individual and society, especially the role of the misfit. It was written out of a desire to give her personal vision to the world, a desire thwarted in poetry, but possible in anthropology. Finally, it was written out of a desire to change ideas of normal and abnormal in American society, partly rising out of the experience of her personal life.

Benedict apparently began writing the book in the summer of 1932. "Aren't you astonished that I should really get some 40,000 words already together for a book?" she wrote Reo Fortune in the field. She wanted his permission to use his field work in Dobu in one of her chapters and outlined her idea of the book then. The theme "of course" was "cultural configurations." Starting with a first chapter on "Anthropology, Old and New," a reprise of her *Century* article, she planned to move to a chapter on the "Diversity of Culture," on "how cultures become so different according to the different aspects of life they capitalize," then to a chapter on the "Integration of Culture," why cultures should be studied as configurations. Then she planned three chapters on specific cultures to make her points clear in context, then one, or perhaps two chapters expanding her "Culture and the Abnormal" paper, "a discussion of the adjustment of the individual to his cultural type." Her working title was "Primitive Peoples: An Introduction to Cultural Types." By October

1932 she had written the first four chapters, confessing to Margaret Mead, "I don't write verses anymore, but in my present mood I can well do without them." Later in October she wrote Mead, "I'm feeling quite bored with my book just now, for it seems fairly elementary." On the positive side it gave good descriptions of Southwest and Northwest Coast cultures, "and the pictures hang together rather well." She added, "Then it gives me a chance to introduce a little sophistication into the discussion of the deviant in a culture." By January Benedict wrote, "I'm awfully off the book just now," the result of not getting much feedback from Papa Franz and getting too much feedback from Otto (probably Otto Klineberg) because "it scares him like anything even to see anybody saying something other people haven't said all their lives," and feeling that Mead and Fortune in the field had doubts and objections about her ideas. But after getting Fortune's letter saying "Of course use the Dobuan material. . . . I'm sure you'll use it interestingly," she worked on the book through the spring and summer of 1933, and it was finally published in 1934.[1]

The book was one of those that appear on the scene as a burst of light. The *New York Times* called it a combination of anthropology, sociology, psychology, and philosophy, "expertly conceived and brilliantly developed." Melville Herskovits, writing in the *New York Herald-Tribune* Books section, praised Benedict's "incisive style," her ability to make complex ideas and ways of life of "singular clarity for the reader." Reviewer Dorothy Hoskins, writing in the *Springfield Republican,* said that *Patterns* belonged with those writings suggesting "intelligent means toward desired social and personal changes. A few of its concepts allowed to germinate in the American consciousness would affect our lives profoundly." The book had already received the imprimatur of Franz Boas when he consented to write an introduction to it. Benedict had written her publisher that most readers would "know and value his name, and most anthropologists will be amazed at his approval of my theme. They have waited for years to have him disavow this type of study," and this would be his first public statement on the subject. Instead, he gave her approach his judicious approval. Kroeber, writing the "official" review in the *American Anthropologist,* called *Patterns* "an important contribution," recognizing that it was written primarily for the "intelligent non-anthropologist." He praised the "distinctive, almost passionately felt, balanced thinking precisely expressed" throughout the book. Speaking as an anthropologist he stated that he did not think Benedict had "carried her configuration approach too far"; rather it remained "to be developed farther, now that this book is done." Kroeber hoped she would "push farther" and give anthropology "new stimuli and insights."[2]

In *Patterns of Culture*, Benedict defined the concept of culture for the non-anthropologist and affirmed its primary importance in human life, stressing the necessity of becoming aware of cultural conditioning even in modern society. She then presented the concept of the "great arc" of all possible human traits and activities, from which each culture chose those it would emphasize and those it would ignore. Some, for example, emphasized adolescence as a period of crisis while others ignored it; some emphasized war, others ignored it. This made each culture unique, although it might share some traits with other cultures. But this diversity did not have to be chaotic. She went on to explain how one could study cultures as wholes or integrated configurations because they tended to be more than just the sum of their parts. Each was like an "individual . . . a more or less consistent pattern of thought and action." She used the Southwestern Pueblos, particularly the Zuñi, and also the Dobu of Melanesia and the Kwakiutl Indians of the Northwest Coast as examples of cultures with configurations that could be treated as wholes. She chose them because she had been to Zuñi and trusted the correctness of the field work of those other anthropologists who had also been there, like Parsons, Kroeber, and Bunzel. She also knew Reo Fortune and trusted his field work on Dobu, and Papa Franz was the acknowledged expert on the Kwakiutl. She not only trusted his field work, he was there at hand to check her interpretation and use of his data. She showed that these three cultures were not chaotic collections of traits but that as cultures they had goals which their institutions and behavioral sanctions fostered. She used the Apollonian/Dionysian contrast concerning the Plains and Pueblo peoples she had discussed in her earlier papers. She spent a chapter discussing the possibilities and also the limitations of her configuration theory. All cultures, she wrote, were not as integrated as her three examples, and this had to be taken into account. There was also a danger of "lopping off" facts to fit a theory about a culture's configuration and it would be easy to generalize too broadly. But in the case of her three examples the field workers had just collected details with no theories in mind. Her theories about the cultures' configurations grew out of patterns present in the field work, she wrote, not the other way around. She did not start with a theory that the Pueblos must be Apollonian and fit her facts to that theory. The field work led her to conclude that this configuration might be at work in the Pueblo culture. Discussing the possibilities of configuration theory, Benedict wrote that configurations were not fixed, that behavior traits and institutions could change and be changed if one knew the essential pattern important to the culture. In the last chapter she looked at the question of the individual in culture, affirming that while the individual was acted on by culture, in turn he or she could influence that culture. She ended by redefining the concept of normality, saying that the normal were those who fit into their culture's arc of accepted behavior and institutions, while the abnormal were those who did not, although they might be perfectly acceptable in another culture.[3]

Patterns of Culture had a multiple impact on American thought. It acted as a signal of and a catalyst for the final acceptance of a profound paradigm change in the social sciences and in American society and set in place the new twentieth-century paradigm or world view which had been taking shape up to that time. In clear, compelling language Benedict drew together the scattered new ideas, filtered them through her own thinking and experience, and articulated a coherent social philosophy, a new set of axioms people could use to give direction to their lives and thoughts. In writing a book about configurations among primitive peoples, Benedict was covertly giving her readers a new underlying configuration for American culture based on the new values and beliefs. As a cornerstone of the new configuration, for the general educated public at large and for the other social sciences as well the book culminated the decade-long debate over biology versus culture. At the beginning of the decade biology was firmly entrenched as the primary motivator of humanity. Biological determinism allowed no leeway for change. One could not change one's gender, or the effects of one's hormones, or one's genes. Social change seemed possible only through rigorous, often cruel, weeding out of the "unfit." Benedict's demonstration of the overwhelming role of culture in creating three different lifestyles, those of the Zuñi, the Dobu, and the Kwakiutl, provided the final important evidence for replacing biology with culture as the major causal factor in human life. But she did not, like Kroeber, rule out the role of biology altogether in a strict cultural determinism. Instead she spoke of "the small scope of biologically transmitted behaviour, and the enormous role of the cultural process" (*Patterns of Culture*, p. 28). Culture, unlike biology, carried within it the potential for and openness toward individual and social change. For culture, though largely unconscious, was human-made and could be modified to suit social demands once the forces of culture were made conscious. Culture seemed the key to a better, more desirable future world. The force of Benedict's argument was helped by the excessive ideas of the eugenics movement in

[209]

the United States by 1934 and the bigoted policies abroad based on supposed racial and biological differences, especially the inferiority and superiority of certain peoples.

As a second important element of the new world view, for the general
educated public at large *Patterns* both parodied the values of Victorian
America and affirmed the end of that era's influence by replacing its absolute, universal standards with cultural relativity. Both Dobu and Kwakiutl
were cultures that honored the worst excesses of the Victorian robber-
baron mind-set. Dobu gave a central place to theft, cheating, and treach-
ery toward others as ways to succeed in life. The Kwakiutl stressed self-
glorification, arrogance, and the consequent humiliation of others. Like
Victorian America, Dobu stressed excessive prudery and fostered sexual
jealousy and suspicion. Among the Kwakiutl, marriage was a business
proposition, as Charlotte Perkins Gilman insisted it had been for many
nineteenth-century women. These were cultures Americans could only
perceive as paranoid and megalomaniac, Benedict wrote, yet her readers
could see the parallels with American society. The absolute standards of
Victorian America had fostered the worst excesses of American society,
her writing implied. They led to extreme selfishness, as in Dobu, or to the
excesses of consumer culture, as among the Kwakiutl. In their place she
offered the standard of cultural relativity. Each culture developed its own
different goals and standards out of a universal pool of possibilities.
There could therefore be no "right" or "wrong" standards, she wrote,
thus affirming ethical relativity as well. For most people relativity had
meant uncertainty, the potential for chaos. But Benedict made cultural
relativity a positive quality, one consistent in important ways with the old
goals and values of American society. "Much profit and enjoyment," she
wrote, could come from "relations with peoples of different standards"
once Americans understood and respected other cultures' mores (p. 25).
She framed the differences in terms of a great arc of possible human interests from which each culture selected those to emphasize, just as language
picked a finite number of sounds from an almost unlimited set of possibilities, or individuals developed their own personalities from the potentials
available to them. "The possible human institutions and motives are le-
gion," she wrote, and "wisdom consists in a greatly increased tolerance
toward their divergencies" (p. 45). This idea of tolerance and acceptance
of others lay close to Jesus' command to "Love one another," and in line
with the American acceptance of different peoples to its shores. She emphasized that with cultural relativity there could still be standards and
order, not necessarily chaos.[4]

To those struggling for a Modern perception of the world, Benedict's greatest contribution to the new world view was her answer to the great problem of Chaos—not an acceptance merely of social dissonance, or the negation of dissonance in a fixed, ordered, and artificial system, but the coexistence of Chaos and Order, as in the paintings of the Cubists, or Modern poetry. Hers was not a closed system. "It would be absurd to cut every culture down to the Procrustean bed of some catchword characterization," she said (p. 200). She called nothing more unfortunate "than an effort to characterize all cultures as exponents of a limited number of fixed and selected types" (p. 208). She accepted the existence of dissonance. Not all cultures achieved a "balanced and rhythmic pattern" (p. 196). Some scattered; for them "lack of integration" seemed as characteristic as extreme integration did for others (p. 198). But even in these cases she suggested an underlying order; dissonance due to a culture's bordering between two or more strong cultures; historical factors such as movement into a different culture's area or the influence of a newly migrated tribe on cultures in an area. Even in the most "disoriented" cultures, she wrote, one could follow "accommodations that tend to rule out disharmonious elements and establish selected elements more securely" (p. 198). Or, she suggested, the possibility existed that the description of the culture was disoriented, not the culture itself. Or "the nature of the integration may be merely outside our experience and difficult to perceive" (p. 200). Sustaining her acceptance of chaos was the belief that there existed underlying order, that within dissonance lay patterns which, if we were only acute enough to perceive them, could reorder our perspective of reality and create a new view of the universe, take people a step beyond the place where they were at that time and place. "Cultures," she wrote, "are more than the sum of their traits." They possess "new potentialities" (p. 53), a new level of complexity not present in their elements, and the same elements in other combinations behave differently. She, more clearly than any of her contemporaries, managed to reconcile the philosophical opposites of her day, and gave her readers a base from which to launch their own elaborations of the new paradigm. She suggested the possibility of a philosophy of the coexistence of Chaos and Order in the integration of seeming cultural dissonance.

Next, for the social sciences and society in general, she dealt with the question of the individual in society. She condemned the nineteenth-century view and advocated a new view of the relationship between the individual and society. They were not antagonists, she wrote, as a misleading "nineteenth-century dualism" proclaimed (p. 218). Because of this old idea of the conflict of the individual and society, "emphasis upon cultural behaviour" was often interpreted as denial of individual autonomy (p. 219). What should be stressed, she wrote, was the pattern of "mutual reinforcement" between the two (p. 220). This idea of individualism, an "unselfish" individualism, formed part of the new twentieth-century American paradigm. To the question of whether individuals changed society or were locked in step with it, she answered that again there was no dualism. Influence flowed both ways. Most people were influenced by culture but had no trouble fitting into it. But some individuals temperamentally were not in tune with their culture and therefore could not accept its standards and goals. She made no judgment of rightness or wrongness. She only described these people as different and implied that they could stop blaming themselves for their inability to fit into society.

As a corollary to the new paradigm she affirmed the relativity of normality, making a clear statement against homophobia in American society. Western culture tended "to regard even a mild homosexual as an abnormal," she wrote (p. 227). The clinical picture of homosexuality stressed neuroses and psychoses arising from it and the "inadequate functioning of the invert" (p. 227). But looking at other cultures showed that homosexuals had functioned well and even been especially acclaimed, as in Plato's *Republic*. When homosexuality was regarded as perversion, she wrote, the person involved became exposed to conflicts. "His guilt, his sense of inadequacy, his failures" thus were actually the result of "the disrepute which social tradition visits upon him." She added, "Few people can achieve a satisfactory life unsupported by the standards of the society" (p. 229). She suggested that other means of dealing with misfits' alienation from society existed beyond "insisting that they adopt the modes that are alien to them" (pp. 234–235). On one hand, the misfits could objectively learn more about their own preferences and how to live with and deal with their "deviation from the type." Learning how much their troubles were due to lack of social support, they could educate themselves to accept their difference, and achieve "a more independent and less tortured" existence (p. 235). Second, education of society to tolerance needed to go hand in hand with individual self-education. In making these assertions concerning homosexuality, however, she was careful to use other examples of deviation with it, such as trance, and insisted on having her name on the cover page as *Mrs.* Ruth Benedict, even though she and Stanley had been separated for four years. Thus she brought to bear on what she had to say not only the authority of science and academia, but also her covert authority in American life as a married woman.[5]

Benedict's philosophy in *Patterns of Culture*, besides the other purposes it fulfilled, remained true to a feminist vision. In stressing the importance of culture and the relativity of cultural practices, Benedict laid the base for a reevaluation of relationships between men and women. If masculine and feminine were perceived as biological, then women could not escape the weakness and inferiority inherent in being female. But if masculinity and femininity were cultural, that is, learned behavior, then women's weaknesses were not inherent, but culturally learned, and could be changed. In the examples that she used of relationships between the sexes among primitive peoples she suggested alternative possible ways for men and women to relate to each other. The implied message was that American ways were not set in concrete—they should be questioned and if necessary changed. The Zuñi, for example, were a matrilineal culture in which women owned and inherited all properties and their husbands worked for them, a radical departure from typical United States male-oriented practices. Benedict talked of the ease of divorce among the Zuñi, the implication being that divorce did not have to be the traumatic experience it was in American society. She wrote of the Dobu, who lived one year with the wife's clan, where she dominated the household, and the next year with the husband's clan, where he dominated. She described the Kwakiutl, with whom inheritance was also matrilineal, but went to the husband of a daughter, and women were bartered like property among men to gain status and power. In choosing these and other examples, Benedict wanted her readers to stop and think about their own culture in contrast and give themselves permission, through the alternate possibilities of anthropology, to free themselves from their own conventional or stereotyped ways of thinking about men and women and to search for new ones.

Patterns of Culture did not initiate the trend but it confirmed anthropology as a source of moral authority in American life, superseding natural history. When one needed the aid of a pithy example to make a point, one would turn not to the insect or mammal worlds as at the turn of the century, but to the case of a "primitive society," and what happened in such societies became intimately linked to the happenings of American life.

The book had a "wave effect" in American culture. The first wave washed over a comparatively small group of people: leaders in the social sciences and among the general educated public who had been groping toward the expression of the new twentieth-century paradigm and for whom *Patterns* acted as a centering device to bring its elements together.

Through these people the ideas of *Patterns* became the guiding principles for a new perspective of the world which became the underlying beliefs of the intellectual community. The second wave began in 1946, when *Patterns* was published as a twenty-five-cent paperback, and when it became "one of the first true anthropological best-sellers in this country." With this *Patterns* moved out of the intellectual community and into the consciousness of the mass reading public. In this way Benedict's ideas truly became "common coin" in the American psyche.[6]

Among her colleagues, Benedict's approach was daring and novel. It took great courage to reintroduce subjectivity as a working tool for anthropologists, since they had spent the first twenty years of the century discrediting it. To the "scientifically minded" it seemed like the introduction of potential chaos into anthropology, with a resulting threat to soundness. But it was a subjective approach based on the verifiable facts of a culture's way of life, a subjectivity that gave promise of actually working to make cultures comprehensible. Some anthropologists saw *Patterns* as a step toward making their discipline a truly predictive science. If one can have a basic idea of *why* people act the way they do, as the configuration approach seemed to promise, one can then predict with a fair measure of success which programs they would accept or how they as a people would react to an issue—a necessary preliminary to workable social engineering. *Patterns* became a catalyst of the Culture and Personality movement in anthropology. But within the discipline the book marked a clear split for the rest of the decade and beyond between what Kroeber, writing in 1934, called "scientific" and "historical" anthropologists.

For Ruth Benedict personally, *Patterns of Culture* represented a summation of the meaning of her life to that point. But it also marked a path into the future: for America, for anthropology, and for herself.

By the mid-1930's Culture and Personality (C&P) studies had become a legitimate field of interest, bolstered by the support of the Social Science Research Council Committee on Personality and Culture and the National Research Council Committee on Culture and Personality, chaired by Edward Sapir. C&P studies had begun institutionally with Sapir's seminar on Culture and Personality at Yale in the fall of 1931, when he first introduced psychoanalytic ideas to anthropology students in an integrated way with the help of psychiatrist Harry Stack Sullivan, who commuted once a week from New York to participate. A showcase seminar in 1932–1933 sponsored by Rockefeller Foundation money generated through the interest of Lawrence Frank gave Sapir the opportunity to conduct his Culture and Personality class for a group of scholars chosen from various European countries. It provided a convincing display of the ability of C&P research to attract big money and tackle serious problems which influenced later SSRC and NRC acceptance.[7]

But the earliest signal event in the emergence of the Culture and Personality movement was the presentation of Ruth Benedict's "Psychological Types in the Cultures of the Southwest" in 1928. "Psychological Types" and later "Configurations of Culture in North America" (1932) were the first papers to use psychological ideas to make anthropological sense in a major way. Previous writers had floundered trying to integrate a basically individual-oriented, biologically rooted psychology with group-oriented, culturally rooted anthropology. Benedict's idea of culture as "personality writ large" pointed a direction anthropologists could follow, a theoretical approach that reached its greatest development in *Patterns of Culture* (1934). But *Patterns of Culture,* after its initial favorable reception, precipitated to the surface a debate that had been latent through the 1920's on what kind of discipline anthropology was and should be. This identity struggle appeared in three different ways: a debate over whether anthropology should consider itself as primarily "historical" or "scientific"; a debate over whether a functional or a structural approach was more important; and, within C&P itself, the question of which was more important—the individual or the culture in which he or she was enmeshed.

During the first quarter of the twentieth century, anthropology in America had developed under Boas to consider itself a "historical science." By this anthropologists meant that they saw their discipline as a "science plus." Science was foremost. Anthropology's roots were in the biological sciences, and physical anthropology was definitely an experimental science in which hypotheses could be proposed and validated in mathematical terms. Ethnology had become scientific through its meticulous and scrupulous collection of masses of raw data and its attention to observable phenomena and to what they revealed rather than to the creation of largely unfounded generalizations common to the nineteenth-century "unscientific" anthropologists. Ethnology had attained scientific objectivity by refraining from direct value judgments on various cultures and from indirect value judgments through the comparison of cultures, both weaknesses of the nineteenth-century anthropologists. In the study of diffusion and the possibility of convergence anthropologists examined processes which held possibilities of explanation and prediction. In the analysis of cultural phenomena into their component parts, anthropologists hoped to be able to discover basic regularities or "laws" of culture as physics and chemistry had done in the inorganic world. The "plus" consisted of two principles concerning space and time taken from history to help the new scientists deal with the unstable human phenomena of their discipline. The first was an insistence that phenomena could not be torn out of their context and used to "prove" positions, as had been done by the nineteenth-century anthropologists. Information always had to be dealt with in context. The second was respect for phenomena as the end result of a sequence of events through time and the necessity of understanding as much of that sequence as was discoverable, by doing as much historical reconstruction as possible. As a result of this approach, Boas and his students were termed, somewhat misleadingly, the "historical school" of anthropology, or the users of a "historical approach."[8]

With the declaration of independence from biological science in the early 1920's and the focus on the ambiguous concept of culture as the material of their discipline, ethnologists set themselves on a collision course with their own standards. To deal with "culture," if it were not to be seen as an endless array of haphazard items, meant opening the Pandora's box of interpretation, comparison, weighing values, all the heresies of the nineteenth century that anthropologists had learned to distrust. For a time this conflict was obscured by the necessity of defining culture and its component parts. But by the late 1920's rumblings had begun within the discipline. By that time it was also becoming apparent that historical reconstruction which relied on the study of diffusion had played itself out and convergence had proved an intellectual dead end. Anthropologists had come to feel the need for some kind of integrative approach to make culture coalesce, to deal with culture as a whole. There was a sense of identity crisis: where do we go from here as a discipline?

With *Patterns of Culture* the identity crisis came out into the open. In responding to the book anthropologists also revealed the way they identified themselves and their discipline and the struggle between various points of view concerning new hopes and old fears. *Patterns of Culture* taught the potential of integrative studies in anthropology. But it also served to reinforce the threat that with them anthropology would lose its status as a science and would fall back into the speculative philosophical realm of the nineteenth-century anthropologists it had spent the last quarter of a century totally discounting. To those who saw the potential, *Patterns of Culture* was an inspiration. They discounted its faults as endemic to any pioneer work, took Benedict's ideas as a direction in which to search for answers, and tried to go on from there. To those who saw mainly the threat, Benedict's work was "unscientific," too subjective, too vague, too interpretive. To an extreme fringe of this second group Benedict seemed a "delusionist" with obsessive investment in her idea, distorting or manipulating facts to support her stance.

The configuration theory of *Patterns of Culture* was extremely influential in anthropology. It established the principle that it was legitimate to deal with culture wholes and gave a working model for doing so, from which others could establish their own working models. For many anthropologists, as Morris Opler later wrote, Benedict's work was "liberating" and a "refreshing influence" on American anthropology. Moreover, while it was a step into the future it retained ties with anthropology as a "historical science." Franz Boas had written in his introduction to her book, "The interest in these socio-psychological problems is not in any way opposed to the historical approach." Boas had the reputation of quickly popping intellectual bubbles and withering practitioners of fragile speculative thinking with a glance. His approval gave assurance that there was substance to Benedict's work and added to the confidence of those who used Benedict's ideas to kindle their own.[9]

Within anthropology, some spent time clarifying the configuration concept and making it more precise. Ralph Linton, for example, in *The Study of Man* (1936) broke down culture patterns into three types: universals, specialties, and alternatives. Universals were common to all adult members of a culture. Specialties meant traits or habits shared by a group within a culture but not by the whole culture. Alternatives were those ways used by individuals within a culture which gave different paths for achieving the same ends. John Gillin at the University of Utah wrote an article called "The Configuration Problem in Culture" (1936), defining configurations more clearly as to their properties, types, how they changed, the relations of configurations and their parts, why anthropology needed them, and possible directions of major configurational research.[10]

One major focus of research, directly inspired by Benedict's section on the Zuñi in *Patterns of Culture,* was the delineation and analysis of "ideal" and "real" patterns: cultural ideals versus actual behavior within a culture. The paradox of Zuñi was that although knowledgeable observers besides Benedict agreed that as a culture it stressed order, restraint, and communal over individual effort, as a society it was rife with factionalism, and acts of disorder by individuals were not unknown. Columbia graduate student Irving Goldman wrote about the Zuñi for *Cooperation and Competition among Primitive Peoples* (1937), edited by Margaret Mead, that "in spite of the formal phrasings of cooperation, non-aggressiveness, and affability, the Zuñi are in the opinion of a number of field workers a rather 'mean people,'" holding grudges and sharp personal animosities "that under the influence of white contact seem to have flowered into full-blown factionalism," especially between Catholics and Protestants, pro-whites and anti-whites. The Zuñi, he wrote, cooperated in all formal and ceremonial situations and did not use violence, except in the few cases of women's quarrels noted by Benedict. But they had "no love for their fellowmen" and were ready "to defame anyone on the least pretext." In short, he wrote, there was discord between the ideals which the Zuñi had laid out for themselves and the way they put those ideals into practice. "Beneath the surface of a cultural norm of benignity and of affability there appears to lie some restless irritability," he wrote. "It is difficult to account for it." [11]

The pro-*Patterns* group in anthropology explained the Zuñi paradox by deciding that Benedict's depiction was that of the ideal pattern of Zuñi life, often violated in actual practice, but setting goals, attitudes, and directions for Zuñi culture to follow. The study of ideal versus real patterns became an important one in anthropology. Clyde Kluckhohn, a pro-Patternist, called Benedict's picture of Zuñi that of her old informants of the pueblo, who told her of the ideal rather than the reality. Kluckhohn elaborated on ideal versus reality in "Patterning as Exemplified in Navaho Culture" (1941), in which he defined "ideal patterns" as those that show what people do and say when they completely conform to cultural standards: in other words, the "musts" and "shoulds" of a culture. Other patterns, "behavior patterns," came from observation of how people actually behaved. Usually, he wrote, there was a difference between the ideal and the behavior patterns. He also suggested five categories of ideal patterns: the compulsory, in which a culture allowed only one way to meet a situation; the preferred, in which out of several possible ways, one was most acceptable; the typical, in which out of several proper ways of behaving one was most usual; the alternative pattern, in which several behaviors were equally acceptable; and the restricted, in which behavior was acceptable only for some members or groups of society, not society as a whole. He proposed that "pattern" be used to talk about overt culture and "configuration" to talk about covert culture in an attempt to clarify terms. In "Covert Culture and Administrative Problems" (1943), Kluckhohn elaborated on the ideas of "covert" and "overt" culture, which he attributed to Ralph Linton, another way of approaching ideal versus reality. Earlier C. S. Ford, in "Society, Culture, and the Human Organism" (1939), defined culture as a set of rules and beliefs that touched on but were not necessarily the same as actual behavior. George Peter

Murdock, in "The Cross-Cultural Survey" (1941), also distinguished between ideal patterns and the behavior of people in a society. He considered real behavior irrelevant to a study of culture. Thus Benedict's work led cultural anthropologists to wrestle with the ideas of real behavior and ideal behavior, and the weight to assign to each.[12]

A second direction that opened to the pro-Patternists was the idea of multi-characterization of culture. Benedict had concentrated on cultures with one dominant integration and had agreed in *Patterns* that most cultures did not have this degree of integration. In a search for ways to deal with more loosely integrated cultures, several anthropologists turned to a multi-causal framework. Morris Opler developed the idea of "themes" in cultures, the presence of several dominant elements interweaving within a culture, both reinforcing and blocking each other in varying degrees. John Gillin formulated the idea of "objectives" as cultural integrators in "Cultural Adjustment" (1944), each objective in turn made up of smaller components such as "trends" or "orientations" within the culture. Clyde Kluckhohn and Dorothea Leighton, in *The Navaho* (1946), used the idea of nine "basic convictions" or "premises" underlying Navaho life. The premises essentially set out a standard of behavior, explained how it worked in related situations, and included alternatives for satisfying the standard.[13]

But the approach that attracted the most attention and gave the movement its name was the study of personality in and of culture. This ranged from James Woodard's rather crude but interesting attempt to explain cultural structure directly in terms of personality structure based on Benedict's idea of culture as "personality writ large," to psychoanalyst Abram Kardiner's very sophisticated formulation of "basic personality structure" in each culture, a concept his anthropological colleague Cora Du Bois later modified to "modal personality." Margaret Mead, writing in 1935 in *Sex and Temperament in Three Primitive Societies,* said her work took Benedict's "approved" personalities one step farther, making hers a study of "approved personalities of each sex." Anthropologists and psychologists together explored culture and personality, searching for "ideal" personalities or later "typical" personalities within cultures, those who conformed more or less to the ideals and standards of their cultures. Benedict had described the "ideal man" of Zuñi, the Plains, Kwakiutl, and Dobu cultures. Following studies attempted to put her ideas on a more scientific foundation.[14]

The conflict point within the profession came at the Zuñi paradox. While both the enthusiastic and the unenthusiastic could accept the idea of real and ideal patterns and of configurations, the latter group balked at Benedict's Apollonian-Dionysian contrast. Many anthropologists had not been comfortable with it from its inception in "Psychological Types." The idea itself was a literary one, deliberately so on Benedict's part in an attempt to neutralize the terminology. As she wrote to Mead about Boas' response to psychoanalytic ideas, "I think Boas would accept all of it but the terminology—but that kills it." However, the idea backfired. To many the Apollonian-Dionysian contrast marked the epitome of the non-scientific method which they were determined to minimize in their discipline. Kroeber made their fears vivid in his article "History and Science in Anthropology" (1935) and subsequent articles on the same theme. The article suggested that anthropology was no longer a "historical *science*," and that the discipline now faced a choice between an identity as "scientific" or "historical" anthropology. By "historical" he did not mean especially concerned with time, but with "a basic and integrative intellectual attitude" imported from history, just as objective analysis had been imported from science. Kroeber's use of the word *historical* was misleading because what he wanted to convey was the idea of an integrated holistic approach rather than scientific analysis into parts. He identified the work of Benedict and Mead, and to a lesser extent Fortune and Bunzel, as deriving from this historical side of anthropology. Critical of the "painstaking analysis and non-selective objectivity of the 'scientific' approach," this group, as did researchers in history, selected elements needed to build up a picture, omitted those not needed, or "slurred" them "with intentional subjectivity." This subjectivity caused a conflict with the "scientific" group, but Kroeber wrote that this was "no longer a defect as soon as its [their work's] essentially historical nature" was accepted.[15]

Kroeber saw the subjective quality of Benedict's and her colleagues' work not as a flaw, but as an acceptable result of a different quality of interpretation. As he had explained in his review of *Patterns of Culture*, the approach, that of finding the "genius" of a culture, could not be "measured or demonstrated." It lay outside the present narrow boundaries of science, which did not admit the validity of a "subjective empirical approach." Estimating the relative importance of a pattern in a culture had to be done "primarily by feeling," and validity depended on "the fit of the pattern parts" and on not leaving a significant part of the culture out of the picture. "Those who will," he wrote, "may quarrel with the approach as 'unscientific.'" But then they also had to quarrel with historian Jacob Burckhardt's *Renaissance*, Lord Bryce's *American Common-*

wealth, or anthropologist Robert Redfield's *Tepoztlan,* all acknowledged and respected, though nonscientific, works of cultural insight, conveying essential truths about their subjects in "historical" style. Kroeber supported Benedict. He found her ideas "original, suggestive, and stimulating." Unfortunately, he wrote, the 1930's decade was a time "which rates science high and history low." [16]

Anthropology was not the only social science experiencing this crisis of approach. In psychology in 1938 well-respected Harvard psychologist Henry A. Murray wrote of two movements in psychology, which he labeled the "peripheralists" and the "centralists," terms that more accurately describe what was also going on in anthropology than Kroeber's split into "history" and "science." The peripheralists equated to those in Kroeber's science category. They were objectivists, desiring to concentrate on the observable and measurable facts, the external data. When they did speculate they used limited conceptual schemes found useful in analyzing parts, not wholes. The culture area in anthropology was that type of scheme. The psychological objectivists saw the concept of personality as their counterparts in anthropology saw culture, as only the "sum total or product of interacting elements rather than a unity," something to analyze into parts. [17]

The centralists, whom Kroeber would have identified under the term *history,* and with whom Ruth Benedict stood, were "attracted to subjective facts" and chiefly concerned with the "governing processes" of the brain (or culture). They found these processes by "listening to the form and content" of the personality (of culture). They used subjective terminology. They were "conceptualists," trying to observe behavior accurately but merging interpretation with perception, referring overt actions to underlying impulses which they conceptualized as there. They were "totalists," seeing the personality (or culture) as a "complex unity, of which each function is merely a partially distinguished integral." They were open to the use of empathic intuition; as "dynamicists" they ascribed action to inner forces rather than external ones. The centralists, unlike the peripheralists, felt "no compulsion to count and measure." Murray defended the need for centralists in psychology as Kroeber defended the need for "historians" in anthropology. In its present stage, Murray said, the study of persons needed people with broad views, who perceived "the interplay of general forces." Psychology in its then fluid state needed people with intuition, for "In the wake of intuition comes investigation directed at crucial problems rather than mere unenlightened fact collecting." Murray's analysis did not threaten his colleagues. But when Kroeber argued for a similar recognition in anthropology his terms were too full of negative connotations for anthropologists to accept.[18]

Boas' response was to deny that such a dichotomy existed. Benedict and others who agreed with her approach, such as Kroeber, saw themselves as scientists, but of necessity forging a new definition and philosophy of science, a more realistic, flexible tool than the rigid ideal of "true" science borrowed erroneously from the physical sciences. Kroeber himself spent the 1930's trying to derive such a philosophy of science. But Kroeber had raised the spectre for other more sensitive readers that anthropology would no longer be accounted scientific in an intellectual milieu where, as Kroeber put it in a later paper, science had become "the god of innumerable laymen" with a "totalitarian realm" claimed for it, where even anthropologists made a "fetish" of science.[19]

Moreover, the values of history were values that anthropologists had learned to discard, to avoid, to view as shoddy work. The "historical approach" was "subjective," the catch-all word in anthropology for worthless work. It depended on the view of the observer rather than the reality of the event or object observed. The historian received recognition for his or her ability at perceiving relations and building "convincing bridges" across gaps in knowledge. The historian was honored most especially for skill in interpretation: for reading between the lines, selecting elements to highlight, omitting or downplaying elements deemed unimportant, giving elements perspective—all scientifically damning practices. Historians did not "prove," as scientists tried to. They "inferred" more likely or less likely "probabilities of fact, of relation, of significance." The historian weighed possibilities, then selected and combined them into the most coherent whole or pattern. This was the method of conceptual integration, wrote Kroeber. If anthropologists were to follow Ruth Benedict's lead, this is how they would end up as a discipline. For many anthropologists this nonscientific projection was hard to stomach.[20]

Benedict had first used the Apollonian/Dionysian comparison in 1928. In the nine years between 1928 and the publication of two major articles on the subject in 1937, the only one to attack it was Paul Radin, and his was an isolated case. Radin was of the first generation of Boas' students. Like the others his family had emigrated to America from Europe. He was an expert on the Winnebago and knew other American Indian tribes as well. But he had a love-hate relationship with academic life and for many years went from one temporary position to another. In 1926 he spent the winter in New York. He gave an informal class to Columbia graduate students and Benedict got to know him. Her diary from that year contains several references to him. She enjoyed him, but their views were not compatible. "Lunch with Radin—," she wrote, "much anthropological divergence." Radin was a Jungian, but paradoxically he believed in the basic historicity of mythology. Like Parsons and Kroeber but to a greater extreme, he saw historical reconstruction, or the piecing together of the historical backgrounds of cultures, as the major way of understanding cultural processes in the present. In quick succession he wrote two books—*Social Anthropology* (1932), which defended historical reconstruction, and *The Method and Theory of Ethnology: An Essay in Criticism* (1933), in which he severely criticized Boasian anthropologists for moving away from it. Benedict's ideas presented an approach to culture that threatened to replace historical reconstruction, which was already under attack, as the chief approach of the discipline. In *The Method and Theory of Ethnology* Radin wrote critically of her "Configurations" article. He talked of her "revolt" against the quantitative method, writing that "her whole temperament is that of a culture historian" even though she protested against historical reconstructions as "naïve and *simpliste.*" He accused her of "dogmatically" including and excluding things "in an unjustifiable and arbitrary manner," and added that since "unpalatable facts" might disturb the "desired harmony," Benedict "not only flies in the face of these facts; she calmly leaves them out." Apart from this, Radin thought it doubtful that "distilled syntheses" like Benedict's were ever really applicable to culture. They were fascinating but of extremely problematical value. They might hold for individuals but not for a specific culture or a culture area. Radin's attack on Benedict was minor compared to that on Boas and others in American anthropology. Kroeber wrote to Boas that Radin made him and Wissler feel like "the two thieves crucified by the side of the True Cross." It was generally recognized at the time that Radin was upholding his own rather extreme point of view in his books.[21]

But after 1935 and the writing of Kroeber's "History and Science" article, the Apollonian-Dionysian configurations of Zuñi and the Plains became a primary focus of anthropological debate. Only Reo Fortune had been to Dobu, and there was no way to either prove or disprove his work. Nobody dared challenge Benedict's Kwakiutl interpretation in the face of Boas' approval. But Zuñi and the Plains lent themselves to an attack. Disproving the Apollonian-Dionysian contrast became the key symbolic activity for disproving or disparaging the historical approach and reaffirming the primacy of science in anthropology.[22]

It took a few years for a serious attack to get going. The objectivists had the problem that Benedict's account of Zuñi was not just based on her own experience there and her own known expertise in Zuñi mythology but also upon the best data available at the time. Even Robert Lowie, a natural skeptic of holistic interpretations, remarked that Benedict's account of Zuñi was "so satisfactory" because it rested on "most ample documentation by herself and other observers." Later investigators also seemingly found corroboration for an Apollonian world view in the Pueblos among the Hopi. It was not until 1937 that two articles appeared, one a direct attack, the other more circumspect, yet seen as more damaging to Benedict's position. This latter was "Zuñi: Some Observations and Queries," written by a young Chinese anthropologist, Li An-che. The article was not a critique of Benedict per se. Li An-che wrote the article with the help of both Ruth Benedict and Ruth Bunzel. He intended to make the article a study of how observations about Zuñi by prior observers, even those aware of the problem, had been colored by unconscious and implicit expectations from Western society which he, being Chinese, could see around. He perceived himself as questioning "official view[s], native or otherwise," in favor of the realities of Zuñi culture. He singled out not only Benedict and Bunzel but also Kroeber for specific criticism and criticized the work of "almost all the students of Zuñi culture" and "the universal idea of the students of the area," adding that observers were "easily led astray by their own background." Of those points of Benedict's and Bunzel's he took exception to, their emphasis on the lack of personal elements in Zuñi religion, the idea of leadership in Zuñi, and the discipline of children, he stressed that they were "oversimplified" and "misleading" because of a "basic fallacy"—reasoning within "the logical implications of one's own culture." He saw research in Zuñi in general as unbalanced due to an unconscious Western point of view.[23]

In Western society, he wrote, prayers as a fixed formula and as a spontaneous outpouring of the heart were antithetical, so Benedict and Bunzel had seen the formulaic religion of the Zuñi as impersonal and detached. But he himself had felt an intensity in the formulaic prayers of the Zuñi. Concerning leadership, he wrote that at least since white contact there had been struggles for individual leadership within Zuñi, stirring up strife between groups. But he also saw Benedict as caught in the Western idea that lack of personal competitiveness implied lack of desire to lead. He saw traditional Zuñi ambition as based in religious knowledge, not personal magnetism or ego. He also challenged the idea held by all Zuñi researchers and used by Benedict, that Zuñi parents did not discipline children. Here again, he wrote, reiterating his main point, it was not the observation that was at fault but "an interpretation based on an incomplete recognition of the factors involved." His own interpretation suggested that verbal discipline of children came from all adults, not just parents, and that adults instilled mental or religious fears in children to make them behave well, as effective as the fear of a spanking. Besides these points, he also challenged Kroeber's "Western" approach to marriage. Thus it was not facts Li An-che challenged in his article but the interpretation put upon the facts by Benedict and others. He did not call it unjustifiable and arbitrary as Radin had, merely uninformed and restricted by Western perceptions. Li An-che spent one summer season in Zuñi before writing his article. In part he was influenced by his own Chinese perspective. But his article provided the first specific ammunition for the view that the interpretation in *Patterns of Culture* was flawed.[24]

The direct attack on the Apollonian-Dionysian contrast occurred when Bernard Aginsky, a graduate of the Columbia Anthropology Department now teaching at New York University, presented a paper before the annual joint American Anthropological Association–American Folk-Lore Society meeting at New Haven, Connecticut, in December 1937, called "Psychopathic Trends in Culture." As Aginsky understood it, Benedict had set up the Apollonian-Dionysian duality to apply to all North America, calling every tribe outside the Pueblos Dionysian. His purpose was to show that the Pomo Indians of California had both Dionysian and Apollonian traits, plus what he called an "Anxiety" pattern, and thus refute the idea that the Pomo were Dionysian, as they would be classified under Benedict's system as he understood it. This paper is the only one to which Benedict replied in print. In her "Reply to Dr. Aginsky," published in the same issue of *Character and Personality* in which the article afterwards appeared, she stated that Aginsky's idea of her Apollonian-Dionysian contrast as "polarities of behavior . . . whereby cultures can be understood in toto" was totally wrong, "completely alien to my own theoretical position." She added that she had "constantly opposed any 'typing' of cultures into which any newly studied culture would have to be arbitrarily fitted." To call her Apollonian-Dionysian contrast such a system was an egregious misreading of her book. The system she espoused was an open and not a closed one. She also charged that he had used *Apollonian* with quite a different meaning than she had, shaping the word to his argument.[25]

Lowie discussed Li An-che's criticisms of Benedict's work in his *His-*

tory of Ethnological Theory (1938). Typical of those troubled by the subjective implications of Benedict's work, he gave "qualified approval" to her configuration approach, agreeing that "cultural *leitmotifs*" existed and should be studied. But he attacked the Apollonian-Dionysian contrast. He argued that in that contrast Benedict had oversimplified a real antithesis. He compared her to a physicist finding out about electricity by looking it up in a dictionary rather than observing the actual phenomena involved. He thought Li An-che had shown that Benedict's emphases threw the picture "out of focus," rather than making it more precise. He argued that Benedict's use of terms like "trance," "frenzy," and "orgy" without giving them "precise and accepted" meanings "largely vitiates Benedict's interesting contrast of non-Pueblo and Pueblo cultures of North America." He argued that so-called Dionysian peoples conformed to that pattern "only to a moderate degree." The Crow, a people he had extensively studied, rarely talked of supernormal phenomena in terms of ecstasy, he wrote. This from the man who in 1922 had written a fictionalized account of a Crow warrior's life that was totally Dionysian. To counteract the idea of the ecstatic vision he cited from an article by Radin, "Ojibwa and Ottawa Puberty Dreams," the nonecstatic, carefully orchestrated case of an Ojibwa boy of seven who after fasting under the eye of his elders acquired "the sort of guardian spirit his instructors permit him to accept." If Lowie had looked he would have discovered that Benedict had talked about this type of vision and where it fit into the Dionysian scheme in *Patterns*.[26]

Elsie Clews Parsons' *Pueblo Indian Religion* came out in 1939. It was the most complete study of the Pueblos to date and is still a comprehensive master source of data. Parsons did not agree with the psychological approach to culture and therefore the book was not a resounding affirmation of *Patterns of Culture*. Although she was against Benedict's subjective approach, her own scientific objectivity led her to confirm Benedict's information on several disputed points: the disinclination to drink; the almost unheard-of quality of suicide and, in Zuñi, the point that it was so foreign to them that it caused laughter; that murder was almost as rare as suicide; that whipping in Pueblo families was infrequent, marginal behavior; whipping as a voluntary public rite of cleansing certain times of the year or in certain ceremonies; the fact of the boys getting to whip the katcinas at the end of their second initiation. At the one whipping rite where Parsons was present, only perfunctory whipping went on and it was a cleansing rite. She confirmed the idea of Zuñi as an orderly society where leaders had to be men of peace, a cooperative society where individuality was frowned upon. She affirmed that the scalp ritual was to cleanse the slayer, not celebrate victory.[27]

But she tried through historical reconstruction to undermine Benedict's position by showing that social aggression had once existed in Zuñi. She suggested war, the threat of war, or internal feuds as bases for Pueblo migrations in early history. She also suggested that kiva groups originated as organizations of war brothers, an idea that provoked a sharp response from Benedict in her review that it would "hardly survive marshalled argumentation." Parsons also suggested that Pueblo children, while not punished into conformity, were frightened into it. She saw punishment as a factor in Pueblo whipping of adults, though not a major factor. All in all, Parsons supplied information that both sides could use to uphold or damn the Apollonian idea, but, if anything, the book tended to confirm Benedict's picture of Zuñi.[28]

The controversy heated up still more in the 1940's. Laura Thompson and Alice Josephs' book, *The Hopi Way* (1944), offered major support to the Apollonian idea, as did Thompson's article, "Logico-Aesthetic Integration in Hopi Culture" (1945). But the objectivists intuitively felt that where there was factionalism and personal animosity there must be aggression in the culture. Benedict had stressed the nonviolence of Zuñi culture. Evidence of violence, aggression, or even a tendency to excess within the Pueblos would shatter the Apollonian idea once and for all. Dissenting research focused on such issues as discipline of children, lack of suicide, and the use of alcohol in Pueblo culture.

Li An-che had raised the question of how children were socialized in Zuñi. Esther Schiff Goldfrank examined this question in 1945 in "Socialization, Personality and the Structure of Pueblo Society (with Particular Reference to Hopi and Zuñi)," which she considered a major attack on Benedict's position on the disciplining of children and the Apollonian view. Though she agreed with Benedict that parents were very lenient, she disagreed with Benedict's statement that ceremonial whippings were so light they did not raise welts. She gave several graphic examples of severe whippings from Hopi, but her one explicit reference from Zuñi revealed that boys were whipped in layers of blankets, taken off one by one after each ceremonial whipping so that only the last touched the skin itself. Where she was most successful in undermining the Apollonian idea was in her point that contrary to Benedict's and Thompson's ideas, Zuñi and Hopi children were not gradually fitted into their cultural patterns, but forcibly coerced. She gave a plausible account of fears instilled into children so that they would behave correctly, positing that these fears led to the molding of children into cooperative adults. But even when attacking the Apollonian idea Goldfrank did it within the Culture and Personality approach, accepting Benedict's idea of the Zuñi configurational pattern, questioning only the supposedly Apollonian means by which Zuñis achieved cooperation. Anthropologist John W. Bennett, trying to explain the difference between Goldfrank's approach and that of Thompson and Benedict, said that Goldfrank's "critical realism" contrasted sharply with the "impressionistic, evocative" approach of Thompson and Benedict. Goldfrank was more the "literal-minded scientist," while Thompson was more subjective. This work followed an article written by Dorothy Eggan, "The General Problem of Hopi Adjustment" (1943), which argued that Hopi Indians in spite of loving infancies developed into adults exhibiting a high degree of anxiety, not Apollonian calm. Earlier, *Sun Chief: The Autobiography of a Hopi Indian* (1942) vividly described Sun Chief's brutal whippings during his initiation ceremonies and the fearsomeness of the scare katcinas. However, the book was criticized in 1945 because it was unclear whether Sun Chief was a misfit or representative of Hopi in general and because only one-fifth of the original data had been used and there was no indication as to the effect of the condensing and editing on the final version.[29]

On the issue of alcohol Benedict had written that unlike the situation with other Indians, alcohol was neither an "administrative problem" nor an "inescapable issue" among the Pueblos, that as a culture drunkenness was "repulsive" to them, in line with their Apollonian bent. The results of inquiry about alcohol were mixed. Studies done in the 1940's showed that some Zuñis did drink, especially around the time of a major festival, the Shalako. But it also seemed clear that there were strong social attitudes against drinking and that drunkenness was not the social problem it was for many American Indian tribes. Concerning Benedict's statement that suicide was almost outside the Pueblo world view, a totally foreign idea, a statement backed up by both Ruth Bunzel and Elsie Clews Parsons, the two anthropologists who had spent the most time in the Pueblos and knew the people best, former Columbia graduate student E. Adamson Hoebel used the principle of the negative instance against her, discovering three cases of suicide committed in Zuñi after 1939 by which he tried to cast doubt on Benedict's information. Hoebel was one of the most active in the 1940's in discounting the Apollonian-Dionysian idea. In *The Cheyenne Way* (1941) he showed that the supposedly Dionysian Cheyenne had what he considered many Apollonian features, such as the restrained behavior expected of chiefs and the low amount of aggressive behavior between members of the tribe. In *Man in the Primitive World* (1949), he argued that the Western Pueblos, Hopi and Zuñi, differed from the Central and Eastern Pueblos; that all could not be considered Apollonian.[30]

The war against the Apollonian-Dionysian contrast went on long after Benedict's death. In a 1954 article Hoebel cited the criticisms by Eggan (1943), Goldfrank (1945), Li An-che (1937), and Bennett (1946), saying exaggeratedly that they "only begin to indicate the extent of the artistic and poetic idealization of Pueblo culture that Benedict presented." He was forced to add however that it was a paradox that with her "highly questionable techniques of observation" she contributed "theory and methodological devices of such great import and lasting value." Even Kluckhohn by the mid-1950's agreed that Benedict's work had to be "qualified in many respects and modified or re-expressed in others if justice is to be done to the variety of behavioral fact" and the Zuñi ideal pattern. Victor Barnouw in 1963 cited "a tendency to overstatement and to ignore inconvenient inconsistent data." By the late 1950's anthropology had successfully relegated the Apollonian-Dionysian idea to the dust heap. In his revised edition of *Man in the Primitive World* (1958), Hoebel deleted the material about the suicides and that about the differences between the Western and Eastern pueblos. He also succinctly summed up the general anthropological position by then about *Patterns of Culture*. He called it the "classic formulation of the idea of cultural configuration in relation to ideal personality types." He called it "persuasively written in fine literary style," but added, "it should not be taken as a reliable ethnography of the cultures discussed, although its major theme is acceptable."[31]

It seems clear in retrospect that people saw in Benedict's work what they needed to fortify their own version of anthropological reality—and also that the Apollonian-Dionysian contrast became a symbol of the underlying value struggle between what was perceived as science versus non-science as the framework of the discipline, with "true" science eventually winning out. Those who opposed the contrast most vehemently were those who believed in the necessity of anthropology being identified as a science in the traditional sense. Each side brought a different set of facts and interpretations to the argument, and on both sides the facts were true; only the viewpoint of the observer differed, and the observers divided at the boundary between a rigid definition of "science" and a flexible definition of science that was interpreted as "non-science." The evidence itself was ambiguous and could be read both ways. If the issue had just been that of the character of the Zuñi people, as it ostensibly seemed, the arguments against Benedict's work should have totally discredited it as a shoddy piece of field work and it should have been forgotten. But again and again in the following decades anthropologists discredited Benedict's cultural description but ended by accepting the premises on which that description was built.

According to their varying lights, both sides were "right." Accepting the values reinforced by the scientific side meant admitting that Benedict's work *was* subjective, literary, overstated, and oversimplified, and thus scientifically damned. From the history-minded side these same qualities became positive values and Benedict's work reinterpreted as integrative, clear writing that established a deeper level of insight into cultures than had been achieved before. This value difference probably accounts for the bafflement and ambiguity of response in the writing of some anthropologists in the 1950's and 1960's, who, after criticizing the description of Zuñi in *Patterns* as useless, still could not discard Benedict's insight into the heart of Zuñi life.[32]

It seems clear that Ruth Benedict did not deliberately leave out information in an arbitrary and unjustified manner. She worked with the best available data of her time, relying on the field work of Ruth Bunzel, who had learned the Zuñi language and spent several years returning to Zuñi to study the culture. This information she supplemented with the work of Elsie Clews Parsons and others, bolstered by her own experience at Zuñi. "Benedict's description of Zuñi has found favor with the best judges," wrote Lowie in 1938. She built her theory on data, not airy speculation. That she selected and highlighted certain information is clear, but only in the humanistic tradition that allowed and encouraged such highlighting if it led to a clearer truth. Those who attacked her were excessive in upholding the rigid "scientific" tradition. She did downplay the tension and factionalism in Zuñi life. She did not omit them. She wrote of culturally sanctioned violence by women, where wives blackened the eyes of rivals and sisters broke furniture or took something from the other's house after quarreling. She spoke of critical village gossip as commonplace; of the war priests, war societies, and scalp ceremonies; of whipping as a common act in Zuñi, although as a "blessing and a cure," not as self-torture or torture. She wrote of witchcraft as an "anxiety complex" among the Zuñi, of people suspecting one another. She gave the example of one famous case of a man among the Zuñi whom she knew who got drunk, boasted he could not be killed (the sign of a witch), and was tortured by being hung up from the rafters by his thumbs for witchcraft, with the result that his shoulders were crippled for life.[33]

She did not try to hide or repress information potentially damaging to her view of Zuñi. Writing to political scientist Harold Lasswell in 1935, she said that judging from her experience in Zuñi there was something "deep-seated in pueblo ethos" that allowed stresses to build up until they released disastrously. "Zuñi is intact," she wrote, "but its history could always be written in terms of factionalisms," and splits in Hopi were "just the logical extension of the usual pueblo situation." Again she wrote in *Zuñi Mythology* (1935), "Grudges are cherished in Zuñi. They are usually the rather generalized expression of slights and resentments in a small community." When graduate student Irving Goldman wrote about the Zuñi in *Cooperation and Competition* (1937), he did so after a number of conversations and discussions with Benedict and Ruth Bunzel. He made a number of revisions in the text at their suggestion. What he wrote about the Zuñi therefore had their stamp of approval. What he wrote suggests that Benedict and Bunzel were then working on answers to the problem of Zuñi factionalism. The paper suggests that Benedict first saw factionalism as a result of white contact and not integral to the Zuñi configuration. Moreover, she was dealing in *Patterns* with the "normal" person of Zuñi society, the approved person the society encouraged everyone to be. Gossip and bickering were not a part of the approved way to live although they were prevalent in reality. They existed outside of the Zuñi ideal.[34]

We perceive this now as a limited idea, but then the configuration approach was a pioneering concept that Benedict felt it necessary to make clear above all else. Like all new ideas it took time for it to unfold in all its ramifications. There were some things Benedict just could not see at the beginning that later became clearer. By 1935 she had begun to see the gossip and factionalism as part of the configuration. By then she was working on the difference between sin and shame and how they act in a society. Goldman's paper suggests she saw a connection between the gossip and defamation in Zuñi and the culture's chief social sanction of shame, which made both public criticism and sensitivity to such criticism necessary. By 1935 she had also begun to see certain facets of Zuñi life as counterbalances and safety valves that helped preserve the amiability of Zuñi social life. Her book *Zuñi Mythology* pointed to mythology as an outlet for vicarious violence and wish fulfillment not allowed by actual Zuñi life that served to defuse actual violence in the society. She wrote to Elsie Clews Parsons in 1937, "Zuñi daily life is full of cherished grudges but no violence; the mythology allows the violent expression of them."[35]

Aside from her reply to Bernard Aginsky's article, Benedict stayed out of the controversy surrounding her work. In a 1936 letter she wrote, "I haven't any claims to describing a culture in one word." Where there was a word available "to point up a discussion," such as Apollonian or Dionysian, she used it. "But," she wrote, "I don't attach any more meaning to it than a historian does to 'feudal' when he has to use that." In her effort "not to be technical" and her "dislike for the passive voice," she wrote, "I often omitted much that seemed to be obvious." If she had realized how her intentions would be misunderstood, she would have "left the clumsy sentences in." In a 1941 letter she called the Apollonian-Dionysian contrast between Plains and Pueblo "as important as the feudal non-feudal contrast is between Europe in the 13th Century and such a trade center as Florence." But the categories were neither universal nor necessarily transferable to other cultures or other times.[36]

She gave her answer to the profession in her outgoing speech as President of the AAA in 1947, and that answer was a vision of an anthropology in which science and "history" did not fight each other, but melded together to create a more complete, complex picture of the life of humankind. She affirmed anthropology as a science but added that anthropology "handicaps itself in method and insight by neglecting the work of the great humanists." The humanist tradition had much to offer discriminating anthropologists, she stated, because humanists had a head start in studying "emotion, ethics, rational insight and purpose," which had become the subjects which with modern anthropologists were wrestling. They could "analyze cultural attitudes and behavior more cogently," she wrote, if they knew George Santayana's *Three Philosophical Poets*, Arthur Lovejoy's *Great Chain of Being*, or Shakespearian criticism. In *Three Philosophical Poets* Santayana studied the contrasting cultures of Lucretius, Dante, and Goethe as characterized by the "cosmic parables" they wove in their work. From both Santayana and Shakespearian criticism, Benedict wrote, she learned "habits of mind which at length made me an anthropologist." She learned from the criticism written in different eras how human thoughts were culturally conditioned. She learned from the standards of good criticism to take into account "whatever is said and done," discarding nothing relevant, to try to "understand the interrelations of discrete bits," to surrender oneself to the data and use all the insights one was capable of. Criticism, she wrote, taught the importance of contextual knowledge of facts, and studies of imagery taught techniques for studying "symbolisms and free associations which fall into patterns and show processes congenial to the human mind in different cultures." The humanities alone, however, provided only partial answers to human questions, as did the sciences alone. "Any commitment to methods which exclude either approach is self-defeating." The anthropologist should not be afraid to belabor the obvious or to be "subjective." For, she concluded, "The anthropologist can use both approaches."[37]

Another controversy split American anthropologists in the 1930's and 1940's. "Two currents are flowing in opposite directions" in anthropology, Alfred Kroeber wrote in 1943. The currents he referred to were the study of configurations or patterns versus function. In 1931 A. R. Radcliffe-Brown was appointed professor of anthropology at the University of Chicago to succeed Sapir, who had gone to Yale. While at Chicago Radcliffe-Brown played an influential role in American anthropology and functionalism vied with the Culture and Personality movement as the major integrative direction in American anthropology. Functionalism and C&P shared several attributes as integrative approaches. Both accepted the idea of the interrelationship of parts. But they differed fundamentally in their placement of emphasis. The Culture and Personality researchers stressed form over function. For them the framework of a culture, whether it was a configuration or a "basic personality," was more important than the interrelation of functions. It was the underlying "structure" that in fact related seemingly unrelated areas of a culture, explaining apparent irrationalities within the culture. Functionalists stressed function over form. For them function, the interrelation of social parts, was more important than the underlying framework. "I submit that form is always determined by function," wrote Malinowski, while the configurationists tended to believe function more determined by form. Radcliffe-Brown emphasized that in using the idea of social structure within which functioning took place he did not mean, using the analogy of society to an organism, that the organism was "itself the structure." He meant it was a collection of units "arranged in a structure, i.e., in a set of relations." Thus he defined structure in terms of function rather than form. He went on to say that "the life of an organism is conceived as the *functioning* of its structure." Malinowski, the other great functionalist leader, concurred in this idea. Most Culture and Personality researchers, though, agreed that the "life" of a people resided in the underlying mental configuration, however they defined it.[38]

Radcliffe-Brown's functionalism also differed from the Culture and Personality approach in its emphasis on society versus culture, its sociological orientation, and its view of anthropology as a potential "true" science eventually comparable to physics and chemistry. For Radcliffe-Brown, "culture" was too amorphous a concept to form the basis of a science. "You cannot have a science of culture," he said in 1937. One could study culture, the area of learned behavior and belief, "only as a characteristic of a social system." Society carried culture, not the other way around. Because of this he stressed methods and ideas developed from a sociological orientation, which helped distinguish social relations and social roles more clearly. Radcliffe-Brown called himself a comparative sociologist and was particularly influenced by the ideas of French sociologist Emile Durkheim. Durkheim gave him the concept of "social facts," which were concrete things like a tabu, or a ceremony, or a language usage, or a food custom—external and binding on people beyond free choice. By relating a custom to all the relevant social facts, a system of relationships between people formed. Understanding the functioning of these systems of relationships and their interrelation with other such systems led ultimately, Radcliffe-Brown believed, to the understanding of society. Since social facts could be treated as objective phenomena, concrete, external, available for observation rather than inference, Radcliffe-Brown constantly emphasized that anthropology could become a "hard" science by using scientific methods paralleling those of the physical sciences. He never doubted that the ultimate outcome of functional anthropological studies would be the discovery of general laws underlying the workings of society.[39]

Boas responded with sharp criticism to Radcliffe-Brown's ideas. A social anthropology with "'laws' of cultural development as rigid as those of physics," he wrote, could not be attained in the present state of knowledge and probably would never be found because of the complexity and uniqueness of cultural phenomena. Any general laws discovered would be so "vague" and "self-evident" they could not lead to deeper understanding. Anthropologists who had grown up in the "historical science" of anthropology criticized Radcliffe-Brown for an overemphasis on the functional approach which Boas had been teaching long before Radcliffe-Brown discovered it. They also criticized his emphasis on present, contemporary relations and functions without regard for past influences, which were often accidental and not caused by function; and they were skeptical of Radcliffe-Brown's organism analogy, which inferred a closed system. Those who had become C&P anthropologists criticized Radcliffe-Brown for his emphasis on sociology, since their main bent was toward a psychological orientation. Both groups of American anthropologists criticized Radcliffe-Brown's criticism of their attempts to build a "science of culture" and his creation of anthropology in the image of the physical sciences instead of in its own image.[40]

But several young American anthropologists fell under Radcliffe-Brown's spell. While at Chicago Radcliffe-Brown drew to himself a talented group of disciples, among them Fred Eggan and Sol Tax. Morris Opler, then a graduate student at Chicago and not so enchanted with Radcliffe-Brown, wrote Benedict of the "wall-eyed youths" who stumbled through the halls murmuring the jargon of functionalism "in awed whispers." The importance of function itself as a concept was easily accepted by both "historical science" and C&P anthropologists, and by the end of the decade had slipped quietly in as an important concept in American anthropology. Where Americans differed with Radcliffe-Brown was in treating function and social relations as only part of the material with which they were concerned, not the major focus. Nor did they see social relations as a distinct, integrated whole, irreducible; instead they scattered the parts to other types of relations. Also, Radcliffe-Brown's personal manner antagonized many American anthropologists who otherwise accepted some of his ideas. Ruth Benedict wrote to Opler after seeing Radcliffe-Brown at the annual AAA meeting in 1933, "In private conversation he was very scornful of all N.[orth] A.[merican] ethnology." But, she continued, "he tells me the world is saved by the studies that Eggen [sic] and Sol have now done." She was "saddened" at his bias for "disciples against non-disciples." [41]

One effect of Radcliffe-Brown's functionalism was to intensify the debate over science in anthropology. In "History and Science," Kroeber had criticized Radcliffe-Brown's search for scientific laws of society. He spent the years after his 1935 article trying to build a philosophy of science that included both the physical and the social sciences without falling into the trap of considering the social sciences analogous to the physical. It seemed clear to him, in spite of Radcliffe-Brown's proselytizing, that this was a standard the social sciences could not meet because their subject matter was complex, unpredictable humans rather than predictable atoms. He was concerned with the question that bothered many in the profession: How then was anthropology a science, if it was not like the physical sciences? He also wanted to incorporate his "historical" approach as a legitimate scientific approach. After analyzing what constituted science and its methodology he found not all inorganic sciences were pure objective sciences. The historical approach was not only used in anthropology and the social sciences but extended to natural history on the organic level and even to astronomy and geology on the inorganic level. Since they existed as historical science, they legitimated the historical approach as belonging in a philosophy of science. Nor were objective and historical methods antithetical, he declared; they often interacted. Thus Kroeber tried to set forth a new flexible idea of science which anthropologists could use to explain their discipline.[42]

Lowie in his *History of Ethnological Theory* (1938) also faced the question of whether anthropology was a science. He affirmed anthropology as essentially scientific, but not in the same way as physics. Some anthropologists, he wrote, postulated and searched for laws in anthropology based on a misunderstanding of the physics model because they feared otherwise anthropology would assume an inferior status. But every science, he wrote, formulated its data according to its own nature. Ethnologists might never discover laws, he concluded, but scientific respectability remained as long as they coordinated, "with a maximum of attainable efficiency," their particular phenomena. This meant "an orderly arrangement of its data, the verifiability of its findings, a logical basis for its conclusions."[43]

Benedict's approach to the problem of anthropology as a science was to accept it as one and, like Kroeber, try to develop a more flexible definition of science than the rigid one usually applied. This was the underlying message of her AAA presidential speech. In advocating a melding of "science" and the "humanities" she looked for the creation of a new idea of science, one which not only analyzed or dissolved phenomena into processes, but also integrated phenomena and preserved them intact in their uniqueness as far as possible; which not only searched for general laws, but tried to understand individual phenomena; which accepted controlled "subjective" findings along with the objective; which accepted as validation not only the ability to predict or explain, but also the fit of an interpretation within the totality of interpretations and phenomena; which accepted not only the quantitative but also the qualitative.

In a social science whose subject matter was subjective, the use of quantification provided a visible sign that anthropology was a science. Statistics were the earliest symbol of true science in the social sciences. Using them came closest to a physical-science approach. But Boas, who understood physical science, said often that anthropology was not amenable to statistics. With the small numbers of people in any given "primitive community" statistics had no meaning. Behind statistics in anthropology lay "unanswered questions," he wrote on "how far the materials enumerated are really comparable." When Mead went to Samoa he advised her against using statistics. Working with statistics would require tearing material out of its setting; without this context the meanings of particular bits of behavior might be lost forever. "A complete elimination of the subjective attitude of the investigator is of course quite impossible in a matter of this kind," he wrote, but he told her to overcome it as far as possible. He advised her to follow the method used by doctors in their analysis of individual cases on which they built the general picture of the illness or bodily pathology they wanted to describe.[44]

Benedict felt the same way about statistics in anthropology. They were essentially useless. When the Kinsey report came out in 1948 her chief objection to it was that it tore sexual experience out of context and reduced it to a mass of measurements and numbers. She told Oscar Lewis the summer before her death "that just as soon as you begin to quantify, you are no longer studying culture." She wanted instead to introduce an alternative standard to that of measurement: pattern rather than numbers. Language study gave her the form. Language research did not operate on statistics; instead it depended on learning the pattern of root and grammatical elements from the spoken language in order to understand it. Language study preserved context and sought interrelationships. Languages had formal patterning just as did cultures. The study of cultures was analogous to the study of languages. By discovering patterns in cultures one moved beyond the need for statistics or other scientific measurement. Language scholar Benjamin Whorf wrote in 1941, "quantity and number play little part in the realm of patterning" where there are no variables but instead "abrupt alterations from one configuration to another." What is required is "patternment," or "an exactness of relation irrespective of dimensions." He continued, "Quantity, dimension, magnitude are metaphors since they do not properly belong in this spaceless, relational world." This sums up Benedict's own philosophy.[45]

In 1937 Radcliffe-Brown left Chicago to take up the first chair of social anthropology established at Oxford University in England. In 1938 Bronislaw Malinowski came to the United States for a sabbatical year. When World War II began, he decided to remain and taught at the New School, then Cornell, and finally at Yale. There he remained until his death in 1942. Malinowski's functionalism differed from Radcliffe-Brown's in important ways and probably had its greatest impact on American anthropology in the 1920's, with his interest in using Freudian psychology in anthropology. By the 1930's Malinowski had developed a theory of functionalism based on biological needs that was not acceptable to most American anthropologists. Benedict wrote in 1934, "Malinowski gets feebler with each public appearance," and she was not talking about his health. In the 1920's Malinowski had laid down the idea that in all societies every custom, belief, or material thing fulfilled some vital function, was an indispensable part of a working whole. Out of the necessity of explaining seemingly non-functioning elements of culture, by 1941 he defined function as "always the satisfaction of a need," either biological or cultural, that is, derived from the needs of the social organism rather than individual biology. Within societies people created institutions to fill basic physical needs, he wrote, defining an institution as a group of people acting for a common purpose within a certain environment, using some technical apparatus, and obeying a set of rules. They also needed to satisfy a second level of needs, derived needs, or cultural imperatives, all related to the wants of the social organism, all linked to the necessity of the organism's survival, these in turn provoked by cultural responses. Function remained need-oriented, whether satisfying hunger directly through eating rituals or filling the derived need expressed in the communion of bread and wine which satisfied another hunger, the cultural need to know God.[46]

Malinowski criticized Ruth Benedict for a concept of culture "so general and vague as to defy any kind of scientific evaluation." He called it "illegitimate to cover our inability to deal with certain facts by such mystic labels as the 'genius of culture,'" whether it were "Apollonian, Dionysiac, megalomaniac or hysterical." But his own selections of what need fit what function seemed wildly speculative to American anthropologists, especially as Malinowski's theories were tied primarily to his knowledge of one people, the Trobrianders, from whose experience he tended to generalize. Nor could Americans accept his return to biology and a seemingly Darwinistic explanation of culture. Kluckhohn later criticized him for his inability to recognize that cultural development came as often from instability as stability and that cultures created problems for people as well as helping to fulfill their needs. Finally, his system was still a closed one. Malinowski assumed a "harmonious master plan" based on a biological determinism.[47]

Because of the critical response of most American anthropologists to functionalism, it never took hold in America as a comprehensive integrative system, although elements of functionalist thought greatly influenced American anthropologists.[48] Instead, in America Culture and Personality became the source of integration because it incorporated the most creative aspects of functionalism within its own point of view. C&P became the most influential movement in American anthropology in the 1930's.

But the Culture and Personality approach could hardly be called unified. It was an umbrella term that encompassed all sorts of experimental combinations of culture with, of, or in personality and vice versa. There were two major strains that vied for preeminence: culture-oriented and individual-oriented. The former concentrated on the influence of culture upon personality formation, with emphasis on an underlying pattern, whether configuration, basic, modal, standard, or typical personality and individual variations from the norm. Ruth Benedict worked from this standpoint. The latter concentrated on the influence of individuals on culture formation, with emphasis on the individual personality in culture, the real person or specific number of persons in actual situations. Edward Sapir led this wing of the movement. "The true locus of culture," he wrote, "is in the interactions of specific individuals" and in the "world of meanings" that individuals abstract for themselves from these interactions. He attacked culture-orientation as impersonal and so abstract as to be valueless, a "ghost-inhabited science." He advocated focusing on real individuals to observe their experience of their culture and what culture traits meant to them, instead of studying the abstract typical or ideal individual in a culture. His goal was "to bring every cultural pattern back to the living context" and "every fact of personality formation back to its social matrix." He felt the dynamics of culture could not be understood without studying actual human beings. He saw psychiatry as the key to this study.[49]

Harry Stack Sullivan's theory of interpersonal relations influenced Sapir. Like Sullivan, he saw psychiatry as primarily concerned not with the human organism but with "the more intangible, and yet more intelligible, world of human relationships and ideas that such relationships bring forth." He advocated that anthropologists adopt an essentially psychiatric way of thinking by analyzing human beings and their interrelationships to find certain permanencies that might be called cultural. This meant studying a "personality organization" and its changes from infancy to death. The life histories of individuals therefore became keys to culture, and the 1930's saw a strong movement to collect life histories and study culture from their viewpoint. Sapir's psychological colleague John Dollard became most visible in the life history movement, writing on the criteria and uses of autobiographies. Even more influential than this idea was Sapir's suggestion that anthropologists study child development, i.e., how culture was acquired by the individual child. He suggested studying the child "minutely and carefully" from birth until around age ten to find the order in which cultural patterns appeared in his or her psychic world and the relevance of these patterns for the growth of her or his personality, to see how much "total official culture" was significant to him or her. In this area Margaret Mead influenced both Sapir and Benedict, for she had focused on the study of children as a locus of research

[239]

from the beginning of her career. This approach was enthusiastically taken up by all varieties of C&P scholars and used to produce studies of significant value.[50]

But Sapir did not succeed in creating a significant integrated "personality" approach within C&P, partly because of his early death in 1939 and comparatively few writings, partly because toward the end of his life he became more psychological than anthropological in approach. He became disenchanted with the idea of culture as an unproductive abstraction and felt that cause and effect in life must ultimately be clarified by a social psychology that was a melding of psychiatry and anthropology, but the necessary understanding of individuals upon which to base such a social psychology was lacking. He moved too far toward the edges of anthropology to attract more than a small number to take up his ideas as a whole. The life history and studies of child development remain his legacy to C&P. They were absorbed by the culture-oriented group, however, and child development studies especially were used to talk about *the* Hopi child, or *the* Zuñi child, an abstraction of which he did not approve. What Sapir did was to get anthropologists to become aware of and deal with the psychiatric side to even the "coldest and most indifferent" cultural pattern.[51] But he could not overcome the traditional idea that the subject of anthropology was primarily the group, not the individual. His point of view went against the anthropological grain.

Sapir as language scholar rather than Sapir's psychology had influenced Benedict's development of the configurations idea in the 1920's. But the life history and child development studies gave her direction in the 1930's.

10

The Psychology of Culture

BY THE MID-1930's Benedict had described the vision and other mystical states as "border-line psychological." In 1940 she planned for her students to research "religion as a psychological projection of the social order." During the 1930's Benedict's strong interest in religion merged with her deepening interest in creating a "psychology" of culture, a way the insights of psychology and psychoanalysis on individual personality could be applied to the study of culture. She contributed to the growth of Culture and Personality (C&P) studies within anthropology itself and the use of the concept of culture within psychoanalysis to challenge established ideas concerning men and women, abnormality, and mental disease. Amid the intellectual dueling of the 1930's, Ruth Benedict walked her own individual path. But her path paralleled the paths of Culture and Personality anthropologists as a group during this period. Her intellectual journey reveals the variety of ways psychology and psychoanalysis influenced anthropology in the 1930's and also how anthropology had an important effect on psychoanalysts. The influence of the culture-conscious Neo-Freudians in psychoanalysis has had significant impact on general ideas underlying American culture into the present time.[1]

The one criticism out of all that were written about *Patterns of Culture* that pointed a future direction for Benedict concerned a certain static quality of her conception. How, for instance, did configurations change, or did they? How did they operate? She sought for ways to make configuration theory dynamic, to deal with processes of change and transmission of configurations by incorporating ideas from psychology and psychoanalysis into anthropology. Notes from a discussion on C&P in November 1934 reflect this concern for dynamic processes. The group, including Benedict, Mead, Lawrence Frank, Otto Klineberg, and others, discussed cultural processes such as transmission, "diffusion," i.e., patterns picked up by individuals because they find them attractive or useful, and assimilation of foreign culture. They discussed processes "resulting in idiosyncratic patterns," and those resulting in "stereotype patterns." They discussed the question "What are the forces that can break up old forms?" Benedict's contribution, taken from evidence on Messiah cults, was that it was not the personality or the program of Messiahs that led to change but the readiness of a culture to receive change that was important.[2]

In her first major project after *Patterns of Culture* and *Zuñi Mythology* she became involved in Margaret Mead's study of cooperation and competition. Although Benedict wrote nothing, Mead credited her with what seems to have been codirectorship of the actual project, writing that Benedict "assumed part of the task of supervision and planning" as well as providing guidance on the Zuñi, Kwakiutl, and Dakota chapters of the book. The subject was timely in those days of the Depression when intellectuals hotly debated the problems of capitalism and the benefits of Marxism. Mead called it a first attempt through information from primitive people to gather background for planning cooperation-competition research in American society. The study occurred under the auspices of the Subcommittee on Competitive-Cooperative Habits of the Social Science Research Council Committee on Personality and Culture. Mead herself saw it as a pioneering Culture and Personality effort.[3]

The study broke new interdisciplinary ground by creating a new way of integrating methods for studying personality with the study of culture. It took two psychological traits, cooperation and competition, and compared their strength, variations, and relationships among thirteen different cultures, much as psychologists studied traits as they appeared from individual to individual. Within anthropological methodology it broke new ground as the first study to attempt contextual comparison between cultures—not the pulling out of information in haphazard fashion that had characterized nineteenth-century comparative studies, but a comparison of traits within the context of the wealth of detail known about a culture itself. This contextual cross-cultural comparison of psychological traits seemed to those involved to hold great promise for future research. But it did not have the impact its planners had hoped, receiving mixed reviews because of the subjectivity it involved. *Cooperation and Competition among Primitive Peoples* (1937) did influence Benedict however. She called it one of the five scholarly works of "outstanding importance" since World War I, the first comparative study of cultures with reference to the influence of "social forms (institutions) upon human behavior." Over the next several years she made plans for her own contextual comparative study, based on the field work her students were doing and with which she was intimately involved, discussing their field notes, editing their manuscripts, using them as informants.[4]

In 1933, Margaret Mead met Sapir's colleague, the psychologist John Dollard, and through her interest Benedict came to learn about the use of life histories in anthropological studies. Mead wrote a life history for Dollard, got her sisters to do so as well, and persuaded Benedict also to write one, apparently not completed, but of which she left at least a partial manuscript. By 1941 Benedict called the collection of life histories one of the two important methods of Culture and Personality research. Through them, she wrote, one could study special cases of the impact of a culture on individuals in both the stalwart upholder of society and the deviant. Life histories provided data on "all kinds of problems of behavior in a tribe."[5]

While involved with the cooperation and competition project Benedict also began working with psychoanalysts in formal and informal ways. She continued her interest in Gestalt psychology, which held the personality to be greater than the sum of its parts, attending the annual Gestalt meeting in 1936. Her ideas profoundly influenced the Cultural School of Psychoanalysis propounded by Karen Horney and Erich Fromm, which will be discussed in more detail further on. In 1936 she became involved with a seminar given by psychoanalyst Abram Kardiner and sponsored by the New York Psychoanalytic Institute. Cora Du Bois, a former undergraduate student of Benedict's from Barnard and a young anthropologist of great promise, collaborated with Kardiner in these seminars. Ruth Bunzel had begun cooperating with Kardiner a year earlier. Benedict contributed information primarily on the Zuñi. The seminar created a sense of breaking intellectual bonds as its shifting membership groped with Kardiner toward the idea of each culture's possessing a basic personality. For two years Benedict participated in the seminar, during the spring of 1937 giving a series of three sessions on the "Constellation of Competition and Rivalry in Primitive Society."[6]

During the first three years the seminar studied seven primitive cultures. First Du Bois presented Malinowski's Trobrianders and Boas' Kwakiutl from the literature. Ruth Bunzel and then Ruth Benedict added a new dimension, presenting the Zuñi culture they knew firsthand. The group then studied the Chuckchee of Siberia, the Eskimos, and with the addition of Ralph Linton in 1937–1938, two cultures he had studied, the Tanala and the Marquesan. Western culture was also constantly analyzed and used as a referent. The idea of the basic personality structure of cultures was an extension of Benedict's configuration theory, truly "personality writ large." Kardiner was a Neo-Freudian who believed the early years of childhood to be crucial to personality formation. Linton, in his foreword to Kardiner's second book, defined the basic personality structure as "that personality configuration which is shared by the bulk of the society's members as a result of the early experiences which they have in common."[7]

For Benedict, working with Kardiner was an attempt to explain what happened in cultures that did not have the focus Zuñi, Dobu, or the Kwakiutl had seemed to possess yet had some integration. Kroeber had named this as the next step for her in his review of *Patterns,* and she herself obviously saw it as an important step. Using the idea of basic personality structure placed the focus of cultural integration in the common denominator of the personalities of individuals within a culture. The first two years were spent developing and clarifying concepts on which analysis of cultures as wholes could proceed and working on methods of procedure. It was in this phase that Benedict participated most and her insights had most impact. In the third year, when Linton took part, Benedict participated less. Linton persuaded Kardiner to analyze his material as the final phase of cultural analysis, and this later formed the basis of Kardiner's book, *The Individual and His Society* (1939), written with Linton's collaboration. Linton coopted Kardiner's program into the Columbia Anthropology Department, and the joint Kardiner-Linton seminars held there over the next few years were a very popular Culture and Personality showcase. Benedict, not willing to see the Kardiner work as an arena of competition with Linton, withdrew into the background. She continued to attend seminars and supported Cora Du Bois' trip to Alor in 1937–1939 to do a psychoanalytic-anthropological field study, but the seminars became Linton and Kardiner's show.[8]

By 1936 Benedict was also involved in Dr. Caroline Zachry's study of adolescents, funded by the Rockefeller Foundation. She probably became involved through Margaret Mead, who had worked with the study since 1934. Other anthropologists were also included at various times. In 1936 Zachry wrote Mead, "Ruth Benedict is helping us with some of our problems." The study brought her together with active child-oriented professionals in education, social work, and counseling. As Sapir had suggested in his 1934 article, and as many other anthropologists were doing by the late 1930's, Benedict studied child development and education in hopes of understanding how culture was transmitted, how the individual child learned the standards and expectations of its culture. By 1941 she was emphasizing the need for information in field work on the way children were raised, an area of study, incidentally, where anthropologists had the advantage.[9]

In 1938 Benedict wrote a remarkable paper about childhood called "Continuities and Discontinuities in Cultural Conditioning." It attacked the idea of "Progress," the ingrained idea of human development as progressive, advancing from one stage to another. Physical growth was progressive; psychological growth was not necessarily. The latter depended on cultural institutions, i.e., fixed modes of thought or behavior, which either promoted or nullified progress. The article emphasized the dissonance of life.

America, she wrote, was a culture that fostered discontinuity for its children, that made of childhood and adulthood two totally contrasting roles and provided few ways of making the transition. So children were either jarred roughly into adulthood or never made it to the adult role, falling ill from the strain or taking refuge in ways learned in childhood that had become inappropriate for them as adults. She presented the American system implicitly as an irrational one, giving examples from cultures that gradually introduced children into adult roles or provided transitions from the conflicting role of childhood that eased the strain of becoming an adult. The message implicit in the article was that life did not have to be the way it was in America. The institutions which created childhood and adulthood as conflicting roles, e.g., the non-responsible status role in American culture of children, who suddenly have to become responsible adults; the expectance of dominance by adults and submission by children; the view of children as asexual or wicked, but adults as pleasantly sexual, could be changed. Social institutions could be developed which taught gradual responsibility to children, in which dominance and submission were cast aside, in which children were not taught sexual attitudes they would have to unlearn.

The development of institutions which furthered a society's basic goals was to become an important topic for her in the study of synergy in the early 1940's. Her later thought on childhood would probe in other directions, but this first paper was a far cry from other anthropologists' descriptions of parental attention, feeding, toilet training, and systems of punishment. It was both Modern in its emphasis on disjunction and nonprogress, yet Progressive in its hope for a better America through knowledge. Discontinuity occurred not because of economic, political, or social necessity but because of "some conceptual dogma," often an irrational belief. She believed the realization of this dogma-like quality would dissipate its power, clear the way for more responsible, intelligent, rational planning. One of the criticisms she had of Kardiner's book was that he saw ideology as passive. She did not make that mistake.[10]

One other development came out of the involvement with the Zachry study for Benedict. She began learning about Rorschach testing. Swiss psychiatrist Hermann Rorschach had created and published the Rorschach Test in 1922. There were ten Rorschach cards containing bilaterally symmetric inkblots, half with some color, and half without, which were shown in the same order to everyone who took the test. The subject told the tester what he or she saw in the cards, and the tester noted these responses as well as how long the response took. After the first run-through the tester went through the answers with the subject to be sure what parts of the blots the subject had used and how the answers were perceived—e.g., if there was a butterfly, whether it was flying or at rest. Then the tester examined the responses for clues to personality makeup, based on certain criteria laid down by Rorschach, e.g., the number of responses, references to color or movement, and how much of an inkblot was used in an answer, the whole of it or large or small details. Dr. Bruno Klopfer, a German refugee immigrant who had come to New York in the 1930's, was one of the most knowledgeable advocates of the Rorschach Test.[11]

In the spring of 1938 a small class formed to learn more about Rorschach testing. Led by Klopfer, it included Ruth Benedict, Caroline Zachry, Ruth Bunzel, anthropological graduate student William Whitman, Zachry's housemate Wilma Lloyd, and Esther Goldfrank. The group met in a classroom in the brownstone that was Zachry's personal residence and headquarters for the Study of Adolescents. The Rorschach interested Benedict and other anthropologists because it seemed to be especially adaptable to "primitive" peoples. There was no literacy requirement, and the test was not culture-bound, since the inkblots did not represent specific things or ideas and responses could be validated within other cultural frameworks. It could also be given to people of different ages. When Cora Du Bois went to Alor, Rorschach testing was one of her tools. Benedict's student Jules Blumensohn (later Henry) also used the Rorschach among South American Indians. Most anthropologists could use the inkblots only in conjunction with a psychologist trained to understand and interpret the results. But in studies where they were used, especially Du Bois' in which the Rorschachs were interpreted blind by a psychoanalyst, the tests seemed to show close agreement with other sources of information about a culture. In addition to the Rorschach, the Thematic Apperception Test (TAT), word association tests, and the Por-

teus maze test were used by Culture and Personality anthropological researchers in an attempt to make the nebulous study of personality more
precise and scientific. For awhile, in the late 1930's and early 1940's, the
use of such psychological tests seemed to be one answer to C&P's critics.

Goldfrank reported that Benedict told her in casual conversation of
her own Rorschach results. She had given only one answer per card and
each answer was a whole. "Quite schizophrenic," Benedict said, adding,
"Klopfer was amazed at the complexity of my integrations of color and
movement." They had learned that one response to a card usually indicated a schizophrenic personality, but what they did not know then was
that later clinical work revealed that people with hearing problems give
far fewer responses on the Rorschach than those with normal hearing.
Hearing problems apparently skew this and other tests dealing with
schizophrenia because what these tests usually measure is isolation and
detachment from interpersonal relationships, a "normal" characteristic
of the deaf or near-deaf person. Keeping in mind Ruth Benedict's hearing
problem, ordinary interpretations for the number of responses were out
of line with the reality of her life. Her use of color and movement within a
single whole did seem to indicate superior talent to juggle and coordinate
very dissimilar items within a single framework, indicating her definite
disposition toward non-Euclidean thinking. Possibly because of her own
experience with the Rorschach and her disagreement with its assessment
of herself, by the early 1940's she had become highly skeptical of the
value of Rorschach testing in field work, an attitude the rest of the profession caught up with in the early 1950's.[12]

Ruth Benedict's search into psychoanalysis took her in one other direction in the 1930's, and that was learning about Harry Stack Sullivan's theory of interpersonal relations. The Neo-Freudians taught the extreme
importance of experiences in infancy and early childhood in shaping
the individual personality. Sullivan emphasized the importance of relations between persons in shaping the personality, whether in regard to
dominance-submission or other responses. In 1933 Sullivan and some
colleagues founded the William Alanson White Psychoanalytic Foundation, which became the umbrella for the Washington School of Psychiatry
and the journal *Psychiatry* which Sullivan founded in 1938. Sullivan encouraged interdisciplinary work by psychoanalysts, giving an example in
his own life through his collaboration with Sapir and his committee work
with anthropologists through the National Research Council. Benedict
had worked with him on an NRC subcommittee to award graduate training fellowships for learning methods of personality study in 1935 and

probably had met him or at least heard of him before that from Sapir. She sometimes visited the Sapir family at its summer home, where Sullivan also spent much time and where the conversation and discussion continued into the night. Her use of ideas on interpersonal relations was clear in "Continuities and Discontinuities," which she wrote for an early issue of *Psychiatry*. At her death Sullivan wrote that he would miss Benedict as a colleague ready for "any new, difficult task in relating psychiatry and the social sciences to the problems of man." In the 1940's she became a Fellow of the Washington School of Psychiatry and during the war taught classes there in an interdisciplinary program.[13]

By the end of the 1930's Benedict had explored the possibilities of cross-cultural correlation of psychologically oriented traits, had interacted with psychoanalysts and been influenced by Neo-Freudian theories and theories of interpersonal psychiatry, had sought in child development and the life history the answer to the dynamic problems of culture change and transmissions, and had seriously studied Rorschach testing for possible use as an anthropological tool. The directions her search took reflect the paths Culture and Personality anthropologists in general took during this time period. The complexities of her own involvements reveal the extent and the directions in which psychoanalysis influenced anthropology during the 1930's. But the influence was not one-way, as a rereading of Benedict's life during this period shows.

In the summer of 1934 Margaret Mead and John Dollard had both attended the Hanover Seminar of Human Relations (sponsored by SSRC), where Mead wrote that they got "a lot of good thinking done." By the New Year of 1935 Mead and Dollard were trying to get together a small but high-powered group to work on Culture and Personality problems. Dollard wrote Mead in January that he had been in touch with psychoanalyst Karen Horney and she wished to invite Mead to her house. After that took place Mead wrote Horney a note saying how much she would enjoy further talk and Horney replied that the "circle was too wide," and perhaps just she, Fromm, Dollard, and Mead could get together at times. By February 1935 Mead had met and liked Erich Fromm, to whom Dollard had apparently steered her. The "next move," she wrote Dollard, was to plan a small gathering, perhaps a dinner party, to get the four together. She also wanted him to meet Ruth Benedict, who was going to give a speech to the Anthropology Club in New Haven, Connecticut, soon. Dollard, then learning to be a lay analyst and doing a control analysis with Abram Kardiner, wrote that he was "a little sour" on the last meeting with Fromm and Horney and wanted to postpone their getting together until late March or early April. He looked forward to meeting Ruth Benedict. Mead replied, "So beit [sic], we'll postpone any more psycho-analytical rapprochments [sic] until April." She liked Fromm "very much," she wrote, hoped to see him again, and thought she could work with Horney.[14]

The proposed meeting did not occur until May, but Dollard found it "delightful." In June Mead wrote him that she had taken Ruth Benedict to a party at Erich Fromm's to which Horney also came. "Now Erich is very eager for some kind of further cooperation between us five on defining problems which should be tackled by ethnologists and analysts." A few days after the meeting Karen Horney wrote Benedict inviting her to dinner. She told her to bring Margaret Mead or come alone. "I like it both ways," she wrote. She also sent a reprint of a paper on masochism they had talked about and was interested in Benedict's response. "Horney. Dinner," entries began to appear in Benedict's appointment book. In July 1935, Mead wrote William Ogburn, "We are really getting a lot of thinking done, Ruth, and Karen Horney, and Erich Fromm, and John and I." They were working on the character formation behind American Indians' sensitivity to shame from group disapproval as a major form of social control. So far they had distinguished four types of social control methods—the character structure that worked on shame (American Indian), guilt (our own, Manus, Samoa), fear (Ifugao, Dobu), and "incongruity" (Samoans, Javanese), in which the individual's sense of security was attached to the perfection of a pattern of ritual and threatened when the pattern was not perfect. That same month Karen Horney published an article in the *Psychoanalytic Review* on masochism "done with anthropological problems specially in mind." Fromm wrote Mead that month that her book *Sex and Temperament* and Ruth Benedict's "excellent" *Patterns of Culture* had stimulated his thinking and he was planning an article as a result. Mead wrote Fromm in August that she and Ruth Benedict were "looking forward to the conferences in the fall, and to getting old points setteled [sic] and new points raised."[15]

Karen Horney was two years older than Ruth Benedict. She had studied medicine in Germany at a time when the question of any form of higher education for women was hotly argued. She married at the age of twenty-four, had three daughters in all, and continued her education while living through the disruptions of World War I, finally setting up in private psychoanalytic practice in 1919. In 1925 she gave some lectures, e.g., "Certain Types of Women's Lives in the Light of Psychoanalysis," that made her a symbol of the liberated woman to young feminist woman students at the Berlin Psychoanalytic Institute with which she was affiliated. That same year she began to rebel against Freud's ideas about the psychology of women and female sexuality. She had begun questioning the castration complex in an article in 1922, not rejecting it then, but suggesting that penis envy was not a basic instinct in itself, but a secondary one; not based on anatomical desire for a penis but on other secondary reasons, such as desire to urinate like a man, or to see and touch genitals as men so easily could. In 1926 her famous paper "Flight from Womanhood" appeared, a much more sophisticated piece which pointed out the male-centered psychoanalytic view of female development. She still saw some unconscious biological influences, but also wrote that actual social conditions contributed to women's feelings of inferiority. She wrote several other papers on women before "The Problem of Feminine Masochism" appeared in 1935. Following her discussions with Benedict and Mead she denied that masochism was an integral part of women's nature or biology. Masochistic symptoms were more likely a reaction to cultural influences such as the blocking of emotional or sexual outlets, the lower status and economic dependency of women, and the low self-esteem in childbearing. She concluded that no woman need be prey to masochistic tendencies.[16]

Horney had separated from her husband in 1926 and had come to America in 1932 as the result of a job offer to become assistant director of the Chicago Psychoanalytic Institute. As conditions worsened in Germany she stayed on, moving to New York in 1934. When she met Benedict and Mead she was ready for the cultural ideas they had to offer. Her own experience with patients in Germany and the United States had shown her important differences in neurotic conflicts between the two cultures. In her papers on women's psychology she had been groping toward a theory about women that included the importance of social factors as well as psychological factors in women's personalities. The anthropological ideas of Benedict and Mead gave her the tools with which to refashion Freudian psychology from a biological to an environmental, cultural base.[17]

In the fall of 1935, after a summer of collaboration with Benedict and Mead, Horney taught her first course for the New School for Social Research, entitled "Culture and Neurosis." She talked and later wrote of the "importance of cultural implications," to what extent neuroses were "moulded by cultural processes," as "normal" character was. This idea, she added, meant modification of Freud's ideas. She talked of neuroses, such as the inferiority complex, nourished by the all-pervasive competition in American society. In the article based on her New School class, she footnoted Benedict's *Patterns of Culture* and Mead's *Sex and Temperament* in her rejection of Freud's idea of a "biologically determined human nature." Although she presented her ideas as a shift of emphasis from Freud's, other psychoanalysts saw it for the fundamental departure it really was. In 1937 Horney published a book that came to be a psychoanalytic classic, summarizing her views on the importance of culture to personality structure. As her preface and footnotes showed, the book was written with input from Benedict, Mead, Dollard, Harold Lasswell, and other social scientists. Originally titled *Culture and Neurosis*, it appeared as *The Neurotic Personality of Our Time*. The book affirmed the principle of cultural relativity, saying there was no absolute definition of what was normal, no unchanging universal human nature, no typical neurosis except in terms of individual cultures. Benedict reviewed the book for the *Journal of Abnormal and Social Psychology* in 1938 and praised Horney for giving Freud the "truest honor" by building on what he had done and going beyond him, discarding ideas of Freud's that were culture-bound to his time and place. Horney went beyond Freud's biological determinism. She rejected the biological base of penis envy, the libido theory as explanation for anxiety, the death instinct as a base for masochism. She held neither the Oedipus complex nor physiological pre-genital stages to be universal. Instead she looked to the "psychic difficulties presented to individuals by the culture in which they live." Benedict praised Horney for stating "so clearly her conviction that the conflicts found in neurotic persons in a given culture correspond to the ways of life laid down in that culture." Benedict looked forward to useful cooperation between social scientists and psychologists coming out of Horney's book.[18]

Horney wrote Benedict, "No reviewer got the essential points of the book as clearly as you did," and asked her to have lunch and a talk. Psychiatrist Clara Thompson also reviewed the book favorably but foresaw that it would be controversial among analysts. It was controversial but acceptable because of Kardiner's well-known seminar work which also suggested the importance of cultural factors in personality, though in a more ethnological rather than psychoanalytical way. The fact that Kardiner had been analyzed by Freud himself gave his ideas a certain status. Horney's second book, *New Ways in Psychoanalysis* (1939), however, became a battle area in psychoanalysis as she went farther and totally rejected the libido theory, Oedipus complex, death instinct, repetition-compulsion, and the superego, all basic to Freud's ideas. The situation was compounded by the influx into America by this time of refugee analysts from Europe. The majority of them were conservative about Freud's ideas and possibly because of the insecurity caused by their own uprooting were deeply against any revision of the master's principles. They stood for strict training, professional standards, and Freudian orthodoxy, and moved against Horney as a heretic. She was voted out of the New York Psychoanalytic Institute in 1941, and a number of liberal psychoanalysts left also and joined with her in the Association for the Advancement of Psychoanalysis with the American Institute for Psychoanalysis as the training arm. The group became affiliated with the New School for Social Research.[19]

The group inaugurated a monthly series of lectures given by members and invited speakers, of whom Ruth Benedict was one. Others were psychoanalysts she had come to know—Kardiner, Abraham H. Maslow, Fromm, Sullivan. There was a sense of excitement at these lectures, a sense that learning was going on. Anything could happen. At one meeting where Fromm was to speak and Benedict to lead the discussion, Harry Stack Sullivan suddenly went to the podium and remarked, "I am a schizophrenic," causing gasps and applause in the audience. In 1943 there was a new controversy, this time between Fromm and Horney. Horney expelled him from her society because he was a lay analyst, not an M.D. This turned Sullivan and his friends away from cooperation with Horney. Benedict, who knew people in both groups, stayed out of the controversies and remained friendly with both sides. In spring 1943, she took part in another New School course for Horney. In 1944 she wrote Hiram Hayden of the *American Scholar* that she thought "very highly" of Karen Horney and recommended the journal ask her for an article. By then Benedict was living and working in Washington, D.C., and had become involved with Harry Stack Sullivan's Washington School of Psychiatry, teaching classes there in 1944 and 1945. She had also refused to become involved in the 1941 schism with the New York Psychoanalytic Institute, supporting Karen Horney with her participation in the monthly groups but accepting an invitation from the New York Psychoanalytic Institute to attend a colloquium in 1942.[20]

Horney's basic premise of the impact of culture on psychoanalysis eventually became an accepted major movement, the Cultural School of Psychoanalysis. The modifications and revisions of Freud's theories suggested by this school and other Neo-Freudians have largely been accepted by psychoanalysts today. By dealing directly with the androcentrism and culture-bound limitations of Freud's psychology, Horney helped free Freud's ideas from their net of biological determinism. Her work widened the perspective of psychoanalysts so that they began to take culture into account. But the greatest effect of Horney's approach was not within the narrow limits of psychoanalysis but in its impact on American culture at large. Acceptance of Freud's psychology in American culture has largely been in the form that Horney gave it. The cultural focus was much more amenable to Americans with their tradition of the "self-made man" and the influence of the Progressive stress on the importance of environment. Horney's ideas have become absorbed into the American intellectual viewpoint, and Ruth Benedict had a hand in their shaping.

Benedict's second major influence on psychiatry was in the encouragement of a relative definition of *normal* and *abnormal*. From the writing of "Anthropology and the Abnormal" this remained a recurring theme for her. Benedict's ideas on abnormality and normality sparked discussion within the psychological community. In her talk at the American Association for the Advancement of Science Symposium on Mental Health in 1938, she reiterated her arguments. Cross-culturally, she said, some acts that were symptoms of mental illness in American society were not so in others. Suicide in Japan, for example, was the sign of an honorable person, not a disturbed one. Other cultures considered acts brushed off in American culture, such as a lack of hospitality or the striking of a child, as signs of mental illness. She did offer one universal criterion for mental illness that took relativity between cultures into account: "the loss of ability to go on functioning." [21]

She spent the rest of the paper giving a concrete example of how cultural factors affected mental health in one area: cultural institutions which singled out a person for public humiliation. Again she emphasized the relativity of what was humiliating and what prestigious from culture to culture. She contended that societies fostering mental health had institutions that allowed for humiliation of individuals only when they transgressed or defaulted. In societies that humiliated even though a person lived up to the mores, people remained healthy if some outlet, some way of wiping out the humiliation, was readily available. She gave the Chuckchee of Siberia as an example of a society that made life a constant series of humiliations, yet did not provide outlets for them. These people had many personality disorders such as kleptomania, nightmares of choking to death in which people actually died, vowed suicides, and running amok with compulsive, murderous rage. However, the most unstable group in terms of hallucination, trance, and other Western signs of mental illness, the shamans, did not have a record of psychic breakdown. Benedict suggested that this was because theirs was an honored profession, they filled a place in society. "The chances of mental health correlate with the social role individuals are allowed to play," she concluded. Any "comprehensive program for social control of mental health" had to take cultural factors into consideration. Harry Stack Sullivan, the panel moderator, in his summary understood Benedict to be asking "whether we might not profitably turn to an overhauling of our heritage of traditions and institutions" rather than go on building mental hospitals.[22]

Her ideas about homosexuality also developed. In the early 1930's she concentrated on the issue of normalcy, defending homosexuality by noting that while it was considered abnormal in American society, other cultures had given it a place. But a question that came to be equally important was why homosexuality occurred. By 1939 she saw homosexuality as linked to gender roles allowed by a society to its members. That year she participated in a discussion of homosexuality, presenting a paper in reply to another written by psychoanalyst J. Wortis. He had argued that the American horror of homosexuality was culturally induced, not instinctive, a sanction against crossing the boundaries of the American moral code, not of human nature. Benedict agreed with him that sex offenses or those sexual practices regarded as wrong varied from culture to culture. Using American Indian examples she made the point that homosexuality went back to "tribal distinctions between the role of men and that of women." The Dakota, who had strong male-female differentiation, had the institution of the berdache and some Lesbianism among women. The Ojibwa, their neighbors, did not culturally differentiate men's and women's roles. Women could go on the warpath, become shamans, and divorce as could men. The Ojibwa had no berdaches. "The aetiology of homosexuality," she wrote, though it might be physiological in a few persons, was "overwhelmingly social."[23]

She stated that the key issue seemed to be self-respect. If a person had a respected or at least accepted role in his or her own society, if that self-respect was there, then the psychic harm which American psychoanalysts insisted must occur would be defused. The gist of her words was that homosexuals were not insane or disturbed, but mentally healthy if given a chance to be by the culture; not biologically determined, but discouraged or encouraged by cultural institutions, especially ideas of masculinity and femininity and male and female accepted social roles. It seems clear that Benedict explained her own sexual preference to herself at least partially as stemming from confusion over her own sex role obligations and her desires as a child for identification with her father and masculine sex roles and the rejection of those of her mother. In changing the definitions of normalcy and abnormality and in trying to gain a new perspective for homosexuality, Ruth Benedict struck a blow for her own self-respect in a time when homosexuality and Lesbianism were on a par with leprosy in American society. In doing so she struck a blow for the self-respect of all gay men and women and helped lay the foundations of the idea of homosexuality as an alternative lifestyle rather than a disease. It took a generation more for her ideas in this respect to become commonly accepted, but in 1974 the American Psychological Association took homosexuality off its list of pathological conditions.

One way Ruth Benedict influenced psychological theory without realizing it was in sparking psychologist Abraham Maslow's theory of the self-actualizing individual. Maslow had gotten his Ph.D. in psychology at the University of Wisconsin. While there he became exposed to the ideas of Benedict and other anthropologists. In 1935 psychologist Edward L. Thorndyke invited him to come to Columbia as a research associate, and he spent the next two years there, then taught at Brooklyn College. He wrote that he sat in on as many anthropology classes and seminars as he could with Ruth Benedict, Alexander Lesser, and George Herzog, learned from conversations with Margaret Mead, Gregory Bateson, Ralph Linton, and others, and became so involved in anthropology that he went on a summer field trip to the Northern Blackfoot near Calgary, Canada, in the late 1930's. Of all the anthropologists, it was Benedict who made the deepest impression on him. He wrote later that his self-actualization studies started in 1935, "as the effort of a young intellectual to try to understand two of his teachers whom he loved, adored, and admired and who were very, very wonderful people." These were Gestalt psychologist Max Wertheimer, teaching at the New School, and Ruth Benedict. He had to understand why these two were "so different from the run-of-the-mill people in the world . . . they were most remarkable human beings." He made notes on them, wrote about them in his journal, thought about them and realized years later "in one wonderful moment that their two patterns could be generalized. I was talking about a kind of person, not about two noncomparable individuals." He lectured to his classes at Brooklyn College on self-actualization but developed his ideas for several years before publishing "Self-Actualizing People: A Study of Psychological Health" in 1950, two years after Benedict's death—an article which he later expanded into a book, *Motivation and Personality*. By self-actualization he meant a need in people for fulfilling their potential, "to become everything that one is capable of becoming." Self-actualization was the sign of the supremely healthy person in any society. That Maslow found in Benedict the prototype of the super-normal person should be enough in itself to confound all the stereotypes concerning Lesbians. Since Benedict was one of the sources of Maslow's theory, his description of self-actualizing people can perhaps give an instructive picture of how she appeared to him and the qualities she projected to the world.[24]

Self-actualizing people, he wrote, were efficiently and comfortably in tune with reality. They were unusually able to judge people perceptively. They saw "concealed or confused realities more swiftly and more correctly than others," in areas from art and science to public affairs. They were less caught up with the superstructure of abstraction, expectations, beliefs, and stereotypes "most people confuse with the world." More than others, they perceived what was really there. They were intrigued rather than threatened by the unknown. Self-actualizing people accepted themselves and their own natures with all their shortcomings and discrepancies. They desired to improve but did not have the sense of unnecessary, unrealistic guilt, shame, or anxiety that affected even normal people in American society. They lacked, to an unusual degree, "cant, guile, hypocrisy, front, face," game-playing.[25]

Their behavior was "marked by simplicity and naturalness, and by lack of artificiality or straining for effect." Not necessarily externally unconventional, they were unusually unconventional thinkers. They went through "the ceremonies and rituals of convention with a good-humored shrug and with the best possible grace," but they never allowed convention to keep them from what they considered important. They enjoyed people who did not demand or expect routine behavior, and they preferred these people as company. Their ethical codes were individual rather than conventional. They tended to be focused on problems outside themselves that called on their energies, usually some responsibility or duty to humankind. They lived "in the widest possible frame of reference." They gave the impression of being "above small things, of having a larger horizon, a wider breadth of vision," which imparted "a certain serenity and lack of worry over immediate concerns." They liked solitude and privacy beyond the average. They found it "easy to be aloof, reserved, and also calm and serene," detached from and undisturbed by what produced turmoil in other people. Their reserve at times shaded over into "austerity and remoteness." They had the ability for intense concentration with its by-products of absent-mindedness and obliviousness of surroundings. In social relations their detachment created problems. It was easily interpreted as "coldness, snobbishness, lack of affection, unfriendliness, or even hostility."[26]

Unlike most people they did not depend on extrinsic satisfactions, but intrinsic ones. They seemed self-contained and self-reliant, in times of trouble depending on their own resources. Their sense of appreciation was constantly renewed. Life remained full of thrilling, exciting, ecstatic moments. They derived "ecstacy, inspiration, and strength from the basic experience of life." Sexual experience for them was not passing pleasure but deeply strengthening and revivifying. They tended to have what Maslow called then "mystic experiences," later "peak experiences." They identified with humanity, although often "saddened, exasperated, and even enraged by the shortcomings of the average person." They had deeper relationships than other adults—capable of "more fusion, greater love," fewer ego boundaries. But their circle of intimates was small. They tended to be kind and patient with everyone and especially tender toward children and easily touched by them. They had compassion for humankind but could speak "realistically and harshly of those who deserve it, and especially of the hypocritical, the pretentious, the pompous, or the self-inflated." Their hostility was external, however, based on situations that occurred. They attracted admirers, even disciples and worshippers, and found this "embarrassing, distressing, and even distasteful." They tried to avoid them "as gracefully as possible." Self-actualizing people were democratic—accepting of everyone regardless of race, politics, class, color. They were also non-authoritarian. They learned from anyone who could teach them, without regard for keeping up dignity or status. In a kind of humility they gave "honest respect" to those who had skills they did not. They selected their friends on the basis of "character, capacity and talent, rather than birth, race, blood, name, family, age, youth, fame, or power." [27]

They tended to believe in a God, but more as a "metaphysical concept than as a personal figure." They tended to be fixed on ends rather than means. They had a different sense of humor. They did not laugh at hostile humor, or humor based on superiority. They enjoyed humor that poked fun at humans being foolish or bombastic. They also liked "thoughtful, philosophical humor." They were creative. They resisted enculturation and maintained a certain detachment from their culture. They had a tolerant acceptance of things they considered unimportant and cut corners in favor of "directness, honesty, saving of energy," when possible. They showed a "calm, long-time concern with culture improvement" that implied "an acceptance of slowness of change" but they emphasized the necessity and desirability of such change. They were "not against fighting, only against ineffective fighting." [28]

[257]

They had their imperfections. They were very strong people, sometimes capable of unexpected ruthlessness, displaying a surgical coldness in cutting themselves off from dishonest relationships. They tended to be independent of the opinions of other people. Their detachment made them uninterested in chatting or light conversation, and this sometimes insulted and hurt others. Kindness sometimes led to mistakes, such as allowing neurotics, bores, or unhappy people to get too close and being sorry for it, or allowing scoundrels and parasites to impose for awhile. They had their own "internal strife, and conflict." Very few understood them, however much they might like them. They were truly like people from a far country.[29]

Benedict's influence on self-actualization, cultural psychoanalysis, and psychologically defined normality and the various ways she explored the use of psychological methods and ideas reflect the complex interaction between psychologists, psychiatrists, and anthropologists in the 1930's. Culture and Personality anthropologists took psychological methodologies related to the individual personality and tried to apply them to culture, or attempted to create a concept of culture based at its roots on Benedict's idea of "personality writ large." In many ways their work was exciting and thought-provoking. But it led anthropology in directions in which a number of anthropologists did not want to go.

11

Academic Politics

ALTHOUGH THE PSYCHOLOGY of culture continued to occupy Benedict's mind, on another level the 1930's became a decade of academic politics for her, a decade of accruing power as a scholar, as a teacher, as an administrator, but also a time for learning the limits of power; a decade which took her to the inner circle of her profession, yet ended by finding her an outcast in the Department that was her intellectual home.

Boas began giving Benedict real authority in the Department in 1930. She had grown increasingly influential during the late 1920's. As Margaret Mead said, students got used to finding her in the seminar room between classes "to talk about all sorts of things, and her gentle, faraway accessibility provided a kind of center in a department in which the professor was harried, shy, and abrupt in first contacts." She became a mediator between the students and Boas, one who interpreted his sometimes oracular words and actions to students and in turn relayed their feelings and problems to Boas. She became someone to turn to for advice. Boas came to regard her as someone with whom he could share his own plans for anthropology, his own ideas, his hopes and fears for students. He had given her increased teaching responsibilities and some administrative experience as the 1920's progressed. He had begun trying to get her a permanent position in the Department in 1927, an effort culminating finally in an assistant professorship in 1931. But in 1930 influence became authority. During that year Boas went on sabbatical, taking the fall to make a return field trip to the Kwakiutl Indians in British Columbia, Canada. He wrote to Dean Howard L. McBain, "During my absence Dr. Ruth F. Benedict will take charge of all the administrative details of the Department of Anthropology." He also gave her control of money, writing the bursar to honor her signature on requisitions, except for the Marcus fund for physical anthropology, which Bruno Oetteking would administer. Benedict's letters to Boas make clear that she held no empty honor but a working position. While he was gone she participated in negotiations to set up a project with the Columbia Council on the Humanities to fund field work on religion and culture in Mexico, a project that ultimately became reality. She administered funds for students in the field. She arranged for summer school funds and took care of the details with former student Melville Jacobs, who was to teach that summer. She also handled a heavy teaching load that fall, and she enjoyed teaching more than she ever had. "Seminar is an enormous gathering," she wrote; "they all seem deeply earnest, but I don't know how good they are." Her religion class was "intelligent and interested," her American Indian class full of "*earnest* special students," and her big extension course turned out to possess "more personality" than it had promised at first.[1]

With spring Boas planned to return and take charge again, but in December he had heart trouble which made him seriously ill, so Benedict continued de facto to run the Department. Boas was seventy-two years old at the time. A car had hit and killed his wife a year earlier, in December 1929, a shock from which he had not fully recovered, and it looked as if he would be forced to retire within a year. Dean of Natural Sciences Howard L. McBain, sympathetic to anthropology, gave Boas the go-ahead to approach Kroeber at Berkeley to succeed him at Columbia, and Edward Sapir to act as his second-in-command, with Ruth Benedict as assistant professor and junior department member. At this time unfortunately Sapir had committed to go to Yale as Sterling Professor of Anthropology. Boas knew that when he wrote, but as he said, within a year Sapir's plans might change. Kroeber was seriously interested, but by March 1931 had made the decision to stay where he was. "If I had been ten years younger," he wrote, "or my children ten years older, I should probably have accepted." He was reluctant to leave a thriving department he had built for one where he would at least for a few years have to be guided by or clash with Boas' wishes. "I seem destined to move more independently of you than some of the men you have started in life," he wrote, and he was reluctant to give up this independence.[2]

Boas did not give up easily however. He persuaded Kroeber to come as visiting professor in hopes that he would change his mind, and Kroeber agreed to come for the spring semester of 1932. The third part of the original plan went forward, and Ruth Benedict became assistant professor of anthropology at Columbia in May 1931. Sapir wrote congratulating her, calling it "a modest and criminally belated acknowledgement of your services, and I hope it won't be long before they raise your rank." That year her *Tales of the Cochiti Indians* came out as a Bureau of

American Ethnology publication, furthering her scholarly reputation in the anthropological community. That summer, as a mark of professional recognition, she was appointed to lead the ethnological study group for the Santa Fe Laboratory in Anthropology. The lab, which Benedict called the "Woods Hole" of anthropology, had been organized in 1927 and each summer groups of students in archaeology and ethnology spent several weeks with various tribes. Group leaders were chosen for their expertise and out of respect for their professional competence, and Benedict was the first woman chosen as a group leader. There had been a certain amount of bias against women at the lab since its organizational meeting, which had excluded Elsie Clews Parsons, the woman who had done much of the detail work on Southwest ethnology herself and financed a good deal of the rest. Alfred Kidder, organizing the original meeting, had not even thought of inviting Parsons, and had made arrangements to meet at the Yale Club, which excluded women. "I am afraid that I cannot manage to include Mrs. Parsons," Kidder wrote Boas. He called himself "incredibly stupid" and hoped Boas would "explain things" when he saw her. As sessions became organized there was also trouble over the exclusion of women students, depending on the attitude of the group leader. In the summer of 1929 women were excluded from the archaeology group. Boas objected to this to Sapir, who wrote back that he thought the "impression that women were not wanted in the field was a very much exaggerated one." Sapir believed that "whether a student is a man or woman should not enter materially into the decision of the Committee." When chair of the planning committee for 1931 himself, he proved it by appointing Benedict as ethnology leader. Kidder considered this an "excellent appointment" and O. S. Halseth, an archaeologist in Arizona, wrote that he had seen the field leader selection with "great personal joy."[3]

The trip was very successful. Benedict chose the Mescalero Apache reservation in New Mexico as the training center and went there with a group composed of four young men, Jules Blumensohn (Henry), Morris Opler, Sol Tax, and John Gillin, and one young woman, Regina Flannery. All later became successful anthropologists. Paul Frank, a student of Sapir's, came along as handyman. Harry Hoijer, a linguist from the University of Chicago, worked with the group on linguistics, while Benedict handled the ethnology. The group apparently stayed in a school. "We are lodged in the girls' dormitory, where the men have one large room together," she wrote. The group worked with informants and attended ceremonies such as the Apache girls' sunrise adolescence ceremony. Benedict tried to arrange for the students to see "the way the culture is lived and their attitudes" besides just gather information, though there was less of that than she had hoped. She felt her students had done good work with results "creditable to any group of ethnologists," and was satisfied that they had "really learned something in the process."[4]

She returned to play her role as Boas' second-in-command and then in December 1931, Boas was again seriously ill with an embolism in the coronary artery that kept him in bed until the end of January and recovering through the spring semester. Again the work of the Department fell on Ruth Benedict's shoulders. As Mead wrote, "letters were sent to her on the assumption that Boas was relinquishing his hold on things—that he would never look at this manuscript now, never take up that issue." Kroeber came as visiting professor that spring, but it was clear by the end of the semester that he would not change his mind. By then also Sapir had firmly settled at Yale, and he too refused the offer to take Boas' place. That summer of 1932 marked a time of significant change in Benedict's life. She learned to drive, bought a car, and took her mother on vacation. She started the manuscript which would eventually be *Patterns of Culture,* and she wrote to Mead that Boas' illness had made her realize "that whatever happens in this department I shall have to do certain things in it if they're done at all." She wrote Mead that the future of the Department was "complete guesswork." She continued, "With finances as they are now Columbia will not bring anyone else so long as Papa Franz holds out." Columbia would probably retire him, she conjectured, before bringing in a full professor to replace him. "So all I can see at the present moment is to consolidate my position. Then when the time comes we'll see."[5]

During the next three years Benedict and Boas ran the Department together. The evolution of Benedict's authority in the Department is clear in a series of letters between Ella Deloria, Ruth Benedict, and Franz Boas. Deloria, a Dakota Sioux, had graduated from Columbia Teachers College in 1927. While a student at Columbia and afterward she worked with Boas on Dakota linguistics. In the 1930's he sent Deloria into the field to collect information on various Indian languages and cultures, paying her for her work. Boas trained her in anthropology and came to regard her work highly. In 1933 her book *Dakota Texts* was published; Jules Blumensohn (Henry), then in the field in Brazil, commented, "it is so good that the time I ought to devote to my own work I spend reading her book." In the summer of 1932 Deloria clashed with Benedict over the issue of authority. Not accepting Benedict as having true authority over her work that summer, Deloria was slow going to the field and harassed Benedict about money arrangements. Benedict, irritated and frustrated, felt Deloria was trying to take advantage of her. On her side Deloria resented working unexpectedly for Benedict rather than Boas. She wrote to him, "I did not know, and you did not tell me, that I was not working for you this summer but for Ruth Benedict." She told him she felt insecure and Benedict had made her feel "uncomfortable" about the money. Boas backed up Benedict's authority and Deloria continued to work for Benedict. By 1935 she had accepted Benedict as authority along with Boas. Communicating with Boas in November of that year she wrote, "Meantime, if Ruth Benedict or you want me to notice anything in particular, I hope you will write back at once." Benedict in turn that year wrote to Lowie of the pleasure she'd had working with Deloria and the beauty of the material Deloria had collected.[6]

During these years Benedict was "flowering into her great self," as anthropologist Ruth Landes wrote. Landes said her own professional life began "when Boas led me into her office in 1932." She added, "She was quite wondrous during the next five years." Beyond teaching ability, students and colleagues look for people who "'profess,' debate, argue, stand for something, live their subject." During the mid-1930's Benedict came into her own in this role. Her work with configurations and the publication of *Patterns* established her as a creator of new directions, one at the cutting edge of her discipline. "It took courage to write *Patterns of Culture*," wrote anthropologist and folklorist Dorothy Lee. It appeared "at a time when we doubted our old methods but had nothing to put in their place" and was "of immediate importance," both to the social sciences and the humanities. *Patterns* introduced "a new approach" to studying society. Lee added that it took Ruth Benedict's "peculiar genius and her brand of courage to apply the theory to the details which comprised most ethnographies at that time." A later student, Sidney Mintz, said that what she had done was "pose in a daring new way . . . formulations of an unusual and original kind" that other people could use to structure their own ideas. She was a risk-taker in the realm of ideas. What impressed Mintz as her student was "her daring and her willingness to work intuitively." Another comment made about her was that "She never turned away from contradictions, from paradox." She searched for coherence, but never denied the possibility of its absence.[7]

Boas had stressed the philosophy of teaching students to tackle problems, not regurgitate facts. He felt that if they had the structure with which to pick up knowledge, they would learn the subject matter they needed as they went along. This reinforced the same philosophy Benedict had learned from John Dewey and the progressive education movement.

Like Boas, Benedict emphasized creative problem-solving as the key to knowledge. She involved her students in the learning process. For example, in a Social Organization class she gave her students lists of kinship terms from selected societies, and they had to figure out the kinship system of a society from the terms. One student wrote that he and a friend "laughed helplessly" over the frustrating complexities and contradictions, "trying to figure out why an Omaha mother's brother's daughter should be called 'mother.'" Benedict had the insight of a great synthesizer, putting others' findings in perspective, seeing implications in colleagues' and students' work which they overlooked. She was a perceptive social critic. She had a gift for summing up ideas in ways that turned students' thinking upside down. Mintz remembered being struck by her comment about colonialism that she thought the English had done well with warlike peoples like the Sikhs and Gurkhas and the Dutch had ruled well over submissive people, but neither had administered wisely those peoples of opposing temperament. She remarked in another context that those who studied mythology in America a hundred years from now would find it in Westerns, detective stories, and even perhaps psychoanalysis, which she did not mean as a put-down. Bringing into play more than a detached perception, she became a "fighter-for-truth" working against the misuse of scientific evidence and pseudo-scientific pronouncements by the Nazis and their allies. She also had the courage to speak out concerning issues at home. When Columbia wanted to fire anthropologist Gene Weltfish, Ruth Benedict stopped a Board of Trustees meeting at Columbia in order to protest.[8]

She not only took risks herself, she also helped her students take necessary risks for intellectual gain. She supported them in the work they wanted to do, beginning with Margaret Mead and Samoa. Boas was having doubts about sending Mead to Samoa due to Sapir's fears for her mental and physical well-being. He sought Benedict's advice, and she advised him to let Mead go. "I credit her with a great deal of common sense," she told him, "and I know she can carry out any precautions she agrees to." She told her students "Go! If this is what you want to do, do it." She worried about them but felt the choice should be theirs. With students in the Department she continued the tradition of responsibility she had learned from the older generation of anthropologists, particularly Boas, who loaned his students money when they needed it, helped them with personal problems when approached, and got them jobs. Benedict too loaned students money or gave it as outright grants, and she passed on the tradition. One graduate student who received fifty dollars from

her remembered that she had told him "the thing to do was to help someone else in my turn." She co-signed loans for student Frieda Hahn in
1930 and 1931, as did Boas. In 1936 when Herbert Halpert, later a well-
known folklorist, brought his collection of children's verses and New
Jersey folksongs to her, she encouraged him to enter graduate school and
found him a scholarship. She loaned him the Department's recording
equipment and *her* car and enabled him to make his first New Jersey
folksong sound recordings. When she found a good student she worked
to find money to keep that student going. Cora Du Bois, later the first
woman appointed in anthropology at Harvard, had graduated from Barnard and taken anthropology there from Benedict the year she taught for
Reichard. She had then gone on to get her Ph.D. in California under
Kroeber. She wrote to Benedict in 1933 that she had run out of funding
and resources. Neither fellowship she had applied for had come through
and renewal of her present appointment was "problematic." Benedict
wrote back within a few weeks offering money for field work in California to keep her going in anthropology the next year—this during the Depression when she had trouble funding students affiliated with Columbia.
But, more than the money, she offered reassurance of her ability and future in anthropology at a low ebb of Du Bois' life. "I can't think of anyone I'd sooner trust than you to do a full-size California monograph,"
Benedict wrote.[9]

Benedict appeared formal and somewhat distant in public, but folklorist
Dorothy Lee said of her that she made her students feel important, remembering even after a ten-minute interview the essential points about
them, their training, their background and special interests. Anthropologist Clyde Kluckhohn remembered meeting her as a graduate student: in
a few moments she had made him feel relaxed and skillfully interviewed
him on his experience with Southwest Indian tribes. Their conversation
went into the small hours of the morning, and both missed their subway
stops on the way home because they were still talking, not about any
"tenuous abstractions" but about a very concrete but obscure point of
Navaho life. Her students were not afraid to joke with her. Blanche
Harper, a graduate student at Columbia, had met Kluckhohn in the
Southwest in the summer of 1934 and wrote of him to Benedict, "He had
heard at Oxford that Papa is the world's greatest anthropologist, and that
you are beautiful." She told him that "Papa is also beautiful, and that
you are the world's second-greatest anthropologist." Another Columbia
graduate student, in California in 1933, wrote her jokingly that he would
trade the California contingent even "for one drink of your Holland gin

in a Cognac bottle—or one twist of your Turkish coffee grinder." The students who had participated in the Santa Fe lab trip also felt free to joke with her in letters. Morris Opler wrote in this vein, adding "Thanks again for the splendid manner in which you have continued your Mescalero role of guardian and director to males aged 2 to 25." One of the qualities Mintz remembered about Benedict was "her extraordinary sense of humor" displayed in classes and in teacher-student conferences. Sociologist and colleague Robert Lynd, author of *Middletown,* praised Benedict's "courtesy and imagination" with students both from anthropology and other disciplines, and added, "student problems were to her as real as her own." Mintz praised her "complete evenhandedness with her male and female students." Landes wrote that she entered anthropology because Benedict and Boas "appeared to distinguish, not the sexes, but only ability. It was their overriding concern." She did have a bias however, and that was toward students who were somewhat out of step with the world around them, who grew up like herself as misfits in American culture. Students noticed that she seemed to take these people especially under her wing.[10]

From the beginning of her academic career her hearing problem had made teaching difficult and exhausting. She was at the mercy of outside circumstances. Varying background noise conditions in a classroom affected what she could hear; the level of lighting affected what she could lip-read. Some days conditions would be optimal and leading discussions or answering questions went well. At other times she would be totally at sea, operating on guesswork, as students' voices became unintelligible mumbles and she missed their lip movements. Hard-of-hearing people often understand the opposite of what a person meant to say, and it was easy for Benedict to make mistakes in understanding. The close concentration needed in every class session was a strain leading to mental and physical exhaustion, and it was too easy to let attention slip for a crucial second. She had trouble lecturing, unsure whether her voice was loud enough, her presentation complicated by a nervous stutter, stumbling miserably with "uhs" and "ums," sometimes blocking at a word or phrase, painfully unable to get beyond it. So during the 1920's teaching was for Ruth Benedict a source of anxiety, insecurity, frustration, deep fatigue, and only very occasionally elation. The new crop of graduate students who began around 1925–1926, including Gene Weltfish, Alexander Lesser, Otto Klineberg, Melville Jacobs, and Thelma Anderson, known as "Jacobs' gang," did not cluster around Benedict as a favored teacher, as they did around anthropologist Paul Radin, spending the year 1926 in

New York. That year, while teaching for Gladys Reichard at Barnard, Benedict determined to try a hearing aid, an "earphone" from Western Electric. She got one but "didn't have nerve to take it out in class!" A hearing aid was an uncongenial solution for her, and she never repeated the experiment. So she spent years developing techniques which worked for her in the classroom. By the mid-1930's she had mastered a style unique to herself which made teaching more enjoyable to her than ever before and learning more accessible to her students.[11]

She learned to stand among her students when she lectured rather than at a rostrum, the close contact more personal for her students, besides making it easier for her to hear, lip-read, and be heard. She gradually learned to "focus attention, lose herself in what she had to say enough, but not too much," as Margaret Mead later wrote. She learned to give positive feedback on students' statements through a smile that accepted the student's general position although she had not caught all the details. She learned to rephrase questions to make sure she had heard correctly and did so in a way that "made the questioner out to be so much more intelligent than had the original question." She had the "rare gift," said Mead, "of taking the half-articulate groping interest of a student and illuminating it with a warmth which was like an accolade." She also learned to supplement her formal teaching with student-teacher conferences, which gave her optimal conditions for communication in a one-on-one situation in the quiet of her office. These techniques did not alleviate all her problems. Students were still occasionally irritated or embarrassed at her stuttering or misunderstanding. But her techniques enabled her to acquire security and poise as a teacher, to relax, to stutter less, to let her sense of humor surface, and to be an effective and admired teacher and scholar.[12]

As a woman in academia she struggled to find a style with which to relate to her predominantly male colleagues. In the early days of women in academic life, most women tried to approach men as equals by assuming a neuter role, dressing plainly in unattractive clothes, not becoming masculine, but denying the feminine side of themselves, a side identified in the public mind with flirting, shallowness, dilettantism. They emphasized the intellectual, rational side of themselves, downplaying the emotional as a source of weakness. When Benedict first entered the academic world in the early 1920's she did this too. She tried to develop a "uniform," just as the suit was the male professor's "uniform." She wore the same dress to class every session, just as Boas wore the same suit. Her clothes appeared unattractive to her female students. But over the years and with input from Margaret Mead, who understood the correlation in American society between dress and image, she developed a style which accepted and displayed her femininity yet underscored her seriousness as a scholar. She developed her own "uniforms," severely styled suits in "tones of grayed blue or green," worn with a frilly blouse, a look which was both professional and feminine, attractive yet comfortable to her male colleagues, and pleasing to herself. During the 1920's she gave up being "beautiful" to be intellectual. By the 1930's she had discovered that she could be both.[13]

She also struggled to find a style of behavior that worked in academia and suited her temperament. Some women tried to breach the "femininity" barrier by using slang or relying on a bluff heartiness. Others cultivated seriousness, gaining reputations for lacking a sense of humor. Instead of neutering herself Benedict developed a style based on her strengths as a woman. She succeeded because she accepted and capitalized on the virtues expected of a woman. Women in American society are expected to be listeners, to sooth emotional hurts and shocks, to "be there," strong and caring, when needed. Benedict raised listening to a high art. The intense, concentrated quality of her listening, a skill made necessary by her hearing difficulties, became a trait students and colleagues remembered and especially appreciated. Her letters to Boas are full of comforting statements as he grew older and had troubles. Students appreciated her soothing quality as they brought their troubles to her and she responded with warmth and concern. She kept a sense of humor and proportion when dealing with students. But if she felt certain students were not working up to potential through laziness or expectation that the world owed them a living, she had little time for them. For those who worked hard and came to her with problems, however, she had sympathy and a willingness to "agonize with" them even if she could not solve their problems.[14]

She succeeded also because she was able to project herself in the work situation into women's roles familiar and acceptable to her male colleagues. With Boas she was not so much a daughter as a granddaughter, a little removed from his direct responsibility and supervision because she was in her thirties and married when she came to Columbia. She in turn apparently regarded him much in the role of her patriarchal grandfather, John Samuel Shattuck. A group of her students called her "Mother Ruth" for a year, just as they called Professor Boas "Papa Franz" or "the Papa," and thought of themselves as an anthropological family.[15] But the woman's role Benedict played best and was most remembered for was that of the "lady," a little formal, a little distant, polite, well-bred, but always gracious, always composed, always generous. The comments after her death reveal this as the primary image her colleagues and students had of her.

It was not the maternal image that survived her, but that of the woman who could manage a castle or a plantation, take care of everyone's wants and needs, and still be the ultimate of womanly virtues. Anthropologist Judith Modell interviewed former students and colleagues of Ruth Benedict's. Most, she reported, commented on her beauty, but all remembered her "delicacy and femininity," and "the gracious manners and tone of a well-bred woman." Sidney Mintz recalled Benedict as "serene, generous and courteous—more so, certainly, than she needed to be." Alfred Kroeber called her "fine-grained" (as opposed to coarse), and "reserved as a person, restrained in expression, yet sympathetic and kindly." Cora Du Bois praised her "unstinting generosity," her "rare sensitivity in matters both of the intellect and of the feelings," her personality "in which malice and aggression were singularly unvoiced," her "compassion" for others, and her dignity which "discouraged the familiarities." Robert Lynd recalled her courtesy with students. He also recalled her strength. She was neither "awed" nor "intimidated" by men, he said. "She had the spunk to get research funds without so much as a 'By your leave'—; and she did distinguished research with those funds." Victor Barnouw, another former student, called her "a tall and slender Platonic ideal of a poetess." Psychoanalyst Abram Kardiner, who did research with her, recalled her "easy but unassailable dignity" which "kept people from getting too close." The qualities these people described were those expected of a great lady. One disgruntled student spoke disdainfully of her in this role as "Princess Ruth." But around her in the mid-1930's was an image of beauty and calm, humor and tolerance, that grew brighter as she grew older and into her last role, that of "wise woman." [16]

Ruth Benedict helped destroy academic stereotypes about women, the covert expectation that a woman academic must be ugly, or "mannish," or perpetually single. As Ruth Landes wrote, she hadn't cared to become a "Ph.D. bluestocking," herself. But in Ruth Benedict she had an example and role model: a woman who was "beautiful and married," and also a lady. Her woman students found her willing and available to talk about the contradictions inherent in being both woman and academic, and the difficulties they faced in the role of "New Women." Landes recalled talking to Benedict one summer about the guilt she felt on leaving her husband for field work, her feeling of deserting her marriage to take a Ph.D., her own troubled feelings about taking her husband's name and being expected to lean on a man for support. Benedict, she recalled, shared her questions. They agreed, jokingly, that the ideal husband would be Chekhov, the Russian playwright, who understood and accepted things with "warm humanness." Boas had the reputation for accepting woman students on an equal level with men, but as anthropologist Virginia Wolf Briscoe has pointed out, it is interesting that between 1901 and 1920, nine men and only three women received Ph.D.'s in anthropology from Columbia. From 1921 through 1940, twenty men and nineteen women received Ph.D.'s in anthropology there, for a total from 1901 through 1940 of twenty-nine men and twenty-two women. Harvard from 1894 through 1939 graduated fifty-three male anthropology Ph.D.'s and no women. From 1897 through 1940 the University of Chicago graduated twenty-eight men and two women Ph.D.'s in anthropology. Even the Department of Anthropology at the University of California at Berkeley, where Kroeber had adopted the open attitude of his mentor Boas toward women, from 1901 through 1940 graduated eighteen male and nine female Ph.D.'s. It is strikingly apparent that something was tipping the scales at Columbia in favor of women finishing their degrees, staying on the track, overcoming the regular academic obstacles and some peculiarly placed difficulties felt only by women. World War I and the movement for women's emancipation had opened paths for women's entry into a professional accreditation hitherto a male province—but entry did not guarantee completion. For that students needed advice, sympathy, a standard to live up to. Women at Columbia found these things in Ruth Benedict.[17]

The standard she represented was a high one. In 1932 J. McKeen Cattell, editor of *Science,* wrote to tell her she had been selected as one of the five top anthropologists among twenty leading anthropologists and one thousand leading scientists in the United States. In 1933 she was selected by *American Men of Science* as one of the three leading women scientists in the country, considered to be the equals of the top rank of male scientists, a distinction that gave her celebrity status and led to interviews with several newspapers and *Time* magazine. That same year she was elected a Fellow of the American Association for the Advancement of Science and the next year a Fellow of the New York Academy of Sciences. Power came to her unasked. In 1935 she was appointed on the recommendation of the American Anthropological Association as a member of the National Research Council Division of Anthropology, one of the top non-academic appointments anyone could receive, at the center of financial power and disbursal of funds. She served until 1938. She was selected to serve on the Advisory Board for the Santa Fe Lab, 1936–1939. In 1937 she was elected a member of the Columbia Council on Research in the Social Sciences, the group in charge of disbursing funds to the social sciences at Columbia and a main source of anthropological research money. Honors and authority accrued naturally to her as she rose in professional esteem.[18]

The Modern perspective pervaded her approach as a teacher. "At a time when we were trying to be scientific in the old Pearsonian sense, deleting the observer from the observed," wrote Dorothy Lee, Benedict was scientific "in the Einsteinian sense, including the observer." Beyond just including the observer, she presented this individual as "a total person," one perceiving not only cognitively with the intellect, but immediately and intuitively through the emotional side. When Benedict studied the mass of details that constituted most ethnographies of that time, she read and reread, studying the details until she could "experience reality" as the group being described did, perceive the world as they perceived it. This is what she tried to teach her students to do, to perceive the world from many different frames of reference. At a time when participant observation was replacing older field methods, Benedict taught her students to be participant observers. As participant observers anthropologists went to live for a long period of time in the midst of a people whose culture they wanted to understand. They tried to immerse themselves in the culture, learning from details how the group thought and felt, how they perceived reality. Benedict's students studied ethnologies as if they were visiting the people described. She taught them to look meticulously at details, for "no detail was trivial," and to examine each one closely "as a clue to society's peculiar expression and arrangement of reality." Understanding came from "a genuine surrender to what the data, derived from the observation of living people, or their words, could give." She strove to get students to immerse themselves totally in the material, to suspend their own beliefs for a time, and to understand deeply other versions of reality. To have her students see life through more than one pair of eyes was her goal. She taught her students the need to ask questions, quoting in class from Archibald MacLeish's *Hamlet,* loosely:

> We know the answers, all the answers
> It is the questions that we do not know.

Asking the wrong question could result in the wrong answer. A wrong question was one, as Boas said, "we construct on the basis of our modern concepts," framing both question and answer within our own parochial perspective. Benedict once told Esther Schiff Goldfrank that nineteenth-century anthropologist Lewis Morgan had not asked the right question on a point because she thought his answer parochial in this way.[19]

During the years Boas and Benedict informally ran the Department together, they split responsibilities. Besides teaching, editing the *Journal of American Folk-Lore,* and sharing Department administrative duties, Benedict became responsible for the development and coordination of ethnology from financing and pre-field-trip advising through publication of field work afterward. She not only continued the study of North American Indian tribes but also initiated field work study of South American peoples and coordinated students from Fiji to Africa. She recognized the importance of good field work from a Culture and Personality point of view and throughout the decade promoted C&P research among the students she sent out. The amount of field work done and published at Columbia in the 1930's testifies to her effectiveness at coordination, work accomplished under the difficult funding problems engendered by the Depression. Benedict was not personally hurt by the Depression. She wrote a friend in 1933 that life seemed happy except when she let herself wonder how students would support themselves. "Jobs are sinking into the discard instead of being newly created." The Boas papers are full of letters from former students telling of jobs lost through funding cuts, or whole programs endangered by loss of funds and research money. Boas wrote to student May Mandelbaum (later Edel) in 1932, "Our greatest trouble is that the University has a big deficit and they are trying to cut expenses in every direction." Because there were few jobs, Benedict and Boas tried to carry as many finished students as possible, providing them with field work opportunities and a small stipend while they wrote up their work. Alexander Lesser, Gene Weltfish, and Jules Blumensohn (Henry) were all among the students benefiting from this policy. Both Boas and Benedict contributed what money they could spare to the Department for students and to pay clerical expenses. So in spite of her increase in power and responsibility over students, she was limited by the struggle to juggle scarce financial resources to keep people working. At times she became discouraged and returned to her dream of a life of the spirit, calling anthropology "busy work I do with my left hand."[20] Moreover, in spite of the steady growth of her reputation and position during the 1930's and her success with students, Benedict also experienced failure. One student, Henrietta Schmerler, was murdered on a field trip, while another, Buell Quain, committed suicide.

Schmerler's murder occurred in the summer of 1931 while Benedict was leading her Santa Fe lab group on another reservation. Boas had described Schmerler in a recommendation two months before her death as "very intelligent and serious," a student particularly interested in African ethnology, working at Columbia with native African informants as a basis for future work on American blacks "and the practical problems confronting us in regard to this part of our population." She was working with Benedict on her Master's degree and Benedict had arranged her field work that summer with the White Mountain Apaches after consulting archaeologist O. S. Halseth in Arizona. Apparently when she arrived at the reservation Schmerler, in a desire to get good results fast, disregarded her instructions to go slow and work with the women alone. In too great a haste to get to know people, she apparently blundered against Apache mores concerning women and seemed "loose," offending people in the white and Indian communities and causing community disapproval. Gladys Reichard called her trusting and said she probably did not sense trouble behind the scene. She went riding with a small group of Apache young men who seemingly misread her intentions, and the result was her murder after probable sexual assault in late July 1931.[21]

Benedict had no inkling that Schmerler was not following instructions. She wrote to Benedict that she was living in a cabin near the mission and working with an old woman who was teaching her how to make a woman's buckskin dress in the old way. The news of her death came as a profound shock. Benedict called it a "nightmare." Gladys Reichard, doing field work among the Navaho in Arizona, when she heard of the murder called it "incomprehensible no matter how hard I try to visualize it or realize it." Benedict wrote to Boas, "I know it is one of those unprecedented things that cannot be foreseen or guarded against, and yet I think of endless points at which I might so easily have made different arrangements." The nightmare continued through the next year, as the responsibility for the Schmerler case fell on her shoulders. She visited the family first to express her deep sorrow and later on business concerning the trial. She handled repercussions from the Bureau of American Ethnology as they tightened up requirements for anthropological field work. She dealt with the university and was involved in the trial of the accused Indian that fall. The newspapers had played the murder for sensationalism. Reichard wrote at the end of August, "I guess everybody in the U.S.A. knows about the one field trip that was a failure. I can't talk to anyone without getting on to the subject." After receiving Reichard's report of what had happened, Boas wrote Benedict, "It is dreadful. How shall we ever dare to send a young girl out after this? And still. Is it not necessary and right?" Benedict also worried that feelings worked up at the trial would cause a backlash against anthropological work. This senseless death was compounded in the fall of 1931, when Benedict's cousins, Aunt Mamie's sons, one twenty-four years old, the other thirty, died in the crash of a private airplane. The effect of these deaths, coming so close together, may have played a role in focusing Benedict's thoughts on achieving goals in this world. That next summer she began writing *Patterns of Culture*.[22]

The Buell Quain incident occurred much later, in 1939. Quain came into the Department as a graduate student in 1934 and had already completed one successful field trip to Fiji when he went to South America to study Indian tribes there. He had a rougher time than he permitted anyone to know and personal problems as well. He wrote that one of the tribes he was working with had prevalent skin diseases caused by syphilis, tuberculosis, and leprosy. He was upset about it, and it could be he thought he had caught something from them. At any rate he wrote Benedict a suicide note saying, "Dear Dr. Benedict, I have a fever that may be contagious *STERILIZE* this letter." He told her he was going to die, wished her luck with future work in Brazil, and said that he was leaving her $4,000, the amount of his Brazilian field trip which he felt he had squandered since his work would be lost, and was leaving the rest of his money to his sister and niece, who needed it. Benedict wrote to his mother "at the moment I can only think of the personal loss and weep at his suffering."[23]

In spite of these deaths she did not become conservative, but continued to help her students take risks. As Gladys Reichard wrote after Henrietta Schmerler's murder, "After all, it is true as Ruth says, that each person going out cannot but be on his own responsibility. That is why we send them." In contrast to those who failed, there were people like Margaret Mead, who went to Samoa alone for one of the important field trips of the century; or May Mandelbaum, who at the age of twenty-two went to Africa alone and did outstanding field work there; or Ruth Bunzel, who worked alone in Guatemala and Mexico; or Ruth Landes, who studied black cults in Brazil; or Jules Blumensohn (Henry), also on his own in South America; or Ruth Underhill, who successfully completed field work alone in Arizona among the Papago the summer Henrietta Schmerler was murdered.[24]

By the mid-1930's Benedict had accumulated authority and status both in the Department and in anthropology. But her future seemed precarious. When Boas retired, her academic life would depend on his successor, and she tried to have input into that choice. For a brief time in the early 1930's she and Boas gave some thought to Radcliffe-Brown as Boas' successor. Margaret Mead wrote to him in 1932 trying to talk him into seeking the position, saying Benedict thought well of him. He came and taught summer school at Columbia in 1931 while Benedict was in the Southwest with her group. But during the annual American Association for the Advancement of Science meeting in 1932 she wrote Mead that she was "terribly disappointed" in him and couldn't "trump up any fellow feeling" for him. She found him condescending and patronizing, his scorn of field work done in America irritating, and his claims for functionalism bombastic. "He seemed to me impenetrably wrapped in his own conceit, and I certainly shan't feel justified in working to have him appointed at Columbia," she wrote. She saw him as approving the work of "disciples over against work done by non-disciples," not on the basis of its actual worth. "I certainly don't feel like signing up with him against all other American anthropologists and nothing less, I think, would make relations endurable," she said. Boas found Radcliffe-Brown too fanatical about his own ideas and did not want his fanaticism at Columbia.[25]

Mead tried again in 1936. This time her choice was W. Lloyd Warner, a former student of Kroeber's and Lowie's in California and later greatly influenced by Radcliffe-Brown. Warner had done field work in Australia in the 1920's, but his goal in studying primitives was, as he wrote, "to know modern man better." Upon returning to the United States he became an instructor at Harvard, where he became interested in applying anthropological methods to studying industry and participated in the famous Hawthorne study, a study of workers in the Hawthorne Plant of the Western Electric Company in Chicago, a social science landmark which showed, among other things, how knowledge of a test skewed its results, and how personal interest and increased interaction among workers improved productivity. From 1931 through 1936 Warner directed his Yankee City study, the first study of a contemporary community by an anthropologist using anthropological methods, and the most comprehensive study of its kind ever done. Mead wrote to him encouragingly, "Of course, Ruth is definitely for you up to the ears." Boas, she told him, was not antagonistic, just knew nothing about him, and was "very anxious to know that it will be alright [sic], and everyone will be safe in your hands." She coached him, "You can manage to convey that." Benedict wrote a letter to Robert Lynd recommending Warner, saying he could be trusted to emphasize good and well-documented field work. For her that was the "main point." Boas wrote to Kroeber, Lowie, and others about

Warner, getting back mixed recommendations. This flurry of activity with regard to a successor occurred because in November 1935, Boas, then seventy-seven years old, received notice from President Butler that he was being retired in June 1936, after forty years at Columbia. By May Benedict wrote that the opposition to Warner seemed fairly widespread. Warner ended up going to the University of Chicago in 1936. Robert Lynd wrote to Benedict that two or three people had mentioned Ralph Linton, professor of anthropology at the University of Wisconsin, as Boas' possible successor.[26]

President Butler, no friend to Boas or the Department, appointed an ad hoc committee to study the Anthropology Department and recommend a successor for Boas. No anthropologists were on the committee and no one from the Department was involved. As Boas wrote to Ruth Bunzel in 1937, "The committee in charge of the matter on which anthropology is not represented do not think it worthwhile to let us know what they are doing." Boas' former students were passed over. When it appeared that a younger man would be appointed, Benedict wrote Lynd that there was no reason she should passively agree just "because I'm disqualified by being a woman." She didn't really see herself as disqualified however. Apparently Dean McBain supported her candidacy for the position. She wrote that he had said "the universities will have to come to it, and he didn't believe it was bad policy to take the bull by the horns and accept the necessity." She concluded, "Of course I know the difficulties." But McBain's sudden death in 1936 shattered any hopes she had of succeeding Boas. With McBain's backing a few years as "acting head" might have turned into "departmental chair." Without it the matter was impossible.[27]

As it was, no one was appointed immediately and Benedict served as acting head of the Department in 1936–1937, while former student Frans Olbrechts from Belgium came over as visiting professor. The next year Linton came as visiting professor and Benedict continued as department executive officer with the understanding that after a trial year Linton would take over the Department. On the surface this seemed like an amicable settlement of the succession. Linton was head of his own successful program at the University of Wisconsin. His widely praised book, *The Study of Man,* had appeared in 1936. He had a reputation as an entertaining and dramatic teacher. His anthropological interests were close to Benedict's, although his field work was mostly in Malaysia and Madagascar. Benedict and he had had friendly relations as distant colleagues, and they had worked together on the American Anthropological Association Nominating Committee in 1932. Linton had even been a poet in his younger days. After his selection Linton wrote Benedict in June 1937 that he hoped his coming did not interfere with her becoming an associate professor. "You certainly have it coming to you," he wrote, and if he got the job he would do all he could to put it through as soon as possible.[28]

But under the surface lay potential problems. Linton had entered anthropology a few years before Benedict but received his degree at around the same time. He had been a graduate student at Columbia before the war, but Boas did not consider him a top student. After the war, when he showed up in the Department in uniform to register, Boas threw him out in a scene that became a Department legend. He then finished his degree at Harvard. Hearing indirectly that the committee had selected Linton, Boas wrote the new dean of the College of Natural Sciences in January 1937 that Linton was good enough "in his place in Madison" but that Boas considered him a "mediocre man without any original ideas who would go on in a routine way" rather than help the Department develop and grow. Boas recommended Benedict, Berkeley-trained archaeologist Duncan Strong, and two former students, Alexander Lesser and George Herzog, as the Department personnel: since Benedict was in charge, presumably she would remain so. So Linton lacked Boas' backing. There was also a lot of resentment in the Department over the selection process. Ruth Bunzel wrote Boas, "You can imagine what I think of the general idiocy of the proceedings and the final solution." Older students in the Department generally felt the same way, so Linton faced the Department as a leader forced on it from the outside. Benedict thought *The Study of Man* a good text in elementary ethnology long needed, full of common sense, "sane and clear." But the key word was elementary—not an idea book out on the edge. Again, Linton had a photographic memory and a large disregard for the trappings of scholarship. *The Study of Man* contained exactly one footnote and no references, and this was the trend of his other articles and books as well. Benedict also had reason to doubt his standards for field work. One of her students who had been with him at a Santa Fe Lab summer session reported his approach to documentation as sloppy. Moreover Linton's emphasis for students was not problem-solving but the memorizing of facts, a change of method distasteful to those familiar with the Boas/Benedict approach. It seemed useless to them to have students "cram and then forget what they have learned."[29]

For Benedict herself the change was a trying one. For several years she had been a decision-maker. Responsibility had been on her shoulders. Soon she would have to defer to Linton as head of the Department. Her disappointment at having been passed over not because she couldn't do the job but because she was a woman must have been intense. Moreover, because she was a woman, although she was given the rank of associate professor, she was paid $1,000 less per year than Duncan Strong, also an associate professor in November 1938. Mead's brother-in-law, Leo Rosten, wrote Mead that he had seen Benedict and she was irritated by Linton's appointment.[30]

When Linton first came to Columbia, Boas told him, "Of course, you know this is not what I wanted." Boas, appointed Professor Emeritus in Residence, continued to use his office, making tension unavoidable. Linton found Benedict "cool and unreceptive" to him, as were many graduate students. Moreover their styles were different. Linton was openly confrontive. Benedict shied away from confrontation by becoming distant or indicating with a smile, a look, or a movement that something was ridiculous or simple, or becoming "bored." Benedict got angry but got over it. Linton tended to brood over situations in which he felt slighted or treated unjustly, and that first year at Columbia must have been full of small episodes. His resentment focused on Benedict, and he built up a grudge against her that he carried to his grave. His hostility crossed the bounds of good taste. According to Mintz, who was a colleague of his at Yale, Linton later used to pull out a Melanesian charm bag and boast that he had used it to help kill Ruth Benedict. He felt threatened by her and in competition with her for power and authority in the Department and in anthropology. In their public relationship they maintained a façade of politeness, but Benedict stopped going to Department lunches, ostensibly because she had a class at one o'clock.[31]

Linton was in deadly, all-out competition with Benedict by 1939, not only over financial aid, but over scholarship. In the late 1930's he entered heavily into the area of Culture and Personality that Benedict had pioneered and worked to wrest its leadership into his own hands. In 1936 Benedict had been working with psychoanalyst Abram Kardiner in his seminar in which participants applied psychoanalytical ideas to culture. Linton became friendly with Kardiner, and it gradually became Kardiner and Linton's seminar while Benedict played a smaller and smaller role. Benedict had planned a book based on the field work done by students in the 1930's through which she hoped to pull together the threads of psychology and culture from an anthropological perspective, possibly in counterpoint to Karen Horney's study of the two from a psychoanalytical viewpoint. But ultimately the field work was edited and published by Linton, not Benedict. He pushed for a different approach in the Department in sharp contrast to Benedict's and Boas', one that emphasized required courses and book knowledge of facts rather than solving problems and original study.

In 1939 Benedict arranged a sabbatical to begin after a teaching field trip to the Blood and the Blackfoot in Canada and the American Northwest. She used it to write *Race: Science and Politics,* and she spent it in California far away from the Department. This did not stop her from getting news however. Ruth Bunzel wrote frantically that Linton and Strong were using her absence to make important policy changes. Benedict wrote Boas, "I know that Linton is a maddening person to work with," but she didn't believe *the* moment of crisis in policy change had come. She respected Linton and Strong's goal to have students learn more facts; the important thing was to see that research standards remained high. That would depend on directing specific projects, and there Linton would not be influential, she wrote. "He will let it go by default because he hasn't many ideas about it." That would be her opportunity, and no schedule of courses would prevent it. "Anyway," she wrote, "I know that I'm in the minority now and certain concessions are necessary." In another letter she wrote to Boas that at worst students might be advised not to take her courses, but "even at that, I have confidence that I can influence the best students and help in their work," while quite willing to let Linton and Strong "sweat over the dull ones." She felt her duty was "to publish and to get my own backing for these best students." [32]

The money that Buell Quain had left had turned out to be $30,000. Benedict had offered it to his mother and sister but they wished the money to be used for publications and field work as a memorial to Quain. Quain's mother, Benedict's lawyer, and Benedict herself formed a committee to choose how to expend the monies. Benedict wrote Boas that she had heard that Linton was "paranoid" about her control of this money. By 1940 she wrote that he was trying to block university appropriations until the Quain money was used up. "To him," she wrote, "it means that if I have money in my hands I will use it to interfere with his power in the Department." By then the committee had decided to use the Quain money to support the writing-up of field notes and publication where other money was not available. The Quain fund gave her back the ability to help students in a basic financial way that she had begun to lose when Linton took over the Department. But it remained a sore spot between Linton and Benedict. [33]

One other event occurred while Benedict was on sabbatical. In a surprise move through a special council session to which she was not invited, Benedict was quite literally dropped as editor of the *Journal of American*

Folk-Lore after fifteen years of service without even the gloss of a sentence of thanks. The issues behind this move were complex and had been building for a series of years. The *Journal* had been chronically underfinanced and at the beginning of Benedict's term as editor the American Folk-Lore Society (AFLS) had made the decision to publish the *Journal* abroad, estimated to save the society three-fourths of the current printing cost. This began a pattern of chronic delays in publishing due to distance that never came under control. The *Journal* was consistently behind schedule.[34]

Moreover, folklore by the late 1930's was gaining a sense of itself as a legitimate discipline in its own right, and not merely a branch of anthropology. There was a movement to draw "literary" and "anthropological" folklorists together into one representative organization. Anthropologists involved in folklore such as George Herzog, Ann Gayton, and Melville Herskovits began to urge that the literary folklorists be given equal say in the American Folk-Lore Society, which had been dominated by anthropologists for so long. In 1936 literary folklorist Stith Thompson from Indiana University was elected AFLS president and he began to move the society out of the anthropological sphere by creating an annual AFLS meeting independent of that of the American Anthropological Association. There was a sense among both anthropological and literary folklorists that folklore, coming into its own, needed positive and forceful leadership to give it necessary direction and purpose. They felt that the *Journal* editor should take a front role in defining and exploring folklore as a discipline in its own right.[35]

Benedict saw herself as an anthropologist first and a folklorist second. Moreover she had too many other irons in the fire to put the *Journal* first. In the 1930's, with her increasing responsibilities in the Department and in anthropology, she gave the *Journal* a minimum of time and attention. As early as 1931 Benedict had made an attempt to give the editorship to someone else. Again in 1936 she had asked Ann Gayton, whom she had persuaded to become book review editor, to take over the *Journal*. Gayton refused, suggesting Stith Thompson as a gesture to the literary folklorists. By 1940 enough folklorists agreed that they wanted stronger leadership from the *Journal* editor: more emphasis on theory, exploration of folklore methodology and future directions, the display of a wider range of interests. They regarded Benedict as a caretaker rather than a leader. Firing Benedict as editor, like the separate annual meeting, was a gesture that further symbolized the independence of folklore as a discipline from anthropology. It did not, however, symbolize a split between anthropological and literary folklorists at that time, as Judith Modell seems to suggest in *Ruth Benedict: Patterns of a Life*. Most of those on the council which ousted Benedict were anthropologists, and Gladys Reichard took over as interim editor. The policy committee which rewrote the policies of the society in 1940 consisted of both anthropological and literary folklorists, working together. In the next few years anthropologist Melville Herskovits emerged as a folklore leader, becoming American Folk-Lore Society president in 1945.[36]

When informed of her dismissal she wrote George Herzog at Columbia that "in view of my years-long effort to get another editor no letter of resignation from me is necessary," asking him to let her know who ended up as *Journal* editor and "whether I'm supposed to feel brokenhearted." Reichard's interim editorship lasted for a year; then the editorship went to literary folklorists Archer Taylor and Erminie Vogelin. After the initial period of indignation and righteousness by which a new guard washes away the influence of the old, peace gestures were made. Reichard wrote toward the end of her year in office that now that she was in a position to consult Ruth, she was surprised at how they came to the same conclusions. Parsons suggested a few months later that she considered Benedict desirable as an assistant editor.[37]

In 1939 the American Anthropological Association selected Benedict as fourth vice-president, a move that revealed the esteem of her colleagues because it put her in direct line for the association presidency in four years. According to the system at that time each vice-president moved one rung up the ladder. Benedict could expect to move in progression from fourth to third to second to first vice-president and then into the presidency—a signal honor. In 1939 she was the first woman ever admitted into the chain-of-command. As the decade ended she looked forward to achieving the highest authority and influence within the profession. At the same time, she had become an outsider in the policy meetings and decision-making of her own Department. The loss of the *Journal* editorship and the circumstances of that loss merely served to reinforce the lesson of the limits of power.[38]

12

The Politics of Culture

ACADEMIC POLITICS were not the only kind that engaged Benedict's time and attention in the 1930's. As the Nazis marshaled ideas into the service of anti-Semitism and the control of "inferior" races, Boas and Benedict responded to the challenge by arraying the ideas and implications of the culture concept against them in the service of anti-Fascism. In the face of the virulence of the attack they gave time and energy to anti-Fascist activism, concerned that America hold to the liberal principles on which it had been founded. In doing so they were attacked as Communists or, even worse, naïve Communist dupes. Ironically while this again reinforced her sense of marginality to American culture, Benedict used her image as a white, Anglo-Saxon descendant of the *Mayflower* Pilgrims and "daughter" of the American Revolution to reinforce the impact of her ideas upon her American audience. The culmination of her efforts was her book *Race: Science and Politics*, published in 1940.

It was Boas who first became involved in the early 1930's. In the spring of 1933, Boas' books were taken out of circulation at the University of Kiel library in Germany because of his liberal beliefs on race issues and his Jewish descent. When the book-burnings began, his were among the books reported burned. Already German liberal and Jewish academics were fleeing or being exiled from Germany, and as he had done after World War I, Boas flung himself into the work of helping refugees, this time finding fellowships and jobs in America for these displaced scholars. That spring he wrote an open letter to German President von Hindenburg condemning the new policies, which was read over the German radio and published in the *Staatszeitung*. He tried to get the National Academy of Science and other scientific and professional organizations to pass resolutions affirming the necessity of academic freedom and protesting trends in Europe. He helped organize and became president of the Lessing League, an organization to combat anti-Semitism in New York. In the war of ideas the League's goals included collecting information on Nazi activities in the United States, preparing articles for newspapers and magazines, establishing a lecture bureau, and monitoring the newspapers and magazines to catch errors and misstatements. He approached non-Jewish colleagues on writing authoritative articles on Nazi pseudo-science, particularly condemning the forced sterilization in Germany of those with hereditary diseases and also Jews. He began gathering evidence on the positive contributions Jews had made to German culture, including the aid of American Jewish philanthropies there. He helped organize and participated in a summer Institute on Race Relations sponsored at Swarthmore by the Society of Friends. He had thought of visiting his relatives, colleagues, and friends in Germany that summer, but wrote May Mandelbaum in Uganda, "With the mess in Germany I do not want to go."[1]

Meanwhile that spring Ruth Benedict put the finishing touches on *Patterns of Culture*. She spent the summer in Norwich at the Shattuck farm with Aunt My. Since the separation from Stanley, the farm had become her summer retreat. From there she wrote to Boas that she was "living in Zuñi," preparing her manuscript on Zuñi mythology, which made her feel like she was off on a long trip. This was a far cry from Boas' burst of activism. But she was not indifferent—"I wonder so often what you are hearing from Germany," she added. She had written to Margaret Mead in March that the news of Hitler and the "terrible plight" of Germany filled the papers. She described Boas in May as "tireder and tireder," but fighting "almost with the old spirit, and giving time and money and emotion to the anti-Hitler campaign." In June she wrote Mead that Boas "runs committees and committees on the German business and doesn't spare himself except at the most extreme points."[2]

By the fall, and Benedict's return to New York, Boas had decided that the most important thing to do was "to undermine the pseudo-scientific theory on which the anti-semitic propaganda is based," first by "careful and unbiased investigations" and second by getting the results popularized and publicized in the mass media. He added pragmatically that for greater credibility the studies should be carried out by a non-Jewish or partially Jewish committee. He wrote to various people into the spring reiterating his basic idea. He also must have talked over his plans with Benedict. To Stephen F. Wise of the American Jewish Congress he wrote that the attack should be two-pronged, scientific and popular, through the launching of both a serious study and a popular book. A few weeks later, writing to Dr. F. P. Keppel of the Carnegie Foundation, he added a third prong to the attack, the writing of pamphlets for discussions by women's clubs and other organizations. That winter Boas himself tried his hand at popularization, writing a paper, "Aryans and Non-Aryans," later made into a pamphlet and distributed covertly in Germany. Aryan, he wrote, first meant a language. Science had found that there was no one pure "German" race, but instead people of a mixture of racial stocks called themselves German. It was the same with Jews. Either group could produce blond, blue-eyed, or dark members. He told his readers that the attempt to ostracize German Jews on racial grounds was scientifically false, based on "ancient prejudice and pseudo-science." There was no Aryan race, he said. The Aryan part of Hitler's program was based on "hate and not fact." "Aryans and Non-Aryans" was distributed by the underground in Germany, was translated into Spanish and distributed in South America, was printed in English in the United States, and also appeared in shorter form in the *American Mercury*.[3]

Boas saw the main struggle with Fascism as an ideological one. Fascism had to be fought and defeated on the plane of ideas, and this could be done most effectively through the rigorous use of science. But he had few illusions that the scientific approach would do much to influence the Fascist movement in Germany. Rather, his basic goal was "to prevent a similar state of mind developing in this country." This was a goal Benedict sympathized with. From 1936 to 1939 Nazism in America was at its most visible, with the German-American Bund sporting paramilitary regalia, sponsoring summer camps for youth, putting out a newspaper and a youth magazine filled with racism and anti-Semitism. Boas was concerned with the spread of racist and anti-Semitic ideas among the American public at large. But even more, as he had been during World War I, he was concerned for the preservation of academic freedom in American universities as well as the maintenance of freedom of speech and belief in the country at large. He saw the dissemination of scientifically verified knowledge as a preventative necessary to nip Nazi tendencies here in the bud. His primary goal was to prevent the spread of Nazism in America.[4]

Boas received funding from various organizations, and by April 1934 the conduit for the serious scientific study, the Committee on Research on Heredity and Environment, made up of non-Jewish scientists, was functioning. In the fall of 1933 he had agreed to do a series of lectures at the Socialist Party's Rand School of Social Science on "Race and Culture." In the fall of 1934 he added a course on "Race and Culture" to the Columbia curriculum. He also started a campaign to get other colleges to teach race courses. No effort was too small. For example, he got New York University to agree to offer "Race and Culture" as an adult education class taught by Alexander Lesser from the Columbia Department because Boas agreed to pay three-fourths of the expense for it. In 1934 Ruth Benedict protested half-seriously to Margaret Mead, "He has given up science for good works. Such a waste!" She herself, while concerned and sympathetic, was not yet ready to become involved. Boas himself had written to A. M. Tozzer of Harvard in November 1933, "My time has been altogether too much distracted from scientific work on account of the crazy conditions in Germany." He had not, of course, given up scholarship. Through these years he and several students continued physical anthropological studies with immigrants and blacks over the crucial question of environment versus heredity. By 1936 he could report that studies showed that the physical development of whites and blacks in the same social circumstances followed the same course. A study of gesture behavior had shown that gestures were environmental and subject to change: both Jews and Italians lost certain striking gestures upon assimilation. Formerly those gestures had been considered biologically and racially determined. Studies of crime and mental diseases among immigrants showed both these factors subject to environment, patterns changing among immigrant groups on contact with American culture. Intelligence test results also changed in different types of environment.[5]

That same year Boas wrote that conditions for refugee scholars were "absolutely desperate." In 1935 he had written that visiting scholars could not return to Germany. Anyone away over a year was "sent to a camp, in order to learn the principles of national socialism, which I presume, means more or less of a concentration camp." Boas had good cause to be alarmed with family and friends in Germany subject to the new laws and restrictions. In 1935 a set of laws called the Nuremberg laws stripped Jews of their German citizenship, prohibited marriage between Jews and "Aryans," and made extramarital relationships between them a criminal offense. At the same time Jewish children were expelled from the elementary school system. The next year the expropriation without reimbursement of Jews' property and bank accounts began.[6]

With his retirement in 1936 Boas wrote to Carl Van Doren that he was going to "take a more active interest in Anti-Nazi activities," particularly by "counteracting similar tendencies in this country." He continued to seek ways of popularizing the scientific studies affirming the influence of environment over heredity. He corresponded with the Progressive Education Association (PEA) and other agencies about writing a book on race for school use to be written "by some popular writer under our direction," and also about preparing a film for spreading knowledge about race. In

1937 Boas reaffirmed his goals. For the last three years, he wrote, he had been working to counteract anti-Semitic propaganda in the United States and had conducted scientific studies on the general problem of race prejudice. But the scientific work "intended to undermine the pseudo-scientific basis of race prejudice is not enough." He considered it absolutely essential "to popularize the results and also to attack the attitude on an emotional basis." He had three plans in mind: "preparation of a small book written in very simple terms intended for school use"; the creation of an educational film for school and college use; and the shooting of a popular film to be shown in movie houses, preferably a biography, possibly of Dr. Paul Ehrlich, the discoverer of Salvarsan for treatment of venereal disease, to show how absurd race prejudice was through the life of one person.[7]

Meanwhile Benedict was slowly being drawn into various activist projects. She had begun in her classes an exercise asking students to pick out the Jews and non-Jews, using their inaccuracies to start discussion on race. In 1936 she became a member of the Progressive Education Association's newly formed Commission on Intercultural Education. This organization was founded to stress the positive points of racial differences and to combat racism and anti-Semitism. She gave a lot of time to the commission and in 1938 became a member of the PEA Advisory Board and chair of the commission. That same year she also became a member of the PEA Committee on Human Relations. But her involvement dramatically increased after 1936. This was the year Stanley Benedict died of a heart attack. Ruth and Stanley had separated but never divorced, and after the separation she continued to use him as a cover for her private life, implying in public that she and Stanley were still together. He, in turn, never repudiated her and left her a trust fund in his will. Little exists concerning her feelings about his death. Her pocket engagement book reads: Monday, December 21, 1936—"Stanley died—"; December 23,—"News of S's death"; December 30—"AM—to S's grave; PM—lecture to Gestalt Psych; To N.Y." There is also a poem, "A Woman to Her Dead Husband," which reveals regret that the speaker cannot remember her husband at his best, but only at his harshest. It is possible that Stanley's death freed Ruth from concern that what she did would affect his reputation as well, a concern she had had when they were living together. The Spanish Civil War also began in 1936, shocking Americans with its violence and brutality. "You may affix my signature to the Open Letter on Culture and Democracy in Spain," she wrote Boas in the spring of 1937, and her name was listed as a member of the Columbia University Faculty Committee for Aid to the Spanish People, along with Boas, John Dewey, Mark Van Doren, Robert Lynd, and twenty-nine others. She and two others on the committee sent out a letter asking for contributions to send an ambulance to Spain from Columbia University. Out of the effort for Spain a more comprehensive organization came into being in December 1937, the University Federation for Democracy and Intellectual Freedom, with Nobel-prize-winning chemist Harold Urey as chair and Ruth Benedict as secretary and head of the Membership Committee. Boas became chair of the organization's Committee on Intellectual Freedom. In a letter addressed to the faculty of Columbia University as secretary of the federation, Benedict urged them to join the organization. "Now more than ever," she wrote, "in view of the fascist threat to world peace and culture, it is imperative that we join in defense of democracy." Within a few months of its founding the University Federation had enrolled four hundred members among students and faculty, had drawn ten other organizations into affiliation, and had become the largest organization on campus.[8]

At the same time she was getting involved with the federation Benedict became treasurer of the newly formed Committee for Austrian Relief with Boas as chair. The winter of 1938–1939 also found her involved as a member of the Executive Committee for the Conference (later National Council) on Pan-American Democracy, which was organized by a former student, David Efron, and of which Boas was the honorary chair. By 1938 sporadic violence against Jews had become general in Germany, culminating November 10 of that year in the night of organized violence against Jews later called Krystallnacht and the farcical edict following that made Jews responsible for all damage and fined them one billion marks. That same year Mussolini in Italy announced a special Aryan race policy like that of Nazi Germany.[9]

For the next few years Benedict's activism took many different turns. As an officer of the University Federation for Democracy and Intellectual Freedom she participated in the planning of the variety of activities carried out. She helped organize the gathering of signatures for a published condemnation of Nazi science and defense of democratic principles in a Manifesto on Freedom of Science, published December 11, 1938, with 1,284 signatures, Benedict's among them. The manifesto was widely reported in the media, including a story in *Time* magazine. She spent time and effort obtaining scholarships in colleges and universities across the country for refugee students, and the federation obtained over seventy scholarships filled by a mixture of Protestant, Catholic, and Jewish students, most from Germany and Austria. She took positions on public issues. On April 22, 1938, she and others sent a letter protesting a suggestion in the American Education Association magazine *Signpost* that teachers spy on one another and report "radicals" to their superiors. Another time she became one of the signers of a telegram to President Roosevelt asking him to rescind the Neutrality Law in Spain's case, pressing for the lifting of the embargo on supplies to the Loyalist government. The federation also continued the work of the Faculty Committee for Aid to the Spanish People by sending medical supplies to Loyalist Spain. Benedict helped plan a mass demonstration across the United States in support of democracy and intellectual freedom through the coordination of rallies held on Lincoln's Birthday in 1939 at various places around the country, especially in New York. That day the leaders of the federation and others working with them founded the American Committee for Democracy and Intellectual Freedom, replacing the University Federation with a national organization meant to rally scientists and educators to "active participation in the struggle to preserve and extend our democratic institutions"; to protect and strengthen democracy and intellectual freedom; to fight propaganda inflaming racial and religious prejudice; and to make schools "fortresses of democracy." Eventually the organization numbered over eleven thousand members nationwide.[10]

That spring Benedict lent the prestige of her name to sponsoring an exhibition of Spanish children's drawings and agreed to sponsor a Student Assembly for Human Rights. The American Committee for Democracy and Intellectual Freedom program included, besides the Lincoln's Birthday demonstration, the gathering of more signatures for a Manifesto of Educators, published April 4, 1939, with 2,535 signatures; the preparation of a radio series of half-hour shows called "Give Me Liberty"; opposition to legislation in the New York legislature potentially restricting freedom of speech; the publication of the pamphlet "Can You Name Them?" on racial and ethnic discrimination in school textbooks and the beginning of a campaign to change this. Finally there were plans for National Rediscovery Week, centered around Columbus Day, October 8–14, for rediscovering the roots of democracy, again calling for the organization of meetings around the country and a massive celebration on the World's Fair grounds with much media coverage. Besides her work on the Executive Committee of the American Committee for Democracy and Intellectual Freedom, Benedict continued to work on the Executive Committee of the National Council for Pan-American Democracy and became a member of the Educational Advisory Committee of the Council against Intolerance in America, working on a high school manual on mutual tolerance and democracy. She also joined the Descendants of the American Revolution, a liberal organization formed to counteract the influence of the conservative Daughters of the American Revolution (DAR) which seemed to promise to use the prestige of America's aristocracy, the Anglo-Saxon descendants of Revolutionary heroes and *Mayflower* pioneers, to work effectively for better race relations.[11]

There had been rumblings of concern over Communism throughout the 1930's. Boas fumed over an *Educational Signpost* article in 1938 which equated "every progressive movement with communism" and identified "every liberal opinion with ill-understood communism." In May 1939, Boas wrote, "Up to this time nobody has accused us [probably the American Committee] of 'red' inclinations," but he saw it as a coming danger. He saw in America "fear of radicalism expressed with increasing vehemence." In 1938 reactionary Congressman Martin Dies, Jr. (D-Texas) engineered the setting up of the House Un-American Activities Committee, with himself as head, to investigate "un-American propaganda" in the United States as well as all other related issues. He began what amounted to a witch hunt, accusing liberal and radical organizations of being Communist-influenced or Communist-dominated, basically using the committee as a forum against the New Deal. Boas joked to Ruth Benedict in the summer of 1939 that since he had received birthday greetings from a number of CIO people "I suppose I am now without a doubt a 'fellow traveller' and may be called before the Dies Committee." He added that he had seen by accident a letter that had called him a Communist "because at a meeting I attended President Roosevelt's position was supported."[12]

Boas was not a Communist and neither was Benedict. Boas *was* a socialist and did not see Communism as the bugbear mainstream America regarded it as. He saw Russia as "the greatest experiment that has ever been made in Social Science with a high ideal in view," and that ideal was "equal rights for every member of humanity." He told a *Pravda* interviewer in 1932, "Humanity can only learn from what you are doing." At the same time he condemned as "intolerable" any condition where "any kind of opinion is held as a dogma . . . whether it is due to capitalism or to communism." In 1936 he declined an invitation to a Communist luncheon, saying, "While I agree with the aims of the Party I cannot agree with their methods." While appreciative of the Russian ideal, he recognized, as he wrote in 1939, that the methods of Russia and the Fascist states had "much in common . . . free expression of opinion is ruthlessly suppressed." He continued, "Intellectual freedom, which I value as one of the highest goods, is alien to countries in which opinion must conform to prescribed tenets, be they Communist or Nazi."[13]

The suppression of intellectual freedom was what he feared most would happen in the United States, and the Dies Committee was its harbinger. His own position during these years is summed up in a statement he made in 1938: "I am condemning fascism, supporting socialism, and am absolutely opposed to any kind of prejudice against races or classes." He was also "willing to discuss matters with extremists from either side." He restated his position in 1940: "I dislike tyranny of any party no matter whether they are reactionaries or Communists." But, he went on, there was no prospect that the Communists would ever be the majority in America, and if it ever happened it would take such a long time that their policies would have changed to conform with American culture. "If therefore, at the present time we can agree in regard to a certain specific subject there is no reason why we should bring other considerations into the situation." Esther Goldfrank reports him as saying during that same period, "I will go along with anyone who is fighting for what I am fighting for." Mead wrote that Boas "believed that he would be able to spot a Communist at once by his lack of intellectual independence which, he felt sure, would show through everything." If people were intellectually independent and affirmed in word and action the ideals of intellectual freedom and civil liberty he espoused, Boas did not particularly care whether they called themselves Communists. He shrugged off attacks on himself and organizations to which he belonged, secure in his own intellectual integrity of purpose.[14]

Benedict also did not care if some of the people she worked with in activist organizations espoused Communist principles. She didn't see the need to take this seriously. As Mead wrote, if she had had a good friend who became a Communist she would have "shrugged her shoulders" and accepted it. Nor were they concerned with the splits among those on the left. Mead wrote that in "battles against race hatred, discrimination, and limitations of freedom of speech and of the press," Benedict and Boas "marched ahead," hardly looking twice at "those who were willing to let a good cause go by default if by chance the 'Stalinists' had also espoused it." Communism was the radicalism of choice among the young in the 1930's. The Columbia Anthropology Department was not immune, so some students quietly became members of a Communist cell. Many of the activists in the anti-Hitler fight were motivated by Communist principles. In 1939, Moses Finkelstein (later Finley), a Ph.D. candidate in history, took over as secretary of the newly created American Committee for Democracy and Intellectual Freedom, although Benedict remained on the Executive Board. In 1938, Finkelstein had held Marxist study group meetings at his apartment, and there were certainly others in the organization with similar Marxist leanings.[15]

In the fall of 1939, several organizations Boas and Benedict belonged to began to be attacked as Communist infiltrated or dominated "fronts." The American Committee for Democracy and Intellectual Freedom was attacked in the *Guild Teacher* in an article that coupled some committee names with the Communist newspaper the *Daily Worker*. On April 8, 1940, Walter Winchell in his column "On Broadway" in the *New York Daily Mirror* said that at a meeting of Communists scheduled that week in Washington, D.C., "The principal commy will be Franz D. Boas, a Columbia University professor." That same month, a report entitled "Stalinist Outposts in the United States," put out by John Dewey and Sidney Hook's Committee on Cultural Freedom, listed the University Federation for Democracy and Intellectual Freedom as under "Outright Communist Party Control"; the Council for Pan-American Democracy as "Under Communist Influence (With Non-Communists Present)"; and the Descendants of the American Revolution as an organization "in Close Collaboration with the Communist Party." This report, put out by an anti-Stalinist committee on the liberal side, espoused intellectual freedom, but condemned Russia's totalitarian practices and saw Stalinists as much the enemy as Nazis. It attacked Boas' and Benedict's public credibility among liberals, as the Dies Committee attacked the credibility of their organizations with the general public. In a report to Congress in 1942 the Dies Committee named the American Committee for Democracy and Intellectual Freedom, the Council for Pan-American Democracy, and the Descendants of the American Revolution as Communist Party fronts, each "nothing more or less than a bold advocate of treason." By that time, however, Benedict had resigned from the Descendants of the American Revolution because their original activist promise concerning race remained unfulfilled and because she disagreed with their policy toward lend-lease. By then too the American Committee had come to the end of its usefulness and that summer merged with another group, at which point Benedict left the organization.[16]

But all these tensions and attacks seemed like distant rumbles of thunder to Benedict in the summer of 1939 as she prepared to go on sabbatical after completion of a student group field trip to the Blackfoot and the Blood in the American Northwest and Canada. That spring Modern Age Publishers had approached her to do a popular book on race. She was ambivalent, since it was not her area of expertise. She was not a physical anthropologist and had not done research on race questions herself. She also felt that it was useless to fight racial prejudice, an emotional state of mind, with scientific accuracy, because those prejudiced paid no attention. But Louis P. Birk, an editor at Modern Age, replied that, without confronting the intolerant directly, "we could, I think, lay a groundwork of sound information, interestingly written, which would serve as an obstacle to the spread of racial intolerance." [17] The Modern Age ideal was to reach intelligent but not well-informed readers with low-cost books and raise their consciousness concerning important issues like race. Modern Age originally promised to publish her book in a fifty-cent edition, which meant it would reach a large and wide-based audience. Benedict was the perfect author for such a book because of her Anglo-Saxon background, her Revolutionary War ancestors, her descent from the Pilgrims on the *Mayflower*. These, combined with her reputation as a scientist and an anthropologist, gave her words an authority few other writers could command. Benedict, knowing Boas' views on the importance of popularization, could not pass up this opportunity that had dropped into her lap. She arranged to take a sabbatical for the year 1939–1940 and originally planned to visit friends in England and Paris and to write the book while overseas.

Benedict wrote Boas from the field that she approved "enormously" of the two brochures on race put out by the committee. "I feel very far out of the world," she concluded on August 16, 1939, "but at least I know no world conflagration has flared up yet." But the outbreak of war two weeks later blocked her plans to spend her sabbatical abroad, so she decided to visit her family in California. From California in September she wrote Boas, "I am writing the Race book now. It goes pretty well, and I take great comfort in knowing that you will read it and criticize it before anyone else sees it." She did not find the book exciting to write. She was not working with her own ideas, but sifting and simplifying the ideas of others. The book was not on the "cutting edge" of knowledge, not an original creative contribution to scholarship, but instead reiterated ideas that had become clichés in anthropology by 1939, although they remained fresh and startling to the largely uninformed general public she was trying to reach. What creativity the book involved came in organizing the material and making it forceful and understandable. To Boas she wrote, "I get bored with it but it's been interesting in spots even though as you know it's a field where all my knowledge is second-hand." Again she wrote him, "I wish I were sure it was worth it to have written this kind of a book. But all one can do is try." She saw her book basically as one that could be used in high schools and in discussion groups in churches and clubs.[18]

The book was a summary of information clearly and stylishly presented, divided into two sections. The first, "Race," discussed the facts of race as science had disclosed them; the second, "Racism," addressed the mythical side of the race issue, which made racial ideas "like a religion" or "a dogma," an important way, she wrote, "of separating the sheep from the goats," the inferior from the superior. She defined race as based on inherited traits. Early in the book she introduced the concept of culture as learned behavior and differentiated heredity from culture, stressing the superiority of culture. A race may die out, but a culture lives on; different races come together to create cultures and those of one race have not all had the same culture, or even the same degree of culture, she wrote. She attacked physical racism, the Aryan myth of the blond, blue-eyed Teutonic race, by discussing human physical properties and stressing the great overlap and ambiguity even in so seemingly clear a differentiation as skin color. Neither blond hair nor blue eyes were the sign of a whole ethnic group, and dark eyes were common to all races, she said. Hair types crossed color lines, with dark Asiatic Indians having smooth, wavy hair. Thus she went through shape of nose, stature, cephalic index, and blood groups, showing the broad range of variation of each feature within a race, individuals having features from one end of the spectrum to the other. She showed that scientifically there were no "pure" races; the aeons-long migrations of peoples had seen to that. She stressed that race mixture was not evil but natural and even positive; that when mixed children were inferior it was due to social discrimination, not physical degeneracy.[19]

One cannot inherit traits from a race, she wrote, only from one's family line. So-called racial traits were learned behavior. She went through the scientific evidence and showed that differences in keenness of sight, for example, occurred through training and environment. On the question of mental superiority, she gave the example of the World War I I.Q. tests, which showed that some whites from the South scored lower than some blacks from the North, and that results of the tests varied by educational opportunity, not innate intelligence. As for the argument that one race was historically destined to lead the rest, she talked of past cultures that had cycled up and then down again.

She then turned to the non-rational side of the race issue, the ideas based on belief and not fact and which all the facts in the world had no power to touch in the minds of believers. This was *racism,* a doctrine based at heart on ethnocentrism, the desire of humans to be the center of the universe. She called racism "a pretentious way of saying that 'I' belong to the Best People . . . 'I belong to the Elect.'" This ethnocentrism, she wrote, first expressed itself among primitive tribes as cultural superiority—"My culture is better than yours"[20]—and tribes designated themselves as human and non-members of the tribe as not human. In Western Civilization superiority expressed itself historically chiefly through religion, non-Christians being regarded as pagans and therefore inferior. By the beginning of the nineteenth century, she wrote, the religious argument had worn thin and a new theory of superiority became necessary. Race became the basis of this new theory of superiority, which by the beginning of the twentieth century had become the doctrine of the superiority of nations as "races."

Here the book became an expression of a broadly encompassing social vision, one that had been implicit in *Patterns of Culture* but was here straightforwardly expressed in clear and simple language. To understand race conflict, she wrote, people needed to understand the roots behind the *conflict* before information about race, for the battleground shifted, but the underlying battle went on. The more one studied European anti-Semitism, the more it appeared that the real source of conflict was "unequal citizenship rights." The cure for anti-Semitism and all minority conflicts, she wrote, was "the extension to all men of full citizenship rights and of full opportunity to make good in any field." For Negroes in America the same was true. The necessary objective in any program concerning blacks, she wrote, was the "ultimate elimination of legal, educational, economic, and social discriminations."[21]

Countries and groups within countries had succeeded in advancing civilization when they had optimum social conditions such as economic sufficiency, opportunity to work, freedom of opinion, and equal civil liberties. When these conditions faltered, "the torch soon fell from their hands." She continued, "If we are serious in our hopes for the human race, we will devote ourselves to providing those social conditions under which they can be realized." Education alone would not do the job. "Social engineering" was necessary, and the government needed to take on increased responsibility for it. Social conditions were not "inescapable facts of nature." There was "no historical reason for fearing the increased role of the state," she wrote, out of the experience of the New Deal, for the past few years had shown that national action decreased economic discrimination and protected civil liberties. Concerning conflict, history and anthropology studies had shown that there existed two primary group codes of ethics: that of the "in-group," an open-handed giving and sharing along with condemnation of members who hurt others within the group; and that of the "out-group," non-members or strangers, outside human consideration. "Death at sight, torture, and the exaltation of robbery" were applied to them. "In-group mutual support" was as native to the human race as "out-group hostility." But it only developed as "all members share in their tribal enterprises and do actually profit from one another's activities." When there was competition for food, when the legal power favored one group over another, when the religious power did the same, persecution developed. Such persecution had often been used unscrupulously by those in power to gain wealth or justify government policies. "Racist doctrines are invoked for political ends" by those who travesty science for authority. "The slogan of 'science' will sell most things today," she wrote, "and it sells persecution as easily as it sells rouge." The way to end persecution and conflict was to work toward ending minority discrimination, but also to help the majority to live decently. Poor whites needed help as much as poor blacks. "Whatever reduces conflict, curtails irresponsible power, and allows people to obtain a decent livelihood will reduce race conflict," she wrote. "Nothing less will." She projected the vision of society becoming one vast "in-group," mutually supportive, sharing, and respectful of one another through the gradual lessening and final disappearance of "out-groups," as social engineering permitted their incorporation into the inner circle. All of this would not be easy. Change produced difficulties and dislocation. "But if we know the direction in which we must move, we can resolve to pay the necessary costs of change." She knew these costs from her own activist experiences, but she and Boas had known the direction in which they had to move, regardless of charges of treason or political naïveté.[22]

Race was widely reviewed. The reviews called it a "most useful book," "an admirable book," "a tract for the times." Professor Bruno Lasker, who had published studies on children and race prejudice, wrote Modern Age that "this is *the* popular book about race if we ever hope to get one," and spent the rest of the letter trying to convince them to put it out in a fifty-cent edition to reach more people rather than sell it for $2.50 as they finally planned. Karen Horney wrote to Benedict calling *Race* a "courageous book," saying she wished everyone in the United States would read it. Hortense Powdermaker, reviewing *Race* for the *American Anthropologist,* praised its "point of view," which she thought should be "shouted from the roof tops." But she doubted the book would be popular, i.e., reach the lowest-common-denominator audience it was supposedly targeted for. It had no pictures, no drama, no personal experiences, limited emotional appeal, and no concrete program for the future. It made no use of any of the "well known devices for selling an idea to large groups of people." This was advice Benedict took to heart in the following years.[23]

On the whole reviewers ignored her social vision and concentrated on her recounting of the facts of race and racism. But Benedict believed in the power of ideas. When it came to cultural change, she wrote a student in 1944, "ideology isn't passive." It was the vision that had made it important for her to write the book, not the facts. Her book was a balanced study of the rational and the irrational, the logical and the emotional bases of the race issue, but she knew that the only way to fight a belief was to replace it with another belief; the only way to uproot a value was to root in its place another value, giving a new direction to social activity. This was her purpose in *Race*. It was a purpose and a vision with which she tried to reach people on the most basic level, which she developed in ever more "popular" ways until her death.[24]

In 1941, in collaboration with a high school teacher, Mildred Ellis, she wrote a Resource Unit for teachers sponsored by the National Association of Secondary School Principals and the National Council for the Social Sciences entitled *Race and Cultural Relations: America's Answer to the Myth of a Master Race*. She repeated the basic arguments of *Race* concerning race and racism but became much more specific on actual racial prejudice in the United States and what needed to be done. She frankly said that blacks had the least attractive and poorest-paid jobs, were paid less than whites for the same work, were last hired, first fired. They were usually excluded from professional associations and trade unions, denied equal opportunity with whites, and segregated to live in less desirable districts. They were often denied access to cultural facilities, discriminated against in religion and political activity, and "forced to accept humiliating segregation" in transportation and restaurants. She used statistics to show that all this was true. Orientals, she continued, faced the same kind of discrimination, but to a lesser degree. However, they also faced restrictive immigration laws. The third form of race prejudice in the United States, she wrote, was anti-Semitism, "generally unofficial, covert rather than overt," which included such things as not hiring Jews; excluding them from fashionable resorts, hotels, social clubs, and residential districts; setting educational quotas; name-calling, threats, and put-downs.[25]

She also became more specific on the program needed to defuse race prejudice. It involved using America's "full manpower for the common benefit," raising housing and labor standards above the "needlessly low standards" in many parts of the country, "enforcing the practice of social responsibility on industry," raising health standards, providing equal educational advantages for all, and extending civil liberties. In a "working democracy" people of all ethnic groups recognized "mutual interdependence with their fellows—and the need and desirability of mutual support." In this type of society, she wrote, there was "an awareness of shared advantages and common benefit created and participated in by all." In a working democracy "a rapidly dwindling chorus of racists would sing its songs of bitterness and hate to an empty house." The draft of the unit was done by the spring of 1941, mimeographed and tested in workshops with teachers during the summer, revised, and was ready for general distribution by May 1942. Paul E. Elicker of the National Association of Secondary School Principals called it a "significant contribution to secondary education."[26]

In 1943, seeking an even broader audience, Ruth Benedict became part of a committee of Columbia professors to write a Public Affairs Pamphlet on race. The other committee members were L. C. Dunn, of zoology; Otto Klineberg, of psychology; and Marion Smith and Gene Weltfish from anthropology. The Public Affairs Committee had been founded in 1936 as a nonprofit organization to make "the results of research on economic and social problems" available in a summarized, inexpensive way, for the broadest possible audience of the American public. The committee thus hoped "to aid in the understanding and development of American policy," although the organization stated that it did not have a policy of its own to promote. *The Races of Mankind* was the eighty-fifth pamphlet put out by the committee and cost ten cents. It was written in conversational rather than scholarly style, with cartoon pictures scattered throughout. The pamphlet, according to legend, was written over one intensive weekend in Washington, D.C., by Gene Weltfish and Ruth Benedict. It repeated the basic information about race and racism, emphasizing the fact that "the whole world has been made one neighborhood . . . Our neighbors now are peoples of all the races of the earth." Since America was at war, winning on the racial front was as important as winning on the production front or the inflation front. Benedict and Weltfish stressed that in spite of seeming physical differences, all humans formed one community—"In their bodies is the record of their brotherhood"— adding the new fact that skin color was caused by chemicals in the skin and even Caucasians had carotene, which made skin yellow, and melanin, which made skin dark. It was just a matter of how much you had of each that determined skin color. They pointed out that Jewishness was not a race but a religion—some blacks and Asians were also Jews. They stressed the superiority of culture over heredity in shaping people. Race prejudice, they stated, was caused by fear because when afraid people picked out scapegoats to blame their fears on. Ending underlying fear was the way to eliminate race prejudice. This would occur when nations had guarantees of collective security, when the laws upheld equal citizenship rights, when labor decisions gave workers security and self-respect in their jobs and farmers had arrangements that secured them from losing their farms to banks. They stressed the necessity of accepting "*differences*" and not treating them as "*inferiorities*." "Our country would be poorer in every phase of its culture," they wrote, "if different cultures had not come together here, sharing and learning the special contributions each had to offer." They ended on a positive note, naming organizations working for better race relations and the work of the government and individuals in that direction.[27]

Races of Mankind had originally been written to be distributed in USO centers and copies had been ordered by the Army for use by leaders of orientation courses. It became a *cause célèbre* when the chair of the House Military Affairs Committee, Congressman Andrew J. May, prohibited its distribution in the Army. May was from Kentucky, and Kentucky was one of three Southern states specifically cited in the pamphlet from the Army World War I intelligence tests to show that Northern blacks had scored higher than Southern whites. Southern whites in Kentucky had median test scores of 41.50; Northern blacks outscored them with median scores of 45.02 in New York, 47.35 in Illinois, and 49.50 in Ohio. The suppression of the pamphlet caused a furor and brought protests from liberals of every stamp. One person wrote Benedict that after May's attack on the pamphlet "people around my office began calling for it from our Bureau library . . . One fighting old liberal ordered ten copies for distribution to his friends." Organizations began buying them up for distribution to their members and especially for distribution in the South. Newspapers around the country carried the story. This one public act of suppression by a powerful bigot did more for the distribution of knowledge about racism than any amount of positive publicity could have. The Public Affairs Committee sold almost a million copies of *Races of Mankind* over the next ten years. The pamphlet was later translated into French, German, and Japanese and distributed in those countries. *True*

Comics did a version of it called "There Are No Master Races." The United Auto Workers of the CIO sponsored an educational cartoon film based on *Races* called *The Brotherhood of Man.*[28]

Its final metamorphosis was into a children's book, *In Henry's Backyard*, by Ruth Benedict and Gene Weltfish, published in 1948. The text of *Races* was adapted for the children's book by Weltfish, Benedict, and Violet Edwards, director of education of the Public Affairs Committee. Weltfish and Edwards did the actual writing while Benedict acted as advisor and approver, but it is her vision that permeates this little book. Henry wakes up one morning and finds the whole world fitted into his backyard and all sorts of people as his neighbors. His first reaction is open curiosity, then his "Green Devil, who lived inside him," makes him suspicious of all the differences. The same thing happens to all his new neighbors too and fighting starts. Then Henry starts thinking and asking questions about skin color. He goes through the old arguments for white superiority and has them refuted one by one, with the stress on people's samenesses, not differences. He discovers that all desire love and a home, a family, and the right to worship their own way. "Sensible people stop kicking *each other* around and apply their boots to the seats of the ugly Green Devils of prejudice, stupidity, hate." People hate and fight each other, the book continues, for quite different reasons than they think, reasons lying deep within themselves. They included fears that caused people to do foolish things: fears from an unhappy childhood, or of loss of jobs or savings, fears of sickness, age, loss of status. "And when people have these fears they are jumpy . . . and suspicious . . . and too ready to take it out on the other fellow . . . especially a *different* kind of fellow." Henry finally concludes, "we're not *born* haters. Our Green Devils of prejudice and fear grow inside us . . . because we are worried and afraid . . ." To get rid of worries, the book goes on, people need to see that every child born has good health care and education and the chance to work at jobs of all kinds. "If we adopt this scientific way of looking at things," the book ends, "we can rid ourselves of useless anxieties and fears, and all get together to contribute to the coming of a better world."[29]

The writing of *In Henry's Backyard* simplified Benedict's social vision and suggested how the personal had become for her the social. Her "Blue Devils" of depression became translated into "Green Devils" of prejudice. The book shows an exploration of inner fears as causes for action but uses these fears as an alternative scapegoat instead of minority peoples. The problem of racism was internal within themselves and not external in the looks or actions of other people, the book told its readers. Benedict also identified the program for equal rights for all with the moral authority of science, a force to conjure with in the twentieth century.

Her writings on race gave Benedict an opportunity to explore her own situation and turn her understanding of self outward toward society. Her exploration of the race issue gave her a forum to call for an end to every form of prejudice, and she alone knew that she was also part of an extremely oppressed group. In ways she explored her own social oppression in her study of race. She wrote of situations harmless in themselves being turned into "social evil[s]." Racial intermarriage was such a social evil—but she might just as well have been thinking about Lesbian cohabiting when she wrote that even sensible people grieved over such alliances, adding "we must live in the world as it is." From her point of view, homosexuality had been artificially turned into a social evil, but with the world as it was she could only chip away at the general concept of "social evil," showing that it did not have to exist, rather than defend homosexuality outright. Her call for the ending of "unequal citizenship rights" for all groups and their chance for equal opportunity in all fields strengthened the hope of extending tolerance to homosexuals as well. She wrote, "To be able to live a decent life and be respected for it, without being subjected to a blanket damnation that one's personal life cannot remove, is a human right." If it were granted it would have "immense social repercussions." She wrote this ostensibly about blacks, but it could also refer to her own life.[30]

Her 1939 sabbatical and the publication of *Race* marked Benedict's commitment to a public position on race, her movement into the forefront as a perceived expert on race, an authority with the rights of critic and commentator. It was a commitment she honored until her death in 1948. But when Benedict made a list of those to whom she wanted complimentary copies sent, Natalie Raymond's name was not among them. Her sabbatical also marked an end to a personal chapter in her life, and a new beginning. In 1937 in her will Benedict left Shattuck Farm and her personal property to Nat upon her death. Yet by that time there must have already been rumblings of discontent, coming out in the open and to a head in the summer of 1938. Benedict wrote that she took a "gambler's chance" that summer, giving Nat Raymond the money to research a traveler's guidebook of Guatemala. "It was the first thing in years that she had wanted to undertake," and so far she seemed to be very businesslike about it, Benedict wrote, taking great care over assembling information. "Of course I'm banking on what putting some one job through might possibly do for her; I am keeping my fingers crossed," Benedict wrote. She went to Guatemala that summer and spent five weeks driving around with Nat, seeing the land and the people. Raymond stayed there through the summer and fall and planned to be back in New York for the winter, but apparently that summer together signaled the end of their relationship. "What of Natalie?" a friend wrote in March 1939. "Is she still very secretive about her whereabouts, or her plans, if she has any?" [31]

The strain of breaking up the relationship, Buell Quain's suicide, and the stress of the Blackfoot field trip caught up with Benedict in the fall, and she lay very sick with pleurisy for awhile. But it was during this time when she was lowest that life started looking up again. While visiting with her sister's family in Pasadena she began a relationship with another woman that lasted until her death. Entries in her Engagement Book catalog events:

Sept. 17, 1939—To Bradleys with Val
Sept. 19, 1939—Val to dinner
Sept. 21, 1939—Val's invitation to stay with her
Sept. 22, 1939—*Cancelled NY trip.*

Ruth Valentine, known as "Val" to her friends, was a psychologist. She had gotten her Ph.D. in psychology at the University of California at Berkeley under behavioral experimentalist Edward C. Tolman, studying rats in mazes, but she practiced as a clinical psychologist. That fall Ruth moved out of her sister's house and into Val's, ostensibly for the peace and quiet in which to work. There she stayed as long as she could, not even returning to New York for the birth of Margaret Mead's baby, although she did send handmade booties. Sometime in the early 1940's Val decided to live with Benedict in New York. [32]

13

The War Years

LONG BEFORE AMERICA actually entered World War II, the war influenced the course of Benedict's life and thought. It intensified her activism; it subtly influenced the direction of her scholarly work; and it plunged her overtly into applied anthropology, a direction that dominated the remaining years of her life.

The war began for Europeans with the German blitzkrieg attack on Poland September 1, 1939. For Americans active war did not begin until almost two years later. In America these years of impending war sharpened an already ongoing examination of the American way of life. People asked themselves what in American life was worth fighting and dying for and, concomitantly, what was worth fighting to change. When Benedict returned from California in the spring of 1940, she came prepared to make an increasing commitment against racism in all its forms, whether it affected Jews, blacks, or Asiatics. Neither by temperament nor by inclination a public speaker, she spoke wherever and whenever she could find a forum. "America's Racial Myths" became a lecture in Iowa; "A Message" about race the topic of a talk to Alpha Kappa Alpha sorority members; "Must We Divide on Race Lines?" a 1942 talk at Vassar. She wrote articles with titles ranging from "The Facts about Race" to "If I Were a Negro" and "We Can't Afford Race Prejudice."[1]

She also came back to New York prepared to uphold the principle of academic freedom that war traditionally undermined. At the start of the 1940–1941 school year Columbia President Nicholas Murray Butler called a special meeting of the faculty to tighten academic freedom of speech. He told them that when an individual's position on an issue clashed with that of the university, that individual should leave the university. He called his position "before and above academic freedom." Students and faculty interpreted Butler's speech as a warning to accept his policy on Columbia's position on the war or get out. Benedict and seven other American Committee for Democracy and Intellectual Freedom members from the faculty immediately wrote an open letter to Butler, publicly confronting him over the issue and sending a copy to the *New York Times*. As a result Butler had to back down and reaffirm the priority of academic freedom. But the fact of war did not only precipitate action; it also caused serious thought.[2]

When she had gone to California in 1939, Benedict had had time to reflect on war and discuss the possibility of war with her family. The result was an article called "The Natural History of War." In an earlier article written in the 1920's she had compared war to cannibalism in a vein of Swiftian satire. She had emphasized the absurdity of war as a method of satisfying human needs. This second article was a more searching and philosophical venture. Implicit in the 1939 article was the expectation that the United States would soon be involved. Benedict, although she detested war, was not a total pacifist. War, she wrote in the *New Republic* in September 1941, was "a last resort, kept in reserve with full knowledge that war in itself never decides crucial issues." But she believed firmly in the value of peace over war. In this article she advocated allowing America's leaders a free hand to win a "pre-war 'peace'" that would make war unnecessary. In 1939 "The Natural History of War," while it developed her thoughts on war, much more overwhelmingly emphasized her ideas on peace, especially the components necessary for a lasting and realistic peace.[3]

She strongly affirmed war as cultural and not an innate biological instinct or drive of human nature. She accepted war as a social institution which, like murder, had taken many different forms through time and varying cultures. She did not mince words. She defined war as "homicide in a blaze of glory," unlike murder, "homicide with penalties." Where no homicide double standard existed, there was no concept of war. War developed, she wrote, when tribes came in contact with other tribes and the idea of in-groups and out-groups formed. Homicide within the tribe or in-group became murder; homicide toward the out-group, to the benefit of the in-group, was glorified. War could exist in socially healthy societies in a "socially nonlethal" way as long as they remained economically self-sufficient, i.e., both societies remained intact, as in the war raiding of North American Indian tribes where one group did not strive to conquer or subjugate another. But when tribes became mutually dependent on one another, wars became "sociologically lethal." They destroyed the societies against which they were waged while seriously damaging if not also destroying the "victors." "We wage the lethal variety of the genus

War," she wrote. Because of the interdependence of the Western nations in finance, goods, services, and intellectual pursuits, war between them had become socially mutilating. Benedict likened the nations to a man trying to cure an infection in his left leg by knifing or shooting it. Like the man, the nations could be cured only when they recognized their life blood circulated throughout the whole body and knifing one area led only to death.[4]

Some tribes in Central Australia, she wrote, had eliminated war by emphasizing their likenesses and making these likenesses a bond rather than a reason for conflict, creating "warm ties of interdependence" among differing tribes and reinforcing them by rites and observances. Other tribes in Melanesia, linked economically, had eliminated war through the Kula Ring in which money, goods, and traders moved in an elaborate pattern which precluded warfare. Like these tribes, a civilization that had to live as a whole had to adopt social institutions that allowed it to function as a whole. The peace had failed after World War I because nations gave lip service to international goals but did not give up nationalistic practices, did not act to create a new international reality to underlie their goals. The creation of a lasting peace meant finding ways of making the whole world an in-group in which war could not be sanctioned, but perceived and penalized as the murder it truly was. The world needed "a common government," she wrote, to end "international anarchy," to create international money, and to provide an international mechanism to deal with colonies; to provide for international rather than national defense; and to create an international trade policy, thus ending national "cutthroat policies." In this conclusion she was at one with a whole generation of intellectuals and policy-makers who, at the war's end, created the United Nations. But building new social institutions working for human good was not good enough in itself, Benedict wrote. They needed to be institutions rooted in the self-interest and not the ideals of humanity. Soon the United States might be involved in this war for reasons both idealistic and non-idealistic. This time, she wrote, let's buy something valuable with the price. True change meant adapting the "social machinery" to international social realities; it meant changing the prevailing nationalistic orientation. "If we fail," she wrote, "it is because we are not sufficiently clear in our analysis and radical in our demands."[5]

The coming war influenced the direction of Benedict's scholarship. For her next anthropological book after *Zuñi Mythology* she had planned a comparative study built on students' and colleagues' field work, work she could trust. Her work with the Cooperation and Competition study had convinced her of the value of contextual comparative studies. She intended to write a book discussing "sociological correlates of different personality developments," i.e., the connection between personality and social institutions. By the late 1930's she had selected cultures that she felt contrasted strongly and struggled to find the words to explain these differences. In the early stages she used words appropriate "over a martini but not in print," calling one group "surly," the other "nice," one anxious, the other not. She took large sheets of newsprint and wrote down all that was known about the cultures she had chosen, all the while trying to decide why they contrasted. On one side, the Zuñi, the Arapesh, the Dakota, an Eskimo group, the Northern Blackfoot were secure cultures, "high-morale" cultures as the war came closer. On the other side, the Chuckchee, the Ojibwa, the Dobu, the Kwakiutl were insecure, low-morale cultures. She kept trying all the generalizations possible to make about these cultures, comparing them on race, wealth, geography, complexity, climate, size—none of the comparisons worked. She tried to classify them as suicidal versus non-suicidal, polygamous versus monogamous, matrilineal versus patrilineal, even large houses versus small. None of the classifications worked.[6]

She looked for help in other people's work. A break seemed to come with the reading of *Explorations in Personality* (1938) by psychologist Henry A. Murray and members of the Harvard Psychological Clinic. She wrote Murray in 1940 that his book was the only one she had read that gave her the "psychological ground-work I need as an anthropologist," especially his press-need formulation which was "basic to my analysis of cultures and the behavior that occurs in them." Murray defined a press as the tendency of a situation to facilitate or obstruct the individual, "a temporal gestalt of stimuli which usually appears in the guise of a *threat of harm* or *promise of benefit*" to the individual. A press could be "nourishing, or coercing, or injuring, or chilling, or befriending, or restraining, or amusing, or belittling" to the individual. The combination of a press with a need within a person caused behavior to occur. The press led to gratification or frustration. Benedict translated Murray's idea from the individual to the cultural level. She also borrowed from psychologist Saul Rosenzweig's studies on frustration and Erich Fromm on self-respect. In her own work she began to speak of the tendency of a social institution to frustrate or benefit individuals. She divided her cultures finally on the basis of those that satisfied their individuals and those that obstructed them. She began to look at concrete behaviors within cultures in these terms. What were the social restraints on individual action, she asked, and what kinds of activities did cultures foster?[7]

In 1940, in a discussion of Jules Henry's article "Hostility in Pilaga Children," she used the question as to why some cultures displayed high interpersonal hostility and others had low hostility to outline the direction her researches were taking. The Pilaga of South America were hostile, she wrote, because their social mechanisms fostered hostility. Low interpersonal hostility occurred in cultures where the social institutions made it possible for a person "to advance the general welfare of the society at the same time and by the same act that advances his own prestige or security." Such societies made a reality of the old *laissez-faire* slogan "private advantage is public gain," she wrote. In such a society all food production benefited the whole society and was rewarded with honor and prestige, while the food was distributed throughout the community. The individual did not encounter humiliation unless lazy or criminal, and had no experience of gaining advantage at someone else's expense. The Pilaga, on the contrary, did not share food, but hoarded it. Private possession of property marked their whole society. The hungry could not rely on hospitality or reciprocal exchanges. They could "only beg, and beg shamefully." In this discussion she expanded on her idea from "The Natural History of War" that the new international government to come needed institutions rooted in self-respect to survive.[8]

Meanwhile later in the spring of 1940 the Nazis took Belgium, Luxembourg, and the Netherlands. They then struck at France. Italy attacked France from the south. By the end of June France had fallen. The war debate intensified in America. As it did, the search for methods of lasting peace intensified in Benedict's work.

In a paper written sometime in 1941–1942 she wrote of the necessity "to find the positive conditions under which desired events take place." She had read and was teaching Emile Durkheim's *The Division of Labor in Society* in which he set out the idea that as division of labor increased, there was a resulting increase in the social solidarity that bound together the units of society. Less advanced societies had "mechanical" solidarity tending to suppress individuality, while in complex societies "organic" solidarity advanced individuality. Durkheim used law as his example, saying that simpler societies had more repressive law by punishment, while complex societies used more restitutive law, to restore rather than punish. Benedict liked Durkheim's ideas but felt he overemphasized law and ignored other parts of society. She liked him not so much for his answers as for the way he raised questions. The job of social scientists, she wrote in her article, was to find "the ways and means of social cohesion—the scientific study of aspects of society which *do* correlate with social cohesion and so with minimizing individual aggression and frustration." Benedict made it her highest priority to study social institutions that made for social cohesion and those that did not.[9]

She was still planning to write her book then. In June 1940, she reported to Columbia on her plans for future research. She planned a study of North American Indians to "compare and contrast the social order in these different cultures from various points of view," a Personality and Culture study based on her students' field work. When the South American field work was complete she planned a book on South American cultures. She also wanted to write a book on religion, this time "as reflecting aggression or lack of aggression set up by the larger social forms" of various cultures. In all of these books she intended to work with comparative material "relevant to sociological and psychological theory" often itself based "too exclusively on the special instances of our own culture."[10]

Working on the book she found that there seemed to be basic differences in social structures between the groups she labeled "secure" and "insecure," "nice" and "surly." The former had comforting religions with gods or spirits having goodwill toward them. The latter had terrifying gods or spirits out to destroy or punish them. The first group used religion to benefit all the people, such as to pray for rain or good crops, health and children. Amulets or individual supernatural power were used to strengthen oneself, call spirits to cure the sick, or guard against enemies. The second group used religion to gain private profit by ruining others' crops, bringing sickness, or calling spirits to hurt others. The one side had social mechanisms to defuse and limit the impact of humiliation. The other did not, and life among these cultures contained a high level of stress from built-in humiliations. Among the Chuckchee, for example, young men had to work for their prospective fathers-in-law, were made the butt of family humor, had to sleep outside in arctic weather, and were fed scraps, all in the ordinary process of taking a wife. The secure group had "siphon" systems of economics in which wealth constantly moved through the community, never concentrated for very long. The other had "funnel" systems of economics which collected and channeled wealth toward the already rich. This was an idea Ruth Bunzel had suggested. She also found that the behaviors among her "secure" group benefited all the people and led to social cohesion while enhancing individual prestige and self-respect, but the behaviors of the "insecure" group benefited the individual at the expense of social cohesion.

She finally chose the word "synergy" to describe what she saw happening. It was an objective, value-neutral word and had its roots in both science and the humanities. The word came from medicine and theology, she wrote, where it described a "combined action," a working together of parts to produce a result greater than the sum of the parts led one to believe possible. One example might be the ability of a person to lift the weight of an automobile off a trapped person using only his or her bare hands. The stress of the moment causes nerves and muscles to combine together to act in a way that ordinarily seems impossible. The same thing occurs in alloys of metals, where combinations of certain metals produce a strength far out of proportion to the strength of the individual metals themselves. The idea of synergy took into account the irrational side of life. Synergy itself was non-logical or perhaps better, beyond logic. Why should things add up to more than they were? Yet it happened, and it seemed to occur in an orderly way, although it was not well understood. Benedict set up her study as one of opposites, yet synergy itself had the potential to transcend polarities, to create a synthesis beyond the potentialities of its parts.[11]

Benedict revealed her theory of synergy publicly in spring 1941, while delivering the Anna Shaw Lectures at Bryn Mawr, in themselves a signal honor for her. The invited Anna Shaw Lecturer taught a six-week seminar while delivering one public lecture per week. The lectures were well received. A student involved in the graduate seminar wrote Margaret Mead that Benedict was "flourishing" at Bryn Mawr and had given a very good lecture on the individual and the social order. "She is beginning to bring a little relevance into our seminar, thereby breaking with tradition." The concept of synergy, although developed out of Benedict's Culture and Personality interests in the 1930's, was subtly shaped by the climate of impending war into an answer to the problem of creating a realistic and lasting peace among the nations of humankind.[12]

Cultures with high synergy have a social structure that reinforces the individual and leads to social cohesion greater than the sum of the individuals, because when the individual gains, society also gains. Cultures with low synergy have social structures that frustrate the individual's needs and desires, where the individual gains advantages only at the expense of others, discouraging social solidarity. A society with high synergy teaches individuals to expect rewards from cooperating with people, not competing against them. High synergy means a low aggression level in society. Benedict wrote, "Societies where nonaggression is conspicuous have social orders in which the individual by the same act and at the same time serves his own advantage and that of the group." This lack of aggression occurs "not because people are unselfish and put social obligations above personal desires, but because social arrangements make these two identical." [13]

Implicit in her concept of synergy was the idea that social science needed to direct its energy into discovering the social structures necessary to create high synergy and embodying them into the new international federation after the war. The coming international government needed to include mechanisms that did not frustrate individual nations' needs and desires, but made their satisfaction a source of greater gain for the whole international group. It needed mechanisms that rewarded nations for cooperating and not for competing. Whether an activity or a rule led to high or low synergy between nations could serve as a necessary, effective guideline for building the actual structure of a working, international United Nations, and creating realistic, lasting peace. The social cohesion thus created meant all peoples could eventually become one huge ingroup in which the folly of war would be outlawed. She saw the future United Nations ultimately as an instrument of synergy.

Ideas implicit in synergy also helped Benedict to answer for herself the question of values confronting educated people in the face of war. Relativity, previously an asset, seemed to become a handicap. If one culture or one set of values was as good as any other, how did one justify standing up for one's own way of life and reconcile it with one's relative beliefs? By 1940 the relative world view had become the majority view among intellectuals and in the social sciences, and the dilemma was widely felt. Anthropologists were especially vulnerable. As Benedict voiced the question for fellow anthropologists in one article, "must we, in this conflict of value systems, take a professional stand of cultural relativity, and no matter how we are involved as citizens write ourselves down as skeptics?" [14] Her own answer to this problem was complex. Her private feeling was that cultures should be left to go their own way, no matter how seemingly pathological, as long as they did not harm other cultures. She could accept Nazi Germany as the zoologist accepted and studied the rattlesnake as a part of the universe. But if a snake hurt others, it had to be defanged or destroyed.

Her immediate stance was to affirm relativity in the face of a conservative movement to return to a system of absolutes. She reviewed *The*

Crisis of Our Age and the fourth volume of the series *Social and Cultural Dynamics* by Harvard sociologist Pitirim Sorokin in the *New Republic* in 1942. Sorokin was one of the best-known voices of the conservatives. Benedict likened him to a Hebrew prophet making a "call for repentance" against the sin of relativism, calling for a "return to God," a turning again to the eternal verities, to "faith again in the absolute." But to do so, she wrote, would be to say "that the values of this day and age are not worth fighting for." We have learned a lot from relativism, she wrote, and will learn more. Only by knowing the relative could one discover any absolute values that might exist. Many institutions formerly thought to be absolute had been shown to be relative. Relativity had to be taken into account "if we are to understand those social problems which lie beyond it." [15]

She affirmed the relative importance of democracy as a way of life. Democracy, she wrote, "*can* be used to promote the individual freedom our ideologies exalt; it does not inherently assure it." Democracy as a political form was imperfect. Like monarchy and other systems it had the potential to be stable and energetic or divided and aggressive. "Political representative government," she wrote, did not necessarily work "automatically and of its own nature to preserve and further the freedom we exalt." Societies were not necessarily free because they were democracies. Submission to authority did not necessarily mean the suffocation of freedom. What was important, she stressed, was not the political form but what it embodied: not a democratic way of life but "the permanent victory of democratic *ways* of life." She referred to ways of life that gave people a sense that they were free to attain their personal goals; that made certain unremovable freedoms the common property of all; that made the world "safe for differences." For Benedict these were embodied in "civil liberties" and were what were worth fighting for, those freedoms "beyond the reach of arbitrary interference by men." Even civil liberties were relative, she wrote, changing from culture to culture. But when societies observed these protections, the people of the culture regarded themselves as free. Such civil liberties, she wrote, were built into cultures with high synergy. [16]

Her most complete statement of her position on values appeared in 1942 in an *Atlantic Monthly* article entitled "Primitive Freedom." She began with a description of the Chuckchee culture of Siberia. They were wealthy and democratic, but that did not make them free. They called themselves "doomed." They did not have freedom to reach out for their own personal goals because their society blocked them at every turn.

Their society had no mechanisms for mutual assistance and gave the master of the herds unrestricted power, whether benevolent or tyrannical, over the household. People gave help grudgingly, humiliating the asker. The only way to get ahead was by overpowering others or becoming a sycophant. Blind, uncontrolled anger was a common cultural response.[17]

Benedict contrasted the Chuckchee with the Canadian Blackfoot Indians among whom she had done field work. They too were rich and democratic, but unlike the Chuckchee they had a sense that they were free. They respected personal desires and their realization as the reason for life. Unlike the Chuckchee, chiefs among the Blackfoot did not have punitive power over followers. The prestige of the chief depended on the prestige of the people who followed him, so it was in his self-interest to provide what they needed to realize their goals. When a chief gave a horse to a horseless brave and the man returned from raiding with more horses (in the old days), or from hunting with more provisions, it enhanced the wealth of the tribe and the prestige of the chief as well as the individual's prestige. Satisfied followers in turn served their leader well. Unlike the Chuckchee, the Blackfoot had a system of mutual advantage between follower and leader, with the leader taking responsibility for the well-being of his followers. Sharing with others was an accepted social mechanism that benefited both individual and tribe.

The Blackfoot had a sense of satisfaction and freedom because theirs was a society with high synergy. The individual, in serving his or her own advantage, automatically served that of the group. Sharing for mutual benefit rather than hoarding for private advantage supported a measure of self-respect among the Blackfoot that the Chuckchee lacked. The Blackfoot had a siphon economy that distributed economic benefits around the community, whereas the Chuckchee had a funnel economy, focusing wealth on the masters of the herds. The Chuckchee did not have civil liberties built into their society, while the Blackfoot did. They were not civil liberties such as our society sponsors, she wrote. Instead they were things like the right to hospitality or the right to subsistence; no one went hungry while there was food in the tribe. Another was the right to an economic start for young adults, giving them the tools or horses or land they themselves could not afford to buy. Another was the open opportunity to become a chief or anything else one wished and for which one had the ability.

Freedom is threatened, she wrote, when "a privileged group can act arbitrarily and without responsibility and still retain its privileges." When that occurs leaders are "split off from responsibility and respect for those upon whose labor the advantages depend." Under such a system there is little respect for individual goals or individual rights. But "societies which make privilege inseparable from trusteeship have been able to perpetuate and extend civil liberties." The society becomes a kind of "joint-stock company . . . with pooled profits and limited liability," in which any curtailment of rights threatens each member. This, she said, is the basis for strong, "zestful" societies and for the individual's feeling of inner freedom.[18]

War, she went on, creates in Western society an artificial state of high synergy because it emphasizes mutual support and sacrifice, the sharing of burdens, and concern for the group over self. That is one of the reasons men like war. "Our social order starves men in peacetime for gratifications they get only in time of war," she wrote. Many Indian tribes, she stated, reversed the conditions of Western society. They provided these conditions in their daily lives, making society "a cooperating group where mutual support brought every man honor." War for them was an area of private advantage sought at the expense of the enemy, who was not considered human.[19]

She concluded her article by saying that one could support democracies in the face of Nazism because, with all their failures, they still based their philosophy "upon freedoms which *can* be made common and provide political frameworks that can be used to extend them." Nazi freedoms could not be made common, because they implied, as among the Chuckchee, "an underdog." The measures the Nazis used "cut civil liberties at their roots." The solid foundation for opposition to Nazism was not therefore democracy versus authoritarian state, but "the social utility of civil liberties, the liberties which can be made common property." These were not possible in a Nazi "New Order" that made so-called lesser breeds slaves, took their possessions, and used "naked force against the helpless." She ended with a warning to Americans on the necessity of protecting civil liberties at home under the war-time temptation to push them aside. Americans would be no better than their enemies if they did not defend their civil liberties. Not only must they not be curtailed, she wrote, "we must extend them to other fields not now recognized."[20]

On December 7, 1941, the Japanese bombed Pearl Harbor and America went to war. In February of the new year Benedict wrote a letter to the *New York Herald-Tribune* on making the ending of race prejudice part of the "victory program." America's enemies used discrimination as propaganda, she wrote, trying to get Asiatics and blacks to see that "the war of the United Nations is a war of white domination." Every refusal of jobs to

blacks, every city ordinance condemning blacks to poor housing, denial
of education to blacks, racial conflict, each was "a handout to our enemies," she wrote. "We need the Negroes and they need us," she stated.
"We can win through together if the whites do not keep erecting barriers
which deny to Negroes the opportunities of decent citizenship." A week
later she wrote a letter to the *New York Times* defending the Japanese-
American community on the West Coast. America had "reason to be
proud" of the loyalty of these people and "their dedication to our war
effort, even at great personal cost." The letter did not question the need
for evacuation and resettlement, a disappointing blindness encouraged
then by the shocking destruction of the American fleet at Pearl Harbor
and the feared possibility of a West Coast invasion by the Japanese. But it
did call for resettlement with dignity, so that people could start a new life
in another part of the country as good as the one they left and be assured
of "insurance from persecution." At a time when xenophobia swamped
reason concerning Japanese-Americans Benedict called for the protection
of their rights as citizens.[21]

As she had before the war, Benedict focused her attention on shaping
the time of peace. She became a member of the Advisory Council of the
Research Institute on Peace and Post-War Problems of the American Jewish Committee. She advocated disarmament after the war in an *American Scholar* editorial. The "unified commands and administrations" the
United Nations were experimenting with needed to be "reinforced and
extended in an international army and in international policy-making,"
because the nations had started to recognize "in peace as we do in war
that fighting in Burma or in Bengazi is the concern of the whole interdependent world." She based her hopes on the future United Nations, her
belief in the practicality of disarmament, and hope in people's ability to
change. In the *New Republic* she wrote that there were two alternatives
to keep order in the world: "Hitler's or a United Nations." She advocated
a "framework within which people can get what they want by conforming to the existing arrangements rather than by destroying them." Again
she called for disarmament.[22]

In 1942 her friendship with Margaret Mead got her involved with the
West Side Citizens' Defense Council. Mead had been active in the council
but was leaving New York for awhile and nominated Benedict to take her
job as director of the council's Leadership Training Institute. During the
spring of 1942 Benedict trained teachers and organized courses on "Home
Making in Wartime" which were held in public schools and settlement
houses for groups of English-speaking and non-English-speaking neigh-

borhood women, with play groups for children provided during the sessions.[23]

Meanwhile, many of her colleagues had begun to take jobs related to the war effort. One of these was Geoffrey Gorer, an Englishman whom Benedict had met in 1935. Gorer, author of *Africa Dances* (1935) and *Bali and Angkor* (1936), later wrote that Benedict and Mead had given him a crash course in anthropology, introduced him to the New York anthropological community, and encouraged him to do field work. His first anthropological study, *Himalayan Village* (1938), received good reviews. While at Yale in 1941 he did a pioneering Culture and Personality study on Japan, "Japanese Character Structure and Propaganda: A Preliminary Survey," which possibly led to his offer of a job at the Office of War Information in Washington, D.C., in 1942. While there he did a study of Burma, later mimeographed as *Burmese Personality*. In 1943 he took a job at the British Embassy and nominated Ruth Benedict for his old job at OWI.[24]

For Benedict the job beckoned as an "Open Sesame" in a life where other doors seemed to be shutting one by one. With Linton as chair, the Department at Columbia had become an increasingly uncomfortable place for her. Petty administrative hassles, disregard for her opinions and ideas concerning the Department, difficulty obtaining funds for students, all wore her down. Then in December 1942, while attending a luncheon for French colleague Paul Rivet, Franz Boas died. Benedict mourned for him but felt relief that he had died at the height of his powers and not after a long decline. She had worried about finding funds to keep his research going in the year or so before his death and had concocted a benefit scheme in which she persuaded Boas to give a talk at which all present contributed a donation in order to help him without offering charity. But his death was a loss no one else could fill. In her obituary for him in *The Nation*, she wrote, "At eighty-four he had not sold out, or stultified himself, or locked himself in a dogmatic cage." Since 1939 Edward Sapir, Alexander Goldenweiser, and Elsie Clews Parsons had also died. The older generation, the generation of anthropologists with whom she identified herself, was slowly being eroded away. The Washington job offered a sense of freedom from surrounding problems, from New York, and from the Department. But more than that, it offered a chance to practice applied anthropology on a major scale.[25]

Benedict had been interested in the idea of applied anthropology as it developed in the 1930's and had agreed to be one of the founding members of the Society for Applied Anthropology when it organized in 1941.

She gave a paper entitled "Personality and Culture" at the first meeting. The idea of applied anthropology began to take form with the publication in 1929 of sociologists Robert and Helen Lynd's *Middletown,* which had led some anthropologists to see the value of applying their skills to present-day American life. The results were anthropologist-led community studies and industry studies in the 1930's and 1940's. Applied anthropology also meant using anthropological insights and techniques to address contemporary Indian problems, and an Indian commissioner sympathetic to this cause led some anthropologists to focus their interest on Indian life in the present rather than in the lost past. Anthropologists began to do acculturation studies and assimilation studies in the mid and late 1930's, focusing on present-day Indian life, exploring the idea that the culture Indians had created on the reservations or in small villages might be worth learning about. In a world increasingly threatened by Fascism during that time, acculturation studies concentrating on the present lives of Indian tribes often took the form of studies of the dominance of one people by another and how this affected the dominated group. In the early 1940's Benedict wrote one such study, "Two Patterns of Indian Acculturation," which dealt with two major ways Indians accommodated to white conquest: survival and integration contrasted with escape or extinction. Her point was that subordination was not an innate quality of Indians but a result of circumstances now reinforced by culture, which could be changed. With the growth of interest in community studies, industry studies, and acculturation studies, by the 1940's the structure was in place for a major effort in applied anthropology. The war provided the incentive.[26]

A review in 1942 reflected Benedict's own growing concern over the present. Paul Radin's book *Indians of South America* was a scholarly anthropological study. But Benedict criticized the book for its lack of awareness that in South America the character and future of the Indians were major social and political concerns. What was needed, she wrote, was a book that gave necessary knowledge for "understanding the social and political problems that center around the South American Indians." Radin's, she wrote, was not the needed book. Benedict's own interest in applied anthropology grew out of work in the area of nutrition. In 1938 M. L. Wilson, an undersecretary in the Department of Agriculture, had invited her to give a talk in the department's Democracy Series and meet with a seminar group the next day. The lecture had an audience of almost a thousand. The seminar included about fifty to seventy-five of the key administrators and policy-makers in the Department. The talk she gave had to do with the funnel and siphon systems of economics. Wilson became a missionary for cultural anthropology, describing the first four chapters of *Patterns* as stating his "fundamental social philosophy better than anything I know." In 1940 Wilson, by then the director of extension work in the Department of Agriculture, wrote Benedict asking advice in the area of nutrition. He had become chief of a federal task force charged with coordinating nutrition programs of all the federal agencies for the coming war effort. About one-third of Americans, he wrote, had an unsatisfactory diet because of the cultural lag between knowledge of nutrition and the actual food habits and ideas about food held by people. He had recommended that the National Research Council set up two committees, one on the biochemical part of nutrition, the other on food habits, and wanted to get her thoughts on the idea.[27]

In the spring of 1939, Benedict had participated with a group of three other college professors, one graduate student, and one new Ph.D., on the New York branch of a study of primitive diets and food habits. Similar affiliated studies took place also at Harvard and on the Pacific Coast. She had developed a genuine interest in this area and wrote back to Wilson that she had "thought often" about problems of nutrition and defense, with war clouding the horizon. She saw future diet programs in America falling into two categories. The first, dealing with biochemistry, included programs such as reinforcing flour or sugar with synthetic vitamins. This would have quick results and be vitally important in defense programs. The second dealt with changing habits, which would not be done in a few months. Family incomes had to increase, she wrote, children become accustomed to healthier foods, young girls given incentives to learn to cook healthier meals. But government programs could be used "to the hilt" to further healthier dietary changes. She saw school lunches as a way to teach new eating habits and also school cooking classes. There would be no immediate results, however.[28]

She amplified her letter January 2, 1941, with an "Anthropological Memorandum on Diet Habits." Here she recommended distributing desired foods at low cost, providing school lunches, and extending rural distribution of milk and oranges under the food stamp plan. As availability increased, use of good foods would increase. School lunches also exposed students to contact with the idea of a healthy meal as well as the reality, an idea that with enough exposure would become part of their lives. But vitamin reinforcement was the easiest plan to implement. There was no need to teach people or for them to learn a new habit, only to accept something new, easily done in America where people wanted the best, especially for their children. The philosophy embodied in this memorandum was also her philosophy of social change: it took time, did not occur all at once. But expose people to ideas, and with enough exposure the ideas became part of the reality of their lives.[29]

The Committee on Food Habits of the National Research Council Division of Anthropology and Psychology organized just a month after Benedict's memorandum, and she accepted the invitation to become a member. The committee's objective was to study food habits and make recommendations to the office of the Coordinator of Health, Welfare and Related Defense Activities. Members met once a month for two days in Washington for a group discussion and the rest of the time worked from their home cities. They decided by September 1941 that they needed someone to open an office in Washington and run it, acting as liaison to various government agencies and programs, compiling data, and preparing written materials. Benedict suggested Margaret Mead for this post and the day the Japanese bombed Pearl Harbor invited her to become executive director of the Committee on Food Habits, which gave her a base in Washington as the war commenced. Benedict remained active on the committee through 1942, helping develop and write position papers on various food problems. The committee dealt with devising ways to get Americans to accept new food practices, rationing, food conservation, and the most efficient, nutritional food utilization. As the war sent Americans overseas, the committee organized material on food practices in countries where U.S. forces found themselves and the adjustment of available American relief food to foreign food practices.[30]

By 1943 Benedict saw as increasingly urgent the need for understanding the foibles and values of different cultures so that they could work together. For the United Nations to become viable as an instrument of synergy this basic understanding and ability to work with cultural differences was a necessary preliminary condition. The creation of a socially cohesive international government depended on it. The danger, she wrote, was that non-understanding of foreign ways of life could lead America into "head-on collision" with other countries and America would "fall back on the old pattern of imposing our own values by force." The American experience with immigrants had given Americans the belief that with half a chance all peoples would take the American way of life as their model. Since democracy in America took the form of mass suffrage and representative government and parties, Americans expected this to be the necessary model for democracy in other countries. Americans' "deep loyalties" to what worked here "will inevitably lead Americans to believe that adoption of our system is the one trustworthy means to democratic government."[31]

The ruling idea of democracy in America through World War II was symbolized by the "melting pot," the giving up of foreign ways and the Americanization of immigrants. Benedict, Mead, and other anthropologists and social scientists attempted to introduce a new idea of democracy. Instead of neutralizing differences, it respected differences and strove to preserve a sense of ethnic pride and heritage. They feared that what would happen after the war was that Americans would take America's as the normative experience in dealing with other countries. This was the way it had happened in America, they saw the rationale going, therefore this was the way it should be in foreign countries, regardless of their own values, experiences, or expectations. They felt an urgent need to open Americans to the idea that what worked in America would not necessarily work in other countries and to instill a respect for cultural differences and for the necessity of cultures to work out their own destinies on their own terms.

In "Recognition of Cultural Diversities in the Postwar World" (1943) Benedict suggested major differences in the idea and practices of democracy between America and most of the rest of the world. The cooperative village, led by a council of elders and organized for mutual services and joint responsibility, was the basic unit in many countries, not the individual. By these other standards even a government viewed by Americans as totalitarian, if it accomplished progressively more for the common welfare, might be viewed locally as democracy. The one criterion for judging the success of each country's efforts at achieving democracy was not their form of government but whether it furthered the general welfare. Making differences between cultures known and respected became a necessity for Benedict superseding her work on synergy, as synergy could not come into existence internationally without respect for and willingness to work with cultural differences as an underpinning.[32]

Her job with the Office of War Information, commencing in the summer of 1943, gave her a forum to do just that. She saw as the challenge of her job, she wrote, "to get policy makers to take into account different habits and customs of other parts of the world." She moved down to Washington, taking the apartment of a former student then leaving Washington, and Ruth Valentine went with her. She joined the Office of War Information as head of the Basic Analysis Section, Bureau of Overseas Intelligence, a grandiose title since she was the only person in the section at the time. She began defining a new discipline, pioneering analyses of contemporary rather than primitive cultures. The Council on Inter-cultural Relations founded by Margaret Mead and Gregory Bateson had sponsored the first such studies in 1942. Benedict took cultural analysis into government and over time made it work on a practical level. Her job was to work on problems of behavior and attitude in enemy and occupied countries. Gorer's OWI work and his earlier paper on Japanese childhood had been more psychoanalytical than practical. There was a lot of skep-ticism within the government concerning the value of such "egghead" re-search. One of the first things Benedict did was write a memo on the im-portance of gathering cultural material on other countries. Then she launched into a C&P study on Thailand, the first of her studies of "cul-ture at a distance," an analysis of Thai culture done without ever having been to Thailand, relying on written reports and the help of Thai infor-mants in America. The purpose of the report was its use as background material to plan a program of psychological warfare on the Thai as allies of the Japanese, and for reconstruction after the war.[33]

The study itself showed that she had come far from *Patterns of Cul-ture*. She did not define the Thai in terms of one label or designation. Her description was multi-thematic, reflecting her acceptance of the use of a multiplicity of patterns in Culture and Personality studies. She identified three major patterns that influenced Thai behavior. The first was "The Enjoyment of Life," an optimistic belief that life was good, that good ulti-mately triumphed over evil, and that accumulated merit had its reward in this world rather than future lives. A second pattern she called "The Cool Heart," living as far as possible without anxiety, but also having sangfroid in times of crisis. This included the ability to estimate consequences ra-tionally and then act. The third pattern was "Male Dominance," or the unconscious expectation that men would prevail over women in life. The national game of kite-flying symbolized the relationship of men and women. Benedict described it as "a 'courtship' of a female kite and a male kite." In a contest played exclusively by men, the holder of the larger, heavier male kite tried to pull the smaller female kite into its orbit. This depended on skilled maneuvering rather than overpowering the other. The male kite had to "catch" the female kite in the air by maneuvering bamboo twigs on the kite into a loop on the female kite so that they could fly together.[34]

Along with her multi-thematic characterization, which emphasized ele-ments of interpersonal relations among the Thai, Benedict described Thai child development and its effects on developing character and culture habits. She concluded that a "psychic security" made the Thai generally cheerful, convivial, and nonviolent in character, the result of a "long and remarkably permissive infancy," with loose feeding, sleeping, and toilet-training routines and lack of concern over childish genital play. Hierarchy based on age in the family easily translated to acceptance of hierarchy in the state. The Thai learned self-reliance as they learned motor skills and their parents threw them on their own responsibility. Buddhism re-inforced this responsibility to oneself, which became among adults the responsibility to bring events to a satisfactory conclusion, to come out ahead, and culturally permitted the use of deceit, flattery, and manipula-tion of others' weaknesses to do so.[35]

By September 1943, she had finished the Thai study and was working on a similar C&P study of Rumania. Benedict considered these two the only real C&P studies she did during her work at OWI. Both works were used to create plans for dealing with Thailand and Rumania after the war. She wrote a thirty-eight-page report on "German Defeatism at the Beginning of the Fifth Winter of War" in December 1943. Then, moving away from the model of the academic research paper, she began writing shorter pieces on specific issues, and it was these that caught the attention of higher-ups in the office. "An Anthropological Note on Finnish Re-gional Directives," only four pages, done in January 1944, impressed Bjarne Braatoy of the OWI, who told her it was "challenging and stimu-lating." He wrote her that "it made the case for analyses of the kind throughout the shop."[36]

The shop was the Bureau of Overseas Intelligence, the arm of OWI for which Benedict worked. Braatoy wanted her to do more on Danish and Norwegian directives, so she began researching those countries. The Fin-nish report gained her the authority to hire one staff person. She also hired people like psychoanalyst Erik Erikson as consultants. She wrote memorandums on post-war rehabilitation in Norway. She collected back-ground material for pamphlets for distribution among the Norwegians and the Dutch about U.S. troops, comparing the Americans with the Dutch and the Norwegians. Through 1944–1945 she wrote three- and four-page memos on various topics: "Note on an Authoritative View of 'The True Danger' to German Morale" (April 1944); "Target-oriented propaganda for European nations" (July 1944); "A Note on Long Range Communications Planning for Europe" (n.d.); "Problems in Japanese Morale Submitted for Study by Psychiatrists" (n.d.). She studied Poland and Italy, collected a lot of material, but did not complete writing it up before the war's end.[37]

Through 1945 she continued working for Basic Analysis, but in 1944 also became a Social Science Analyst of the Foreign Morale Division of OWI under Alexander Leighton, a psychological colleague from New York. The division assigned her to the study of Japan in June 1944. She was asked to use all her skills as a cultural anthropologist "to spell out what the Japanese were like." She read translated Japanese books and books about Japan by Westerners. She interviewed Japanese in this country who had been brought up in Japan. She watched movies written and produced in Japan, checking her idea of them with Japanese informants. The immediate result was a series of memos on Japan. She wrote on Japanese suicide, Japanese myths, and Japanese behavior patterns, which she called a study in Japanese ethics. What she thought of as her most influential memo was one entitled "What Shall Be Done about the Emperor?" in which she recommended that instead of deposing the Japanese emperor the Americans make use of his position as a "sacred chief," above politics, the "spiritual" leader of the nation, to promote their own programs. This was what ultimately occurred. She worked on other projects and programs as well during the war years. She participated in the OSS Far East Orientation School, acquainting participants with problems and future critical issues in the Far East. She started a project never finished to teach Japanese women about women in Japanese history who had acted in ways of which Americans approved.[38]

Applied anthropology did not go on only at the office during these years. A significant number of Benedict's anthropological and psychological colleagues from New York and other places held jobs in Washington. They met frequently after work and often ended up having spirited discussions in someone's living room, analyzing American culture and discussing the war and the post-war world. Benedict's Rumanian memorandum acted as a catalyst to this semi-formal study of contemporary cultures. It was the precursor of small meetings in Washington where people tried to pool ways to use informants and analyze films, literary plots, and other material to make models of nations' cultural characters. Her war work and the networking stimulated Benedict and provided her with the least stressful environment she had had in years. OWI left her fairly free to work as she liked because she produced results people could use and understand and because her bosses did not know much about anthropology. While working in Washington she did not make speaking engagements or sponsor activities. She did teach at the Washington School of Psychiatry, but it was an interdisciplinary setting working with mature men and women on issues related to culture. When she needed time to herself she sat at home and read Shakespeare. This was important because she had begun having problems with her health: high blood pressure, dizzy spells, and cardiac stress.[39]

Just a month after V-J Day Benedict had begun writing *The Chrysanthemum and the Sword*. Her working title was *Japanese Character*. She told Ferris Greenslet at Houghton Mifflin that she was writing it "as humanly as I can."[40] *The Chrysanthemum and the Sword* came out in the fall of 1946 with an immediate impact on the general educated public at which it was aimed, including policy-makers within the U.S. government and occupation forces in Japan. It was a timely, practical book on several levels. For the general public it explained seemingly incomprehensible Japanese behavior by showing the foundations upon which it rested. These were often totally alien to Americans but, once understood, enabled Americans to see the Japanese as "human," rather than incomprehensibly barbarous and cruel. Its second impact was as a tool for policy-making. It provided an understanding of the wellsprings of Japanese behavior which could be manipulated to promote American designs for post-war Japanese reconstruction. Finally, by comparing American usages and beliefs to Japanese, it explained to astute readers almost as much about America as about Japan.

The Japanese had seemed barbaric to many Americans, committing atrocities such as the Death March at Bataan. They had seemed inhuman in their fanaticism, especially the kamikazes. Prior to the war they had seemed too easily insulted for no reason Americans could see. Their international behavior had seemed illogical by American standards. They were a people of bewildering contradictions to Americans, polite yet insolent and arrogant, rigid yet flexible, loyal and generous yet treacherous and spiteful, brave yet timid, giving high honor to the arts of peace such as Noh drama, tea ceremonies, or growing chrysanthemums, yet equally high honor to the cult of the sword and warrior. As Benedict wrote, many Americans regarded the Japanese as "the most alien enemy" the United States had ever fought in declared war.[41]

Benedict made their alienness familiar and understandable by explaining the reasons behind the behavior and by linking Japanese actions to American standards. She showed that there was a consistent system of reasoning behind the seeming irrationality of the Japanese. Concerning the prisoners of war, Benedict explained that the Japanese treated them in general no worse than they treated their own soldiers. Forced marches and sardine conditions in transport were exacted from Japanese soldiers, and they applied their own standards to POW's. The soldiers were expendable, and honor was bound with fighting to the death. Surrender was shameful. There were no litter-bearers at the front for Japanese soldiers, and the wounded were often killed or left to suicide with grenades when the Japanese had to retreat from a place where there was a hospital. Medical facilities were seen as interference with heroism. Just so medical treatment and supplies were not deemed important for POW's. The Japanese in general, Benedict said, did not ask of their prisoners anything they did not ask of themselves. But their self-expectations were much harsher than those of Westerners. This was a situation that Americans could finally understand, if not accept.

Benedict showed that the place Americans gave to equality, the Japanese gave to hierarchy, or filling one's proper station in life. As the Americans applied the standard of democracy to international affairs, the Japanese applied the standard of hierarchy, wanting to enable each nation to find its proper station in the world, striving to gain the top of the ladder for themselves. While Americans gave high esteem to the "self-made man," Japanese lived in a vast network of indebtedness to others, some of which, such as indebtedness to the Emperor or parents, could never be fully repaid, and other parts, due to peers and coworkers, had to be repaid exactly in certain proportions and sometimes with interest. Being debtors made the Japanese quick to take offense. The system worked by not allowing too much resentment to build up, basically by emphasizing politeness in general and sympathy for those in debt from those holding debts. For Americans to understand this she suggested they look on each human interaction as Americans viewed financial transactions, where the attitudes were comparable. Love, kindness, and generosity to the Japanese had strings attached, some of which they accepted justly, some of which they resented. What Americans regarded as a casual favor the Japanese saw as an obligation to be repaid in a greater way than the original favor. Defaulting against a moral debt had the same penalties that in America attached to defaulting on a loan: disgrace before the community.

Benedict explained the complexities surrounding the Japanese feeling of moral indebtedness, which involved *gimu*, or one's debt to the Emperor and to parents and unrepayable; and *giri*, one's debt to others and to one's name and repayable. She explained that America was a country where social controls stemmed from internal guilt and sense of sin, while in Japan they stemmed from shame, or external ridicule and contempt. With shame there was no absolute standard of right and wrong. The important thing was to be accepted by others, and she stressed that a people with this as a wellspring could change easily. The Japanese did not have a golden rule. They moved in different circles, and each circle had its prescribed code and approved behavior. The rules could be changed within a circle, resulting in entirely transformed behavior, whereas the American approach to life was "either-or": one was either one way or another and not liable to change quickly or easily. The Japanese saw life as a careful balancing of the needs of one circle against another, like a debtor owing too many debts, who ignores some and pays others, trying not to fall into bankruptcy. The Japanese system strove to minimize competition, which caused strains and tensions among the Japanese, while to Americans competition was a way of life. Americans, she wrote, learned that discipline means self-sacrifice, for example, to eat "healthy," less palatable foods instead of junk foods one liked. In Japanese culture discipline meant gaining the power to live more fully, to enlarge life. After explaining all these differences from the way Americans perceived life, Benedict spent a chapter showing how they all grew out of childhood learning and how this too differed from American standards. Japanese duality, she argued, grew out of the discontinuity between their early, extremely permissive childhood and their later life with its restraints. Benedict also suggested in a well-argued way that the Japanese could change from a seemingly warlike and aggressive people to a peaceful one. The Japanese, she wrote, had an "ethic of alternatives." When the Japanese failed, they abandoned that course for an alternative one. This could be seen in the Meiji Reform of the nineteenth century. They had tried to achieve their "proper place" in the world through war and had lost. Because of this utter failure, they had to "henceforth tread the path of a peaceful nation"[42] and find their proper place in the world along this path. In all these ways Benedict showed the Japanese indeed to be human, and deserving of a place eventually within the circle of the United Nations.

As a Culture and Personality study *The Chrysanthemum and the Sword* was on the cutting edge of scholarship. The book was an unparalleled melding of all the techniques Culture and Personality researchers had been struggling to use without concentrating too heavily on any one element as *the* determining force. Benedict's brilliant analysis of Japanese interpersonal relations remains the heart of the book. But she also included child study, an analysis of Rorschach tests, analysis of Japanese films and literature, and information gathered from interviewed Japanese in America on their life histories, supplemented with information on recent Japanese general history. The book pointed the direction for Culture and Personality studies of the future.

The *Chrysanthemum and the Sword* was read enthusiastically in Washington. For one thing, it praised the work of the American occupation administration in Japan. Americans had good reason to be proud of the administration of Japan since V-J Day, Benedict wrote, "administered with skill" by General MacArthur. The American administration had kept the Emperorship and the Japanese government intact and allowed that government to take over reconstruction in the country, while the MacArthur administration set goals for the Japanese to work toward. Doing this removed humiliation from defeat and challenged the Japanese to chart a new course. She especially praised MacArthur's handling of the situation with the Emperor and the promotion of labor organization in Japan which made many Japanese feel that they had won something from the war after all. Beyond her praise for the reconstruction, *The Chrysanthemum and the Sword* was popular in Washington because, as Margaret Mead later wrote, "It was the kind of book that colonels could mention to generals and captains to admirals without fear of producing an explosion against 'jargon,'" and also a book "safe to put in the hands of congressmen alert to resist the 'schemes of long-haired intellectuals.'" Benedict left out psychiatric and technical social science language because she saw it as culture-bound, with too many connotations for American readers that would stop them from understanding the reality of Japanese perceptions.[43]

She recommended Japanese disarmament as the best future course in order to reconstruct the Japanese economy, a course which was ultimately followed and which helped accrue such benefits as to make Japan one of the top five peacetime economies in the world. The United States, she wrote, could not "by fiat" create a free and democratic Japan. The Japanese had to create their own version, based on their own models, ethics, and past. MacArthur's headquarters invited Benedict for a consulting tour of Korea and Japan in December 1946, and she wanted to go, but this fell through. The Chief of the Advisory Study Group, Plans and Operations Division, War Department General Staff, wrote to her that the ASG had studied *The Chrysanthemum and the Sword* with interest and gained "insight into pertinent problems now facing the U.S." He asked her advice on other books and studies that could give insight into European cultures, especially Russia, and expressed the wish to meet with her and discuss "the broad aspects" of applying the knowledge of the patterns of various cultures to long-range concepts of national security.[44]

The Chrysanthemum and the Sword was widely reviewed. The general response was extremely positive. The *New York Times* called it a "scholarly and fascinating study." The *Christian Science Monitor* called it "provocative and unusual . . . An illuminating interpretation of immediate importance and permanent value." In *Social Studies* reviewer Erna Fergusson called it a book of "the utmost significance and one that could herald a new approach to international relations." For some old Far East hands, the fact that Benedict had never been to Japan was a deterrent. One wrote, "as a result it has a bookish quality that puts it at a long remove from the realities of present-day Japan." Another said it pictured "a Japan that exists more in tradition than in reality," and consigned it to the heap of books of historical interest. But the book had a great impact on the Japanese themselves after it was translated. It was widely read there. Roger Baldwin of the American Civil Liberties Union found the book in great demand among both Americans and Japanese in Japan in 1947. He reported that Japanese who read it thought it "a superb job. It opened their own eyes as to what makes them tick as a people." The only criticism he reported from Japanese was that they thought it leaned too heavily on practices of the middle-class Japanese in trade and generalized too greatly from their patterns of loyalty. They thought a large segment of Japan freed for a long time from those constraints. One Nisei woman wrote Benedict, "It's like a fog clearing." She had fought all her life against some of the Japanese ways of life Benedict explained. Now she could see why there was so much frustrating conflict in the personal life of a westernized Nisei. "Some of the old ways simply cannot be compromised with the western ways and if one tries, the result is confusion." Over the years the chief criticisms of *The Chrysanthemum and the Sword* have been that Benedict failed to take into account class and regional variations and differences between pre- and post-Meiji Japan through time. Her view of Japan has also been perceived as static rather than dynamic. Nonetheless, in spite of various criticisms, the book is recognized as a classic, and is still considered by both Japanese and knowledgeable Americans as a good place to begin in understanding the Japanese. Two writers, after criticizing the book in 1961, wrote, "No synthetic analysis approaching the stature of Benedict's work has, however, yet emerged." This is still true.[45]

The Chrysanthemum and the Sword had one more important result. It made the case for cultural studies like it. It launched Ruth Benedict's last great project, the project that filled her life in the last two years before her death.

14

The Last Great Vision

IN 1947 RUTH BENEDICT embarked on her last and, in the idiom of the 1940's, her "grandest" project. It was grand in concept, proposing to tackle and unravel the complexities of modern Western and Eastern civilizations, a job many considered impossible. It was bold in organization, at once both feminist and synergistic. With a budget of $90,000 a year and a work force of over a hundred it was "Big Science" and promised the chance to have a major impact in anthropology and in the intellectual and policy-making community. It was also grand in spirit. People volunteered their time and expertise and spent thousands of hours beyond those they were paid for because they believed in the project. It became a crusade tied together by camaraderie. On Benedict's part, it was grand in goal. She saw this work as paving the way for a synergistic United Nations through the creation of new forms of international relations. It embodied Benedict's last great vision and pulled together in concrete form important themes in her life. Officially named Columbia University Research in Contemporary Cultures (RCC), the project became known popularly as the study of National Character.

The idea of "national character" was as old as the founding of the first nation-state and came from the question of what set a certain group of people apart from another—what made them special. Defining what it was to be an American, for example, became part of American intellectual musings around the time of the Revolution and had continued with greater or lesser emphasis into the twentieth century. It received new impetus immediately before and during World War II, when people needed to reaffirm their unique national identity as they moved forward into conflict with other nations. But what had been written on national character was intuitive, impressionistic, overly general, and often biased by the writer's own cultural expectations. It often degenerated into describing the crudest stereotypes as fact, such as avowing that all Germans were aggressive, or all Frenchmen great lovers. But by the early 1940's the social sciences were approaching the idea of national character with some rigor and a group of anthropologists took up the concept of national character as a study of learned cultural behavior with the purpose of turning it into a branch of scientific knowledge with applied possibilities.

In 1942 Margaret Mead wrote the first popular anthropological national character study, on American character, entitled *And Keep Your Powder Dry*. That same year, Mead, along with her husband, Gregory Bateson, and others, had founded the Council on Intercultural Relations. They viewed the council as a nonprofit clearing house for the study of Culture and Personality in contemporary Eastern and Western cultures. In the war context the council wanted to study the unexpressed but powerful beliefs and ideas underlying overt behavior in different countries in order to find factors that might speed victory and provide the best chance for peaceful post-war rebuilding. The council planned to provide this information to organizations even then planning for the post-war period, and became a pioneer in the genre of what would later be termed "think tanks," hoping to influence policy through information and ideas. Mead later wrote that the council began the study of national character.[1]

At first Benedict was involved only peripherally with the council. But when she joined the Office of War Information in 1943 she soon assumed a position of leadership in the study of contemporary cultures. She taught an interdisciplinary seminar at the Washington School of Psychiatry on "National Character." She also became involved in the affairs of the council, which incorporated and changed its name to the Institute for Intercultural Studies in 1944. With Benedict as vice-chair and member of the institute's Board of Directors, the organization now openly became a clearing house "for research and theoretical contributions to the understanding of national character." As before, the institute encouraged analysis of contemporary cultures, and institute members pioneered in developing new methods in interviewing and film analysis to facilitate this. But there was a new focus on understanding cultural differences in order to aid international cooperation during the war but especially in constructing world order after the war. Besides international relations, the institute also became concerned with the problems of American minorities. The institute continued to try to make its work available to people actually in policy-making positions. The new emphasis on cultural differences, international relations, and American minorities seems to reflect Benedict's own vision of the post-war world. The belief in the applied use of anthropological analysis on major contemporary civilizations flowed from Benedict's and Mead's own experience in such research during the war.[2]

Benedict's post-war plans centered on continuing this work begun during the war, and thereby influencing the shape of the post-war world. In 1946, Mead wrote later, their positions were reversed. Benedict had been "skeptical" as Mead and the council had worked to get the study of contemporary cultures started. After the war the others went in different directions, leaving Benedict to keep such study going almost single-handedly. Her first step was to continue her leave of absence from Columbia in order to write her classic national character study of Japan, *The Chrysanthemum and the Sword.* During this time she won both the $1,000 American Design Award for her war services and the $2,500 Achievement Award of the American Association of University Women. In her speech to the AAUW she revealed the next phase of her program. She planned to teach a seminar at Columbia composed of European students, both those fresh to and those long familiar with the United States. The seminar had a threefold purpose: to study American culture through the eyes of outsiders; to gain insights into the students' own cultures; and to "try out in little," she told her audience, "some of the problems which face the United Nations," perhaps for her the seminar's most important contribution. Benedict returned to Columbia in the fall semester of 1946 with a $3,500 project fund. *The Chrysanthemum and the Sword* came out that fall. The book's timeliness and clarity created a favorable climate for more such contemporary studies. Benedict's nomination as President of the American Anthropological Association at the December annual meeting in 1946 increased her prestige as an anthropologist.[3]

That fall Benedict had found another potential source of funding. In the spring of 1946 Benedict had told a group including Margaret Mead at a party that she had discovered where they could get a hundred thousand dollars. "She was unaccountably gay and mischievously refused to tell us anything more," wrote Mead. The Office of Naval Research had set up funds for human behavior studies and had contacted Benedict as one of those to design the first projects. The money available to Benedict was indeed close to $100,000 a year. Never had so much money been available to the Columbia-based anthropologists at one time. In June 1946, Benedict wrote Mead that she had gone down to Washington and was putting together the project. In October 1946, Benedict wrote Geoffrey Gorer that she was glad he was coming back from England to work on the new project, Research in Contemporary Cultures. She had only asked for a two-year contract, she wrote him, feeling that after that further work should be carried out under other sponsorship than the Armed Forces. Because of these "strange auspices" she had worded the project as a study of foreign-origin groups in the United States, stressing that they would work with persons actually from the country studied in each group. "It won't change what we actually do on the project," she wrote, "but it provides a 'security' I couldn't get in any other way." It bypassed the necessity for security clearances and "secret"/"non-secret" classifications of material. All project work was thus unclassified and available for general use.[4]

Ruth Valentine, Margaret Mead, Ruth Benedict, and Ruth Bunzel became the project organizers. Valentine handled administrative planning, Mead took over the technical design for interviewing and protecting informants, and Bunzel started to build a preliminary project manual from materials prepared during the war and in the 1930's Yale seminar on "The Impact of Culture and Personality" led by Edward Sapir and John Dollard. They contacted various people to get together a team of workers. The spring of 1947 was one of alternate frustration and celebration as they worked to get the project accepted by the Navy and actually operating. Benedict wrote Gorer that she was frustrated by the "painful delays" and cuts in the research budget. "My patience is completely gone," she told him. She later wrote to Nathan Leites and Martha Wolfenstein [Leites], "You wouldn't believe all the messy details of getting the thing started but Ruth Valentine and Ruth Bunzel have put their shoulders to that wheel."[5]

Research in Contemporary Cultures began officially April 1, 1947. By the summer seventeen people were working for the project, with Ruth Valentine as executive secretary and Benedict as director. In July Benedict wrote Gorer, who was to join the project in the fall, that he and Margaret Mead would take on the study of Russia. "The real problems of today will be your dish," she told him. By September the project had taken shape. A staff had been assembled and consultants and other investigators lined up. A project manual of about 350 pages had been completed for use by project workers and as a basis for seminar discussions. Office space had been established. Project members had begun interviewing immigrants and nationals from other countries recently arrived in the United States who could report on their countries. A system had been established in which all material obtained was typed and three copies made, analyzed, then indexed in the office for use by other workers. A general seminar had been established for the meeting of all workers, at first once a month, but by September, every two weeks. These seminars came to be held on alternate Thursday evenings at the Viking Fund library, a donated space. Research groups had begun meeting and preparing comparative materials for the general seminars.[6]

In September another, more formal project inauguration took place. By December 1947, sixty-two people had worked for the project: fifteen graduate students, twenty-six professional anthropologists, folklorists, psychologists, psychiatrists, sociologists, and economists; and twenty-one native speakers from various countries. Research groups had been set up to study the cultures of France, Czechoslovakia, Russia, East European Jews, and China, plus a group on the acculturation of Europeans in the United States and one on clinical problems that guided the use of projective tests such as the Rorschach. The study groups met on their own schedules, which varied from three times a week to once every two weeks, to discuss findings, phrase problems, consider new data needed, and organize already collected material. The groups used a combination of interviewing, literature and film analysis, and analysis of other forms of communication, supplemented by the use of projective tests.[7]

The scope and potential impact of Research in Contemporary Cultures set up the last stage of the anthropological identity struggle between the patternists and the empiricists begun in the 1930's. This time it would be played out between Culture and Personality as National Character and cultural materialism embodied in the cultural ecology of Julian Steward and the neo-evolutionism of Leslie White. C&P had been very successful in the 1940's. The largest anthropological study of that decade had been Culture and Personality oriented: the Research on Indian Education and Personality Study cosponsored by the Bureau of Indian Affairs and the Committee on Human Development of the University of Chicago. In the early 1940's the project had undertaken a massive interdisciplinary study of education programs on twelve Indian reservations representing five Indian tribes, involving the testing of over one thousand Indian children and analysis of the tests and cultural context in C&P terms. Attacks on Benedict's Apollonian-Dionysian idea blended with attacks on the findings of Laura Thompson from this study, because her work on the Hopi tended to confirm Benedict's basic argument. Benedict, in fact, had been an advisor to this project. Now the visibility of RCC and the prestige of Benedict pressured anthropologists to make some decisions concerning their own values and direction as a discipline.

If Research in Contemporary Cultures were spectacularly successful, as by its size and the enthusiasm of its members it showed promise of being, its driving values could be expected to set the direction of anthropology for the foreseeable future. These included a central commitment to interdisciplinary work; an emphasis on the study of complex modern civilizations; an adherence to the idea of cultural relativity; and a commitment to a Culture and Personality approach. All of these values ran counter to the desires of major portions of the anthropological community in the 1940's.

After the war many anthropologists rejected a commitment to interdisciplinary work. One of the reasons cultural ecology became so important during the post-war period was its focus on doing anthropology rather than interdisciplinary research. The reorganization of the American Anthropological Association after the war also reflected this retreat from the decentralization and diffusion of interdisciplinary work.

During the 1930's anthropology had grown until specialization had become the rule, and this had decentralized the profession. Archaeologists, linguists, and physical anthropologists had formed their own societies. Growth in numbers had caused anthropologists to begin to lose their sense of themselves as a close familial community. Interdisciplinary work with psychologists, psychiatrists, sociologists, and others in the 1930's contributed to the sense of scatter, of professional diffusion. A sensed lack of order in the profession had intensified in the disorder of war. By the 1940's the American Anthropological Association had become an umbrella organization whose chief duties were editing a scholarly magazine and keeping anthropologists in touch with each other and their research once a year at the annual meeting. The AAA presidency had become a largely honorary position reflecting the esteem of one's colleagues and status in the profession. There was a felt need for a centering organization, one that would reintegrate anthropology and provide it with a cohesive identity. Beyond that, anthropologists wanted an organization to speak for and protect the interests of the discipline in the already-begun post-war scramble for research funds and university positions.

At the December 1945 AAA annual meeting, members agreed to explore reorganization. Ralph Linton was elected president for 1946, and he appointed a Committee on Reorganization and made Julian Steward chair. During the year, when various plans were being considered, Benedict and Mead argued for decreased centralization in anthropology, Benedict proposing a federation, while Mead suggested a new society just for cultural and social anthropologists. But their suggestions were passed over because most anthropologists wanted a center. As George Stocking wrote, if anthropology was to receive its share of the post-war research spoils, "an integrative, embracive discipline claiming for itself the status of a 'science'" seemed better than "a congeries of subdisciplines in some of whom the humanistic orientation was quite strong." The AAA after the reorganization was charged with making sure anthropology had a place in the new post-war research organization (later the National Science Foundation), with exploring possibilities of applying anthropological ideas in United Nations research and policy-making, with development of anthropological public relations, and with establishing a permanent office to further the professional interests of anthropologists. With the reorganization the AAA had become a lobby for anthropological interests with the president expected to be the chief lobbyist.[8]

At that same December 1946 meeting that approved constitutional reorganization, Benedict was elected as the last president of the American Anthropological Association under the old constitution. This meant she would serve only half a year as interim president until the new constitution went into effect. After talking the situation over with Margaret Mead, Benedict declined to run for a full term as president. As the last president under the old system, "I was chosen as a person to fill a position of honor," she wrote. In the new circumstances, "officers are to be chosen to carry out a job," she concluded. She did not need more jobs and found the materialistic values represented by the winners of the reorganization controversy repugnant.[9]

Cultural relativity, the idea that each culture was unique and measurable only in terms of itself and that only by recognizing these cultural differences was cooperation between peoples possible, so integral to Research in Contemporary Cultures, had become a sore point in post-war anthropology. Many anthropologists were in the process of modifying their stance on cultural relativity after the war. The publication of a twenty-five-cent edition of *Patterns of Culture* led to an outright attack on the book's cultural relativism in an article in the *American Anthropologist*, "Anthropology for the Common Man," by Elgin Williams. With emotional overtones the article charged Benedict with doing a great disservice to her readers by advocating cultural relativism, a pernicious idea after Hiroshima, Hitler, and the concentration camps of Europe. The reissuing of *Patterns* as a thirty-five-cent paperback a few years later led Benedict's former student Victor Barnouw to attack her cultural relativism in the same vein. Research in Contemporary Cultures adhered to cultural relativity and tried to show that cross-cultural comparison was possible in those terms. The members did this by analyzing similarities and differences between cultures in terms of what they communicated in each culture and how they differentiated value structures between cultures. They could be compared if the "unique pattern of organization" of each culture was "taken into account." [10]

During the same period Julian Steward and Leslie White's reanalyses of the idea of cultural evolution contained a veiled reaction to cultural relativity. Although their approaches to cultural evolution differed, they both postulated a process of evolution operating in all cultures and looked for signs of how evolution worked itself out in societies. This denied the uniqueness of each culture, measurable only in terms of itself. In an article written after Ruth Benedict's death, Steward contrasted the ideas of "relativism" and "evolutionism." Relativists, he wrote, emphasized cultures as having unique cultural patterns to be dealt with case by case, emphasizing cultural *differences*. Evolutionists believed there were patterns within cultures that crossed cultures and therefore emphasized *similarities* between cultures. Evolutionism, he concluded, seemed to lend itself more easily to cross-cultural comparison which might lead to the discovery of cultural laws in the "true" science sense. Cultural ecology also reaffirmed the importance of the study of primitive peoples, one of the key markers of professional identity. Cultural ecology was centristic rather than centrifugal. It reaffirmed the boundaries of the discipline. In the post-war climate this was an important point. [11]

But the issue that caused the most problems was the question of the commitment to a Culture and Personality approach that had already been labeled in the 1930's as "historical," or subjective, or "soft," that dealt with inferred findings over actual observed data, that sought standards and values over facts. It was an approach that seemed to many anthropologists to confer the dubious label of an "art" rather than a "true science," that emphasized qualitative over quantitative methods, that was not easily replicated if at all. In contrast, cultural ecology was objective, based on facts. It was aligned with biology in its theoretical orientation. It concentrated on the importance of material factors: the environment, technology, the means of production, external factors that could be evaluated in objective terms. His approach, Steward claimed, held promise of resolving the tensions between anthropology and the true science model. Steward called it "avowedly scientific and generalizing rather than historical or particularizing" in its search for "cultural regularities or laws." In physics and biology, he wrote, hypotheses were usually "approximations of observed regularities," and so long as cultural laws formulated "recurrences of similar inter-relationships of phenomena," they expressed cause and effect in the same way the law of gravity did. Also like the law of gravity which relativity had modified, any suggested cultural laws might be useful as a working hypothesis even though with further research they had to be qualified or reformulated.[12]

RCC, on the other hand, was aligned with psychoanalytic theory, highly suspect as speculative. Moreover the anthropologists involved did not do field work in the countries they studied and did not have the experience of first-hand observation indispensable to "true" anthropology. The RCC counter argument to this objection was, first, that most of the countries they studied were closed to field work and, second, that direct observation and "field work" were carried out "face to face" through extensive interviews with and observation of human beings from each culture. A key objection stemmed from the complexity of the civilizations studied, which meant overwhelming amounts of data to organize and coordinate. Another objection came from the partial nature of the research: the comparatively small number of non-random informants not being significant enough to give "the" national character of a country or instead giving a biased view of the culture concerned. To that Benedict replied that "Vast quantities of material are a handicap only when the crucial problems to be investigated are not formulated," and those studying national character had taken care in this area. As for the second objection, Benedict answered that no one would look for "the" national character of a multicultural state like Yugoslavia and the solution to the limited number of subjects was to multiply investigations multiculturally or regionally to the desired point. To the criticism that class differences in contemporary societies made using anthropological methods impossible, Benedict stated that there were ways to look at classes, both as to attitudes they held in common and as to conflicts. Instead of trying to follow the true science model, RCC advocates continued to try to structure an alternative to it. Concerning criticisms about sampling, Benedict's position had been stated in *The Chrysanthemum and the Sword*. There she wrote that in this type of study, "one quickly reaches the point where the testimony of great numbers of additional informants provides no further validation. Who bows to whom and when, for instance, needs no statistical study of all Japan"; to find what was "approved and customary" it was "not necessary to get the same information from a million Japanese." Mead later argued that anthropological sampling differed from sociological sampling. The sample validity depended not on the number of cases but on the proper specification of the informant regarding variables like age, sex, birth order, family, life experiences, temperament, political and religious positions, and so forth. This method with informants grew up historically to deal with the survivors of Indian cultures, she said. She compared it with experiments in medicine where a large number of measurements were made on a few cases.[13]

Sociologists and social psychologists asked "how much," Mead wrote, whereas anthropologists were interested in pattern. For example, in the case of surveying resistance to parents' authority, sociologists would be interested in the distribution of the resistance; anthropologists would study instead the pattern of resistance and respect in regard to parents, grandparents, siblings, and other sets of relationships. The anthropologist in dealing with culture, she wrote, assumed she was dealing with a "system which can be delineated by analysis of a small number of very highly specified samples." How many were necessary was a purely "structural decision." "Any member of a group," Mead said, provided the member's position in the group was specified, was "a perfect sample of the group-wide pattern on which he is acting as an informant." Thus, she went on, a twenty-one-year-old Chinese-American boy from a small New York town just graduated summa cum laude from Harvard and a tenth-generation deaf-mute born in Boston were equally good examples of American national character, provided their individual positions and characteristics were taken into account. A person from one region, such as New England, still manifested American national character, but with its own flavor. Mead here was exploring an alternative to quantification for anthropologists that was tied in with an alternative definition of science that most anthropologists were not ready to listen to or explore.[14]

Another criticism was that there was no way to replicate the observations. Again Mead countered that the criticism failed to take pattern into account. The pattern, she wrote, could be replicated. Seemingly impressionistic statements, such as "these are a very oral people," had precise meaning when supported by detailed descriptions of type of oral play, photos of such play, text and material from observation, the definite theoretical meaning of "oral," and the comparative experience the anthropologist had with other peoples. Moreover, she wrote, validation was available from other types of organized data, cross-disciplinary validation and the testing of pattern for cultural and psychic fit. In these ways Mead tried to explain national-character research as qualitative but rigorous.[15]

But Research in Contemporary Cultures was too deep a threat to "true" scientific identity to become the mainstream of anthropology. Ultimately, cultural materialism won, and various forms of ecological anthropology derived from cultural ecology became the mainstream of anthropology in the 1950's. One of the important contributing factors was the death of Ruth Benedict in the middle of the project and its underlying controversy.

Benedict had made plans to wind up the Naval version of RCC during the winter of 1948–1949. In the spring of 1948 she had started negotiating with the RAND Corporation for a second Russian project and signed a book contract with Carnegie, intending to use the advance to further the project. Apparently this book would have been on anthropology and international relations. In May 1948, she was promoted to full professor at Columbia, the first woman so honored in the Faculty of Political Science. That spring she was also invited to lecture at a six-week UNESCO Seminar on Childhood Education July 21–August 25, at Poděbrady, Czechoslovakia. Her health had been poor, but she decided to attend. It was a chance to see Czechoslovakia and other European cultures she had studied from a distance first-hand. Also the workload expected of her at the seminar was comparatively light: four lectures in a two-week period. Before she left she went to California to visit her sister's family and her mother during June and early July. While in Czechoslovakia she visited David and Elizabeth Rodnick, who had worked with her in the RCC Czech group and who had gotten a grant to do field work in Czechoslovakia. She attended a conference in Poland and there visited Sula Benet, a former Columbia graduate student and RCC colleague doing field work in Poland. She visited Holland and attended the International Anthropological Meetings in Brussels, Belgium. She went to Paris and saw Otto Klineberg, who was there working for UNESCO. She wrote that she was enjoying the whole trip and found it worthwhile as well. She felt good about how accurate her "blind" work had been, and that Poles, Czechs, and the Dutch actually behaved as her research had led her to expect.[16]

Her words from the UNESCO seminar suggest that had she lived, she might have found a way to make the project methods acceptable to the anthropological community. One of the things RCC faltered on after Benedict's death was the issue of swaddling, or tying a baby to a cradleboard. Because of the way it was presented, non-project anthropologists perceived swaddling to be RCC's deterministic and simplistic answer to what created the elements of Russian character. Benedict spoke of swaddling practices at the UNESCO seminar. But she used it neither simplistically nor as a causal determiner of national character. Instead she used it, as a custom of child rearing common to many countries, to delineate value differences between these countries and to show the cultural communication within countries between parents and infants. She cited six different varieties of expectations concerning swaddling which indicated different values.[17]

France, England, and the United States, she wrote, did not swaddle and indeed avoided restraining children, American doctors going so far as to say that swaddling caused tics. Swaddling was tightest and longest among Great Russians and regarded as protecting children from hurting themselves through excess energy. In Poland parents justified swaddling because babies were so fragile. Finally, Southern Italians, she wrote, viewed swaddling as a pleasure of life babies should not miss. These different rationales concerning swaddling pointed up cultural values which were communicated to the infant by the interaction between parent and child. Americans, who did not swaddle, valued freedom from restriction. Russian swaddling, she wrote, laid the basis for a strong feeling for the distinction between inner spontaneity, which was not seen as curbed by bodily restraint, and the restrictions of external life, which were to be expected. Great Russians thus had a high capacity for being free spirits in their souls while accepting external limitations. Polish children learned from swaddling that suffering was a part of their lives that they needed to accept and be strengthened against. Southern Italian parents saw swaddling as a bodily gratification for babies, part of teaching them the naturalness of everything having to do with the body. They say that babies "cry to be swaddled," she wrote.[18]

The last of her four lectures at the UNESCO seminar she devoted to answering questions raised by seminar participants. Her remarks displayed her philosophy and research directions in this last summer of her life. She was asked if her work was limited to child-rearing. "Certainly not," she replied. Her "usual stock-in-trade" was "much wider" than children's education, though that was a "favourite subject" of hers. Her work covered "all social arrangements and the whole of adult life, including economics" as well. The seminar, she said, was concerned with only one problem area, education. But things did not have only one cause. It was better to visualize "a circle or a web of causes."[19]

During the UNESCO seminar she had reaffirmed her belief that "recognition of cultural differences among civilized nations can promote international cooperation." Answering questions, she stressed the necessity of accepting the "different ideals and alternative social arrangements" of the world's nations. In her lecture she said that usually people working for world cooperation minimized fundamental differences between nations and emphasized human similarities. Those who opposed international cooperation saw differences as signs that other nations were "evil and have evil intentions." Both types wanted other nations to accept the values of their own culture as the mainspring of a peaceful world. Americans, especially, she warned again, as she had done several times in these last years, because of the cultural experience of assimilating millions of immigrants, felt the whole world should and if given a chance would want to become Americans. The melting pot had served America well as domestic policy, she wrote, but as an international policy it was "inadequate" and "destructive." Americans needed to learn to "accept and respect national differences." All nations had to learn that "respecting the culture of another nation does not mean devaluing the culture in which one has been reared."[20]

She affirmed the basic principles of anthropology she had spent her life setting in place—that ways of life, even aggression, were learned, not innate. She stressed objectivity and tolerance in comparing cultures. She told the seminar participants that cultures had consistency within themselves, but patterns had to be taught anew to each generation. In the question-and-answer period she distinguished two different types of social change: that brought about by external conditions, and change through internal influences, that is, "through the inner evolution of a given culture." As people learned to know their own cultures, she told her listeners from many nations, they might learn to understand the process of development, and begin a critical survey of previous social changes which "in its turn will lead to *planned* social changes within the culture of the country concerned." Child-rearing was a place to begin if internal changes in a culture were to be planned, for children were flexible and trainable. But this must go far beyond curriculum revision and into the informal education received in the family. However, first it was necessary to collect observations on child-rearing in order to understand the patterns actually occurring before they could be changed.[21]

In the question session she was asked whether absolute judgments of cultural differences were possible. She again affirmed relativity because those espousing absolutes were too often " 'neurotics' that want others to be faithful replicas of themselves." The only cross-cultural principle she committed herself to was the primary importance of balancing rights with responsibilities. To go beyond relativity was "dangerous" with the limited material and small number of workers in comparative culture.[22]

She talked of how knowledge of other cultures led to understanding how different moral values were brought to bear on international situations and negotiations, and the need of finding a path amenable to every set of values. Knowledge of other cultures also helped those dealing with a culture to learn to distinguish between those willing to help and those who would obstruct. Such knowledge made it easier for people to live together. One questioner asked if it was enough to understand other people's ways of life in order to end war. Benedict said no. Building peace, she said, was like building a railroad track; studying different cultures was like observing the different types of locomotive using the track. The first thing to do was to "organize a world where there can be discussion and compromise between all nations," using the weight of the world's powers to see that agreed-on arrangements became reality. "Once this organization is achieved," she told them, then the study of different cultures could be most useful in achieving respect for all nations and understanding of their problems.[23]

In Europe Benedict found herself increasingly fatigued. For two years, since the war's end, she had lived intensely and stressfully. Project details had called for unceasing amounts of time and energy. As Mead wrote, "Evenings in which we used to discuss poetry and the novelistic aspects of real life were now filled with petty details." The uncertain future of the project involved her time in seeking alternative sources of future funding. Besides the project, Benedict had another full-time job in her teaching and work with students at Columbia. Linton had left Columbia in 1946 to accept the Sterling Professorship at Yale and Julian Steward had replaced him as professor, while Duncan Strong became executive officer of the Department. But the Department, even with Linton gone, never regained the old sense of embracive community it had had for her with Boas. Though he and Benedict got along personally, Steward made no secret of his low regard for C&P work in favor of cultural ecology. Columbia after the war seemed to her like "a great factory."[24]

The students after the war differed significantly from pre-war students. Many of them were lower-middle-class young men who had seen combat as enlisted men and had come back to school on the G.I. Bill. They were children of the Depression and turned most readily to ideas like Steward's that dealt with material concepts. There was a definite anti-female bias among them. Some of these students, whom Benedict thought "sometimes good in their own way," she classified privately as her "barbarians." Among these students Benedict was perceived in her last two female roles, two opposite sides of the same mask applied generally to older women in America: as "wise woman" and as "witch." There were students who regarded her with awe, reverence, and delight. But there were also students whose materialistic values or temperament clashed with hers, who, when working with her, saw her as obstructive because their standards were not her standards, and who resented her power over them as students.[25]

When it came to her own standards, Benedict did not compromise, and she could be blunt about ideas in a way she seldom was about people. She asked student Richard Chase to arrange to drop her from his dissertation committee because the dissertation seemed written in "misery and boredom" and she had "serious theoretical objections" to his ideas on the nature and purpose of myth. A series of letters in Benedict's papers shows that she was personally sympathetic to his finishing, but she thought his work was intellectual junk. Chase later went on to have a successful academic career, but when *An Anthropologist at Work* came out, he wrote a critical review in which his resentment toward her was apparent. Chase was not the only student to have dissertation problems. Victor Barnouw, who admired Benedict, later wrote of his dissertation troubles with her. She was assigned as his dissertation advisor while she was on leave from Columbia during the war. He worked for two years on his own and felt he had put together a good dissertation. When she returned, however, he found his work did not meet her standards. It had no thesis, she told him. He was "stunned" and numbed by the thought that he almost had to begin all over again. She gave his final draft, when completed, "qualified approval." When he wrote about this Barnouw acknowledged that he had written a better dissertation because of her direction, but at the time his problems with Benedict must have seemed catastrophic and unnecessary, since the other committee members "seemed to think well" of his work. In 1949 he wrote a critique of *Patterns of Culture* that demonstrated his mixed feelings toward her. Differences in expectation led to frustration and stress for both students and Benedict. Finally, in the summer of 1948, Benedict's relationship with Ruth Valentine was under stress. That summer a friend of both Benedict's and Valentine's had lost her husband to cancer and Val had stayed in California to help her out. There was some question of Val's making a choice between this friend and Benedict, but by the end of the summer she had decided to return to New York and Benedict.[26]

All of these sources of stress led to increasing fatigue, insomnia, and high blood pressure, culminating in a heart attack two days after her return from Europe. The thought of dying did not frighten her. In her last years, her sister Margery wrote after her death, Ruth's "blue devils" had vanished and she had developed "a true love of life." She continued, "Her old accustomed love of death merged with her newfound love of life, and she could be utterly at peace." She had spent her life coming to terms with death and accepted its imminence with great grace. When told of her condition she "smiled peacefully," Mead wrote, saying "My friends will take care of everything." She detached herself from the webbing of life, never mentioning work again. She gave up thinking about the future and concentrated on staying "quietly alive" until Ruth Valentine, summoned by telegram, arrived from California. Ruth Bunzel and Margaret Mead spent as much time with her as they could in the remaining five days of her life. When Valentine arrived, the two spent the afternoon talking, and Benedict died that evening. Coincidentally, or not so coincidentally, Benedict died on September 17, 1948, the anniversary of her father's birth. She was sixty-one years old.[27]

Margaret Mead took over management of Research in Contemporary Cultures and brought it to a conclusion in 1951. If Benedict had lived, and had written her book on anthropology and international relations, the project might have had the broad impact all the participants had hoped for. As it was, in the years following Benedict's death, the reaction to RCC dissipated any significance of its findings. The anthropology community reaffirmed its identity as a science by rejecting RCC. Cora Du Bois, reviewing *The Study of Culture at a Distance* (1953), edited by Margaret Mead and Rhoda Métraux, admitted that national character study had not gained acceptance because it was not considered scientific. She added that whether "esthetic, intuitive, and perceptual gifts" were "any more irrelevant to science than 'intelligence' is certainly open to debate." John W. Bennett, reviewing the book in the *American Journal of Sociology,* wrote, "this national culture material unquestionably has validity—often a very great deal." But this validity was gained from "intuitive methods which from any 'scientific' standpoint absolutely lack reliability." RCC was perceived as unbalanced in the direction of child-rearing as a causal deterministic force and larded with the jargon and the suspect techniques of psychoanalysis. The reaction to RCC was distinguished by its emotional tone, a sure sign that the issue in hand was not the true issue being addressed. Colleagues caricatured actual RCC findings by oversimplification. Swaddling was the key target for this attack. An oversimplification like "Swaddling them as infants makes Russians incapable of freedom" could easily be dismissed by any anthropologist, while a statement that the "prolonged and very tight" swaddling of Russian child-rearing practice "is one of the means by which Russians communicate to their infants a feeling that a strong authority is necessary" required serious and possibly ineffectual logical refutation. The emphasis on child-rearing in RCC was satirized and trivialized as "diaperology."

Through such trivialization RCC was placed outside the professional boundaries of the anthropological community. Its chief findings were denigrated by the anthropological community, which used it as a lever to discredit Culture and Personality research in general. It took the 1960's to revive C&P as "psychological anthropology," a subdiscipline of mainstream anthropology. The cultural impact of RCC on its own time was also small. A few anthropologists were hired by the American government and the United Nations, but anthropology in general did not have much effect on American policy. America through the 1950's and 1960's did just what Ruth Benedict had warned against—tried to fit other countries into the American scheme of values and ignored basic cultural differences with costly international consequences.[28]

On the surface, Research in Contemporary Cultures as a memorial to Ruth Benedict's life seems hardly fitting. But upon re-examination the important legacy of RCC was not, after all, its content, but its structure. This structure remains in itself Benedict's last great vision, an attempt to concretize her ideas of the "New Earth" in a structural reality. It combines within itself a feminist, synergistic, and potentially Post-Modern view of the world.

The project design was unique—deliberately so, for design experimentation had been written into the terms of the contract. The project was not just interdisciplinary. Like the European seminar at Columbia, RCC was designed to create the effect of a United Nations in miniature. Each research group represented a country or culture of the world, and they all came together in the general seminar, where they had to learn to understand each other's frame of reference, confront and learn from their different cultural reactions to the same material, and cooperate with each other for the furtherance of RCC's common goals. The institutional frame of the project was set up synergistically to facilitate this interaction. First, there were no "outsiders." Instead of creating in-groups and out-groups based on status, prestige, or work, the project created one huge in-group that emphasized mutual concerns, shared goals and problems, and concern for the project as a whole over the work of any individual group. The general seminar, described by one member as "that wonderful cauldron of people," was the institutional locus for this effect. It met every two weeks, everybody belonged to it, including secretaries and typists, and everybody was obliged to attend. Each person, from the rawest new student to the most seasoned professional, had equal respect and status there. Reports on individual group work were given in the general seminar, and work on particular themes was compared and contrasted among the groups. There people got to know each other and how each of them worked and established a common language. There they received a sense that they belonged to a whole that was indeed greater than the sum of its parts, for which they all shared a common loyalty. One result was that the project workers had "the zeal of Crusaders" and the conviction that they were "the most brilliant army ever assembled." [29]

RCC created high synergy also by teaching people through its organization to expect rewards from cooperation with people, not competition with them. Sharing with others was emphasized. Everybody was expected to read what everybody else had written and to circulate their own notes on interviews and other material. This was made easier by the provision of clerical help in writing-up and automatic carbon copying of material for each of the project offices. People coordinated with each other and became colleagues and teammates rather than rivals. Gaining advantage at someone else's expense was minimized. Competition for secretarial help was minimized by providing it on the basis of need rather than status and by decentralizing the clerical staff. The organizational design was non-hierarchical. Instead of the usual pyramiding organization with its narrowing ladder of increasing power and status embodying the necessity of competing with fellow workers for ever fewer positions of authority, the research groups, all "coequal circles," radiated out from a central circle, which was the general seminar that included everyone in the project.[30]

RCC tried to eliminate competition for status and prestige roles by minimizing them and downplaying their importance. Research groups did not have bosses; they had "conveners" who facilitated the group's work by taking responsibility for necessary group organization and communication with other groups and project staff but had no dictatorial authority. All project administrators also worked in a research group so that they would be in constant touch with what was actually going on and to discourage their identification by themselves and by the groups with pyramidal status roles. Thus Benedict appeared as director on the organizational chart, but was not the director of the general seminar, only a member of it, and also first a member, then convener of the Czech group. Valentine was executive secretary, but also a member of the Czech group. Mead served as research director and thus directed the general seminar, as co-convener with Geoffrey Gorer of the Russian group, and as a member of the French group. As Mead later wrote, "There were no titles that indicated prestige, but only those indicating different types of responsibility." [31]

Leadership in RCC embodied the synergistic concept that leaders gave away power to get results, which Benedict had elaborated in her article "Primitive Freedom" (1942). No differentiation of status was made between volunteers and paid workers, novices or professionals, full or part-time workers. Benedict did not give herself a salary and so made volunteer project work respectable on the one hand and subject to her own high standards on the other. Mead also contributed her time on a voluntary basis. Space was organized, partly out of exigency, in non-hierarchical fashion. There was no central, high-status project office. The general seminar met in space loaned by the Viking Fund. Individual groups met in members' homes. Typing and collating of materials, informal message-leaving and meetings went on at the Kipps Bay–Yorkville Health Center, Columbia, the American Museum of Natural History, and the French Cultural Mission the first year; in the second year the project lost the French Mission space and gained other space from Columbia University.[32]

In synergistic fashion the group framework was organized to *extend* and complement the abilities of individual members. The complexity of the material on modern civilizations was too great for one person alone to absorb. Optimally, Benedict and the other planners had wanted groups containing members of at least three cultures, both sexes, several disciplines, and several types of mind, with varying experience levels and age range. The range of group members would compensate for the limitations of each individual member, and the interactions and exchange of knowledge between members would speed up the individual creative process and lead to insights by individuals that they otherwise could not have had. This group design was rooted in the idea suggested by Ruth Benedict that the synergistic community reinforced individual needs and desires and enhanced individual self-respect, thus rooting the work in self-interest and not abstract ideals. RCC was a social structure designed as an experiment in creating high synergy as it reinforced individual needs and desires while using them to create a project greater than the sum of its individuals.[33]

The result of this experiment was a low aggression level among project workers and a high degree of social cohesion. Mead wrote that the many diverse workers "never had an important argument about methods or concepts" during the time of the project.[34] They generated an enormous amount of work. In the back of *The Study of Culture at a Distance*, Mead and Métraux listed fifty publications that had resulted from the project by 1953, and that listing was not inclusive.

RCC was feminist in a rather subtle way. To understand this element it is necessary to understand Ruth Benedict's own philosophy as a feminist. Like Olive Schreiner, she agreed that feminism took many forms, public and private. Benedict's own form of feminism dealt with the "depths of the individual consciousness." Hers was an internal feminism. Like Ellen Key she believed it necessary to clear away the "dead rubbish of conventionalism" concerning women in society that each individual both male and female had internalized. This would give woman her own relativistic freedom—as Key wrote, "the absolute right to believe, to feel, to think and to act in her own way, if it does not interfere with the rights of others." Key called this "the psychological sphere" of feminism.[35]

By the end of World War I Benedict's feminism had its focus in this mental sphere, in the changing of attitudes, beliefs, and expectations about women and by this means creating a "feminist" society. This meant for her a society in which gender did not matter; in which, as Olive Schreiner had written, each individual could find the work that most contributed to his or her "development, happiness, and health," and in which his or her special gifts benefited society as well. She desired to create a world where, as Key wrote, men and women could be complete personalities: people who cultivated their strength as human beings without neutralizing the characteristic of sex. In the 1920's Benedict's feminism became what she might have called with Ellen Key a Woman's Movement of the spirit, both in its desire to change women's individual "spirits," that is, their internal consciousness and makeup, and also the "spirit" or "genius" of the culture. As Key wrote, this new feminism began with men and women who "did not follow the call of the spirit of the time; no, who from lonely heights sent out their awakening call *to* the time," who fought to "give their age new ideals." The first goal, freeing women from convention, Benedict saw as becoming possible when men and women embraced a new, liberating, relativistic philosophy of life, such as she advocated in *Patterns of Culture*. She was aware of the value of the concept of culture in changing internalized beliefs and values concerning men and women. In the 1930's she encouraged Margaret Mead to explore the relativity of seemingly innate qualities of masculinity and femininity. The results of Mead's field work in *Sex and Temperament* seemed to show decisively the role of culture in setting male and female standards. During that time she also worked with psychoanalyst Karen Horney to create a cultural rather than an instinct-based psychology. With Freud's ideas that women's inferior position in society stemmed from biology, women were caught in a trap. If this position were shown to be cultural, the inferiority of women could be changed. All this work and the work with cultural relativity fulfilled other purposes besides these, but along with them they also worked to change negative internalized values, beliefs, and attitudes about women. This side of feminism, changing ideas about men and women in society, continued to be important to her. But along with it grew the desire also to change the "spirit" of American culture by substituting for the underlying "male" perspective of American society a "female" one, such a radical new point of view that it would change the direction of the culture itself.[36]

Ellen Key had talked in general about women bringing "new points of view . . . new means . . . and new ends" to social problems. Olive Schreiner had hinted at the possibility when talking of women and war. The day women took their place beside men in public affairs, Schreiner wrote, would also be "that day that heralds the death of war as a means of arranging human differences." This would not occur because of some natural moral superiority on women's part, but as a result of experiences women had that were not shared by men. Women, she wrote, knew the preciousness of human flesh, having given it birth. "Men's bodies are our women's works of art," she wrote, not to be thrown away cheaply. Women could kill, she stated, but not lightly. "Arbitration and compensation" would seem to women "cheaper and simpler methods of bridging the gaps in national relationships." In her poetry in the 1920's one of Benedict's goals had been to present the realm of the spirit from a woman's point of view, in relation to a woman's insights and a woman's experience. More and more toward the last part of her life she seemed to concentrate on the introduction of *women's* values and a woman's perspective into American culture. When Benedict received a letter asking for an article from a feminine point of view, she sent the editor her "Natural History of War." Her research concentrated on the benefits of cooperation, traditionally a woman's value complex, over competition, traditionally a male value complex. Intuition had been identified as a "woman's" quality. In her American Anthropological Association presidential speech Benedict held up the insight of intuition as being just as important as the findings of science.[37]

Research in Contemporary Cultures was intended to be a living example of the effectiveness of organization and research conducted within the underlying premises of a woman's perspective on society. Many aspects that were synergistic also overlapped as feminist. Ellen Key had pinpointed cooperation as a feminine value before World War I, urging mothers to educate their children in the naturalness of cooperation, not competition. When women gained power, she saw them using it for cooperative purposes such as more humane working conditions and a more just distribution of profits. RCC stressed a "feminine" non-hierarchical circular structure over a "masculine" pyramidal hierarchical one. Part-time work and volunteerism had traditionally been women's areas. In the 1940's Benedict wrote about the feelings of inferiority volunteer women often internalized. She recognized volunteerism as a problem area for women's self-esteem because of the lack of respect given to volunteers, yet it was an important and essential element in American life. RCC gave volunteers the same status as paid workers, the part-time worker the same respect as the full-time.[38]

RCC treated workers, in the tradition of women's socialization toward concern with interpersonal relations, as full human beings. As Mead wrote, the project took into account each worker's "special skills and defects," culturally inculcated and job-related strengths and weaknesses, "his blind spots, his babies, his love affairs, and his psychoanalysis." The emphasis on the importance of interpersonal relations built an organization that did not make workers keep rigid hours; that gave people "time off to deal with personal crises without question"; that recognized that some people "will sleep until ten in the morning and work until two in the morning"; and that accepted that going to a party given by a group member "may be more important at a given moment than recording another interview." Interpersonal relations had normally been viewed as a woman's area and especially as a component of the home. RCC treated interpersonal relations as an important component of productivity.[39]

Another important undervalued area for women in American society was parenthood and nurturing. Benedict spoke of this in a talk on "The Psychology of Love." Most societies, she said, gave to raising a family the social rewards America gave to ownership of property and high income. She talked of how society discriminated against the family compared to business or government and of the necessity of revaluing parenthood in American society until it gained the esteem given to public careers, and nurturing had gained a place in American public life as well as private life. RCC provided an opportunity for valuing child study as highly as other, more prestigious areas of anthropological study such as social organization or the study of religious ceremonials.[40]

One last theme important to Benedict ran through the project—a Modern perspective on life which had begun to take on elements of the Post-Modern, or as some prefer to call it, the second stage of Modernism. RCC was Modern in its attempt to foster multi-perspectivity as the focal element of insight. In the general seminar, by listening and participating, members got a multi-perspective look at cultures, as Mead wrote, "now as Greeks, now from the viewpoint of a French education, now as Russians, now recalling Polish training—about a Chinese problem." The scrambled nature of the groups also encouraged multiple-perspective realizations from members, as they utilized the insights from different cultures, disciplines, sexes, temperaments, levels of experience, and ages present within their group. RCC was characterized by its acceptance of diversity.[41]

None of the research groups were alike. Each had different task organization, met at different times on different schedules, and was differently composed. Each group met the spirit of the project's original ideal of group makeup in its high degree of diversity. Each group was expected to have a member or members of the culture being studied in it, but that was the only regularity, and these differed by class, education, and time away from the culture. Each group planned its own work in its own sequence. The whole diversified structure was held together by the regularity of the general seminar and the necessity of preparing general seminar presentations on topics and questions common to all groups for cross-cultural comparison. Finally RCC was Modern in its acceptance of cultural differences without feeling the necessity of remodeling them, only of working with them. Benedict described her work and implicitly RCC not as the study of national character, but as the study of national *differences*. "The diversities do not confuse the picture," she wrote; "they enrich it."[42] For a world that hoped for the success of the United Nations yet doubted that order and harmony could occur out of such wide diversity of cultures and seeming chaos of values, RCC offered a working example that it could be done.

RCC began to go beyond the Modern in its creative use of "chaos," its tolerance for disorder, its movement away from formal constraints, and its acceptance of dissonance and diversification as integral to the functioning of the structure. Benedict was willing "to let anyone—of no matter how unorthodox an approach or a professional background—work in the project if that person was motivated to do so," wrote Mead. Their organization gave them a structure within which to use the talents of every type of person drawn to the project: the steady worker and the erratic, the eccentric, the busy, the skilled and the non-skilled. Participation included full-time work by professionals as well as temporary and long-term part-time work; committed volunteer work by both students and professionals; paid student work; and student involvement through university courses, ranging from the giving of a few weeks' time to signing up for the project's duration. RCC accepted and used the talents of the gifted who did not fit into a peacetime mold: "the aberrant, the unsystemic, the people with work habits too irregular ever to hold regular jobs." [43]

Another area where RCC verged beyond Modernism was in its incorporation of chance elements. Both the research groups and the general seminar were open-ended. Anyone could come to one meeting or several, depending on his or her interest and interaction with the group. Groups were encouraged to incorporate a novice whose naïve viewpoint might bring fresh insights that the trained mind overlooked. Benedict herself in her last years seemed to be moving to an acceptance of contradictions as a natural feature of life: not just artificial contradictions that one proceeds to solve, but contradictions for which there were as yet no answers. She seemed to be groping toward a higher-order synthesis that did not nullify contradiction as the Moderns had done, but worked through contradiction to a new integration. She manifested this view in her idea of moving "beyond relativity" to an intellectual position where absolute and relative would not be contradictory opposites, but would somehow integrate in a new higher-order synthesis. She shared this vision in her AAA presidency speech in her acceptance of the scientific and humanistic contradictions of anthropology and her belief that both were necessary to the development of the discipline.[44]

Although the cultural impact of RCC in its own time was small, it remains a great vision of how humankind can create a unified world out of dissonant reality.

Benedict ended her life as she had lived it, reaching beyond the boundaries of most of her contemporaries, boundaries she had regarded as narrow and constricting. She spent her life trying to enlarge and ultimately eliminate those boundaries, not by eliminating differences, but by respecting them. Perhaps her best epitaph lies in words she herself wrote on the death of her mentor, Franz Boas. Like him she had not sold out, or stultified herself, or locked herself in a dogmatic cage. Her sister wrote after her death that Ruth had so often "stirred up my mind and exploded so many conventional notions and given me a new point of view." [45] This was her gift to America as well.

The holism of Ruth Benedict's anthropology, which influenced a generation of anthropologists, has fallen into the past for most contemporary members of the discipline. But for American society the challenge of the ideas she proposed and the changes woven into the American pattern of values and beliefs remain. They are her enduring legacy.

Notes

Abbreviations Used

AA	*American Anthropologist,* New Series
AW	*An Anthropologist at Work: Writings of Ruth Benedict,* ed. Margaret Mead
AW2	Ms. of *AW,* "Supplementary Copy No. Two of Correspondence Only," in ECP Papers (see Chapter 6, note 35)
ECP Papers	Elsie Clews Parsons Papers, American Philosophical Society Library, Philadelphia
FB Papers	Franz Boas, Professional Correspondence, microfilm of original collection at American Philosophical Society Library, Philadelphia (see Chapter 4, note 13)
HRC	Harry Ransom Center, University of Texas at Austin
JAFL	*Journal of American Folk-Lore*
LB Papers	Louise Bogan Collection, Amherst College Library, Amherst, Mass.
MM Papers	Margaret Mead Papers, Library of Congress, Washington, D.C.
RFB Papers	Ruth Fulton Benedict Papers, Vassar College Library, Poughkeepsie, N.Y.

Prologue: The "Simple Theme"

1. Benedict wrote, "It is curious to see how the basic patterns of our lives hold from babyhood to decrepitude. All the tale could be told if we could set down the simple theme and the more and more significant terms in which we work it out in our different stages of growth." Journal fragment, "Dec. 3" [n.d., c. 1935], in the Ruth Fulton Benedict Papers, Vassar College Library, Poughkeepsie, New York. [The collection is cited hereafter as RFB Papers.]

2. "The Story of My Life . . . ," in *An Anthropologist at Work: Writings of Ruth Benedict,* ed. Margaret Mead, reprint ed., p. 99. Except for a few fragments I was unable to find a handwritten original of this partial autobiography in the RFB Papers at Vassar, although there is a typewritten copy of *An Anthropologist*

at Work. ["The Story of My Life . . ." is cited hereafter by page number in the text. *An Anthropologist at Work* is cited as *AW.*]

The RFB Papers also contain other autobiographical fragments on Benedict's childhood that were not included in *AW.*

3. Experts writing about children and death today concur with Benedict's psychological analysis, agreeing that exposure to death can lead to emotional and behavioral problems, that small children's reactions to death are largely influenced by their observations of adult reactions, that children sometimes feel responsible for deaths around them, and that withdrawal and anger are not uncommon reactions to death among children. See Robert Kastenbaum and Ruth Aisenberg, *The Psychology of Death*, pp. 15, 23; Erna Furman, *A Child's Parent Dies: Studies in Childhood Bereavement*, pp. 14, 15, 18, 21, 111, 112, 122, 168; Charles E. Hollingsworth, et al., *The Family in Mourning*, pp. 71, 72, 80, 101, 103.

4. On the normality of small children running away, see Elinor Verville, *Behavior Problems of Children*, p. 185.

5. Journal fragment, "July 12, 1930," RFB Papers.

Although Benedict understood Nietzsche's own meanings for Apollonian (critical-rational) and Dionysian (creative-passionate) and used them more in her sense to apply to the Pueblo and Plains Indians, in the context of her childhood she viewed Dionysian as destructive and Apollonian as creative. Her mother's world was a world of confusion and destruction, and her father's world was the place where the greatest beauty and insight were possible.

On identification with the dead parent, see Furman, *A Child's Parent Dies*, pp. 59, 65, 98, 169; Hollingsworth et al., *The Family in Mourning*, p. 102.

Verville, *Behavior Problems*, p. 165, says the "peak age" for imaginary friends is three and a half, and they are usually created by children of "superior intelligence, especially girls." The imaginary playmate gives children "great pleasure." She continues, "No harm is done when a child creates an imaginary playmate and he usually disappears when the child starts to school and exchanges his private world for the real one."

6. "Dec. 3" [n.d.], RFB Papers.

7. On anger at death and children's response, see Furman, *A Child's Parent Dies*, p. 122; Hollingsworth et al., *The Family in Mourning*, p. 103; Verville, *Behavior Problems*, pp. 110, 128, 182, 188, 276. On children's developmental stages, see Arnold Gesell et al., *Infant and Child in the Culture of Today*, rev. ed., pp. 43–44, 145–146; *The Child from Five to Ten*, rev. ed., pp. 37–42, 82–83, 98, 101, 108, 287. On depression see Felix Brown, "Depression and Childhood Bereavement," *Journal of Medical Science* 107 (1961): 775; David Moriarty, *The Loss of Loved Ones*, pp. 67–89.

8. On discipline and the hard-of-hearing child, see Beryl Lieff Benderly, *Dancing without Music: Deafness in America*, pp. 47, 64; Lily Brunschwig, *A Study of Some Personality Aspects of Deaf Children*, pp. 10, 16, 19.

9. Benderly, *Dancing without Music*, p. 101; Helmer R. Myklebust, *The Psychology of Deafness*, pp. 49–50, 116, 136, 144, 151, 357–359; Henry Hunter Welles, *The Measurement of Certain Aspects of Personality among Hard of Hearing Adults*, p. 10; Verville, *Behavior Problems*, p. 168.

10. On vomiting and psychophysical illness, see Verville, *Behavior Problems,* pp. 138, 234–235.

11. On the servant girl's suicide, see autobiographical fragment beginning "When I was a little girl nine years old," RFB Papers. On children's death play see Hollingsworth et al., *The Family in Mourning,* pp. 72, 78; Kastenbaum and Aisenberg, *The Psychology of Death,* p. 149. It is also possible to view the cave in the hay as a womb image.

12. See Marvin Meyers, *The Jacksonian Persuasion: Politics and Belief,* pp. 33–56; Paul E. Johnson, *A Shopkeeper's Millennium: Society and Revivals in Rochester, New York, 1815–1837,* pp. 38–48.

13. For more on Colonial women's roles see Laura Thatcher Ulrich, *Good Wives,* especially the chapter on "Deputy Husbands," and pp. 37–38.

Catharine Beecher, *Treatise on Domestic Economy for the Use of Young Ladies at Home and at School,* pp. 28–29.

14. See Kathryn Kish Sklar, *Catharine Beecher,* pp. 134–137, 151–167.

15. In "Our Last Minority: Youth," *New Republic* 104 (February 24, 1941): 271, Benedict wrote, "Our latest minority group is Youth. When I was young it was women; they were special animals who belonged in the home."

16. Barbara Welter, "The Cult of True Womanhood: 1800–1860," in *Dimity Convictions: The American Woman in the Nineteenth Century,* pp. 21–41. Ann Douglas, *The Feminization of American Culture,* pp. 84–85. John S. Haller, Jr., and Robin M. Haller, *The Physician and Sexuality in Victorian America,* especially Chapter 2, "The Lesser Man."

17. Harriot Stanton Blatch and Alma Lutz, *Challenging Years: The Memoirs of Harriot Stanton Blatch,* p. 9.

Douglas, *The Feminization of American Culture,* pp. 240–272. See also Barbara Welter, "Coming of Age in America: The American Girl in the Nineteenth Century," in *Dimity Convictions,* pp. 10–13; Thomas Bender, *Toward an Urban Vision: Ideas and Institutions in Nineteenth Century America,* pp. 80–93; Kastenbaum and Aisenberg, *The Psychology of Death,* p. 151; James J. Farrell, *Inventing the American Way of Death, 1830–1920,* pp. 4–5, 34; Robert W. Habenstein and William M. Lamers, *The History of American Funeral Directing,* pp. 392, 413–416.

Helen Swick Perry, *Psychiatrist of America: The Life of Harry Stack Sullivan,* pp. 47, 117, 118, 120, 123, 9. Perry noted a "continuous and major preoccupation with suicide" (p. 123) in the *Norwich Sun* from 1890 to 1910.

1. Inner Circle, Outer Circle

1. On Ruth Benedict's perception of herself as an outsider see Margaret Mead, "Anne Singleton, 1889–1934," *AW,* p. 83, and "Patterns of Culture, 1922–1934," *AW,* p. 201. Anthropologists themselves have acknowledged the pattern in their discipline that draws those somehow on the edge of society to its ranks, the type of person who prefers to look at societies with an outsider's eye. See Margaret Mead and Ruth Bunzel, eds., *The Golden Age of American Anthropology,* p. 5; Hortense Powdermaker, *Stranger and Friend: The Way of an Anthropologist,* pp. 20, 21.

2. Homeopathy (spelled "homoeopathy" in the nineteenth century) was the creation of German Dr. Samuel C. F. Hahnemann (1755–1843). Homeopathy came to America around 1825 and by mid-century formed a significant part of American medicine. The other two major medical sects were allopathy and eclecticism. See William G. Rothstein, *American Physicians in the Nineteenth Century,* pp. 152–162, 177, 230–239, 246.

3. "In Memory of Fred S. Fulton," *Chenango Union* (Norwich, N.Y.), April 25, 1889; reprinted from *North American Journal of Homoeopathy,* April 1889 [hereafter cited as Fulton obit.].

4. Fulton obit.

5. A letter from Peggy Freeman Courtney, Ruth Benedict's niece, October 1982, related the story of the engagement.

6. Date is from "Obituary. Dr. S. J. Fulton," in file at Guernsey Memorial Library, Norwich, N.Y. [hereafter referred to as Norwich Library file]. This obituary of Frederick Fulton's father comes from a local newspaper, of which there were two at the time: the *Chenango Union* (also at times known as the *Chenango Semi-Weekly Telegraph*), and the *Norwich Sun* (also known as the *Morning Sun*). The obituary ran sometime in December 1896, probably in the *Chenango Union.* [Hereafter cited as S. J. Fulton obit.]

"Obituary. Hetty D. Shattuck," in Norwich Library file, local newspaper, probably the *Chenango Union,* n.d., 1900 [hereafter cited as Hetty Shattuck obit.].

On the Phi Beta Kappa, see *The Vassarion, being a Record of College Life during the Senior Year of the Class of 1906, Edited by the 1906 Vassarion Board,* p. 214. [*The Vassarion* is cited from here on as *Vassarion,* year.] On Miss Mittleberger's, see the Vassar Biographical Questionnaire filled out by Bertrice Shattuck Fulton, dated December 1, 1929, in the possession of the Vassar Alumnae Association. On Ruth as Class Baby, see *Vassar Alumnae Monthly* 1 (1910): 183. There were thirty-five members in the Class of 1885.

7. Letter from Peggy Freeman Courtney, October 1982.

8. Fulton obit. On neurasthenia, see Haller and Haller, *The Physician and Sexuality,* pp. 5, 6, 14.

9. S. J. Fulton obit.; see also typed page titled "Shattuck and Allied Families L929S," Norwich Library file.

10. "Mrs. S. J. Fulton," obituary from June 1897, in the Norwich Library file, local newspaper, probably the *Chenango Union* [hereafter cited as Harriet Fulton obit.]; see also "Obituary, Ella L. Fulton," Norwich Library file, local newspaper, n.d., probably January 1927; reprinted from the *Colorado Springs Gazette,* December 29 [1926].

11. "Death of a Well-Known Farmer," *New York Farmer,* Thursday, October 23, 1913 [hereafter cited as John Samuel Shattuck obit.]. Information on the Shattucks' early life and the Shattuck farm comes from what looks like a family journal page, handwritten, Norwich Library file.

12. "Mrs. John Samuel Shattuck," in the Norwich Library file, n.d., local newspaper (after November 23, 1909, the date of death) [hereafter cited as Joanna Terry Shattuck obit.]. Information on the children is from the handwritten page mentioned above in the Norwich Library file.

13. Hetty Shattuck obit.; see also "Obituary," in *The Searchlight*, church paper of the Delaware Avenue Baptist Church, Buffalo, September 1900.

14. "Mary Shattuck Ellis who passed away December 20, 1930," a tribute written and read by Mrs. James R. Spraker at the meeting of the Abigail Fillmore Chapter, Daughters of the American Revolution, January 23, 1931, copy in Norwich Library file. "Obituary, Mary Shattuck Ellis," by E. G. W. in a local Norwich newspaper, n.d., after December 20, 1930, the date of death, copy in Norwich Library file. "In Memoriam," *Town Club Bulletin*, Buffalo, n.d., c. January 1931, copy in Norwich Library file.

15. "In Memoriam," *Chenango Union*, September 13, 1945. "Obituary. Myra Shattuck," *Chenango Union*, August 31, 1945.

16. Fulton obit. "The Story of My Life," *AW*, p. 97. [As in the Prologue, page numbers from this work are cited in the text.]

17. Lemuel Shattuck, *Memorials of the Descendants of William Shattuck*, p. 16. Family information from an interview with Ruth Benedict, "Who's News Today—Red Man's Culture Is Her Specialty," by Delos W. Lovelace, 1946, unidentified newspaper clipping, possibly *New York Sun*, RFB Papers.

18. Mary M. DeBolt, ed., *Lineage Book: National Society of the Daughters of the American Revolution*. Vol. 67, 67001–68000, 1908, pp. 36–37. The DAR came into existence in 1890 and reflected increasing nativism in turn-of-the-century America.

S. J. Fulton obit. "Benedict, Ruth." In *Current Biography* (1941), p. 66.

19. "In Memoriam," *Chenango Union*, September 13, 1945. Ruth Benedict to Chard Powers Smith, April 2, 1947, RFB Papers. On her grandfather, see Ruth Benedict, Interview by Oliver Pilat, *New York Post*, April 8, 1944, clipping in RFB papers.

20. "Old Esther Dudley" and "The Perseverance of Sir William Phipps" are both stories in the RFB Papers.

21. Judith Schachter Modell, in *Ruth Benedict: Patterns of a Life*, pp. 31, 39, makes a point of Benedict's disliking pea-shelling, but Benedict's own writings show just the opposite. "May 20" [1913], in "Journal: 1912–1916," *AW*, p. 126, speaks of the family's common sense.

22. Autobiographical fragment [n.d., c. 1935], which begins, "We have been talking," RFB Papers.

23. Ibid.

24. "July 12, 1930," RFB Papers.

25. "The Passing of Gabriel—Regent's Composition, Jan. '01," "The Home of Evangeline," "A Blessed Incident," "The Happiest Evening of My Life—Writer: Evangeline," and "How the Acadian Men Were Entrapped—Writer: Father Felican," are all in the RFB Papers.

26. "We have been talking," RFB Papers.

27. Autobiographical fragment, "When I was a little girl nine years old" (two versions in same fragment), RFB Papers.

28. Margery Fulton Freeman to Margaret Mead, September 18 [1948], RFB Papers. On nervous diseases, see Haller and Haller, *The Physician and Sexuality*, pp. 59, 15, 37, 38. On Vassar women's reputations, see Henry Noble MacCracken, *The Hickory Limb*, p. 164.

29. Blatch and Lutz, *Challenging Years*, p. 9. Farrell, *Inventing the American Way of Death*, pp. 34, 133. See also Habenstein and Lamers, *The History of American Funeral Directing*, pp. 389, 344; Douglas, *The Feminization of American Culture*, pp. 240–272.

30. Letter from Peggy Freeman Courtney, October 1982.

31. Psychologists today find this pattern an expected reaction among children who have lost a parent. When a parent dies the child depends all the more on the surviving parent. Furman, in *A Child's Parent Dies*, p. 169, says: "The children tended to direct their anger at the dead parent against the living one so that the latter would receive more than double the amount of anger. Yet the children's intense dependency on the only living parent made it particularly difficult for them to tolerate any anger against this parent."

32. On lying in young children, see Verville, *Behavior Problems*, p. 174.

33. Bertrice Shattuck Fulton, in Associate of Vassar College 1938 Biographical Register Questionnaire, in the possession of the Vassar Alumnae Association.

34. Ibid. See also the *Thirty-Second Annual Report of the Board of Education of the City of St. Joseph, Mo., for the Year 1895–96*, p. 25.

35. On Norwich, see *The National Atlas of the United States*, U.S. Department of the Interior Geological Survey (1970), pp. 6, 389, and J. H. Mather and L. P. Brockett, M.D., *A Geographical History of the State of New York . . .* , pp. 269, 272. On St. Joseph, see R. A. Campbell, ed., *Campbell's Gazetteer of Missouri . . .* , p. 77, and Howard L. Conrad, ed., *Encyclopedia of the History of Missouri*, pp. 439, 442, 517–518. St. Joseph was the county seat of Buchanan County.

For her remarks on her early education, see Ruth Fulton Benedict, "The Challenge of the Elementary Schools," *Vassar Quarterly* 3 (July 1918): 269–270.

36. Larry Dean Pettegrew, *The History of Pillsbury Baptist Bible College*, pp. 36, 34, 35. Edgar Bruce Wesley, *Owatonna: The Social Development of a Minnesota Community*, pp. 70–71, 139–140.

37. Wesley, *Owatonna*, pp. 101, 126–128. See also W.P.A. Federal Writers' Project, *Minnesota: A State Guide*, p. 399.

38. William M. Case, ed., *The Sibyl*, Vol. 4 (1898), pp. 15, 16.

39. Although he was kind to Ruth he was later discharged under a cloud, accused of "soliciting young girls" ("The Story of My Life," *AW*, p. 107).

40. "Eager to Fight," *People's Press* (Owatonna, Minn.), April 29, 1898, p. 1. "Academy Gleanings," *Owatonna Journal*, April 29, 1898. On declining enrollment, see Pettegrew, *History of Pillsbury*, p. 37.

On the invitation from Aunt Mamie, letter from Peggy Freeman Courtney, October 1982. On salaries, see Philip S. Foner, *Women and the American Labor Movement*, p. 264, and June Sochen, *Herstory: A Record of the American Woman's Past*, p. 200. On Bertrice Fulton's salary in Norwich and St. Jo, see Perry, *Psychiatrist of America*, p. 62.

41. Brenda K. Shelton, *Reformers in Search of Yesterday: Buffalo in the 1890's*, p. 4. Karl Baedecker, ed., *The United States with an Excursion into Mexico*, p. 193, and *The United States with Excursions to Mexico, Cuba, Porto* [sic] *Rico, and Alaska*, 4th rev. ed., pp. 136–137.

42. "Dec. 3" [n.d., c. 1935], RFB Papers.

43. In *Madisonensis,* the Madison University school newspaper, for June 21, 1882, Vol. 14, No. 17, p. 1, F. S. Fulton was listed as one of the editors.

44. "Lulu's Wedding (A True Story)," RFB Papers.

45. "The Greatest of These," RFB Papers. Myklebust, *The Psychology of Deafness,* p. 116, suggests that people with hearing problems don't acquire the same biases and tabus that mark the "normal" population.

46. "Obituary," *The Searchlight,* September 1900.

47. School averages from letter from Peggy Freeman Courtney, September 19, 1982. Information on Mrs. Thompson from the above letter and Margery Fulton Freeman, quoted in *AW,* pp. 537–538n.3.

2. Vassar

1. Margery Fulton Freeman, quoted in *AW,* p. 538. Robert A. Smith, *A Social History of the Bicycle,* pp. 75–82, 97–109. Vassar graduate, quoted in Agnes Rogers, *Vassar Women,* p. 216.

2. Mabel Newcomer, *A Century of Higher Education for American Women,* pp. 46, 49.

"Madcap Frolics of College Girls," *Ladies Home Journal,* October 1905, pp. 17, 62–63; S. T. Rorer, "What College Girls Eat," *Ladies Home Journal,* November 1905, pp. 13–14; "When College Girls Make Merry," *Ladies Home Journal,* November 1908, p. 34; February 1909, p. 22; May 1909, p. 23; November 1909, p. 34; "College Girl Follies," *Good Housekeeping,* September 1909, pp. 238–241.

Margery Fulton, in *Class Day Book, Vassar Class of 1909,* p. 6; copy in possession of the Vassar Alumnae Association.

3. G. Stanley Hall, quoted in "Educational Questions of the Day," *Current Literature,* September 1904, p. 273. A. L. Smith cited in Haller and Haller, *The Physician and Sexuality,* p. 59. Frances M. Abbott, "Three Decades of College Women," *Popular Science Monthly,* August 1904, pp. 350–352. I determined the figure given for Vassar women by dividing the number of married women by the total number of graduates given in the article. Professor D. Collin Wells, "Some Questions Concerning the Higher Education of Women," *American Journal of Sociology* 14 (May 1909): 735.

4. Elsie Clews Parsons, "Higher Education of Women and the Family," *American Journal of Sociology* 14 (May 1909): 759–762.

5. Newcomer, *A Century of Higher Education,* p. 22. James Monroe Taylor and Elizabeth Hazleton Haight, *Vassar,* pp. 137, 159, 183. Blatch and Lutz, *Challenging Years,* p. 42. Mary Caroline Crawford, *The College Girl of America,* p. 69. Pamphlet, "Welcome to Vassar College, Poughkeepsie, New York: A Map of the Campus," n.d. [1980's], "Campus Landmarks" section, n.p.

6. "Dec. '15," in "Journal: 1912–1916," *AW,* p. 135. Crawford, *The College Girl,* p. 63. Taylor and Haight, *Vassar,* p. 186.

7. Lillian L. Stroebe, "The Teaching of German at Vassar College in Peace and War: A Retrospect, 1905–1943," *Bulletin of Vassar College* 34, No. 2 (March 1944): 6, 8, 9. In her first semester of German Benedict received a B, in her second semester an A, and another B in sophomore year. She also received an A in music.

Modell, in *Ruth Benedict,* p. 58, says Benedict got a D in German and in music but that is wrong according to Benedict's transcript. Also, she could not have graduated Phi Beta Kappa with two D's. On Benedict's classes and grades, see Ruth Fulton, Vassar College Transcript, RFB Papers.

The information about Benedict's hearing comes from a letter from Margaret Mead to her grandmother, Martha Adeline Mead, February 19, 1924, Margaret Mead Papers, Library of Congress, Washington, D.C. [hereafter cited as MM Papers]. On the major in English literature, see Margaret Mead, *Ruth Benedict,* p. 7.

8. Taylor and Haight, *Vassar,* p. 183. *Class Day Book,* p. 6. Taylor and Haight, *Vassar,* p. 180.

9. Crawford, *The College Girl,* pp. 65, 68, 69.

10. Taylor and Haight, *Vassar,* pp. 179, 185; see also pp. 182, 183.

11. *Class Day Book,* pp. 15–16. Crawford, *The College Girl,* p. 67.

12. Crawford, *The College Girl,* p. 63. *Class Day Book,* p. 15. The class of 1909 chose new officers each semester for their freshman, sophomore, and junior years, then one president for the entire senior year, but there were six presidents in all. Tyer served not only as second-semester sophomore president, but also as senior-year president.

13. Crawford, *The College Girl,* pp. 60–62.

14. MacCracken, *The Hickory Limb,* pp. 20, 22, 24, 25. Abbott, "Three Decades of College Women," p. 359.

15. MacCracken, *The Hickory Limb,* p. 25; see also p. 34. *Vassarion,* 1909, p. 53. Blatch and Lutz, *Challenging Years,* p. 271; see also p. 108. MacCracken, *The Hickory Limb,* p. 26. Margery Fulton Freeman, "100th Anniversary Questionnaire," Vassar College Alumnae Association, November 1956. Constance Dimock Ellis, *The Magnificent Enterprise: A Chronicle of Vassar College,* p. 43.

See also Taylor and Haight, *Vassar,* pp. 190–191; *Vassarion,* 1907, pp. 114, 118, 138, 173; 1908, pp. 86, 88, 96, 99, 222; 1909, pp. 122, 135, 136, 140, 142.

16. "The Sense of Symbolism," *AW,* p. 116; ms. also in RFB Papers. Friedrich Wilhelm Nietzsche, *Thus Spake Zarathustra,* in *The Philosophy of Nietzsche,* p. 162. See also Freeman, "100th Anniversary Questionnaire"; Blatch and Lutz, *Challenging Years,* pp. 109, 113, 133.

17. Rogers, *Vassar Women,* p. 118. MacCracken, *The Hickory Limb,* pp. 25, 33, 70. Ruth Fulton [Benedict] to Florence V. Keys, a letter written c. 1910 in her European trip notebook, probably unsent, expressing schoolgirl admiration for Keys' teaching, RFB Papers. Edith Finch, quoted in Jesse Bernard, *Academic Women,* p. 311n.15. See also Freeman, "100th Anniversary Questionnaire"; Interview with Gerald Blank, *PM Daily,* c. February 1948, copy in RFB Papers.

18. Rogers, *Vassar Women,* p. 170. Bernard, *Academic Women,* p. 114.

19. "Dec. '15," *AW,* pp. 134–135. Walter Pater, *The Renaissance: Studies in Art and Poetry,* 5th ed., pp. 234, 236–238.

20. "Dec. '15," *AW,* p. 134.

21. Walter Pater, *Marius the Epicurean: His Sensations and Ideas,* Vol. 2, p. 218; *The Renaissance,* p. 213; "A Study of Dionysius: The Spiritual Form of Fire and Dew," in *Greek Studies,* pp. 9–52.

22. On discovering Nietzsche, see Benedict to Margaret Mead, April 1926, *AW*, p. 548n.35. Friedrich Wilhelm Nietzsche, *The Birth of Tragedy from the Spirit of Music,* in *The Philosophy of Nietzsche,* pp. 953, 967, 984, 999, 1033, 951. Anthony Ward, *Walter Pater: The Idea in Nature,* p. 82. "Dec. 3" [n.d.], RFB Papers.

23. Benedict to Mead, April 1926, in *AW*, p. 548. Nietzsche, *Thus Spake Zarathustra,* pp. 92, 144, 239, 238, 18, 25.

24. Nietzsche, *Thus Spake Zarathustra,* pp. 75, 73, 69, 70.

25. Blatch and Lutz, *Challenging Years,* p. 108. Charlotte Perkins Gilman, *Women and Economics,* pp. 38, 222, 237, 178.

26. Margaret Deland, "The Change in the Feminine Ideal," *Atlantic Monthly,* March 1910, p. 292.

27. John Burroughs, quoted in H. A. Haring, "John Burroughs' Own Story of Slabsides," in H. A. Haring, ed., *The Slabsides Book of John Burroughs,* p. 30. MacCracken, *The Hickory Limb,* p. 85. See also *Vassarion,* 1909, p. 181; Caroline E. Furness, "John Burroughs and Some Bird Lovers from Vassar," in Haring, ed., *The Slabsides Book of John Burroughs,* pp. 145–168.

28. Vassar student, quoted in Furness, "John Burroughs and Some Bird Lovers from Vassar," p. 168. MacCracken, *The Hickory Limb,* p. 85. "The Sense of Symbolism," *AW*, p. 117.

John Burroughs, "Literary Values," pp. 3, 5, and "The Secret of Happiness," pp. 244, 249, 250, 253, in *Literary Values and Other Papers.*

Nietzsche, *Thus Spake Zarathustra,* p. 368.

See also Haring, "John Burroughs' Own Story of Slabsides," pp. 45–46.

29. John Burroughs, *Whitman: A Study,* p. 1. Ruth Fulton [Benedict], "Walt Whitman," *Vassar Miscellany* 37 (March 1908): 306, 305. At this time the *Miscellany* was a literary magazine published bimonthly. It later became a newspaper, published weekly.

30. Ruth Fulton [Benedict], "*Lena Rivers,* by Mary J. Holmes," *Vassar Miscellany* 37 (May 1908): 422; "Literature and Democracy," *Vassar Miscellany* 38 (March 1909): 292, 293, 294.

31. *Vassarion,* 1908, p. 148.

32. *Vassarion,* 1909, pp. 32, 55; see also pp. 84, 173, 236; 1911, p. 77; 1907, p. 75. Agnes Naumberg Bass to Margaret Mead, September 26 [1948], in RFB Papers.

On a page headed "Chicago—Aug. 12–28, 1909," in her European trip notebook Ruth listed the names of people she met, some of them from Hull House, including "Aunt Harriet—Miss Monroe." Although she did not say whom she was visiting, her friend Polly Root lived in Chicago. European trip notebook in RFB Papers.

33. Freeman to Mead, September 18 [1948], RFB Papers. Freeman, "100th Anniversary Questionnaire." On Margery's school activities, see *Vassarion,* 1906, pp. 19, 26, 118; 1907, p. 85; 1908, p. 82; 1909, p. 115.

34. Bruce Barton, "Dr. R. Freeman Says We Have Influence," *Buffalo Times,* January 3, 1926. "Dr. Robert Freeman Dies in California," *Buffalo News,* June 29, 1940. "Rev. Robert Freeman, D.D.," in *History of Pasadena and the San Gabriel Valley, California* (S. J. Clarke Pub. Co., 1930), Vol. 2, p. 194.

Priscilla Leonard, "The Joys of Jiu-Jitsu for Women," *Current Literature*, August 1904, p. 144.

35. Ruth Fulton [Benedict], "The Fool in King Lear," *Vassar Miscellany* 38 (November 1908): 47. On Margery, see *Vassarion*, 1908, p. 90; 1909, pp. 126, 84, 43; on Ruth, see *Vassarion*, 1909, p. 84; 1913, p. 244.

36. Ruth Fulton [Benedict], "The Racial Traits of Shakespeare's Heroes," *Vassar Miscellany* 38 (June 1909): 480–486; "The Sense of Symbolism," *AW*, pp. 113–117. Other essays by Benedict published in the *Miscellany* not already mentioned include: "The High Seriousness of Chaucer," 37 (October 1907): 1–6; "*The Trojan Women* of Euripedes," 37 (November 1907): 53–57; "Charles Lamb: An Appreciation," 37 (January 1908): 193–198.

37. *Vassarion*, 1909, p. 43. Freeman to Mead, September 18 [1948], RFB Papers.

38. Crawford, *The College Girl*, p. 70. Rogers, *Vassar Women*, p. 216.

3. The Limits of the Possible

1. Ruth explains the suddenness of the trip in Fulton to Keys, RFB Papers. Information on the other young women comes from a handwritten note on the back of a picture from the European trip called "The Three at Certosa—Betty on the wall and Katherine below her," RFB Papers. The note also stated that C. M. Pratt of Glen Cove, Long Island, a boyhood friend of Katherine Norton's father and Dean of Pomona College at that time, paid all expenses for the trip. On Pratt as a Vassar trustee, see MacCracken, *The Hickory Limb*, p. 11. Probably the trip was offered to the top graduates of the Class of 1909, and the woman who graduated first had other plans. Margery, who graduated second, had married Robert Freeman in June. That left Ruth, who graduated third.

Ruth's account of the trip comes from the *First Annual Bulletin, Class of 1909*, June 1910, p. 23, copy in possession of the Vassar Alumnae Association, Vassar College, Poughkeepsie, N.Y. [hereafter referred to as *Class Bulletin*].

2. Fulton to Keys, c. 1910, RFB Papers. "The Switzerland without a Baedecker," pages of description of a two-day walking tour the girls took through little Swiss villages, in Ruth's European trip notebook, c. 1910, RFB Papers. *Class Bulletin*, p. 23.

3. European trip notebook, pages of description of the Swiss family the three young women stayed with, RFB Papers.

4. Joanna Terry Shattuck obit. details death of grandmother, November 23, 1909. On C.O.S. work see Ruth Benedict, "Questionnaire for Biographical-Address Register," Alumnae Office, Vassar College, May 10, 1919 [cited hereafter as "Questionnaire"]; also "Chronology," *AW*, p. 524. Benedict got the dates wrong on her questionnaire for the years she taught and did social work, but she showed her social work as paid, not volunteer. On the Charity Organization Society, see Paul Boyer, *Urban Masses and Moral Order in America, 1820–1920*, pp. 145, 150.

5. Boyer, *Urban Masses*, p. 152. Roy Lubove, *The Professional Altruist*, p. 80.

6. Fulton to Keys, c. 1910. "Dec. '15," *AW*, p. 135.

7. Unpublished mss., "The Chance for Life" and "The Last Bluff," RFB Papers. Jacob Riis, *How the Other Half Lives*, p. 207.

8. "The Chance for Life," p. 1. "The Last Bluff," pp. 2, 3.

9. "Douglaston—Nov. '14," in "Journal: 1912–1916," *AW*, p. 132. [Page numbers for published journal entries are given in the text hereafter.] This depression was not an unusual reaction for educated women of Ruth Benedict's generation as they struggled to find a use for their education and an outlet for their energies after college. See Rogers, *Vassar Women*, p. 101, and Barbara Ehrenreich and Deirdre English, *For Her Own Good: 150 Years of the Experts' Advice to Women*, pp. 1–3.

Freeman to Mead, September 18 [1948], RFB Papers.

"Mary Wollstonecraft," c. 1914–1917, *AW*, p. 499. Benedict wrote this about Mary Wollstonecraft, but it applies to her own life as well.

Los Angeles City Directory (1912), p. 1616 (on the Westlake School for Girls). Bertrice Shattuck Fulton, "Questionnaire for Biographical-Address Register," Alumnae Office, Vassar College, May 10, 1919. Benedict to Mr. Warren [first name unknown], May 23, 1946, RFB Papers.

10. Sochen, *Herstory*, p. 200.

11. On the California suffrage campaign, see Eleanor Flexner, *Century of Struggle: The Woman's Rights Movement in the United States*, pp. 255, 257.

Olive Schreiner, *The Story of an African Farm*, p. 167. Benedict mentions this book in a draft of a letter to Houghton Mifflin concerning publication of her women's biographies, c. 1918, RFB Papers.

12. Olive Schreiner, *Woman and Labor*, 8th ed., pp. 75, 79, 81, 172.

13. Ibid., pp. 258, 19, 65, 62, 69, 184.

14. Ibid., pp. 125, 129, 141, 142, 265, 273.

15. Stanley Benedict to Ruth Fulton [Benedict], January 14, 1913, *AW*, p. 539.

16. William H. Summerson, "Benedict, Stanley Rossiter," *Dictionary of American Biography, under the Auspices of the American Council of Learned Societies,* Vol. 22, Supplement 2 [to December 31, 1940], pp. 35–36; Elmer Verner McCollum, "Stanley Rossiter Benedict, 1884–1936." *Biographical Memoirs*, National Academy of Sciences, Vol. 27, pp. 155–177.

17. Stanley Benedict to Ruth Fulton [Benedict], 1913, quoted in *AW*, p. 537.

18. Stanley Benedict to Ruth Fulton [Benedict], January 14, 1913, *AW*, pp. 539–541.

19. "The Bo-Cu Plant," unpublished ms., RFB Papers. The pseudonym "Edgar Stanhope" could have many meanings. My guess is that the Edgar is after Edgar Allan Poe, a favorite of both Ruth and Stanley, and "Stanhope" could be a pun on Stanley's hopes for the story genre of chemical detective stories, and also a pun on Ruth's aspirations, because Lady Mary Stanhope was a famous bluestocking in eighteenth-century England.

20. Freeman to Mead, September 18 [1948], RFB Papers.

21. "Mary Wollstonecraft," *AW*, p. 491.

22. Handwritten note on back of picture of Ruth Benedict in canoe, RFB Papers. Dr. Jeanette A. Behre, quoted in McCollum, "Stanley Rossiter Benedict," p. 169.

23. Ellen Key, "The Morality of Woman," in *The Morality of Woman and*

Other Essays, trans. Mamah Bouton Borthwick, pp. 28, 32. Schreiner, *Woman and Labor,* p. 19.

The chess story comes from Esther S. Goldfrank, *Notes on an Undirected Life,* p. 223.

24. Autobiographical fragment, n.d.[c. 1930's] beginning, "~~I shrink from love~~," RFB Papers.

25. Ibid.

26. On Benedict's childlessness, see Margaret Mead, *Ruth Benedict,* p. 18. The major writers are Mead herself, Kardiner and Preble (*They Studied Man*), and Jessie Bernard (*Academic Women*). See note 28 below.

27. "Thursday, February 8," in "Diary: 1923," *AW,* p. 65; "Monday, January 15," in "Diary: 1923," *AW,* p. 60.

28. "The Woman-Christ," n.d., RFB Papers. Anne Singleton [Ruth Benedict], "To My Mother," *Poetry* 31 (January 1928): 192. Kardiner and Preble, *They Studied Man,* p. 180. Mead, *Blackberry Winter,* p. 269. See also Bernard, *Academic Women,* p. 24; she says that, denied motherhood, Benedict's life became a "torturous search" for meaning—but it already was before this fact became known. Apparently other friends of Ruth Benedict did not agree with Mead's emphasis on Benedict's childlessness; see *Blackberry Winter,* p. 313. Mead sometimes misread what Benedict said (see *Blackberry Winter,* pp. 131, 214), and Mead wrote that Benedict shaped her responses to the needs and interests of her friends (*AW,* p. xix).

29. Goldfrank, *Notes on an Undirected Life,* p. 36.

30. Ellen Key, *The Woman Movement,* trans. Mamah Bouton Borthwick, pp. 175, 181, 182, 171, 163, and "The Morality of Woman," in *The Morality of Woman and Other Essays,* pp. 5, 15.

31. Key, *The Woman Movement,* pp. v, xv, 68, and "The Woman of the Future," in *The Morality of Woman and Other Essays,* pp. 54, 66, 72.

32. Schreiner, *Woman and Labor,* pp. 141–142.

33. Notebook on *Adventures in Womanhood,* RFB Papers.

34. Ibid.

35. Notebook on Margaret Fuller, attached note and p. 5, RFB Papers.

36. "Mary Wollstonecraft," unpublished ms., RFB Papers. "Mary Wollstonecraft," *AW,* pp. 493–494, 515, 518, 519.

37. Notebook on Margaret Fuller, p. 39, RFB Papers. "Mary Wollstonecraft," *AW,* p. 494. Title page of ms. "Mary Wollstonecraft," RFB Papers.

38. Margaret Mead, *Ruth Benedict,* p. 18; McCollum, "Stanley Rossiter Benedict," p. 165.

39. "Foreword" [to *Adventures in Womanhood*], RFB Papers.

4. The Search for Place

1. "May, 1917," in "Journal Fragments: 1915–1934," *AW,* p. 142. "Rupert Brooke, 1914–1918," *AW,* p. 6. Ellen Key, "The Conventional Woman," in *The Morality of Woman and Other Essays,* pp. 68, 62, 67.

2. Benedict, "The Challenge of the Elementary Schools," pp. 272, 271. Bene-

dict, "Questionnaire." The entry under "Graduate Study; professional and technical training," begins "1918–1919 with John Dewey Columbia University."

3. Kastenbaum and Aisenberg, *The Psychology of Death*, pp. 104, 105.

4. Psychology in recent years has begun the study of "script theory," the idea that some people's lives are predisposed to travel certain paths as a result of forced, premature early childhood decisions about who they are. One of these "scripts" concerns life expectancy. A person, according to this theory, can give him or herself unconscious permission to live only until a certain age. If the person lives beyond this age he or she may experience a release of energy or gradually begin to enjoy life. This seems to have been the case with Ruth Benedict. For popular presentations of this theory, see Claude Steiner, *Scripts People Live* and *Games Alcoholics Play;* also Eric Berne, *Beyond Games and Scripts,* especially pp. 190–191.

5. Kastenbaum and Aisenberg in *The Psychology of Death* say that ideas about death undergo "developmental transformations" throughout life (p. 43). A letter from Benedict's sister, Margery Fulton Freeman, to Margaret Mead, September 18 [1948], RFB Papers, indicates that this occurred for Ruth Benedict. Freeman spoke of Benedict's preoccupation with death turning into a love of life in her later years.

Benedict, on living to fifty, quoted in photo section, hardcover edition of *An Anthropologist at Work* (Boston: Houghton Mifflin Company, 1959), n.p. On needing a career, Benedict, quoted in Margaret Mead, "Search," *AW,* p. 3.

"Some new lovelier life . . ." is from an early, unpublished poem called "(Printemps) Deridens," RFB Papers (discussed by Mead, "Anne Singleton 1889–1934," *AW,* p. 86), which can be read as a veiled comment on World War I.

6. Alvin Johnson, *Pioneer's Progress: An Autobiography,* p. 278. Mead, "Search," *AW,* p. 7.

7. Leslie Spier, "Elsie Clews Parsons, I," *American Anthropologist* [hereafter cited as *AA*] 45 (1943): 244, 246. Alfred L. Kroeber, "Elsie Clews Parsons, II," ibid., pp. 252–255. Gladys Reichard, "Elsie Clews Parsons," *Journal of American Folk-Lore* [hereafter cited as *JAFL*] 56 (1943): 45, 47. Peter H. Hare, *A Woman's Quest for Science: Portrait of Anthropologist Elsie Clews Parsons,* pp. 11–13, 19. Elsie Clews Parsons, *The Family: An Ethnographical and Historical Outline . . . ,* pp. 49, 346, 349, 350, 354. Goldfrank, *Notes on an Undirected Life,* p. 21.

8. Wilson D. Wallis, "Alexander A. Goldenweiser," *AA* 43 (1941): 250, 253. Margaret Mead, in section labeled "June 12, 1957," p. 9, "Draft of *An Anthropologist at Work* 1957," RFB Papers (material deleted from the final version). Benedict, "A. A. Goldenweiser," manuscript, RFB Papers; later published as part of an article, "Alexander Goldenweiser: Three Tributes, Sidney Hook, Ruth Benedict, Margaret Mead," *Modern Quarterly* 11 (1940): 31–34. Class notes, "History of Anthropological Thought," taught by Goldenweiser in 1924, MM papers. Titles of talks in a six-lecture series given by Goldenweiser in April 1923, *AA* 25 (1923): 129.

9. Benedict, "A. A. Goldenweiser," RFB Papers. Benedict ultimately took four courses from Goldenweiser: "Groundwork of Civilization" (Spring 1920), "Early

Society and Politics" (Fall 1920), "Early Economics and Knowledge" (Spring 1921), and "The Diffusion of Civilization" (Fall 1921). Information from a pink sheet noted "Information on Ruth Benedict's courses as student at New School, given by Miss de Lima of the New School," RFB Papers.

Judith Modell, *Ruth Benedict*, p. 117, says that Elsie Clews Parsons accompanied Benedict to her admissions interview with Franz Boas. Sidney W. Mintz, "Ruth Benedict," in *Totems and Teachers*, ed. Sydel Silverman, p. 144, also says Boas accepted Benedict "on Parsons' urging." But relations between Parsons and Benedict always remained formal and a little strained. Although she came to address Alfred Kroeber in letters as "Kroeber," and Lowie as "Robert," with Elsie Clews Parsons it remained "Mrs. Parsons" to her death. See Margaret Mead, "The Years as Boas' Left Hand," *AW*, p. 342; Goldfrank, *Notes on an Undirected Life*, p. 94.

On Lowie, see *Robert H. Lowie, Ethnologist: A Personal Record*, pp. 168, 170; Mead and Bunzel, eds., *Golden Age*, pp. 342, 485; Robert F. Murphy, *Robert H. Lowie*, pp. 10, 11, 20; Paul Radin, "Robert H. Lowie, 1883–1957," *AA* 60 (1958): 358, 359.

10. Benedict, Autobiographical fragment beginning "When I was a little girl nine years old," RFB Papers.

11. Edward B. Tylor, "How the Problems of American Anthropology Present Themselves to the English Mind," *Science* 4, No. 98 (December 19, 1884): 550. Nancy Oestreich Lurie, "Women in Early Anthropology," in *Pioneers of American Anthropology*, ed. June Helm, pp. 38, 39. Mead and Bunzel, eds., *Golden Age*, pp. 205, 227.

12. Franz Boas, quoted in Gladys Reichard, "Franz Boas and Folklore," in Alfred L. Kroeber et al., *Franz Boas, 1858–1942*, p. 53. Alfred L. Kroeber, "Franz Boas: The Man," in ibid., pp. 22, 7. (On the scars see also Abram Kardiner and Edward Preble, *They Studied Man*, p. 136; Mead, *Blackberry Winter*, p. 122. The different descriptions of the scarring between Kroeber and Mead can be explained by a facial operation Boas had for cancer in 1915.) Robert H. Lowie, "Franz Boas (1848–1942)," *JAFL* 57 (1944): 64. Franz Boas, "An Anthropologist's Credo," in "Living Philosophies, II," *Nation* 147 (August 27, 1938): 201.

13. Eight-page statement headed "Nov. 1917," numbered 219–226, "Barnard College 1917" handwritten at the top, pp. 219, 220; Boas to Sylvester Viereck, June 19, 1917; Boas to Tozzer, June 6, 1917; all in Franz Boas, Professional Correspondence, 44 reels, 35 mm. (Wilmington, Del.: Scholarly Resources, Inc., 1972); microfilm of the original collection at the American Philosophical Society Library, Philadelphia [hereafter referred to as FB Papers].

14. See George W. Stocking, Jr., "The Scientific Reaction against Cultural Anthropology, 1917–1920," in *Race, Culture, and Evolution*, pp. 270–307. This essay deals in depth with the covert issues behind Boas' censure in 1919. They included hyperpatriotism and post-war xenophobia, especially anti-Germanic: a regional power struggle between Washington and Boas in New York; and the struggle to create a professional anthropological identity and what that identity would be.

15. C. W. Weiant, "Bruno Oetteking, 1871–1960," *AA* 62 (1970): 676. Mead, "Search," *AW*, p. 10. Alfred L. Kroeber, "Pliny Earle Goddard," *AA* 31

(1929): 3–4, 5. Boas to Nicholas Murray Butler, November 28, 1928, FB Papers. Lowie, *Robert H. Lowie*, p. 136. Mead and Bunzel, eds., *Golden Age*, p. 342. Murphy, *Robert H. Lowie*, p. 32.

16. Peter Hare calculated just from adding up sums mentioned in *JAFL* that Parsons had given over $30,000 through the years to *JAFL* alone (Hare, *A Woman's Quest*, p. 21). Boas' papers contain letters thanking her for her secretarial fund over the years. See also Goldfrank, *Notes on an Undirected Life*, p. 4. For information on the Southwest Society, see Hare, *A Woman's Quest*, p. 148.

17. Lowie, "Franz Boas," p. 60. Mead, "Search," *AW*, p. 13. On the students, see Gladys Reichard to Boas, May 18, 1919, FB Papers; Marian W. Smith, "Gladys Amanda Reichard," *AA* 58 (1956): 913, 914; Alan P. Merriam, "Melville Jean Herskovits, 1895–1963," *AA* 66 (1964): 83; Goldfrank, *Notes on an Undirected Life*, pp. 1, 2, 19.

Boas' then-secretary Esther Schiff (Goldfrank) first used "Papa Franz" on the Southwest field trip to Laguna in 1920 (Goldfrank, p. 39), and it gradually circulated in the Department. It became a mark of inside status in the Department to be able to speak or write to Boas as "Papa Franz," and both men and women did it.

18. Mead, "Search," *AW*, p. 8; Goldfrank, *Notes on an Undirected Life*, p. 37.

19. Mead, "Search," p. 9. Robert Lowie to Boas, February 21, 1923, FB Papers. Alexander Goldenweiser, *Early Civilization*, pp. 191–192. Edward Sapir to Benedict, June 25, 1922, *AW*, p. 49. Boas to Professor Charles Cooley, November 7, 1922, FB Papers.

Modell cites publication of the dissertation as a key focal point, but I believe the dissertation defense to have been the actual rite of passage. During that time one became a colleague within the profession and entitled to be called "Dr." after the final defense. The Ph.D. was not conferred officially until after publication of the dissertation, which sometimes took years because of lack of funds. Margaret Mead, for example, defended in 1925 before she went to Samoa. But she did not receive her Ph.D. officially until 1929, when her dissertation was finally published. This occurred after the publication of *Coming of Age in Samoa* and while Mead was on her second field trip. According to "Chronology," *AW*, p. 524, Benedict defended at the end of the spring semester, 1922. Sapir congratulated her in June 1922, and Boas called her "Dr. Benedict" in an official report on anthropological work to Columbia President Nicholas Murray Butler in October 1922 (Boas to N. M. Butler, October 1, 1922, FB Papers).

On the number of Ph.D.'s, see Bernard, *Academic Women*, p. 71. The use of the maiden name was a feminist code at the turn of the century just as hyphenating the maiden and married names became in the 1970's. Anyone who used that form of her name was advertising her feminist leanings.

20. Mead, "Ruth Fulton Benedict, 1887–1948," *AA* 51 (1949): 458.

Benedict, "A Brief Sketch of Serrano Culture," *AA* 26 (1924): 366. Modell says that Benedict stayed with her sister's family in Pasadena and not at the reservation and that her informant, Rosa Morongo, came to work with her there (*Ruth Benedict*, p. 170). This can't be the whole truth, however. Benedict wrote that just after World War I "I was living with the Serrano Indians of Southern California" ("The Natural History of War," *AW*, p. 371), and Mead (*Blackberry Winter*,

p. 147) talked of Benedict taking her mother along for a vacation when she worked with the Serrano.

Theodora Kroeber, *Alfred Kroeber*, pp. 86–87. (She calls the syndrome Meunier's disease.) Boas to Dean Walter Morris Hart [of Berkeley], October 31, 1921, agreeing to teach summer school June 26 to August 5, FB Papers.

21. Boas to Benedict, September 17, 1922, RFB Papers. Goldfrank, *Notes on an Undirected Life*, p. 36.

22. Benedict to Boas, September 16, 1923, FB Papers (reprinted in *AW*, p. 399). "Diary: 1923," *AW*, p. 60. Kardiner and Preble, *They Studied Man*, p. 141. Benedict, "A. A. Goldenweiser," RFB Papers. Modell (*Ruth Benedict*, p. 117) suggests this was her pattern with Parsons.

23. "Diary: 1923," *AW*, p. 65.

24. Boas to Robert Lowie, February 13, 1923, and to Elsie Clews Parsons, February 9, 1923; Parsons to Boas, February 10, 1923; all in FB Papers.

25. "Diary: 1923," *AW*, pp. 65–66.

26. Benedict to Boas, September 16, 1923, FB Papers (reprinted in *AW*, p. 400). Sapir to Benedict, September 10, 1923, *AW*, p. 54. Melville Herskovits to Margaret Mead, August 23, 1923, MM Papers. On the concordance, see Benedict to Erna Gunther, June 28, 1928, RFB Papers.

27. Ruth Bunzel to Boas, August 6 [1924], FB Papers. Triloki Nath Pandey, "Anthropologists at Zuñi," *Proceedings of the American Philosophical Society* 116 (1972): 332, 331. "Dr. Ruth Bunzel," a vita collected in the MM Papers. "Ruth L. Bunzel," in Margaret Mead, *Anthropologists and What They Do*, p. 88. For nickname, see "Index of Personal Names," *AW*, p. 566.

28. Pandey, "Anthropologists at Zuñi," p. 333. Benedict to Mead, September 3, 1925, *AW*, p. 299. Ruth Bunzel, *The Pueblo Potter*, "Acknowledgements," n.p. The eleven hours of dictation came from Mead to Benedict, September 13, 1924, *AW*, p. 287. "They Dance for Rain in Zuñi," *AW*, pp. 222–225.

29. Benedict to Mead, August 6, 15, 24, and 29, September 1, 3, 5, 8, 13, and 16, 1925, *AW*, pp. 291–303.

30. "Preliminary Report of Anthropological Fieldwork, Summer of 1927," RFB Papers.

The concordance was never completed. In 1926 Benedict handed the work to a woman hired to complete it, since she herself was hard pressed for time. This did not work out, so she and Boas arranged to give the concordance work to anthropologist Erna Gunther [Spier] in 1927. Gunther, because of changes in her life and the press of other work, never completed it either.

31. Rexmond C. Cochrane, *The National Academy of Sciences*, p. 246. Frank R. Lillie to Elsie Clews Parsons, May 23, 1924, RFB Papers. Merriam, "Melville Jean Herskovits," p. 84. Mead, *Blackberry Winter*, p. 140.

32. Sapir to Benedict, October 21, 1926, *AW*, pp. 184–185. Benedict, "Application for Small Grant in Aid of Research in the Humanistic and Social Sciences" (given by the American Council of Learned Societies in 1926, 1927, and 1928), denied; see Edward C. Armstrong to Benedict, April 23, 1926, RFB Papers. Smith, "Gladys Amanda Reichard," p. 914, on the Guggenheim. Frank Fackenthal to Ruth Benedict, May 10, 1926, on the job and salary, RFB Papers.

33. "Chronology," *AW*, p. 524. Mead (*AW*, p. 524) says Benedict became an

anthropology lecturer in 1923, but I have found nothing to substantiate this and there is a letter in the FB Papers that appears to be the original request for her first appointment, Franz Boas to Dean F. J. E. Woodbridge, December 29, 1924. Copies of the "Budget, Anthropology Department, 1925–1926," list Melville Herskovits, P. E. Goddard, and Ruth Benedict as lecturers with no salary, FB Papers; also "Annual Budget 1927–28," FB Papers.

On Boas' *JAFL* assistant, see Boas to Tozzer, October 9, 1923, FB Papers, and "Thirty-Fifth Annual Meeting of the American Folk-Lore Society," *JAFL* 37 (1924): 245; p. 246 shows Benedict elected Assistant Editor. *JAFL* 38 was edited by Ruth Benedict. For the other honors, see "Annual Meeting, January 2, 2:30 p.m.," in "Anthropology at the Washington Meeting and Proceedings of American Anthropological Association," *AA* 27 (1925): 191, Benedict elected to the 21-member council for 1928; and "American Anthropological Association, Proceedings of the American Anthropological Association for the Year Ending December, 1928," *AA* 31 (1929): 324, Benedict elected a member of the Executive Committee.

34. Boas to Dr. Beardsley Ruml, March 16, 1927, and to Dean Frederick J. E. Woodbridge, November 30, 1927, FB Papers. Mead, in "The Years as Boas' Left Hand," *AW*, p. 347, states that it was not until her separation from Stanley that Boas began trying to get Benedict a permanent job. The evidence shows that this is just not true. Mead, *Ruth Benedict*, p. 29. Woodbridge to Boas, February 21, 1928, FB Papers.

35. Benedict to Professor John J. Coss, February 21, 1928, RFB Papers.

36. John Coss to Benedict, October 16, 1930, RFB Papers. Boas to Nicholas Murray Butler, November 15, 1929, FB Papers. Frank Fackenthal to Benedict, February 7, 1928, February 5, 1929, and February 4, 1930, RFB Papers.

37. Boas to Alfred Kroeber, February 27, 1931, and Dean Howard McBain to Boas, May 12, 1931, FB Papers. Benedict to Frank Fackenthal, June 3, 1931, RFB Papers.

5. The Social Quest

1. "Aug. 15, 1919," in "Journal Fragments: 1915–1934," *AW*, pp. 142–143.

2. Mead, "Search," *AW*, p. 5. "[Undated]," in "Journal Fragments," *AW*, p. 144.

3. Sapir to Benedict, December 12, 1924, *AW*, p. 166. Franz Boas, "Aims of Ethnography (1888)," in *Race, Language, and Culture*, p. 629. Benedict, "Franz Boas as an Ethnologist," in Kroeber et al., *Franz Boas*, p. 33.

4. Clark Wissler, "Opportunities for Coordination in Anthropological and Psychological Research," *AA* 22 (1920): 8–9. Wissler was a former student of Boas from the first generation who remained at the American Museum of Natural History after Boas' resignation in 1905 and took Boas' former job there, a seeming disloyalty that rankled for years. Wissler also held ideas of Nordic racial superiority with which Boas thoroughly disagreed. See George W. Stocking, Jr., "Wissler, Clark," *Dictionary of American Biography*, Supplement 4, 1946–1950, pp. 906–909.

Clark Wissler, *Man and Culture*, pp. 328, 336. Franz Boas, *Anthropology and*

Modern Life, p. 11. Benedict, "Franz Boas as an Ethnologist," p. 31. Franz Boas, "Anthropology," in *Encyclopaedia of the Social Sciences,* Vol. 2, p. 110.

5. William Fielding Ogburn, *Social Change,* pp. 364–365.

6. J. Donald Butler, *Four Philosophies and Their Practice in Education and Religion,* 3d ed., pp. 385, 387.

7. Nels Anderson, *The Hobo.*

For a good account of objectivity, particularism, and function in the social sciences see Edward A. Purcell, Jr., *The Crisis of Democratic Theory,* pp. 21–24.

8. Ruth Fulton Benedict, *The Concept of the Guardian Spirit in North America,* p. 85; italics added. A. R. Radcliffe-Brown took these words by Benedict as a "rags and tatters" approach to culture (see Mead, "Patterns of Culture," *AW,* p. 204). It was not her intent here to deny interconnections and relations but to deny culture as *a closed system.* Her own vision, when she elaborated it in *Patterns of Culture,* was a marvelously open system.

Sapir to Benedict, June 25, 1922, *AW,* p. 50. "Diary: 1923," *AW,* p. 58. Ogburn, *Social Change,* pp. 200–201, 206. John Dewey, *Human Nature and Conduct,* p. 108.

9. Margaret Mead to Grandma [Mrs. Martha Adaline Ramsay Mead], March 11, 1923, MM Papers.

10. Ruth Benedict, *Patterns of Culture,* p. 33. "Diary: 1923," *AW,* pp. 60, 63, 69. Mead, note 3 to "Two Diaries," *AW,* p. 534. Benedict tried to get "Cups of Clay" published in *Century Magazine* but was unsuccessful.

11. Edward Burnett Tylor, *The Origins of Culture,* Vol. 1, p. 1.

12. Stocking, "Lamarckianism in American Social Science, 1890–1915," in *Race, Culture and Evolution,* p. 264. Franz Boas, "Eugenics," *Scientific Monthly* 3 (1916): 472.

13. Alfred Kroeber, "The Superorganic," *AA* 19 (1917): 183, 179, 180, 188. Edward Sapir, "Do We Need a Superorganic?" *AA* 19 (1917): 441. Alexander Goldenweiser, "The Autonomy of the Social," *AA* 19 (1917): 448. ("Superorganic" was a word Kroeber borrowed from nineteenth-century social scientist Herbert Spencer with conscious irony, for Spencer was a staunch defender of the inheritance of acquired characteristics.)

14. Robert H. Lowie, *Culture and Ethnology,* pp. 1, 5, 39–40; see also pp. 16, 35, 38–39.

15. For a thorough development of this thesis, see Stocking, "Lamarckianism in American Social Science, 1890–1915," in *Race, Culture and Evolution.*

16. Alfred Kroeber, "The Superorganic," pp. 193, 201, 202, and "On the Principle of Order in Civilization as Exemplified by Changes of Fashion," *AA* 21 (1919): 263.

17. Sapir, "Do We Need a Superorganic?" pp. 443, 442. Sapir to Benedict, June 25, 1922, *AW,* p. 50. Goldenweiser, "The Autonomy of the Social," p. 449.

18. Robert H. Lowie, *Primitive Society,* p. 441. Franz Boas, "In Memoriam: Herman Karl Haeberlin," *AA* 21 (1919): 73, and "The Methods of Ethnology," *AA* 22 (1920): 315.

19. Benedict, "A Brief Sketch of Serrano Culture," pp. 366–368 [map page between], 375, and *Patterns of Culture,* p. 34.

Nietzsche wrote, "Bless the cup that is about to overflow that the water may flow golden out of it, and carry everywhere the reflection of thy bliss! Lo! This cup is again going to empty itself and Zarathustra is again going to become a man," in *Thus Spake Zarathustra*, p. 4.

20. Franz Boas, *The Mind of Primitive Man*, p. 204. Benedict, "Myth," in *Encyclopaedia of the Social Sciences*, Vol. 11 (1933), p. 180, and "Folklore," in ibid., Vol. 6 (1931), p. 288.

21. Hermann Weyl, quoted by G. H. Whitrow, *The Nature of Time*, p. 125. *Modernism* is a term used in the study of literature of the early twentieth century which describes a changed world view. It has been expanded by some historians in true non-Euclidean fashion to describe a cultural epoch. It is not original with me and it has its imperfections, but it is the best term in use now for what I am trying to describe.

22. Franz Boas, "Changes in Bodily Form of Descendants of Immigrants" (1910–1913), in *Race, Language and Culture*, pp. 60–75. (Preliminary report 1910; final report later.) Melville Herskovits, "Franz Boas as Physical Anthropologist," in Kroeber et al., *Franz Boas*, pp. 39, 47.

23. Walter Pater, "Coleridge," in *Appreciations: An Essay on Style*, p. 65. Nietzsche, *Thus Spake Zarathustra*, p. 60. Gilman, *Women and Economics*, p. 274.

24. Robert H. Lowie, "Reflections on Goldenweiser's 'Recent Trends in American Anthropology' (*AA* 43 [1941], pp. 151–163)," p. 6, ms. in the Elsie Clews Parsons Papers at the American Philosophical Society Library in Philadelphia, Pennsylvania [hereafter cited as ECP Papers]. Butler, *Four Philosophies*, pp. 390–392.

25. Sigfried Giedion, *Space, Time and Architecture*, 5th ed., rev. and enl., p. 14.

26. Guillaume Apollinaire, "Pure Painting" (1913), in *The Modern Tradition: Backgrounds of Modern Literature*, ed. Richard Ellmann and Charles Feidelson, Jr., p. 116.

27. Ezra Pound, "In a Station of the Metro," in *Ezra Pound, Selected Poems*, p. 35. F. S. Flint and Ezra Pound, "Imagism," in *The Modern Tradition*, ed. Ellmann and Feidelson, p. 143.

28. "Mary Wollstonecraft," *AW*, p. 492. Benedict to Robert Redfield, November 20, 1930, RFB Papers. (Marcel Proust was a Modern French writer who wrote from a multiplicity of views.) Purcell, *The Crisis of Democratic Theory*, pp. 51–52.

29. Purcell, *The Crisis of Democratic Theory*, pp. 49–51. "Mary Wollstonecraft," *AW*, p. 491.

30. John M. Clark, quoted in Purcell, *The Crisis of Democratic Theory*, p. 62. Robert Lowie, quoted in ibid., p. 66. Edward Sapir, "The Grammarian and His Language," *American Mercury* 1 (1924): 158.

31. Alexander Goldenweiser, "The Principle of Limited Possibilities in the Development of a Culture," *JAFL* 26 (1913): 263, 259, 270.
The idea of culture areas began in the 1890's as a device for classifying museum collections, attributed in this context to Boas. Anthropologists used the term loosely through the early years of the twentieth century until Wissler gave it clarity and definition. Alfred Kroeber gives him credit for it in his *Encyclopaedia of the Social Sciences* article, "Culture Area," Vol. 5, pp. 646–647.

32. Benedict, "The Vision in Plains Culture," *AA* 24 (1922): 21.

33. Benedict, *Concept of the Guardian Spirit*, pp. 84, 85.

34. Benedict, "The Religion of the North American Indians" (I), Chapter 1, unpublished ms., RFB Papers. Benedict talks of the study of primitives as an area in which "to reestablish our faith in the range of human cultural inventions and imaginings," and to study "the almost limitless potentialities of man's beliefs and adjustments" (p. 4).

6. Mythology, Religion, and Culture

1. Benedict, "Folklore," pp. 288, 289. Benedict wrote, "For the purposes of study mythology can never be divorced from folklore" ("Myth," p. 179). She also wrote that distinctions of folklore and mythology were "inappropriate" when studying North American Indians ("North American Folklore," unpublished ms., p. 1, RFB Papers). The two terms are used together here with the understanding that mythology refers to tales of the supernatural and folklore refers to tales of the natural world.

2. Benedict, "Folklore," pp. 288–290.

3. Ibid., p. 291. Benedict, "Franz Boas as an Ethnologist," p. 33.

4. Tyler, *The Origins of Culture,* Vol. 1, p. 16, and Chapters 3 and 4.

5. Benedict, "A Matter for the Field Worker in Folk-Lore," in "Notes and Queries," *JAFL* 36 (1923): 104. Sapir to Benedict, September 10, 1923, *AW,* p. 54.

On archetypes, see Benedict, "Folklore," pp. 290–291. Benedict remained skeptical about Jung. She once referred to him derogatorily as "the great god Jung" (Benedict to Mead, March 5, 1926, *AW,* p. 305). Mead wrote to her in 1924, "If you'll forgive a Jungian reference . . ." (Mead to Benedict, September 8, 1924, *AW,* p. 286).

6. Boas to Dean F. J. E. Woodbridge, March 21, 1925, FB Papers. Notes on Ruth Benedict's class reports by Margaret Mead, MM Papers.

7. Benedict, Review of *The North American Indian* by Edward S. Curtis, Vol. 12, *The Hopi, AA* 27 (1925): 460; "North American Folklore," p. 6, RFB Papers (written for the *Encyclopaedia Britannica,* May 1928, paid for but not printed because received too late); "Introduction to Zuñi Mythology," in *Zuñi Mythology,* Vol. 1, p. xiii; "The Primitive and His Ego," review of *The 'Soul' of the Primitive* by Lucien Lévy-Bruhl, *New Republic* 57 (March 6, 1929): 77.

8. A. R. Radcliffe-Brown, *The Andaman Islanders,* p. 330. Benedict to Mead, March 5, 1926, *AW,* p. 306. On myths as novelistic tales, see Benedict, *Tales of the Cochiti Indians,* pp. ix, 202. Benedict was so impressed by Rivers' book that she attended a special memorial service for Rivers in New York after his death in 1922 (Jane Howard, *Margaret Mead: A Life,* p. 93).

9. Benedict, *Tales of the Cochiti Indians,* p. 221; "Folklore," pp. 292, 291; *Zuñi Mythology,* p. xvi. See also Modell, *Ruth Benedict,* pp. 202–205, and Virginia Wolf Briscoe, "Ruth Benedict, Anthropological Folklorist," *JAFL* 92 (1979): 470, 471.

10. Benedict, "Folklore," p. 291.

11. Ibid., pp. 292–293.

12. Benedict, "The Science of Custom," p. 648. Boas, "Anthropology," p. 101.

Benedict, "The Religion of the North American Indians" (I), 4-page synopsis, p. 3, and Chapter 1, p. 6, RFB Papers. (There are two versions of this manuscript.)

13. Benedict, "Myth," p. 179.

14. Dewey, *Human Nature and Conduct*, p. 331. George Santayana, *Platonism and the Spiritual Life*, p. 84. Benedict, "Religion," in *General Anthropology*, ed. Franz Boas, pp. 663, 664.

15. Sapir to Benedict, November 26, 1924, AW, p. 164, and February 7, 1925, AW, p. 172 (on Knopf). Gilbert Loveland [Henry Holt & Company] to Benedict, August 7, 1930; Benedict to Loveland, August 16, 1930; Edward Sapir, note attached to ms. of "The Religion of the North American Indians"; all in RFB Papers.

16. Benedict, "The Religion of the North American Indians" (I), Chapter 2, p. 1; Chapter 1, pp. 6, 7; (II) Chapter 5, p. 9, RFB Papers. John Dewey, "Anthropology and Ethics," in *The Social Sciences and Their Interrelations*, ed. William Fielding Ogburn and Alexander Goldenweiser, p. 34. Seminar notes taken by Margaret Mead, Fall 1924, Ruth Benedict report, "Sanctions for Instructions Found in Mythology," MM Papers. Dewey, *Human Nature and Conduct*, p. 294.

17. Edward Sapir, "Culture, Genuine and Spurious," *American Journal of Sociology* 29 (1924): 410.

18. Boas, *Anthropology and Modern Life*, p. 219.

19. Radcliffe-Brown, *The Andaman Islanders*, p. 230.

20. Benedict to Mead, March 5, 1926, AW, p. 305. Powdermaker, *Stranger and Friend*, p. 35.

21. Clyde Kluckhohn, "Bronislaw Malinowski, 1884–1942," *JAFL* 56 (1943): 208. See also Benedict to Mead, March 5, 1926, AW, p. 305.

22. Kurt Koffka, *The Growth of the Mind: An Introduction to Child Psychology*, trans. Robert Morris Ogden, pp. 131, 140, 137–139.

23. Wissler, *Man and Culture*, pp. 188, 78, 77. Goldenweiser in 1913 had suggested the idea of a universal pattern in "The Principle of Limited Possibilities," p. 271, but attributed it to the psychic unity of humankind, not biological innateness.

Alfred L. Kroeber, *Anthropology: Race, Language, Culture, Psychology, Prehistory*, rev. ed., p. 311. Melville J. Herskovits and Malcolm M. Willey, "The Cultural Approach to Sociology," *American Journal of Sociology* 29 (1924): 197.

24. Alexander Goldenweiser, "The Principle of Limited Possibilities," pp. 267, 270. Boas, "In Memoriam: Herman Karl Haeberlin," p. 73. Wissler, *Man and Culture*, pp. 3, 51–53.

25. Wilson D. Wallis, "Mental Patterns in Relation to Culture," *Journal of Abnormal and Social Psychology* 19 (1924): 179–184. Sapir, "Culture, Genuine and Spurious," p. 410.

26. Sapir to Benedict, March 5, 1926, AW, p. 177.

Benedict, "Dress," *Encyclopaedia of the Social Sciences*, Vol. 5, p. 235. Here Benedict speaks of work by Köhler not described in Koffka.

Benedict, "A Study in the Stability of Culture Traits among a Primitive People," ms. for Social Science Research Council grant application (6 pp.), pp. 1, 3, 5, RFB Papers.

Wilson D. Wallis, "History and Psychology," in *The Social Sciences and Their*

Interrelations, ed. Ogburn and Goldenweiser, p. 217. Edward Sapir, "Anthropology and Sociology," in ibid., p. 108. Goldenweiser, "Anthropology and Psychology," in ibid., pp. 84–85.

27. Benedict to Boas, n.d. [1927], quoted in Mead, "Patterns of Culture," *AW,* p. 206; Benedict, *Patterns of Culture,* p. 84.

28. Benedict, "Psychological Types in the Cultures of the Southwest" (1928), *AW,* pp. 249, 261.

29. Benedict to Mead, September 21, 1928, *AW,* p. 308; December 29, 1928, *AW,* p. 311. Elsie Clews Parsons, Review of *Primitive Religion* by Robert Lowie, *AA* 27 (1925): 563.

30. Boas, "Anthropology," pp. 101, 102.

31. Benedict, "Configurations of Culture in North America," *AA* 34 (1932): 2–4.

32. Ibid., pp. 13, 18, 19.

33. Ibid., pp. 24, 25, 26.

34. Elsie Clews Parsons, *The Old-Fashioned Woman,* p. 25. Benedict, "Counters in the Game," *AW,* pp. 40–43.

35. Benedict, "The Uses of Cannibalism," *AW,* pp. 44–48; "They Dance for Rain in Zuñi," *AW,* pp. 222–225.

Benedict to Mead, January 30, 1929, in ms. of *An Anthropologist at Work,* "Supplementary Copy No. Two of Correspondence Only: Letters of Ruth Benedict and Franz Boas; Letters from Ruth Benedict to Margaret Mead re Franz Boas; Correspondence with Margaret Mead and Reo F. Fortune" [hereafter cited as *AW*2], ECP Papers. This ms. contains a larger selection from unavailable letters than appears in the published version.

36. Benedict, "The Science of Custom: The Bearing of Anthropology on Contemporary Thought," *Century Magazine* 117 (April 1929): 641, 644, 646–648.

37. Ibid., pp. 642, 648, 649.

7. The Personal Vision

1. "[Undated]," in "Journal Fragments: 1915–1934," *AW,* pp. 149–150. Internal evidence suggests this was written c. 1917 and the experience occurred c. 1914.

Mead, "Search," *AW,* p. 6.

2. Benedict, "Jan. 7 [1913]," in "Journal: 1912–1916," *AW,* p. 126; "[Undated]," in "Journal Fragments," *AW,* pp. 136–137.

Mead, "Anne Singleton," *AW,* p. 87. The last name remained the same as in her detective-story pseudonym, connoting the same meanings (see Chapter 3, note 19). Interestingly Benedict retained her own first name, indicating possibly that poetry came from her deepest self. The use of a pseudonym probably came not only from her own inclinations, but also from a need, as the wife of Stanley Benedict, to protect his privacy as well.

Benedict, quoted in Mead, "Search," *AW,* p. 6.

3. "Undated," in "Journal Fragments," *AW,* p. 152. Benedict, *The Concept of the Guardian Spirit in North America,* pp. 24, 28. Pater, *The Renaissance,* p. 236.

4. Benedict, "Religion," in *General Anthropology,* ed. Boas, p. 630. This ar-

ticle was not published until 1938, but a reading of articles in the *Encyclopaedia of the Social Sciences* ("Magic," "Animism," "Myth," "Folklore") shows that the ideas in the article formed the basis of Benedict's approach to religion by 1930.

5. Benedict, "Religion," pp. 656, 659, 660, 663.

6. Benedict, quoted in Mead, "Anne Singleton," *AW*, p. 85. The poem is "Dead Star," *Poetry* 35 (1930): 306–307, later renamed "Ripeness Is All," and reprinted in *AW*, pp. 85–86. In the last line, "at length" in the *AW* version replaces "at last" in the *Poetry* version.

7. Benedict, "Application for Small Grant in Aid of Research in the Humanistic and Social Sciences" [given by ACLS, 1926–1928], mentions the "Origin of Death" as in press at *AA*, but it was never published. See also Benedict, class outline, "Mythology of Primitive Peoples," 1st term, 1925–1926, which mentions the Origin of Death as a topic. Both in RFB Papers. Benedict, "Psychological Types," *AW*, p. 260.

8. Benedict, "Configurations of Culture," pp. 4, 13. In "Configurations" Benedict wrote about cultures. But the "psychological sets" she spoke of were first individual and personal; they became cultural when institutionalized by the culture. Given her background, her search for personal answers in scholarship, and the information in this paper, this interpretation of Benedict's ideas seems legitimate.

On Bertrice Fulton as a realist, see "June 15," in "Journal," *AW*, p. 127: "Even Mother always tells me somewhere in the conversation that life isn't all cake."

9. Benedict, "Configurations of Culture," pp. 18–23.

10. Benedict, "The Science of Custom," p. 648. Louis Untermeyer, *American Poetry since 1900*, pp. 6–7.

11. Adam Smith, *An Inquiry into the Nature and Causes of the Wealth of Nations*, ed. Edwin Cannon, p. 423. Charles Eliot, *The Conflict between Individualism and Collectivism in a Democracy*, pp. 99–100.

12. Sapir to Benedict, June 14, 1925, *AW*, p. 180.

13. Review of *Dreams and Gibes* by Edward Sapir, *Poetry* 15 (1919): 170. Sapir to Benedict, June 25, 1922, *AW*, p. 53.

14. Sapir to Benedict, November 26, 1924, *AW*, pp. 163–164; October 19, 1925, *AW*, p. 181; March 11, 1926, *AW*, p. 182; December 20, 1924, *AW*, p. 168; February 7, 1925, *AW*, p. 172; February 27, 1925, *AW*, p. 173.

Edward Sapir, "Signal (To A. S.)," *AW*, p. 164; also published in *Poetry* 27 (1926): 175–176 (this version is two lines longer than the one in *AW*). A. S. referred to Benedict's pseudonym, Anne Singleton. This poem could easily be misread as referring to a personal relationship between Sapir and Benedict, but that this would not be correct is evident from references to the poem in other letters. On June 10, 1928, Sapir wrote Benedict to congratulate her on having her work included in Louis Untermeyer's anthology, saying "I take satisfaction in having my 'Signal' come prophetic" (*AW*, p. 192); also on November 26, 1924, talking of poetry, Sapir had written, "Let the smoke gradually give way to flame" (*AW*, p. 163).

15. Sapir to Benedict, November 26, 1924, *AW*, p. 161; March 3, 1925, *AW*, p. 174.

16. Mead, "Anne Singleton," *AW*, p. 90. As a measure of Benedict's delight in

Léonie Adams' verse, Margaret Mead went so far as to leave her own manuscript copies of Adams' verse to Benedict when she wrote her will before going to Samoa (MM Papers).

Sapir to Benedict, December 12, 1924, *AW*, p. 166. Louise Bogan, quoted in Elizabeth Frank, *Louise Bogan*, p. 75.

17. Frederick J. Hoffman, Charles Allen, and Carolyn F. Ulrich, *The Little Magazine*, p. 263. Louis Untermeyer, in "Notes and Comments," *The Measure* No. 57 (1925), p. 17, Harry Ransom Center, University of Texas at Austin [hereafter cited as HRC].

18. Sapir to Benedict, April 16, 1928, *AW*, p. 191. Louis Untermeyer, quoted in Mead, "Anne Singleton," *AW*, p. 92. Amy Lowell, "Two Generations in American Poetry," *New Republic* 37, Pt. 2 (1923): 3.

19. Louise Bogan, quoted in Frank, *Louise Bogan*, p. 91.

The Lyricists have been dismissed in American literary history as the last gasp of the late-nineteenth-century art-for-art's-sake school of writers, a conservative poetic reaction rather than a radical avant-garde (see Marsha Brown, "Elinor Wylie and the Religion of Art: Poetry and Social Attitudes in the 1920's," Ph.D. dissertation, Emory University, and Thomas A. Grey, *Elinor Wylie*). But Dada itself is also a logical extreme of the "religion of art" philosophy. The Dada Manifesto stated, "Art is a private matter; the artist does it for himself; any work of art that can be understood is the product of a journalist" (Dada Manifesto, quoted in Malcolm Cowley, *Exile's Return*, rev. ed., p. 149). Dadaists showed contempt for the mass public and popular writing through their extreme obscurity. They carried nineteenth-century individualism to its absurd extreme as they created poetry in which no one could understand anyone else's work. In fact, both Dadaism and Lyricism were Modern responses to a changed world on different ends of the spectrum.

20. Gerhard Hoffman, Alfred Hornung, and Rüdiger Kunow, "'Modern,' 'Postmodern' and 'Contemporary' as Criteria for the Analysis of 20th Century Literature," *Amerika Studien* 22, 1 (1977): 20. T. S. Matthews, "Elinor Wylie's Poems," *New Republic* 54 (April 4, 1928): 77–78. M. D. Z. [Morton Dauwen Zabel], "The Mechanism of Sensibility," *Poetry* 34 (1929): 151. Frank, *Louise Bogan*, p. xv. Edward Sapir, "Symbolism" (1934), in *Selected Writings of Edward Sapir in Language, Culture and Personality*, ed. David G. Mandelbaum, p. 566. Louise Bogan, quoted in Frank, *Louise Bogan*, p. 24.

21. "The Sense of Symbolism," *AW*, p. 116 (written c. 1909). Louise Bogan, "The Springs of Poetry," *New Republic* 37, Pt. 2 (December 5, 1923): 9. A. Donald Douglas, Review of *Body of This Death* by Louise Bogan, *New Republic* 37, Pt. 2 (December 5, 1923): 20. Llewellyn Jones, "Louise Bogan" (1925), in *Critical Essays on Louise Bogan*, ed. Martha Collins, p. 29.

22. Mead, *Blackberry Winter*, p. 178. William Jay Smith, *Louise Bogan: A Woman's Words*, pp. 6–7. Louise Bogan, *Journey around My Room: The Autobiography of Louise Bogan*, ed. Ruth Limmer, pp. 115, 72. Jean Gould, *American Women Poets*, p. 288. Theodore Roethke, quoted in Frank, *Louise Bogan*, p. 58. Margaret Mead, quoted in ibid., p. 89. Louise Bogan, "The Springs of Poetry," p. 9.

23. Lowell, "Two Generations in American Poetry," p. 3.

For a more detailed reading of the critical view of *Body of This Death* as woman's inner journey to selfhood, see Deborah Pope, "Music in the Granite Hill: The Poetry of Louise Bogan," in *Critical Essays*, ed. Collins, pp. 149–166.

24. Elinor Wylie, "Let No Charitable Hope," in *Collected Poems of Elinor Wylie*, p. 65.

25. Elinor Wylie, "Jewelled Bindings," *New Republic* 37, Pt. 2 (December 5, 1923): 14. Louise Bogan to R. Humphries, July 31, 1924, in *What the Woman Lived: Selected Letters of Louise Bogan, 1920–1970*, ed. Ruth Limmer, p. 9.

26. "New Year," in "Diary: 1923," *AW*, p. 56. Anne Singleton [Ruth Benedict], "Toy Balloons," *Poetry* 28 (August 1926): 245, and "Withdrawal," *The Measure*, No. 51 (May 1925): 7; both also in "Selected Poems: 1941," *AW*, pp. 488–489, 482.

27. "Of Graves," *AW*, p. 84. Anne Singleton [Ruth Benedict], "Death Is the Citadel," *Nation* 128 (February 20, 1929): 231; "She Speaks to the Sea," *Palms* 3 (March 1926): 164 (also in *AW*, pp. 487–488). Ruth Benedict, "Resurrection of the Ghost," *New York Herald-Tribune*, Books, August 26, 1934, p. 6; also in *AW*, p. 490.

28. Louise Bogan to Benedict, August 23, 1926; December 16, 1926; October 11, 1928; [March] 1929; March 13, 1927; all in the Louise Bogan Collection, Amherst College Library, Amherst, Mass. [hereafter cited as LB Papers]; also in *What the Woman Lived*, pp. 28, 29, 37, 44. (In *What the Woman Lived* some of the letters were edited to leave out information non-pertinent to Bogan's life that adds to a view of Benedict's; cf. December 16, 1926, LB Papers, on "But the Son of Man.")

"Diary: 1926," *AW*, p. 77. Sapir to Benedict, May 11, 1926, *AW*, p. 183.

29. Louis Untermeyer, quoted in Benedict to Mead, August 5, 1930, quoted in Mead, "Anne Singleton," *AW*, p. 92.

Judith Modell suggests Benedict took the name Anne from her grandmother's name, Joanna, and Singleton from "single tone" (Modell, *Ruth Benedict*, p. 129).

Mead, "Anne Singleton," *AW*, p. 94.

Rivers might have given her the idea that a double personality could call elements of the unconscious to the surface, freeing elements suppressed by the other consciousness. See Rivers, *Instinct and the Unconscious*, Chapters 2 and 10.

30. Benedict, "The Story of My Life," *AW*, p. 102. On the Grand Canyon, see Margaret Mead to Grandma, August 3, 1925, MM Papers.

31. Adams and Benedict quoted in Mead, "Anne Singleton," *AW*, p. 91.

32. George Santayana, *The Life of Reason or the Phases of Human Progress*, Vol. 3, *Reason in Religion*, p. 272.

8. The Personal Search

1. Sapir to Benedict, September 29, 1927, *AW*, p. 186. "Diary: 1923," pp. 59, 66, 67. Goldfrank, *Notes on an Undirected Life*, p. 35. Go-bang was an American version of the Japanese game of go (Goldfrank, p. 223n.13).

2. "We'll have no crumb in common," in "Diary: 1923," *AW*, p. 58. Howard in *Margaret Mead*, p. 52, and Mary Catherine Bateson in *With a Daughter's Eye: A Memoir of Margaret Mead and Gregory Bateson*, p. 125, read this poem as

referring to Margaret Mead, but it is written between two paragraphs concerning Stanley, and the timing seems wrong for any but a student-teacher relationship between Benedict and Mead at that time.

Nietzsche, *Thus Spake Zarathustra*, pp. 73–74. Benedict, quoted in Modell, *Ruth Benedict*, p. 126; see also p. 186. "March 22, 1930," RFB Papers.

"The Worst Is Not Our Anger," at the end of "Diary: 1923," *AW*, pp. 70–71, dated 1925; published in *The Measure*, No. 63 (May 1926): 10, as Anne Singleton.

"Sight," in Sapir to Benedict, January 19, 1925, *AW*, p. 170; published in *Palms* 3 (March 1926): 166, as Anne Singleton.

On the stamp episode, see Mead, "Anne Singleton," *AW*, p. 93.

Engagement Book, 1930: November 5—"Stanley overnight—separated—," RFB Papers.

3. Mead, *Blackberry Winter*, pp. 109–115; "Search," *AW*, p. 4. Howard, *Margaret Mead*, p. 47.

4. Mead, *Ruth Benedict*, p. 3; *Blackberry Winter*, pp. 122, 123; "Ruth Fulton Benedict," p. 459; "Search," *AW*, p. 4.

5. Mead, "Search," *AW*, pp. 4–5. Benedict, "Diary: 1923," *AW*, p. 65.

6. Mead, *Blackberry Winter*, pp. 123–124.

7. Raymond Firth, quoted in Howard, *Margaret Mead*, p. 124; on dance, see p. 299.

8. Benedict, ms. of "Speech at Presentation of the Chi Omega National Achievement Award to Margaret Mead," published in *The Eleusis of Chi Omega* 42 (1940), RFB Papers. Mead to Grandma, March 11, 1923, MM Papers. Benedict, "Diary: 1923," *AW*, pp. 67, 68. Mead, *Blackberry Winter*, p. 129.

9. Mead, "Anne Singleton," *AW*, p. 84; "Search," *AW*, p. 9. Bateson, *With a Daughter's Eye*, p. 125.

10. Ellen Key, *The Morality of Women*, p. 16. Lillian Faderman, *Surpassing the Love of Men*, p. 190. On women's romantic friendships see Faderman's book and Carroll Smith-Rosenberg, "The Female World of Love and Ritual: Relations between Women in Nineteenth Century America," in *Disorderly Conduct*, pp. 53–76. On men's romantic friendships, see Robert Abzug, *Passionate Liberator: Theodore Dwight Weld and the Dilemma of Reform*.

11. Stories quoted in Faderman, *Surpassing the Love of Men*, pp. 302–304. Lorine Pruette, "The Flapper," in *The New Generation*, ed. V. F. Calverton and Samuel D. Schmalhausen, p. 575.

12. Helen Lefkowitz Horowitz, *Alma Mater*, pp. 166, 65–68, 190.

13. Benedict, "The Story of My Life," *AW*, p. 109; "Mary Wollstonecraft," *AW*, pp. 496, 497. Margaret Fuller, quoted in Faderman, *Surpassing the Love of Men*, p. 160. Mabel Dodge Luhan, *Intimate Memories*, pp. 213–221. Elizabeth Atkins, *Edna St. Vincent Millay and Her Times*, pp. 37–38. Benedict to Florence Howe, c. 1910, probably never sent, RFB Papers.

14. Wanda Fraiken Neff, quoted in Faderman, *Surpassing the Love of Men*, pp. 298–299. Mead, *Blackberry Winter*, p. 111.

15. Ellen Key, *The Woman Movement*, p. 79.

16. Katharine Bement Davis, *Factors in the Sex Life of Twenty-Two Hundred Women*, pp. 247, 298 (percentages figured from the tables on these pages).

17. "West Alton Weekend, July 26, 1930," RFB Papers; "March 22, 1930," RFB Papers; "New Year," in "Diary: 1923," AW, p. 56. Howard, in *Margaret Mead*, p. 51, and Bateson, in *With a Daughter's Eye*, p. 125, suggest this poem was written for or about Margaret Mead. I see it as an imaginative fantasy not directed at any one person when written.

18. A series of letters, 1922–1923 from "Lee," suggest a warm, intimate, possibly physical relationship that apparently ended on friendly terms, with best wishes for Margaret's wedding; in MM Papers. Bateson, *With a Daughter's Eye*, p. 93.

19. "St. Paul sur Nice, August, 1926," in "Journal Fragments: 1915–1934," AW, p. 153. Mead, *Blackberry Winter*, p. 176; "Anne Singleton," AW, p. 85. On England, Mead to Grandma, August 26, 1926, MM Papers.

20. Mead, "Anne Singleton," AW, p. 87. Benedict, "Reprieve," AW, p. 480; "This Breath," AW, p. 474; "Journal Fragments," AW, p. 149. Anne Singleton [Benedict], "Preference," *The Measure*, No. 52 (June 1925): 13; also in AW, pp. 177–178; "Love That Is Water," *Poetry* 35 (1930): 306; also in AW, p. 474; "Earthborn," *Poetry* 31 (1928): 192–193, written by 1926 (Bogan to Benedict, December 16, 1926, LB Papers); also in AW, p. 487; "This Gabriel," *Palms* 3 (March 1926): 167; also in AW, p. 486. "This Gabriel" was written in 1924 (Sapir to Benedict, November 26, 1924, AW, p. 162). Mead wrote that this poem was written for her in "Anne Singleton," AW, p. 88. The interpretation is my own.

21. Anne Singleton [Benedict], "Unicorns at Sunrise," *Poetry* 35 (March 1930): 305–306; also in AW, pp. 481–482; written in 1925 (Sapir to Benedict, April 3, 1925, AW, p. 176). "I Shall Not Call," *Poetry* 31 (1928): 193–194.

22. Anne Singleton [Benedict], "For the Hour after Love," *Poetry* 31 (1928): 193; also in AW, p. 480. "Burial," *The Measure*, No. 52 (June 1925): 13, HRC; also in AW, p. 483.

23. "In Parables," *Palms* 3 (March 1926): 165; written in 1924 (Sapir to Benedict, November 15, 1924, AW, p. 160). "Our Task Is Laughter," *Palms* 3 (March 1926): 168; written in 1924 (Sapir to Benedict, December 12, 1924, AW, pp. 165, 167–168).

24. Mead, "Patterns of Culture," AW, p. 208; *Coming of Age in Samoa*, pp. 102, 103, 104n (italics added).

25. Mead, *Coming of Age in Samoa*, p. 104n. Benedict, "Configurations of Culture," p. 25.
Robert Lowie, "On the Principle of Convergence in Ethnology," *JAFL* 25 (1912): 39. Boas, "Anthropology," p. 85. Edward Sapir, "The Discipline of Sex," *American Mercury* 16 (1929): 417; "Observations on the Sex Problem in America," *American Journal of Psychiatry* 8 (1928): 529.

26. "Diary: 1923," AW, p. 57. See also Modell, *Ruth Benedict*, pp. 126–142. Richard Handler, "Vigorous Male and Aspiring Female: Poetry, Personality, and Culture in Edward Sapir and Ruth Benedict," in *Malinowski, Rivers, Benedict and Others*, ed. George W. Stocking, Jr., p. 143. "West Alton Weekend, July 26, 1930," RFB Papers.

27. Howard, *Margaret Mead*, pp. 67, 73–75, 87. Mead, *Blackberry Winter*, pp. 140–142. Bateson, *With a Daughter's Eye*, p. 125. Sapir to Benedict, April 29, 1929, AW, p. 196.

28. Benedict, "Configurations of Culture," pp. 13, 16, 26, 14. Sapir to Benedict, March 23, 1926, *AW*, p. 182; August 18, 1925, quoted in Mead, "Anne Singleton," *AW*, p. 85. Luther Cressmann, quoted in Howard, *Margaret Mead*, p. 100. This is important because Mead controlled the interpretation of Benedict's life after she died and projected her own tendency to dramatize and find symbolic meanings onto Benedict's life.

29. Mead, "Patterns of Culture," *AW*, pp. 206–207; "Dominant Cultural Attitudes in Manu'a," *AW*, p. 247.

30. Mead to Mother [Emily Fogg Mead], April 19, 1928, MM Papers. Mead, quoted in Howard, *Margaret Mead*, p. 293—"I've only excluded other people if the person who loved me just couldn't abide my caring for other people. I would honor that feeling." Mead, *Blackberry Winter*, p. 125. Bateson, in *With a Daughter's Eye*, pp. 117–118, suggests the physical relationship continued in Mead's marriage to Gregory Bateson, but if so it must have been largely attenuated by Benedict's other relationships and Mead and Bateson's long absences from the United States.

31. Mead, quoted in Howard, *Margaret Mead*, pp. 293, 57. Mead, *Blackberry Winter*, p. 119. Bateson, *With a Daughter's Eye*, p. 124. Radclyffe Hall, *The Well of Loneliness*.

32. "West Alton Weekend, July 26, 1930"; Morris Opler to Benedict, March 22 [1932]; Benedict, "June 15, 1934"; all in RFB Papers.

Modell writes that Raymond was a research chemist (*Ruth Benedict*, p. 189), but I think from remarks in letters that she was a medical student at Cornell Medical for the first few years of their relationship. She apparently did not finish and could settle to no purpose in life until she decided to write a travel guide to Guatemala in 1938. See Opler to Benedict, October 26 [1931], Benedict to Regina Flannery, January 30, 1932, and April 11, 1932, and Benedict to David Levy, October 24, 1938, RFB Papers; also Benedict to Boas, July 3, 1938, FB Papers.

33. Benedict to Henry J. Wegrocki, July 2, 1936, RFB Papers. "Anthropology and the Abnormal," *Journal of General Psychology* 10 (1934): 60, 64, 66, 69, 72; reprinted in *AW*, pp. 276–278.

34. Benedict, "Anthropology and the Abnormal," pp. 73, 74, 75.

35. Ibid., pp. 75, 79.

9. Patterns of Culture: Between America and Anthropology

1. Benedict to Reo Fortune, August 2, 1932, *AW*, pp. 320–321. Benedict to Mead, August 10, 1932, *AW*, p. 322; October 9, 1932, *AW*, p. 323; October 16, 1932, *AW*, p. 324; January 6, 1933, *AW*, p. 329. Fortune to Benedict, November 21, 1932, *AW*, pp. 329–330.

2. *New York Times*, October 21, 1934, p. 24. Melville Herskovits, *New York Herald-Tribune*, Books, October 28, 1934, p. 6. Dorothy Hoskins, *Springfield Republican*, November 18, 1934, p. 7e. Benedict to Ferris Greenslet [Houghton Mifflin], December 8, 1933, RFB Papers. Alfred Kroeber, Review of *Patterns of Culture*, AA 37 (1935): 689–690.

3. Benedict, *Patterns of Culture*; quotes from pp. 35, 53, 200. Subsequent

quotations from *Patterns of Culture* are noted by page numbers in the text in this chapter.

4. George W. Stocking, Jr., "Benedict, Ruth Fulton," in *Dictionary of American Biography*, Supplement 4, 1946–1950, p. 72.

5. Benedict to R. N. Linscott [Houghton Mifflin], June 28, 1934, RFB Papers.

6. Walter Goldschmidt, "Anthropology in America," in *Social Science in America*, ed. Charles M. Bonjean, Louis Schneider, and Robert L. Lineberry, p. 167. *Patterns of Culture* was issued in paperback first by Pelican Books, an American spin-off company from the British Penguin Books, in 1946. Pelican Books in 1948 became The New American Library of World Literature, Inc., and later printings were issued as Mentor Books (Piet Schreuders, *Paperbacks, U.S.A.: A Graphic History, 1939–1959,* trans. Josh Pachter [San Diego, Calif.: Blue Dolphin Enterprises, 1981], pp. 45, 46).

7. Perry, *Psychiatrist of America,* p. 344. Clyde Kluckhohn and Henry A. Murray, eds., "Introduction to the First Edition," in *Personality in Nature, Society, and Culture,* 2d ed., p. xvi.

8. Edward Sapir, "Time Perspective in Aboriginal American Culture: A Study in Method" (1916), in *Selected Writings,* ed. Mandelbaum, p. 391.

9. Morris Edward Opler, "Some Recently Developed Concepts Relating to Culture," *Southwestern Journal of Anthropology* 4 (1948): 111. Boas, "Introduction," in *Patterns of Culture,* p. xiv.

10. Ralph Linton, *The Study of Man,* pp. 272–274. John Gillin, "The Configuration Problem in Culture," *American Sociological Review* 1 (1936): 373–386.

11. Irving Goldman, "The Zuñi Indians of New Mexico," in *Cooperation and Competition among Primitive Peoples,* ed. Margaret Mead, p. 345.

12. Clyde Kluckhohn, statement in E. Adamson Hoebel, "Contributions of Southwestern Studies to Anthropological Theory," *AA* 56 (1954): 724; "Patterning as Exemplified in Navaho Culture," in *Language, Culture and Personality,* ed. Leslie Spier, A. Irving Hollowell, and Stanley S. Newman, pp. 117, 121, 129; "Covert Culture and Administrative Problems," *AA* 45 (1943): 213–227.

Ford and Murdock's articles are cited in Morris Opler, "Some Recently Developed Concepts Relating to Culture," pp. 115, 116.

13. Morris Opler, "Themes as Dynamic Forces in Culture," *American Journal of Sociology* 51 (1945): 198–206. John Gillin, "Cultural Adjustment," *AA* 46 (1944): 443. Clyde Kluckhohn and Dorothea Leighton, *The Navaho.*

14. James Woodard, "The Relation of Personality Structure to the Structure of Culture," *American Sociological Review* 3 (1938): 637–651. Abram Kardiner, *The Individual and His Society.* Cora Du Bois, *The People of Alor.* Mead, *Sex and Temperament in Three Primitive Societies,* pp. 263, 259.

15. Benedict to Mead, March 5, 1926, *AW,* p. 306. Alfred Kroeber, "History and Science in Anthropology," *AA* 37 (1935): 558, 556–557; "So-Called Social Science" (1936), pp. 66–78, "Historical Context, Reconstruction and Interpretation" (1938), pp. 79–84, and "Structure, Function and Pattern in Biology and Anthropology" (1943), pp. 85–94, in *The Nature of Culture.*

16. Kroeber, Review of *Patterns of Culture,* p. 689; "History and Science in Anthropology," p. 557.

17. Henry A. Murray et al., *Explorations in Personality,* pp. 6, 8, 7.

18. Ibid., pp. 8, 9, 21. George W. Stocking, Jr., in *Selected Papers from the American Anthropologist, 1921–1945*, pp. 31–33, suggests the terms "romanticist" and "progressivist" to characterize these two major trends, calling Benedict a romanticist. I think progressivist accurately describes the objectivists, but would prefer to call Benedict a Modernist rather than a romanticist.

19. Kroeber, "So-Called Social Science," p. 72; "Historical Context, Reconstruction and Interpretation," p. 79. Franz Boas, "History and Science in Anthropology: A Reply" (1936), in *Race, Language and Culture*, pp. 305–311.

20. See Kroeber, "Historical Context, Reconstruction and Interpretation," p. 79.

21. "Diary: 1926," *AW*, p. 76. Radin, *The Method and Theory of Ethnology*, pp. 179, 180. Kroeber to Boas, January 30, 1934, FB Papers.

22. Geza Roheim later worked in Dobu and provided some corroboration of Fortune's views—see Benedict to Robert Lowie, April 17, 1935, in the Robert Lowie Papers, Bancroft Library, University of California at Berkeley. Rumors later circulated that Fortune did not approve of Benedict's use of his work, and years later he said that he did not. But at the time, as his letters to Benedict show, he certainly did and rather enthusiastically (see Fortune to Benedict, November 21, 1932, and January 5, 1934, *AW*, pp. 329–330, 338). For further information on this issue see Margaret M. Caffrey, "Stranger in This Land: The Life of Ruth Benedict" (Ph.D. thesis, University of Texas at Austin, 1986), pp. 695–696n.50.

Not until the 1950's was the Kwakiutl section challenged. See Helen Codere, "The Amiable Side of Kwakiutl Life," *AA* 58 (1956): 334–351; also Melville Jacobs, *Pattern in Cultural Anthropology*, p. 58.

23. Robert Lowie, *The History of Ethnological Theory*, p. 278. Li An-che, "Zuñi: Some Observations and Queries," *AA* 39 (1937): 62n.1, 65, 69, 70, 63, 68. See also Laura Thompson and Alice Josephs, *The Hopi Way;* Laura Thompson, "Logico-Aesthetic Integration in Hopi Culture," *AA* 47 (1945): 540–553.

24. Li An-che, "Zuñi," pp. 70, 72.

25. B. W. Aginsky, "Psychopathic Trends in Culture," *Character and Personality* 7 (1939): 331–343. Benedict, "A Reply to Dr. Aginsky," *Character and Personality* 7 (1939): 344–345.

26. Lowie, *History of Ethnological Theory*, pp. 279, 278, 273, and "Takes-the-pipe, a Crow Warrior," in *American Indian Life by Several of Its Students*, ed. Elsie Clews Parsons, pp. 17–43. Benedict, *Patterns of Culture*, p. 84.

27. Elsie Clews Parsons, *Pueblo Indian Religion*, Vol. 1, pp. 23, 75, 150, 53, 467, 468, 473, 107–109, 153; Vol. 2, pp. 1155, 621.

28. Ibid., Vol. 1, pp. 14–15, 50–55, 30–33. Benedict, Review of *Pueblo Indian Religion, Review of Religions* 4 (1940): 439.

29. Esther Goldfrank, "Socialization, Personality, and the Structure of Pueblo Society" (1945), in *Personal Character and Cultural Milieu*, rev. ed., ed. Douglas Haring, pp. 262–263, 247–271.

John W. Bennett, "The Interpretation of Pueblo Culture: A Question of Values," *Southwestern Journal of Anthropology* 2 (1946): 373.

Dorothy Eggan, "The General Problem of Hopi Adjustment," in *Personality*, ed. Kluckhohn and Murray, pp. 276–291.

Leo W. Simmons, ed., *Sun Chief, The Autobiography of a Hopi Indian*. Clyde

Kluckhohn, "The Personal Document in Anthropological Science," in *The Use of Personal Documents in History, Anthropology, and Sociology*, ed. L. Gottschalk, C. Kluckhohn, and R. Angell, pp. 97, 99.

30. Benedict, *Patterns of Culture*, pp. 88, 110–111.

Donald Horton, "The Functions of Alcohol in Primitive Society: A Cross Cultural Study" (1943), in *Personality*, ed. Kluckhohn and Murray, pp. 680–690, agreed with Benedict. E. Adamson Hoebel, in *Man in the Primitive World* (1949), p. 452, talked of the "uncontrollable drunkenness" in the Central Pueblos between 1945 and 1947.

Karl N. Llewellyn and E. Adamson Hoebel, *The Cheyenne Way*. Hoebel, *Man in the Primitive World* (1949), p. 450.

See also Marvin Harris, *The Rise of Anthropological Theory*, where these arguments come up again, and Alfred L. Kroeber, *Anthropology: Race, Language, Culture, Psychology, Prehistory*, rev. ed., p. 553, defending Benedict.

31. Hoebel, "Major Contributions of Southwestern Studies," p. 724. Clyde Kluckhohn, "Southwestern Studies of Culture and Personality," *AA* 56 (1954): 690. Victor Barnouw, *Culture and Personality*, p. 57. Hoebel, *Man in the Primitive World*, 2d. ed. (1958), p. 592.

32. See, for instance, Hoebel, *Man in the Primitive World* (1958), p. 592, and "Major Contributions of Southwestern Studies," p. 724; Barnouw, *Culture and Personality*, pp. 42, 51, 52, and "The Amiable Side of 'Patterns of Culture,'" *AA* 59 (1957): 532–535; Edward P. Dozier, *The Pueblo Indians of North America*, pp. 117, 180 (ideal personality type), 200–201, 211 (world view).

33. Lowie, *History of Ethnological Theory*, p. 278. Benedict, *Patterns of Culture*, pp. 98–99, 113, 102, 64, 95, 74–75, 107–108, 114, 95, 96, 225–226.

Benedict also wrote about the clowns (see "Psychological Types," *AW*, p. 259), although in *Patterns of Culture* they are minimized.

34. Benedict to Harold Lasswell, May 1, 1935, MM Papers. Benedict, *Zuñi Mythology*, Vol. 1, pp. xix–xx. Goldman, "The Zuñi Indians of New Mexico," pp. 353, 345, 346.

35. Benedict to Elsie Clews Parsons, June 19, 1937, ECP Papers. Goldman, "The Zuñi Indians of New Mexico," p. 346. Benedict, *Zuñi Mythology*, pp. xviii–xxi. On shame, see Mead to William Fielding Ogburn, July 1, 1935, MM Papers.

36. Ruth Benedict to Miss Lindgren [no first name], July 27, 1936, and to Dr. Jessie Bernard, May 17, 1941, RFB Papers.

37. "Anthropology and the Humanities" (1947), *AW*, pp. 463, 465, 467, 468, 470.

38. Kroeber, *The Nature of Culture*, p. 87. Bronislaw Malinowski, *A Scientific Theory of Culture and Other Essays*, p. 149. A. R. Radcliffe-Brown, "On the Concept of Function in Social Science," *AA* 37 (1935): 395; italics in original.

39. A. R. Radcliffe-Brown, *A Natural Science of Society*. This material is from a 1937 discussion in Chicago.

40. Boas, *Race, Language, and Culture*, pp. 311, 258.

41. Opler to Benedict, December 1 [1931], and Benedict to Opler, January 8, 1933, RFB Papers. See also Benedict to Mead, December 28, 1932, *AW*, pp. 326–327.

42. Kroeber, *The Nature of Culture*, pp. 66–69.

43. Lowie, *History of Ethnological Theory*, pp. 288, 279–280.

44. Boas, *Race, Language, and Culture*, p. 309. Boas to Mead, February 15, 1926, copies in both MM Papers and FB papers. (Boas copy says "subjective use" rather than "attitude.")

45. Benedict on WMCA (N.Y.) radio panel show discussing Kinsey's *Sexual Behavior of the Human Male*, Friday, February 27, 1948, notes, RFB Papers. Oscar Lewis, "Controls and Experiments in Field Work," in *Anthropology Today*, ed. A. L. Kroeber, p. 454. Benjamin Whorf, "Linguistics as an Exact Science," *Technology Review* 43 (1940): 61–63, 80–83.

On the influence of linguistics theory on Benedict's approach, derived, I believe, as much from Boas as from Sapir, see David F. Aberle, "The Influence of Linguistics on Early Culture and Personality Theory," in *Essays in the Science of Culture*, ed. Dole and Carneiro, pp. 1–29.

46. Benedict to Leslie Spier, January 10, 1934, RFB Papers. Malinowski, *A Scientific Theory of Culture*, pp. 159, 83, 91, 96.

47. Malinowski, quoted in Kardiner and Preble, *They Studied Man*, p. 173. Kluckhohn, "Bronislaw Malinowski, 1884–1942," p. 264. Kroeber, *Anthropology*, p. 287; see also Lowie, *History of Ethnological Theory*, p. 235.

48. Adam Kuper, *Anthropology and Anthropologists*, rev. ed., p. 48.

49. Edward Sapir, "Cultural Anthropology and Psychiatry" (1932), in *Selected Writings*, ed. Mandelbaum, p. 515; "Psychiatric and Cultural Pitfalls in the Business of Getting a Living," in *Mental Health*, ed. Forest Ray Moulton, p. 238; "The Emergence of the Concept of Personality in a Study of Cultures," in *Selected Writings*, ed. Mandelbaum, p. 592.

50. Sapir, "Cultural Anthropology and Psychiatry," p. 512; "Why Cultural Anthropology Needs the Psychiatrist," *Psychiatry* 1 (1938): 11; "The Emergence of the Concept of Personality in a Study of Cultures," in *Selected Writings*, ed. Mandelbaum, p. 597.

See John Dollard, "The Life History in Community Studies," in *Personality*, ed. Kluckhohn and Murray, pp. 532–544.

51. Sapir, "Why Cultural Anthropology Needs the Psychiatrist," p. 11.

10. The Psychology of Culture

1. Benedict, "Religion," in *General Anthropology*, ed. Boas, p. 656. Benedict to Frederica de Laguna, February 28, 1940, RFB Papers.

2. "Culture and Personality—Notes on discussion, November 23, 1934," 4 pp., RFB Papers. Benedict, "A Reply to Dr. Aginsky," pp. 344–345.

3. Mead, "Preface," in *Cooperation and Competition*, ed. Mead, p. viii.

4. Benedict to Redfield, February 24, 1938, RFB Papers. Wilson D. Wallis, Review of *Cooperation and Competition among Primitive Peoples*, AA 39 (1937): 710–711.

5. Benedict, "Synergy: Some Notes of Ruth Benedict," ed. A. Maslow and John Honigmann, AA 72 (1970): 321. The other important method was child study. Mead to William Fielding Ogburn, December 3, 1934, MM Papers.

6. Benedict to W. Lloyd Warner, May 7, 1938, and A. Kardiner to Benedict, February 26, 1937, RFB Papers.

7. Ralph Linton, "Foreword," in Abram Kardiner, *Psychological Frontiers of Society*, p. viii. Kardiner, "Author's Preface," in *The Individual and His Society*, p. xxiii.

8. Goldfrank, *Notes on an Undirected Life*, p. 112, says Benedict was attending seminars in 1939; see Project 134—"Malasia," begun in September 1937. Kardiner contributed $3,500 and Columbia gave 25 percent matching funds for Cora Du Bois, under Benedict's direction, RFB Papers.

9. Caroline [Zachry] to Mead, December 11, 1936, MM Papers. Benedict, "Synergy," p. 321.

10. Benedict, "Continuities and Discontinuities in Cultural Conditioning," *Psychiatry* 1 (1938): 166. Benedict to Thelma Herman, July 12, 1944, RFB Papers.

11. Goldfrank, *Notes on an Undirected Life*, p. 125.

12. Ibid., p. 126. Myklebust, *Psychology of Deafness*, pp. 124, 157. Barnouw, "Ruth Benedict," *American Scholar* 49 (1980): 507.

13. Harry Stack Sullivan to Benedict, December 2, 1935, and Benedict to Sullivan, December 6, 1935, RFB Papers. On visiting Sapir, see Powdermaker, *Stranger and Friend*, pp. 131–135. Harry Stack Sullivan, "Ruth Fulton Benedict, Ph.D., D.Sc. 1887–1948," *Psychiatry* 11 (1948): 402.

14. Mead to William Fielding Ogburn, December 3, 1934, MM Papers. John Dollard to Mead, January 14, 1935; Mead to Dollard, February 11, 1935, and February 15, 1934 [actually 1935]; Dollard to Mead, February 20, 1935; Mead to Dollard, February 25, 1935; all in MM Papers.

15. Dollard to Mead, May 22, 1935, and Mead to Dollard, June 20, 1935, MM Papers.

Karen Horney to Benedict, June 24, 1935, RFB Papers.

Mead to Ogburn, July 1, 1935 (Mead wrote *Psychoanalytic Quarterly* but it was *Psychoanalytic Review*); Erich Fromm to Mead, July 28, 1935; Mead to Fromm, August 11, 1935; all in MM Papers.

16. Jack Rubins, *Karen Horney: Gentle Rebel of Psychoanalysis*, pp. 5–59, 111, 143–144, 151. Karen Horney, "On the Genesis of the Castration Complex in Women" (1922), "Flight from Womanhood" (1926), and "The Problem of Feminine Masochism" (1935), in *Feminine Psychology*, ed. Harold Kelman, pp. 37–53, 54–70, 214–233.

17. Rubins, *Karen Horney*, pp. 114, 139, 186. Karen Horney, *New Ways in Psychoanalysis*, p. 12. Benedict and Mead were not the only sources of Horney's ideas. She also belonged to Harry Stack Sullivan's "Zodiac" group, which she joined in 1934 and which met informally Monday evenings in New York. It included Billy Silverberg, Clara Thompson, and sometimes Erich Fromm. But it is clear from her work that Benedict's and Mead's ideas on culture as determinant were the ones she ultimately followed, rather than the idea of the individual as shaper of culture that Sapir stressed. For information on the Zodiac group, see Perry, *Psychiatrist of America*, p. 354.

18. Karen Horney, "Culture and Neurosis," *American Sociological Review* 1 (1936): 221, 229. Benedict, Review of *The Neurotic Personality of Our Time*, *Journal of Abnormal and Social Psychology* 33 (1938): 133–135. Horney, *The Neurotic Personality of Our Time*, pp. viii, 14–17.

19. Horney to Benedict, October 1, 1937, RFB Papers. Horney, *New Ways in Psychoanalysis,* p. 39, Chaps. 3, 7. Rubins, *Karen Horney,* pp. 210, 234, 239, 248. Perry, *Psychiatrist for America,* pp. 379, 386.

20. Rubins, *Karen Horney,* p. 248. Benedict to Hiram Hayden, April 19, 1944; Horney to Benedict, June 17, 1943; Benedict to Lawrence S. Kubie, January 20, 1942; all in RFB Papers.

21. Benedict, "Some Comparative Data on Culture and Personality with Reference to the Promotion of Mental Health," in *Mental Health,* ed. Moulton, p. 246. See John P. Foley, Jr., "The Criterion of Abnormality," *Journal of Abnormal and Social Psychology* 30 (1935): 279–291; Henry J. Wegrocki, "A Critique of Cultural and Statistical Concepts of Abnormality" (1939), in *Personality,* ed. Kluckhohn and Murray, pp. 691–701; and Joseph Wortis, "Sex Taboos, Sex Offenders, and the Law," *American Journal of Orthopsychiatry* 9 (1939): 554–564.

22. Benedict, "Some Comparative Data," p. 249. Harry Stack Sullivan, "Formal Discussion Summary and Critique," in *Mental Health,* ed. Moulton, p. 277.

23. Benedict, "Sex in Primitive Society," *American Journal of Orthopsychiatry* 9 (1939): 572, 573.

24. Abraham H. Maslow, *The Farther Reaches of Human Nature,* pp. 41, 42; *Motivation and Personality,* p. 92. Chapter 12, from which these observations are taken, was originally written in 1943 (Maslow, *Motivation and Personality,* p. xiii). Richard J. Lowry, *A. H. Maslow: An Intellectual Portrait,* pp. 3, 4, 7, 8.

25. Maslow, *Motivation and Personality,* pp. 204, 205, 208.

26. Ibid., pp. 208, 209, 212, 213.

27. Ibid., pp. 215–220.

28. Ibid., pp. 221, 222, 225, 226.

29. Ibid., p. 229.

11. Academic Politics

1. Mead, "The Years as Boas' Left Hand," *AW,* p. 344. Boas to Dean Howard L. McBain, October 15, 1930, and Mr. Danielson [Bursar], October 11, 1930; Benedict to Boas, November 3, 1930; November 21, 1930; December 8, 1930; all in FB Papers.

2. Alfred Kroeber to Franz Boas, March 10, 1931; Boas to Kroeber, February 16, 1931, and to Sapir, February 16 and 26, 1931; all in FB Papers. Mead in *AW,* p. 347, says Mrs. Boas died in 1930, but the year was 1929 (cf. Waldemar Bogoras to Boas, January 13, 1930, FB Papers).

3. Sapir to Benedict, March 16, 1931, RFB Papers. Benedict to Mead, December 29, 1930, quoted in Mead, "Anne Singleton," *AW,* p. 95. Alfred Kidder to Boas, May 31, 1927; Sapir to Boas, March 7, 1930; Kidder to Boas, February 13, 1931; all in FB Papers. Odd S. Halseth to Benedict, May 29, 1931, RFB Papers.

4. Benedict to Boas, June 31 [*sic*], 1931; July 28, 1931; August 24, 1931; all in FB Papers. Sapir to Benedict, April 2, 1931, RFB Papers.

5. Mead, "The Years as Boas' Left Hand," *AW,* pp. 347–348. Benedict to Mead, February 20, 1932, AW2. Benedict to Mead, August 17 [1932], *AW,*

p. 322; January 29, 1932, *AW*2. Sapir to Benedict, March 16, 1931, and Gladys Reichard to Benedict, July 8 [1932], RFB Papers. Benedict to Boas, July 24, 1932, FB Papers.

6. Jules Blumensohn [Henry] to Boas, August 8, 1933; Ella Deloria to Franz Boas, July 11, 1932; November 11, 1935; see also Deloria to Boas, August 25, 1935; Boas to Deloria, September 26, 1932; Benedict to Boas, June 30, 1932; all in FB Papers. For information on Ella Deloria, see "Who's Who among the Sioux: Ella C. Deloria," *University of South Dakota Bulletin, Institute of Indian Studies* 76 (August 1976), News Report No. 68, p. 3. Benedict to Lowie, April 17, 1935, Robert H. Lowie Papers, Bancroft Library, University of California, Berkeley.

7. Ruth Landes to Mead, February 4, 1977, MM Papers. Bernard, *Academic Women,* p. 115. Dorothy Lee, "Ruth Fulton Benedict (1887–1948)," *JAFL* 62 (1949): 346, 347. Sidney W. Mintz, "Ruth Benedict, Discussion," in *Totems and Teachers,* ed. Silverman, pp. 165, 163. Unidentified commentator, quoted in ibid., p. 163.

8. Victor Barnouw, "Ruth Benedict," *American Scholar* 49 (1980): 504. Mintz, "Ruth Benedict," p. 155. Remark on westerns and detective stories in Benedict to Richard Chase, January 6, 1946, RFB Papers; also in newspaper interview carried by papers across the country, e.g., "'Zuñi Mythology' by Ruth Benedict," *Madison Times,* June 28, 1936; *New York Herald-Tribune,* December 13, 1936. Gene Weltfish in Mintz, "Ruth Benedict, Discussion," p. 161.

9. Benedict to Boas, July 18, 1925, FB Papers; reprinted in *AW,* p. 291. Mead, "The Postwar Years: The Gathered Threads," *AW,* p. 437. Dick Slobodin to Benedict, July 9 [c. 1943–1945], RFB Papers. W. Emerson Gentzler [Bursar] to Boas, January 24, 1939, FB Papers.

Neil V. Rosenberg, "Herbert Halpert: A Biographical Sketch," in *Folklore Studies in Honor of Herbert Halpert,* ed. Kenneth S. Goldstein and Neil V. Rosenberg, pp. 2, 3.

Cora Du Bois to Benedict, June 21, 1933 and Benedict to Du Bois, July 10, 1933, RFB Papers.

10. Lee, "Ruth Fulton Benedict," p. 347. Clyde Kluckhohn in Viking Fund, *Ruth Fulton Benedict: A Memorial,* pp. 18–19.

Blanche Harper to Benedict, August 6, 1934; Joe D. [unreadable last name] to Benedict, January 3, 1933; Morris Opler to Benedict, November 5 [1931]; all in RFB Papers.

Mintz, "Ruth Benedict," pp. 155, 156. Robert Lynd, in Viking Fund, *Memorial,* p. 22. Ruth Landes, "A Woman Anthropologist in Brazil," in *Women in the Field,* ed. Peggy Golde, p. 120. Modell, *Ruth Benedict,* pp. 165–166.

11. Welles, *Measurement,* p. 153. Mead, *Ruth Benedict,* p. 25. "Diary: 1926," *AW,* p. 74. Judith Modell, "A Biographical Study of Ruth Fulton Benedict" (Ph.D. dissertation, University of Minnesota, 1978), pp. 121–123.

12. Mead, "Ruth Fulton Benedict," pp. 459, 458. Lee, "Ruth Fulton Benedict," p. 347.

13. "Benedict, Ruth," in *Current Biography: 1941,* p. 66; also *Vassar Miscellany News,* May 10, 1944, news clip, RFB Papers. See picture with Lee article in *JAFL* for this look. Bernard, *Academic Women,* p. 311. Mead, *Ruth Benedict,* p. 3.

14. Mead, "The Postwar Years," *AW,* p. 437. Modell, *Ruth Benedict,* pp. 162, 164.

15. Frans M. Olbrecht to Benedict, December 24, 1926, RFB Papers. Mead, "The Years as Boas' Left Hand," *AW,* p. 346.

16. Judith Modell, "Ruth Benedict, Anthropologist: The Reconciliation of Science and Humanism," in *Toward a Science of Man,* ed. Timothy H. H. Thoresen, p. 198. Mintz, "Ruth Benedict," p. 156. Alfred Kroeber, Cora Du Bois, and Robert Lynd, in Viking Fund, *Memorial,* pp. 11, 12–13, 22, 23. Victor Barnouw, "Ruth Benedict: Apollonian and Dionysian," *University of Toronto Quarterly* 18 (1949): 242. Kardiner and Preble, *They Studied Man,* pp. 205, 204. Bernard Mishkin to Mead, June 1, 1936, MM Papers.

17. Landes, "Woman Anthropologist," in *Women in the Field,* ed. Golde, pp. 120, 123. Virginia Wolf Briscoe, "Ruth Benedict, Anthropological Folklorist," *JAFL* 92 (1979): 472.

18. J. McKeen Cattell to Benedict, June 13, 1932; "Data on Ruth Benedict"; Henry B. Ward to Benedict, August 26, 1933; Roy Waldo Miner to Benedict, April 10, 1934; W. W. Campbell to Benedict, June 3, 1935, on the National Research Council; List, "Laboratory of Anthropology Advisory Board," and Philip Hayden to Benedict, January 27, 1937, on Columbia Council for Research in the Social Sciences; all in RFB Papers.

19. Lee, "Ruth Fulton Benedict," p. 346. Mead, "Ruth Fulton Benedict," p. 461. Archibald MacLeish, quoted by Benedict in class. See John L. Champe to Benedict, January 18, 1941, and Benedict to Champe, January 27, 1941, RFB Papers. The lines are slightly misquoted in Champe's letter. Boas to Dr. Yovan Erdeljanovic, September 30, 1937, FB Papers. Goldfrank, *Notes on an Undirected Life,* p. 161.

20. Benedict to Elizabeth [no last name], November 28, 1933, RFB Papers. Boas to May Mandelbaum [Edel], December 6, 1932, FB Papers. "June 9, 1934," in "Journal Fragments," *AW,* p. 154. Benedict to Mead, March 23, 1933, AW2.

Boas to Roscoe Pound, May 23, 1933; to Philip Hayden, December 21, 1932, and December 21, 1933; "Memorandum to Executive Officers of Departments," April 16, 1934; Boas to Hayden, May 4, 1934; all in FB Papers.

"For Radvanyi-11/47," pp. 2, 3, RFB Papers. There Benedict states that between 1930 and 1939 about twenty North American expeditions were carried out and results published, and seven major Central and South American projects between 1935 and 1940, "under my direction."

For examples of problems caused by the Depression, see Mel Jacobs to Boas, October 17, 1932, and March 6, 1933; F. G. Speck to Boas, March 29, 1933; Louis E. King to Boas, October 1, 1932; Frederica de Laguna to Boas, January 15, 1934; Jaime de Angulo to Boas, October 9, 1932; Paul Radin to Boas, October 6, 1932; all in FB Papers.

21. Boas to Mr. Wilbur K. Thomas, May 29, 1931, FB Papers.

Jesse Nusbaum to Benedict, July 27, 1931; Benedict to Odd S. Halseth, May 22, 1931; Halseth to Benedict, May 29, 1931; Ruth Underhill to Benedict, n.d. [note says 8-7-31]; Henry Carr to Benedict, February 27, 1933; Benedict to Carr, March 9, 1933; all in RFB Papers.

See also Gladys Reichard to Boas, July 26, 1931, and Mead to Boas, August 14, 1931, FB Papers.

22. Benedict to Nusbaum, July 29, 1931, RFB Papers.

Reichard to Boas, July 26, 1931; Benedict to Boas, July 28, 1931; Reichard to Boas, August 29, 1931; all in FB Papers.

Boas to Benedict, August 27, 1931, and Benedict to Nusbaum, November 4, 1931, RFB Papers.

See *Buffalo Courier*, September 28 and 29, 1931; also the *Buffalo Times*, September 28, 1931, for stories of the plane crash.

Benedict to Opler, October 8, 1931, RFB Papers.

23. Buell Quain to Benedict, August 2, 1939; Benedict to Fannie Quain, n.d. [draft]; Nathaniel P. Davis to the Department of Anthropology, August 22, 1939; Professor Heloisa Alberto Torres to Benedict, January 2, 1939, all in MM Papers. William Lipkind to Boas, September 30, 1939, FB Papers.

24. Reichard to Boas, August 29, 1931, FB Papers.

25. Benedict to Mead, December 28, 1932, *AW*, pp. 327, 326. Mead to Radcliffe-Brown, May 15, 1932, MM Papers. A. Tozzer to Boas, December 1, 1932, and Boas to Tozzer, December 2, 1932, FB Papers.

26. W. Lloyd Warner and Paul S. Lunt, *The Social Life of a Modern Community*, p. 3. Mead to W. Lloyd Warner, January 14, 1936, MM Papers. Benedict to Bob [Lynd], February 5, 1936, RFB Papers.

Robert Lowie to Boas, January 31, 1936; Boas to Kroeber, February 11, 1936; Tozzer to Boas, February 27, 1936; Nicholas Murray Butler to Boas, November 7, 1935; all in FB Papers.

Benedict to Bob Lynd, May 29, 1936, and Bob [Lynd] to Benedict, February 9, 1936, RFB Papers.

William L. Partridge and Elizabeth M. Eddy, "The Development of Applied Anthropology," in *Applied Anthropology in America*, ed. Elizabeth M. Eddy and William L. Partridge, pp. 16–18.

27. Boas to Bunzel, February 11, 1937, FB Papers. Benedict to Lynd, May 29, 1936, RFB Papers.

28. Ralph Linton to Benedict, June 19, 1937, RFB Papers.

29. Boas to Dean George B. Peagram, January 28, 1937, and Bunzel to Boas, April 30, 1937, FB Papers. Benedict, ms. of review of *The Study of Man* by Ralph Linton, and Boas to Benedict, October 27, 1939, RFB Papers. Adelin Linton and Charles Wagley, *Ralph Linton*, pp. 13, 34, 75. On field work, see [Jeanette Mirsky] to Mead, June 26, 1935, MM Papers.

30. Frank Fackenthal to Benedict, April 5, 1937, RFB Papers. Leo [Rosten] to Mead, November 8, 1938, MM Papers.

31. Linton and Wagley, *Ralph Linton*, pp. 48, 49, 6. Mintz, "Ruth Benedict, Discussion," p. 161.

When told Ruth Benedict had died of angina, Linton said, "Goddammit, she can't even *die* of a woman's disease!" (Howard, *Margaret Mead*, p. 281).

Benedict to Elsie Clews Parsons, December 7, 1940, ECP Papers.

32. Benedict to Boas, November 5, 1939, FB Papers, and October 24, 1939, RFB Papers.

33. Benedict to Boas, December 3, 1939, and March 16, 1940, RFB Papers. Benedict to Dutchy [her lawyer]. November 22, 1939, and Marion Q. Kaiser [Quain's sister] to Benedict, September 13, 1939, MM Papers.

34. "Thirty-fifth Annual Meeting of the American Folk-Lore Society," *JAFL* 37 (1924): 245; "Thirty-seventh Annual Meeting of the American Folk-Lore Society," *JAFL* 39 (1926): 209.

35. Stith Thompson, "Reminiscences of an Octogenarian Folklorist," ed. Hari S. Upadhyaya, *Asian Folklore Studies* 27 (1968): 118.

36. Boas to Professor Dean Fansler, May 13, 1931, FB Papers.

[Ann Gayton] to Benedict, April 6, 1937; Gayton to Elsie Clews Parsons, April 23, 1937; Melville Herskovits to Parsons, February 21, 1940; and to Members of the AFLS Policy Committee, December 2, 1940; Report on the Committee on Policy, AFLS, December 11, 1940; all in ECP Papers.

Modell, *Ruth Benedict*, pp. 220, 221.

After his election as president of the American Folk-Lore Society Herskovits wrote an article the next year on "Folklore after a Hundred Years: A Problem in Redefinition," *JAFL* 59 (1946): 89–100; other articles on the problems and state of folklore by both literary and anthropological folklorists also appeared in *JAFL* in the mid-1940's.

37. Benedict to George Herzog, February 24, 1940, RFB Papers. Gladys Reichard to Parsons, October 2, 1940, and Parsons to A. I. Hallowell, January 4, 1941, ECP Papers.

38. Elsie Clews Parsons actually became the first woman president of the AAA. She was inserted into the chain-of-command for this purpose in 1940. Due to administrative reorganization and politics, Benedict did not become president until 1946 (see Chapter 14).

12. The Politics of Culture

1. Boas to May Mandelbaum [later Edel], May 26, 1933, FB Papers.

On Boas' books, see J. McKeen Cattell to Alfons Dampf, July 13, 1933, FB Papers.

"Faculty Fellowship Committee—Minutes," August 11, 1933; Boas to Dr. Charles G. Abbott, April 17, 1933; to Nicholas Murray Butler, May 3, 1933; to Dr. Alfred Plaut, May 11, 1933; to Louis Posner, May 26, 1933; to Albert Frosch, August 12, 1933 (see letterhead and signature); Clarence Lewis to Boas, August 15, 1933; Boas to Professor H. S. Jennings, July 8, 1933; "Summary of Minutes of Organizational Meeting of Institute of Race Relations, Columbia University, March 25, 1933," 4 pp.; all in FB Papers. There was much correspondence on the institute during March and April 1933. On the positive contributions of German Jews, see correspondence scattered through May 1933.

2. Benedict to Boas, August 29, 1933, FB Papers. Benedict to Mead, March 23, 1933, May 19, 1933, and June 16, 1933, AW2.

3. Boas to Jacob Billikopf, October 23, 1933; ms., "Aryans and Non-Aryans," 12 pp.; Boas to Rev. Stephen S. Wise, February 19, 1934; to Dr. Frederick P. Keppel, February 27, 1934; to Frida Kirchway, September 17, 1935; Jay Lovestone to Boas, May 21, 1934; Boas to W. S. Schwabacher, May 22, 1934; all in FB Papers.

4. Boas to Dr. Elisha Friedman, November 24, 1933, FB Papers. Leland Bell, *In Hitler's Shadow: The Anatomy of American Nazism,* pp. 19, 22, 24, 27–30, 31.

5. Benedict, quoted in Mead, "The Years as Boas' Left Hand," *AW,* p. 348. Boas to Tozzer, November 16, 1933, FB Papers.

Boas to Paul Rivet, November 15, 1937, FB Papers. There was much correspondence on the serious scientific study, especially in 1937.

William E. Bohn to Boas, August 8, 1933, FB Papers. Correspondence on the NYU course is spread through December and January 1934–1935.

Boas to B. W. Huebsch, March 21, 1935; to Sidney Wallach, December 7, 1936, and April 24, 1937; all in FB Papers.

6. Boas to Leonard Bloomfield, March 10, 1936, and to Livingston Farrand, April 17, 1935, FB Papers. Benedict, *Race: Science and Politics,* rev. ed., p. 211.

7. Boas to Carl Van Doren, July 1, 1936; to Sidney Wallach, December 7, 1936; to Ira A. Hirschmann, February 4, 1937; all in FB Papers.

8. Engagement Book, 1936, and "A Woman to Her Dead Husband," unpublished poem, RFB Papers.

Benedict to Boas, n.d., filed end of May 1937, and Benedict to the Faculty of Columbia University, n.d., filed at the end of 1938, FB Papers.

Thirteenth Annual Class Bulletin, Class of 1909, p. 62.

Edith Laekin to Benedict, December 21, 1936; Benedict to Dr. W. Carson Ryan, May 7, 1938, and June 3, 1938; all in RFB Papers.

Robert Lynd to Sir [form letter], October 14, 1937, listing Benedict on the letterhead as a member of the committee, and Benedict, Professor Leslie C. Dunn, and Selig Hecht to the Faculty of Columbia University, n.d. [form letter], about an ambulance [filed end of 1938], FB Papers.

"University Federation for Democracy and Intellectual Freedom," printed 4-page circular on the federation and its activities; second letter by Benedict to the Faculty of Columbia University, n.d.; both filed at the end of 1938, FB Papers.

9. "Committee for Austrian Relief," March 31, 1938; Boas to David Efron, January 3, 1939; "Minutes Executive Committee, National Council for Pan-American Democracy, Jan. 3, 1939"; Albert O. Bassuk to Boas, July 21, 1938; all in FB Papers. Benedict, *Race,* p. 211.

10. "Record * Program * Needs" of the American Council for Democracy and Intellectual Freedom (ACDIF), pamphlet; copy of "Manifesto on Freedom of Science"; Benedict to Miss Kiel, November 1, 1938; all in RFB Papers.

J. McKeen Cattell to Boas, December 10, 1938; I. Van Meter [*Time*] to Boas, December 15, 1938; Harold Urey, Leslie Dunn, Franz Boas, Ruth Benedict, and Irwin H. Kaiser to Chair, Board of Education, New York City, April 22, 1938; Boas to Editors, *New York Sun* and *World-Telegram,* May 5, 1938, on the telegram to Roosevelt signed by Benedict among others; "University Federation for Democracy and Intellectual Freedom," p. 2; MLF to Franz Boas, February 3, 1939 (letterhead); all in FB Papers.

Emily Fogg Mead to Margaret Mead, February 7, 1939, MM Papers. Alexander Lesser, "Franz Boas," in *Totems and Teachers,* ed. Silverman, p. 20.

11. Belle Boas and Charles Martin to Benedict, February 27, 1939; Benedict to

Joseph P. Lash, June 3, 1939; "Record * Program * Needs" of ACDIF; all in RFB Papers. Benedict to Boas, August 16, 1939, FB Papers.

"Minutes of Continuations Committee of Conference on Pan-American Democracy, December 19, 1938," and "Minutes Executive Committee, National Council for Pan-American Democracy, January 3, 1939," FB Papers. G. A. MacCormick to Benedict, June 8, 1939, and Benedict to Mrs. Sylvia Wilcox Razey, February 18, 1939, RFB Papers.

12. Boas to Charles J. Hendley, March 28, 1938; to Harry Schneiderman, May 15, 1939; to The Initiating Committee of "A Call to All Active Supporters of Democracy and Peace," July 20, 1939; all in FB Papers.

Boas to Benedict, July 23, 1939, RFB Papers. William Gellerman, *Martin Dies,* pp. 61, 163–164; the whole book gives a good picture of the work of the Dies Committee.

13. Boas to Moissaye J. Olgin, November 5, 1932; to The Initiating Committee of "A Call to All Active Supporters of Democracy and Peace," July 20, 1939; to Rockwell Kent, September 25, 1936; all in FB Papers.

14. Boas to Henry Salasin, April 22, 1938; to Professor Clyde R. Miller, January 9, 1939; to Alice Dodge, August 5, 1940; all in FB Papers. Goldfrank, *Notes on an Undirected Life,* p. 117. Mead, "The Years as Boas' Left Hand," *AW,* p. 349.

15. Mead, "The Years as Boas' Left Hand," *AW,* p. 349. Goldfrank, *Notes on an Undirected Life,* pp. 114, 116.

16. M. I. Finklestein to Dr. Abraham Lefkowitz, October 21, 1939; clip of Winchell's column, "On Broadway," April 8, 1940, from the *New York Daily Mirror;* "Stalinist Outposts in the United States," April 1940, a report by the Committee on Cultural Freedom about Communist front organizations, 8 pp.; all in FB Papers.

Dies Committee report quoted in Gellerman, *Martin Dies,* p. 157.

Benedict to Paul Allen, October 10, 1941, RFB Papers.

On the fate of the ACDIF, see Boas to Professor Ernest M. Patterson, July 30, 1942; M. I. Finkelstein to Franz Boas, August 18, 1942; George Marshall to Boas, September 12, 1942; all in FB Papers. Boas to Benedict, August 18, 1942, and Bob Lynd to Benedict, August 18 [1942], RFB Papers.

17. Louis P. Birk to Benedict, May 15, 1939, RFB Papers.

18. Benedict to Boas, August 16, 1939; September 26, 1939; November 5, 1939; January 18, 1940; all in FB Papers. Benedict to Louis Birk, October 27, 1939, RFB Papers.

19. Benedict, *Race;* quotes from pp. 153, 5.

20. Ibid., pp. 154–155.

21. Ibid., pp. 241, 242.

22. Ibid., pp. 249, 251, 216, 232, 237, 255.

23. *Christian Century* 57 (October 30, 1940): 1345; *New Republic* 104 (January 13, 1941): 62; *Nation* 151 (October 19, 1940): 372.

Bruno Lasker to Modern Age Publishers, November 20, 1940, RFB Papers. Some reviewers criticized sloppiness and errors in the Modern Age edition. These were corrected in the revised edition put out by Viking Press in 1943, and this has since become the standard edition and a classic text on race issues.

Karen Horney to Benedict, August 22 [c. 1940–1941], RFB Papers. Hortense Powdermaker, Review of *Race: Science and Politics, AA* 43 (1941): 474–475.

24. Benedict to Thelma Herman, July 12, 1944, and Oliver Pilat, "She's a Reluctant Celebrity," *New York Post,* April 8, 1944, clipping, in RFB Papers.

25. Benedict and Mildred Ellis, *Race and Cultural Relations,* pp. 8–11.

26. Ibid., pp. 42–43. Paul E. Elicker to Benedict, May 16, 1942, and Louis Wirth to Benedict, July 31, 1941, RFB Papers.

27. Luther Gulick to Most Reverend Edward F. Hoban, Bishop of Cleveland, May 13, 1948, RFB Papers. Benedict and Gene Weltfish, *The Races of Mankind,* quotes from pp. 32, 2, 3, 26, 24. Alice Payne Hackett, *60 Years of Best Sellers, 1895–1955,* pp. 72, 73.

28. Sam Schmerler to Benedict, March 22, 1944, RFB Papers. Benedict and Weltfish, *Races of Mankind,* p. 18. Oliver Pilat, "She's a Reluctant Celebrity," *New York Post,* April 8, 1944, clipping in RFB Papers. Hackett, *60 Years,* p. 73—966,997 copies sold by 1955. On translations, see J. Max Bond to Benedict, April 29, 1947, and G. Gunnerson to Benedict, June 19, 1947, RFB Papers. On *True Comics,* see Harold C. Field to Violet Edwards, February 17, 1944, RFB Papers. Information on the film is from the unnumbered page at the beginning of Benedict and Gene Weltfish, *In Henry's Backyard: The Races of Mankind.*

29. Benedict and Weltfish, *In Henry's Backyard,* pp. 9, 40, 41, 42, 44, 49. Violet Edwards to Benedict, January 10, 1947, RFB Papers.

30. Benedict, *Race,* pp. 80, 241, 243.

31. Benedict to Dr. David Levy, October 24, 1938; Lyle Smith to Benedict, March 31, [1939]; Benedict to David Zablodowsky, September 10, 1940; Engagement Book, 1938; "Last Will and Testament of Ruth Fulton Benedict," July 16, 1937; all in RFB Papers. Benedict later sold Shattuck Farm after the death of Auntie My and made a new will, naming Ruth Valentine and not mentioning Raymond.

32. Engagement Book, 1939, RFB Papers.

On the field trip there was an automobile accident in which an Indian guide was killed while the husband of one of the field trip participants was driving. See Benedict to Boas, July 12, 1939, FB Papers.

Valentine is listed as a clinical psychologist in "Index of Personal Names," *AW,* p. 572. See also Ruth Valentine, "The Effects of Punishment for Errors on the Maze Learning of Rats," *Journal of Comparative Psychology* 10 (1930): 35–53, an abridgment of her Ph.D. thesis.

Mead to Gregory Bateson, January 9, 1940, MM Papers.

13. The War Years

1. All of these talks and manuscripts are filed in the RFB Papers.

2. "Dr. Butler's Address to the Columbia Faculties," *New York Times,* October 4, 1940, p. 14.

News release from the American Committee for Democracy and Intellectual Freedom, October 6, 1940—open letter by eight ACDIF members including Ruth Benedict to Columbia President Nicholas Murray Butler; Butler to Benedict, October 8, 1940, backing off; J. Russell Smith to Benedict, October 7, 1940, thanks her "for getting up and signing that very much needed letter" to Butler; all in RFB Papers.

3. Benedict, "The Uses of Cannibalism," *AW,* pp. 44–48; in "On Declaring War," *New Republic* 105 (September 1, 1941): 279–280; "The Natural History of War," *AW,* pp. 369–382.

4. "The Natural History of War," *AW,* pp. 371, 373, 377, 378.

5. Ibid., pp. 375, 379–382.

6. Benedict, "Reply to Dr. Aginsky," p. 345. Maslow, *The Farther Reaches of Human Nature,* pp. 200–201.

7. Benedict to Dr. H. A. Murray, July 30, 1940, RFB Papers. Murray et al., *Explorations in Personality,* pp. 40, 42.

8. Benedict, "Hostility in Pilaga Children—Discussion," *American Journal of Orthopsychiatry* 10 (1940): 120–121.

9. "Ideologies in the Light of Comparative Data," *AW,* p. 385. Barnouw, "Ruth Benedict," p. 504.

10. Benedict to Philip Hayden, June 13, 1940, RFB Papers.

11. Benedict, "Synergy: Some Notes of Ruth Benedict," ed. A. Maslow and John Honigmann, *AA* 72 (1970): 326. The idea of synergy particularly influenced the theories of psychoanalyst Abraham Maslow, who made it an integral part of his later work. Anthropologist John Honigmann also used the idea in his writings. Mead taught a seminar at Vassar in 1941 using synergy as the grounding concept. It is remotely possible Benedict's concept of synergy influenced R. Buckminster Fuller's use of the idea in the 1960's. But probably its most important impact was in Benedict's own post-war research (see Chapter 14).

12. Judith [Stephen] to Mead, February 24, 1941, MM Papers.

13. Benedict, "Synergy," p. 325.

14. "Ideologies in the Light of Comparative Data," *AW,* p. 383.

15. Benedict, Review of *The Crisis of Our Age* and *Social and Cultural Dynamics, New Republic* 106 (February 2, 1942): 154–155.

16. "Ideologies in the Light of Comparative Data," *AW,* p. 384; in "On Declaring War," p. 280 (italics added); "Franz Boas: An Obituary" (1943), *AW,* p. 420; "Primitive Freedom," (1942), *AW,* p. 393.

17. Benedict, "Primitive Freedom," *AW,* pp. 386–389.

18. Ibid., pp. 389–391, 393–396.

19. Ibid., pp. 396, 397.

20. Ibid., pp. 398, 397.

21. Benedict, "Race Prejudice in War," *New York Herald-Tribune,* February 25, 1942; "Plea for American-Born Japanese," *New York Times,* March 6, 1942.

22. Moses Moskowitz to Benedict, April 15, 1941, RFB Papers. Benedict, "Editorial," *American Scholar* 12 (1942–1943): 3, 4. Benedict to Dr. Charles A. Shull, December 11, 1942, RFB Papers. Benedict, "Pre-War Experts," *New Republic* 107 (October 5, 1942): 411.

23. Benedict to Professor Allison Davis, June 27, 1942, RFB Papers. See also Benedict, "A New York City Experiment in Home Making in Wartime," unpublished ms. in RFB Papers.

24. Geoffrey Gorer, "Foreword to the First Edition," in *Himalayan Village: An Account of the Lepchas of Sikkim,* 2d ed., p. 12. Mead, "The Years as Boas' Left Hand," *AW,* p. 352.

25. In her Engagement book for December 21, 1942, Benedict wrote, "Lunch with Boas, Rivet—; Papa Franz died," which seems to indicate that she was there (RFB Papers); but Goldfrank has reported that Boas' secretary recalled calling both Benedict and Ruth Bunzel to tell them of his death (Goldfrank, *Notes on an Undirected Life,* p. 122).

"Franz Boas: An Obituary," *AW,* p. 422.

26. On Benedict as a founding member of the Society for Applied Anthropology, see Benedict to Eliot Chapple, April 5, 1941, RFB Papers. Also, Eddy and Partridge, eds., *Applied Anthropology in America,* p. 33. Benedict, "Two Patterns of Indian Acculturation," *AA* 45 (1943): 207–212.

27. Benedict, Review of *Indians of South America* by Paul Radin, *New York Herald-Tribune,* Books 18 (April 26, 1942): 16. M. L. Wilson to Benedict, February 16, 1938, RFB Papers, and November 6, 1940, MM Papers.

28. Benedict to Wilson, December 7, 1940, MM Papers. Benedict to Father Natallana, March 30, 1939, RFB Papers.

29. Benedict, ms. "Anthropological Memorandum on Diet Habits," January 2, 1941, MM Papers.

30. "Suggestions for Father Cooper to use in discussing role of Social Science in connection with the Kilgore Bill," October 2, 1945; "Memo Margaret Mead from Ruth Benedict," April 8, 1942, on vitamin word usage; "Memorandum to M. L. Wilson, Asst. Dir. Office of Defense Health and Welfare Services," March 20, 1942, by Ruth Benedict, among others; all in MM Papers.

31. "Recognition of Cultural Diversities in the Post-War World" (1943), *AW,* p. 442.

32. Ibid., pp. 443, 444.

33. Benedict to Rev. Richard Henry, August 8, 1946, RFB Papers. Mead, *AW,* p. 558n.19. Benedict, "Memo to Mr. Katz," July 2, 1943, RFB Papers. Benedict, *Thai Culture and Behavior,* p. 1.

34. Benedict, *Thai Culture and Behavior,* pp. 42, 43, 33, 38.

35. Ibid., pp. 44, 45.

36. Mead, in "The Years as Boas' Left Hand," *AW,* pp. 352–353, says that the Rumanian study was done first, but actually the Thai report was done first. See Benedict to Esther [Goldfrank], September 11, 1943, RFB Papers.

See "Basic Plan for Rumania: Background and Suggestions for Psychological Warfare," 16 pp., and "Background for a Basic Plan for Thailand," September 4, 1943, 16 pp., RFB Papers. How or whether these were used I don't know.

"Memorandum," by Bjarne Braatoy to Benedict, January 22, 1944, RFB Papers.

37. Benedict to Isabelle [no last name], January 15, 1944; Benedict to Erik Erikson, March 7, 1944; Erikson to Benedict, March 23, 1944; "Memo—Ruth Benedict to Samuel Williamson—Re Background Material for pamphlet for the Dutch on American troops"; Benedict, "Note on an Authoritative View of 'The True Danger' to German Morale," April 4, 1944; "Target-oriented propaganda for European nations," memo to Wallace Carroll from Benedict, July 24, 1944; Benedict, "Problems in Japanese Morale submitted for Study by Psychiatrists,"

2 pp.; Benedict to Carl Withers, March 13, 1946; all in RFB Papers.

38. Benedict, *The Chrysanthemum and the Sword: Patterns of Japanese Culture*, pp. 3, 6, 7. "Japanese Behavior Patterns," 59 pp.; "Japanese Origins: Official Versions vs. Science," 5 pp.; "What Shall Be Done about the Emperor?" 3 pp.; F. Theodore Cloak to Benedict, August 30, 1945; Benedict to Mrs. Alex C. Dick, August 8, 1946; all in RFB Papers.

39. Gertrude Grimwood Cameron to Benedict, n.d., post-war, RFB Papers. Mead, *Ruth Benedict*, p. 61; "The Years as Boas' Left Hand," *AW*, p. 353.

40. Benedict to Ferris Greenslet, November 14, 1945, RFB Papers.

41. Benedict, *The Chrysanthemum and the Sword*, p. 1.

42. Ibid., p. 304.

43. Ibid., p. 297. Mead, "The Postwar Years," *AW*, p. 428.

44. On the proposed tour, see Major D. Donald Klous to Benedict, December 26, 1946, RFB Papers. Colonel Don Z. Zimmerman to Benedict, February 26, 1948, MM Papers.

45. *New York Times*, November 24, 1946, p. 4. *Christian Science Monitor*, December 16, 1946, p. 16. Erna Fergusson, Review of *The Chrysanthemum and the Sword*, *Social Studies* 38 (1947): 48. Robert Peel, Review of *The Chrysanthemum and the Sword*, *Booklist* 43 (1947): 131. Harold Strauss, Review of *The Chrysanthemum and the Sword*, *New Republic* 116 (January 6, 1947): 38.

Roger Baldwin to Benedict, September 17, 1947, and T. Muriel Kitagawa to Benedict, August 16, 1947, RFB Papers.

See J. W. Bennett and M. Nagai, "Echoes: Reactions to American Anthropology," *AA* 55 (1953): 404–411, on criticisms of *The Chrysanthemum and the Sword*. Also Takao Sofue, "Japanese Studies by American Anthropologists: Review and Evaluation," *AA* 62 (1960): 306–317.

Edward Norbeck and George DeVos, "Japan," in *Psychological Anthropology: Approaches to Culture and Personality*, ed. Francis L. K. Hsu, p. 21.

14. The Last Great Vision

1. Mead, n. 19, in "Notes," *AW*, p. 558. On the council's purpose, see "The Council on Intercultural Relations," in "Current Items," *American Sociological Review* 8 (1943): 223. Sometimes called Council for Intercultural Relations.

2. "Institute for Intercultural Studies," [June 1945], MM Papers.

There has been some confusion as to the chronology of the founding of these organizations. The "1947 Report of the work of the Institute for Intercultural Studies," p. 5, says the institute came into existence at an informal luncheon meeting in Philadelphia in 1941, organized originally as the Council for Intercultural Relations in 1942, and incorporated into IIS in 1943 (actually 1944 according to Benedict to Fannie Quain, January 6, 1945, MM Papers), and other information agrees with Benedict; all in MM Papers.

3. Mead, "The Postwar Years," *AW*, p. 432. Benedict, "Remarks on Receiving the Annual Achievement Award of the American Association of University Women" (1946), quoted in Mead, "The Postwar Years," *AW*, p. 431.

4. Mead, "The Postwar Years," *AW*, p. 433; here Mead says this party took

place in winter 1946–1947, but in *Ruth Benedict,* she says it took place in spring 1946. This latter seems to be correct—see letters cited below.

Benedict to Geoffrey [Gorer], October 21, 1946, and Benedict to Mead, June 26, 1946, MM Papers. Officially the contract title was "Office of Naval Research Contract for Cultural Study of Certain Minorities of European and Asiatic Origin in New York City" (Mead, "Chronology," *AW,* p. 525).

5. Benedict to Geoffrey [Gorer], March 23, 1947, and Benedict to Nathan and Martha [Wolfenstein] Leites, July 4, 1947, MM Papers. Mead, "The Postwar Years," *AW,* p. 433.

6. Benedict to Geoffrey [Gorer], July 4, 1947; "RCC Admin. Summer 1947 plans. Memorandum of meeting of Ruth Benedict, Margaret Mead, and Ruth Valentine"; "RCC Progress Report, September 1, 1947," on the first six months of the program; all in MM Papers.

7. "RCC Progress Report, December 1, 1947," MM Papers.

8. George W. Stocking, Jr., "Ideas and Institutions in American Anthropology: Toward a History of the Interwar Period," in *Selected Papers from the American Anthropologist 1921–1945,* ed. Stocking, p. 42. For a clear exposition of the AAA reorganization see this article, especially pp. 37–42.

9. Benedict to Father John Cooper, January 22, 1947, RFB Papers. There was an attempt to cheat Benedict out of the honor of an AAA presidency. There was a proposal that Linton continue as president during the interim, which would have meant bypassing Benedict as president, but this was successfully opposed (Mead, *Ruth Benedict,* p. 68).

10. Mead, "National Character," in *Anthropology Today,* ed. Kroeber, p. 647. Elgin Williams, "Anthropology for the Common Man," *AA* 49 (1947): 85. Victor Barnouw, "Ruth Benedict: Apollonian and Dionysian," pp. 248–250.

11. Julian Steward, "Evolution and Process," in *Anthropology Today,* ed. Kroeber, p. 314. White's cultural evolutionism differed from Steward's. Steward called White's approach, and that of V. Gordon Child, "universal" evolution, focusing on "world embracing schemes and universal laws." Steward called his own approach "multilinear" evolution, a search for parallels occurring in limited ways across cultures, rather than for universals. Both believed in successive stages of development in cultures: White on a universal scale, Steward on a limited one by searching for forms, processes, and functions recurring similarly cross-culturally (Steward, "Evolution and Process," pp. 316–318). White's work was controversial because of his scathing attack on Boas in the process of explaining his own ideas and for its uncomfortable closeness to nineteenth-century unilinear evolution in its vastness of scale. But White did stir up re-examination of the idea of cultural evolution, although probably more anthropologists were comfortable with Steward's usage.

12. Steward, "Evolution and Process," p. 315; "Cultural Causality and Law: A Trial Formulation of the Development of Early Civilization," *AA* 51 (1949): 5.

13. Benedict, "The Study of Cultural Patterns in European Nations" (1946), in Mead, *Ruth Benedict,* pp. 161, 162. Benedict, *The Chrysanthemum and the Sword,* pp. 16–17. Mead, "National Character," pp. 654–655.

14. Mead, "National Character," p. 655, 648.

15. Ibid., pp. 656, 658, 659.

16. On the book, see Benedict to Professor Grayson L. Kirk, July 17, 1947, MM Papers. Mead, "The Postwar Years," *AW*, pp. 437–438. Benedict to Mrs. V [unreadable], August 15, 1948, MM Papers.

17. Actually seven—she talked about American Indians as well, but used them to show the range of results from swaddling, from extreme passivity to extreme energy, depending upon the culturally or tribally expected result (Benedict, ms. of "The Study of Cultural Continuities in the Civilized World," Lecture given at UNESCO Seminar on Childhood Education in Podêbrady, Czechoslovakia, July 21–August 25, 1948, RFB Papers).

18. Ibid., pp. 6–7.

19. "Answering a Few Questions," Fourth Lecture by Ruth Benedict at the UNESCO Seminar, p. 3, RFB Papers.

20. Benedict, "The Study of Cultural Continuities in the Civilized World," pp. 1, 2; "Answering a Few Questions," p. 8; both in RFB Papers.

21. Benedict, "Answering a Few Questions," p. 2.

22. Ibid., p. 2.

23. Ibid., p. 1.

24. Mead, *Ruth Benedict,* p. 74. Benedict to Alfred Kroeber, October 19, 1947, Alfred L. Kroeber Papers, Bancroft Library, University of California, Berkeley.

25. Benedict to Clyde Kluckhohn, December 7, 1947, MM Papers. Mintz, "Ruth Benedict," p. 156.

26. Benedict to Richard Chase, January 6, 1946, RFB Papers. There is a series of letters on this subject around this time period. The article Chase later wrote was "Ruth Benedict: The Woman as Anthropologist," *Columbia University Forum* 2 (1959): 19–22.
Barnouw, "Ruth Benedict," pp. 507, 508; see Barnouw, "Ruth Benedict: Apollonian and Dionysian" for critique of *Patterns of Culture.* Margery Fulton Freeman to Benedict, September 7, 1948, RFB Papers.

27. Freeman to Mead, September 18 [1948], RFB Papers. Mead, "The Postwar Years," *AW*, p. 438. Leila Lee to Lottie [no last name], September 13, 1948, MM Papers. On the date, see Modell, *Ruth Benedict,* p. 309.

28. Cora Du Bois, Review of *The Study of Culture at a Distance, Annals of the American Academy of Political and Social Sciences* 292 (1954): 176–177. John W. Bennett, Review of *The Study of Culture at a Distance, American Journal of Sociology* 60 (1954): 92. Mead, "National Character," p. 644. Howard, *Margaret Mead,* p. 278.

29. Howard, *Margaret Mead,* p. 276.

30. Margaret Mead and Rhoda Métraux, eds., *The Study of Culture at a Distance,* provides a picture of the RCC organization, especially pp. 85–104. See also Mead, "The Postwar Years," *AW*, pp. 434–437.

31. Mead and Métraux, eds., *The Study of Culture at a Distance,* p. 89.

32. Mead, "The Postwar Years," *AW*, pp. 434–435. On Mead as volunteer see Ruth Valentine to Mead, April 19, 1947, MM Papers.

33. Mead and Métraux, eds., *The Study of Culture at a Distance,* pp. 86–87.

34. Mead, "The Postwar Years," *AW*, p. 435.

35. Schreiner, *Woman and Labor,* pp. 141–142. Key, *The Morality of Woman and Other Essays,* pp. 52, 54; *The Woman Movement,* p. v.

36. Schreiner, *Woman and Labor,* p. 226. Key, *The Woman Movement,* pp. 65, 126.

37. Key, *The Woman Movement,* p. 132. Schreiner, *Woman and Labor,* pp. 176, 180. Molier Harris Fisher to Benedict, November 28, 1940, and Benedict to Fisher, December 7, 1940, RFB Papers.

38. Key, *The Woman Movement,* pp. 132, 41. Benedict to Edward L. Bernays, March 4, 1946, RFB Papers.

39. Mead, "The Postwar Years," *AW,* p. 437. Mead and Métraux, eds., *The Study of Culture at a Distance,* p. 94n.

40. Benedict, ms., "The Psychology of Love," RFB Papers.

41. Mead and Métraux, eds., *The Study of Culture at a Distance,* p. 91.

42. Benedict, "Child Rearing in Certain European Countries" (1948; published posthumously 1949), *AW,* p. 458.

43. Mead and Métraux, eds., *The Study of Culture at a Distance,* p. 87. Mead, "The Postwar Years," *AW,* p. 434.

44. Benedict, "Ideologies in the Light of Comparative Data," *AW,* p. 385.

45. Freeman to Mead, September 18 [1948], RFB Papers.

A Bibliographical Note on Sources

THE MOST IMPORTANT SOURCE for information on Ruth Benedict is the Ruth Fulton Benedict Papers, Special Collections, Vassar College Library, Poughkeepsie, New York. This collection contains the bulk of Ruth Benedict's known personal papers, published and unpublished manuscripts, letters, and pictures. The collection is not complete. Some items published in *An Anthropologist at Work* (1959), edited by Margaret Mead, seem to have disappeared, such as the original of "The Story of My Life," Benedict's account of her childhood. Though there are handwritten autobiographical fragments, the only copy of "The Story of My Life" is a typewritten one in a draft copy of *An Anthropologist at Work*. Other things seemingly missing include some published Journal segments, the published Diary from 1923, and the letters from Edward Sapir published in *An Anthropologist at Work*. Some letters are sealed until 1990, however, and these may be among them. Treasures in the collection include the stories Benedict wrote as a child and young adult; her unpublished poetry; a partial unpublished book manuscript, "The Religion of the North American Indians," that is a precursor to *Patterns of Culture;* unpublished Journal fragments; a notebook from Benedict's 1910 European trip; the notes and drafts for her feminist biographies; her Office of War Information and Research in Contemporary Cultures material; and the insights contained in hundreds of "public" letters, i.e., letters from colleagues, acquaintances, students, and strangers along with the few letters from good friends and family. Special Collections also contains the Martha Beckwith and Dorothy Lee collections. Both were colleagues of Benedict's, and Lee wrote an excellent obituary of Ruth Benedict for the *Journal of American Folk-Lore* (JAFL 62 [1949]: 345–347).

Besides Special Collections, the main library at Vassar has what is left of Ruth Benedict's personal book collection scattered on its shelves. If one looks in the anthropology section one can find some of them, a few even annotated. The *Vassar Miscellany* and *Vassar Quarterly,* available on the library shelves, yielded unexpected articles written by Benedict while she was a student at Vassar and a young married woman: "The High Seriousness of Chaucer," *Miscellany* 37 (October 1907): 1–6; "*The Trojan Women* of Euripides," *Miscellany* 37 (November 1907): 53–57; "Charles Lamb: An Appreciation," *Miscellany* 37 (January 1908): 193– 198; "Walt Whitman," *Miscellany* 37 (March 1908): 304–309; "*Lena Rivers,* by Mary J. Holmes," *Miscellany* 37 (May 1908): 419–422; "The Fool in King Lear," *Miscellany* 38 (November 1908): 46–51; the prize-winning "Literature and Democracy," *Miscellany* 38 (March 1909): 292–295; "The Racial Traits of Shakespeare's Heroes," *Miscellany* 38 (June 1909): 480–486.

The Vassar Alumnae Association, headquartered at Vassar, is a repository of information on past classes. There I found the Class Day Book for the Class of 1909, several questionnaires filled out by Benedict, her sister, and her mother, all Vassar graduates, and the annual reports for the Class of 1909 through the years. The Vassar yearbook, the *Vassarion,* 1905–1909, proved a storehouse of information on Ruth and Margery's activities while they were students at Vassar and provided glimpses of their classmates and teachers.

The Margaret Mead Papers at the Library of Congress, Washington, D.C. yielded good information on Research in Contemporary Cultures, the Buell Quain suicide, and the connection with Neo-Freudian psychoanalysts Karen Horney and Erich Fromm. There are also class notes by Mead from seminars in the 1920's containing notes of reports by Ruth Benedict, and all varieties of background information on anthropology and anthropologists during Ruth Benedict's lifetime. This collection also contains sealed Benedict letters. Mead was an intimate friend whose book, *An Anthropologist at Work: Writings of Ruth Benedict* (1959) is *the* classic reference work on Ruth Benedict. It remains the most comprehensive source of published information by and about Benedict available. It includes important published articles by Benedict and previously unpublished work by her from different periods of her life, such as "The Sense of Symbolism" (c. 1909), "Counters in the Game" (c. 1925), "The Uses of Cannibalism" (c. 1925), "They Dance for Rain in Zuñi" (c. 1920's), "The Natural History of War" (1939), "Ideologies in the Light of Comparative Data" (c. 1941–1942); her earlier manuscript of "Mary Wollstonecraft" (c. 1914–1917); private journal entries, diaries for 1923 and 1926, and a collection of her poetry, most not published before this time; letters to Margaret Mead and from Edward Sapir, not otherwise available; and letters to and from Franz Boas, which are also available in the Benedict or Boas Papers. All of the selections are tied together by four biographical essays on Benedict written by Mead from various perspectives of Benedict's life.

An Anthropologist at Work is a remarkable book, and it is indispensable to any biographer of Ruth Benedict. It broke new ground in biography when it appeared. But of necessity it was selective, and this very selectivity suggested things about Benedict, concealed other things, and reflected Mead's own imperatives as well as those of the late 1950's when it was written. To give an example of each: Mead subtly suggested that Benedict and Sapir had an affair during the early 1920's, which does not seem to have been true; in fact, it was Mead herself who had such an affair. The suggestion itself helped to conceal or cast doubt on Benedict's Lesbianism. By including "Child Rearing in Certain European Countries" as the last selection, the book suggested this as her primary interest at the end of her life when in fact other articles written during that last year show that it was one interest among many. The selection of emphasis reflected the return of American women to domesticity in the 1950's and Mead's own driving interest in children and her own streak of dramatic sentimentalism. Thus the Journal selections were chosen to reflect the struggle over home and career and the seeming overemphasis on the importance of Benedict's childlessness by Mead, who had felt that emphasis in her own life. (Not only Mead in the late 1950's, also Abram Kardiner and Edward Preble, *They Studied Man* [1961] and Jessie Bernard, *Academic Women* [1964] reflect the 1950's emphasis on "Momism.") In *An Anthropologist at Work* one can also feel an undertone of emphasis on Benedict's existential angst, a crucial element in the intellectual world of the late 1950's. When Mead next wrote about Benedict in the short book *Ruth Benedict* (1974), she readjusted the emphases for the more feminist 1970's, focusing on Benedict's struggle to find an independent path for herself. This little book also contains a few more published Benedict articles not included in *An Anthropologist at Work*.

A third archival collection of importance is the Franz Boas Papers at the American Philosophical Society, Philadelphia. I read these papers on microfilm (Wilmington, Del.: Scholarly Resources, 1972) at the Perry-Castaneda Library of the University of Texas at Austin. These papers are fascinating for the picture they build of the massive personality that was Franz Boas. They also contain much good background material on issues in anthropology and the Anthropology Department at Columbia, on students, and on Ruth Benedict herself, along with letters from her to Franz Boas. The papers were especially good on the political activism of the 1930's and the gradual turnover of responsibility to Benedict in the Department.

Also at the American Philosophical Society, Philadelphia, are the Elsie Clews Parsons Papers. They were especially useful on the ouster of Benedict as editor of the *Journal of American Folk-Lore* in 1940, and the reorganization of the American Folk-Lore Society that took place at that time. This collection also contains a draft version of *An Anthropologist at Work* that includes more quoting from unavailable Benedict letters than was later published. The Stanley Benedict Papers are also at the American Philosophical Society, but I did not find any helpful information there.

An excellent source of information on Benedict's relatives and family history is the Guernsey Memorial Library, Norwich, New York, which keeps a file of original obituaries and papers which have come into its hands on local families, including the Shattucks and the Fultons. Some of the newspaper clippings of family members' obituaries in this collection were not identified as to the local newspaper from which they were taken, but they are all from one of two local newspapers of the time: the *Chenango Union* (also at times known as the *Chenango Semi-Weekly Telegraph*), and the *Norwich Sun* (also known as the *Morning Sun*). The Buffalo Public Library was not able to supply anything on Bertrice Shattuck Fulton's job there, but did have some newspaper reports on Aunt Mamie's family, particularly the tragedy of her two sons' death together in the crash of a private plane. The Owatonna [Minnesota] Public Library provided knowledge of the Pillsbury Academy yearbook, *The Sibyl,* and local newspaper reports from the time Ruth Benedict lived there as a child. Information on Miss Orton's school and the Westlake School for Girls where Benedict taught in California came from the Pasadena Public Library and the Los Angeles Public Library.

Concerning Ruth Benedict's poetry, the Harry Ransom Center at the University of Texas at Austin has a collection of the little magazine *The Measure,* while the Latin American Collection at the University of Texas has a collection of *Palms.* The Louise Bogan Papers, Amherst College Library, Amherst, Massachusetts, provided some insight into Benedict and Bogan's poetic interaction, but Benedict's letters to Bogan had been destroyed in a fire c. 1930 in which Bogan lost most of her personal papers. Excerpts from Bogan's letters to Benedict have been published in *What the Woman Lived: Selected Letters of Louise Bogan, 1920–1970* (1973), edited by Ruth Limmer. The Barker Texas History Center at the University of Texas at Austin houses the David Rodnick Papers. Rodnick was a student of Sapir's who worked with Benedict at the Office of War Information and later worked in Research in Contemporary Cultures with her. A memo by Benedict turned up there, plus good background information.

Most of Benedict's poetry comes from the Benedict Papers at Vassar or from work published during her lifetime in *Poetry, The Measure, Palms,* or after her death in *An Anthropologist at Work.* When a poem is mentioned I have given the full citation in the relevant note rather than including the poetry in the bibliography. The same is true for newspaper articles or reviews. The full citation is given in the relevant note.

The alphabetical list of sources that follows this essay includes those articles and books that appeared in the notes. Because of the volume of material available it cannot cover everything, but it is to be hoped that it includes the most important sources.

Selected Bibliography

Works by Ruth Fulton Benedict (in Chronological Order)

1918 "The Challenge of the Elementary Schools." *Vassar Quarterly* 3 (July): 269–272.

1922 "The Vision in Plains Culture." *American Anthropologist* 24: 1–23.

1923 *The Concept of the Guardian Spirit in North America.* Memoirs of the American Anthropological Association, No. 29. Menasha, Wis.
"A Matter for the Field Worker in Folk-Lore." In "Notes and Queries." *Journal of American Folk-Lore* 36: 104.

1924 "A Brief Sketch of Serrano Culture." *American Anthropologist* 26: 366–392.

1925 Review of *The North American Indian* by Edward S. Curtis, Vol. 12, *The Hopi. American Anthropologist* 27: 458–460.

1929 "The Primitive and His Ego." Review of *The 'Soul' of the Primitive* by Lucien Lévy-Bruhl. *New Republic* 57 (March 6): 77.
"The Science of Custom: The Bearing of Anthropology on Contemporary Thought." *Century Magazine* 117 (April): 641–649.

1930 "Psychological Types in the Culture of the Southwest." In *Proceedings of the Twenty-third International Congress of Americanists, 1928,* pp. 527–581. New York.
"Animism." In *Encyclopaedia of the Social Sciences,* general editor Edwin R. A. Seligmann, Vol. 2, pp. 65–67. New York: Macmillan.

1931 *Tales of the Cochiti Indians.* Bureau of American Ethnology, Bulletin 98. Washington, D.C.: Smithsonian Institution.
"Dress." In *Encyclopaedia of the Social Sciences,* general editor Edwin R. A. Seligmann, Vol. 5, pp. 235–237. New York: Macmillan.
"Folklore." In *Encyclopaedia of the Social Sciences,* Vol. 6, pp. 288–293.

1932 "Configurations of Culture in North America." *American Anthropologist* 34: 1–27.

1933 "Magic." In *Encyclopaedia of the Social Sciences,* Vol. 10, pp. 39–44.
"Myth." In *Encyclopaedia of the Social Sciences,* Vol. 11, pp. 178–181.

1934 "Ritual." In *Encyclopaedia of the Social Sciences,* Vol. 13, pp. 396–397.
"Anthropology and the Abnormal." *Journal of General Psychology* 10: 59–82.

1934/ *Patterns of Culture.* With an introduction by Franz Boas and a new
1960   preface by Margaret Mead. New York: Mentor Book, New American
         Library of World Literature, 1960; orig. paperback, 1946; orig. hard-
         back, 1934.
1935 *Zuñi Mythology.* 2 vols. New York: Columbia University Press.
1938 "Continuities and Discontinuities in Cultural Conditioning." *Psychia-
         try* 1: 161–167.
         Review of *The Neurotic Personality of Our Time* by Karen Horney.
         Journal of Abnormal and Social Psychology 33: 133–135.
         "Religion." In *General Anthropology,* edited by Franz Boas, pp. 627–
         665. Boston: D. C. Heath and Co.
1939 "A Reply to Dr. Aginsky." In "News and Notes." *Character and Per-
         sonality* 7: 344–345.
         "Sex in Primitive Society." *American Journal of Orthopsychiatry* 9:
         570–573.
1940 Review of *Pueblo Indian Religion* by Elsie Clews Parsons. *Review of
         Religions* 4: 439.
         "'Hostility in Pilaga Children'—Discussion." *American Journal of
         Orthopsychiatry* 10: 120–121.
1940/ *Race: Science and Politics.* New York: Modern Age Publishers, 1940.
1943   Rev. ed., New York: Viking Press, 1943.
1941 "Our Last Minority—Youth." *New Republic* 104 (February 24):
         271–272.
         In "On Declaring War." *New Republic* 105 (September 1): 279–280.
1942 Review of *The Crisis of Our Age* and *Social and Cultural Dynamics* by
         P. A. Sorokin. *New Republic* 106 (February 2): 154–155.
         Review of *Indians of South America* by Paul Radin. *New York Herald-
         Tribune Books* 18 (April 1926): 16.
         "Pre-War Experts." *New Republic* 107 (October 5): 410–411.
         "Primitive Freedom." *Atlantic Monthly* 169: 756–763.
1942/ (and Mildred Ellis). *Race and Cultural Relations: America's Answer to
1949   the Myth of a Master Race.* Analysis by Ruth Benedict. Teaching Aids
         by Mildred Ellis. Problems in American Life Series, Unit 5. Washing-
         ton, D.C.: National Council for the Social Studies and National Asso-
         ciation of Secondary-School Principals, Departments of the National
         Education Association, 1942. Rev. ed., 1949.
1942–1943   "Editorial." *American Scholar* 12: 3–4.
1943 "Two Patterns of Indian Acculturation." *American Anthropologist* 45:
         207–212.
         "Recognition of Cultural Diversities in the Post-War World." *Annals of
         the Academy of Political and Social Science* 228: 101–107.
         (and Gene Weltfish). *The Races of Mankind.* Public Affairs Pamphlet
         No. 85. Public Affairs Committee.
1946/ *The Chrysanthemum and the Sword: Patterns of Japanese Culture.*
1954   Rutland, Vt., and Tokyo, Japan: Charles E. Tuttle Co., 1954; orig.
         1946.

1948 "Anthropology and the Humanities." *American Anthropologist* 50: 585–593.

(and Gene Weltfish). *In Henry's Backyard: The Races of Mankind.* New York: Henry Schuman.

1952 *Thai Culture and Behavior: An Unpublished War-time Study Dated September, 1943.* Data Paper 4, Southeast Asia Program. Department of Far Eastern Studies, Cornell University. February 1952. 3d printing, May 1963.

1959 *An Anthropologist at Work.* See Mead, Margaret, ed.

1970 "Synergy: Some Notes of Ruth Benedict," edited by A. Maslow and John Honigmann. *American Anthropologist* 72: 320–333.

Other Sources

Abbott, Frances M. "Three Decades of College Women." *Popular Science Monthly,* August 1904, pp. 350–359.

Abzug, Robert. *Passionate Liberator: Theodore Dwight Weld and the Dilemma of Reform.* New York: Oxford University Press, 1980.

Aginsky, B. W. "Psychopathic Trends in Culture." *Character and Personality* 7 (1939): 331–343.

Anderson, Nels. *The Hobo: The Sociology of the Homeless Man.* Chicago: University of Chicago Press, 1923.

Atkins, Elizabeth. *Edna St. Vincent Millay and Her Times.* Chicago: University of Chicago Press, 1936.

Baedecker, Karl, ed. *The United States with an Excursion into Mexico: Handbook for Travellers.* Leipzig: Karl Baedecker; New York: Charles Scribner's Sons, 1893.

———. *The United States with Excursions to Mexico, Cuba, Porto* [sic] *Rico, and Alaska: Handbook for Travellers.* 4th rev. ed. Leipzig: Karl Baedecker; New York: Charles Scribner's Sons, 1909.

Barnouw, Victor. "The Amiable Side of 'Patterns of Culture.'" *American Anthropologist* 59 (1957): 532–535.

———. *Culture and Personality.* The Dorsey Series in Anthropology and Sociology, edited by Robin M. Williams. Homewood, Ill.: Dorsey Press, 1963.

———. "Ruth Benedict." *American Scholar* 49 (1980): 504–509.

———. "Ruth Benedict: Apollonian and Dionysian." *University of Toronto Quarterly* 18 (1949): 241–253.

Bateson, Mary Catherine. *With a Daughter's Eye: A Memoir of Margaret Mead and Gregory Bateson.* New York: William Morrow and Company, 1984.

Beecher, Catharine. *Treatise on Domestic Economy for the Use of Young Ladies at Home and at School.* New York: Harper and Brothers, 1856.

Bell, Leland. *In Hitler's Shadow: The Anatomy of American Nazism.* National University Publication Series in American Studies, general editor James P. Shenton. Port Washington, N.Y.: Kennikat Press, 1973.

Bender, Thomas. *Toward an Urban Vision: Ideas and Institutions in Nineteenth*

Century America. Baltimore: Johns Hopkins University Press, 1982; orig. 1975.

Benderly, Beryl Lieff. *Dancing without Music: Deafness in America*. Garden City, N.Y.: Anchor Press, Doubleday, 1980.

"Benedict, Ruth." In *Current Biography: Who's News and Why*, edited by Maxine Block, pp. 65–66. New York: H. W. Wilson Co., 1941.

Bennett, John W. "The Interpretation of Pueblo Culture: A Question of Values." *Southwestern Journal of Anthropology* 2 (1946): 361–374.

———. Review of *The Study of Culture at a Distance*, edited by Margaret Mead and Rhoda Métraux. *American Journal of Sociology* 60 (1954): 91–94.

Bennett, J[ohn] W., and M. Nagai. "Echoes: Reactions to American Anthropology." *American Anthropologist* 55 (1953): 404–411.

Bernard, Jessie. *Academic Women*. New York: New American Library, 1964.

Berne, Eric. *Beyond Games and Scripts. with Selections from His Major Writings*. Introduced by Claude M. Steiner and Carmen Kerr. New York: Grove Press, 1976.

Blatch, Harriot Stanton, and Alma Lutz. *Challenging Years: The Memoirs of Harriot Stanton Blatch*. New York: G. P. Putnam's Sons, 1940.

Boas, Franz. "An Anthropologist's Credo." In "Living Philosophies, II." *Nation* 147 (August 27, 1938): 201–205.

———. "Anthropology." In *Encyclopaedia of the Social Sciences*, general editor Edwin R. A. Seligmann, Vol. 2, pp. 73–110. New York: Macmillan, 1930.

———. *Anthropology and Modern Life*. New York: W. W. Norton & Company, 1928.

———. "Eugenics." *Scientific Monthly* 3 (1916): 471–478.

———. "In Memoriam: Herman Karl Haeberlin." *American Anthropologist* 21 (1919): 71–74.

———. "The Methods of Ethnology." *American Anthropologist* 22 (1920): 311–321.

———. *The Mind of Primitive Man*. A Course of Lectures Delivered before the Lowell Institute, Boston, Mass., and the National University of Mexico, 1910–1911. New York: Macmillan Company, 1929; orig. 1911.

———. *Race, Language and Culture*. New York: Free Press, 1966; orig. 1940.

Bogan, Louise. *Journey around My Room: The Autobiography of Louise Bogan*. Edited by Ruth Limmer. New York: Viking Press, 1980.

———. "The Springs of Poetry." *New Republic* 37, Pt. 2 (December 5, 1923): 9.

———. *What the Woman Lived: Selected Letters of Louise Bogan, 1920–1970*. Edited by Ruth Limmer. New York: Harcourt Brace Jovanovich, 1973.

Bonjean, Charles M., Louis Schneider, and Robert L. Lineberry, eds. *Social Science in America: The First Two Hundred Years*. Austin: University of Texas Press, 1976.

Boyer, Paul. *Urban Masses and Moral Order in America, 1820–1920*. Cambridge, Mass.: Harvard University Press, 1978.

Briscoe, Virginia Wolf. "Ruth Benedict, Anthropological Folklorist." *Journal of American Folklore* 92 (1979): 445–476.

Brown, Felix. "Depression and Childhood Bereavement." *Journal of Medical Science* 107 (1961): 754–777.

Brown, Marsha. "Elinor Wylie and the Religion of Art: Poetry and Social Attitudes in the 1920's." Ph.D. dissertation, Emory University, 1979. Ann Arbor,
Mich.: University Microfilms International.

Brunschwig, Lily. *A Study of Some Personality Aspects of Deaf Children.* Teachers College, Columbia University, Contributions to Education, No. 687. New
York: Bureau of Publications, Teachers College, Columbia University, 1936.

Bunzel, Ruth. "Introduction to Zuñi Ceremonialism," pp. 467–544, "Zuñi Origin Myths," pp. 545–609, "Zuñi Ritual Poetry," pp. 611–835, and "Zuñi
Katcinas: An Analytical Study," pp. 837–1086. In *Forty-Seventh Annual Report of the Bureau of American Ethnology to the Secretary of the Smithsonian
Institution, 1929–1930.* Washington, D.C.: Government Printing Office, 1932.

———. *The Pueblo Potter: A Study of Creative Imagination in Primitive Art.*
New York: Dover Publications, 1972; orig. 1929.

Burroughs, John. *Literary Values and Other Papers.* Boston: Houghton Mifflin
Company, 1902.

———. *Whitman: A Study.* Boston: Houghton Mifflin Company, 1896.

Butler, J. Donald. *Four Philosophies and Their Practice in Education and Religion.* 3d ed. New York: Harper and Row, 1968.

Calverton, V. F., and Samuel D. Schmalhausen, eds. *The New Generation: The
Intimate Problems of Modern Parents and Children.* New York: Macaulay
Co., 1930.

Campbell, R. A., ed. *Campbell's Gazetteer of Missouri from Articles Contributed
by Prominent Gentlemen in Each County of the State, and Information Collected and Collated from Official and Other Authentic Sources by a Corps of
Experienced Canvassers.* St. Louis, 1874.

Case, William M., ed. *The Sibyl,* Vol. 4. Owatonna, Minn.: Published by the Senior Class of Pillsbury Academy, 1898.

Chase, Richard. "Ruth Benedict: The Woman as Anthropologist." *Columbia
University Forum* 2 (1959): 19–22.

Child, C. M., Kurt Koffka, John E. Anderson, John B. Watson, Edward Sapir,
W. I. Thomas, Marion E. Kenworthy, F. L. Wells, and William A. White. *The
Unconscious: A Symposium.* With an Introduction by Ethel S. Dummer. New
York: Alfred A. Knopf, 1929.

Cochrane, Rexmond C. *The National Academy of Sciences: The First Hundred
Years, 1863–1963.* Washington, D.C.: National Academy of Sciences, 1978.

Codere, Helen. "The Amiable Side of Kwakiutl Life: The Potlatch and the Play
Potlatch." *American Anthropologist* 58 (1956): 334–351.

"College Girl Follies." *Good Housekeeping,* September 1909, pp. 238–241.

Collins, Martha, ed. *Critical Essays on Louise Bogan.* Boston: G. K. Hall and
Company, 1984.

Conrad, Howard L., ed. *Encyclopedia of the History of Missouri: A Compen-
dium of History and Biography for Ready Reference.* New York: Southern History Company, 1901.

"Council on Intercultural Relations." In "Current Items." *American Sociological
Review* 8 (1943): 223.

Cowley, Malcolm. *Exile's Return: A Literary Odyssey of the 1920's.* Rev. ed.
Harmondsworth, Middlesex, England: Penguin Books, 1969; orig. 1934.

Crawford, Mary Caroline. *The College Girl of America.* Boston: L. C. Page and Company, 1904.

Davis, Katharine Bement. *Factors in the Sex Life of Twenty-two Hundred Women.* Publications of the Bureau of Social Hygiene. New York: Harper and Brothers, 1929.

DeBolt, Mary M., ed. *Lineage Book: National Society of the Daughters of the American Revolution.* Vol. 67, 67001–68000, 1908. Washington, D.C.: Judd and Detweiler, 1924.

Deland, Margaret. "The Change in the Feminine Ideal." *Atlantic Monthly,* March 1910, pp. 291–296.

Dewey, John. *Human Nature and Conduct: An Introduction to Social Psychology.* New York: Henry Holt and Company, 1922.

Dole, Gertrude E., and Robert L. Carneiro, eds. *Essays in the Science of Culture in Honor of Leslie A. White.* New York: Thomas Y. Crowell Co., 1960.

Douglas, A. Donald. Review of *Body of This Death* by Louise Bogan. *New Republic* 37, Pt. 2 (December 5, 1923): 20.

Douglas, Ann. *The Feminization of American Culture.* New York: Avon Books, 1977.

Dozier, Edward P. *The Pueblo Indians of North America.* Case Studies in Cultural Anthropology Series, general editors George and Louise Spindler. New York: Holt, Rinehart and Winston, 1970.

Du Bois, Cora. *The People of Alor: A Social-Psychological Study of an East Indian Island.* With analysis by Abram Kardiner and Emil Oberholzer. Minneapolis: University of Minnesota Press, 1944.

———. Review of *The Study of Culture at a Distance,* edited by Margaret Mead and Rhoda Métraux. *Annals of the American Academy of Political and Social Sciences* 292 (1954): 176–177.

Eddy, Elizabeth M., and William L. Partridge, eds. *Applied Anthropology in America.* New York: Columbia University Press, 1978.

"Educational Questions of the Day." *Current Literature: A Magazine of Contemporary Thought,* September 1904, p. 273.

Ehrenreich, Barbara, and Deirdre English. *For Her Own Good: 150 Years of the Experts' Advice to Women.* Garden City, N.Y.: Anchor Books, Doubleday, 1978.

Eliot, Charles. *The Conflict between Individualism and Collectivism in a Democracy.* New York: Books for Libraries Press, 1967; orig. 1910.

Ellis, Constance Dimock, ed. *The Magnificent Enterprise: A Chronicle of Vassar College.* Compiled by Dorothy A. Plum and George B. Dowell. Illustrated by Julia Cuniberti. Poughkeepsie, N.Y.: Vassar College, 1961.

Ellmann, Richard, and Charles Feidelson, Jr., eds. *The Modern Tradition: Backgrounds of Modern Literature.* New York: Oxford University Press, 1965.

Faderman, Lillian. *Surpassing the Love of Men: Romantic Friendship and Love between Women from the Renaissance to the Present.* New York: William Morrow and Company, 1981.

Farrell, James J. *Inventing the American Way of Death, 1830–1920.* Philadelphia: Temple University Press, 1980.

Fergusson, Erna. Review of *The Chrysanthemum and the Sword* by Ruth Benedict. *Social Studies* 38 (1947): 48.

Flexner, Eleanor. *Century of Struggle: The Woman's Rights Movement in the United States.* New York: Atheneum, 1974; orig. 1959.

Foley, John P., Jr. "The Criterion of Abnormality." *Journal of Abnormal and Social Psychology* 30 (1935): 279–291.

Foner, Philip S. *Women and the American Labor Movement: From Colonial Times to the Eve of World War I.* New York: Free Press, Macmillan Publishing Company, 1979.

Frank, Elizabeth. *Louise Bogan: A Portrait.* New York: Alfred A. Knopf, 1985.

Fulton, Margery [Freeman], Helen Lee McCulloch, Cora Ballard Edgcomb, Ruth Flanigan, Frances Louise Tyer, and Inez Milholland. *Class Day Book, Vassar College, Class of 1909.* N.p., n.d.

Furman, Erna. *A Child's Parent Dies: Studies in Childhood Bereavement.* New Haven, Conn.: Yale University Press, 1974.

Gellerman, William. *Martin Dies.* New York: John Day Company, 1944.

Gesell, Arnold, Frances L. Ilg, and Louise Bates Ames, in collaboration with Glenna E. Bullis. *The Child from Five to Ten.* Rev. ed. New York: Harper and Row, 1977.

Gesell, Arnold, Frances Ilg, and Louise Bates Ames, in collaboration with Janet Learned Rodell. *Infant and Child in the Culture of Today.* Rev. ed. New York: Harper and Row, 1974.

Giedion, Sigfried. *Space, Time, and Architecture: The Growth of a New Tradition.* 5th ed., rev. and enl. Cambridge, Mass.: Harvard University Press, 1967.

Gillin, John. "The Configuration Problem in Culture." *American Sociological Review* 1 (1936): 373–386.

———. "Cultural Adjustment." *American Anthropologist* 46 (1944): 429–447.

Gilman, Charlotte Perkins. *Women and Economics: A Study of the Economic Relation between Men and Women as a Factor in Social Evolution.* 9th ed. London: G. P. Putnam's Sons, 1920; orig. 1899.

Golde, Peggy. *Women in the Field: Anthropological Experiences.* Chicago: Aldine Publishing Company, 1970.

Goldenweiser, Alexander. "The Autonomy of the Social." *American Anthropologist* 19 (1917): 447–449.

———. *Early Civilization: An Introduction to Anthropology.* New York: Alfred A. Knopf, 1922.

———. "The Principle of Limited Possibilities in the Development of a Culture." *Journal of American Folk-Lore* 26 (1913): 259–290.

Goldfrank, Esther S. *Notes on an Undirected Life: As One Anthropologist Tells It.* Queen's College Publications in Anthropology, No. 3. Flushing, N.Y.: Queen's College Press, 1978.

Goldschmidt, Walter, ed. *The Anthropology of Franz Boas: Essays on the Centennial of His Birth.* Memoir No. 89 of the American Anthropological Association. *American Anthropologist* 61, No. 5, Pt. 2 (October 1959).

Goldstein, Kenneth S., and Neil V. Rosenberg, eds., with the assistance of Richard E. Buchler, Sonia Paine, and Leslie Prosterman. *Folklore Studies in Honor of Herbert Halpert: A Festschrift.* St. John's, Newfoundland: Memorial University of Newfoundland, 1980.

Gorer, Geoffrey. *Himalayan Village: An Account of the Lepchas of Sikkim.* 2nd ed. With a new Foreword by the author. New York: Basic Books, 1967; orig. 1938.

Gould, Jean. *American Women Poets: Pioneers of Modern Poetry.* New York: Dodd, Mead and Company, 1980.

Grey, Thomas A. *Elinor Wylie.* New York: Twayne Publishers, 1969.

Habenstein, Robert W., and William M. Lamers. *The History of American Funeral Directing.* Milwaukee, Wis.: Bulfin Printers, 1955.

Hackett, Alice Payne. *60 Years of Best Sellers, 1895–1955.* New York: R. R. Bowker Company, 1956.

Hall, Radclyffe. *The Well of Loneliness.* With a commentary by Havelock Ellis. New York: Blue Ribbon Books, 1928.

Haller, John S., Jr. and Robin M. Haller. *The Physician and Sexuality in Victorian America.* New York: W. W. Norton and Company, 1974.

Hare, Peter. *A Woman's Quest for Science: Portrait of Anthropologist Elsie Clews Parsons.* Buffalo: Prometheus Books, 1985.

Haring, Douglas, ed. *Personal Character and Cultural Milieu: A Collection of Readings.* Rev. ed. Syracuse, N.Y.: Syracuse University Press, 1949; orig. 1948.

Haring, H. A., ed. *The Slabsides Book of John Burroughs.* Boston: Houghton Mifflin Company, 1931.

Harris, Marvin. *The Rise of Anthropological Theory: A History of Theories of Culture.* New York: Harper and Row, 1968.

Helm, June, ed. *Pioneers of American Anthropology: The Uses of Biography.* Seattle: University of Washington Press, 1966.

Herskovits, Melville J. "Folklore after a Hundred Years: A Problem in Redefinition." *Journal of American Folk-Lore* 59 (1946): 89–100.

Herskovits, Melville J., and Malcolm M. Willey. "The Cultural Approach to Sociology." *American Journal of Sociology* 29 (1924): 188–199.

Hoebel, E. Adamson. "Contributions of Southwestern Studies to Anthropological Theory." *American Anthropologist* 56 (1954): 720–727.

———. *Man in the Primitive World.* New York: McGraw-Hill Book Company, 1949. 2d ed., 1958.

Hoffman, Frederick J., Charles Allen, and Carolyn F. Ulrich. *The Little Magazine: A History and a Bibliography.* Princeton, N.J.: Princeton University Press, 1946.

Hoffmann, Gerhard, Alfred Hornung, and Rüdiger Kunow. "'Modern,' 'Postmodern,' and 'Contemporary' as Criteria for the Analysis of 20th Century Literature." *Amerika Studien/American Studies* 22 (1977): 19–46.

Hollingsworth, Charles E., Robert O. Pasnau, and Contributors. *The Family in Mourning: A Guide for Health Professionals.* Seminars in Psychiatry Series. New York: Grune and Stratton, 1977.

Horney, Karen, M.D. "Culture and Neurosis." *American Sociological Review* 1 (1936): 221–235.

———. *Feminine Psychology.* Edited and with an Introduction by Harold Kelman, M.D. New York: W. W. Norton and Company, 1967.

———. *The Neurotic Personality of Our Time*. New York: W. W. Norton and Company, 1937.

———. *New Ways in Psychoanalysis*. New York: W. W. Norton and Company, 1939.

Horowitz, Helen Lefkowitz. *Alma Mater: Design and Experience in the Women's Colleges from Their Nineteenth Century Beginnings to the 1930s*. New York: Alfred A. Knopf, 1984.

Howard, Jane. *Margaret Mead: A Life*. New York: Simon and Schuster, 1984.

Hsu, Francis L. K., ed. *Psychological Anthropology: Approaches to Culture and Personality*. The Dorsey Series in Anthropology and Sociology, edited by Peter H. Rossi and William Foote Whyte. Homewood, Ill.: Dorsey Press, Inc., 1961.

Jacobs, Melville. *Pattern in Cultural Anthropology*. Dorsey Series in Anthropology and Sociology, edited by R. M. Williams, Jr., and William Foote White. Homewood, Ill.: Dorsey Press, 1964.

Johnson, Alvin. *Pioneer's Progress: An Autobiography*. New York: Viking Press. 1952.

Johnson, Paul. *A Shopkeeper's Millennium: Society and Revivals in Rochester, New York, 1815–1837*. New York: Hill and Wang, 1978.

Kardiner, Abram. *The Individual and His Society: The Psychodynamics of Primitive Social Organization*. With a Foreword and Two Ethnological Reports by Ralph Linton. New York: Columbia University Press, 1939.

———. *Psychological Frontiers of Society*. With the collaboration of Ralph Linton, Cora Du Bois, and James West [pseud.]. New York: Columbia University Press, 1945.

Kardiner, Abram, and Edward Preble. *They Studied Man*. Cleveland: World Publishing Company, 1961.

Kastenbaum, Robert, and Ruth Aisenberg. *The Psychology of Death*. New York: Springer Publishing Company, 1972.

Key, Ellen. *The Morality of Woman and Other Essays*. Translated from the Swedish by Mamah Bouton Borthwick. Chicago: Ralph Fletcher Seymour Co., 1911.

———. *The Woman Movement*. Translated by Mamah Bouton Borthwick. With an introduction by Havelock Ellis. New York: G. P. Putnam's Sons, 1912.

Kluckhohn, Clyde. "Bronislaw Malinowski, 1884–1942." *Journal of American Folk-Lore* 56 (1943): 208–219.

———. "Covert Culture and Administrative Problems." *American Anthropologist* 45 (1943): 213–227.

———. "The Personal Document in Anthropological Science." In *The Use of Personal Documents in History, Anthropology, and Sociology*, edited by L. Gottschalk, C. Kluckhohn, and R. Angell, pp. 77–173. SSRC Bulletin 53. New York, 1945.

———. "Southwestern Studies of Culture and Personality." *American Anthropologist* 56 (1954): 685–697.

Kluckhohn, Clyde, and Dorothea Leighton. *The Navaho*. Cambridge, Mass.: Harvard University Press, 1946.

Kluckhohn, Clyde, and Henry A. Murray, eds., with the collaboration of David M.

Schneider. *Personality in Nature, Society, and Culture.* 2d ed., rev. and enl. New York: Alfred A. Knopf, 1955.

Koffka, Kurt. *The Growth of the Mind: An Introduction to Child Psychology.* Translated by Robert Morris Ogden. New York: Harcourt, Brace and Company, 1924.

Kroeber, Alfred L. *Anthropology: Race, Language, Culture, Psychology, Prehistory.* Rev. ed. New York: Harcourt, Brace and World, 1948.

———. "Culture Area." In *Encyclopaedia of the Social Sciences,* general editor Edwin R. A. Seligmann, Vol. 5, pp. 646–647. New York: Macmillan, 1931.

———. "Elsie Clews Parsons, II." *American Anthropologist* 45 (1943): 252–255.

———. "History and Science in Anthropology." *American Anthropologist* 37 (1935): 539–569.

———. *The Nature of Culture.* Chicago: University of Chicago Press, 1952.

———. "On the Principle of Order in Civilization as Exemplified by Changes of Fashion." *American Anthropologist* 21 (1919): 235–263.

———. "Pliny Earle Goddard." *American Anthropologist* 31 (1929): 1–8.

———. Review of *Patterns of Culture. American Anthropologist* 37 (1935): 689–690.

———. "The Superorganic." *American Anthropologist* 19 (1917): 163–213.

———, ed. *Anthropology Today: An Encyclopedic Inventory.* Chicago: University of Chicago Press, 1953.

Kroeber, Alfred L., Ruth Benedict, Murray B. Emeneau, Melville J. Herskovits, Gladys A. Reichard, and J. Alden Mason. *Franz Boas, 1858–1942.* Memoir No. 61 of the American Anthropological Association Series. *American Anthropologist,* n.s. 45, No. 3, Pt. 2 (1943).

Kroeber, Theodora. *Alfred Kroeber: A Personal Configuration.* Berkeley: University of California Press, 1970.

Kuper, Adam. *Anthropology and Anthropologists: The Modern British School.* Rev. ed. London: Routledge and Kegan Paul, 1983.

Lee, Dorothy. "Ruth Fulton Benedict (1887–1948)." *Journal of American Folk-Lore* 62 (1949): 345–347.

Leonard, Priscilla. "The Joys of Jiu-Jitsu for Women." *Current Literature: A Magazine of Contemporary Thought,* August 1904, pp. 144–145.

Lévy-Bruhl, Lucien. *The 'Soul' of the Primitive.* Translated by Lilian A. Clare. New York: Macmillan, 1928.

Li An-che. "Zuñi: Some Observations and Queries." *American Anthropologist* 39 (1937): 62–76.

Limmer, Ruth, ed. See Bogan, Louise.

Linton, Adelin, and Charles Wagley. *Ralph Linton.* New York: Columbia University Press, 1971.

Linton, Ralph. *The Study of Man: An Introduction.* Student's Edition. New York: D. Appleton-Century Company, 1936.

Llewellyn, Karl N., and E. Adamson Hoebel. *The Cheyenne Way.* Norman: University of Oklahoma Press, 1941.

Lowell, Amy. "Two Generations in American Poetry." *New Republic* 37, Pt. 2 (December 5, 1923): 1–3.

Lowie, Robert H. *Culture and Ethnology.* With an Introduction by Fred Eggan. Classics in Anthropology Series, edited by Stanley Diamond. New York: Basic Books, 1966; orig. 1917.

———. "Franz Boas (1848–1942)." *Journal of American Folk-Lore* 57 (1944): 59–64.

———. *The History of Ethnological Theory.* New York: Farrar and Rinehart, 1938.

———. "On the Principle of Convergence in Ethnology." *Journal of American Folk-Lore* 25 (1912): 24–42.

———. "Plains Age Societies," *Anthropological Papers of the American Museum of Natural History* 2 (1916): 881ff.

———. *Primitive Society.* New York: Boni and Liveright, 1920.

———. *Robert H. Lowie, Ethnologist: A Personal Record.* Berkeley: University of California Press, 1959.

Lowry, Richard J. *A. H. Maslow: An Intellectual Portrait.* Written for The International Study Project, Inc. Monterey, Calif.: Brooks/Cole Publishing Company, 1973.

Lubove, Roy. *The Professional Altruist: The Emergence of Social Work as a Career, 1880–1930.* New York: Atheneum, 1971; orig. 1965.

Luhan, Mabel Dodge. *Intimate Memories: Background.* New York: Harcourt, Brace and Company, 1933.

McCollum, Elmer Verner. "Stanley Rossiter Benedict, 1884–1936." In *Biographical Memoirs,* National Academy of Sciences, Vol. 27, pp. 155–177. Washington, D.C.: National Academy of Sciences, 1952.

MacCracken, Henry Noble. *The Hickory Limb.* New York: Charles Scribner's Sons, 1950.

"Madcap Frolics of College Girls." *Ladies Home Journal,* October 1905, pp. 17, 62–63.

Malinowski, Bronislaw. *Argonauts of the Western Pacific.* New York: E. P. Dutton, 1961; orig. 1922.

———. *A Scientific Theory of Culture and Other Essays.* With a Preface by Huntington Cairns. Chapel Hill, N.C.: University of North Carolina Press, 1944.

Maslow, Abraham H. *The Farther Reaches of Human Nature.* New York: Viking Press, 1971.

———. *Motivation and Personality.* New York: Harper and Brothers, 1954.

Mather, J. H., and L. P. Brockett, M.D. *A Geographical History of the State of New York Embracing Its History, Government, Physical Features, Climate, Geology, Mineralogy, Botany, Zoology, Education, Internal Improvements, etc., with a Separate Map of Each County: The Whole Forming a Complete History of the State.* Utica: Hawley, Fuller and Company, 1851.

Matthews, T. S. "Elinor Wylie's Poems." *New Republic* 54 (April 4, 1928): 77–78.

Mead, Margaret. *Anthropologists and What They Do.* New York: Franklin Watts, 1965.

———. *Blackberry Winter: My Earlier Years.* New York: Pocket Books, 1975; orig. 1972.

————. *Coming of Age in Samoa: A Psychological Study of Primitive Youth for Western Civilization*. Foreword by Franz Boas. New York: Mentor Book, New American Library, 1949; orig. 1928.

————. *Growing Up in New Guinea: A Comparative Study of Primitive Education*. New York: Dell Publishing Company, 1968; orig. 1930.

————. *Ruth Benedict*. Leaders of Modern Anthropology Series, general editor Charles Wagley. New York: Columbia University Press, 1974.

————. "Ruth Fulton Benedict, 1887–1948." *American Anthropologist* 51 (1949): 457–463.

————. *Sex and Temperament in Three Primitive Societies*. New York: Dell Publishing Company, 1963; orig. 1935.

————, ed. *An Anthropologist at Work: Writings of Ruth Benedict*. Reprint ed. New York: Avon Books, Equinox Books, 1973; orig. 1959.

————, ed. *Cooperation and Competition among Primitive Peoples*. New York: McGraw-Hill Book Company, 1937.

Mead, Margaret, and Ruth Bunzel, eds. *The Golden Age of American Anthropology*. New York: George Braziller, 1960.

Mead, Margaret, and Rhoda Métraux, eds. *The Study of Culture at a Distance*. Chicago: University of Chicago Press, 1953.

Merriam, Alan P. "Melville Jean Herskovits, 1895–1963." *American Anthropologist* 66 (1964): 83–91.

Meyers, Marvin. *The Jacksonian Persuasion: Politics and Belief*. Stanford, Calif.: Stanford University Press, 1957.

Modell, Judith Schachter. "A Biographical Study of Ruth Fulton Benedict." Ph.D. dissertation, University of Minnesota, 1978.

————. *Ruth Benedict: Patterns of a Life*. Philadelphia: University of Pennsylvania Press, 1983.

Moriarty, David. *The Loss of Loved Ones*. Springfield, Ill.: Charles C. Thomas Company, 1967.

Moulton, Forest Ray, ed. *Mental Health*. Publication of the American Association for the Advancement of Science, No. 9. Lancaster, Pa.: Science Press, 1939.

Murphy, Robert F. *Robert H. Lowie*. Leaders of Modern Anthropology Series, general editor Charles Wagley. New York: Columbia University Press, 1972.

Murray, Henry A., and the Workers at the Harvard Psychological Clinic. *Explorations in Personality: A Clinical and Experimental Study of Fifty Men of College Age*. New York: Oxford University Press, 1938.

Myklebust, Helmer R. *The Psychology of Deafness: Sensory Deprivation, Learning, and Adjustment*. New York: Grune and Stratton, 1960.

Newcomer, Mabel. *A Century of Higher Education for American Women*. New York: Harper and Brothers, Publishers, 1959.

Nietzsche, Friedrich Wilhelm. *The Philosophy of Nietzsche: Thus Spake Zarathustra, Beyond Good and Evil, The Genealogy of Morals, Ecce Homo, The Birth of Tragedy*. Introduction by Willard Huntington Wright. New York: Modern Library, Random House, 1927.

Ogburn, William Fielding. *Social Change, with Respect to Culture and Original Nature*. New York: B. W. Huebsch, 1922.

Ogburn, William Fielding, and Alexander Goldenweiser, eds. *The Social Sciences and Their Interrelations.* Boston: Houghton Mifflin Company, 1927.

Opler, Morris Edward. "Some Recently Developed Concepts Relating to Culture." *Southwestern Journal of Anthropology* 4 (1948): 107–122.

———. "Themes as Dynamic Forces in Culture." *American Journal of Sociology* 51 (1945): 198–206.

Pandey, Triloki Nath. "Anthropologists at Zuñi." *Proceedings of the American Philosophical Society* 116 (1972): 321–337.

Parsons, Elsie Clews. *The Family: An Ethnographical and Historical Outline with Descriptive Notes, Planned as a Textbook for the Use of College Lecturers and of Directors of Home-Reading Clubs.* New York: G. P. Putnam's Sons, 1912; orig. 1906.

———. *Fear and Conventionality.* New York: G. P. Putnam's Sons, 1914.

———. "Higher Education of Women and the Family." *American Journal of Sociology* 14 (May 1909): 758–763.

———. *The Old-Fashioned Woman: Primitive Fancies about the Sex.* New York: G. P. Putnam's Sons, 1913.

———. *Pueblo Indian Religion.* 2 vols. Chicago: University of Chicago Press, 1939.

———. Review of *Primitive Religion* by Robert Lowie. *American Anthropologist* 27 (1925): 562–564.

———, ed. *American Indian Life by Several of Its Students.* Illustrated by C. Grant LaFarge. New York: B. W. Huebsch, 1922.

Pater, Walter. *Appreciations: An Essay on Style.* London and New York: Macmillan and Company, 1889.

———. *Greek Studies: A Series of Essays.* London: Macmillan and Company, 1914; orig. 1895.

———. *Marius the Epicurean: His Sensations and Ideas.* 2 vols. London: Macmillan and Company, 1914; orig. 1885.

———. *The Renaissance: Studies in Art and Poetry.* 5th ed., 1901. Reprint, London: Macmillan and Company, 1914. (1st ed., 1873.)

Perry, Helen Swick. *Psychiatrist of America: The Life of Harry Stack Sullivan.* Cambridge, Mass.: Belknap Press, Harvard University Press, 1982.

Pettegrew, Larry Dean. *The History of Pillsbury Baptist Bible College.* Owatonna, Minn.: Pillsbury Press, 1981.

Pound, Ezra. *Ezra Pound, Selected Poems.* New York: New Directions, 1957.

Powdermaker, Hortense. Review of *Race: Science and Politics* by Ruth Benedict. *American Anthropologist* 43 (1941): 474–475.

———. *Stranger and Friend: The Way of an Anthropologist.* New York: W. W. Norton and Company, 1966.

Purcell, Edward A., Jr. *The Crisis of Democratic Theory: Scientific Naturalism and the Problem of Value.* Lexington: University Press of Kentucky, 1973.

Radcliffe-Brown, A. R. *The Andaman Islanders.* Glencoe, Ill.: Free Press, 1948; orig. 1922.

———. *A Natural Science of Society.* With a Foreword by Fred Eggan. Glencoe, Ill.: Free Press, 1957; orig. 1948.

————. "On the Concept of Function in Social Science." *American Anthropologist* 37 (1935): 394–402.

Radin, Paul. *The Method and Theory of Ethnology: An Essay in Criticism*. New York: McGraw-Hill Book Company, 1933.

————. "Robert H. Lowie, 1883–1957." *American Anthropologist* 60 (1958): 358–361.

————. *Social Anthropology*. New York: McGraw-Hill Book Company, 1932.

Reichard, Gladys. "Elsie Clews Parsons." *Journal of American Folk-Lore* 56 (1943): 45–48.

Riis, Jacob. *How the Other Half Lives*. New York: Hill and Wang, 1957; orig. 1890.

Rivers, W. H. R. *Instinct and the Unconscious*. London: Cambridge University Press, 1920; 2d ed., 1922.

Rogers, Agnes. *Vassar Women: An Informal Study*. Poughkeepsie, N.Y.: Vassar College, 1940.

Rorer, S. T. "What College Girls Eat." *Ladies Home Journal*, November 1905, pp. 13–14.

Rothstein, William G. *American Physicians in the Nineteenth Century: From Sects to Science*. Baltimore: Johns Hopkins University Press, 1972.

Rubins, Jack. *Karen Horney: Gentle Rebel of Psychoanalysis*. New York: Dial Press, 1978.

Santayana, George. *The Life of Reason or the Phases of Human Progress*. 5 vols. New York: Charles Scribner's Sons, 1905.

————. *Platonism and the Spiritual Life*. New York: Charles Scribner's Sons, 1927.

Sapir, Edward. "Culture, Genuine and Spurious." *American Journal of Sociology* 29 (1924): 401–429.

————. "The Discipline of Sex." *American Mercury* 16 (1929): 413–420.

————. "Do We Need a Superorganic?" *American Anthropologist* 19 (1917): 441–447.

————. "The Grammarian and His Language." *American Mercury* 1 (1924): 149–155.

————. *Language: An Introduction to the Study of Speech*. New York: Harcourt, Brace and Company, 1921.

————. "Observations on the Sex Problem in America." *American Journal of Psychiatry* 8 (1928): 519–534.

————. *Selected Writings of Edward Sapir in Language, Culture, and Personality*. Edited by David G. Mandelbaum. Berkeley: University of California Press, 1949.

————. "Why Cultural Anthropology Needs the Psychiatrist." *Psychiatry* 1 (1938): 7–12.

Schreiner, Olive. *The Story of an African Farm*. New York: Fawcett Premier, 1968; orig. 1883.

————. *Woman and Labor*. 8th ed. New York: Frederick A. Stokes Company, 1911.

Shattuck, Lemuel. *Memorials of the Descendants of William Shattuck, The Progenitor of the Families in America That Have Borne His Name; including an*

Introduction, and an Appendix containing Collateral Information. Boston: Dutton and Wentworth, 1855.

Shelton, Brenda K. *Reformers in Search of Yesterday: Buffalo in the 1890's.* Albany: State University of New York Press, 1976.

Silverman, Sydel, ed. *Totems and Teachers: Perspectives on the History of Anthropology.* New York: Columbia University Press, 1981.

Simmons, Leo W., ed. *Sun Chief: The Autobiography of a Hopi Indian.* New Haven, Conn.: Yale University Press, 1942.

Sklar, Kathryn Kish. *Catharine Beecher: A Study in American Domesticity.* New York: W. W. Norton and Company, 1973.

Smith, Adam. *An Inquiry into the Nature and Causes of the Wealth of Nations.* Edited by Edwin Cannon, with a second Introduction by Max Lerner. New York: Modern Library, 1937; orig. 1796.

Smith, Marian W. "Gladys Amanda Reichard." *American Anthropologist* 58 (1956): 913–916.

Smith, Robert A. *A Social History of the Bicycle: Its Early Life and Times in America.* New York: American Heritage Press, McGraw-Hill, 1972.

Smith, William Jay. *Louise Bogan: A Woman's Words.* A lecture delivered at the Library of Congress May 4, 1970, by William Jay Smith, Consultant in Poetry in English at the Library of Congress, 1968–70. With a bibliography. Washington, D.C.: Library of Congress, 1971.

Smith-Rosenberg, Carroll. *Disorderly Conduct: Visions of Gender in Victorian America.* New York: Oxford University Press, 1985.

Sochen, June. *Herstory: A Record of the American Woman's Past.* 2d ed. Sherman Oaks, Calif.: Alfred Publishing Company, 1981; orig. 1974.

Sofue, Takao. "Japanese Studies by American Anthropologists: Review and Evaluation." *American Anthropologist* 62 (1960): 306–317.

Spier, Leslie. "Elsie Clews Parsons, I." *American Anthropologist* 45 (1943): 244–251.

———. "The Sun Dance of the Plains Indians: Its Development and Diffusion." *Anthropological Papers of the American Museum of Natural History,* 16, Pt. 7 (1921).

Spier, Leslie, A. Irving Hallowell, and Stanley S. Newman, eds. *Language, Culture and Personality: Essays in Memory of Edward Sapir.* Menasha, Wis.: Sapir Memorial Publication Fund, 1941.

Stanton, Elizabeth Cady. "The Solitude of Self" (1892). In *The History of Woman Suffrage,* edited by Susan B. Anthony and Ida Husted Harper, Vol. 4, pp. 189–191. Indianapolis: Hollenbeck Press, 1902.

Steiner, Claude M. *Games Alcoholics Play: The Analysis of Life Scripts.* New York: Grove Press, 1971.

———. *Scripts People Live: Transactional Analysis of Life Scripts.* New York: Grove Press, 1974.

Steward, Julian. "Cultural Causality and Law: A Trial Formulation of the Development of Early Civilization." *American Anthropologist* 51 (1949): 1–27.

Stocking, George W., Jr. "Benedict, Ruth Fulton." In *Dictionary of American Biography,* Supplement 4, 1946–1950, pp. 70–73.

————. *Race, Culture, and Evolution: Essays in the History of Anthropology.* London: Collier-Macmillan; New York: Free Press, 1968.

————, ed. *Malinowski, Rivers, Benedict and Others: Essays on Culture and Personality.* Vol. 4 of *History of Anthropology.* Madison: University of Wisconsin Press, 1986.

————. *Selected Papers from the American Anthropologist, 1921–1945.* Washington, D.C.: American Anthropological Association, 1976.

Stroebe, Lillian L. "The Teaching of German at Vassar College in Peace and War: A Retrospect, 1905–1943." *Bulletin of Vassar College* 34, No. 2 (March 1944).

Sullivan, Harry Stack. "Ruth Fulton Benedict, Ph.D., D.Sc., 1887–1948." *Psychiatry* 11 (1948): 402.

Taylor, James Monroe, and Elizabeth Hazelton Haight. *Vassar.* New York: Oxford University Press, 1915.

Thirty-second Annual Report of the Board of Education of the City of St. Joseph, Mo., for the year 1895–96. St. Joseph, Mo.: Nelson Printing Company, 1897.

Thompson, Laura. "The Logico-Aesthetic Integration in Hopi Culture." *American Anthropologist* 47 (1945): 540–553.

Thompson, Laura, and Alice Josephs. *The Hopi Way.* Chicago: University of Chicago Press, 1944.

Thompson, Stith. "Reminiscences of an Octogenarian Folklorist (An Interview of Dr. Hari S. Upadhyaya with Dr. Stith Thompson)." Edited by Dr. Hari S. Upadhyaya. *Asian Folklore Studies* 27 (1968): 107–145.

Thoresen, Timothy H. H., ed. *Toward a Science of Man: Essays in the History of Anthropology.* The Hague: Mouton, 1975.

Tylor, Edward B. "How the Problems of American Anthropology Present Themselves to the English Mind." *Science* 4, No. 98 (December 19, 1884): 545–551.

————. *The Origins of Culture* and *Religion in Primitive Culture.* 2 vols. With an Introduction by Paul Radin. New York: Harper and Brothers, 1958; orig. pub. as *Primitive Culture* (1871).

Ulrich, Laura Thatcher. *Good Wives: Image and Reality in the Lives of Women in Northern New England, 1650–1750.* New York: Oxford University Press, 1980.

Untermeyer, Louis. *American Poetry since 1900.* New York: Henry Holt and Co., 1923.

Vassar Alumnae Association. *First Annual Class Bulletin, Class of 1909.* Poughkeepsie, N.Y., June 1910.

Verville, Elinor. *Behavior Problems of Children.* Philadelphia: W. B. Saunders Company, 1967.

Viking Fund. *Ruth Fulton Benedict: A Memorial.* New York, 1949.

W.P.A. Federal Writers Project. *Minnesota: A State Guide.* American Guide Series. New York: Viking Press, 1937.

Wallis, Wilson D. "Alexander A. Goldenweiser." *American Anthropologist* 43 (1941): 250–255.

————. "Mental Patterns in Relation to Culture." *Journal of Abnormal and Social Psychology* 19 (1924): 179–184.

————. Review of *Cooperation and Competition among Primitive Peoples,* edited by Margaret Mead. *American Anthropologist* 39 (1937): 710–711.

Ward, Anthony. *Walter Pater: The Idea in Nature.* London: Macgibbon and Kee, 1966.

Warner, W. Lloyd, and Paul S. Lunt. *The Social Life of a Modern Community.* New Haven, Conn.: Yale University Press, 1941.

Weiant, C. W. "Bruno Oetteking, 1871–1960." *American Anthropologist* 62 (1960): 675–680.

Welles, Henry Hunter. *The Measurement of Certain Aspects of Personality among Hard of Hearing Adults.* Teachers College, Columbia University, Contributions to Education, No. 545. New York: Bureau of Publications, Teachers College, Columbia University, 1932.

Wells, D. Collin. "Some Questions Concerning the Higher Education of Women." *American Journal of Sociology* 14 (May 1909): 731–739.

Welter, Barbara. *Dimity Convictions: The American Woman in the Nineteenth Century.* Athens, Ohio: Ohio University Press, 1976.

Wesley, Edgar Bruce. *Owatonna: The Social Development of a Minnesota Community.* Minneapolis: University of Minnesota Press, 1938.

"When College Girls Make Merry." *Ladies Home Journal,* November 1908, p. 34; February 1909, p. 22; May 1909, p. 23; November 1909, p. 34.

Whitrow, G. J. *The Nature of Time.* New York: Holt, Rinehart and Winston, 1972.

Whorf, Benjamin. "Linguistics as an Exact Science." *Technology Review* 43 (1940): 61–63, 80–83.

"Who's Who among the Sioux: Ella C. Deloria." *University of South Dakota Bulletin, Institute of Indian Studies* 76 (August 1976), New Report No. 68, p. 3.

Williams, Elgin. "Anthropology for the Common Man." *American Anthropologist* 49 (1947): 84–90.

Wissler, Clark. *Man and Culture.* Crowell's Social Science Series, edited by Seba Eldridge. New York: Thomas Y. Crowell Company, 1923.

————. "Opportunities for Coordination in Anthropological and Psychological Research." *American Anthropologist* 22 (1920): 1–12.

Woodard, James. "The Relation of Personality Structure to the Structure of Culture." *American Sociological Review* 3 (1938): 637–651.

Wortis, Joseph, M.D. "Sex Taboos, Sex Offenders, and the Law." *American Journal of Orthopsychiatry* 9 (1939): 554–564.

Wylie, Elinor. *Collected Poems of Elinor Wylie.* New York: Alfred A. Knopf, 1960.

————. "Jewelled Bindings." *New Republic* 37, Pt. 2 (December 5, 1923): 14.

Zabel, Morton Dauwen. "The Mechanism of Sensibility." *Poetry* 34 (1929): 150–155.

Index

Adams, Léonie, 171, 172, 175, 176, 179, 180, 181–182, 373–374n16
Aginsky, Bernard, 225, 231
America
—nineteenth-century: and absolute sense of right and wrong, 29; and Anglo-Saxon nativism, 21; and death, 13, 31; and Doctrine of Spheres, 9–11, 188–189; and farm life for women, 23; and individualism, 167–168, 211–212; in *Patterns of Culture*, 210; and practicality, 25, 26; and self-control, 24; and True Woman ideal, 11–12
—Progressive-era: and feminism, 69, 78; and beginnings of Modernism, 130–134; and idea of environment shaping character, 123 (*see also* Anthropology, American: development of concept of culture); and importance of the expert, 120; and importance of objectivity, 118, 121; and importance of physical science model and of scientific approach to social change and social control, 120–121, 222; and organic model, 151; in *Patterns of Culture*, 209–210, 212; and Pragmatism, 120; and political Progressivism in social activism and the Social Gospel, xi, 59, 116–117, 137–138, 159; and search for regularities and laws, 118–119; and "unselfish" individ-

ualism, 168, 169. *See also* Benedict, Ruth Fulton; Boas, Franz
—1920's: and covert or cultural Progressivism, 119–122; and materialism, 159–160; and non-Euclideanism, 134–135; and question of self versus society, 143–144, 168–169, 182; and resurgence of fundamentalism, 146
—1930's: and acceptance of primary role of culture over biology, 209–210; and Communism, 290–291; and debate over capitalism versus Marxism, 242; and Depression, 181, 272; and German-American Bund, 284; and New Deal, 289, 294
—1940's: an interconnected world, 304, 313; World War II, 302, 312. *See also* Benedict, Ruth Fulton
American Anthropological Association (AAA), 100, 103, 111, 112, 113, 225, 235, 280, 281; reorganization of, 332–333
American Committee for Democracy and Intellectual Freedom, 288, 291, 302–303
American Council of Learned Societies (ACLS), 112
American Folk-Lore Society (AFLS), 101, 280–281. *See also Journal of American Folk-Lore*
Anderson, Thelma, 266
Anthropology:

[421]

161; and Progressivism, xi, 58–59,
62–63, 66, 116–117, 121–122,
159–160, 169, 245; and psychophysical vomiting or bilious attacks,
8; and Quain fund, 279; and Quain
suicide, 274; and race, writings on,
291–300, 312–313; reaction of, to
World War II relocation of Japanese-Americans, 312–313; and redefining normality, 203–205, 253,
255; relationships of, with women,
185–203, 300–301, 378n32; and
relativity of democracy, 310–312,
317–318; and Research in Contemporary Cultures, 317, 329–332,
335–337, 342–350; and respect
for cultural differences, 298, 317–
318, 338–340; and Rorschach testing, 246–247; and Rumanian
study, 320; and Schmerler murder,
272–274; as self-actualized person,
255–258, 384n24; and Southwest
concordance work, 107–108, 111,
139, 366n30; and smoking, 51;
striving of, for national fellowship
recognition, 111–112; and synergy,
245, 308–312, 317, 318, 392n11;
and Thai study, 319–320; at
UNESCO seminar (1948), 337–
340; at Washington School of Psychiatry, 248, 252, 321–322, 328;
at Westlake School for Girls, 67,
68, 69; as wise woman and witch,
340–341; and Woman-Christ idea,
83, 84
—academic career of, at Columbia:
academic rank, 112–115, 260,
278, 337; anthropological rites of
passage, 103–106; desire for a
regular academic position, 107,
114; as teacher, 263–267, 271; as
a woman in academia, 267–271
—and American Anthropological Association: offices in, 113, 281; as
president of, 232–233, 236, 329,
333, 347, 350, 388n38, 395n9
—anthropological writings of: ar-

ticles, 103, 137, 155–161,
166–167, 203–205, 245–246,
310–312, 318; books—see The
Chrysanthemum and the Sword,
Patterns of Culture, Race: Science
and Politics, Tales of the Cochiti Indians, Zuñi Mythology; dissertation, 103–104, 121–122, 137,
152, 368n8; reviews, 309–310,
315; unpublished works, 122,
147–148, 316, 320–321, 337–
340, 348
—and Culture and Personality studies,
238–248, 272, 308, 319–320. See
also Research in Contemporary
Cultures
—and family: childhood comparison
with sister, 24–28; Fulton family
members, 18; Great-Uncle Justin
Fulton, 3, 26; importance of grandfather, 27; influence of father's early
death, 1–9, 53, 94; pioneer heritage, 15, 21–22; relationship with
mother, 2–3, 30–33, 38; Shattuck
family members, 19–20. See also
Freeman, Margery Fulton
—and feminism: as cultural feminist,
86–87, 92–93, 117–118, 345–
348, 365n19; feminist biographies
by, 78, 87–91, 169; feminist influences on, 55–56, 69–72, 85–86;
in Patterns of Culture, 213; in poetry, 175–177; and rejection of
True Woman ideal, 12–13; in Research in Contemporary Cultures,
347–348; and temporary rejection
of Woman's Rights ideas, 76–78
—field work of: Blood and Blackfoot,
279, 291, 301, 391n32; Cochiti,
110–111; Mescalero Apache,
261–262; Mohave, 111; Pima,
110–111, 154–155; Serrano,
104–105, 128–129, 365–366n20;
Zuñi, 108–110
—and Japan: early interest in, 61, 68;
war work on, 321. See also The
Chrysanthemum and the Sword